COMPUTERS IN THE
COMPOSITION CLASSROOM

COMPUTERS IN THE COMPOSITION CLASSROOM

A Critical Sourcebook

EDITED BY

Michelle Sidler
Auburn University

Richard Morris
Parkland College

Elizabeth Overman Smith
Tennessee State University

BEDFORD / ST. MARTIN'S Boston • New York

For Bedford / St. Martin's

Executive Editor: Leasa Burton
Developmental Editor: Joanna Lee
Senior Production Supervisor: Joe Ford
Senior Marketing Manager: Karita dos Santos
Text Design: Anna George
Project Management: Diana Puglisi George
Cover Design: Donna L. Dennison
Composition: LinMark Design
Printing and Binding: RR Donnelley & Sons, Inc.

President: Joan E. Feinberg
Editorial Director: Denise B. Wydra
Director of Marketing: Karen Melton Soeltz
Director of Editing, Design, and Production: Marcia Cohen
Manager, Publishing Services: Emily Berleth

Library of Congress Control Number: 2006940456

Manufactured in the United States of America.

2 1 0 9 8 7
f e d c b a

For information, write: Bedford / St. Martin's, 75 Arlington Street, Boston, MA 02116 (617-399-4000)

ISBN-10: 0-312-45844-4
ISBN-13: 978-0-312-45844-7

ACKNOWLEDGEMENTS
Acknowledgments and copyrights are continued at the back of the book on pages 509–12, which constitute an extension of the copyright page.

ACKNOWLEDGMENTS

We greatly appreciate all the hard work and commitment of Bedford/ St. Martin's and its staff, who have made the Critical Sourcebook series such a success. We believe that, like the other books in this series, our collection is a much-needed resource for composition teachers, especially those who want to improve their teaching by reflecting upon the impact of computer technology. We are most grateful for the enthusiasm and hard work of Leasa Burton, executive editor, without whom this project would not have succeeded. We also thank Joanna Lee, associate editor, for her editorial contributions and Jimmy Fleming, English marketing specialist, for his help in orchestrating this project in its early stages.

We are also grateful for the support of the computers and writing community who gave us guidance throughout the project, especially Gail Hawisher and Cynthia Selfe, who were immediately enthusiastic and gracious with their help. Several others members of the community offered input and support along the way, including Heidi McKee and our manuscript reviewers: William P. Banks, Christy Desmet, Dànielle Nicole DeVoss, Dene Grigar, Rich Rice, and Rebecca Rickly. Their many insightful comments and suggestions enriched the project and provided a greater depth of knowledge about the field. We also thank the publishers, editors, and authors whose works are represented in this collection. The articles and book chapters included here are thoughtful explorations of important issues for teachers in computer classrooms, and we hope the works receive even more attention from this collection.

Finally, we thank our friends and family—Jason Kneip, the whole Sidler clan, Robert Smith, Nancy Overman, Madonna, and Rich's faithful dog, Spike—for their encouragement and patience. Their support makes this collection possible.

CONTENTS

ACKNOWLEDGMENTS   *v*

INTRODUCTION

Reflecting on Technology and Literacy in the Composition
Classroom   *1*

**Part One FOUNDATIONS OF COMPUTERS
AND COMPOSITION**   *9*

Introduction   *11*

1 CCCC Position Statement on Teaching, Learning,
   and Assessing Writing in Digital Environments   *15*

2 Literacy, Technology, and Monopoly Capital   *20*
   RICHARD OHMANN

3 The Rhetoric of Technology and the Electronic
   Writing Class   *35*
   GAIL E. HAWISHER AND CYNTHIA L. SELFE

4 Distant Voices: Teaching and Writing in a Culture
   of Technology   *46*
   CHRIS M. ANSON

5 The Politics of the Interface: Power and Its Exercise
   in Electronic Contact Zones   *64*
   CYNTHIA L. SELFE AND RICHARD J. SELFE JR.

Part Two   LITERACY AND ACCESS   *87*

Introduction   *89*

6   Technology and Literacy: A Story about the Perils
of Not Paying Attention   *93*
CYNTHIA L. SELFE

7   From Pencils to Pixels: The Stages of Literacy
Technologies   *116*
DENNIS BARON

8   Champing at the Bits: Computers, Copyright,
and the Composition Classroom   *135*
JOHN LOGIE

9   "It wasn't me, was it?": Plagiarism and the Web   *151*
DÀNIELLE DEVOSS AND ANNETTE C. ROSATI

10   Reading Hypertext: Order and Coherence
in a New Medium   *165*
JOHN M. SLATIN

Part Three   WRITERS AND IDENTITY   *179*

Introduction   *181*

11   Feminist Research in Computers and Composition   *185*
LISA GERRARD

12   Out of the Closet and into the Network: Sexual
Orientation and the Computerized Classroom   *207*
JONATHAN ALEXANDER

13   The Persistence of Difference in Networked Classrooms:
Non-negotiable Difference and the African American
Student Body   *218*
TODD TAYLOR

14   Reversing Notions of Disability and Accommodation:
Embracing Universal Design in Writing Pedagogy
and Web Space   *228*
PATRICIA A. DUNN AND KATHLEEN DUNN DE MERS

Part Four   WRITERS AND COMPOSING   *231*

Introduction   *233*

15   Pedagogy in the Computer-networked Classroom   *239*
JANET M. ELDRED

16   Contrasts: Teaching and Learning about Writing
in Traditional and Computer Classrooms   *251*
MIKE PALMQUIST, KATE KIEFER, JAMES HARTVIGSEN,
AND BARBARA GOODLEW

17   Rethinking Validity and Reliability in the Age
of Convergence   *271*
DIANE PENROD

18   Looking for Sources of Coherence in a Fragmented
World: Notes toward a New Assessment Design   *293*
KATHLEEN BLAKE YANCEY

19   The Politics of the Program: MS Word as the Invisible
Grammarian   *308*
TIM MCGEE AND PATRICIA ERICSSON

20   The Computer and the Inexperienced Writer   *326*
CHRISTINE A. HULT

21   Web Literacy: Challenges and Opportunities
for Research in a New Medium   *333*
MADELEINE SORAPURE, PAMELA INGLESBY,
AND GEORGE YATCHISIN

22   Web Research and Genres in Online Databases:
When the Glossy Page Disappears   *350*
MICHELLE SIDLER

Part Five   INSTITUTIONAL PROGRAMS   *367*

Introduction   *369*

23   The Debate about Online Learning: Key Issues
for Writing Teachers   *373*
PATRICIA WEBB PETERSON

24 Why OWLs? Value, Risk, and Evolution   *385*
STUART BLYTHE

25 The Best of Both Worlds: Teaching Basic Writers in Class
and Online   *389*
LINDA STINE

26 The Impact of the Computer in Second
Language Writing   *404*
MARTHA C. PENNINGTON

27 WAC Wired: Electronic Communication across
the Curriculum   *425*
DONNA REISS AND ART YOUNG

Part Six **THE RHETORIC OF NEW MEDIA WRITING**   *449*

Introduction   *451*

28 Negative Spaces: From Production to Connection
in Composition   *454*
JOHNDAN JOHNSON-EILOLA

29 Part 2: Toward an Integrated Composition Pedagogy
in Hypertext   *469*
SEAN D. WILLIAMS

30 Some Notes on Simulacra Machines, Flash in First-Year
Composition, and Tactics in Spaces of Interruption   *482*
ANTHONY ELLERTSON

31 Re: The Future of Computers and Writing: A Multivocal
Textumentary   *485*
BILL HART-DAVIDSON AND STEVEN D. KRAUSE

SUGGESTED READINGS   *499*

ABOUT THE EDITORS   *507*

CREDITS   *509*

INDEX   *513*

COMPUTERS IN THE
COMPOSITION CLASSROOM

INTRODUCTION

Reflecting on Technology and Literacy in the Composition Classroom

No technology, not even the apparently autonomous computer, can ever function as a writing space in the absence of human writers and readers.

—JAY DAVID BOLTER, *WRITING SPACE*

For it is inescapable that every culture must negotiate with technology, whether it does so intelligently or not. A bargain is struck in which technology giveth and technology taketh away.

—NEIL POSTMAN, *TECHNOPOLY*

It almost seems unnecessary to say that we live in a digital age. It's something we take for granted even as we live more and more with and through our cell phones, conduct business and stay in touch with friends and family through e-mail, fearlessly shop and bank online, check the news, weather, and sports with the click of a mouse, and compactly tote thousands of songs wherever we go. But as we embrace what Todd Gitlin has called a digital tsunami and leave old technologies and the ways we related to them behind, have we thought about how the new technologies have changed us and why? Have we really begun to consider, as Neil Postman prods us to, what we have gained and what we have lost?

As we ponder these questions, we must also step back and remember a fundamental principle: At its core, writing itself is a technology of literacy, one that philosophers, rhetoricians, and teachers have debated throughout recorded history (Ong). Plato himself bemoaned the spread of written literacy, fearing it would lead to false realities and lazy minds. Gutenberg's Bible set off a revolution in literacy and epistemology—and shoved aside oral traditions. As Dennis Baron recounts in this collection, Thoreau disparaged the invention of the telegraph, wondering why people would even want to communicate long distances—despite the fact that he and his family were manufacturers of another communication technology, the pencil.

In looking at television and computers today, many modern critics have echoed Plato's fears and Thoreau's disdain; however, many writing theorists and teachers argue that computer technologies reflect our students' own literacies, which are increasingly visual, multimedia, and fast-paced. In fact, Jay David Bolter and Richard Grusin contend that digital writing spaces are appropriately and increasingly "hypermediate" because they allow for transparent, interactive engagement with the tools of communication. These polar viewpoints underscore another point made by Postman: Technologies are the product of culture at the same time that they influence the culture in which they reside.

Questions about technology, literacy, and culture are not just the domain of philosophers. Teachers in every discipline, but especially teachers of writing, must eventually grapple with these issues if we are to uphold our historical roles as teachers who prepare students for civic as well as academic discourse. Teaching students to become citizen-rhetors in the digital age enacts a critical awareness of what Laura Gurak calls "cyberliteracy," an understanding of the power that occurs in all interactions with technology. To be truly literate, students must know more than keystrokes and Web design; they must be reflective, responsible users of technology. As Bolter reminds us, there is always a human ghost behind the composing machine.

But how do we, as teachers, many of whom grew up in the generation before digitized writing, teach a literacy that was unheard of in our childhoods and seems to change with every passing year? How do we negotiate the jolt of moving from what seems like a static or stable print/image culture to a society where messages and images are zapped into our consciousness in a nanosecond? The tactile days of writing out drafts in pencil or ink are almost gone. Students can hardly believe the stories we tell about literally cutting out paragraphs with scissors to rearrange an essay or marking up pages with inserted words and phrases. Typewriters—and the nightmare of editing a typo or finding an error after carefully typing in our script—have largely been relegated to the junk heap or museum. The VCRs we fought to get in our classrooms are on their last leg, and CD players may not be far behind. Old technologies have yielded to new, and teachers and students today experience, use, and understand the world differently from the way students and teachers did three decades ago. In less than thirty years digital technology has become an integral part of higher education. In that short time, computer technologies have literally electrified writing instruction, and it has been the job of composition studies to respond with new pedagogies, research, and scholarly communities.

Even if we teach in traditional classrooms, it is now difficult to imagine writing instruction without computer technology and impossible to ignore its impact on literacy. At the very least, most of us ask our students to word-process final drafts and use the Internet in many facets of research. Moreover, students in computer and writing classes interact with technology every day: editing drafts, checking e-mail, downloading and exchanging information—and even creating multimedia writing projects. In addition to word processing and e-mail, other software has made its way into our classrooms: PowerPoint and similar presentation software facilitates (and breathes new life into) student presentations; drawing programs provide a more flexible approach to brainstorming and document design; hypertext allows students to explore new rhetorics and literacies.

Computer technologies also allow for a range of digital texts, including multi-media writing that integrates visuals, sound, and interactivity. And, of course, the Internet expands the reach of composition beyond the single classroom to a network of connected communities and resources: Synchronous (real-time) chat can be used to hold class discussions, even across many miles; asynchronous (near-real time) postings and e-mails offer alternatives to handwritten reading responses and even draft response groups; and of course, online research brings not only the school library, but the culture and information of the world, into our classrooms, instantaneously expanding our horizons.

How do we begin to assess the impact of this technological revolution? From our experience, when writing instructors first teach in computer class-rooms, one point becomes abundantly clear: computer technology changes the environment in which learning and writing occur. Computers have be-come much more than simply a writing tool; they create an interconnected, fluid communication space. Moreover, the Internet lets the "outside" world in, supplying students with access to many types of information, including sophisticated academic research and unpredictable cultural discourse. As many of the writers in this collection remind us, these changes require intelli-gent negotiation and planning, which may make the task of teaching in this environment seem daunting at first. Computers may seem to undermine teachers' authority, create a constant distraction, and disenfranchise those un-derprepared students whose college experience is already full of difficult challenges. The tradeoff, however, is that our new classroom technology can foster more student engagement, facilitate hands-on writing experiences, and provide a myriad of tools with which students can develop literacy skills for this century. Such classroom complexities make for both a more dynamic and less controlled pedagogical approach to writing instruction, reflecting the ex-citement and unpredictability of writing itself.

Accordingly, theorists and practitioners in rhetoric and composition have grappled with the impact of this digital age on our pedagogy, on our students, and on our lives. Like the rise of composition studies itself, the field of com-puters and writing grew out of social and economic necessity. The wide-spread acceptance of personal computers (PCs) in the 1980s led to their gradual implementation in composition classrooms, while government sup-port for "computer literacy" in the 1990s prompted political and economic support for more computer access across all levels of education (Selfe, *Tech-nology and Literacy*). Reacting to this socioeconomic climate, college and uni-versity administrators poured money into expanding their institutions' technological resources, and writing classrooms eventually (though not im-mediately) participated in the technology boom. Rooms that once housed small writing desks (able to accommodate only a pad of paper and perhaps a print book) were suddenly equipped with standalone computers, which in the earliest days acted as little more than word processors and, often, elec-tronic babysitters, performing style checks on students' written works or prompting students to complete drill-and-grill grammar exercises.

During the last two decades of the 20th century, many composition class-rooms were transformed into networked computer centers with PCs, Internet connections, and monitors alive with color, images, and even sound. More-over, as desktop publishing and networked technologies arose, they became integrated into process theories of writing, and computer classrooms came to be seen as workshop space wherein students composed, exchanged, and re-searched. It became possible to communicate about writing, not only with classmates, but with peer editors, colleagues, and audiences outside the class-room—and anywhere in the world.

Research within the computers and writing community expanded as well; by the early 1990s, computers and composition (as a pedagogical ap-proach and a scholarly community) had "come of age" (Hawisher et al. 171). *Computers and Composition,* a journal devoted to the teaching of writing in computerized environments, matured in the mid-1980s from an intermittent newsletter to a well-subscribed scholarly quarterly. The annual Computers and Writing conference, which began in the early 1980s as an ad hoc gathering sponsored by volunteers, blossomed into a well-attended yearly event by the turn of the 21st century. Along with these professional developments, com-puters and writing research became both more diverse in its topics and more critical of the computer's role as teacher within the classroom. Teachers and researchers encouraged effective computer-assisted pedagogies based in process theory and rhetorical principles while emphasizing the need for criti-cal understandings of technology's constructive, collaborative—and exclu-sionary—tendencies.

Since this collection centers on the digital enterprise of writing with com-puters, we admit the irony of laying out this collection in print. In a more dig-ital age—perhaps in the near future—this collection would appear as a Web site or a downloadable PDF or even a graphic podcast, complete with links to all the articles and discussions on these issues, easily accessible in one virtual place. It might even offer an interactive blog or discussion board. We believe that such a day will soon come, but for now, we are still in the late age of print where most of us read extended text in print, where even our computer-netted classes often use textbooks with paper pages and covers, and where the distribution of teaching materials occurs primarily through traditional publishing. Moreover, we offer this collection in one print volume because, as many of the writers represented in this collection contend, not everyone has access to cutting-edge digital technologies that are mobile and easy to read and allow us to leave notes in the margins. Nevertheless, we appreciate an-other theme expressed by many of the authors in this collection: the meaning and import of texts are determined not just by the author's words but also by the medium used to express those words. Therefore, we have chosen to in-clude only screen shots of several *Kairos* webtext articles with the introduc-tion, and hope that readers visit them online. These works are intended to be read in a digital environment that we cannot duplicate, and we respect that intention. All are freely available on the Web, and while we acknowledge the limits of access, we hope that as digital technology permeates the social fabric, more people will have access through such institutions as public libraries and community centers.

It is our intention here to acknowledge research from the past while looking toward the future. We include a set of articles that have shaped past conversations and have been often cited, used, and discussed in tackling thorny pedagogical and composing issues related to computers and writing. Although many of the pieces collected in this volume were written before contemporary technologies existed, the themes and issues they raise remain relevant today and are particularly important in helping teachers become more effective in using computerized, digitized classrooms for the benefit of all their students. These readings not only reflect a selection of topics that teachers and graduate students considering these issues for the first time will find useful, but also remind teachers at all levels of experience about the real-world negotiation of technology in the classroom. Looking toward the future, we offer a representative sampling of the current research and pedagogy concerning composition instruction in computer classrooms. As many other thoughtful publications are available, we have also included at the end of this book a list of Suggested Readings that will point you toward more of those works.

We have divided this collection into six parts. Part One establishes the theoretical framework of the field of computers and writing, reaching back to some of the earliest critical work to be published in major composition journals, and Part Six highlights recent research that speaks to multimedia composition pedagogies that are arguably already in place, but certainly are on the horizon. The middle four parts take up specific areas of inquiry and application in the field: literacy and access, identity, writers and composing strategies, and the ongoing relationship between computers and affiliated writing programs within institutions.

Part One: Foundations of Computers and Composition surveys the most influential of the early critical works, exploring the role of technology in society, politics, and the economy. The writers establish a thoughtful framework for subsequent research, one that operates at the intersection of technology, power, literacy, and culture. Major themes emerge from these critical works and provide a framework for the rest of the collection: the role of economic interests in fostering computer competency, the often-touted link between computers and other tools of literacy, the complex relationship between culture and technology, and the importance of working within local institutional sites to implement responsible technologies while understanding our own institutions' investments in the greater society. The collection's next four parts address each of these themes in turn, offering more detailed accounts of critical pedagogies in technological spaces.

Part Two: Literacy and Access shows how literacy has become "inextricably linked" to technology (Selfe, *Technology and Literacy*), making access to technologies an integral component of literacy acquisition. These works explode many myths, including the fear of new technologies, the guarantee of technology's role in student success, and the liberal assumption that technology supplies the necessary tools for upward mobility. The readings also explore technology's tendency to develop new literacies, both expanding and complicating the role of writers through copyright restrictions and new forms such as hypertext and multimedia. Because technologies are a double-edged sword, these literacy opportunities are often reserved for students of privilege while excluding the most disenfranchised.

Building on this critical awareness of multiple literacies and opportunities, Part Three: Writers and Identity further explores the role of students' subjectivity and its relationship to technology. The authors show how computer technologies tend to reflect straight, white, able-bodied male epistemologies, interests, and literate practices. They challenge the myth of universal computer access, which presumes that technology will lead to advanced literacy for all students and citizens, by delineating a myriad of technological challenges faced by nontraditional students and the disenfranchised, including minorities, women, gays and lesbians, and persons who are physically challenged. However, the readings also underscore that technology opens up online spaces of representation for these communities, describing alternative literate practices enabled by the Internet well as classroom strategies to promote students' success. As with all forms of writing technology, computers require composition teachers to attend to the needs of diverse student populations.

Part Four: Writers and Composing presents a series of practical strategies for implementing computer technologies in the composition classroom, focusing on major components of traditional composition courses, such as research, drafting, workshopping, and proofreading. In addition, the readings explore how computer technologies alter the role of the teacher from one of evaluator to one of guide, a threatening transition for some new teachers. All of the writers emphasize that implementing technology does not simply add a computer tool to the classroom—it changes the writing, learning, and teaching environment in which we conduct composition instruction. Moreover, technologies alter students' literate practices, mediating how they compose, communicate, and research.

The works in Part Five: Institutional Programs explore additional concerns about the implementation of technology. Readings in this section discuss technology's role in various institutional programs related to composition instruction, including online education, writing centers, developmental and second-language (ESL) instruction, and writing across the curriculum (WAC) programs. Computer technologies expand the instructional options for these fields, offering flexible tools for nontraditional students and combining "real-world" writing experiences with academic inquiry. The writers urge teachers and administrators to survey their own institutions carefully before initiating technological changes, catering those interventions to the needs of the local student community. Though all the writers represented in Part Five are proponents of computer technology, they also offer concrete cautionary guidelines for teachers and administrators to consider as they go forward.

Looking forward with reflection and critique is perhaps the most prevalent theme throughout this collection, and it is a motto that any teacher in computerized classrooms should espouse. Thus, we conclude with Part Six: The Rhetoric of New Media Writing, a glimpse into the near-future (or, for some, the present day) of computers and writing, wherein composition courses integrate not only print texts but also multimodal rhetorics and literacies. The tools of composition are increasingly more complex, integrating multimedia software that records, edits, and transmits images, sound, and video. Writing programs that seem experimental now, particularly those that concentrate on this "new-media writing," will again change the environment in which we teach. Several authors in this section explore how we can make that transition in our classrooms and in our teaching community, while still valuing composition's core commitment to composing processes. Others argue that computers are quickly changing the way we view literacy, requiring a new label for this type of pedagogy and research: rhetoric and technology.

And so, we end as we began, addressing our roles as teachers of writing in the digital age, preparing students as responsible citizen-rhetors in a fast-paced technoculture. Certainly, teachers of computers and writing can look forward to better computer-enhanced teaching, emerging communication technologies, and new forms of literacy. However, the field is also committed to preparing literate citizens and thoughtful academics, and we should always be mindful of the critical framework laid out by the writers in this collection. We should heed the words of Donna Haraway and help our students take control of technology before they become slaves to the machine: "We can be responsible for machines; they do not dominate or threaten us. We are responsible for boundaries; we are they" (180). Computers, like writing, are powerful technologies, but they do not have to be more powerful than students' own discourse, so we must continue to foster our students' critical voices with and through the tools of communication. As teachers of "critical technological literacy" (Selfe, *Technology and Literacy*), we can help students approach composing decisions with rhetorical savvy and critical awareness.

REFERENCES

Bolter, Jay David. *Writing Space: Computers, Hypertext, and the Remediation of Print,* 2nd ed. Mahwah: Erlbaum, 2001.

Bolter, Jay David, and Richard Grusin. *Remediation: Understanding New Media.* Cambridge: MIT P, 1999.

Gitlin, Todd. "The Liberal Arts in an Age of Info-glut." *Chronicle of Higher Education* 44. 1988. (June 28, 2006) <http://chronicle.com/colloquy98/liberalarts/re.shtml>.

Gurak, Laura. *Cyberliteracy: Navigating the Internet with Awareness.* New Haven: Yale UP, 2003.

Haraway, Donna. "A Cyborg Manifesto: Science, Technology, and Socialist-feminism in the Late Twentieth Century." *Simians, Cyborgs and Women: The Reinvention of Nature,* Ed. Donna Haraway. New York: Routledge, 1991. 149–81.

Hawisher, Gail, Paul LeBlanc, Charles Moran, and Cynthia L. Selfe, eds. *Computers and the Teaching of Writing in American Higher Education, 1979–1994: A History.* Greenwich: Ablex, 1996.

Ong, Walter. *Orality and Literacy.* London: Methuen, 1982.

Postman, Neil. *Technopoly: The Surrender of Culture to Technology.* New York: Vintage, 1993.

Selfe, Cynthia. *Technology and Literacy in the Twenty-First Century: The Importance of Paying Attention.* Carbondale: Southern Illinois UP, 1999.

PART ONE

*Foundations
of Computers
and Composition*

Introduction to Part One

The earliest computers each filled a large room and were more high-priced toys than functional machines. And even when computers became more manageable and functional, they were mostly the domain of business, not the general populace, and certainly not the classroom. Likewise, the early Internet was created by and the domain of the American Defense Department and not comprehensible to the general public, much less accessible. But as these technologies evolved and moved into the educational realm in the early 1980s, theorists began to ponder what this meant for us, as human beings and as teachers. At first, this research entailed classroom-based accounts of pedagogies and software, but a major turning point came in the mid-1980s when Richard Ohmann and others started to observe cultural, ethical, and social implications of computers themselves. These researchers contended that technology can make our lives more convenient and challenge us to learn new skills. They also found that computers can be a space of liberation and resistance for students if we prepare them with appropriate skills and critical awareness. Unfortunately, such computer literacy is often more difficult for those already struggling with disenfranchisement.

Consequently, the authors in this section remind us that writing is a complex interaction between peoples, cultures, and classes, one that should be approached with rhetorical skill, humanist critique, and ethical awareness. The works collected here represent some of the most often cited and most influential texts of the field because they critically examine "big picture" aspects of technology in the classroom, including issues of epistemology, economics, culture, access, and postmodernism. Many were the first articles to do so, laying the groundwork for major areas of inquiry in the field. These themes include computers' connection to economics, politics, working conditions, and culture, situating classroom research as an endeavor of pedagogical improvement, institutional awareness, and cultural sensitivity. While praising the great potential of technology to liberate students, authors in this section remind us that technologies can marginalize them as well.

To set the pedagogical context, both for this section and for the collection as a whole, we have included the Conference on College Composition and

Communication (CCCC) Position Statement on Teaching, Learning, and Assessing Writing in Digital Environments. Like other position statements from CCCC and the National Council of Teachers of English (NCTE), this document offers policies and guidelines for computerized instruction, encouraging teachers and administrators to reflect on technology's complex relationship to composing before implementing computer-assisted curricula. The position statement reminds us that like any literacy tool, computers are best employed in conjunction with other "best practices" for writing instruction. Reflecting the sentiment of other articles in this section, the statement emphasizes that relying on computers as electronic babysitters or drill-and-grill evaluators is not an effective educational use of technology. Instead, computers radically change the teaching and writing environment, requiring careful planning and implementation. By including the CCCC statement on writing in digital environments, we hope that teachers at all levels will reflect on their best teaching practices when they employ technology in the classroom.

Richard Ohmann's 1985 *College English* article, "Literacy, Technology, and Monopoly Capital," provides another opportunity to reflect on the relationship between literacy and technology. The article marks the historical beginning of critical discussions about technology in major composition journals, taking a "decidedly theoretical turn" (Hawisher et al., p. 83) away from earlier classroom-based research. While previous published work tended to concentrate on word processors, grading programs, and other instructional technology, Ohmann brings his well-known Marxist analytical framework to bear on the issue of technology and literacy. Briefly surveying the history of the term "literacy," he argues that new technologies, like other forms of literacy, do not necessarily empower those of less privilege; instead, new technologies tend to sustain preexisting systems of power, especially that of monopoly capitalism. As teachers and scholars, we should critically analyze the ways new technologies and literacies are employed by governments and corporations, aiming to reconstitute them as tools for resistance and liberation rather than tools of capitalism.

Though Ohmann's article shows its age—having been written before the Internet and before many writing programs even had access to computer technology—the critical questions Ohmann poses have become strong undercurrents in the field. His link between technology and literacy—and their place within larger social and economic forces—continues to challenge teachers and researchers over twenty years later. His concern about the changing workplace owing to technology has become a reality, with computer skills becoming a necessity in virtually every field. And his call for the democratization of technology has been heeded by many teachers and researchers, especially those whose writings make up the rest of this section.

Bringing this analysis more directly to previous research on computers and composition, Gail Hawisher and Cynthia Selfe examine what were often laudatory accounts of computer successes in composition classrooms in their 1991 piece, "The Rhetoric of Technology and the Electronic Writing Class." Citing their own observations within classrooms, they believe this "rhetoric of technology" portrays a misleading, overly positive assessment of computers in the classroom. Though early teachers of computerized composition were well-intentioned when they praised technology's ability to support student-centered classrooms, more hands-on writing in the classroom, and more direct communication media, they also tended to overlook technology's tendency to sustain authority and control and to turn the classroom into a disconnected writing factory. Echoing Ohmann's earlier call for more critical awareness, Hawisher and Selfe maintain that we must think critically about our roles as teachers in computerized classrooms: We have the potential to change classrooms into spaces where we "become learners within a community of other learners, our students" (44).

Nearly ten years later, Chris Anson updates Hawisher and Selfe's call in his article, "Distant Voices: Teaching and Writing in a Culture of Technology." Anson foresees a future of rapid technological expansion, including mobile technologies that replace many classroom environments. To prepare for this future, he states that we must manage our classrooms and technology carefully by becoming involved with administrative decisions about computers, ensuring that technology is chosen because it is pedagogically effective, not just fiscally efficient. He also connects technology to faculty hiring practices, arguing that distance education and other instructional media applications tend to support the ongoing trend toward part-time, adjunct, and provisional faculty positions.

To help faculty and administrators make wise choices about technology, Anson offers seven guiding questions about the impact of technology on education, including issues such as online communication and classroom discussions, changes in collaborative learning facilitated by network discourse, the increasing presence of distance education, the relationship of humans to technology, the conditions of work (including the impact of telecommuting), and the rise of corporate education. He believes that if we as teachers engage in thoughtful discussions about these issues, we can more fully prepare for our technological future and guide institutional decisions about instructional media.

In their insightful article, "The Politics of the Interface: Power and Its Exercise in Electronic Contact Zones," Cynthia Selfe and Richard Selfe Jr. draw on Mary Louise Pratt's concept of "contact zones" to describe cultural, ideological, and linguistic features of computer interfaces, including desktops, languages, menus, and images. Contact zones are social spaces wherein various cultures, languages, and classes mix, often creating imbalanced power relations. Selfe and Selfe argue that computer interfaces are also social spaces that reflect power relations, generally as a result of economic and political colonialism. Drawing on examples from online discussion boards and educational software, Selfe and Selfe maintain that early researchers in computers and composition painted an overly optimistic picture of technology's positive impact on writing instruction. They also argue that we should "teach students and ourselves to recognize computer interfaces as non-innocent physical borders (between the regular world and the virtual world), cultural borders (between the haves and the have-nots), and linguistic borders" (495). To address the potentially hegemonic power of technology, Selfe and Selfe suggest that teachers should become "technology critics" as well as "technology users" (496); teachers should also contribute to technology design and re-vision computer interfaces as texts that can be critiqued and re-conceived.

Writers in this section stress that teaching composition in computer classrooms requires more than technical skill. It necessitates a critical, reflective—and forward-looking—approach to instructional technology. Computers impact genders, cultures, and classes in different, often inequitable ways, and composition courses must always be attuned to those differences. Whereas most of these articles include examples from the early days of computerized classrooms, the number and type of computer-assisted classes has expanded greatly. Some are specialized labs with desktop computers and long tables; some are wireless rooms that facilitate students' own laptops; some are personal computers spread throughout the country (and the world), linked only by the virtual Internet connection of distance education. The next twenty years will bring even more changes, and the writers in this section provide a critical framework through which we can understand and address the "promise (and peril)" of that future (Tuman, 1992).

REFERENCES

Hawisher, Gail, Paul LeBlanc, Charles Moran, and Cynthia L. Selfe, eds. *Computers and the Teaching of Writing in American Higher Education, 1979–1994: A History.* Greenwich: Ablex, 1995.
Tuman, M, ed. *Literacy Online: The Promise (and Peril) of Reading and Writing with Computers.* Pittsburgh: U of Pittsburgh P, 1992.

1

CCCC Position Statement on Teaching, Learning, and Assessing Writing in Digital Environments

CONFERENCE ON COLLEGE COMPOSITION AND COMMUNICATION, FEBRUARY 2004

[In the spring of 2003, then-Chair of CCCC Shirley Wilson Logan appointed a CCCC Committee whose purpose was to create a position statement governing the teaching, learning, and assessing of writing in digital environments. This is the document this group produced; it was adopted by the CCCC Executive Committee as of February 25, 2004.]

Submitted by the CCCC Committee on Teaching, Learning, and Assessing Writing in Digital Environments (Kathleen Yancey, Chair; Andrea Lunsford; James McDonald; Charles Moran; Michael Neal; Chet Pryor; Duane Roen; Cindy Selfe)

Increasingly, classes and programs in writing require that students compose digitally. Such writing occurs both in conventional "face-to-face" classrooms and in classes and programs that are delivered at a distance. The expression "composing digitally" can refer to a myriad of practices. In its simplest form, such writing can refer to a "mixed media" writing practice, the kind that occurs when students compose at a computer screen, using a word processor, so that they can submit the writing in print (Moran). Such writing may not utilize the formatting conventions such as italics and boldfacing available on a word processor; alternatively, such writing often includes sophisticated formatting as well as hypertextual links. Digital composing can take many other forms as well. For example, such composing can mean participating in an online discussion through a listserv or bulletin board (Huot and Takayoshi). It can refer to creating compositions in presentation software. It can refer to participating in chat rooms or creating webpages. It can mean creating a digital portfolio with audio and video files as well as scanned print writings. Most recently, it can mean composing on a class weblog or wiki. And more generally, as composers use digital technology to create new genres, we can expect the variety of digital compositions to continue proliferating.

From National Council of Teachers of English.
<www.ncte.org/cccc/resources/positions/123773.htm>

The focus of writing instruction is expanding: the curriculum of composition is widening to include not one but two literacies: a literacy of print and a literacy of the screen. In addition, work in one medium is used to enhance learning in the other.

As we refine current practices and invent new ones for digital literacy, we need to assure that principles of good practice governing these new activities are clearly articulated.

ASSUMPTIONS

Courses that engage students in writing digitally may have many features, but all of them should

a. introduce students to the epistemic (knowledge-constructing) characteristics of information technology, some of which are generic to information technology and some of which are specific to the fields in which the information technology is used;

b. provide students with opportunities to apply digital technologies to solve substantial problems common to the academic, professional, civic, and/or personal realm of their lives;

c. include much hands-on use of technologies;

d. engage students in the critical evaluation of information (see American Library Association, "Information Literacy"); and

e. prepare students to be reflective practitioners.

As with all teaching and learning, the foundation for teaching writing digitally must be university, college, department, program, and course learning goals or outcomes. These outcomes should reflect current knowledge in the field (such as those articulated in the "WPA Outcomes Statement"), as well as the needs of students, who will be expected to write for a variety of purposes in the academic, professional, civic, and personal arenas of life. Once programs and faculty have established learning outcomes, they then can make thoughtful decisions about curriculum, pedagogy, and assessment.

Writing instruction is delivered contextually. Therefore, institutional mission statements should also inform decisions about teaching writing digitally in the same ways that they should inform any curricular and pedagogical decisions.

Regardless of the medium in which writers choose to work, all writing is social; accordingly, response to and evaluation of writing are human activities, and in the classroom, their primary purpose is to enhance learning.

Therefore, faculty will

1. incorporate principles of best practices in teaching and learning. As Chickering and Ehrmann explain, those principles are equally applicable to face-to-face, hybrid, and online instruction.

   a. Good Practice Encourages Contacts Between Student and Faculty

    b. Good Practice Develops Reciprocity and Cooperation Among Students

    c. Good Practice Uses Active Learning Techniques

    d. Good Practice Gives Prompt Feedback

    e. Good Practice Emphasizes Time on Task

    f. Good Practice Communicates High Expectations

    g. Good Practice Respects Diverse Talents and Ways of Learning

2. provide for the needs of students who are place-bound and time-bound.

3. be guided by the principles outlined in the CCCC "Writing Assessment: A Position Statement" for assessment of student work in all learning environments—in face-to-face, in hybrid, and in online situations. Given new genres, assessment may require new criteria: the attributes of a hypertextual essay are likely to vary from those of a print essay; the attributes of a weblog differ from those of a print journal (Yancey). Because digital environments make sharing work especially convenient, we would expect to find considerable human interaction around texts; through such interaction, students learn that humans write to other humans for specific purposes. Good assessment requires human readers.

Administrators with responsibilities for writing programs will

1. assure that all matriculated students have sufficient access to the requisite technology, thus bridging the "digital divide" in the local context. Students who face special economic and cultural hurdles (see Digital Divide Network) as well as those with disabilities will receive the support necessary for them to succeed;

2. assure that students off campus, particularly in distance learning situations, have access to the same library resources available to other students (see American Library Association, "Guidelines for Distance Learning");

3. assure that reward structures for faculty teaching digital writing value such work appropriately. Department, college, and institutional policies and procedures for annual reviews and for promotion and tenure should acknowledge the time and intellectual energy required to teach writing digitally (see CCCC "Promotion and Tenure" and "Tenure and Promotion Cases for Composition Faculty Who Work with Technology"). This work is located within a new field of expertise and should be both supported—with hardware and software—and recognized. Similarly, institutions that expect faculty to write for publication must have policies that value scholarly work focused on writing in digital environments—the scholarship of discovery, application/engagement, integration, and teaching (see Boyer; Glassick, Huber, and Maeroff; Shulman);

4. assure that faculty have ready access to diverse forms of technical and pedagogical professional development before and while they teach in digital environments. Such support should include regular and just-in-time workshops, courses, individual consultations, and Web resources;

5. provide adequate infrastructure for teaching writing in digital environments, including routine access to current hardware; and

6. develop equitable policies for ownership of intellectual property that take effect before online classes commence.

Writing Programs, in concert with their institutions, will

1. assess students' readiness to succeed in learning to write in digital environments. Programs should assess students' access to hardware, software and access tools used in the course, as well as students' previous experience with those tools. In order to enhance learning, programs may also assess students' attitudes about learning in online environments; and

2. facilitate the development of electronic portfolios where such programs are in place or are under consideration. As important, writing programs will work to help develop the infrastructure and the pedagogy to assist students in moving their portfolios from one course to another, one program to another, one institution to another, as well as from educational institutions to the workplace, working to keep learning at the center of the enterprise and to assure that students learn to use the technology, not just consume it. To accomplish this goal, institutions need to work with professional organizations and software manufacturers to develop portfolio models that serve learning.

A CURRENT CHALLENGE: ELECTRONIC RATING

Because all writing is social, all writing should have human readers, regardless of the purpose of the writing. Assessment of writing that is scored by human readers can take time; machine-reading of placement writing gives quick, almost-instantaneous scoring and thus helps provide the kinds of quick assessment that helps facilitate college orientation and registration procedures as well as exit assessments.

The speed of machine-scoring is offset by a number of disadvantages. Writing-to-a-machine violates the essentially social nature of writing: we write to others for social purposes. If a student's first writing-experience at an institution is writing to a machine, for instance, this sends a message: writing at this institution is not valued as human communication—and this in turn reduces the validity of the assessment. Further, since we can not know the criteria by which the computer scores the writing, we cannot know whether particular kinds of bias may have been built into the scoring. And finally, if high schools see themselves as preparing students for college writing, and if college writing becomes to any degree machine-scored, high schools will begin to prepare their students to write for machines.

We understand that machine-scoring programs are under consideration not just for the scoring of placement tests, but for responding to student writing in writing centers and as exit tests. We oppose the use of machine-scored writing in the assessment of writing.

WORKS CITED

American Library Association, "Guidelines for Distance Learning Library Resources." http://www.ala.org/ala/acrl/acrlstandards/guidelinesdistancelearning.htm.

American Library Association, "Information Literacy Competency Standards for Higher Education." http://www.ala.org/ala/acrl/acrlstandards/informationliteracycompetency.htm.

Boyer, Ernest. *Scholarship Reconsidered: Priorities of the Professoriate.* Princeton, NJ: Carnegie Foundation for the Advancement of Teaching, 1990.

CCCC. "Promotion and Tenure Guidelines for Work with Technology." http://www.ncte.org/groups/cccc/positions/107658.htm.

CCCC. "Writing Assessment: A Position Statement." http://www.ncte.org/about/over/positions/category/write/107610.htm.

Chickering, Arthur W., and Stephen C. Ehrmann. "Implementing the Seven Principles: Technology as Lever." *AAHE Bulletin* (October 1996): 3–6. http://www.tltgroup.org/programs/seven.html.

Digital Divide Network. http://digitaldividenetwork.org.

Glassick, Charles, Mary Huber, and Gene Maeroff. *Scholarship Assessed: Evaluation of the Professoriate.* San Francisco: Jossey-Bass, 1997.

Moran, Charles. "The Winds, and the Costs, of Change." *Computers and Composition* 10.2 (April 1993): 33–44.

Shulman, Lee. "From Minsk to Pinsk: Why a Scholarship of Teaching and Learning. *"The Journal of Scholarship of Teaching and Learning* (JoSoTL). 1.1 (2000): 48–53. 22 August 2003 http://www.iusb.edu/~josotl/Vol1No1/shulman.pdf.

Takayoshi, Pamela and Brian Huot, eds., *Teaching Writing with Computers.* Boston: Houghton Mifflin: 2003.

"Tenure and Promotion Cases for Composition Faculty Who Work with Technology." http://www.hu.mtu.edu/~cyselfe/P&TStuff/P&TWeb/Introduction.htm.

"WPA Outcomes Statement for First-Year Composition." http://www.ilstu.edu/~ddhesse/wpa/positions/outcomes.htm.

Yancey, Kathleen Blake. Looking for Coherence in a Postmodern World: Notes toward a New Assessment Design. *Computers and Composition* 21.1 (March 2004): 89–102.

2

Literacy, Technology, and Monopoly Capital

RICHARD OHMANN

My late, lamented colleague Vernon Dibble once told me this rule of thumb: if a title comprises three words or phrases in a series, and their order makes no difference, then the lecture or article will be nonsense. (Vernon used a stronger word than "nonsense," actually.) I hope to make some sense in this essay, although the three terms of my title could as well come in any sequence.[1] In fact, the five sections of the essay might themselves be rearranged. They represent five pieces of what I take to be a Big Picture, so big that to fill it all in would require a fat volume which I do not plan to write. So I ask the courteous reader to bear with my somewhat fragmentary method, here, and with an argument that cannot be decisive, only suggestive.

It may help if I indicate where I am heading. I claim that exhortations about the need for "computer literacy" have much in common with longer-standing debates about literacy itself; that both kinds of discussion usually rest on a serious misconception of technology and its roles in history; and that we can best understand the issues that trouble us by situating them within the evolution of our present economic and social system—a very recent historical process, going back little more than a hundred years. The whole discussion presumes that questions of literacy and technology are inextricable from political questions of domination and equality.

1. HISTORY

The earliest citations for the word "literacy" in the OED come from the 1880s. The word "illiteracy," in the common modern sense, appears only a bit earlier. (Before that, it referred to lack of cultivation, or to ignorance.) The adjectives "literate" and "illiterate" have a much longer history; but again, before the late nineteenth-century they had a global, qualitative meaning—well-read and civilized, or the reverse—rather than indicating a line that divided those who could read and write from those who could not.

From *College English* 47.7 (1985): 675–89.

If this were 1850, we could not talk about literacy in the language we use now, nor with the same concepts. Of course people had been discussing for centuries the ability to read and write, and who should have it. But they did so without a mass noun that isolated that ability from other human practices and that referred to it as a measurable attribute of individuals, groups, or whole societies. That seems odd to me. Why did the concept and the term "literacy" come into play just when they did, toward the end of the last century?

We can get a hint by looking at the discourse within which writers (and doubtless speakers) began to use the words "literacy" and "illiteracy." One of the OED's earliest citations for "literacy" points us to *The New Princeton Review*, Nov., 1888.[2] The word turns up in an article by George R. Stetson, called "The Renaissance of Barbarism," which laments and analyzes the rise in crime—statistically documented—since mid-century. He sees this quite specifically as a class phenomenon. There has been a widening "separation of those who have, from those who have not, a complete control of their appetites and passions"; the latter, he calls "the brutalized class," and to them he attributes almost all "the outrageous, inhuman, and barbarous crimes." That is why, although "Education is more general, our literacy greatly increased," moral degeneracy is also on the rise—with immigrants and Negroes contributing far more than their share (336–7).

A companion article in the same issue, by James P. Munroe, ponders "The Education of the Masses." Munroe, like Stetson, worries about moral degeneration, idleness, and crime: like Stetson, he writes of these dangers in terms of class. There is a "dangerous class," composed mainly of immigrants, which may easily contaminate the class next to it, "the so-called working class." (His theory of class interaction: "Below a certain stratum of the social structure, all populations have a tendency toward degeneration—a tendency enormously increased by contact with classes upon a still lower plane.") Munroe's concern is to provide the right education for these "slowly-plodding millions, without fame, almost without identity. . . ."

In this context he, too, uses one of the new words. He does *not* advocate repeal of compulsory education laws: "Not for one moment would I advocate illiteracy," he writes, even though at the moment, "the evils of mal-education" are "perhaps greater . . . than those of illiteracy. . . ." His solution: take the children of the masses—who are "unfitted or indisposed" to educate their children—from the parents at age two or three, put them in "kindergartens," and train them "to habits of cleanliness, order, neatness, and punctuality." To offset the cost of such education, Munroe advocates the abolition of free high schools, whose "higher education" is wasted upon most of the lower classes (348–52 *passim*). I would note that Stetson also fixes upon education as a cause, and possible cure, for crime: a purely "intellectual" schooling has pushed out "religious and manual training," expanding literacy but not moral character (342–3).

I don't want to make these two articles bear too much weight, but I suggest that we think about the soil in which our main concept took root. The argument over education for poor people had been joined long before the 1880s, of course. What catches my attention is how easily the new idea slid into that discourse. For it was a top-down discourse from the start, and its participants almost invariably took the underlying question to be: how can we keep the lower orders docile? Thus, for instance, Bernard de Mandeville: "Going to School . . . is Idleness, and the longer Boys continue in this easy sort of Life, the more unfit they'll be when grown up for downright Labour. . . ." (180). And, on the other side, Adam Smith: "An instructed and intelligent people . . . are always more decent and orderly than an ignorant and stupid one" (269; see Altick for a useful treatment of this debate). Once the lower orders came to be seen as masses and classes, the term "literacy" offered a handy way to conceptualize an attribute of theirs, which might be manipulated in one direction or the other for the stability of the social order and the prosperity and security of the people who counted.

From these origins, the concept evolved naturally to serve purposes of social diagnosis and reform. One could *measure* literacy scientifically. The first study of illiteracy in the United States was published in 1870 (Leigh),[3] but it was not until World War I, when thirty percent of recruits were unable to take the written intelligence test, that a movement toward systematic literacy testing got underway (Resnick and Resnick 381–82). Literacy *tests* and census questions become evidence to fix the literacy *rate* of a society. After that, of course, we may thrill to periodic literacy *crises*, followed by back-to-basics movements. And international agencies may attack low literacy rates in third world countries with literacy *campaigns* designed to hasten modernization. (Modernization theory held that a literacy rate of forty percent was necessary for "take-off" to occur.)

All of this—the analytic division of people into measurable quantities, the attempt to modify these quantities, the debate among professionals and political leaders over what's good for the poor—all this legacy still inheres in the discourse of literacy, even now, when almost everyone takes it for granted that literacy is a Good Thing, and when it would be hard to find a Mandeville to argue that the poor should be kept illiterate in order to keep them content.

2. MONOPOLY CAPITAL

By coincidence—or maybe not—the term "literacy" came into use roughly at the beginning of the epoch of monopoly capital.[4] A word about the transformation I have in mind: in the mid- and late-nineteenth century, *competitive* capitalism ran its energetic course, building a huge industrial system with unparalleled speed. The familiar movement from farm and shop to factory, from country to city, can be expressed in any number of statistics. For instance, the value of manufactured goods increased seven-fold in the last four decades of the century, far outdistancing the value of farm products. The number of factories quadrupled, and the number of people working in them tripled. Profits were large, and most of them went into the building of more industrial capacity: industrial capital quadrupled just in the last three decades of the century, and the *rate* of capital formation reached the highest point before or since, in the 1890s. Production changed utterly, and businessmen were in command of the nation's future.

But as they raced ahead, making fortunes and transforming the society, they were experiencing painfully the contradictions of the system they had built. Every decade between 1870 and 1900 brought a major depression: cries of overproduction were apparently untamable. Within this volatile *system*, individual businesses led precarious existences: competition was fierce, and none of the legal or illegal attempts to restrain it worked. The rate of profit began to decline. And attempts on the part of businessmen to counter these dangers by reducing wages led to all but open class warfare in 1877, 1885, and the early 1890s. (These conflicts sponsored the discourse of dangerous classes, and what to do about them, to which I referred earlier: just as in England the Hyde Park riots provided an impetus for Arnold's *Culture and Anarchy*.) By concentrating their energies on production and on price competition, businessmen had built an empire, but one they could not govern, either as a class or individually—one whose anarchy led to great instability, killing risk, falling profits, and social rebellion.[5]

What emerged from this extended crisis—and partially resolved it—was the system I am calling monopoly capitalism. This is no time to characterize it in detail; it is, in any case, the ocean in which we now swim, as familiar to all of us as our bodies. I will mention only a few of its main features, as they bear on the themes of this essay. Please keep in mind that every aspect of monopoly capitalism was a response to the crisis of which I have spoken, and an effort to control and rationalize processes that felt—to businessmen as well as to most other people—chaotic and threatening. In fact, one might characterize monopoly capitalism by its powerful drive toward *planning*—its attempt to replace Adam Smith's invisible hand with the visible hand of management.

I take that phrase from Alfred D. Chandler's *The Visible Hand: The Managerial Revolution in American Business*, a classic study of monopoly capitalism's main institutional form, the giant corporation, which emerged in the last two decades of the nineteenth century. Where before, entrepreneurs had built factories and concentrated on getting out the goods, from the 1880s on, the impersonal corporation became dominant. Characteristically, it brought the entire economic process within its compass, from extraction of raw materials through manufacturing through distribution. Far too complex for the supervision of a single businessman (and his family), it brought into existence the modern table of organization, with divisions and subdivisions and layers of hired management. It attempted to coordinate every stage of making and selling, so as to eliminate uncertainty from the process. That project never succeeded entirely, of course, but it did establish an economic order that has proved supple enough through our century.

Before redirecting these large, pear-shaped thoughts toward technology and literacy, I want to mention two ways in which the new corporations carried out this design. First, monopoly capital took control of the labor process, far more precisely and intrusively than had been done before. It developed the approach that came to be known as scientific management, following that magical moment when Frederick Winslow Taylor, overseeing the work of a "Dutchman" named Schmidt, got him to move far more pigs of iron in a day than had previously been thought possible. Taylor analyzed labor into its minutest components, divided the process among various workers, and created the techniques which culminated in Ford's assembly line. He built on three principles: (1) dissociate the labor process from the vested skills and knowledge of workers; (2) separate conception from execution; and (3) reserve understanding for management, and use it to control each step of production. (As Studs Terkel's workers put it, one way and another, "a robot could do my job.") Harry Braverman, from whom I draw this understanding, sums up the role of management thus:

> to render conscious and systematic, the formerly unconscious tendency of capitalist production. It was to ensure that as craft declined, the worker would sink to the level of general and undifferentiated labor power, adaptable to a large range of simple tasks, while as science grew, it would be concentrated in the hands of management (120–21).

The second main movement of monopoly capital was to add control of *sales* to control of production. This was a change of great complexity and unevenness, working through the evolution of department stores, chain stores, mail order houses, the railroads, the telegraph, and the postal system, as well as the new corporate structure and its sales division. The outcome was a universal, national market, increasingly managed by the same corporations that produced the goods. To enter national markets successfully, they quickly developed a number of new practices: uniform packaging (as opposed to the barrel of anonymous pickles or crackers); brand names to help form habits of loyalty among buyers; trademarks to link a *second* sign to the product and enhance its aura; slogans, jingles, and cartoon characters to penetrate every buyer's mind. In short, they came to depend on advertising as a direct channel of instruction from manufacturer to customer. And piggy-back on the new advertising industry, there arose for the first time a national mass culture, whose main product was not the magazine, the newspaper, the radio or TV broadcast, but the *attention of the audience,* sold in blocks to advertisers. I assert that this characteristic feature of modern society and contemporary humanity—mass culture—derives from exactly the same forces that transformed labor. In fact, the two are obverse and reverse, in a social mode that had polarized work and leisure, production and consumption, worker and consumer.

3. TECHNOLOGY

Against this background, I will now marshal some reflections on technology—unsystematic, but I hope suggestive. First, as a kind of loosening-up exercise, I ask you to imagine some instances of the almost unimaginable.

   a. Suppose that writing (a technology, as Walter Ong rightly insists) had been invented by slaves—say, in the Roman Empire—and for purposes of survival, resistance, and rebellion. How might they have devised a writing system to advance those purposes? Might it have been a shifting code, to preserve its secrets from masters? Might there have been a common form that could encode the different languages spoken by slaves? I don't know, but my guess is that writing would not have evolved as it did, had its inventors wanted it as an aid to solidarity and revolt.

b. What about printing? You may recall that when Raphael Hythloday, Thomas More's traveler, showed European books to the Utopians, they quickly reinvented printing and papermaking: their sole purpose was to make available thousands of copies of the Greek classics, so that all who wished might pursue wisdom and the study of nature. Shortly after More wrote, the English adapted printing to a different use, in the *Great Boke of Statutes:* organizing the laws for their more rational administration and enforcement.[6] Would the Utopians, with their purely humanistic and relatively egalitarian aims, have developed the technology of printing in ways different from those that served state power? Certainly the printing technology that served English radicals of the 1790s, with their plethora of small presses, pamphlets, and journals was sharply different from the technology developed for mass circulation magazines, with gigantic rotary presses and photoengraving, to address people as a mass audience rather than as participants in a common discourse. (The 1790s term, "corresponding societies," suggests a very different setting for technology than does our term, "mass communications.")

c. Suppose that wireless communication had evolved, not under the guidance and for the needs of the British Navy, the United Fruit Company, and commercial advertisers, but among women tinkering in their homes, sharing knowledge about domestic production, establishing networks of childcare and concern. Every receiver is in principle a transmitter as well. Might we have had electronic systems that actually merited the name "communication," rather than or in addition to *broadcasting?*

d. And what if the computer . . .? I don't even know the right bizarre question to ask, but I do know that computers are an evolving technology like any other, shaped within particular social relations, and responsive to the needs of those with the power to direct that evolution. I will return to this subject shortly, for a mixture of anxiety and excitement about computers inevitably surrounds any discussion of literacy and technology today.

First, though, let me state the point of the in-some-ways absurd thought experiments I just asked you to conduct. Following Raymond Williams's helpful clarifications (10–14), I have meant to call into question technological determinism (the idea that, e.g., TV somehow got invented, and from that accident many consequences have inexorably followed), and also what Williams calls "symptomatic technology" (the idea that TV was invented on the margins of the social process, and was simply deployed by other forces that dictate the direction of society—so that it is a *symptom* of consumerism, mass culture, passivity, or whatever). This second view is close to what I might call "neutral technology"—the idea that every invention, still thought of as appearing independently, can be put to an infinite number of uses—humane and inhumane, tyrannical and democratic.

I agree with Williams that these views err in abstracting technology from society, sometimes in a way that makes it seem like a miraculous intervention in history. The history of radio and television, as told by Williams, or by Eric Barnouw in *Tube of Plenty*, reveals quite a different process. The technology developed over a century and more, in ways far from accidental. Those with the vision, the needs, the money, and the power gradually made it what they wanted—a mass medium. (I exaggerate only a bit.) Technology, one might say, is itself a social process, saturated with the power relations around it, continually reshaped according to some people's *intentions*. The point is borne out with respect to electric lighting, the telephone, the chemical industry, etc., in David Noble's fine study, *America by Design*. As a recent TV commercial aptly put it: "The future is being driven by technology, and Martin Marietta is masterminding it."

Perhaps I can make the point another way by entering a friendly objection to some characteristic formulations of Walter Ong, one of our most stimulating and learned writers on these matters. In *Interfaces of the Word*, for instance, he writes of "technological devices . . . which enable men to . . . shape, store, retrieve, and communicate knowledge in new ways" (44). Again, "writing and print and the computer enable the mind to constitute within itself . . . new ways of thinking. . . ." (46). And, "the alphabet or print or the computer enters the mind, producing new states of awareness there. . . . the computer actually releases more energy for new kinds of exploratory operations by the human mind itself . . ." (47). My objections are, first, to phrases like "*the* computer," as if it were one, stable device: second, to these phrases used as grammatical agents ("the computer enables the mind . . ."), implying that the technology somehow came before *someone's* intention to enable *some* minds to do *some* things: and third, to phrases like "man," "the mind," and "the human mind," in these contexts, suggesting that technologies interact with people or with "culture" in global, undifferentiated ways, rather than serving as an arena of interaction among classes, races, and other groups of unequal power. Certainly Fr. Ong is no stranger to such ideas, and he may well agree with most of what I am saying. My point is just that technological determinism is a powerful ideology which tends to infiltrate our minds when we look the other way. I think we need to be on guard against it, when thinking about literacy or any other technology, including:

4. COMPUTERS

About which I know remarkably little—so that I may now air my prejudices with only slight interference from the facts.

We are told (in the language of technological determinism) that computers will transform the workplace and the home, not to mention the school, and that in anticipation of this change, we need to provide "computer literacy" for everyone, or at least for the young. Paul A. Strassmann, vice president for "strategic planning" at Xerox's Information Products Group, holds that we are now at the end of the Gutenberg era and "the beginning of the 'electronic display' era." Adults ignorant of computers will soon be as restricted as those who today are unable to read. Software will become the language of the future, and "the dominant intellectual asset" of the human race, so that an "understanding of software ... will be a primary component of literacy in the electronic age" (116, 119). Many of those who worry about education see things the same way. The National Council of Teachers of Mathematics committed itself a few years ago to the proposition that "an essential outcome of contemporary education is computer literacy." The National Science Foundation then funded a study to define computer literacy: its findings appeared in *Mathematics Teacher* (Johnson, et al.).[7] The article lists sixty-four objectives for computer education (including forty "core" objectives), ranging from a grasp of how computers work to familiarity with computer crime. The authors acknowledge that achievement of these objectives would require more than a single course. There is already a lot of pressure on schools to provide such education.

Behind such pressure, of course, is the fear of parents and students that computer literacy will be required for many or most good jobs in the future. People like Strassmann encourage that view. He predicts that almost 30 million people—roughly one-quarter of the workforce—will have "electronic workstations" by 1990, and use this means of communication about one-half the time they are at work (117). I don't know just what Strassmann has in mind, but one may perhaps allay one's anxiety *or* euphoria, in anticipating this revolution, by looking around oneself right now.

For example, in my own department of 23 full-time workers, only one has an electronic workstation, and is required to possess a small degree of computer literacy. She is the junior secretary, and, at $10,000 a year, the worst paid of the 23. (I don't believe that the computer has improved her life or her temperament.) All the workers at my travel agency have electronic workstations, which have considerably routinized (and dehumanized) their work. So does the baggage agent at the airline. So does the teller at my bank. And I wonder if Strassmann's count included the check-out clerks at my supermarket, with their recently installed, computerized scanners, which have reduced the skill required to an almost entirely manual one of the most repetitive kind. Or how about the young people behind the fast-food counter, whose computer keyboards no longer carry numbers and letters, but pictures of food items, so that the work could be done by someone who is both computer-illiterate and just plain illiterate? Predictions that 50 to 75 percent of jobs will be "computer-related" by 1990 sound intimidating, but how many of those jobs will call for even the slightest understanding of computers?[8]

I am suggesting that, seen from the side of production and work, the computer and its software are an intended and developing technology, carrying forward the deskilling and control of labor that goes back to F. W. Taylor and beyond, and that has been a main project of monopoly capital. As Taylor consciously sought to transfer all understanding of production to management and reduce the worker's role to that of a conduit for the transfer of commands into physical energy, engineers are shaping computers now so that those who work at them will be only keyboard operators. As Phil Kraft puts it, "all the skill is embodied in the machines" — in fact, that could be a definition of the term "user-friendly." ("Designing for idiots is the highest expression of the engineering art," in David Noble's words.)[9] In a special irony, engineers are programming some of their *own* skill into obsolescence, along with that of technicians, in the booming field of Computer-Assisted Design/Computer-Assisted Manufacture—"CAD/CAM." And predictably, there begin to be programs for *programming*, aimed at reducing the need for intelligent programmers even as schools and colleges scramble to train them.

Of course there will be more jobs in the computer field itself. But that doesn't amount to much, as against the deskilling that is underway (or indeed, against the number of jobs *eliminated* through computerization). It seems that a decade from now there will be only half a million or so additional jobs in this field, compared to 800,000 new jobs for janitors (Pincus 7). Furthermore, the field is layered into specialties, which will be dead ends for most people in them. Operators seldom become programmers: programmers seldom become systems analysts; analysts seldom become designers or computer scientists (Corson 35). Graduates of MIT will get the challenging jobs: community college grads will be technicians; those who do no more than acquire basic skills and computer literacy in high school will probably find the way to electronic workstations at McDonald's. I see every reason to expect that the computer revolution, like other revolutions from the top down, will indeed expand the minds and the freedom of an elite, meanwhile facilitating the degradation of labor and the stratification of the workforce that have been hallmarks of monopoly capitalism from its onset.[10]

After this brief look at production, an even briefer glance now at consumption, before I skip back to literacy. Microcomputers *will* be in the homes of most people, without question (some forecasts see them penetrating the home market almost as universally as television has done). And to judge from some of my friends who are buffs, hobbyists, and addicts, some people *will* have their horizons widened and their minds challenged. (Though I also forecast even more broken marriages from this cause than have resulted from TV football coverage.) But I remain skeptical about the import of the change. Apparently, eighty percent of home computers are used *exclusively* for games (Douglas Noble 42, another helpfully critical source). I bet many of them will fall into disuse, like other new toys. Yet the manufacturers are selling them hot and heavy, often appealing to the hopes and anxieties of parents in quite unscrupulous ways. Thus, a radio commercial that I often heard last year featured a dad saying to a mom that if they bought a personal computer it could change their daughter's whole life. To Mom's incredulity, Dad explained that their daughter would get an edge on other kids at school that could get her into a prestigious college, and *that* could even affect whom she might *marry!* Mom was convinced. This appeal to hope and anxiety calls to mind strongly the pitch of door-to-door encyclopedia salespeople, thirty years ago.

Seen from *this* side of the market, computers are a commodity, for which a mass market is being created in quite conventional ways. And their other main use in the home, besides recreation, most likely will be to facilitate the marketing of still *more* commodities, as computerized shopping becomes a reality. Thus our "age of technology" looks to me very much like the age of monopoly capital, with new channels of power through which the few try to control both the labor and the leisure of the many.

And the education? That is not my subject here: but a brief aside may be in order, to connect the instructional use of computers to my argument. Only two years ago, Stanley Pogrow lamented that schools were not responding well to the new "information economy." There were only 96,000 microcomputers in the schools, and they were not being used to improve learning for most students. He saw a high likelihood that in this decade, the dissatisfaction of parents and employers will go beyond "political activism" to *abandonment* of public schools, and to "environmental collapse" of a school system unable to adapt, with industry taking over this side of education (92–94). Two other specialists in this area—Tim O'Shea and John Self—are confident that computers will become standard furniture in classrooms, but pose the danger and the choices in this way:

> Computers will cause great changes in education. Already there are examination halls in American universities where rows of nervous students type answers to multiple-choice questions at computer consoles and anxiously await their grade. There are also experimental classrooms where young children happily and confidently command a computer to draw pictures or play music, and articulately explain their latest computer program. Motivated by cost-effectiveness and efficiency, educators may try to use computers to turn classrooms into human battery farms. But there is a possibility that computers will be used to enhance the educational process and equip each learner with an exciting medium for problem-solving and individual tuition. (1)

Most people I've asked agree that O'Shea and Self's first alternative is ascendant at the moment, with computers being used as little more than electronic workbooks and data banks. That the liberatory possibilities explored by O'Shea and Self lag behind may have something to do with the way that Pogrow's forecast is already proving to be wrong. There are now about 500,000 computers in American schools, many of them gifts or nearly so from the manufacturers and from other companies. The motives for such generosity are not hard to imagine. Apparently, business will take care that its needs are met without the "environmental collapse" of public schools, and one cannot expect those needs to include many of the liberatory classrooms mentioned by O'Shea and Self. This is the first area of public education to be so stimulated and directed by business. Most likely, the technology of classroom computers—especially software—will serve purposes I have already described.

Now, none of these developments is foreordained. The technology is malleable; it does have liberatory potential. Especially in education, we have something to say about whether that potential is realized. But its fate is not a technological question: it is a political one.

5. Literacy

I have stated my outlook on these themes in enough ways, now, that you will know whether you find it congenial or not. I will not develop it in detail, with respect to the prospects for literacy in the United States today, but will just reflect on some of its implications.

Plainly, from this perspective it is not helpful to think of literacy as an invariant, individual skill, or as a skill whose numerically measurable distribution across a society (as in "literacy rate") will tell us much of scholarly interest or human relevance. Literacy is an activity of social groups, and a necessary feature of some kinds of social organization. Like every other human activity or product, it embeds social relations within it. And these relations always include *conflict* as well as cooperation. Like language itself, literacy is an exchange between classes, races, and sexes, and so on. Simply recall the struggle over black English, or think on the continuing conflict over the CCCC statement, "Students' Right to Their Own Language," or the battle over generic male pronouns, for times when the political issues have spilled out into the open. But explicit or not, they are always there, in every classroom and in every conversation—just as broadcasting technology is an exchange which has up to now been resolved through control by the dominant classes, and participation by the subordinate classes in the form of Neilson ratings and call-in shows.

That means that we can usefully distinguish between literacy-from-above and literacy-from-below.[11] From the 1790s to roughly the 1830s, popular literacy in England was broad and vigorous (among men, at least), as artisans and the new industrial working class taught one another to read, formed corresponding societies, drafted petitions, put out pamphlets and books, held meetings. *The Rights of Man* sold 1.5 million copies by the time of Paine's death—equivalent to sales of 25 million in the United States today. This happened in a context where, as Donald puts it,

> what we now specify as politics, education, literacy, journalism and recreation were still bound inextricably together. Their division into separate institutions was one effect of the ruling bloc's new techniques of power. (56)

Those techniques won out, both in England and in the United States, as literacy was subsumed within state-run school systems. As we well know, the results here have been such as to provoke both patriotic self-congratulation and repeated literacy "crises" over the last 75 years—the latter meaning a periodic rediscovery by those at the top and their allies that after ten or twelve years of instruction in "English," very many citizens read and write badly.

But why should it be otherwise? Isn't the functional literacy rate just about what you'd except, given how schooling relates to the needs and life chances of the working class? (Shouldn't we expect similar results in computer literacy, once people understand the false promises behind that movement?) Likewise, top-down literacy campaigns in "developing" countries have been almost universally failures. In Cuba, on the other hand, during the single year of 1961, 750,000 illiterate adults learned to read and write, leaving only 250,000 illiterates there, or about four percent of the population. I've suggested that a literacy *rate* is in itself mystifying: but you can sense the *kind* of literacy and the context that supported it by reading some of the letters that "students" wrote to Castro, as their final "exam."

> Dr. Fidel Castro Ruz
>
> Dear Comrade:
>
> I write this to let you know that now I know how to read and write thanks to our Socialist and democratic Revolution. That's why I'm writing to you, so that you can see with your own eyes. I take leave with a firm Revolutionary and democratic salute.
>
> I used to be illiterate
>
> *Patria o Muerte*
>
> Teaching, we shall triumph.
>
> Comrade Fidel Castro:
>
> I am very thankful because I know how to write and read. I would like you to send me the Follow-Up books to improve my knowledge more in the reading and in the writing. To be an educated people is to be free. (Kozol, "A New Look at the Literacy Campaign in Cuba" 358–59)

These peasants had learned to read and write in the context of a revolution, and with the aim of becoming full participants in it, not of passing from third grade into fourth or of meeting a college requirement. Their learning was saturated with politics, an activity of conscious liberation. Of course it did not happen spontaneously, and it *began* at the top in that Castro initiated the campaign. But he spoke for nearly all the people of Cuba when he articulated the goal of full literacy, and those people responded with energy because they saw the revolution as theirs, and literacy as contributing to it.

Cuba at that time had only 35,000 teachers, and they stayed in their classrooms teaching kids. The *brigadistas* who went out into the hills to live and work with peasant families were students, ninety percent of them between ten and nineteen years old, mainly from the cities. Over 100,000 volunteered after Castro's call, in spite of the distances they would travel from home, the crude shacks they would live in, and the strangeness of their task (after just ten days of training). "I knew nothing about reading" (said a woman who was 16 in 1961). "My first motive . . . was not to teach. It was to be part of a great struggle. It was my first chance to take a stand" (Kozol, *Children of the Revolution* 31). They learned to use a primer and a book of readings, which began, not with "See Jane run," but with key political terms: "OEA," Spanish acronym for the Organization of American States; "INRA," the National Institute of Agrarian Reform. From the first day, the project of literacy was for these *campesinos* connected to their needs and their situation in the world. As David Harman (an adult literacy worker in Israel) said to Kozol, the pedagogical theories and classroom techniques don't matter a lot: "None of it works . . . unless it is allied with something else. That 'something else' is what they did in Cuba. It is the promise of a better life for every man and woman in the land" (*Children of the Revolution* 77). The more recent literacy campaign in Nicaragua, which also offered "something else," used similar methods with similar results (Arnove).

Technique is less important than context and purpose in the teaching of literacy: and the *effects* of literacy cannot be isolated from the social relations and processes within which people become literate.

Enough. The age of computer technology will bring us some new tools and methods for teaching literacy. I hope we (or rather, those of us teachers who are on my side!) will manage to shape that technology to democratic forms.

But this age of technology, this age of computers, will change very little in the social relations—the *class* relations—of which literacy is an inextricable part. Monopoly capital will continue to saturate most classrooms, textbooks, student essays, and texts of all sorts. It will continue to require a high degree of literacy among elites, especially the professional-managerial class. It will continue to require a meager literacy or none from subordinate classes. And yet its spokesmen—the Simons and Newmans and Safires and blue ribbon commissions on education—will continue to kvetch at teachers and students, and to demand that all kids act out the morality play of literacy instruction, from which the moral drawn by most will be that in this meritocracy they do not merit much.

But then monopoly capital will *also* continue to generate resistance and rebellion, more at some times than at others. I hope many of us will find ways to take part in that resistance, even in our daily work. Apparently we must learn to fight mindless computer literacy programs, as we have sometimes fought mindless drills in grammar and usage. We should remember that most programmed instruction, in addition to being mindless, builds in imperatives other than ours and other than those of our students. Computerized testing is likely to be undemocratic, not because the computer is, but because it will help realize the impulse toward inequality that is implicit in all standardized testing. We should be critically analyzing the politics of all these tendencies, trying to comprehend them historically, and engaging our students in a discussion of literacy and technology that is both historical and political. It's worth trying to reconstitute literacy as a process of liberation—but also to remember that work for literacy is not in itself intrinsically liberating. The only way to have a democracy is to make one.

NOTES

1. This essay is a revised talk, given at the Wyoming Conference on Freshman and Sophomore English, June, 1984. The theme of the conference was "Literacy in an Age of Technology," and my original title, implying a critique of that conceptualization, was "Literacy in an Age of Monopoly Capital."

2. Actually, the OED says *December.* It had never occurred to me that the OED could be wrong about something.

3. Thanks to my colleague, Gerald Burns, for this reference. Burns also tells me that Horace Mann referred to the "stigma of illiteracy" as early as 1838, in his *Second Annual Report,* but I think this was the older usage of the term.

4. I follow Baran and Sweezy and many other Marxises in the use of this term and in my characterization of our economic system. Other terms — "advanced capitalism," "late capitalism," etc. — imply different theories of history, but point to the same social formation. Terminology aside, almost everyone agrees that a new stage of capitalism emerged around the turn of the century.

5. Here and at the end of this section. I adapt the argument and some phrasing from Ohmann, 1981.

6. See Eisenstein (58–59) for some of the social consequences of this printing innovation. I'm suggesting that social purposes like this had an impact on the technology as well.

7. Thanks to Marilyn Frankenstein and Bob Rosen for pointing me to this and other articles on computers, and to Rosen for helpfully reading a draft of this article.

8. Corson (35) reports these predictions (by the U.S. Labor and Commerce Departments and by corporations like IBM) and discusses this question.

9. Corson (35) is my source for both of these quotations.

10. Pincus (7) reports Bureau of Labor statistics suggesting that however much high tech *gear* may be around, high tech *employment* may be no more important in 1995 than it is today.

11. As does James Donald, whose discussion I found particularly helpful, both for its historical account and for its theoretical position, and I have drawn upon it here, Myron Tuman also offers a good discussion of literacy as cause and effect.

WORKS CITED

Altick, Richard D. *The English Common Reader: A Social History of the Mass Reading Public 1800–1900.* Chicago: U of Chicago P, 1957.

Arnove, Robert F. "The Nicaraguan National Literacy Crusade of 1980." *Comparative Education Review* 25 (1981): 244–60.

Baran, Paul A., and Paul M. Sweezy. *Monopoly Capital: An Essay on the American Economic and Social Order.* New York: Modern Reader Paperbacks, 1966.

Barnouw, Eric. *Tube of Plenty: The Evolution of American Television,* New York: Oxford UP, 1982.

Braverman, Harry. *Labor and Monopoly Capital: The Degradation of Work in the Twentieth Century.* New York: Monthly Review, 1974.

Chandler, Alfred D. *The Visible Hand: The Managerial Revolution in American Business.* Cambridge, MA: Harvard UP, 1977.

Corson, Ross. "Computer Revolution." *The Progressive* Sept. 1982: 32, 34–36.

Donald, James. "Language, Literacy and Schooling." *The State and Popular Culture 1,* a unit in the Open University course on popular culture, Milton Keynes: The Open University, 1982.

Eisenstein, Elizabeth L. "Some Conjectures About the Impact of Printing on Western Society and Thought: A Preliminary Report," *Literacy and Social Development in the West: A Reader.* Ed. Harvey J. Graff. Cambridge, Eng.: Cambridge UP, 1981. 53–68.

Johnson, David C., Ronald E. Anderson, Thomas P. Hansen, and Daniel L. Klassen, "Computer Literacy — What Is It?" *Mathematics Teacher* 73 (1980): 91–96.

Kozol, Jonathan. *Children of the Revolution: A Yankee Teacher in the Cuban Schools.* New York: Delacorte, 1978.

————. "A New Look at the Literacy Campaign in Cuba." *Harvard Educational Review* 48 (1978): 341–77.

Leigh, Edwin. "Illiteracy in the United States." *Annual Report of the Commissioner of Education,* 1870: 467–502.

Mandeville, Bernard de. "Essay on Charity and Charity Schools." *The Fable of the Bees.* 1723. London, 1795.

Munroe, James P. "The Education of the Masses," *The New Princeton Review.* Nov. 1888: 346–54.

Noble, David. *America by Design: Science, Technology, and the Rise of Corporate Capitalism.* New York: Knopf, 1977.

Noble, Douglas. "The Underside of Computer Literacy." *Raritan* 3 (1984): 37–64.

Ohmann, Richard. "Where Did Mass Culture Come From? The Case of Magazines." *Berkshire Review* 16 (1981): 85–101.

Ong, Walter J. *Interfaces of the World: Studies in the Evolution of Consciousness and Culture.* Ithaca: Cornell UP, 1977.

O'Shea, Tim, and John Self. *Learning and Teaching with Computers.* Englewood Cliffs, NJ: Prentice, 1984.

Pincus, Fred. "Students Being Groomed for Jobs That Won't Exist." *The Guardian* 9 May 1984: 7.

Pogrow, Stanley. *Education in the Computer Age: Issues of Policy, Practice, and Reform*. Beverly Hills: Sage, 1983.

Resnick, Daniel P., and Lauren B. Resnick. "The Nature of Literacy: An Historical Exploration." *Harvard Educational Review* 47 (1977): 370–85.

Smith, Adam. *The Wealth of Nations*, 2 vols. London: J. M. Dent and Sons. 1910. Vol. 2.

Stetson, George R. "The Renaissance of Barbarism." *The New Princeton Review*. Nov. 1888: 336–345.

Strassmann, Paul A. "Information Systems and Literacy." *Literacy for Life: The Demand for Reading and Writing*. Ed. Richard W. Bailey and Robin Melanie Fosheim. New York: Modern Language Association, 1983. 115–21.

Tuman, Myron. "Words, Tools, and Technology." *College English* 45 (1983): 769–79.

Williams, Raymond. *Television: Technology and Cultural Form*. New York: Schocken, 1975.

3   The Rhetoric of Technology
and the Electronic Writing Class

GAIL E. HAWISHER AND CYNTHIA L. SELFE

Since the mass production of the first fully-assembled microcomputer in 1977, technological change has influenced not only the ways in which we write but also, for many of us, the ways in which we teach writing.[1] Increasing numbers of writing instructors now depend on computer-supported classrooms and use on-line conferences that take place over computer networks as reaching environments. Writing instructors who hope to function effectively in these new electronic classrooms must assess ways in which the use of computer technology might shape, for better and worse, their strategies for working with students. Along with becoming acquainted with current composition theory instructors, for example, must learn to recognize that the use of technology can exacerbate problems characteristic of American classrooms and must continue to seek ways of using technology that equitably support all students in writing classes. All too frequently, however, writing instructors incorporate computers into their classes without the necessary scrutiny and careful planning that the use of any technology requires.

Such scrutiny will become increasingly important with computers, given the considerable corporate and community investment accompanying this technology as its use expands within our educational system. Unfortunately, as writing instructors, we have not always recognized the natural tendency when using such machines, as cultural artifacts embodying society's values, to perpetuate those values currently dominant within our culture and our educational system. This tendency has become evident as we continue to integrate computers into our efforts at writing instruction. In many English composition classes, computer use simply reinforces those traditional notions of education that permeate our culture at its most basic level: teachers talk, students listen; teachers' contributions are privileged; students respond in predictable, teacher-pleasing ways.

With the new technology, these tendencies are played out in classrooms where students labor at isolated workstations on drill-and-practice grammar software or in word-processing facilities where computers are arranged, rank

---

From *College Composition and Communication* 42.1 (1991): 55–65.

and file, so that teachers can examine each computer screen at a moment's notice to check on what students are writing. What many in our profession have yet to realize is that electronic technology, unless it is considered carefully and used critically, can and will support any one of a number of negative pedagogical approaches that also grow out of our cultural values and our theories of writing.

As editors of *Computers and Composition,* a professional journal devoted to the exploration of computer use in English classes, we read primarily of the laudatory influence of computers in promoting a social construction of knowledge. Scant attention is paid, either in the manuscripts we receive or in the articles we read in other journals, to the harmful ways in which computers can be used even by well-meaning teachers who want to create community and social awareness within their classrooms. If electronic technology is to help us bring about positive changes in writing classes, we must identify and confront the potential problems that computers pose and redirect our efforts, if necessary, to make our classes centers of intellectual openness and exchange. We offer our critical perspectives as members of the composition community who strongly support the use of computers and electronic conferences for writing instruction. Our objections lie not in the use of computer technology and on-line conferences but rather in the uncritical enthusiasm that frequently characterizes the reports of those of us who advocate and support electronic writing classes.

In this paper, we examine the enthusiastic discourse that has accompanied the introduction of computers into writing classes and explore how this language may influence both change and the status quo in electronic classrooms. We do this by looking at published reports of computer use that appear in professional journals, by examining data about computer use collected through questionnaires completed by writing instructors at the 1988 Conference on Computers in Writing and Language Instruction (sponsored by the University of Minnesota at Duluth), and by comparing these analyses with a series of onsite classroom observations. After comparing these accounts of computer use, described through what we call the "rhetoric of technology," and our observations of electronic writing classes, we discuss how electronic technology can intensify those inequitable authority structures common to American education. Finally, we argue that computer technology offers us the chance to transform our writing classes into different kinds of centers of learning if we take a critical perspective and remain sensitive to the social and political dangers that the use of computers may pose.

All too often, those who use computers for composition instruction speak and write of "the effects of technology" in overly positive terms as if computers were good in and of themselves. As editors of a journal devoted to studies in computers and composition, we are most often sent glowing reports that fail to reconcile the differences between a visionary image of technology—what we want computers to do—and our own firsthand observations of how computers are being used in many classrooms around the country. Indeed, this distinctive "rhetoric" of technology seems to characterize more conference presentations, as well as many articles on computer use in other journals. This rhetoric—one of hope, vision, and persuasion—is the primary voice present in most of the work we see coming out of computers-and-composition studies,[2] and it is positive in the sense that it reflects the high expectations of instructors committed to positive educational reform in their writing classes. This same rhetoric, however, may also be dangerous if we want to think critically about technology and its uses.

THE RHETORIC OF TECHNOLOGY AND ELECTRONIC CONFERENCES

For an example of what we call the rhetoric of technology and of how it influences our perceptions and use of technology, we can turn to one specific computer application: electronic bulletin boards and conferences (i.e., conversing over networked computers). Among the claims made about using these electronic conference exchanges in writing classes are the following representative examples:

> Networks create an unusual opportunity to shift away from the traditional writing classroom because they create entirely new pedagogical dynamics. One of the most important is the creation of a written social context, an online discourse community, which presents totally new opportunities for effective instruction in writing. (Batson 32)

> Although I thought I might resent students intruding into my own time after school hours, I find instead that I enjoy our correspondences [over the network]—that I get to know students better and they know me better, too, a benefit that transfers to our classroom. (Kinkead 41)

> All the instructors in the pilot project [using an electronic conference for writing instruction] reported never having seen a group of first-year students, thrown randomly together by the registrar's computer, become as close as their students had. Students set up meetings in the library and in campus computer labs, came early to class and stayed late, made plans together for the next semester, and exchanged addresses. The computer, far from making the class more impersonal, fostered a strikingly close community in one of the nation's largest universities. (Shriner and Rice 476)

> Once people have electronic access, their status, power, and prestige are communicated neither contextually . . . nor dynamically. . . . Thus, charismatic and high status people may have less influence, and group members may participate more equally in computer communication. (Kiesler, Siegel, and McGuire 1125)

> On the network, students can work collaboratively to brainstorm, solve problems, experience writing as real communication with real people. . . . (Thompson 92)

> Those people with powerful ideas will have more influence than those with powerful personalities. . . . The democratization fostered by computer conferencing has other consequences as well. Just as nonverbal cues are missing in conferencing, so too are clues about an individual's status and position. (Spitzer 20)

The above comments represent a number of claims about writing instruction and how it can improve in carefully designed electronic settings: students experience different kinds of intellectual "spaces" in which they can learn differently and sometimes more effectively than in more traditional academic forums; instructors can become better acquainted with their students; many of the status cues marking face-to-face discourse are eliminated, thus allowing for more egalitarian discourse, with greater attention to the text at hand. Collaborative activities increase along with a greater sense of community in computer-supported classes.

Although these remarks reflect claims that we have also made and emphasize pedagogical goals that we too are committed to as specialists in computers and composition, they foreground positive benefits of using networked computers without acknowledging possible negative influences as well. The preceding comments suggest what the use of such networks should encourage, and in the best cases *is* encouraging, but they do not necessarily describe the less desirable outcomes that networks are also capable of supporting. More importantly, we have observed that this highly positive rhetoric directly influences the ways in which teachers perceive and talk about computer use in their classes. When we ask computer-using teachers about word processing in their writing classes (with and without networking) more often than not we again hear echoes of these same optimistic reports.

THE RHETORIC OF TECHNOLOGY AND COMPUTER-SUPPORTED WRITING CLASSES

At the 1988 Conference on Computers in Writing and Language Instruction, we distributed lengthy open-ended questionnaires to writing instructors in an attempt to learn how the environment of a writing class—its social structures, discourse, and activities—might be shaped by the use of computers. Although we cannot claim that the answers regarding teaching and technology are representative of the profession as a whole, when considered with other commentary from publications and presentations we have seen, they seem typical of the rhetoric of computer-using instructors and are similar to the language that we ourselves use when talking of our electronic classrooms.[3]

Specifically, the instructors responding to our survey were asked the question, "Do you prefer teaching writing with traditional methods or with computers? Why?" As might be expected at a computers-and-writing gathering, all the respondents preferred teaching writing with computers and gave the following as their reasons, listed in order of their frequency:

1. Students spend a great deal of time writing.
2. Lots of peer teaching goes on.
3. Class becomes more student-centered than teacher-centered.
4. One-on-one conferences between instructor and students increase.
5. Opportunities for collaboration increase.

6. Students share more with other students and instructor.

7. Communication features provide more direct access to students, allowing teachers to "get to know" students better.

These comments are remarkably similar to the published claims about the use of on-line conferences that we have already examined. Note that these writing teachers, like their colleagues, also concluded that positive changes such as increased student participation and collaboration occurred in classes when they are computer-supported.

These comments illustrate the commitment of the teachers we surveyed to establishing a new kind of cooperative activity in their writing classes, one in which teaching and learning are shared by both instructors and students and through which traditional notions of teaching are altered. These instructors consider themselves not primarily as dispensers of knowledge but rather as collaborators within a group of learners supported by technology. In this sense, we considered the rhetoric of these instructors to be a reflection of their commitment to positive educational change; the survey respondents used the rhetoric of technology to describe a new cooperative electronic classroom shaped by a theory of teaching in which we understand knowledge as socially constructed by both teachers and students rather than as traditionally established. These teachers had come to see and talk about their classrooms in terms of groups of learners-in-progress working with instructors who are also learners (Lunsford and Glenn 186).

As we continued to analyze the open-ended responses to the questionnaires, however, it became clear that when instructors foregrounded the beneficial influences of using computers, they often neglected to mention any negative effects of using the new technology. We recognized, as well, that this perspective was widespread and that the observations the survey teachers made were the same as those we had heard from writing instructors at our own institutions. Moreover, at workshops we have conducted during the past two years, we continue to hear similar, positive reports that correspond to these earlier, more formal analyses.

TEACHING PRACTICES AND THE COMPUTER-SUPPORTED WRITING CLASS

Neither the published claims nor the survey responses, however, helped us to explain the less positive, more problematic uses of computers that we encountered during the past five years as we visited many other electronic writing classes around the country and made informal observations. Notes from a sampling of computer-supported classes we observed more formally in 1988 provided us with information about some of the more problematic social and pedagogical changes in electronic classes.[4] Both the formal and informal observations we made supported neither the teachers' responses in the questionnaires nor the published rhetoric of technology that had been our impetus for this study. In other words, we began to see that the language teachers used when they wrote about using computers sometimes provided incomplete stories that omitted other possible interpretations. Let us explain by using examples from those representative classes we formally observed in stand-alone computer classrooms.

First, however, it is important to note that our observations were limited and that we may well have missed day-to-day classroom dynamics. On other days, in some of the classes, the use of computers may indeed have fostered positive changes in the intellectual climate of the classroom. But we hope that by concentrating on some of the problematic aspects of these electronic classes, we can emphasize that computers do not automatically create ideal learning situations. This is not to say that electronic technology cannot encourage social interaction and cooperative undertakings but rather to stress, in Michel Foucault's words, that a technology cannot "guarantee" any behavior alone "simply by its nature" ("Space" 245); according to Foucault, the "architecture" of such electronic spaces is a highly political act in itself. Like the traditional classroom, the architecture of electronic spaces can put some students at a disadvantage, thwarting rather than encouraging learning.

In each of the ten classes we observed, with a few exceptions, there was a lot of writing going on. In fact, there was so much writing that we wondered sometimes why the time was set aside as class time, rather than as time that students could spend on their writing in a computer lab. We looked for exchanges and talk between instructor and student, and between students—but what we commonly saw were not careful, two-way discussions of the writing problems students were encountering in their papers. Rather the instructors answered a series of one-time queries often having to do with mechanics or coming from the "does-this-sound-right" category. There were exceptions: sometimes an instructor moved from student to student and spent several minutes with each, talking about specific writing problems highlighted on the computer screen. For the most part, though, instructors walked around the room, looking eager, we might add, for someone in the class to need them in some capacity. Although this observation seems to fit with one of the more frequent claims that teachers made for electronic writing classes—students do a lot of writing—the claim does not completely represent the classes we observed. The use of computers in these classes seemed to come between teachers and students, pre-empting valuable exchanges among members of the class, teachers and students alike.

Another kind of computer-supported class we observed reflected traditional practices of writing instruction in American classrooms. The instructor projected a student paper on an overhead projection system, and students critiqued various aspects of the paper. In each instance, classmates seemed to be searching for answers to the instructor's preset questions. And only three or four students were participating in these rather contrived discussions. This sort of class we saw as a variation on George Hillocks's presentational mode. Although the instructors were not lecturing, they had in mind answers that the students were to supply; hence, the discussion, in effect, became the instructor's "presentation." At these times we wondered about the advantage of having computers in the classroom. The use of technology in these classes, far from creating a new forum for learning, simply magnified the power differential between students and the instructor. Ostensibly computers were being used to "share" writing, but the effect of such sharing was to make the class more teacher-centered and teacher-controlled. Hence, describing technology as a mechanism for increasing the sharing of texts or bringing students and teachers together on a more equal basis again told only a part of the story.

Still another typical class we observed was one in which students were meeting in groups, often focusing on something written on the monitor or producing text on the screen. Yet the conversations we overheard only sometimes related to the task at hand—and often, once again, the effort put forth by students seemed to be one aimed at pleasing the instructor rather than one illustrative of active engagement with their classmates or the texts. This type of class seemed to fit with responses from the questionnaires that credited technology with encouraging "lots of peer teaching" or "more opportunities for collaboration." While such claims seemed outwardly to reflect the electronic writing class, they did not take into account the groups that we observed in which neither peer teaching nor collaboration among students occurred.

This realization, then, leads us to believe that it is not enough for teachers to talk about computer use in uncritical terms. We can no longer afford simply, and only, to dwell on the best parts, to tell stories about the best classroom moments, and to feature the more positive findings about computers. Rather, we must begin to identify the ways in which technology can fail us. We need to recognize the high costs of hardware and software, recognize that computers can, and often do, support instruction that is as repressive and lockstep as any that we have seen. We need to be aware of the fact that electronic classrooms can actually be used to dampen creativity, writing, intellectual exchanges, rather than to encourage them. We need to talk about the dangers of instructors who use computers to deliver drill-and-practice exercises to students or of instructors who promote the use of style analyzers to underscore student errors more effectively than they did five years ago with red pens.

How do we proceed then? We do not advocate abandoning the use of technology and relying primarily on script and print for our teaching without the aid of word processing and other computer applications such as communication software; nor do we suggest eliminating our descriptions of the positive learning environments that technology can help us to create. Instead, we must try to use our awareness of the discrepancies we have noted as a basis for constructing a more complete image of how technology can be used positively *and* negatively. We must plan carefully and develop the necessary critical perspectives to help us avoid using computers to advance or promote mediocrity in writing instruction. A balanced and increasingly critical perspective is a starting point: by viewing our classes as sites of both paradox and promise we can construct a mature view of how the use of electronic technology can abet our teaching.

TEACHING PRACTICES AND ELECTRONIC ON-LINE CONFERENCES

As a more specific example of how a critical perspective can help us to identify, and we hope avoid, the dangers that can accompany computer technology in writing classes, we turn again to the use of electronic conferences and bulletin boards. A critical re-examination of these on-line exchanges suggests that while conferences can help teachers create new and engaging forums for learning, they can also serve in ways that might inhibit open exchanges, reduce active learning, and limit the opportunities for honest intellectual engagement.

In the context of Foucault's description of disciplinary institutions as presented in *Discipline and Punish,* we can speculate as to how such conferences might work to the detriment of students and their learning. The electronic spaces created through networking, we learn by reading Foucault, might also be used as disciplinary technologies, serving to control students and their discourse. Of such technologies, Foucault writes:

> [They are] no longer built simply to be seen . . . , or to observe the external space . . . , but to permit an internal, articulated and detailed control—to render visible those who are inside it; in more general terms, an architecture that would operate to transform individuals: to act on those it shelters, to provide a hold on their conduct, to carry the effects of power right to them, to make it possible to know them, to alter them. (172)

This particular theoretical perspective, while it is highly incongruent with existing interpretations of conferences and what goes on in them, may at the same time enrich and problematize those interpretations.

A powerful metaphor to help us critically examine the uses of electronic forums is further elaborated in Foucault's discussion of Bentham's Panopticon, the perfect disciplinary mechanism for the exercise of power.[5] Originally designed as a circular prison building with a guard tower in the middle and the prisoners' cells arranged along the outside, the Panopticon, writes Foucault, is a "mechanism of power reduced to its ideal form" (*Discipline* 205), making it possible for wardens and guards to observe the behavior of inmates without they themselves being observed. Foucault argues that within such a space, because inmates do not know when they are being observed or ignored, prisoners are constantly and unrelentingly self-disciplining. Moreover, because surveillance is "unverifiable," it is all the more effective and oppressive. Although panoptic space differs from electronic bulletin boards and conferences in that students, unlike Bentham's inmates, can converse with one another over networks, those who have conversed over computers will recognize how eavesdropping and watching are made easy through the architecture of an electronic network.

Writing instructors can use networks and electronic bulletin boards as disciplinary mechanisms for observing students' intellectual contributions to written discussions. The institutional requirement of student evaluation contributes to this practice as instructors seek ways "to give students credit" for conference participation. Under certain conditions, without carefully thinking out the theoretical consequences, instructors enter conferences to read and monitor students' conversations without revealing themselves as readers and evaluators. We know after all that electronic conferences are, in some ways, spaces open to public scrutiny, places where individuals with the power of control over technology can observe conversations and participants without being seen and without contributing. When instructors take samples from network discussions into the classroom and use these as positive or negative examples, they are employing electronic conferences to discipline, to shape the conversations and academic discourse of their students.

Such a theoretical perspective reminds us that electronic spaces, like other spaces, are constructed within contextual and political frameworks of cultural values, a point that Shoshana Zuboff makes in her study of computer networking in the corporate environment. As in corporate settings, the architecture of computer networking may encourage "surveillance" of participants. Writing instructors praise on-line communication programs for helping them "get to know" students better, a phrase that survey instructors used in a positive sense but that Fousault includes to describe an architecture of control. Teachers who have easy access to students through a network can also "keep tabs" on student participation, blurring the thin line between "evaluating" contributions students make to electronic conferences and "inspecting" conversations that occur electronically.

Instructors inspecting electronic spaces and networked conversation have power that exceeds our expectations or those of students. In addition, many students who know a teacher is observing their conversation will self-discipline themselves and their prose in ways they consider socially and educationally appropriate. Constructing such spaces so that they can provide room for positive activities—for learning, for the resistant discourse characteristic of students thinking across the grain of convention, for marginalized students' voices—requires a sophisticated understanding of power and its reflection in architectural terms.

CONCLUSION

In this paper, we have suggested that the current professional conversation about computer use in writing classes, as evidenced in published accounts, is incomplete in at least one essential and important way. While containing valuable accounts of electronic classes, this conversation fails to provide us with a critical perspective on the problematic aspects of computer use and thus with a full understanding of how the use of technology can affect the social, political, and educational environments within which we teach. In making this point, we are not arguing against the use of computers in general or, more specifically, against the promising use of electronic conferences and bulletin boards. The central assumption underlying our argument is that writing instructors, by thinking critically and carefully about technology, can succeed in using it to improve the educational spaces we inhabit.

Our view of teaching and of how students learn invariably shapes our behavior in the classroom. The metaphors we build to house our professional knowledge exert powerful influence over us. Few of us, we would argue, construe our role as that of "controller," "gatekeeper," or "guard." We are more likely in the context of the writing class to think of ourselves as "teacher," "writer," and perhaps "expert." If we plan carefully and examine our integration of technology critically, computers have the potential for helping us shift traditional authority structures inherent in American education. We can, if we work at it, become learners within a community of other learners, our students. But the change will not happen automatically in the electronic classroom any more than in a traditional classroom. We have to labor diligently to bring it about.

As teachers we are authority figures. Our culture has imbued us with considerable power within the confines of the classroom: we are the architects of the spaces in which our students learn. Although the use of computer technology may give us greater freedom to construct more effective learning environments, it may also lead us unknowingly to assume positions of power that contradict our notions of good teaching. Unless we remain aware of our electronic writing classes as sites of paradox and promise, transformed by a new writing technology, and unless we plan carefully for intended outcomes, we may unwittingly use computers to maintain rigid authority structures that contribute neither to good teaching nor to good learning.

NOTES

1. We gratefully acknowledge the insightful comments and excellent advice provided by Marilyn Cooper, Michigan Technological University, and Ron Fortune, Illinois State University.

2. Exceptions to this optimistic discourse exist, of course, but these critical voices are less pervasive. For an interesting discussion of how an electronically networked writing class "mutinied" and lost "all sense of decorum about what [was] appropriate to say or write in an English class," see Marshall Kremers's article, "Adams Sherman Hill Meets *ENFI*."

3. The open-ended questionnaires we analyzed were completed by 25 instructors from 10 different states, in addition to Washington, DC. Seventeen of the instructors taught in four-year colleges, four in community colleges, and four in high schools. First-year college writing classes were most frequently given as the course conducted on computers, but instructors also used computers to reach advanced composition, technical writing, business writing, pedagogy courses in composition instruction, and high-school writing courses. Although the majority of the 25 respondents taught in classrooms where stand-alone computers were the rule, several taught in networked environments in which students and instructors shared writing through electronic mail and bulletin boards.

4. We observed ten first-year writing classes taught on computers during the summer and fall of 1988. All instructors had taught composition with computers for at least one year, and several had taught composition for five years or more. Some were teaching assistants, and some were full-time composition instructors.

5. We are grateful to Vicki Byard, Purdue University, for bringing Foucault's treatment of Bentham's Panopticon to our attention at the 1989 CCCC in Seattle. In her insightful paper, "Power Play: The Use and Abuse of Power Relationships in Peer Critiquing," she suggested that even those approaches we use with the most liberating intentions may well prove disciplinary in nature.

WORKS CITED

Batson, Trent. "The ENFI Project: A Networked Classroom Approach to Writing Instruction." *Academic Computing* Feb.-Mar. 1988: 32–33.

Byard, Vicki. "Power Play: The Use and Abuse of Power Relationships in Peer Critiquing." Conference on College Composition and Communication Convention. Seattle, Mar. 1989.

Foucault, Michel. *Discipline and Punish: The Birth of the Prison.* Trans. Alan Sheridan. New York: Vintage, 1979.

———. "Space, Knowledge and Power." *The Foucault Reader.* Ed. Paul Babinow. New York: Pantheon, 1984. 239–56.

Hillocks, George. Jr. *Research on Written Composition.* Urbana: NCTE, 1986.

Kiesler, Sara, Jane Siegel, and Timothy W. McGuire. "Social Psychological Aspects of Computer-Mediated Communication." *American Psychologist* 39 (Oct. 1984): 1123–34.

Kinkead, Joyce. "Wired: Computer Networks in the English Classroom." *English Journal* 77 (Nov. 1988): 39–41.

Kremers, Marshall. "Adams Sherman Hill Meets *ENFI*." *Computers and Composition* 5 (Aug. 1988): 69–77.

Lunsford, Andrea A., and Cheryl Glenn. "Rhetroical Theory and the Teaching of Writing." *On Literacy and Its Teaching: Issues in English Education.* Ed. Gail E. Hawisher and Anna O. Soter. Albany: State U of New York, 1990. 174–89.

Shriner, Delores K., and William C. Rice. "Computer Conferencing and Collaborative Learning: A Discourse Community at Work." *College Composition and Communication* 40 (Dec. 1989): 472–78.

Spitzer, Michael. "Writing Style in Computer Conferences." *IEEE Transactions on Professional Communications* 29 (Jan. 1986): 19–22.

Thompson, Diane P. "Teaching Writing on a Local Area Network." *T.H.E. Journal* 15 (Sept. 1987): 92–97.

Zuboff, Shoshana. *In the Age of the Smart Machine: The Future of Work and Power.* New York: Basic, 1988.

4

Distant Voices: Teaching and Writing in a Culture of Technology

CHRIS M. ANSON

> With the development of the Internet, and . . . networked computers, we are in the middle of the most transforming technological event since the capture of fire.
> —JOHN PERRY BARLOW, "FORUM: WHAT ARE WE DOING ONLINE?" (36)

Augustus 3, Les Agettes, Switzerland. I am sitting on a veranda overlooking the town of Sion some three thousand feet below, watching tiny airplanes take off from the airstrip and disappear over the shimmering ridge of alps to the north. Just below us is another chalet, the home of a Swiss family. At this time of day, they gather at the large wooden table on the slate patio behind their home to have a long, meandering lunch in the French Swiss tradition. Madame is setting the table, opening a bottle of Valais wine, which grandpère ritually pours out for the family and any friends who join them. As they sit to eat, the scene becomes for me a vision of all that is most deeply social in human affairs. They could not survive without this interconnectedness, this entwining of selves, the stories passed around, problems discussed, identities shared and nourished. For weeks, away from phones, TVs, computers, and electronic mail, a dot on the rugged landscape of the southern Alps, I have a profound sense of my own familial belonging, of how the four of us are made one by this closeness of being. Just now Bernard, the little boy who lives on the switchback above, has run down with his dog Sucrette to see if the kids can play. He is here, standing before us, his face smudged with dirt, holding out a toy truck to entice the boys. For now, it is his only way to communicate with them, poised here in all his Bernard-ness, his whole being telling his story.

Not long after writing this journal entry and reflecting on how different my life had become during a summer without access to computers, I came across an issue of *Policy Perspectives*, a periodical issued by the Pew Higher Education Roundtable, which was intriguingly titled "To Dance with Change." When the

---

From *College English* 61.3 (1999): 261–80.

Policy Perspectives began in 1988, the roundtable members believed that "the vitality of education would be defined by its ability to control costs, its capacity to promote learning, and its commitment to access and equity" (1). Less than a decade later, they had shifted their attention to forces beyond academia, realizing that they had been thinking of the institution itself without considering its connection to broader social pressures and movements. They conclude that "among the changes most important to higher education are those external to it" —economic, occupational, and technological. In particular, the electronic superhighway

> may turn out to be the most powerful external challenge facing higher education, and the one the academy is least prepared to understand. It is not that higher education institutions or their faculties have ignored technology. The academy, in fact, is one of the most important supporters and consumers of electronic technology. . . . The problem is that faculty—and hence the institutions they serve—have approached technology more as individual consumers than as collective producers. For the most part the new capacities conferred by electronic means have not enhanced the awareness that teaching might be conceived as something other than one teacher before a classroom of students. While academicians appreciate the leverage that technology has provided in the library and laboratory, they have not considered fully how the same technology might apply to the process of teaching and learning—and they have given almost no thought to how the same technologies in someone else's hands might affect their markets for student-customers. The conclusion that has escaped too many faculty is that this set of technologies is altering the market for even most traditional goods and services, creating not only new products but new markets and, just as importantly, new providers. (3A)

In the context of our beliefs about how students best learn to write, many educators are haunted, like the Pew members, by a sense that bigger things are happening around us as we continue to refine classroom methods and tinker with our teaching styles. Theorists or researchers or just plain teachers, we spend much of our time working within the framework of certain fairly stable educational conditions. These conditions include physical spaces that define the social and interpersonal contexts of teaching: classrooms where we meet large or small groups of students, offices where we can consult with students face-to-face, and tutorial areas such as writing centers. We expect students to come to these places—even penalizing them for not doing so—and also to visit other physical spaces on campus such as libraries, where they carry out work connected with our instruction. The textual landscape of writing instruction also has a long and stable history: students write or type on white paper of a standard size and turn in their work, adhering to various admonitions about the width of their margins and the placement of periphera such as names, dates, and staples. Teachers collect the papers, respond in predictable places (in the margins or in the spaces left at the end) and return the papers at the institutional site. Innovations like portfolios are extensions of the use of this textual space, but the spaces themselves remain the same.

While the Pew Roundtable members may be concerned that faculty are not attentive to the frenzy of innovation in computer technology, it is difficult for them to make the same claim about academic administrations. Searching the horizon for signs of educational and institutional reform, administrators are often the first to introduce new campus-wide initiatives to the professoriate, who react with delight, resistance, apathy, or outrage to various proposals for change. In the climate of burgeoning developments in technology that have far-reaching consequences for teaching and learning, such changes will no doubt challenge existing ideologies of writing instruction, in part because of the assumed stability on which we have based our curricula and pedagogies.

In this essay, I will consider two of the ways in which teaching and responding to student writing are pressured by rapidly developing technologies now being introduced into our institutions. The first—the increasing replacement of face-to-face contact by "virtual" interaction—is the product of multimedia technology, email communication systems, and the recently expanded capabilities of the Word Wide Web. The second, somewhat more institutionally complex development is distance education, in which students hundreds or even thousands of miles apart are connected via interactive television systems. While these technologies offer an endless array of new and exciting possibilities for the improvement of education, they also frequently clash with some of our basic beliefs about the nature of classroom instruction, in all its communal richness and face-to-face complexity. Of even greater urgency is the need to understand the motivation for these developments. More specifically, new technologies introduced with the overriding goal of creating economic efficiencies and generating increased revenues may lead to even greater exploitation in the area of writing instruction, the historically maligned and undernourished servant of the academy. The key to sustaining our pedagogical advances in the teaching of writing, even as we are pulled by the magnetic forces of innovation, will be to take control of these technologies, using them in effective ways and not, in the urge for ever-cheaper instruction, substituting them for those contexts and methods that we hold to be essential for learning to write.

THE ALLURE: TECHNOLOGY AND INSTRUCTIONAL ENHANCEMENT

Until recently, writing instruction has experienced the greatest technological impact from the personal computer, a tool that had an especially powerful effect on the teaching and practice of revision. The integration of the microcomputer into writing curricula seemed a natural outcome of our interests and prevailing ways of teaching: it offered students a screen on which they could manipulate texts, but they could still print out their writing and turn it in on paper.

Throughout the 1980s and 1990s, many writing programs experimented with labs or computerized classrooms where students could write to and with each other on local area networks. (For a historical account of computers in the teaching of writing, see Hawisher, Selfe, Moran, and LeBlanc.) Simultaneously, an array of computer-assisted instructional programs became available, allowing students to work through guided activities (typically alone) on a personal computer. Computer-generated questions could prompt students to invent ideas; style checkers could give them an index of their average sentence length or complexity; and outline programs could help them to map out the structure of their essays as they wrote. But even with all the cut-and-paste functions and floating footnotes that eased the writing process and facilitated revision, the "textuality" of academic essays remained relatively unchanged: students continued to meet in classrooms to work on their assignments, and teachers reacted to and assessed their products in conventional ways, by carrying the papers home and grading them. Personal computers offered students and teachers a new tool to practice the processes of writing, but the outcome still emerged, eventually, on paper.

In the field of composition studies, the development of more reasoned, theoretically informed methods of response to students' writing has been framed by assumptions about the perpetuation of these physical and textual spaces. Recent studies of response analyze marginal comments written on students' papers for various rhetorical or focal patterns (see, e.g., Straub; Straub and Lunsford; Smith). Studies that deliberately attend to the contextual factors that influence teachers' responses continue to do so within the traditional parameters of typed or handwritten papers turned in for (usually handwritten) response or assessment (e.g., Prior). While such work is much needed in the field, it largely ignores the sweep of change in the way that many students now create, store, retrieve, use, and arrange information (including text) in their academic work. Artificial intelligence expert Seymour Papert pictures a scenario in which a mid-nineteenth century surgeon is time-warped into a modern operating theater. Bewildered, the doctor would freeze, surrounded by unrecognizable technology and an utterly transformed profession, unsure of what to do or how to help. But if a mid-nineteenth century schoolteacher were similarly transported into a modern classroom, the teacher would feel quite at home. Recounting Papert's anecdote, Nicholas Negroponte points out that there is "little fundamental difference between the way we teach today and the way we did one hundred and fifty years ago. The use of technology is at almost the same level. In fact, according to a recent survey by the U.S. Department of Education, 84 percent of America's teachers consider only one type of information technology absolutely 'essential' to their work—a photocopier with an adequate paper supply" (220). Yet most statistics show the use of computers, particularly by students in high school and college, increasing at lightning speed. Today, more than one-third of American homes already have a computer, and it is predicted that by 2005 Americans will spend more time on the Internet than watching TV.

That personal computers have done little to disrupt our decades-old habits of working with and responding to students' writing is partly because the channels of electronic media have been separate and discrete. Video has been kept apart from computer text, audio systems, and still pictures, requiring us to use different equipment for each technology (and allowing us to focus on computer text to the exclusion of other media). Whether teachers focus on text to the exclusion of other media is not really the point; as Pamela McCorduck points out, "knowledge of different kinds is best represented in all its complexity for different purposes by different kinds of knowledge representations. Choosing *la représentation juste* (words, images, or anything else) is not at all an obvious thing: in fact, it's magnificently delicate. But we have not had much choice until now because text, whether the best representation for certain purposes or not, has dominated our intellectual lives" (259).

The introduction of hypertext and multimedia refocused attention on the relationship between text and other forms of representation. Experimenting with new technology, teachers of literature dragged laptops and heavy projection equipment into their classrooms and displayed stored multimedia Web sites to students reading *Emma* or *King Lear,* linking such texts to their social and political contexts, revealing connections to pieces of art of the time, playing segments of music that the characters might have heard, or showing brief video clips of famous stage presentations. Early advocates of multimedia in teaching and learning clearly framed its advantages in terms that emphasized the process of absorbing information, however innovatively that information might be structured, and however freely the user might navigate through multiple, hierarchically arranged connections (see, for example, Landow). Multimedia was something *presented* and perhaps *explored,* but it was not "answerable." In all their activity as creators of their own knowledge, students remained relatively passive, now receiving deposits of knowledge from automatic teller machines that supplemented the more direct, human method.

But that situation, as Negroponte has suggested, is rapidly changing, creating potentially profound implications for the delivery and mediation of instruction in schools and colleges. Within a few years, the disparate channels of video, audio, and computerized text and graphics—channels that come to us via airwaves, TV cable, phone cable, CD-ROM and computer disks—will merge into a single set of bits sent back and forth along one electronic highway at lightning speed. Our equipment will selectively manipulate this information to produce various outputs, a process already visible in the rapidly developing multimedia capabilities of the World Wide Web. In turn, users can assemble information and send it back (or out) along the same highway. The effect on both the production and reception of writing may be quite dramatic. Modern newspapers, for example, which are already produced electronically, may largely disappear in their paper form:

> The stories are often shipped in by reporters as e-mail. The pictures are digitized and frequently transmitted by wire as well. And the page layout . . . is done with computer-aided design systems, which prepare the data for transfer to film or direct engraving onto plates. This is to say that the entire conception and construction of the newspaper is digital, from beginning to end, until the very last step, when ink is squeezed onto dead trees. This step is where bits become atoms. . . . Now imagine that

the last step does not happen . . . but that the bits are delivered to you as bits. You may elect to print them at home for all the conveniences of hard copy. . . . Or you may prefer to download them into your laptop, palm-top, or someday into your perfectly flexible, one-hundredth-of-an-inch thick, full-color, massively high resolution, large-format, waterproof display. (Negroponte 56)

In the educational realm, the new capabilities emerging from multimedia technology offer many alternatives for teaching and learning, and for assigning and responding to writing, particularly as "papers" and "written responses" are replaced by electronic data. Imagine, for example, a college student (call her Jennifer) coming into the student union a few years from now. She pulls from her backpack a full-color, multimedia computer "tablet," just half an inch thick, plugs it into a slot on a little vending machine, puts three quarters into the machine, and downloads the current issue of *USA Today*. Over coffee, she reads the paper on the tablet, watching video clips of some events and listening to various sound bites. She finds a story of relevance to a project she is working on and decides to clip and save it in the tablet's memory. Then she deletes the paper.

Jennifer's first class of the day is still remembered as a "lecture course" in history, but the lecture material has been converted into multimedia presentations stored on CD-ROM disks (which the students dutifully buy at the bookstore or download onto massive hard drives from a server, paying with a credit card). Students experience the lectures alone and meet collectively only in recitation sections. Because her recitation begins in an hour and she did not finish the assignment the night before, Jennifer heads for one of the learning labs. There, she navigates through the rest of a multimedia presentation while handwriting some notes on her tablet and saving them into memory. She is impressed with the program, and justifiably: the institution is proud to have an exclusive contract with a world-famous historian (now living overseas) for the multimedia course.

The recitation is held in a room fully equipped for distance learning. Cameras face the students and teacher. Enormous, high-resolution monitors provide a view of two distant classes, each located a hundred miles away on smaller campuses. Jennifer sits at one of seventy-five computer stations. The first half of the class involves a discussion of some of the multimedia course material. The recitation coordinator (a non-tenure-track education specialist) brings the three sites together using artful techniques of questioning and response. After raising a number of issues which appear on a computerized screen from his control computer, the coordinator asks the three classes to discuss the issues. Students pair off electronically, writing to each other; some students at the main site pair with students at the distant sites, selected automatically by the instructor using an electronic seating chart and a program that activates the connections for each pair.

After the recitation, Jennifer remembers that she is supposed to send a revised draft of a paper to her composition instructor. She heads for another lab, where she accesses her electronic student file and finds a multimedia message from her instructor. The instructor's face appears on her screen in a little window, to one side of Jennifer's first draft. As Jennifer clicks on various highlighted passages or words, the instructor's face becomes animated in a video clip describing certain reactions and offering suggestions for revision. After working through the multimedia commentary and revising her draft, Jennifer then sends the revision back electronically to her instructor. Jennifer has never actually met her teacher, who is one of many part-time instructor/tutors hired by the semester to "telecommute" to the institution from their homes.

Because Jennifer is a privileged, upper-middle-class student who has a paid subscription to an online service, her own high-end computer system and modem, and the money to buy whatever software she needs for her studies, she can continue her schoolwork at home. There, she uses her multimedia computer to study for a psychology course offered by a corporation. On the basis of nationally normed assessments, the corporation has shown that its multimedia course achieves educational outcomes equal to or greater than those provided by many well-ranked colleges and universities. Jennifer will be able to transfer the course into her curriculum because the corporation's educational division has been recently accredited. She also knows that, as multimedia courses go, this one is first-rate: the corporation is proud to have an exclusive contract with its teacher-author, a world-famous psychologist. As she checks the courseline via email, she notices that a midterm is coming up. She decides to schedule it for an "off" day, since she will have to go to one of the corporation's nearby satellite centers to take the test at a special computer terminal that scores her answers automatically and sends the results to her via email.

Later that day, Jennifer decides to spend an hour doing some research for her history project. From her home computer, she uses various Internet search programs to find out more about the Civil War battle of Manassas. On her high-resolution, 30-inch monitor (which also doubles as a TV and video player), she reads text, looks at drawings, opens video and audio files, and locates bibliographic material on her topic. She also finds some sites where Civil War aficionados share information and chat about what they know. She sends and receives some messages through the list, then copies various bits of information and multimedia into her computer, hoping to weave them into her report, which itself may include photos, video clips, and audio recordings. Due in less than three weeks, the report must be added (quite simply) to a privately accessed course Web site so that one of the several teaching assistants can retrieve it, grade and comment briefly on it, and send it back to Jennifer with an assessment. Just before she quits her research to watch some rock videos from the massive archives in a subscription server, Jennifer locates a Web site at another college where the students had researched the Civil War. The site includes all twenty-six projects created by the students; one focuses for several electronic pages on the battle at Manassas. Intrigued, Jennifer copies the pages into her computer, intending to look at them carefully the next day and perhaps use parts of them in her own multimedia project.

While this scenario may seem futuristic, much of the technology Jennifer experiences is already here or soon to be. The Knight-Ridder Corporation, for example, has recently developed a prototype of Jennifer's multimedia news "tablet" weighing about two pounds (Leyden). The Web now has the capability to send software to the receiver along with the actual information requested, and this software enhances the user's capacities to work with the information. Programs are currently available that allow teachers to open a student's paper onscreen and scroll through it to a point where a comment might be made to the student. At that point, an icon can be deposited that starts up a voice-recording device. The teacher then talks to the student about the paper. Further marginal or intertextual icons encase further voice comments. Opening the paper on disk at home, the student notices the icons and, activating them, listens to the teacher's response and advice. Computers with tiny videocameras are already enabling a picture-in-picture window that shows the teacher's image talking to the student as if face-to-face. The technology that now provides teleconferencing, when merged with Web-like storage and retrieval devices, will easily facilitate "one-way" tutorials that project audio and video images from a teacher, superimposed over typed text on which marks, corrections, and marginal notes can be recorded "live," like the replay analyses during televised football games.

When demonstrated, such advances may dazzle teachers because we see them as a promise to simplify our lives and streamline our work. New technologies often seem to improve our working conditions and provide better ways to help our students (seasoned teachers, as they stand at the computer-controlled reducing/collating/stapling photocopier, have only to reminisce about the old fluid-and-ink ditto machines to feel these advantages quite tangibly). Teaching, too, seems if not eased, affected in ways that enhance students' experiences. Positive accounts already show that email can help students to form study groups, interact with their teachers, or carry on academic discussions with students at other locations all over the world. In one experiment, students in an all-black freshman composition course at Howard University teamed up with a class of predominantly white students in graphic design at Montana State University to create a 32-page publication, *On the Color Line: Networking to End Racism.* Using digital scanners and email, the students and teachers were able to bring together two classes 1,600 miles apart to critique each other's work, discuss race-related views, and collaboratively produce a pamphlet (Blumenstyk). Many other accounts of networked classrooms suggest increased participation among marginalized groups (see, for example, Selfe, "Technology"; Bump).

Curiously, these and other positive accounts almost always describe adaptations of new technologies as ancillary methods within classrooms where students interact with each other and with their teacher. In a typical computerized grade-school class, for example, a student might use email to ask kids around the world to rank their favorite chocolates as part of a project focusing on *Charlie and the Chocolate Factory*; but then the entire class tallies the results and shares the conclusions (Rector). At the college level, Rich Holeton describes his highly networked electronic writing classroom and its advantages, especially in the area of electronic groups and discussions, yet still sees face-to-face interaction as the "main action" of the course and electronic techniques as "supplementary." Similarly, Tom Creed discusses the many ways he integrates computer technology into his classrooms, but finds it essential to create cooperative learning groups and build in time for students to make stand-up presentations to the class. Electronic innovations, in other words, appear to be carefully controlled, integrated into the existing curriculum in principled ways that do not erode the foundations on which the teacher-experimenters already base their instructional principles. Recognizing the importance of this configuration, some educators much prefer the term "technology-enhanced learning" to other terms that imply a radical shift in the actual delivery of education, such as "technologized instruction."

Because of improvements in educational software and hardware, however, our profession will feel increased pressure to offer technologically enhanced "independent study" courses. Some campuses are already experiencing dramatic differences in students' use of communal spaces with the introduction of dorm-room email. Clifford Stoll, a former Harvard University researcher and author of *Silicon Snake Oil: Second Thoughts on the Information Highway,* claims that by turning college into a "cubicle-directed electronic experience," we are "denying the importance of learning to work closely with other students and professors, and developing social adeptness" (qtd. In Gabriel). Students may be psychodynamically separated from one another even while inhabiting the same campus or dorm building; even more profound effects may be felt when students and faculty use advanced technologies to link up with each other in a course without ever meeting in person. Although many studies and testimonials affirm the ways that Internet chat lines, listservs, email, and other "virtual spaces" can actually increase the social nature of communication, there is no doubt that the physical isolation of each individual from the others creates an entirely different order of interaction.

DISTANCE, INDEPENDENCE, AND THE TRANSFORMATION OF COMMUNITY

The teaching of writing, unlike some other disciplines, is founded on the assumption that students learn well by reading and writing with each other, responding to each other's drafts, negotiating revisions, discussing ideas, sharing perspectives, and finding some level of trust as collaborators in their mutual development. Teaching in such contexts is interpersonal and interactive, necessitating small class size and a positive relationship between the teacher and the students. At the largest universities, such classes taken in the first year are often the only place where students can actually get to know each other, creating and participating in an intimate community of learning. Large lecture courses, driven by the transmission and retrieval of information, place students in a more passive role. In her book on the effect of college entrance examinations on the teaching of English, Mary Trachsel points out that the "factory" model of education, which privileges standardized testing and

the "input" of discrete bits of information, is at odds with our profession's instructional ideals, which align more comfortably with those of theorists like
Paulo Freire:

> The model for [authentic education] is that of a dialogue in which hierar-
> chical divisions are broken down so that teachers become teacher-
> learners, and learners become learner-teachers. Educational values are
> thus determined not by a mandate to perpetuate an established academic
> tradition but by local conditions and by the emerging purposes and real-
> izations of educators and learners in social interaction with one another.
> This socially situated version of education stands in opposition to the
> "banking concept" of traditionally conceived schooling. (12)

For such ideological reasons, the teaching of writing by correspondence
or "independent study" has always lived uneasily within programs that also
teach students in classrooms. Although such instruction can be found at many
institutions, few theorists strongly advocate a pedagogy in which students
write alone, a guide of lessons and assignments at their elbows to provide the
material of their "course," a remote, faceless grader hired by the hour to read
assignments the students send through the mail and mail back responses.
Next to classrooms with rich face-to-face social interaction—fueled by active
learning, busy with small groups, energized by writers reading each other's
work, powered by the forces of revision and response—independent study in
writing appears misguided.

But in the context of our convictions about writing and response, new
technologies now offer educational institutions the chance to expand on the
idea of individualized learning. Online communication with students is an
idea that seems stale by now but is by no means fully exploited; only some
teachers eagerly invite email from students, and only some students end up
using it when invited. Those faculty who value their autonomy and privacy
find that email makes them better able to control when and where students
enter their lives. Departments at many universities are requiring faculty to
use email by giving them computers, hooking them up, offering workshops
on how to use them, and then saying that faculty have no excuse for not voting on such and such an issue or not turning in their book orders on time. The
results have already been felt on many campuses, as meetings give way to
electronic communion, turning some departments into ghost haunts. Very
few universities have developed policies that disallow the use of online office
hours in place of physical presence on campus. As teachers across the country
realize the tutorial potential of electronic media, such media may come to
substitute for direct contact with students. For faculty busy with their own
work, the gains are obvious: consultation by convenience, day or night; freedom from physical space; copyable texts instead of ephemeral talk.

From a more curricular perspective, the concept of independent study is
rapidly changing from its roots in study manuals and the US Postal Service to
a technology-rich potential for students to learn at their own pace, in their
own style, with fingertip access to an entire world of information. Multimedia

computers using text, sound, video, and photos provide opportunities to bring alive old-fashioned text-only materials. But it is not just independent-study programs, usually seen as ancillary to "real" education, that will change: multimedia could transform the very essence of classroom instruction. At many institutions, administrators are realizing that creating a state-of-the-art multimedia course out of, for example, "Introduction to Psychology," which may enroll up to five hundred students, represents a major improvement. The quality of faculty lectures is uneven; they come at a high cost; and they are often delivered in settings not conducive to learning—hot, stuffy lecture halls with poor sound systems and ailing TV monitors hung every few rows. In the converted version, a student can choose when to work through a multimedia presentation in a computer lab, can learn at her own pace, can review fundamental concepts, can download some information for later study, and can even test her developing knowledge as she learns. In such situations, as journalist Peter Leyden writes, "the time-honored role of the teacher almost certainly will change dramatically. No longer will teachers be the fonts of knowledge with all the answers that [students] seek. They can't possibly fill that role in the coming era" (2T).

In itself, multimedia technology has not directly challenged the field of composition. True, many educators are working on integrating into their research-paper units some instruction on citing electronic sources, searching the Web, or using online databases. The prospect of a teacherless and "community-less" course, however, creates much debate in the composition community, where many see computers as poor substitutes for old-fashioned forms of human interaction. In areas involving context-bound thinking, Stanley Aronowitz maintains, "knowledge of the terrain must be obtained more by intuition, memory, and specific knowledge of actors or geography than by mastering logical rules. . . . Whatever its psychological and biological presuppositions, the development of thinking is profoundly shaped and frequently altered by multiple determinations, including choices made by people themselves" (130–31). In the face of the trend to increasing "indirectness" of teaching, Charles Moran argues, "we will need to be more articulate than we have yet been in describing the benefits of face-to-face teaching, or what our British colleagues call 'live tuition'" (208).

New technologies are also giving a strong boost to distance learning. Like the concept of independent study, distance learning too may powerfully affect the way in which we teach and respond to students. In distance learning, students actually participate in the classroom—they are just not there, physically. Beamed in by cable or broadcast, their personae are represented on TV monitors, which, as the idea expands, are becoming larger and gaining in resolution. As classrooms become better equipped, students at several sites will work in virtual classrooms, writing to and for each other at terminals. Teachers can pair students, using small cameras and monitors at their desks, and then regroup the classes at the different sites for larger discussions using the bigger screens.

Institutions are attracted to the concept of distance education for reasons obvious in times of fiscal constraint. Students register for a single course from two or more sites, generating tuition revenue for the parent institution. A course previously taught by several salaried faculty (each on location, hundreds of miles apart) now needs only one main teacher, aided by non-tenure-track staff "facilitator-graders" or teaching assistants hired inexpensively at the different locations. If small satellite sites are created, sometimes in available spaces such as public schools, community centers, or libraries, new revenue sources can be exploited in remote areas. Even after the cost of the interactive television equipment and link-up is calculated, distance education can generate profit for the institution at reduced cost, using its existing faculty resources as "lead teachers." Such an arrangement is especially attractive to institutions used to delivering instruction via the traditional "banking" model of lectures and objectively scorable tests.

Distance learning is also allowing some pairs or groups of institutions to consolidate resources by sharing programs with each other. Imagine that University A realizes that its Swahili language program does not have the resources to compete with the Swahili language program at University B; but it does have a nationally recognized Lakota language program. Unfortunately, the Lakota program is not very cost-effective, in spite of its standing, because its student cohort is so small. Likewise, University B recognizes that its own Lakota language program pales by comparison with University A's, yet it boasts a particularly strong Swahili program similarly suffering from its inability to generate profits for the school. Using sophisticated interactive television and multimedia resources, the two institutions team up to exchange programs, swapping the tuition revenues along with their instructional programs. As technology keeps expanding and becoming refined, collaborations like these will become increasingly popular, even necessary. In part, these ideas save money. In part, they also respond to growing competition from non-academic providers of education, a major threat to our present institutions. By collaborating to deliver the "best" programs possible, the institutions protect themselves against the intrusion of industry, of what the Pew Roundtable calls "high-quality, lower-cost educational programming conjoined with the rising demand for postsecondary credentials that creates the business opportunity for higher education's would-be competitors" (3). But the result is almost certain to be a continued reduction in full-time, tenure-track faculty and an increased reliance on modes of instructional delivery that physically distance students from each other and from their mentors.

Practically speaking, the idea of distance learning seems reasonable in the context of Lakota and Swahili—it saves duplication of effort, it cuts costs, it may lead to increased institutional collaboration, and it offers students at different locations the chance to be taught, in some sense of the word, by high-quality teachers. It is when the prospect of fully interactive, technologically advanced distance learning conflicts with our most principled educational theories that we feel an ideological clash. Long privileged in composition instruction, for example, is the interactive teaching style. Writing teachers arrange and participate in small groups in the classroom, talk with students before and after class, walk with them to other buildings, meet them in offices, and encourage students to respond to each other instead of through the teacher. Distance learning has yet to overcome the virtuality of its space to draw all students into such interpersonal relationships. Teachers often report feeling detached from the students at the distant sites, unable to carry on "extracurricular" conversations with them. The savings promised by distance education come from the elimination of trained professionals who reduce teacher-student ratios and offer meaningful consulation with students, face to face. If distance learning becomes the norm in fields where general education courses are usually delivered in large lectures with little chance for students to learn actively or interact with each other or the teacher, it will not be long before writing programs are encouraged to follow suit.

In exploring the concept of humans in cyberspace, we can find, as Anna Cicognani has found, many of the same conditions as those we experience in physical space: social interaction; logical and formal abstractions; linguistic form; corresponding organizations of time; the possibility for rhetorical action; and so on. But it is, finally, a "hybrid space, a system which is part of another but only refers to itself and its own variables." It belongs to the main system of space, but "claims independence from it at the same time." Cicognani's representation of cyberspace as a hybrid, which still allows communities to form and develop but relies for its existence on the physical space from which it has been created, offers a useful metaphor for the continued exploration of the relationships between education and computer technology, as the latter is carefully put to use in the improvement of the former. Yet to be considered, however, are broader questions about the role of teachers in technology-rich educational settings.

RESPONSE, TECHNOLOGY, AND THE FUTURE OF TEACHING

The quality of faculty interaction with students is a product of our *work*—our training, the material conditions at our institutions, how much support we get for developing our teaching and keeping up on research. While to this point we have been reflecting on the possible effects of new technologies on the quality of students' learning experiences and contexts, we must also consider ways in which colleges and universities, as places of employment, may change.

Teachers of composition continue to argue that writing programs provide an important site for active and interactive learning in higher education. Our national standards have helped to keep classes small; our lobbying continues to call attention to the exploitation of part-time faculty. We argue the need for support services, such as writing centers, tutors, and ESL programs. And, in writing-across-the-curriculum programs, we have helped to integrate the process approach in various disciplines and courses with considerable success. But the current cost-cutting fervor will continue to erode these principles. Massy and Wilger argue, for example, that "most faculty have yet to internalize the full extent of the economic difficulties facing higher education institutions, both public and private. . . . [F]ew faculty take seriously the current fiscal constraints. Most believe that the problems are not as significant as administrators and others warn, or that the conditions are only temporary" (25).

As teachers, our own occupational space is clearly defined. We "belong" to a particular institution, which pays us, and the students get our instruction, consultation, expertise, and time in exchange for their tuition or, in public schooling, the revenues generated by local taxes and other local, state, and federal funds. Yet technology will soon change not only how we work within our institutions but also how "attached" we may be to an institution, particularly if we can work for several institutions at some physical (but not electronic) remove from each other. In an article in the Information Technology Annual Report of *Business Week,* Edward Baig lists by category the percentage of sites that plan additional "telecommuters"—"members of the labor force who have chosen to, or have been told to, work anywhere, anytime—as long as it's not in the office" (59). Higher education is placed at the very top of the heap, with over 90 percent of sites planning to increase telecommuting.

Universities once looked upon computer technology as an expense and a luxury; increasingly it is now seen as an investment that will lead to increased revenues and reduced expenses. The standards of work defined by the Conference on College Composition and Communication have not anticipated a new vision of writing instruction involving low-paid reader-responders, tutorial "assistants" for CD-ROM courses taken "virtually" by independent study, or coordinators at interactive television sites where students from many campuses link to a single site requiring only one "master professor." Robert Heterick, writing for Educom, predicts a major shift in resource allocation across institutions of higher education:

> The infusion of information technology into the teaching and learning domain will create shifts in the skill requirements of faculty from instructional delivery to instructional design . . . with faculty being responsible for course content and information technologists being responsible for applying information technology to the content. These changes will increase the number of students the institutions can service without corresponding increases in the need for student daily-life support facilities. (3)

In the area of composition, part-time telecommuters, supplied with the necessary equipment, could become the primary providers of instruction to many students. At some locations, private industry is already exploring the possibility of supplying writing instruction, using technology, to institutions interested in "outsourcing" this part of their curriculum. In the *Adjunct Advocate,* a newsletter for part-time and temporary writing teachers, instructors have expressed considerable concern about administrators' requests that they teach sections of introductory composition via the Internet (see Lesko; Wertner). The "profound change in work" represented by advanced technology may also further isolate women. Although the computer once promised to level gender discrimination by removing direct identity from online forums, some social critics are now seeing the potential for new inequities in the labor force. In her contribution to Susan Leigh

Star's *The Cultures of Computing,* for example, Randi Markussen takes up the question of "why gender relations seem to change so little through successive waves of technological innovation" (177). Technology promises the "empowerment" of workers, but it also reinforces and more strongly imposes the measurement of work in discrete units. In her analysis of the effects of technology on practicing nurses, Markussen notes that instead of "empowering" employees by making their work more visible or supporting their demands for better staffing and pay, new computer technology actually places greater demands on nurses to account for their work in "categories of work time," decreasing the need for "interpersonal task synchronization" and cooperation with other people. "The transformation of work," Markussen writes, "puts new demands on nurses in terms of relating the formalized electronic depiction of work to caregiving activities, which may still be considered residual and subordinate" (172).

Like nursing, composition has been positively constructed through its preoccupation with the development of the individual and the creation of an engaging, student-focused classroom. Yet composition likewise suffers from higher education's continued attitude that it serves a "residual and subordinate" role, necessary for "remediation." This gross misconception of the value of writing instruction is directly linked to employment practices at hundreds of colleges and universities, where large numbers of "service professionals," a majority of them women, are hired into low-paid non-tenurable positions with poor (or no) benefits. With the potential for the further automation of writing instruction through the use of telecommuting and other technology-supported shifts in instructional delivery, composition may be further subordinated to the interests of powerful subject-oriented disciplines where the conception of expertise creates rather different patterns of hiring and material support.

Our key roles—as those who create opportunities and contexts for students to write and who provide expert, principled response to that writing—must change in the present communications and information revolution. But we cannot let the revolution sweep over us. We need to guide it, resisting its economic allure in cases where it weakens the principles of our teaching. The processes of technology, even when they are introduced to us by administrations more mindful of balancing budgets than enhancing lives, will not threaten us as long as we, as educators, make decisions about the worth of each innovation, about ways to put it to good use, or about reasons why it should be rejected out of hand. More sustained, face-to-face discussion—at conferences and seminars, at faculty development workshops, and in routine departmental and curricular meetings—can give us hope that we can resist changes that undermine what we know about good teaching and sound ways of working. Such discussions are often difficult. They are highly political, painfully economic, and always value-laden and ideological. But as teachers of writing and communication, we have an obvious investment in considering the implications of technology for working, teaching, and learning, even as that technology is emerging.

Because technology is advancing at an unprecedented rate, we must learn to assess the impact of each new medium, method, or piece of software on our students' learning. Most of the time, such assessments will take place locally (for example, as a genetics program decides whether it is more effective for students to work with real drosophila flies or manipulate a virtual drosophila world using an interactive computer program). But we also urgently need broader, institution-wide dialogues about the effect of technology on teaching, particularly between students, faculty, and administrators. Deborah Holdstein has pointed out that as early as 1984 some compositionists were already critiquing the role of computers in writing instruction; "caveats regarding technology . . . have always been an important sub-text in computers and composition studies, the sophistication of self-analysis, one hopes, maturing with the field" (283). Among the issues she proposes for further discussion are those of access, class, race, power, and gender; she questions, for example,

> those who would assert without hesitation that email, the Net, and the Web offer us, finally, a nirvana of ultimate democracy and freedom, suggesting that even visionaries such as Tuman and Lanham beg the question of access, of the types of literacies necessary to even gain access to email, much less to the technology itself. What *other* inevitable hierarchies—in addition to the ones we know and understand . . .—will be formed to order us as we "slouch toward cyberspace"? (283)

While it is impossible to overlook not only that advanced learning technologies are here to stay but that they are in a state of frenzied innovation, Holdstein's admonishments remind us of the power of thoughtful critique and interest punctuated by caution. In addition to the issues she raises, we can profit by engaging in more discussions about the following questions:

1. What will multimedia do to alter the personae of teachers and students as they respond to each other virtually? How do new communication technologies change the relationships between teachers and students? Recent research on small-group interaction in writing classes, for example, shows labyrinthine complexity, as demonstrated in Thomas Newkirk's study of students' conversational roles. What do we really know about the linguistic, psychosocial, and pedagogical effects of online communication when it replaces traditional classroom-based interaction? (See Eldred and Hawisher's fascinating synthesis of research on how electronic networking affects various dimensions of writing practice and instruction.)

2. How might the concept of a classroom community change with the advent of new technologies? What is the future of collaborative learning in a world in which "courseware" may increasingly replace "courses"?

3. What are the consequences of increasing the distance between students and teachers? Is the motivation for distance education financial or pedagogical? Will the benefits of drawing in isolated clients outweigh the disadvantages of electronically "isolating" even those who are nearby?

4. What will be the relationship between "human" forms of response to writing and increasingly sophisticated computerized responses being developed in industry?

5. How will the conditions of our work change as a result of increasing access to students via telecommunications? Who will hire us to read students' writing? Will we work at home? Will educational institutions as physical entities disappear, as Alvin Toffler is predicting, to be replaced by a core of faculty who can be commissioned from all over the world to deliver instruction and response via the electronic highway? What new roles will teachers, as expert responders, play in an increasingly electronic world?

6. What are the implications of telecommuting for the hiring and support of teachers? Could technology reduce the need for the physical presence of instructors, opening the door to more part-time teachers hired at low wages and few benefits?

7. How will writing instruction compete with new, aggressive educational offerings from business and industry? What will be the effects of competing with such offerings for scarce student resources?

If we can engage in thoughtful discussions based on questions such as these, we will be better prepared to make principled decisions about the effect of new technologies on our students' learning and the conditions of our teaching. And we will be more likely, amid the dazzle of innovation, to reject those uses of technology that will lead to bad teaching, poor learning, unfair curricular practices, and unjust employment.

August 21, Les Agettes, Switzerland. I have met the family below. They tell me grandpère has lost some of his memory. He often spends part of the day breaking up stones, clack, clack, clack, behind the chalet. It's not disturbing, they hope. We haven't noticed, I say. We talk almost aimlessly, wandering around topics. Have we met the priest who rents an apartment below the chalet? Can they tell me what the local school is like? We talk about learning, about computers. As if scripted by the ad agency for IBM, they tell me they are interested in the Internet; their friends have computers, and they may get one too, soon. Later, gazing down toward the bustling town of Sion, I wonder how their lives will change. I imagine them ordering a part for their car over the computer without ever catching up on news with Karl, the guy at the garage near the river. Yet I'm also optimistic. They will use email someday soon, and I can get their address from my brother and write them messages in bad French, and they can share them during their long lunches on the patio, where they still gather to eat and laugh, turning my text back into talk.

WORKS CITED

Aronowitz, Stanley. "Looking Out: The Impact of Computers on the Lives of Professionals." Tuman 119–38.

Baig, Edward C. "Welcome to the Officeless Office." *Business Week* (Information Technology Annual Report, International Edition) 26 June 1995: 59–60.

Barlow, John Perry, Sven Birkerts, Kevin Kelly, and Mark Slouka. "Forum: What Are We Doing Online?" *Harper's Magazine* Aug. 1995: 35–46.

Blumenstyk, Goldie. "Networking to End Racism." *Chronicle of Higher Education* 22 Sept. 1995: A35–A39.

Bump, Jerome. "Radical Changes in Class Discussion Using Networked Computers." *Computers and the Humanities* 24 (1990): 49–65.

Cicognani, Anna. "On the Linguistic Nature of Cyberspace and Virtual Communities." <http://www.arch.usyd.edu.au/~anna/papers/even96.htm>

Creed, Tom. "Extending the Classroom Walls Electronically." *New Paradigms for College Teaching.* Ed. William E. Campbell and Karl A. Smith. Edina, MN: Interaction, 1997. 149–84.

Eldred, Janet Carey, and Gail E. Hawisher. "Researching Electronic Networks." *Written Communication* 12.3 (1995): 330–59.

Gabriel, Trip. "As Computers Unite Campuses, Are They Separating Students?" *Minneapolis Star Tribune* 12 Nov. 1996: A5.

Hawisher, Gail E., Cynthia L. Selfe, Charles Moran, and Paul LeBlanc. *Computers and the Teaching of Writing in American Higher Education, 1979–1994: A History.* Norwood, NJ: Ablex, 1996.

Heterick, Robert. "Operating in the 90's." <http://ivory.educom.edu:70/00/educom.info/html>

Holdstein, Deborah. "Power, Genre, and Technology." *College Composition and Communication* 47.2 (1996): 279–84.

Holeton, Rich. "The Semi-Virtual Composition Classroom: A Model for Techn-Amphibians." *Notes in the Margins* Spring 1996: 1, 14–17, 19.

Landow, George. "Hypertext, Metatext, and the Electronic Canon." Tuman 67–94.

Lesko, P. D. "Adjunct Issues in the Media." *The Adjunct Advocate* March/April 1996: 22–27.

Leyden, Peter. "The Changing Workscape." Special Report, Part III. *Minneapolis Star Tribune* 18 June 1995: 2T–6T.

Markussen, Randi. "Constructing Easiness: Historical Perspectives on Work, Computerization, and Women." *The Cultures of Computing.* Ed. Susan Leigh Star. Oxford: Blackwell, 1995. 158–80.

Massy, William F., and Andrea K. Wilger. "Hollowed Collegiality: Implications for Teaching Quality." Paper presented at the Second AAHE Annual Conference on Faculty Roles and Rewards, New Orleans, 29 Jan. 1994.

McCorduck, Pamela. "How We Knew, How We Know, How We Will Know." Tuman 245–59.

Moran, Charles. "Review: English and Emerging Technologies." *College English* 60.2 (1998): 202–9.

Negroponte, Nicholas. *Being Digital.* New York: Knopf, 1995.

Newkirk, Thomas. "The Writing Conference as Performance." *Research in the Teaching of English* 29.2 (1996): 193–215.

Pew Higher Education Roundtable. "To Dance with Change." *Policy Perspectives* 5.3 (1994): 1A–12A.

Prior, Paul. "Contextualizing Writing and Response in a Graduate Seminar." *Written Communication* 8 (1991): 267–310.

———. "Tracing Authoritative and Internally Persuasive Discourses: A Case Study of Response, Revision, and Disciplinary Enculturation." *Research in the Teaching of English* 29 (1995): 288–325.

Rector, Lucinda. "Where Excellence is Electronic." *Teaching and Technology* Summer 1996 10–14. <http://www.time.com/teach>

Selfe, Cynthia. "Literacy, Technology, and the Politics of Education in America." Chair's Address, Conference on College Composition and Communication, Chicago 2 April 1998.

———. "Technology in the English Classroom: Computers Through the Lens of Feminist Theory." *Computers and Community: Teaching Composition in the Twenty-First Century.* Ed. Carolyn Handa. Portsmouth, NH: Boynton/Cook, 1990. 118–39.

Smith, Summer. "The Genre of the End Comment: Conventions in Teacher Responses to Student Writing." *College Composition and Communication* 48.2 (1997): 249–68.

Stoll, Clifford. *Silicon Snake Oil: Second Thoughts on the Information Highway.* New York: Doubleday, 1995.

Straub, Richard. "The Concept of Control in Teacher Response: Defining the Varieties of 'Directive' and 'Facilitative' Commentary." *College Composition and Communication* 47.2 (1996): 223–51.

Straub, Richard, and Ronald F. Lunsford. *Twelve Readers Reading: Responding to College Student Writing.* Cresskill: Hampton, 1995.

Trachsel, Mary. *Institutionalizing Literacy.* Carbondale, IL: Southern Illinois UP, 1992.

Tuman, Myron C., ed. *Literacy Online: The Promise (and Peril) of Reading and Writing with Computers.* Pittsburgh: U of Pittsburgh P, 1992.

Wertner, B. "The Virtual Classroom" (letter to the editor). *The Adjunct Advocate* May/June 1996: 6.

5

The Politics of the Interface: Power and Its Exercise in Electronic Contact Zones

CYNTHIA L. SELFE AND RICHARD J. SELFE JR.

Over a casual lunch at a recent professional conference, Trent Batson, a professor at Gallaudet University, told us a story that made us think about borders and their effects. He had been visiting Mexico on a short day trip in the company of an academic colleague who taught at Mt. Holyoke but had been born in India. On the way back into the United States, these colleagues entered two separate lines at the stations marking the official re-entry point to this country. Border guards, observing the darker skin of the one colleague stopped him—as they did all people who, in Batson's words, "looked vaguely Mexican." The Indian colleague, having lived and worked in this country for a number of years, had made the mistake of thinking that this border, this country, was an open one. He carried only a photocopy of the green card that identified him as a "resident alien," rather than the card itself, as required by United States law.

Given these relatively unexceptional circumstances, what followed seemed significant to us—the Indian-born colleague was detained by officials and eventually fined—even though he carried additional materials identifying him as a professor at Holyoke. Batson was not stopped or questioned. He was also not allowed to accompany his friend, who was taken to an office by the border guards where he was detained for half an hour. Batson was allowed to watch the proceedings through a window, to gaze on the administration and application of American law.

On the surface of the story, no real harm was done: the detainment was short term, the fine minimal, the laws for resident aliens clear. But for us, as citizens of the United States, the telling of this story had a chilling effect. We were ashamed not only about the assumptions that the border guards seem to have made but also of the cultural values that the story revealed. As Midwesterners who live relatively far from the border in question, we were taken aback by the story—by the guards' reactions, by the feelings these reactions suggest about Mexican nationals, and by the treatment that people of color

From *College Composition and Communication* 45.4 (1994): 480–504.

receive every day in our own country. We should not, of course, have been surprised at all. It is at the geopolitical borders of countries that the formations of social power, normally hidden, are laid embarrassingly bare—where power in its rawest form is exercised.

If at the time of this story's original telling we didn't like what it made us think about our country, it was not until we had reflected more closely on the incident that we began to unpack the various ways in which it seemed meaningful and bothersome to us—in general, for our own professional lives as teachers and, in specific, for the more specialized instructional work that we do in computer-supported writing and learning environments. The longer we thought about it, the more we realized that the borders represented in this story, the values built into them and constituted continually by them, were—and are—present in our own classrooms as well. These borders are represented and reproduced in so many commonplace ways, at so many levels, that they frequently remain invisible to us. One place in which such borders remain quite visible, we realized, is in the computers that we, and many other teachers of English, use within classrooms. When re-considering this story in light of our own experiences, we began to see how teachers of English who use computers are often involved in establishing and maintaining borders themselves—whether or not they acknowledge or support such a project—and, thus, in contributing to a larger cultural system of differential power that has resulted in the systematic domination and marginalization of certain groups of students, including among them: women, non-whites, and individuals who speak languages other than English.

This article represents our further thinking about these realizations. In it, we begin the task of describing some of the political and ideological boundary lands associated with computer interfaces that we—and many other teachers of composition—now use in our classrooms. We also talk about the ways in which these borders are at least partly constructed along ideological axes that represent dominant tendencies in our culture, about the ways in which the borders evident in computer interfaces can be mapped as complex political landscapes, about the ways in which the borders can serve to prevent the circulation of individuals for political purposes, and about the ways in which teachers and students can learn to see and alter such borders in productive ways. At the end of the paper, we talk about tactics that teachers can use to enact a radical pedagogy of electronic borders and borderlands.

As a way into this examination, we look at computer interfaces as linguistic contact zones, in Mary Louise Pratt's words, "social spaces where cultures meet, clash, and grapple with each other, often in contexts of highly asymmetrical relations of power, such as colonialism, slavery, or their aftermaths as they are lived out in many parts of the world today" (34). Within this context, we talk about computer interfaces as maps that enact—among other things—the gestures and deeds of colonialism, continuously and with a great deal of success. This is not to claim, of course, that the *only* educational effects computers have is one of re-producing oppression or colonial mentalities. Indeed, from the work of computers and composition specialists, it is clear that computers, like other complex technologies, are articulated in many ways with a range of existing cultural forces and with a variety of projects in our educational system, projects that run the gamut from liberatory to oppressive. However, because recent scholarship on computers has tended to focus in overoptimistic ways on the positive contributions that technology can make to English composition classrooms, our goal in this piece is to sketch the outlines of an alternative vision for teachers, one that might encourage them to adopt a more critical and reflective approach to their use of computers.[1] Such a picture provides a necessary balance, we believe. An overly optimistic vision of technology is not only reductive, and, thus, inaccurate, it is also dangerous in that it renders less visible the negative contributions of technology that may work potently and effectively against critically reflective efforts of good teachers and students. Our goal is to help teachers identify some of the effects of domination and colonialism associated with computer use so that they can establish a new discursive territory within which to understand the relationships between technology and education.

COMPUTERS AS LEARNING ENVIRONMENTS: HISTORY AND MOTIVATION

For the last decade, English composition teachers have been using computers in classrooms to create electronic forums—on local-area networks (LANs) and wide-area networks (WANs)—within which writers and readers can create, exchange, and comment on texts. These spaces, it has been noted, have the potential for supporting student-centered learning and discursive practices that can be different from, and—some claim—more engaging and democratic than those occurring within traditional classroom settings.[2] Such a vision is all the more tantalizing given our recognition that the education taking place in traditional classrooms—despite our best intentions—contributes, in part, to a continuing cultural tendency to marginalize and oppress groups of people due to their race, gender, or ethnic background. Gomez, for example, citing Wheelock and Dorman, compares the 12% dropout rate for white students to the 17% rate for African American students, 18% for Hispanic students, and 29.2% for Native American students (319–20). Giroux notes that "in many urban cities the dropout rate for nonwhite children exceeds 60% (with New York City at 70%)" (111). As teachers of English, we recognize, in other words, that we work in an educational system that instructs students about oppression and inequity, by example, even as we strive to erase such lessons from the official curriculum. This situation and these figures, as June Jordan notes, are all the more dramatic in light of the fact that only 15% of the entrants into the American workforce will be white males by the year 2000 and that some states like California will have 61% non-white students in their populations by the year 2010 (22). And as Mary Louise Gomez further reminds us, most schools can expect 30–40% of their student population to come from a non-English language background by the end of this decade (319).

This continuing pattern has encouraged many teachers of English to turn to—among other things—computer-supported writing environments as places within which they and students can try to enact educational practices that are more democratic and less systematically oppressive: for example, student-centered, on-line discussion groups in which individuals discover their own motivations for using language; on-line conferences in which students' race, gender, age, and sexual preference may not figure in the same ways that they do in more conventional face-to-face settings; collaborative groups in which students learn to negotiate discursive power. To create and maintain these communities—to defend their use and value—we have often used what Hawisher and Selfe have identified as an overly positive "rhetoric of technology" (55) that portrays computer-supported forums— among ourselves, to administrators, to students—as democratic spaces, what Mary Louise Pratt might call "linguistic utopias" (48) within which cues of gender, race, and socioeconomic status are minimized; students speak without interruption; and marginalized individuals can acquire more central voices. And if this rhetoric is helpful in that it describes what we *want* to happen—and sometimes, to some extent, *does* happen—in our classrooms, it is also dangerous. Through its use, we legitimate the status quo of computer use and, as Hawisher and Selfe note, "de-legitimate critique" (53)—thus allowing ourselves to think erroneously that the use of computers and networks provides discursive landscapes that are, in Mary Louise Pratt's words, "the same for all players" (38).

The rhetoric of technology obscures the fact that, within our current educational system—even though computers are associated with the potential for great reform—they are not necessarily serving democratic ends. Computer interfaces, for example, are *also* sites within which the ideological and material legacies of racism, sexism, and colonialism are continuously written and re-written along with more positive cultural legacies.[3] Perhaps the most salient evidence for this claim lies in the different uses to which computers are put in minority classrooms and majority classrooms. Sheingold, Martin, and Endreweit, for example, note that "in schools with large minority enrollments computers are used primarily to provide basic skills instruction delivered by drill-and-practice software . . . In contrast, computer use in majority schools is characterized by its emphasis on the use of computers as tools to develop higher order literary and cognitive skills as objects of study (e.g., instruction focused on computer literacy and programming" (89). Charles Piller, in a recent article in *MacWorld,* notes that minority populations and lower socioeconomic populations are America's growing "technological underclass" (218) and, thus, that these students are the least likely to gain skills during their public schooling experience that will serve them well in a world increasingly dependent on technology.

The recognition of this situation, for many computer-using teachers of English, is not possible without a great deal of pain. It demands our realization that—while we, as individual English teachers, may very strongly support democratic reform, broad involvement, or egalitarian education, and while our teaching and computer use may be aimed toward these ends—we are also simultaneously participating in a cultural project that, at some level and to some degree, seems to support racist, sexist, and colonial attitudes. This is true even as our profession broadly supports more productive and progressive forms of educational action. If we hope to get English composition teachers to recognize how our use of computers achieves both great good and great evil—often at the same time, as Joseph Weizenbaum points out— we have to educate them to be technology *critics* as well as technology users. This recognition requires that composition teachers acquire the intellectual habits of reflecting on and discussing the cultural and ideological characteristics of technology—and the implications of these characteristics—in educational contexts. With such a realization, we maintain, English composition teachers can begin to exert an increasingly active influence on the cultural project of technology design.

MAPPING THE INTERFACE OF COMPUTERS AS EDUCATIONAL SPACE

The project that we have described is not a simple one, nor is it one that we can describe fully here. We can, however, provide an extended example of the agenda we want to pursue by focusing in particular ways on computer *interfaces*, those primary representations of computer systems or programs that show up on screens used by both teachers and students. Within the virtual space represented by these interfaces, and elsewhere within computer systems, the values of our culture—ideological, political, economic, educational—are mapped both implicitly and explicitly, constituting a complex set of material relations among culture, technology, and technology users. In effect, interfaces are cultural maps of computer systems, and as Denis Wood points out, such maps are never ideologically innocent or inert. Like other maps that Wood mentions—the medieval *mappaemundi* that offer a Christian-centered vision of the 13th century world or the Mercater projection that provides a Euro-centric view of the Earth's geography in the 20th century—the maps of computer interfaces order the virtual world according to a certain set of historical and social values that make up our culture. The users of maps, as a result, read cultural information just as surely as they read geographical information—through a coherent set of stereotyped images that the creators of maps offer as "direct testimony" (Berger 69) of the world, of social formations and socially organized tendencies, of a culture's historical development (Wood 145). The enhanced power of maps, growing out of their long association with the projects of science and geography, resides in the fact that they purport to represent fact—the world, a particular space—as it is in reality, while they naturalize the political and ideological interests of their authors (Wood 2).

Given this background, we can better understand why it is important to identify the cultural information passed along in the maps of computer interfaces—especially because this information can serve to reproduce, on numerous discursive levels and through a complex set of conservative forces, the asymmetrical power relations that, in part, have shaped the educational system we labor within and that students are exposed to. What is mapped in computer interfaces — just as what is mapped in other social and cultural artifacts such as our educational system — is both "ownership" and opportunity (Wood 21). In this sense, we maintain, the "ferocious" (Wood 25) effectiveness of computer interfaces as maps is established as much by what they do *not* show about American culture as by what they *do*. Primary computer interfaces do not, for example, provide direct evidence of different cultures and races that make up the American social complex, nor do they show much evidence of different linguistic groups or groups of differing economic status. It is only when we recognize these gestures of omission for what they are, as interested versions of reality, that we can begin to examine the naturalizing functions of computer interfaces and, as educators, break the frame to extend the discursive horizon (Laclau and Mouffe 19) of the landscape we have created and that, in turn, creates us and the students in our classes.

Once we recognize these functions, we also begin to understand the ideological gesture of the interface's map as a "flawed, partial, incomplete" (Wood 26) and interested vision of reality, at least partly constructed from the perspective of, and for the benefit of, dominant forces in our culture. In particular — given that these technologies have grown out of the predominately male, white, middle-class, professional cultures associated with the military-industrial complex — the virtual reality of computer interfaces represents, in part and to a visible degree, a tendency to value monoculturalism, capitalism, and phallologic thinking, and does so, more importantly, to the exclusion of other perspectives. Grounded in these values, computer interfaces, we maintain, enact small but continuous gestures of domination and colonialism. To examine these claims, we have to turn directly to examples that illustrate the ways in which such maps "name, marginalize, and define difference as the devalued Other" (Giroux 33) — not in a totalizing fashion but through many subtly potent gestures enacted continuously and naturalized as parts of technological systems. Such examples are not difficult to come by if we examine the borderland of the interface from the perspective of non-dominant groups in our culture.

Interfaces as Maps of Capitalism and Class Privilege

In general, computer interfaces present reality as framed in the perspective of modern capitalism, thus, orienting technology along an existing axis of class privilege. The graphically intuitive Macintosh interface provides a good example of this orientation. That interface, and the software applications commonly represented within it, map the virtual world as a *desktop* — constructing virtual reality, by association, in terms of corporate culture and the values of professionalism. This reality is constituted by and for white middle- and upper-class users to replicate a world that they know and feel comfortable within. The objects represented within this world are those familiar primarily to the white-collar inhabitants of that corporate culture: manila folders, files, documents, telephones, fax machines, clocks and watches, and desk calendars. We can grasp the power of this ideological orientation—and thus sense its implications—by shifting our perspective to what it does *not* include, what it leaves unstated. The interface does not, for example, represent the world in terms of a kitchen counter top, a mechanic's workbench, or a fast-food restaurant—each of which would constitute the virtual world in different terms according to the values and orientations of, respectively, women in the home, skilled laborers, or the rapidly increasing numbers of employees in the fast-food industry.

Built into computer interfaces are also a series of semiotic messages that support this alignment along the axes of class, race, and gender. The white pointer hand, for example, ubiquitous in the Macintosh primary interface, is one such gesture, as are the menu items of the Appleshare server tray and hand, calculator, the moving van (for the font DA mover), the suitcase, and the desk calendar. Other images—those included in the HyperCard interface commercial clip art collections, and in the Apple systems documentation—include a preponderance of white people and icons of middle- and upper-class white culture and professional, office-oriented computer use. These images signal—to users of color, to users who come from a non-English language background, to users from low socio-economic backgrounds—that entering the virtual worlds of interfaces also means, at least in part and at some level, entering a world constituted around the lives and values of white, male, middle- and upper-class professionals. Users of color, users from a non-English language background, users from a low socio-economic class who view this map of reality, submit—if only partially and momentarily—to an interested version of reality represented in terms of both language and image.

When users recognize the corporate orientation of the interface, they also begin to understand more about how computers as a technology are ideologically associated with capitalism. Computer interfaces, for example, can serve to reproduce a value on the commodification of information. On the Macintosh desktop, for instance, the raw material of information is gathered in databases and files, stored in folders and on hard drives, accumulated within artificially expanded memory spaces, and finally manipulated and written in the form of documents that acquire their own authority and value within a capitalist economy.

All of these information products—following the prevailing model of text-as-commodity established in what Jay D. Bolter calls the "late age of print" (1)—are "owned" by an author who can protect work with a "password" and accord "privileges" to readers according the relationship and involvement she would like them to have with a text. This commodification of information is also played out at additional levels within computer interfaces. Through interfaces, for example, students now learn to access and depend on sources like BITNET or Internet, library systems in other states, and information bases around the world for the information they need. These electronic spaces—which are subject to increasing legislation and control—are at the same time becoming more expensive and more rigidly aligned along the related axes of class privilege and capitalism. The refinement and use of packet charging technologies, for example, and the increasing exploitation of large-scale commercial networks that appeal to the public will continue to support such an alignment. Recent figures published in a recent *New York Times* article indicate that commercial public networks such as Prodigy and Compuserve charge approximately $50 for starter kits on their systems, between $8 and $15 for basic use each month, and some additional per-message or per-minute charges as well. The capital stake that commercial groups have in promoting these electronic systems to citizens is not a small one: Information-as-commodity is big business—approximately 3.4 million people subscribe to commercial networks at the rates we have mentioned (Grimes 13–15).

Interfaces as Maps of Discursive Privilege

The orientation of the interface along the axis of class privilege is made increasingly systematic by the application of related discursive constraints. Primary interfaces, for example, also generally serve to reproduce the privileged position of standard English as the language of choice or default, and, in this way, contribute to the tendency to ignore, or even erase, the cultures of non-English language background speakers in this country. Although the global expansion of technology is exerting an increasingly strong influence on the computer industry—and thus interfaces in other languages are becoming more common—these influences are resisted at many levels and in many ways, and this resistance is represented vividly in the maps of computer interfaces. A more particular example of this orientation exists in most word-processing programs—those tools we present students with so that they can "express" themselves in the language of our choosing. Many such programs commercially distributed in this country present their menued items only in English, despite the fact that, as Mary Louise Gomez reminds us, most schools can expect 30–40% of their student population to come from a non-English language background by the end of the decade (319). Those word-processing programs that *do* present an alternative-language interface market their non-English language background products separately, adding additional cost; or market them only in other countries, making them difficult to obtain especially with education discounts; or retain the privileged position of English simply by default. WordPerfect 5.1 for the IBM, for instance, which presents English menus as the default interface, does allow users operate in other languages—among them three versions of English (Australian, Great Britain, and United States) and only one of Spanish, in addition to Catalan (*WordPerfect for DOS* 325). To write or edit in another language, users must go to a "Layout" pull-down menu and then select—with some irony, we hope—the item labeled "Other" (324). As the manual for WordPerfect notes, moreover, the thesaurus and spell checkers accompanying the regular WordPerfect package come only in English. One can order versions of this thesaurus and spell checker in other languages, but they come at an additional cost. The telephone number which one uses to place such an order, the *Reference* manual notes, further, is "not toll-free" (326).

This decision to use English as a default language—articulated, as we have pointed out, with the custom of identifying non-English language background speakers as a marginalized "Other" and the socio-economic forces that limit access to software in other languages—clearly has important implications for our educational system, for teachers and for students. In schools, this default position means that students from other races and cultures who hope to use the computer as a tool for empowerment must—at some level—submit to the colonial power of language and adopt English as their primary means of communication, even if this submission is only partial or momentary. Few schools and few teachers can find a realistic perspective from which to resist the tendential forces associated with this default to English as a standard. Certainly, those schools that may most need fully functional bi- and trilingual interfaces are the *least* likely to have the monies available to purchase additional packages. This characteristic focus of interfaces on Standard English is further supported and exacerbated by the fact that style and grammar packages are generally based on an overly narrow—and erroneous—vision of "correct" language use and spelling checkers that exert a continuously normative influence (LeBlanc) within the setting of colonial discourse. Both kinds of software can serve to de-value linguistic diversity and inscribe nonstandard language users as Other within the interface, the classroom, the educational system, and the culture.

We got an idea of just how powerful and evenly dispersed this cultural inscription is—how systemically it operates when we attended the 1992 convention of the National Council of Teachers of English. At that gathering, a software company demonstrated a word-processing package designed to present a bilingual (Spanish/English) interface. The package was available in a low-cost, school-edition package for approximately $300 and in a site-license, networkable version for approximately $1500. As the package's literature pointed out, users could employ a pull-down menu system to select the Spanish mode—where all menus, dialog boxes, help, and messages appear in Spanish. When we tested the software in the Spanish mode, however, we found the keystroke options did not change correspondingly to the same language. In fact those options, which depend, for the most part on mnemonic aids—apple-D for "delete"—remain keyed to the English words even when the corresponding Spanish menu items—"eliminar," for example—start with different letters. A student using this program, then, should she want to use the keystroke options, might be able to write in Spanish, but would have to think at some level in English.

This value on English as the privileged language of computer interfaces—and the effects of the design decisions that support this system—are certainly not limited to the United States. For example, a recent international gathering on computer-based instruction (Teleteaching '93) sponsored by the International Federation for Information Processing and focused on the use of computers for global distance education projects, required all sessions and discussions to be conducted in English—even though the conference was held in Norway and many representatives from non-English speaking countries were in attendance. This decision, presented to participants as a necessary convenience, recognized the extent to which Americans have influenced computer design, computer use, and computer applications over the past decade, and the fact that English has been, during this same period, the world language of science and technology. The language of computers has thus become English by default: The majority of standard interfaces are English, much of the documentation for these interfaces and the machines they operate on is in English, and the systems that currently support global computing networks rely on English as a standard exchange language. At the conference in question, several presenters from non-English speaking countries, for instance, noted that the educational conversations and projects they set up for French, German, Russian, or Slovakian students were conducted in English because these exchanges relied on the ability to link computers and systems through a common exchange standard called American Standard Code for Information Interchange (ASCII) that does not adequately support languages other than English. ASCII—because it was originally based on a 7-bit code—can handle, as Charles Petzold points out, only "26 lowercase letters, 26 uppercase letters, 10 numbers, and 33 symbols and punctuation marks" unless it is extended by 8-bit byte computer systems that allow it to handle 128 additional characters. Even with these additional characters, ASCII's alphabetic limitations preclude the full and adequate representation of Greek, Hebrew, Cyrillic, and Han characters (374–75).

In a recent article about Unicode—a proposed international replacement for ASCII—Petzold explores some of the implications of relying solely on ASCII:

> There's a big problem with ASCII and that problem is indicated by the first word of the acronym. ASCII is truly an *American* standard, but there's a whole wide world outside our borders where ASCII is simply inadequate. It isn't even good enough for countries that share our language, for where is the British pound sign in ASCII? . . . ASCII . . . is not only inadequate for the written languages of much of the world, but also for many people who live right in my own neighborhood. . . . We simply can't be so parochial as to foster a system as exclusive and limiting as ASCII. The personal computing revolution is quickly encompassing much of the world, and it's totally absurd that the dominant standard is based solely on English as it is spoken in the U.S. (375)

Although this limitation may not represent a large problem to academic professionals, such a limited system makes global computer communications unnecessarily difficult for student learners who speak languages other than English. What remains most interesting about this situation—especially given that teachers, scholars, and computer designers generally acknowledge the limitations of ASCII—is that the change to a more broadly accommodating system has been so slow, even though the technological means for representing other alphabetic systems (e.g., the memory, the programming mechanics, the computer hardware) have been available for some time now. To change ASCII, however, is to work against a complex set of tendential forces encouraging inertia—because changing ASCII means changing existing software, hardware, documentation, and programming approaches. It also requires that individuals and groups in the computer industry abandon English as the *natural* language of, the natural standard for, computer technology. Such changes do not happen easily or quickly.

Interfaces as Maps of Rationalism and Logocentric Privilege

If the map of the interface is oriented simultaneously along the axes of class, race, and cultural privilege, it is also aligned with the values of rationality, hierarchy, and logocentrism characteristic of Western patriarchal cultures. IBM's DOS environment, for example, is fundamentally dependent on an hierarchical representation of knowledge, a perspective characteristically—while not exclusively—associated with patriarchal cultures and rationalistic traditions of making meaning. This way of representing knowledge within computer environments, although not essentially limiting or exclusive by itself, becomes so when linked to a positivist value on rationality and logic as *foundational* ways of knowing that function to exclude other ways of knowing, such as association, intuition, or bricolage. This validation of positivism, rationality, hierarchy, and logic as the only authorized contexts for "knowing" and representing knowledge continues to inform—and limit—many formal aspects of computer programming and technology design. As Winograd and Flores note, the current rationalistic framework that informs the design of computers and their interfaces is "based on a misinterpretation of the nature of human cognition and language," one that provides "only impoverished possibilities for modeling and enlarging the scope of human understanding" (78). As a result, these authors continue, "We are now witnessing a major breakdown in the design of computer technology—a breakdown that reveals the rationalistically oriented background of discourse within which our current understanding [of technology] is embedded" (78–79). A similar case has been made by Ted Nelson, a pioneer in the design of hypertext interfaces, who has referred to the conceptual structure of hierarchical file systems as an "enormous barrier" to creative thinking. Nelson has characterized the effects of such systems as both "oppressive and devastating." The "tyranny" of hierarchical systems, Nelson contends, "imposes intricate, fixed pathways that we must commit to memory" and "forbid acting on inspiration." He adds, further, that such systems cause programmers to "oversimplify" their representation of data and the uses of such data within computer interfaces (83–84).

As Sherry Turkle and Seymour Papert point out, this conventional validation of—and dependence on—hierarchy, rationality, and logic is all the more potent because it is operative at all levels of computer interface design and programming. Computer programmers are educated to solve problems using hierarchical approaches to problem solving and to represent relationships in programs abstractly, within a strict syntactical system of linear prepositional logic. This "formal, propositional" way of constructing knowledge (129) has come to constitute a "canonical style" (133) for programmers who are solving problems and representing information, a privileged way of relating ideas one to the other that has become "literally synonymous with knowledge" (129) in computer science. So synonymous has this way of thinking become with knowledge, in fact, that computer scientists have come to see propositional thinking not as *one* way of knowing, but as the *only* way of knowing. It has become equated with "formal" and "logical" thinking, and given "a privileged status" (133) within computer science.

Recently, however, increasing numbers of computer specialists have begun to identify the limitations inherent in relying on hierarchical approaches and data representations — in dealing with learners who have varying levels and kinds of visualization skills, in training programmers to apply epistemologically diverse approaches to programming problems, and in representing non-hierarchically organized information structures like *wicked* or *fuzzy* problems (complex problems with no definitive formulations or solutions), and in coping with natural language input.[4] Several programming paradigms have been suggested as alternatives and supplements to hierarchical representations of knowledge, such as object-oriented programming systems (OOPS) and iconic interfaces that represent knowledge, concepts, or programs through small pictures, called *objects* or *icons*. Such methods of programming and designing computer interfaces, some computer designers contend, can support alternative approaches to constructing meaning — though "bricolage," for example, a term that Turkle and Papert (135) use in reference to the work of Claude Levi-Strauss. Bricolage, as Turkle and Papert employ the term, refers to the construction of meaning through the arrangement and re-arrangement of concrete, well-known materials, often in an intuitive rather than logical manner. Bricoleurs get to know a subject by interacting with it physically, by manipulating materials, or symbols, or icons in rich associative patterns, by arranging and re-arranging them constantly until they fit together in a satisfying or meaningful way. Bricoleurs reason "from within" (144) to come to an understanding of a problem through a direct "physical path of access" (145) rather than reasoning with the help of a traditionally validated pattern of logical representation that depends on objective distancing.

Turkle and Papert contend that allowing for bricolage as a way of representing knowledge will encourage an "epistemological pluralism" within the "computer culture" (153) that might especially benefit individuals who feel "more comfortable with a relational, interactive, active, and connected approach to objects" (150). In particular, Turkle and Papert link bricolage with approaches to problem solving that are culturally determined and articulated with gender. Drawing on the work of Carol Gilligan, Evelyn Fox Keller, and Sandra Harding and Merrill Hintikka, these authors suggest that women, in particular, might benefit from conceptual frameworks that would support bricolage, but not exclude rationalistically determined approaches such as hierarchical representations. It could be a mistake, however, as Judith Butler points out, to see gender itself in such fixed terms or to consider the continual construction and re-constructions of gender identities as other than complex, momentary, and contradictory "intersections" (3) of cultural and political forces.

As played out realistically within the maps of computer interfaces, Turkle and Papert's suggestions prove more problematic. The Macintosh interface, for instance, allows for both bricolage and rationalistically determined representations of hierarchy—that is documents, folders, and text nodes can be arranged and re-arranged according to alternative relations of space, time, association, and intuition *or* according to more traditional logical relations of hierarchy and classification. As we have tried to indicate, however, the alignment of these cultural maps along the articulated axes of capitalism, class, gender, and race creates a set of tendential forces that continues to value approaches associated primarily with dominant ideological positions.

Given the characteristics of the interface as a linguistic contact zone, our uses of computers in English classrooms certainly seem capable of supporting what Henry Giroux calls "imperialist master narratives" (57) of colonial dominance, even as they make the promise of technological liberation and progress. Students who want to use computers are continually confronted with these grand narratives which foreground a value on middle-class, corporate culture; capitalism and the commodification of information; Standard English; and rationalistic ways of representing knowledge. These values simultaneously do violence to and encourage the rejection of the languages of different races and the values of non-dominant cultural and gender groups. When students from these groups enter the linguistic borderlands of the interface, in other words, they often learn that they must abandon their own culture or gender and acknowledge the dominance of other groups. As Pratt and Said, among others, note, such individuals are forced, at some level, into "simultaneously identifying with dominant groups" and disassociating themselves from the colonial values of these groups (Pratt 59, citing Moreau).

This is, as we see it, one of the ways in which educators use computers—albeit unconsciously—to enact what Elspeth Stuckey calls "the violence of literacy." Each time we ask students from a marginalized cultural group to use computers, we ask them—require them—to learn a system of literacy that "distance[s] them from the ways of equality" (94). When we connect the regularly dispersed violence of literacy education to the use of computers, as technology critics like C. Paul Olson and Andrew Feenberg point out, we get more than the sum of the parts. We get, indeed, a master narrative that resonates all too successfully with modernist myths of technological progress: Civilization and reason, as manifested in a increasingly literate people, are supported in their historical evolution by continual improvements of industry and science. If teachers hear this resonance, we think they understand the need to identify and correct the tone.

WHAT TO DO?

Scholars who use technology and educators who teach with technology will, no doubt, find it difficult to study the maps of computer interfaces in a critical light to identify the many layers of culture and ideology they represent. As Denis Wood suggests, the greatest difficulty of all comes when we understand that we must locate ourselves in relation to the map. At this point, we end up asking ourselves where we stand in this colonial landscape, how we have cast our own multiple subjective positions within the territory that we have created and examined. Are we the cartographers who compose the map in our own cultural image—as white-collar professionals, many of us white or privileged? Are we members of a dominant group that profits from the map's reproductive function—as official representatives of an educational system and, in the case of many institutions of higher learning, the State? In part, of course, we do (already and always, as they say) stand in these places, but we can also—by revealing the partial and flawed nature of the map, by acknowledging our own role in composing the map—claim other vantage places as well. In particular, we can take with increasing seriousness the role of serving as technology critics when we use computers in the classroom and when we work with other teachers to integrate technology within these learning spaces. As Elspeth Stuckey, in *The Violence of Literacy,* says of literacy education in general—when we finally get around to "seeing" how a system supports repression, we can also find ways to alter the nature of our involvement in it:

> A system takes a lot of trouble. A system must be devised and implemented. To be sure, much of its design is tacit, its implementation an extension of usual modes of comfortable life. That is why uncomfortable people can often change a system. They can see it. (126)

So what do we do as educators and as the teachers of teachers? In our own classrooms, the continuing process has to be centered on a continuing foregrounding of the problems we have sketched out here, which leads us to suggest some related strategies for re-drawing the territory of the interface with students. To begin, however, we have to learn to recognize—and teach students to recognize—the interface as an interested and partial map of our culture and as a linguistic contact zone that reveals power differentials. We need to teach students and ourselves to recognize computer interfaces as non-innocent physical borders (between the regular world and the virtual world), cultural borders (between the haves and the have-nots), and linguistic borders. These borders, we need to recognize as cultural formations "historically constructed and socially organized within rules and regulations that limit and enable particular identities, individual capacities, and social forms" (Giroux 30). We also need to teach students and ourselves useful strategies of crossing—and demystifying—these borders. It is important to understand that we continually re-map and renegotiate borders in our lives.

One of the ways to come to this understanding is through working with students and computer specialists to re-design/re-imagine/re-create interfaces that attempt to avoid disabling and devaluing non-white, non-English language background students, and women. Our goal in creating these new interfaces should be to help rewrite the relationships between the center and the margins of our culture and, in Henry Giroux's words, "extend rather than erase the possibility for enabling human agency" (27) among currently marginalized and oppressed groups represented within the culture and the educational system. Although it is important to recognize—given the strong tendential forces of our cultural and the regularly dispersed nature of ideological systems—that any progress we make toward these goals will be partial, temporary, and contradictory, there are a few practices (what de Certeau might call *tactics*) that could help us enact a border pedagogy in computer-supported writing environments. We would like to spend the last part of this article identifying a few of these practical approaches that might be of use in composition programs at the college and university level.

Becoming Technology Critics as Well as Technology Users

One tactic for responding to the interested nature of computer interfaces has to do with encouraging a general level of critical awareness about technology issues on the part of both pre-service and in-service teachers. Currently, most teachers of composition studies at the collegiate level are educationed to deal with technology not as critics but as users—if, indeed, they are educated to deal with it at all. Few programs that educate college-level teachers of composition, for example, require students to take coursework in technology studies. If they are lucky, new faculty or graduate teaching assistants at an institution may be introduced—during an orientation for instructors or during a graduate course in teaching composition—to a computer facility that they can use for their teaching. Often, these introductions accomplish nothing more than exposing teachers to one or more software programs available for use in the classroom, and allowing time for some minimal hands-on practice with the software. Few composition programs or English departments, however, make a systematic effort to provide parallel instruction on technology issues as they touch on educational projects—stressing readings and discussions on technology criticism, or on the growing body of scholarship and research associated with computers and composition studies.[5] As a result, teachers of composition—and prospective teachers of composition—may learn to use technology, but not to think carefully about the implications of its use within their own classrooms.

Influencing this situation is an additional set of forces that encourage relatively conservative teaching strategies in connection with technology and relatively little room for reflection on these strategies. Given the costs involved in computing, most composition programs and English departments must depend on access to generic *computing* environments rather than facilities designed specifically to provide computer-supported *writers'* environments. Such generic facilities, because they are administered and maintained by computer specialists rather than teachers of English, foreground an emphasis on the machine and its use rather than on a critical approach to teaching composition with computer support. Characteristic of these facilities, often located in interior rooms or basements, are rows of numbered machines arranged to look very much like traditional classrooms and often networked so that they can be controlled from a single teacher's workstation at the front of the room. In such settings, and often armed with very little preparation or training, teachers of composition also have little encouragement to make changes in conventionally influenced teaching approaches they observe in regular classrooms, as Klem and Moran note (5–22). In such an environment, for example, it may become difficult to have students working in flexible groupings, to avoid a teacher-centered classroom, or to provide students room to take some charge of their own learning.

Operating within these parameters, it is recognizably difficult to educate teachers of composition as technology critics and to inculcate the intellectual habit of reflecting critically on the effects that technology might have within composition classrooms. Writing program administrators and individual teachers can, however, take some steps toward this goal by making sure that their programs—whether pre-service or in-service—are spending at least as much time educating teachers about important technology issues (access to technology, design of technology, ideologies associated with technology) as they are on training them to use technology. Among the efforts that might be undertaken by teachers and program administrators in support of this goal are collecting and circulating articles and books that provide critical as well as optimistic visions of technology, setting up research groups and teaching observations to encourage reflective teaching habits in computer-supported writing facilities, encouraging faculty to participate in e-mail lists that discuss technology issues as they are manifested in English composition classrooms, and sponsoring talks by informed scholars who examine technology issues from critical perspectives.[6]

Contributing to Technology Design

A second tactic for addressing the interested nature of computer interfaces is more narrowly and specifically focused on the efforts of those faculty who are computers and composition specialists. Given the embryonic state of this field and the traditional educational reward structures within which computers and composition specialists must function to earn tenure, promotion, and professional recognition, these colleagues have focused most of their efforts during the past fifteen years on identifying, exploring, and testing pedagogical uses of available computer technologies—suggesting, for example, effective ways to integrate the use of word-processing packages, on-line conferences, or idea generation packages into the teaching of English composition classes.[7] Less effort, therefore, has been available to invest in software design efforts—which can be costly in terms of resources and professional advancement, as LeBlanc points out—and almost no involvement has been encouraged in the design of primary interfaces. Without such an involvement by humanist scholars and teachers— especially those individuals who are familiar with language and learning theory, who understand issues raised by technology studies and cultural studies—interface design will continue to be dominated primarily by computer scientists and will lack perspectives that could be contributed by humanist scholars.

Fortunately, avenues for involvement in software design efforts are becoming more accessible. Computers and composition specialists who find the penalties associated with the effort to design specific software packages to be overly costly in terms of tenure, promotion, and advancement, can also influence software design through collective professional action aimed at general technology design efforts. Professional organizations such as the Alliance for Computers in Writing,[8] International Federation of Information Processing, and even the National Council of Teachers of English (through committees like the Instruction Technology Committee, and the CCCC Committee on Computers) currently influence the design of software through various formal and informal strategies of collective action: by identifying groups of teachers and professional educators who can engage directly in conversations with software manufacturers and vendors, by charging committees to take on the task of making systematic suggestions to these manufacturers after consulting with reflective computer-using teachers, by identifying outstanding efforts in software design, by publishing papers and reviews that include critical examinations of design implications in the classroom, and by identifying the kinds of products that are limited in their classroom usefulness. Many of these committees and organizations also hold ongoing discussions of computer issues of interest to teachers of composition on the Internet. Within these forums—which often are global in their participation and include a mix of computer scientists, educators, software designers, and content specialists—computers and composition specialists can encourage discussions that focus on interfaces, language issues, cultural reproduction, learning theories, and critical theories of language use. Through these conversations, computers and composition specialists can contribute to an increasingly critical awareness of technology issues on the part of individuals involved directly in the design of technology. Such conversations—if they can serve to extend and transform the existing intellectual and political terrain for various groups of people—could have, in Laclau and Mouffe's words, a "profound subversive power" (155).

Re-Conceiving the Map of the Interface

A third suggestion for addressing the interested map of reality offered by computer interfaces is to involve composition teachers and students in composition classes in an ongoing project to revise interfaces as *texts.* The purpose of these map-making sessions would be to come up with ideas for changing the interface to reflect a range of cultural, linguistic, and ideological perspectives. Faculty who specialize in computers and composition studies can serve as key resource people in this effort, although the goal is to involve *all* computer-using teachers and students in conceptualizing alternative maps of computer interfaces. The outcome of such sessions should not be to redesign interfaces in a technical sense, but rather to reconceive of them according to the experiences of a broad range of writers and teachers of writing: identifying desirable features generally unavailable in primary interfaces (a light pen for writing in the margins of documents, or a highlighter for color coding related documents), suggesting ways of customizing interfaces for the needs of various writers and readers (adding a read-aloud option for writers who want to hear how their text sounds), or imagining productive metaphors around which interfaces can be built (mechanics' workbenches, kitchen countertops, garages). In these sessions—to further reduce the focus on technical expertise—teachers and students can represent their interface re-revision ideas either through prose descriptions or pencil-and-pen drawings.

For those faculty and teachers who are more adventurous in terms of technology, some relatively simple computer-based tools already exist that could support these projects at a level accessible to non-specialists. Teachers and students can use the computer-based drawing and illustration packages they are already familiar with, for example, to create representations of redesigned interface screens to which they add new features. In addition, software designers for the Macintosh have already published scores of alternative icons and images that can be used by English composition teachers, and students, to customize primary computer interfaces. Matrix Communication Associates of Pittsburgh, for instance, is now marketing a package of African American computer graphics and has plans to market graphics packages that more adequately represent other ethnic groups as well (Creedy). With such packages, faculty and graduate students who have very little familiarity with computers can illustrate how they would like to incorporate various features into primary interfaces—creating icons for bulletin boards, on-line conferences, multiple user dimensions, or other student-centered learning spaces that they would like to include in an interface. It is possible that the representations identified by writing teachers and students can later be used by software and hardware design specialists as the basis for more technical projects that might actually produce working versions of alternative interfaces.

To support these conceptual redesign efforts, computers and composition specialists can also work with both teachers and students to assemble expanded libraries of images that appeal to writers of different ages, races, sexual preferences, classes, and lifestyles. These icons should be chosen to resonate with a range of different cultural and ideological positions—delicatessens and 7-Elevens, babies and rocking chairs, rosetta stones and piñatas, apartment buildings and subway maps, powwow dances and storytellers—which can be used to customize systems for different groups of writers. The goal in identifying these images and icons, in Henry Giroux's words, would be to help students and teachers focus on the act of crossing borders, "moving in and out of borders constructed around coordinates of difference and power," learning and negotiating "the shifting parameters of place, identity, history, and power" (136). This project may help us and students to see that the interests represented within maps are "neither singular nor simple" (Wood 94) and that interests concealed in one map, one representation of a culture, can be revealed and foregrounded in another.

TOWARD A CRITICAL READING OF INTERFACES

For both teachers and students, Giroux notes, the project of eliminating oppression based on class, race, and gender involves "an ongoing contest within every aspect of daily life," a continual project of mapping and re-mapping the educational, political, and ideological spaces we want to occupy." He continues, "no tradition should ever be seen as received in this project" (155–156). In this sense, English teachers cannot be content to understand the maps of computer interfaces as simple, uncomplicated spaces. Rather, we need to prepare ourselves and the students with whom we work to map these virtual spaces as sites of "multiple and heterogeneous borders where different histories, languages, experiences, and voices intermingle amidst diverse relations of power and privilege" (Giroux 169). At the same time, it is prudent to acknowledge the complications and contradictions inherent in such work. As Winograd and Flores point out, our continuing efforts toward revealing the interested nature of computer interfaces will, in part, contribute to concealment because "as carriers of a tradition, we cannot be objective observers of it." This realization, however, cannot provide an excuse for inaction. We must also, as these authors note, take on the responsibility of continuing to "work towards unconcealment . . . and let our awareness guide our actions in creating and applying technology" (179).

Acknowledgments:

We owe a great deal of gratitude to colleagues who helped us work through the ideas in this article. The generosity and intellectual contributions of Marilyn Copper, Jim Sosnoski, and Joe Janangelo are evident in the best aspects of this paper.

NOTES

1. For more critical discussions of the overly optimistic rhetoric associated with computer use in composition classrooms, see Faigley's description of a synchronous network conversation (*Fragments* 163–99), Barton's discussion of the dominant discourses associated with technology, ("Interpreting the Discourses of Technology"), Hawisher and Selfe's exploration of teachers' claims about computer use ("The Rhetoric of Technology"), and Romano's discussion of bias in online conversations ("The Egalitarianism Narrative").

2. Readers who want to explore the potential of electronic forums on WANs or LANs may want to consult: Barker and Kemp's "Network Theory"; Bruce, Peyton, and Batson's *Networked Classrooms;* Cooper and Selfe's "Computer Conferences"; Eldred's "Computers, Composition and the Social View"; Faigley's "Subverting the Electronic Notebook"; Handa's *Computers and Community;* Kiesler, Siegel, and McGuire's "Social Psychological Aspects"; and Spitzer's "Computer Conferencing."

3. Discussions of the ways in which racism, sexism, and power relationships related to colonialism are enacted in connection with technology use can be found in Gomez's "The Equitable Teaching of Composition," Hawisher and Selfe's "Rhetoric of Technology," Jessup's "Feminism and Computers," and LeBlanc's "Competing Ideologies."

4. For descriptions of the challenges associated with wicked problems and fuzzy logic, readers may want to refer to: Ambler, Burnett, and Zimmerman; Kurzweil; Seagull and Walker; Turkle and Papert; and Winograd and Flores.

5. For criticism related to technology, we recommend the works of Feenberg, Kramare, Olson, Ohmann.

6. Several such lists exist for teachers of composition. Megabyte University (MBU), for instance, focuses on issues surrounding the use of computers in writing-intensive classrooms and BreadNet serves to connect English teachers who have attended Breadloaf seminars. To obtain information on Megabyte University, contact Fred Kemp, the founder of MBU, at Texas Tech University (YKFOK@TTACS1.TTU.EDU). To obtain additional information about BreadNet, contact Bill Wright (BWRIGHT@TMN.COM). The National Council of Teachers of English is currently engaged in designing a computer network that will connect teachers of English across the country. For additional information on NCTENet, contact Tharon Howard, Chair of the NCTE Instructional Technology Committee, at Clemson University (THARON@HUBCAP.CLEMSON.EDU).

7. The advent of computers and composition studies is typically dated from 1975, when Ellen Nold's *CCC* article, "Fear and Trembling," gave voice to the concerns English composition teachers had about technology (and thus gave impetus to focused work in this area), or from 1979, when Hugh Burns published the first dissertation that systematically examined the effects of computer-assisted instruction on student writers' invention efforts. The first fully assembled microcomputer, the Apple II, marketed in 1976, provided the actual technological means of introducing computers into composition classrooms in a meaningful way. These machines provided composition teachers with word-processing systems that were far easier to teach and far less difficult to use than the clumsy line-editors offered on mainframe computers in the seventies.

8. The Alliance for Computers in Writing is a national coalition of teachers, publishers, professional organizations, and educational institutions interested in promoting the effective use of computers in English composition classrooms. For more information on the Alliance for Computers and Writing, contact Trent Batson, Gallaudet University (TWBATSON@GALLUA.BITNET).

WORKS CITED

Ambler, Allen L., Margaret M. Burnett, and Betsy A. Zimmerman. "Operational Versus Definitional: A Perspective on Programming Paradigms." *Computer* (September 1992): 28–43.

Barker, Thomas. T. and Fred O. Kemp. "Network Theory: A Postmodern Pedagogy for the Writing Classroom." *Computers and Community: Teaching Composition in the Twenty-First Century.* Ed. Carolyn Handa. Portsmouth, NH: Boynton 1–27.

Barton, Ellen. "Interpreting the Discourses of Technology." *Literacy and Computers: The Complications of Teaching and Learning on Technology.* Ed. Cynthia L. Selfe and Susan Hilligoss. New York: MLA, 1994. 56–75.

Batson, Trent. "The ENFI Project: A Networked Classroom Approach to Writing Instruction." *Academic Computing* (February/March 1988): 32–33, 55–56.

Berger, John. *Ways of Seeing.* New York: Penguin Books, 1972.

Bolter, Jay D. *Writing Space: The Computer, Hypertext, and the History of Writing.* Hillsdale, NJ: Erlbaum, 1991.

Bruce, Bertram, Joy Freeft Peyton, and Trent Batson. *Network-Based Classrooms: Promises and Realities.* New York: Cambridge UP, 1993.

Butler, Judith. *Gender Trouble: Feminism and the Subversion of Identity.* NY: Routledge. 1990.

Burns, Hugh, "Stimulating Rhetorical Invention through Computer-Assisted Instruction." Diss. U of Texas at Austin, 1979.

Copper, Marilyn M., and Cynthia L. Selfe. "Computer Conferences and Learning: Authority, Resistance, and Internally Persuasive Discourse." *College English* 52 (1990): 847–69.

Creedy, Steve. "Local Firm's African-American Computer Graphics Fill Void." *Pittsburgh Post Gazette* 23 August 1993: B8.

de Certeau, Michel. *The Practice of Everyday Life.* Trans. Steven Randall. Berkeley: U of California P, 1984.

Deleuze, Gilles, and Félix Guattari. *A Thousand Plateaus: Capitalism and Schizophrenia.* Trans. Brian Massumi. Minneapolis, MN: of Minnesota, 1987.

Eldred, Janet C. "Computers, Composition, and the Social View." *Critical Perspectives on Computers and Composition Studies.* Ed. Gail E. Hawisher and Cynthia L. Selfe. New York: Teachers College P, 1989. 201–18.

Faigley, Lester. "Subverting the Electronic Notebook: Teaching Writing Using Networked Computers." *The Writing Teacher as Researcher: Essays in the Theory and Practice of Class-Based Research.* Ed. Donald A. Daiker and Max Morenberg. Portsmouth, NH: Boynton, 1990. 290–311.

Faigley, Lester. *Fragments of Rationality: Postmodernity and the Subject of Composition.* Pittsburgh: U of Pittsburgh P, 1992.

Freenberg, Andrew. *Critical Theory of Technology.* New York: Oxford UP, 1991.

Flores, Mary J. "Computer Conferencing: Composing a Feminist Community of Writers." *Computers and Community: Teaching Composition in the Twenty-First Century.* Ed. Carolyn Handa. Portsmouth, NH: Boynton, 1990. 106–17.

Foucault, Michel. "Space, Knowledge, and Power." *The Foucault Reader.* Ed. Paul Rabinow. New York: Pantheon, 1984. 239–56.

Gilligan, Carolyn. *In A Different Voice: Psychological Theory and Women's Development.* Cambridge, MA: Harvard UP, 1982.

Giroux, Henry A. *Border Crossings: Cultural Workers and the Politics of Education.* New York: Routledge, 1992.

Gomez, Mary L. "The Equitable Teaching of Composition." *Evolving Perspectives on Computers and Compositions Studies.* Ed. Gail E. Hawisher and Cynthia L. Selfe. Urbana, IL: NCTE, 1991. 318–35.

Grimes, William. "Computer as a Cultural Tool." *New York Times* 1 December 1992: C13–15.

Handa, Carolyn, ed. *Computers and Community: Teaching Composition in the Twenty-First Century.* Portsmouth, NH: Boynton, 1990.

Harding, Sandra and Merrill B. Hintikka, eds. *Discovering Reality: Feminist Perspectives on Epistemology, Metaphysics, Methodology, and Philosophy of Science.* London: Reidel, 1983.

Hawisher, Gail E. and Cynthia L. Selfe. "Voices in College Classrooms: The Dynamics of Electronic Discussion." *The Quarterly* 14 (Summer 1992): 24–28, 32.

———. "The Rhetoric of Technology and the Electronic Writing Class" *CCC* 42 (1991): 55–65.

———. "Tradition and Change in Computer-Supported Writing Environments." *Theoretical and Critical Perspectives on Teacher Change.* Ed. P. Kahaney, J. Janangelo, and L. A. M. Perry. Norwood, NJ: Ablex, 1993. 155–86.

Janangelo, Joseph. "Technopower and Technoppression: Some Abuses of Power and Control in Computer-Assisted Writing Environments." *Computer and Composition* 9 (November 1991): 47–64.

Jessup, Emily (1991). "Feminism and Computers in Composition Instruction." *Evolving Perspectives on Computers and Composition Studies: Questions for the 1990s.* Ed. Gail E. Hawisher and Cynthia L. Selfe. Urbana, IL: 1991. 336–55.

Jordan, June. *ON CALL: Political Essays.* Boston, MA: South End 1985.

———. "Toward a Manifest New Destiny." *The Progressive* (February 1992): 18–23.

Keller, Evelyn F. *Reflections on Gender and Science.* New Haven: Yale UP, 1985.

Kiesler, Sara, Jane Siegel, and Timothy W. McGuire. "Social Psychological Aspects of Computer-Mediated Communication." *American Psychologist* 39 (1984): 1123–34.

Klem, Elizabeth, and Charles Moran. "Teachers in a Strange LANd: Learning to Teach in a Networked Writing Classroom." *Computers and Composition* 9 (August 1992): 5–22.

Kremers, Marshall. "Adams Sherman Hill Meets ENFI: An Inquiry and a Retrospective." *Computers and Composition* 5 (August 1988): 69–77.

Kramarae, Cheris, ed. *Technology and Women's Voices: Keeping in Touch.* New York: Routledge, 1988.

Kurzweil, Raymond. *The Age of Intelligent Machines.* Cambridge, MA: MIT P, 1990.

Laclau, Ernesto, and Chantel Mouffe. *Hegemony and Socialist Strategy: Towards a Radical Democratic Politics.* London: Verso, 1985.

LeBlanc, Paul. "Competing Ideologies in Software Design for Computer-Aided Composition." *Computers and Composition* 7 (April 1990): 8–19.

Moreau, N. B. "Education, Ideology, and Class/Sex Identity." *Language and Power.* Ed. Cheris Kramarae. Beverly Hills, CA: Sage, 1984. 43–61.

Nelson, Theodor H. "The Tyranny of the File." *Datamation* 15 December 1986: 83–86.

Nold, Ellen. "Fear and Trembling: A Humanist Approaches the Computer." *CCC* 26 (1975): 269–273.

Ohmann, Richard. "Literacy, Technology, and Monopoly Capitalism." *College English* 47 (1985): 675–689.

Olson, C. Paul. "Who Computes?" *Critical Pedagogy and Cultural Power.* Ed. David Livingstone. South Hadley, MA: Bergin, 1987. 179–204.

Petzold, Charles. "Move Over, ASCII! Unicode is Here." *PC Magazine* 12 (26 October 1993): 374–376.

Piller, Charles. "Separate Realities: The Creation of the Technological Underclass in America's Public Schools." *MacWorld* (September 1992): 218–30.

Pratt, Mary Louise. "Linguistic Utopias." *The Linguistics of Writing.* Ed. Nigel Fabb. Et al. Manchester: Manchester UP, 1987. 48–66.

———. "Arts of the Contact Zone." *Profession* 91: (1991) 33–40.

Romano Susan. "The Egalitarianism Narrative: Whose Story? Which Yardstick? *Computers and Composition* 10 (August 1993): 5–28.

Said, Edward. "Reflections on Exile." *Out There: Marginalization and Contemporary Cultures.* Ed. Russell Fergeson, Martha Gever, Trinh T. Minh-ha, and Cornell West. Cambridge, MA: MIT P, 1990. 357–368.

Seagull, J. F. and N. Walker. "The Effects of Hierarchical Structure and Visualization on Computerized Information Retrieval." *International Journal of Human-Computer Interaction* 4 (1992): 369–485.

Selfe, Cynthia L. "English Teachers and the Humanization of Computers: Networking Communities of Readers and Writers." *On Literacy and Its Teaching: Issues in English Education.* Eds. Gail E. Hawisher and Anna O. Soter. 1990. Albany, NY: State U of New York P, 1990. 190–205.

———. "Technology in the English Classroom: Computers through the Lens of Feminist Theory." *Computers and Community: Teaching Composition in the Twenty-First Century.* Ed. Carolyn Handa. Portsmouth, NH: Boynton, 1990. 118–39.

Selfe, Cynthia L., and Paul R. Meyer. "Testing Claims for On-Line Conferences." *Written Communication* 8 (1991): 163–92.

Sheingold, Karen, L. M. Martin, and M. W. Endreweit. "Preparing Urban Teachers for the Technological Future." *Mirrors of the Mind: Patterns of Experience in Educational Computing.* Ed. Roy D. Pea and Karen Sheingold. Norwood, NJ: Ablex, 1987. 67–85.

Spitzer, Michael. "Computer Conferencing: An Emerging Technology." *Critical Perspectives in Computers and Composition Instruction.* Ed. Gail E. Hawisher and Cynthia L. Selfe. New York: Teachers College P, 1989. 187–200.

Springer, Claudia. "The Pleasure of the Interface." *Screen* 32 (1991): 303–23.

Stuckey, Elspeth. *The Violence of Literacy.* Portsmouth, NH: Boynton, 1991.

Turkle, Sherry, and Papert, Seymour. "Epistomological Pluralism: Styles and Voices within the Computer Culture." *Signs* 16 (1990): 128–57.

Virilio, Paul. *Speed and Politics: An Essay on Dromology.* Trans. Mark Polizzotti. New York: Semiotext(e), 1987.

Weizenbaum, Joseph. "Not Without Us: A Challenge to Computer Professionals to Use Their Power to Bring the Present Insanity to a Halt." *Fellowship* (October/November 1986): 8–10.

Wheelock, Ann and Gail Dorman. *Before It's Too Late.* Boston, MA: Massachusetts Advocacy Commission, 1989.

Winograd, Terry and Fernando Flores. *Understanding Computers and Cognition: A New Foundation for Design.* Reading, MA: Addison, 1986.

Wood, Denis, *The Power of Maps.* New York, NY: Guilford, 1992.

WordPerfect for DOS: Reference for IBM Personal Computers and PC Networks, 1989.

PART TWO

Literacy and Access

Introduction to Part Two

Some students will walk into our classrooms loaded up with the latest digital technology, some will have outdated hardware and software, and still others may have no computer at all. And the same is true for Internet literacy. Some students will have technological skills beyond ours as teachers while others may have used a computer rarely or not at all. The issues of access and literacy are inextricably entwined and embedded in every computerized-netted composition classroom and impact every student and teacher. The lessons are as clear to students as they should be to us: If you don't have access to computers or other media, you're at a disadvantage—economically, socially, and politically—even if you know how to use the technology. Moreover, the same is true if you don't know how to use computers: Students who come to college with little training in technology struggle to keep up with peers who have been raised with it. If you have neither digital access nor literacy, you risk being marginalized even further in this increasingly digitized society.

Working from her landmark book, *Technology and Literacy in the 21st Century: The Perils of Not Paying Attention,* Cynthia Selfe's 1997 Conference on College Composition and Communication (CCCC) Chair's Address, "Technology and Literacy: A Story about the Perils of Not Paying Attention," directly assesses the issues of access and literacy in the computers and writing classroom. Selfe finds that technology is "inextricably linked to literacy and literacy education in this country" (96). She warns composition teachers that if we use computers but fail to pay attention to the technology, "we share in the responsibility for sustaining and reproducing [an] unfair system that . . . enacts social violence and ensures continuing illiteracy under the aegis of education" (96). After examining the Technology Literacy Challenge implemented by President Clinton in the 1990s as well as research about other literacy campaigns, Selfe further assaults our institutional myth about literacy and technology: that "a national program will provide all citizens equal access to an improved education and, thus, equal opportunity for upward social mobility" (101). She finds that, historically, such literacy campaigns have served only to reinscribe inequalities that plague our society according to positions of class and gender and most particularly in regard to race.

Selfe offers several suggestions for action, many of which have been pursued by composition teachers since the original publication of this address. She urges writing teachers to approach technology as humanists, critically examining not just the constructive power of technologies, but also their impact on citizen-workers. Selfe believes that action must begin at the local level, with teachers observing and analyzing our own institutions to determine where technologies are distributed and integrated unfairly. As both professionals and citizens, we also need to engage in more social activism and socially responsible research. All of this work, of course, must also occur in our classrooms, where we teach students to be critical thinkers and users of technology, encouraging not just computer literacy, but "critical technological literacy" (111).

In examining the issues of access and literacy that teachers walking into computers and composition classrooms need to consider, Dennis Baron, in the second article in this section, reminds us that since writing itself became a literacy technology, scholars have contemplated the power and importance of language tools. Baron's article, "From Pencils to Pixels: The Stages of Literacy Technologies," leads us through the stages of technological development, starting with writing itself as the first technology and ending with the idea that "the computer is simply the latest step in a long line of writing technologies" (118). Along the way, Baron unites the earliest writing technologies with the latest by situating the first writers as "cuneiform geeks" (121) and positing pencils attached to ancient notebooks as the first laptops. As radical as we may sometimes feel the digital age is, Baron asserts that often the latest technology replicates the products of the old, as we see in the case of the many on-screen computer documents that replicate typewritten texts. Surveying the computer age, Baron lays out the new technology's issues with authentication, authority, and access. He fears that for many low-income workers, technological literacy and access comes only in the form of a checkout scanner, a condition of technology's place in social and economic systems. Baron reminds us that "technology has a trailing edge as well as a down side, and studying how computers are put to use raises serious issues in the politics of work and mechanisms of social control" (132), an awareness that computers and writing teachers need.

If we asked our students about issues of access in the digital age, their responses would probably involve questionably downloaded music. But copyright, though not a glamorous topic, is a crucial issue of access for composition teachers as well as students as we strive to involve our students in the social, political, and cultural issues of our world. As John Logie tells us in his 1998 article, "Champing at the Bits: Computers, Copyright, and the Composition Classroom," copyright law in the United States has always been a balancing act between the public's right of access and the creator's rights of ownership. Logie gives us a brief but fascinating history of copyright law, cues us to recent developments in copyright law, and ends with an annotated list of online resources for teachers (which we have checked and updated). In particular, Logie discusses the principle of "fair use," reminding us that we need to teach composing strategies that "balance our sense of what is right against the developing global definitions of what is legal—and to insure that when the gap between the two is too large, we take action and use our close proximity to the composing process to inform the development of future policies" (146).

To help remind us all of the changing copyright climate, we have placed an Editors' Addendum at the end of Logie's article; it includes the Web address for The Digital Millennium Copyright Act enacted in 1998 and a brief summary of four points of the Act of interest to computers and composition teachers. These guidelines will help us to interpret difficult issues of copyright and plagiarism to our students—and ourselves.

As students discover how relatively easy it is to access, gather, and use information online, copyright and plagiarism are becoming ever more evident in our composition classes. Students learn quickly that cutting and pasting require only a few keystrokes—but this ease of use also leads to confusion about textual ownership. In the fourth essay of this section, Dànielle DeVoss and Annette C. Rosati address the issues surrounding the ease of copying information in their article " 'It wasn't me, was it?' Plagiarism and the Web." They encourage linking plagiarism with discussions of intellectual property and making a connection to workplace writing (not just academic essays). Making this connection will help students better understand the nature and seriousness of plagiarism. The authors suggest that discussing intellectual property provides more opportunities to include ethics and responsibility in a discussion of plagiarism because it ties the argument to the workplace and the legal ramifications associated with stealing. To help students and teachers understand what is and is not plagiarism, they provide a set of questions students might use to evaluate Web sites and information gathered from the Web and provide eleven student activities for developing awareness of plagiarism. DeVoss and Rosati end by arguing that although teaching students about plagiarism and intellectual property may take a lot of class time, we must continue to adjust our curricula to engage current academic and virtual discourse spaces.

Echoing DeVoss and Rosati's concerns about online research, we feel safe in saying that more reading of Internet texts is done on any given day than is done with traditional texts. Commercial Web sites, professional Web sites, educational Web sites and interfaces, sites for the news, entertainment, and weather, personal Web sites and blogs, Face Book, and on and on: The world of hypertext is a fact of American life that most of us may take for granted and we may not have looked at critically. In our fifth and final selection in this section, "Reading Hypertext: Order and Coherence in a New Medium," John M. Slatin examines this brave new world of literacy and access: hypertext. It is easy to see that access to many of our society's institutions and its concomitant privileges may well depend upon our students' literacy as both readers and writers of hypertext. Slatin begins by contrasting traditional text to hypertext, noting that while traditional text is fixed, sequential, continuous, and predictable as well as strongly determined by an author, hypertext is discontinuous; exhibits and utilizes multiple pathways, points of entry, and exit; and is open to a series of jumps based on the whim or interest of the reader. Slatin further contends that hypertext systems envision three different types of readers: the browser, the user, and the coauthor. After guiding us through the hyperworld of linkages and nodes, Slatin then gives us a "how-to" guide highlighting what hypertext writers need to consider in reaching hypertext readers. Slatin cues us to what may be hypertext's greatest strength: the ability to link huge quantities of material that could not be linked conventionally, but he also alerts us to its greatest weakness: its inability to spell out what the relationships entail, a responsibility, we believe, that falls upon teachers.

6

Technology and Literacy: A Story about the Perils of Not Paying Attention

CYNTHIA L. SELFE

Technological literacy—meaning computer skills and the ability to use computers and other technology to improve learning, productivity and performance—has become as fundamental to a person's ability to navigate through society as traditional skills like reading, writing and arithmetic . . . In explicit acknowledgment of the challenges facing the education community, on February 15, 1996, President Clinton and Vice President Gore announced the Technology Literacy Challenge, envisioning a 21st century where all students are technologically literate. The challenge was put before the nation as a whole, with responsibility . . . shared by local communities, states, the private sector, educators, local communities, parents, the federal government, and others. . . .

—GETTING AMERICA'S STUDENTS READY FOR THE 21ST CENTURY (5)

We know, purely and simply, that every single child must have access to a computer. . . .

—BILL CLINTON, QTD. IN GETTING AMERICA'S STUDENTS READY FOR THE
21ST CENTURY (4)

A central irony shaping my experience with the CCCC as a professional organization goes something like this: I consider it a fortunate occurrence and a particular point of pride that many of the best ideas about teaching and learning writing, the most powerfully explanatory theoretical insights about language and discourse and literacy that inform education today, grow directly out of conversations among CCCC members. Given this situation, however, I find it compellingly unfortunate that the one topic serving as a focus for my own professional involvement—that of computer technology and its use in teaching composition—seems to be the single subject best guaranteed to inspire glazed eyes and complete indifference in that portion of the CCCC membership which does not immediately sink into snooze mode.

From *College Composition and Communication* 50.3 (1999): 411–36.

This irony, I am convinced, has nothing to do with collegial good will. CCCC colleagues have been unerringly polite in the 17 years of discussions we have had about technology. After all this time, however, I can spot the speech acts that follow a turn of the conversation to computers—the slightly averted gaze, the quick glance at the watch, the panicky look in the eyes when someone lapses into talk about microprocessors, or gigabytes, or ethernets. All these small potent gestures, as Michel de Certeau would say, signify pretty clearly—technology is either boring or frightening to most humanists; many teachers of English composition feel it antithetical to their primary concerns and many believe it should not be allowed to take up valuable scholarly time or the attention that could be best put to use in teaching or the study of literacy. I have, believe me, gotten the message—as subtle as it is.

These attitudes toward technology issues, of course, aren't shared by everyone in this organization—there are pockets of technology studies scholars and teachers here and there among us; notable occasions when an individual CCCC leader does speak about technology; and, every now and again, a professional conversation among us about the array of challenges associated with technology. These occasions remain exceptions, however, and anybody familiar with the values of traditional humanism knows that, as a group, we tend to hold in common a general distrust of the machine, that a preference for the non-technological still characterizes our community.

Our tendency to avoid focusing on the technological means that—while we are tolerant of those colleagues interested in the "souls of machines," to use Bruno Latour's term—we assign them to a peculiar kind of professional isolation "in their own separate world" of computer sessions and computer workshops and computers and writing conferences that many CCCC members consider influenced more by the concerns of "engineers, technicians, and technocrats" (vii) than those of humanists. It is this same set of historically and professionally determined beliefs, I think, that informs our actions within our home departments, where we generally continue to allocate the responsibility of technology decisions—and oftentimes the responsibility of technology studies—to a single faculty or staff member who doesn't mind wrestling with computers or the thorny, and the unpleasant issues that can be associated with their use. In this way, we manage to have the best of both worlds—we have computers available to use for our own studies, in support of our classes and our profession—but we have also relegated these technologies into the background of our professional lives. As a result, computers are rapidly becoming invisible, which is how we like our technology to be. When we don't have to pay attention to machines, we remain free to focus on the theory and practice of language, the stuff of real intellectual and social concern.

WHY WE ALLOW OURSELVES TO IGNORE TECHNOLOGY

As humanists, we prefer things to be arranged this way because computer technology, when it is too much in our face (as an unfamiliar technology generally is), can suggest a kind of cultural strangeness that is off-putting. We are much more used to dealing with older technologies like print, a technology conventional enough so that we don't have to think so much about it, old enough so that it doesn't call such immediate attention to the social or material conditions associated with its use. Books, for example, are already and always—almost anyway—there. At this point in history, books are relatively cheap, they are generally accessible to students and to us, and they are acknowledged by our peers to be the appropriate tools of teaching and learning to use. As a result, our recognition of the material conditions associated with books have faded into the background of our imagination. Thus, although we understand on a tacit level that the print technology in which we invest so readily (and in which we ask students to invest) contributes to our own tenure and promotion, to our own wallets, and to our own status in the profession and in the public eye—this understanding is woven into the background of our professional attention, and we seldom pay attention to it on a daily basis. If we did, we'd go mad.

There are other things that don't occur to us, as well. When we use the more familiar technology of books, for instance, it is mostly within a familiar ideological system that allows us to ignore, except for some occasional twinges of conscience, the persistence of print and our role in this persistence. It allows us to ignore the understanding that print literacy functions as a cultural system—as Lester Faigley noted two years ago—not only to carry and distribute enlightened ideas, but also as a seamless whole to support a pattern of continuing illiteracy in this country.

I provide this example to suggest that composition studies faculty, educated in the humanist tradition, generally prefer our technologies and the material conditions associated so closely with them to remain in the background for obvious reasons, and the belief systems we construct in connection with various technologies allow us to accomplish this comfortable process of naturalization.

In the case of computers—we have convinced ourselves that we and the students with whom we work are made of much finer stuff than the machine in our midst, and we are determined to maintain this state of affairs. This ideological position, however, has other effects, as well. As a result of the inverse value we generally assign to discussions about computers, our professional organizations continue to deal with technology in what is essentially a piecemeal fashion. We now think of computers, for instance, as a simple tool that individual faculty members can use or ignore in their classrooms as they choose, but also one that the profession, as a collective whole—and with just a few notable exceptions—need not address too systematically. And so we have paid technology issues precious little focused attention over the years.

WHY COMPOSITION SPECIALISTS NEED TO PAY ATTENTION TO TECHNOLOGY ISSUES

Allowing ourselves the luxury of ignoring technology, however, is not only misguided at the end of the 20th century, it is dangerously shortsighted. And I do not mean, simply, that we are all—each of us—now teaching students who must know how to communicate as informed thinkers and citizens in an increasingly technological world—although this is surely so. This recognition had led composition faculty only to the point of *using* computers—or having students do so—but not to the point of *thinking* about what we are doing and understanding at least some of the important implications of our actions.

I believe composition studies faculty have a much larger and more complicated obligation to fulfill—that of trying to understand and make sense of, to *pay attention* to, how technology is now inextricably linked to literacy and literacy education in this country. As a part of this obligation, I suggest that we have some rather unpleasant facts to face about our own professional behavior and involvement. To make these points more persuasively, I offer a real-life story about what has happened in American schools and literacy instruction as a result of our unwillingness to attend to technological issues.

An honest examination of this situation, I believe, will lead composition studies professionals to recognize that these two complex cultural formations—technology and literacy—have become linked in ways that exacerbate current educational and social inequities in the United States rather than addressing them productively. The story will lead us to admit, I believe, that we are, in part, already responsible for a bad—even a shameful—situation, and, I hope, will require us to do something more positive in the future.

I'll provide readers the moral of this story up front so that no one misses it. *As composition teachers, deciding whether or not to use technology in our classes is simply not the point—we have to pay attention to technology.* When we fail to do so, we share in the responsibility for sustaining and reproducing an unfair system that, scholars such as Elspeth Stuckey and Mike Rose have noted in other contexts, enacts social violence and ensures continuing illiteracy under the aegis of education.

I know, however, that it is not easy for composition teachers to pay attention to technology. As Anthony Giddens would say, our tendency to ignore technology—to focus on humans rather than on machines—is "deeply sedimented" (22) in our culture, in the history of our humanist profession. And the sedimentation of this belief system is so deep that it has come to comprise a piece of what Pierre Bordieu might call *doxa* (166)—a position everyone takes so much for granted, is so obvious, that people no longer even feel the need to articulate it. But by subscribing to this attitude, we may also be allowing ourselves to ignore the serious social struggles that continue to characterize technology as a cultural formation in this country.

Nowhere are these struggles and debates rendered in more complex terms in the United States—and nowhere are they more influential on our own work—than they are in the link between literacy and computer technology that has been established in increasingly direct ways over the last decade. This potent linkage is sustained and reproduced by a complexly related set of cultural influences: workplaces in which approximately 70% of jobs requiring a bachelors degree or an advanced college degree now require the use of computers (*Digest of Education Statistics* 458); a corporate sector focused on exploiting the 89% of "teachers and the public" who believe that the Internet adds value to teaching and learning specifically because it "reduces the costs teachers spend on classroom activities" ("MCI Nationwide Poll"); schools in which 87% of high school students are now writing on computers by Grade 11 (Coley, Crandler, and Engle 27); and homes in which 86% of parents are convinced that a computer is *the* one "most beneficial and effective product that they can buy to expand their children's opportunities" for education, future success, and economic prosperity (*Getting America's Students Ready* 10).

The tendential force generated by these complexly related formations — which magnify our country's economic dependence on technology — is considerable. However, because it is always easier to ascribe responsibility for such a situation to others — to blame the greed of the corporate representatives who sell computers, or the blindness of school administrators who mandate the use of computers, or the shortsightedness of parents who consider technology a guarantor of learning for their children, I want to focus primarily on our own professional roles and responsibilities associated with this social dynamic.

It is, after all, partly a result of the involvement of English composition specialists, or lack of involvement, in some cases, that the linkage between literacy and technology has come to inform most of the official instruction that goes on within the United States' educational system, most official definitions and descriptions of literacy featured in the documents we write and read, and many of the criteria used to gauge literacy levels within this country. Few government documents about educational goals; few documents outlining national or state educational standards, including our own NCTE standards document; and few corporate job descriptions now fail to acknowledge a citizen's need to read, write, and communicate in electronic environments.

And certainly, like most Americans, we have not felt a responsibility to involve ourselves directly in some of the more public discussions about technology and educational policy because many of us unconsciously subscribe to a belief — both culturally and historically determined — that technology is a productive outgrowth of Science and Innovation (cf. Winner; Virilio; Feenberg; Johnson-Eilola). As a result, we take comfort when the linkage between literacy and computer technology is portrayed as a socially progressive movement, one that will benefit American citizens generally and without regard for their circumstances or backgrounds. Such a belief releases us from the responsibility to pay attention.

It is this last point, however, that makes the American cultural narrative about technology and literacy a particularly potent force in our lives, and that provides a jumping off point for our real-life story about technology.

AN AMERICAN NARRATIVE ABOUT COMPUTER TECHNOLOGY AND ITS GROWING LINKS TO LITERACY INSTRUCTION

This story about technology and literacy could be dated by any number of historical events, but for the purposes of this paper, we turn to June of 1996, when the Clinton-Gore administration — with direct reference to the larger cultural narrative of social-progress-through-technology that I have just identified—published a document entitled *Getting America's Students Ready for the Twenty-First Century,* which announced an official national project to expand *technological literacy,* the "ability to use computers and other technology to improve learning, productivity and performance" (5).

The purpose of this large-scale project—as outlined by Secretary of Education Richard Riley—was, and is, to help "all of our children to become technologically literate" so that each "will have the opportunity to make the most of his or her own life," to "grow and thrive" within the "new knowledge- and information-driven economy" (3–4). By "technologically literate," this document refers to the use of computers not only for the purposes of calculating, programming, and designing, but also for the purposes of reading, writing, and communicating (15–19)—at least for the officially-sponsored academic tasks required in schools across the country.

Estimates indicate that this particular literacy project may cost up to $109 billion dollars—averaging either $11 billion annually for a decade or between $10 and $20 billion annually for five years—from a variety of sources at the national, state, and local levels (*Getting America's Students Ready* 6). Where has his money come from and where has it gone? As Todd Oppenheimer notes:

> New Jersey cut state aid to a number of school districts this past year and then spent $10 million on classroom computers. In Union City, California, a single school district is spending $27 million to buy new gear for a mere eleven schools. . . . in Mansfield, Massachusetts, administrators dropped proposed teaching positions in art, music and physical education, and then spent $333,000 on computers. (46)

Secretary of Education Richard Riley, in *Getting America's Students Ready,* lists other funded projects from various states—here is a sampling:

California

$279 million (one time, State Board) for "instructional materials, deferred maintenance, technology. . . ."

$13.4 million (State Board) for educational technology.

$10 million (State budget) to "refurbish and update used or donated computers."

$100 million (current year, Governor Wilson) for "educational technology."

$35 million (Pacific Telesis) for rate overcharges. (60)

Delaware

$30 million (State, three years) to fund "infrastructure initiative." (61)

District of Columbia

$9 million for "hardware and software purchases." (61)

Idaho

$10.4 million (Idaho Educational Technology Initiative) for "technology in the classroom." (62)

Maine

$15 million (Governor) to "establish a distance learning network." (63)

Montana

$2.56 million (NSF) to support "SummitNet."

$100,000 (State) "for technology." (65)

Texas

$150 million (State, Telecommunications Infrastructure Fund).

$30/student (State) for "purchasing electronic textbooks or technological equipment . . . , training educational personnel directly involved in student learning, . . . access to technological equipment." (67)

Wisconsin

$10 million (State) for "improve[d] access to advanced telecommunications and distance education technologies." (68)

[Telecommunications providers] have provided unidentified funds for Advanced Telecommunications Foundation. (68)

In comparison to the miserly federal funding this country is allocating to other literacy and education projects, these amounts stagger the imagination.

To put these expenditures for technology into perspective, we can look at the 1999 budget for the Department of Education that President Clinton has recently sent to the United States Congress. In this budget, the President has requested $721 million of direct federal funding for educational technology but less than half of that amount, $260 million, for the America Reads Challenge and less than one-tenth of that amount, $67 million, for teacher recruitment and preparation (Community Update, No. 56, p. 3).

And we are already in the midst of this project—the administration's deadline for creating such a technologically literate citizenry, one that will think of official, school-sponsored literacy practices as occurring primarily in technological contexts, is "early in the 21st century" (*Getting America's Students Ready* 3).

This project, and the extensive influence it has had on our national understanding of officially-sponsored literacy practices, is a phenomenon that deserves close study not only because of the considerable attention that individual teachers and school districts around the country have already paid to its goals, but, interestingly and conversely, because of the utter lack of systematic and considered attention that our profession as a whole and our professional organizations have accorded it. And so I will move the story forward a bit more.

Since 1996, although our professional standards documents now reflect the core values of this project in that they assume the necessity of computer *use* by communicators in the 21st century, they do not provide adequate guidance about how to get teachers and students *thinking critically about such use.* Moreover, in a curious way, neither the CCCC, nor the NCTE, nor the MLA, nor the IRA—as far as I can tell—have ever published a single word about our own professional stance on this particular nationwide technology project: not one statement about how we think such literacy monies should be spent in English composition programs; not one statement about what kinds of literacy and technology efforts should be funded in connection with this project or how excellence should be gauged in these efforts; not one statement about the serious need for professional development and support for teachers that must be addressed within the context of this particular national literacy project.

Nor have these organizations articulated any official or direct response to the project's goals or the ways in which schools and teachers are already enacting these goals within classrooms. And this is true despite the fact that so many literacy educators in a range of situations — including all English and Language Arts teachers in primary, secondary, and college/university classrooms — have been broadly affected by the technology-literacy linkage for the past decade and will continue to be so involved well into the next century.

In other words, as members of these professional organizations, we need to do a much better job of paying critical attention to technology issues that affect us. Now why is this particular task so important? By paying critical attention to lessons about *technology,* we can re-learn important lessons about *literacy.* It is the different perspective on literacy that technology issues provide us that can encourage such insights. In the sections that follow, I point out just a few of these lessons.

Remembering the Truth about Large-Scale Literacy Projects and the Myth of Literacy

The first lesson that the national project to expand technological literacy can teach us has to do with the efficacy of large-scale literacy projects, in general, and with the myth of literacy. One of the primary arguments for the project to expand technological literacy rests on the claim that such an effort will provide all Americans with an education enriched by technology, and, thus, equal opportunity to access high-paying, technology-rich jobs and economic prosperity after graduation. The truth of this claim, however, has not been borne out and is not likely to be so. This fact is one of the primary reasons why we need to pay attention to technology issues.

Scholars such as Brian Street, Harvey Graff, and James Paul Gee note that such claims are not unusual in connection with large-scale, national literacy projects. Indeed, our willingness to believe these claims contributes to the potency of what Graff has called the "literacy myth," a widely held belief that literacy and literacy education lead autonomously, automatically, and directly to liberation, personal success, or economic prosperity. This myth, however, is delusory in its simplicity, as Street says:

> The reality [of national literacy movements] is more complex, is harder to face politically. . . . when it comes to job acquisition, the level of literacy is less important than issues of class, gender, and ethnicity; lack of literacy is more likely to be a symptom of poverty and deprivation than a cause. (18)

In the specific case of the project to expand technological literacy, the claim is that a national program will provide all citizens equal access to an improved education and, thus, equal opportunity for upward social mobility and economic prosperity. If we *pay attention* to the facts surrounding the project's instantiation, however, we can remind ourselves of the much harder lesson: in our educational system, and in the culture that this system reflects, computers *continue to be distributed differentially along the related axes of race and socioeconomic status* and this distribution contributes to ongoing patterns of racism and to the continuation of poverty.

It is a fact, for instance, that schools primarily serving students of color and poor students continue to have less access to computers, and access to less sophisticated computer equipment than do schools primarily serving more affluent and white students (Coley et al. 3). And it is a fact that schools primarily serving students of color and poor students continue to have less access to the Internet, less access to multimedia equipment, less access to CD-ROM equipment, less access to local area networks, less access to videodisc technology than do schools primarily serving more affluent and white students (Coley et al. 3).

This data, which is profoundly disturbing, becomes all the more problematic if we trace the extended effects of the technology-literacy linkage into the country's workplaces and homes. There, too, the latest census figures indicate, the linkage is strongly correlated to both race and socioeconomic status. It is a fact, for instance, that Black employees or Hispanic employees are *much* less likely than white employees to use a range of computer applications in their workplace environments (*Digest* 458). It is also a fact that employees who have not graduated from high school are much less likely to use a range of computer applications than are employees who have a high school degree or have some college experience (*Digest* 458). And it is a fact that poor families in both urban and rural environments and Black and Hispanic Americans are much less likely to own and use computers than individuals with higher family incomes and white families (*Condition* 212; *Digest 1996* 458; *Getting America's Students Ready* 36).

In other words, the poorer you are and the less educated you are in this country—both of which conditions are correlated with race—the less likely you are to have access to computers and to high-paying, high-tech jobs in the American workplace.

The challenges associated with the unequal distribution and use of computer technology along the related axes of socioeconomic status, education, and race have proven embarrassingly persistent for a number of related reasons. Secretary of Education Richard Riley, for example, citing a 1995 General Accounting Office Survey, notes that

> half of all schools do not have adequate wiring (such as outlets) to handle their technology needs. More than half do not have sufficient telephone lines, and 60 percent consider the number of conduits for network cable unsatisfactory. Schools that have all of these infrastructure elements are clearly the exception to the rule. Strikingly, schools in large central cities

are even less equipped to meet the demands of technology than other schools; more than 40 percent do not even have enough electrical power to use computers on a regular basis. . . . Classrooms in older buildings, for example, may require expensive renovations to improve electrical systems before computers and networks can be installed, discouraging the community from making a commitment. (*Getting America's Students Ready* 34–35).

As a result of this overdetermined system, the differential distribution of technology and technological literacy continues—albeit, with some complex new variations. In a recent article published in *Science,* for examples, Hoffman and Novak identified the following findings:

- Overall whites were significantly more likely than African Americans to have a home computer in their household. Whites were also slightly more likely to have access to a PC at work. (390)

- Proportionately, more than twice as many whites as African Americans had used the Web in the past week. As of January 1997, we estimate that 5.2 million (±1.2 million) African Americans and 40.8 million whites (±2.1 million) have ever used the Web, and that 1.4 million (±0.5 million) African Americans and 20.3 million (±1.6 million) whites used the Web in the past week. (390)

- As one would expect . . . increasing levels of income corresponded to an increased likelihood of owning a home computer, regardless of race. In contrast, adjusting for income did not eliminate the race differences with respect to computer access at work. . . . Notably . . . , race differences in Web use vanish at household incomes of $40,000 and higher. (390)

- 73% of white students owned a home computer, only 32% of African American students owned one. "This difference persisted when we statistically adjusted for students' reported household income." (390)

- White students were significantly more likely than African American students to have used the Web, especially in the past week. (391)

- White students lacking a home computer, but not African American students, appear to be accessing the Internet from locations such as homes of friends and relatives, libraries, and community centers. (391)

Acknowledging these facts, we might understand better why the rhetoric associated with national literacy projects serves to exacerbate the dangers that they pose. When Secretary of Education Richard Riley states, for example, that "Computers are the 'new basics' of education . . ." or that the project of technological literacy can help us give "all of our young people" an "opportunity to grow . . . and thrive" in the "new knowledge- and information-driven economy" (*Getting America's Students Ready* 3), he erroneously suggests, in Brian Street's words, "that the acquisition of literacy" will by itself "lead to 'major' impacts in terms of social and cognitive skills and 'development'" within a population (14). As Street reminds us, these "simple stories" that "both politicians and the press" tell about literacy to justify and sustain the momentum of such major programs, frequently "deflect attention from the complexity and real political difficulties" (17). The ultimate effect, according to Street, is an overly narrow understanding of literacy—usually in terms of a single official literacy—and the development of accompanying "patronizing assumptions about what it means to have difficulties with reading and writing in contemporary society. Such rhetoric also serves to raise false hopes about what the acquisition of literacy means for job prospects, social mobility, and personal achievement" (17).

In the specific case of computers and literacy, these stories serve to deflect our attention from the fact that "every single child" does *not* now have access to technology, and some students, especially those who are poor and of color, have less access than others. And so, *if* access to and use of technology in school-based settings *is* now a fundamental skill of literacy and *if* such skills *do* help prepare graduates for the jobs they will be asked to do, these same students can expect less opportunity to assume high-tech and high-paying jobs, not more. As Richard Ohmann described the underlying dynamic in a prescient 1985 *College English* article about the general relationship between technology, literacy, and economic conditions:

> Of course there will be more jobs in the computer field itself. But. . . . the field is layered into specialties, which will be dead ends for most people in them. . . . Graduates of MIT will get the challenging jobs; community college grads will be technicians; those who do no more than acquire basic skills and computer literacy in high school will probably find their way to electronic workstations at McDonald's. I see every reason to expect that the computer revolution, like other revolutions from the top down, will indeed expand the minds and the freedom of an elite, meanwhile facilitating the degradation of labor and the stratification of the workforce that have been hallmarks of monopoly capitalism from its onset. (683)

The frustrating cycle associated with this situation is so dismally clear and sickeningly familiar because it mirrors exactly the dynamics associated with more traditional literacy efforts in our country. As Graff notes, official literacies usually function in a conservative, and reproductive, fashion—in favor of dominant groups and in support of the existing class-based system:

> Hegemonic relationships have historically involved processes of group and class formation, recruitment, indoctrination, and maintenance at all levels of society. For most of literacy's history, these functions have centered upon elite groups and their cohesion and power. For them, the uses of literacy have been diverse but have included common education, culture, and language. . . . shared interests and activities; control of scarce commodities, such as wealth, power, and even literacy; and common symbols and badges, of which literacy could be one. (*Legacies* 12)

Thus, the national project to expand technological literacy has *not* served to reduce illiteracy—or the persistent social problems that exacerbate illiteracy. Rather, it has simply changed the official criteria for both "literate" and "illiterate" individuals, while retaining the basic ratio of both groups.

In sum, we have little evidence that any large-scale project focusing on a narrowly defined set of officially sanctioned literacy skills will result in fundamental changes in the ratio of people labeled as literate or illiterate. These categories are socially constructed identities which our current educational system reproduces rather than addresses. Similarly, we have no specific evidence that the current project to expand technological literacy will change the patterns of literacy and illiteracy in this country. Rather, this project is likely to support persistent patterns of economically-based literacy acquisition because citizens of color and those from low socioeconomic backgrounds continue to have less access to high-tech educational opportunities and occupy fewer positions that make multiple uses of technology than do white citizens or those from higher socioeconomic backgrounds.

LITERACY EDUCATION IS A POLITICAL ACT

Given the effects we have just described, the national project to expand technological literacy can also serve to re-teach us a second lesson — that literacy is always a political act as well as an educational effort. In this context, we can understand that the national project to expand technological literacy is motivated as much by political and economic agenda as it is by educational values and goals. To trace the concrete forms of political agenda, one relatively easy starting place is 1992. At that time in history, the Clinton-Gore team was preparing to enter Washington, and this administration had already identified technology as a key factor in both its domestic and international economic policies. At home, the Clinton-Gore team was facing a long-standing slowdown in manufacturing and productivity, persistent poverty, and an increasing income gap between the rich and the poor. As the 1997 *Economic Report to the President* tells the story:

> For more than two decades America has faced serious problems: productivity growth has been slower than in the past, income inequity has increased, and poverty has persisted. In addition, serious challenges loom for the future, such as the aging of the baby boom, which threatens to create severe fiscal strains in the next century. (Council 18)

The administration knew well that its ability to address these problems and to inject new vigor into the domestic economy — or to convince the American public that it had done so — would be a deciding factor in the way the effectiveness of their administration was judged. On the international scene, the Clinton-Gore team faced three important and related changes in the world's economic picture: the end of the Cold War and the fall of Communism in the Soviet Union, the emergence of growing markets among the developing countries of East Asia and Latin America that threatened to capture an increasingly large percentage of the world's consumers, and the threatening increase in competition due to the global scope of the international economy.

To kill these two economic birds with one stone, the Clinton-Gore administration focused on the idea of expanding America's technology efforts — the design, manufacturing, and consumption of both technology and technological expertise. On the international scene, the administration took three steps to expand technology efforts. The first step involved defining America's focused area of specialization in the world marketplace as technology and information services:

> The Administration's economic policy has been an aggressive effort to increase exports through the opening of markets abroad . . . The United States will certainly gain, both as a major exporter of information technology and as an importer, as American industries take advantage of new foreign technologies that will lower their costs and increase their productivity. (*Economic Report* 27)

The second and third steps involved exerting leadership in the development of a Global Information Infrastructure (GII) built on the back of the country's own National Information Infrastructure (NII). As part of this effort, the United States offered other countries—especially those with emerging markets that were hungry for technological involvement—the opportunity to buy American goods and services exported in connection with the GII. As Gore described the plan to the International Telecommunications Union in Buenos Aires in 1994:

> We can use the Global Information Infrastructure for technical collaboration between industrialized nations and developing countries. All agencies of the U.S. Government are potential sources of information and knowledge that can be shared with partners across the globe. . . . The U.S. can help provide the technical know-how needed to deploy and use these new technologies. USAID and U.S. businesses have helped the U.S. Telecommunications Training Institute train more than 3500 telecommunications professionals from the developing world, including many in this room.

Such a system also set up the possibility of continued reliance on American goods and services. Technicians trained in the deployment and use of American technology and American-designed operating systems, and American software, and American networks, for example, would tend to continue to rely on—and purchase—those products and components with which they were most familiar. Gore articulated the economic reasoning behind this plan:

> For us in the United States, the information infrastructure already is to the U.S. economy of the 1990s what transportation infrastructure was to the economy of the mid-20th century.
>
> The integration of computing and information networks into the economy makes U.S. manufacturing companies more productive, more competitive, and more adaptive to changing conditions . . .

The benefits associated with the GII expansion had political as well as economic effects. If the GII was constructed according to the Clinton-Gore plan, it would not only re-vitalize the American economy, it would also help promote the spread of democracy and capitalism around the globe within the context of a liberalized global economic system. The GII would accomplish this goal by providing forums for democratic involvement and expanded freedom of speech, by increasing privatization of technology resources, and by decreasing government regulation. As Gore noted:

> The GII will not only be a metaphor for a functioning democracy, it will in fact promote the functioning of democracy by greatly enhancing the participation of citizens in decision-making. And it will greatly promote the ability of nations to cooperate with each other. I see a new Athenian age of democracy forged in the fora the GII will create. . . .
>
> The integration of computing and information networks into the economy makes U.S. manufacturing companies more productive, more competitive, and more adaptive to changing conditions and it will do the same for the economies of other nations. . . .
>
> To promote; to protect, to preserve freedom and democracy, we must make telecommunications development an integral part of every nation's development. Each link we create strengthens the bonds of liberty and democracy around the world. By opening markets to stimulate the development of the global information infrastructure, we open lines of communication.
>
> By opening lines of communication, we open minds.

The international effort to expand technology, however, was only one part of the Clinton-Gore agenda. The other—and, in some ways, the more important—effort occurred in the domestic arena and focused on the revitalization of the American domestic economy through the expansion of the American computer industry. The Clinton-Gore team saw this particular industry as an economic "engine" (*Global Information* 3) that would, by increasing technological efforts at home, in turn, jump-start the international effort: providing the resources—the additional technology and the technological expertise—required to exploit emerging world markets.

To carry out this complex plan, the domestic engine of technology had to be cranked up and, to accomplish this goal, the Clinton-Gore administration knew that it had to accomplish two tasks:

- educate a pool of technologically sophisticated workers and technology specialists who could assist in the effort to reach new global markets and export more American manufactured equipment and specialized technology services to the rest of the world; and

- provide an influx of resources into the domestic computer industry so that it could simultaneously support the international effort and assume an increasingly important role in re-vitalizing the domestic economy.

And it was in response to these complexly related economic and political agendas that the national project to expand technological literacy was born. The dynamics that underlie this project were ideally and specifically suited to the economic and political goals we have just sketched out. Touted as an educational effort designed to improve citizens' literacy levels and, thus, their opportunities for future prosperity, the project was targeted at producing a continuing supply of educated workers who both had the skills necessary to design and manufacture increasingly sophisticated technological goods at home, and could offer sophisticated and specialized technological services in international arenas. Central to the task of achieving these targeted goals, the Clinton-Gore team recognized, was its ability to levy the power of the national educational system to reach large numbers of Americans in relatively short order. It was only within such a national system, they recognized, that an appropriately large proportion of the country's population could quickly acquire the training necessary to boost high-tech industries.

Importantly, such a plan was pretty close to self-fueling—citizens who learned the habits of reading, writing, and communicating on computers early in their lives within high-tech schools would tend to demand and consume such goods later in life when they graduated, thus injecting an increasingly continuous flow of money into the computer industry. And the plan's effects in the public sector promised to resonate effectively with its effects in the private sector: when citizens used, or were exposed to, cutting-edge technologies in their workplaces, or in school settings, they would desire them, as well, in their homes—and they would purchase updated technologies more frequently. Further, to ensure the continuation of the same high-tech careers and industries that have served them so well, such citizens would also tend to vote in support of political and economic programs that involved the further expansion of technology markets both domestically and internationally. Such citizens, moreover, would recognize the key role that technological literacy plays in their own success, and, so, demand a similar education for their children.

From our perspective today, of course, we can see a darker side of this dynamic. The economic engine of technology must be fueled by—and produce—not only a continuing supply of individuals who are highly *literate* in terms of technological knowledge, but also a ongoing supply of individuals who fail to acquire technological literacy, those who are termed *"illiterate"* according to the official definition. These latter individuals provide the unskilled, low-paid labor necessary to sustain the system I have described—their work generates the surplus labor that must be continually re-invested in capital projects to produce more sophisticated technologies.

The people labeled as "illiterate" in connection with technology—as expected—are those with the least power to effect a change in this system. They come from families who attend the poorest schools in this country and they attend schools with the highest populations of students of color. In part because of such facts, these students have less access to technology, in general, and less access to more sophisticated technology during their educational years. Partially as a result of their educational backgrounds, such individuals are hired into less desirable, lower-paid positions that demand fewer official technological literacy skills.

Moreover, because skills in *technological* communication environments are so closely linked with literacy instruction *in general,* and because students who come from such backgrounds are afforded the poorest efforts of the educational system and the lowest expectations of many teachers, the label of "illiterate" has broader implications for these individuals' ability to acquire other skills through their formal schooling years.

REMEMBERING OUR OWN ROLE IN THE LITERACY/ILLITERACY CYCLE

The danger associated with such an extensive ideological system, as Terry Eagleton points out, is the effective processes of naturalization that it engenders. Successful ideological systems, "render their beliefs natural and self evident" by so closely identifying them with "common sense" of a society so that nobody could imagine how they might ever be different (58). More importantly, as Eagleton continues,

> This process, which Pierre Bourdieu calls *doxa,* involves the ideology in creating as tight a fit as possible between itself and social reality, thereby closing the gap into which the leverage of critique could be inserted. Social reality is redefined by the ideology to become coextensive with itself, in a way which occludes the truth that the reality in fact generated the ideology. . . . The result, politically speaking, is an apparently vicious circle: the ideology could only become transformed if the reality was such as to allow it to become objectified; but the ideology processes reality in ways which forestall this possibility. The two are thus mutually self-confirming. On this view, a ruling ideology does not so much combat alternative ideas as thrust them beyond the very bounds of the thinkable. (58)

It is within this effectively naturalized matrix of interests, I would argue, that English teachers all over this country have become the unwitting purveyors of technology and technological literacy—even as we try to avoid a technological focus by attending to more traditionally conceived topics within the humanities.

The paradoxical dynamics at the heart of this situation are difficult to wrap our minds around especially because they function at so many different levels. Because we fail to address the project to expand technological literacy in focused, systematic, and critical ways within the professional arenas available to us, English composition teachers have come to understand technology as "just another instructional tool" that they can choose either to use or ignore. And, working from this context, we divide ourselves into two perfectly meaningless camps—those who use computers to teach classes and those who don't. Both groups feel virtuous about their choices, and both manage to lose sight of the real issue. Computer-using teachers instruct students in how to *use* technology—but, all too often, they neglect to teach students how *to pay critical attention* to the issues generated by technology use. Teachers who choose *not* to use technology in their classes content themselves with the mistaken belief that their choice to avoid technology use absolves them and the students in their classes from *paying critical attention* to technology issues. In other words, both groups contribute to the very same end. And when such things happen, when we allow ourselves to ignore technological issues, when we take technology for granted, when it becomes invisible to us, when we forget technology's material bases—regardless of whether or not we use technology—we participate unwittingly in the inequitable literacy system I have just described.

PAYING ATTENTION TO ACTION

So can composition teachers address the complex linkages among technology, literacy, poverty, and race? The primary factors determining any individual's involvement, of course, must necessarily start with the local and specific—with social agents' own deep and penetrating knowledge of the specific colleges and universities in which they work; the particular families, communities, cultures within which we live and form our own understanding of the world; the individual students, teachers, administrators, board members, politicians, and parents whose lives touch ours.

As Donna Haraway reminds us, this kind of "situated knowledges-approach" (175) leads to a kind of "coyote" (189) way of knowing—one different from the traditional perspective of Science, but in that difference, capable of offering a "more adequate, richer, better account of the world" that makes it possible to "live in it well and in critical, reflexive relation to our own as well as others' practices" (178). Such an approach may provide "only partial perspective" (181), Haraway cautions, but it allows us to avoid the trap of claiming a scientific objectivity that invites a false sense of closure and overly simple answers.

This kind of paying attention can serve as a collective effort to construct a "larger vision" of our responsibilities as a profession, one that depends on a strong sense of many *somewheres* (e.g., schools, classrooms, districts, communities) "in particular" (187)—especially when such a project is undertaken with a critical understanding of what we are trying to accomplish with such work and a collective commitment to seeing social problems "faithfully from another's point of view" (181) and even when it is clear that such a vision must remain partial, distorted, and incomplete. In this way, our profession can assemble, from many local understandings "stitched together imperfectly" (183), a picture of technological literacy—as it now functions within our culture—that might allow us to act with more strategic effectiveness and force, both collectively and individually.

A situated knowledges-approach to paying attention also honors a multiplicity of responses to technological literacy. Given the constraints of local and specific contexts, and a commitment to engaging with the lives of individual students, for example, some teachers will find their best avenue of involvement to reside in individual agency, others will find increasing effectiveness when they work with other colleagues. Some educators will find work within their own classroom to be the most immediately pressing and others will find the action in local communities to offer the most immediate and successful venue for their work. Indeed, the appreciation of local situations and variations may help composition studies professionals understand the power of large-scale projects when they are built on the critical understandings and active participation of a diverse group of educators.

Operating from this understanding of the local and particular, suggestions for critical engagement with technological literacy issues must allow for wide variations in social, political, economic, and ideological positionings, and wide variations in teachers, students, administrators, citizens, and communities. In deference to this approach, the suggestions that follow focus on the typical *sites* for critically informed action on technological literacy (and on general areas of attention within such sites) rather than on specific projects that should be undertaken within these sites. Individual teachers and groups of teachers, students, parents, and school administrators must determine within such sites how best to pay increased and critical attention to the linkage between technology and literacy—recognizing as fully as possible the local conditions affecting the work they do.

In Curriculum Committees, Standards Documents, and Assessment Programs

We need to pursue opportunities for resisting projects and systems that serve to establish an overly narrow, official version of literacy practices or skills. Such projects and systems simply serve to reward the literacy practices of dominant groups and punish the practices of others. They serve to reproduce a continuing and oppressive cycle of illiteracy, racism, and poverty in this country and in others.

Within these venues, composition specialists can lead the way in insisting on a diverse range of literacy practices and values, rather than one narrow and official form of literacy. We have made a start at this effort in the 1996 NCTE *Standards for the English Language Arts*, but CCCC needs to go much further in helping both future teachers and those already in classrooms understand why this work is so important and what implications their successes and failures may have.

In Our Professional Organizations

We need to recognize that if written language and literacy practices are our professional business, so is technology. This recognition demands a series of carefully considered and very visible professional stands on a variety of technological issues now under debate in this country: for example, on the access issues we have discussed, on the issue of technology funding for schools, on the issue of multiple venues for students' literacy practices, on the national project to expand technological literacy, and so on. We need to engage in much more of this kind of professional activism, and more consistently.

In Scholarship and Research

We also need to recognize that technological literacy is our responsibility. We need not only additional examinations of the ideological systems and cultural formations currently informing the literacy-technology link, but also the historical patterns established by other literacy technologies. And we need research like that Regina Copeland has just completed in West Virginia that takes a hard look at the access that individuals in various population groups—students of color, poor students, women—have to computer-support literacy instruction, and of the expenditure of government and schools and family funds in support of technology and literacy. We also need additional research on how various technologies influence literacy values and practices and research on how teachers might better use technologies to support a wide range of literacy goals for different populations. We need work like that Nancy Guerra Barron has completed in LA to examine the bilingual online discussions of Latino students in a Chicano studies class and trace the ways in which these students manage to shape and use electronic environments productively to mirror the linguistic richness of their lives outside the classroom. These projects represent only some of the many that we can encourage.

In Language Arts and English Studies Classrooms, and in First-Year and Advanced English Composition Courses

We need to recognize that we can no longer simply educate students to become technology users—and consumers—without also helping them learn how to become critical thinkers about technology and the social issues surrounding its use. When English/language arts faculty require students to use computers in completing a range of assignments—without also providing them the time and opportunity to explore the complex issues that surround technology and technology use in substantive ways—we may, without realizing it, be contributing to the education of citizens who are habituated to technology use but who have little critical awareness about, or understanding of, the complex relationships between humans, machines, and the cultural contexts within which the two interact.

Composition teachers, language arts teachers, and other literacy specialists need to recognize that the relevance of technology in the English studies disciplines is not simply a matter of helping students work effectively with communication software and hardware, but, rather, also a matter of helping them to understand and to be able to assess—to pay attention to—the social, economic, and pedagogical implications of new communication technologies and technological initiatives that affect their lives. Knowledgeable literacy specialists at all levels need to develop age-appropriate and level-appropriate reading and writing activities aimed at this goal. This approach—which recognizes the complex links that now exist between literacy and technology at the end of the twentieth century—constitutes a *critical technological literacy* that will serve students well.

In Computer-Based Communication Facilities

We have to put scholarship and research to work as praxis. These technology-rich facilities can serve not only as teaching environments for students completing literacy assignments — as sites within which both faculty and students can develop their own critical technological literacy — but also as sites within which students and faculty can formulate guidelines and policies for critically informed practices that put these understandings to work in complicated social situations. Feenberg offers the possibility of considering such sites in terms of their *underdetermined* potential, a potential which can be exploited by interested and knowledgeable social agents determined to make a difference in their own and others' lives. Technology-rich communication facilities are already replete with such interested agents — the English/language arts teachers involved in designing and teaching within them, the students involved in using them and learning within them, the staff members (often students) responsible for keeping them operational, and the administrators who help to fund them.

In technology-rich communication facilities, students and teachers can develop a more critically-informed sense of technology by actively confronting and addressing technology issues in contexts that matter — contexts that involve real people (peers, faculty, community members, staff members) engaged in a range of daily practices (making decisions about software and hardware purchases, hiring individuals who can help teachers and students deal more effectively with technology, setting lab fee levels for students, deciding on etiquette and use guidelines, identifying access problems) within their various lived experiences and in light of their own goals. When confronted and addressed in these complicated and often contradictory contexts, technology and technological issues become connected with social issues, human values, and material conditions — rather than naturalized and separated from such experiences.

These sets of issues and others are all part of the process of managing technology-rich environments, and each is a component of the critical technological literacy we believe students must develop as they become effective social agents and citizens. Our culture will need these activists — in school board and PTO meetings, in small businesses, on corporate boards, and in government agencies where decisions about communication technologies will influence the personal and professional lives of citizens.

In Districts and Systems and States That Have Poor Schools, Rural Schools, and Schools with Large Populations of Students of Color

We need to resist the tendential forces that continue to link technological literacy with patterns of racism and poverty. We need to insist on and support more equitable distributions of technology.

In Our Voting for School Board Elections, in Committee Meetings, in Public Hearings, at National Conventions, in the Public Relations Statements of Our Professional Organizations

We have to argue—at every chance that we can get—that poor students and students of color get more access to computers and to more sophisticated computers, that teachers in schools with high populations of such students be given more support.

In Pre-Service and In-Service Educational Programs and Curricula

We need to help all English composition teachers get more education on both technology use and technology criticism. In the curricula comprising our own graduate programs and the educational programs that prepare teachers for careers in our profession, we need to make sure these programs don't simply teach young professionals to *use* computers—but rather, that we teach them how to pay attention to technology and the issues that result from, and contribute to, the technology-literacy linkage. It is no longer enough, for instance, simply to ask graduate students or colleagues to use computers in composition classes. Instead, we need to help them read in the areas of technology criticism, social theories, and computer studies and, then, provide them important opportunities to participate in making hard decisions about how to pay attention to technology issues in departments, colleges, and local communities; how to address the existing links between literacy and technology in undergraduate curricula; how to provide more access to technology for more people and how to help individuals develop their own critical consciousness about technology.

In Libraries, Community Centers, and Other Non-Traditional Public Places

We need to provide free access to computers for citizens at the poverty level and citizens of color—not only so that such individuals have access to computers and, thus, can become proficient in computer use for communication tasks, but also so that these citizens have access to the Internet and to online sites for collective political [action] (Oppel; Hoffman and Novak).

TOWARD AN END . . .

The lessons I have outlined in the preceding pages, as I am sure readers understand, are as much about literacy as they are about technology. But, as Bruno Latour notes, real-life stories *always* lack richness and accuracy when they are told from a single perspective. We require multiple perspectives if we hope to construct a robust and accurate understanding of the ways in which technology functions in our culture. Our profession's occasional respectful attention to technology and the social issues that surround technology may allow us to see things from a slightly different point of view, even if for only a moment in time. And from such a perspective, as Latour reminds us, our interpretations of issues "take on added density" (viii).

I might add that this occasional merging of the technological and the humanist perspectives—into a vision that is more robustly informed—has as much value for scientists and engineers as it does for humanists. Margaret Boden, an early pioneer in artificial intelligence, notes in the Introduction to her landmark 1977 book, that she was drawn to the study of artificial intelligence for its potential in "counteracting the dehumanizing influence of natural science" and for its ability to "clarify the nature of human purpose, freedom, and moral choice," those "hidden complexities of human thinking" (4) that machines cannot replicate, that have always concerned us most within this profession.

One technology writer, Mark Weiser, has said that "The most profound technologies are those that disappear," that "weave themselves into the fabric of everyday life until they are indistinguishable from it" (94). I agree, but with a slightly different interpretation—these technologies may be the most *profound* when they disappear, but—it is exactly when this happens that they also develop the most potential for being *dangerous*. We have, as a culture, watched the twin strands of technology and literacy become woven into the fabric of our lives—they are now inscribed in legislation, in the law—in the warp and woof of our culture. But, recognizing this context, we cannot allow ourselves to lose sight of either formation. We must remind ourselves that laws write the texts of people's lives, that they constantly inscribe their intent and power on individuals—as Michel de Certeau says, "making its book out of them" (140).

It is our responsibility, as educators, to commit ourselves every day that we teach to reading and analyzing these texts, these lives of students—honestly, with respect, and to the very best of our collective and personal abilities. The alternative—of ignoring them, of perceiving students only in terms of their numbers in our schools or as members of undifferentiated groups—is simply unacceptable. As Elspeth Stuckey, Mike Rose, Harvey Graff, Brian Street, James Paul Gee, and many others have told us, when we participate in unthinking ways in political agendas, legislative initiatives, or educational systems that support an overly narrow version of official literacy, we all lose, and we are all implicated in the guilt that accrues to a system of violence through literacy.

It is my hope that by paying some attention to technology, we may learn lessons about becoming better humanists, as well.

WORKS CITED

Barron, Nancy Guerra. "Egalitarian Moments: Computer Mediated Communications in a Chicano Studies (ChS 111) Course." MA Thesis. California State U at Los Angeles, 1998.
Boden, Margaret. *Artificial Intelligence and Natural Man.* New York: Basic, 1977.
Bourdieu, Pierre. *Outline of a Theory of Practice.* New York: Cambridge UP, 1977.
Coley, R. J., J. Crandler, and P. Engle. *Computers and Classrooms: The Status of Technology in U.S. Schools* Princeton: ETS, 1997.

Copeland, Regina. "Identifying Barriers to Computer-Supported Instruction." Diss. West Virginia U, 1997.

Council of Economic Advisors. *Economic Report of the President.* Washington, DC: US Government Printing Office, 1997.

de Certeau, Michel. *The Practice of Everyday Life.* Trans. Steven Randall. Berkeley: U of California P, 1984.

Digest of Education Statistics 1996. Washington, DC: National Center for Education Statistics, Office of Educational Research and Improvement, 1996.

Eagleton, Terry. *Ideology: An Introduction.* London: Verso, 1991.

Faigley, Lester. "Literacy After the Revolution." *CCC 48* (1987): 30–43.

Feenberg, Andrew. *The Critical Theory of Technology.* New York: Oxford UP, 1991.

Gee, James. *Social Linguistics and Literacies: Ideology in Discourses.* New York: Falmer, 1990.

Getting America's Students Ready for the 21st Century: Meeting the Technology Literacy Challenge: A Report to the Nation on Technology and Education. Washington, DC: US Dept. of Education, 1996.

Giddens, Anthony. *The Constitution of Society: Outline of the Theory of Structuration.* Berkeley: U of California P, 1985.

Gore, Albert Jr. "VP Remarks—International Telecommunications Union." Buenos Aires, Argentina, 21 March 1994. <http://www.whitehouse.gov/WH/EOP/OVP/html/telunion.html>.

———. *Global Information Infrastructure: Agency for Cooperation.* Washington, DC: Government Printing Office, 1995.

Graff, Harvey J. *The Legacies of Literacy: Continuities and Contradictions in Western Cultures and Society.* Bloomington: Indiana UP, 1987.

———. *The Literacy Myth: Cultural Integration and Social Structure in the Nineteenth Century.* New Brunswick: Transaction, 1991.

Green, Kenneth C. "The Campus Computing Project: The 1995 National Survey of Desk-top Computing in Higher Education." 1996. <http://ericir.syr.edu/Projects/Campus_computing/1995/index.html>.

Haraway, Donna. "Situated Knowledges: The Science Question in Feminism and the Privilege of Partial Perspective." *Technology and The Politics of Knowledge.* Ed. Andrew Feenberg and Alastair Hannay. Bloomington: Indiana UP, 1995. 175–94.

Hoffman, Donna L., and Thomas P. Novak, "Bridging the Racial Divide on the Internet." *Science* 17 April 1998: 390–91.

Johnson-Eilola, Johndan. *Nostalgic Angels: Rearticulating Hypertext Writing.* Norwood: Ablex, 1997.

Latour, Bruno. *Aramis or the Love of Technology.* Trans. C. Porter. Cambridge: Harvard UP, 1996.

"MCI Nationwide Poll on Internet in Education." National Press Club. Washington, DC, March 1998.

Michigan Curriculum Framework: Content Standards and Benchmarks. Lansing: Michigan Dept. of Education, 1995.

Ohmann, Richard. "Literacy, Technology, and Monopoly Capital." *College English* 47 (1985): 675–89.

Oppel, Shelby. "Computer Lab Offers Escape from Poverty." *St. Petersburg Times* 17 Sept. 1997; 3B.

Oppenheimer, Todd. "The Computer Delusion." *Atlantic Monthly,* July 1997: 45–62.

"Public Law 102–73, the National Literacy Act of 1991." House of Representatives Bill 751, 25 July 1991. <http://novel.nifl.gov/public-law.html>.

Rose, Mike. *Lives on the Boundary: The Struggles and Achievements of America's Underprepared.* New York: Free P, 1989.

Smith, Thomas M. *Condition of Education, 1997.* Washington, DC: National Center for Education Statistics, U.S. Government Printing Office, 1997. NCES 97–388.

Standards for the English Language Arts. Urbana: NCTE, 1996.

Street, Brian V. *Social Literacies: Critical Approaches to Literacy Development, Ethnography, and Education.* London: Longman, 1995.

Stuckey, J. Elspeth. *The Violence of Literacy.* Portsmouth: Boynton, 1990.

US Dept. of Education. Community Update, No. 56. "President Clinton Sends 1999 Budget to Congress." Office of Intergovernmental and Interagency Affairs, 1998.

Virilio, Paul, *Speed and Politics: An Essay on Dromology.* Trans. Mark Polizzotti. New York: Semiotex(e), 1986.

Weiser, Mark. "The Computer for the 21st Century." *Scientific American* 265.3 (Sept. 1991): 94–104.

Winner, Langdon. *The Whale and the Reactor: A Search for Limits in an Age of High Technology.* Chicago: U of Chicago P, 1986.

From Pencils to Pixels: The Stages of Literacy Technologies

DENNIS BARON

The computer, the latest development in writing technology, promises, or threatens, to change literacy practices for better or worse, depending on your point of view. For many of us, the computer revolution came long ago, and it has left its mark on the way we do things with words. We take word processing as a given. We don't have typewriters in our offices anymore, or pencil sharpeners, or even printers with resolutions less than 300 dpi. We scour *MacUser* and *PC World* for the next software upgrade, cheaper RAM, faster chips, and the latest in connectivity. We can't wait for the next paradigm shift. Computerspeak enters ordinary English at a rapid pace. In 1993, "the information superhighway" was voted the word—actually the phrase—of the year. In 1995, the word of the year was "the World Wide Web," with "morph" a close runner-up. The computer is also touted as a gateway to literacy. The Speaker of the House of Representatives suggested that inner-city school children should try laptops to improve their performance. The Governor of Illinois thinks that hooking up every school classroom to the Web will eliminate illiteracy. In his second-term victory speech, President Clinton promised to have every eight-year-old reading, and to connect every twelve-year-old to the National Information Infrastructure. Futurologists write books predicting that computers will replace books. Newspapers rush to hook online subscribers. The *New York Times* will download the Sunday crossword puzzle, time me as I fill in the answers from my keyboard, even score my results. They'll worry later about how to get me to pay for this service.

I will not join in the hyperbole of predictions about what the computer will or will not do for literacy, though I will be the first to praise computers, to acknowledge the importance of the computer in the last fifteen years of my own career as a writer, and to predict that in the future the computer will be put to communication uses we cannot now even begin to imagine, something quite beyond the word processing I'm now using to produce a fairly conventional text, a book chapter.

Passions, Pedagogies, and 21st Century Technologies. Eds. Gail E. Hawisher and Cynthia L. Selfe. (Logan: Utah State P, 1999), 15–33.

I readily admit my dependence on the new technology of writing. Once, called away to a meeting whose substance did not command my unalloyed attention, I began drafting on my conference pad a memo I needed to get out to my staff by lunchtime. I found that I had become so used to composing virtual prose at the keyboard I could no longer draft anything coherent directly onto a piece of paper. It wasn't so much that I couldn't think of the words, but the physical effort of handwriting, crossing out, revising, cutting and pasting (which I couldn't very well do at a meeting without giving away my inattention), in short, the writing practices I had been engaged in regularly since the age of four, now seemed to overwhelm and constrict me, and I longed for the flexibility of digitized text.

When we write with cutting-edge tools, it is easy to forget that whether it consists of energized particles on a screen or ink embedded in paper or lines gouged into clay tablets, writing itself is always first and foremost a technology, a way of engineering materials in order to accomplish an end. Tied up as it is with value-laden notions of literacy, art, and science, of history and psychology, of education, of theory, and of practicality, we often lose sight of writing as technology, until, that is, a new technology like the computer comes along and we are thrown into excitement and confusion as we try it on, try it out, reject it, and then adapt it to our lives—and of course, adapt our lives to it.

New communications technologies, if they catch on, go through a number of strikingly similar stages. After their invention, their spread depends on accessibility, function, and authentication. Let me first summarize what I mean, and then I'll present some more detailed examples from the history of writing or literacy technologies to illustrate.

THE STAGES OF LITERACY TECHNOLOGIES

Each new literacy technology begins with a restricted communication function and is available only to a small number of initiates. Because of the high cost of the technology and general ignorance about it, practitioners keep it to themselves at first—either on purpose or because nobody else has any use for it—and then, gradually, they begin to mediate the technology for the general public. The technology expands beyond this "priestly" class when it is adapted to familiar functions often associated with an older, accepted form of communication. As costs decrease and the technology becomes better able to mimic more ordinary or familiar communications, a new literacy spreads across a population. Only then does the technology come into its own, no longer imitating the previous forms given us by the earlier communication technology, but creating new forms and new possibilities for communication. Moreover, in a kind of backward wave, the new technology begins to affect older technologies as well.

While brave new literacy technologies offer new opportunities for producing and manipulating text, they also present new opportunities for fraud. And as the technology spreads, so do reactions against it from supporters of what are purported to be older, simpler, better, or more honest ways of writing. Not only must the new technology be accessible and useful, it must demonstrate its trustworthiness as well. So procedures for authentication and reliability must be developed before the new technology becomes fully accepted. One of the greatest concerns about computer communications today involves their authentication and their potential for fraud.

My contention in this essay is a modest one: the computer is simply the latest step in a long line of writing technologies. In many ways its development parallels that of the pencil—hence my title—though the computer seems more complex and is undoubtedly more expensive. The authenticity of pencil writing is still frequently questioned: we prefer that signatures and other permanent or validating documents be in ink. Although I'm not aware that anyone actually opposed the use of pencils when they began to be used for writing, other literacy technologies, including writing itself, were initially met with suspicion was well as enthusiasm.

HUMANISTS AND TECHNOLOGY

In attacking society's growing dependence on communication technology, the Unabomber (1996) targeted computer scientists for elimination. But to my chagrin he excluded humanists from his list of sinister technocrats because he found them to be harmless. While I was glad not to be a direct target of this mad bomber, I admit that I felt left out. I asked myself, if humanists aren't harmful, then what's the point of being one? But I was afraid to say anything out loud, at least until a plausible suspect was in custody.

Humanists have long been considered out of the technology loop. They use technology, to be sure, but they are not generally seen as pushing the envelope. Most people think of writers as rejecting technological innovations like the computer and the information superhighway, preferring instead to bang away at manual type writers when they are not busy whittling new points on their no. 2 quill pens.

And it is true that some well-known writers have rejected new-fangleness. Writing in the *New York Times*, Bill Henderson (1994) reminds us that in 1849 Henry David Thoreau disparaged the information superhighway of his day, a telegraph connection from Maine to Texas. As Thoreau put it, "Maine and Texas, it may be, have nothing important to communicate." Henderson, who is a director of the Lead Pencil Club, a group opposed to computers and convinced that the old ways are better, further boasts that Thoreau wrote his anti-technology remarks with a pencil that he made himself. Apparently Samuel Morse, the developer of the telegraph, was lucky that the only letter bombs Thoreau made were literary ones.

In any case, Thoreau was not the complete Luddite that Henderson would have us believe. He was, in fact, an engineer, and he didn't make pencils for the same reason he went to live at Walden Pond, to get back to basics. Rather, he designed them for a living. Instead of waxing nostalgic about the good old days of hand-made pencils, Thoreau sought to improve the process by developing a cutting-edge manufacturing technology of his own.

The pencil may be old, but like the computer today and the telegraph in 1849, it is an indisputable example of a communication technology. Henderson unwittingly concedes as much when he adds that Thoreau's father founded "the first quality pencil [factory] in America." In Thoreau's day, a good pencil was hard to find, and until Thoreau's father and uncle began making pencils in the New World, the best ones were imported from Europe. The family fortune was built on the earnings of the Thoreau Pencil Company, and Henry Thoreau not only supported his sojourn at Walden Pond and his trip to the Maine woods with pencil profits, he himself perfected some of the techniques of pencil-making that made Thoreau pencils so desirable.

The pencil may seem a simple device in contrast to the computer, but although it has fewer parts, it too is an advanced technology. The engineer Henry Petroski (1990) portrays the development of the wood-cased pencil as a paradigm of the engineering process, hinging on the solution of two essential problems: finding the correct blend of graphite and clay so that the "lead" is not too soft or too brittle; and getting the lead into the cedar wood case so that it doesn't break when the point is sharpened or when pressure is applied during use. Pencil technologies involve advanced design techniques, the preparation and purification of graphite, the mixing of graphite with various clays, the baking and curing of the lead mixture, its extrusion into leads, and the preparation and finishing of the wood casings. Petroski observes that pencil making also involves a knowledge of dyes, shellacs, resins, clamps, solvents, paints, woods, rubber, glue, printing ink, waxes, lacquer, cotton, drying equipment, impregnating processes, high-temperature furnaces, abrasives, and mixing (Petroski 12). These are no simple matters. A hobbyist cannot decide to make a wood-cased pencil at home and go out to the craft shop for a set of instructions. Pencil-making processes were from the outset proprietary secrets as closely guarded as any Macintosh code.

The development of the pencil is also a paradigm of the development of literacy. In the two hundred fifty years between its invention, in the 1560s, and its perfection at John Thoreau and Company, as well as in the factories of Conté in France, and Staedtler and Faber in Germany, the humble wood pencil underwent several changes in form, greatly expanded its functions, and developed from a curiosity of use to cabinet-makers, artists and note-takers into a tool so universally employed for writing that we seldom give it any thought.

THE TECHNOLOGY OF WRITING

Of course the first writing technology was writing itself. Just like the telegraph and the computer, writing itself was once an innovation strongly resisted by traditionalists because it was unnatural and untrustworthy. Plato was one leading thinker who spoke out strongly against writing, fearing that it would weaken our memories. Pessimistic complaints about new literacy technologies, like those made by Plato, by Bill Henderson, and by Henderson's idol, Henry David Thoreau, are balanced by inflated predictions of how technologies will change our lives for the better. According to one school of anthropology, the invention of writing triggered a cognitive revolution in human development (for a critique of this so-called Great Divide theory of writing, see Street 1984). Historians of print are fond of pointing to the invention of the printing press in Europe as the second great cognitive revolution (Eisenstein 1979). The spread of electric power, the invention of radio, and later television, all promised similar bio-cultural progress. Now, the influence of computers on more and more aspects of our existence has led futurologists to proclaim that another technological threshold is at hand. Computer gurus offer us a brave new world of communications where we will experience cognitive changes of a magnitude never before known. Of course, the Unabomber and the Lead Pencil Club think otherwise.

Both the supporters and the critics of new communication technologies like to compare them to the good, or bad, old days. Jay Bolter disparages the typewriter as nothing more than a machine for duplicating texts—and as such, he argues, it has not changed writing at all. In contrast, Bolter characterizes the computer as offering a paradigm shift not seen since the invention of the printing press, or for that matter, since the invention of writing itself. But when the typewriter first began to sweep across America's offices, it too promised to change writing radically, in ways never before imagined. So threatening was the typewriter to the traditional literatus that in 1938 the *New York Times* editorialized against the machine that depersonalized writing, usurping the place of "writing with one's own hand."

The development of writing itself illustrates the stages of technological spread. We normally assume that writing was invented to transcribe speech, but that is not strictly correct. The earliest Sumerian inscriptions, dating from ca. 3500 BCE, record not conversations, incantations, or other sorts of oral utterances, but land sales, business transactions, and tax accounts (Crystal 1987). Clay tokens bearing similar marks appear for several thousand years before these first inscriptions. It is often difficult to tell when we are dealing with writing and when with art (the recent discovery of 10,000-year-old stone carvings in Syria has been touted as a possible missing link in the art-to-writing chain), but the to-

FIGURE 7.1   Clay Tokens and Sumerian Inscriptions

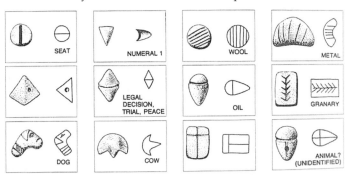

Clay tokens. Some of the commonest shapes are here compared with the incised characters in the earliest Sumerian incriptions (only some of which have been interpreted) (Crystal 1987, 196).

kens seem to have been used as a system of accounting from at least the 9th millennium BCE. They are often regarded as the first examples of writing, and it is clear that they are only distantly related to actual speech (see figure 7.1).

We cannot be exactly sure why writing was invented, but just as the gurus of today's technology are called computer geeks, it's possible that the first writers also seemed like a bunch of oddballs to the early Sumerians, who might have called them cuneiform geeks. Surely they walked around all day with a bunch of sharp styluses sticking out of their pocket protectors, and talked of nothing but new ways of making marks on stones. Anyway, so far as we know, writing itself begins not as speech transcription but as a relatively restricted and obscure record-keeping shorthand.

As innovative uses for the literacy technology are tried out, practitioners may also adapt it to older, more familiar forms in order to gain acceptance from a wider group. Although writing began as a tool of the bean counters, it eventually added a second, magical/religious function, also restricted and obscure as a tool of priests. For writing to spread into a more general population in the ancient world, it had first to gain acceptance by approximating spoken language. Once writers—in a more "modern" sense of the word—discovered what writing could do, there was no turning back. But even today, most written text does not transcribe spoken language: the comparison of script and transcript in figure 7.2 makes this abundantly clear.

Of course writing never spread very greatly in the ancient world. William Harris (1989) argues convincingly that no more than ten percent of the classical Greek or Roman populations could have been literate. One reason for this must be that writing technology remained both cumbersome and expensive: writing instruments, paints, and inks had to be hand made, and writing surfaces like clay tablets, wax tablets, and papyrus had to be laboriously prepared. Writing therefore remained exclusive, until cheap paper became

FIGURE 7.2   Script and Transcript

Scripted Dialogue:

Thersites: The common curse of mankind, folly and ignorance, be thine in great revenue! heaven bless thee from a tutor, and discipline come not near thee! Let thy blood be thy direction till thy death! then, if she that lays thee out says thou art a fair corpse, I'll be sworn and sworn upon't she never shrouded any but lazars. Amen.

Shakespeare, *Troilus and Cressida,* II, iii, 30.

Unscripted Dialogue (Ostensibly):

Lt. Col. North: I do not recall a specific discussion. But, I mean. It was widely known within the CIA. I mean we were tracking that sensitive intelligence. I—I honestly don't recall, Mr. Van Cleve. I mean it—it didn't seem to me, at the time, that it was something that I was trying to hide from anybody. I was not engaged in it. And one of the purposes that I though we had that finding for was to go back and ratify that earlier action, and to get on with replenishing. I mean, that was one—what I understood one of the purposes of the draft to be.

from *Taking the Stand: The Testimony of Lt. Col. Oliver North,* 15 available, and the printing press made mass production of written texts more affordable and less labor-intensive.

What Writing Does Differently

As a literacy technology like writing begins to become established, it also goes beyond the previous technology in innovative, often compelling ways. For example, while writing cannot replace many speech functions, it allows us to communicate in ways that speech does not. Writing lacks such tonal cues of the human voice as pitch and stress, not to mention the physical cues that accompany face to face communication, but it also permits new ways of bridging time and space. Conversations become letters. Sagas become novels. Customs become legal codes. The written language takes on a life of its own, and it even begins to influence how the spoken language is used. To cite an obvious example, people begin to reject traditional pronunciations in favor of those that reflect a word's spelling: the pronunciation of the "l" in falcon (compare the l-less pronunciation of the cognate name Faulkner) and the "h" in such "th" combinations as *Anthony* and *Elizabeth* (compare the nicknames *Tony* and *Betty,* which reflect the earlier, h-less pronunciation).

In order to gain acceptance, a new literacy technology must also develop a means of authenticating itself. Michael Clanchy (1993) reports that when writing was introduced as a means of recording land transfer in 11th-century England, it was initially perceived (and often rightly so) as a nasty Norman trick for stealing Saxon land.

As Clanchy notes, spoken language was easily corroborated: human witnesses were interactive. They could be called to attest whether or not a property transfer had taken place. Doubters could question witnesses, watch their eyes, see whether witnesses sank when thrown bound into a lake. Written documents did not respond to questions—they were not interactive. So the writers and users of documents had to develop their own means of authentication. At first, seals, knives, and other symbolic bits of property were attached to documents in an attempt to give them credibility. Medieval English land transfers also adopted the format of texts already established as trustworthy, the Bible or the prayer book, complete with illuminations, in order to convince readers of their validity.

Questions of validity came up because writing was indeed being used to perpetrate fraud. Monks, who controlled writing technology in England at the time, were also responsible for some notorious forgeries used to snatch land from private owners. As writing technology developed over the centuries, additional ways of authenticating text came into use. Individualistic signatures eventually replaced seals to the extent that today, many people's signatures differ significantly from the rest of their handwriting. Watermarks identified the provenance of paper; dates and serial numbers further certify documents, and in the absence of other authenticators, stylistic analysis may allow us to guess at authorship on the basis of comparative and internal textual evidence. In the digital age, we are faced with the interesting task of reinventing appropriate ways to validate cybertext.

THE PENCIL AS TECHNOLOGY

Just as writing was not designed initially as a way of recording speech, the pencil was not invented to be a writing device. The ancient lead-pointed stylus was used to scribe lines—the lead made a faint pencil-like mark on a surface, suitable for marking off measurements but not for writing. The modern pencil, which holds not lead but a piece of graphite encased in a wooden handle, doesn't come on the scene until the 1560s.

The 16th-century pencil consists of a piece of graphite snapped or shaved from a larger block, then fastened to a handle for ease of use. The first pencils were made by joiners, woodworkers specializing in making furniture, to scribe measurements in wood. Unlike the traditional metal-pointed scribing tools, pencils didn't leave a permanent dent in the wood. By the time Gesner observed the pencil, it had been adopted as a tool by note-takers, natural scientists or others who needed to write, sketch, or take measurements in the field. Carrying pens and ink pots outdoors was cumbersome. Early pencils had knobs at one end so that they could be fastened with string or chain to a notebook, creating the precursor to the laptop computer.

Pencils were also of use to artists. In fact the word pencil means "little tail," and refers not only to the modern wood-cased pencil but to the artist's brush. Ink and paint are difficult to erase: they must be scraped off a surface with a knife, or painted over. But graphite pencil marks were more easily erased by using bread crumbs, and of course later by erasers made of rubber—in fact the eraser substance (caoutchouc, the milky juice of tropical plants such as ficus) was called rubber because it was used to rub out pencil marks.

THOREAU AND PENCIL TECHNOLOGY

It is true that Thoreau rejected modern improvements like the telegraph as worthless illusions. In *Walden* he says, "They are but improved means to an unimproved end." Thoreau did not write much of pencils. He even omitted the pencil in his list of items to take into the Maine woods, though like naturalists before him, he certainly carried one on his twelve-day excursion in order to record his thoughts. Despite this silence, Thoreau devoted ten years of his life to improving pencil technology at his family's pencil factory. It was this pencil technology, not inherited wealth or publication royalties, that provided the income for one of the greatest writers of the American renaissance.

As Petroski tells it, the pencil industry in the eighteenth century was buffeted by such vagaries as the unpredictable supply of graphite, dwindling cedar forests, protective tariffs, and, for much of its history, an international consumer preference for British-made pencils. All of this affected John Thoreau and Co., manufacturers of pencils. Until the nineteenth century, the

Figure 7.3   De Figuris Lapidum

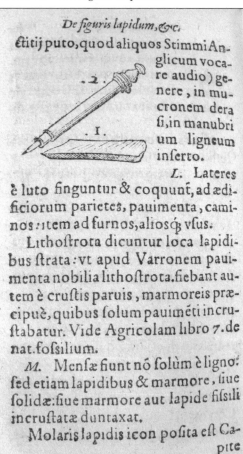

De figuris lapidum, &c.

étitij puto, quod aliquos StimmiAn-
glicum voca-
re audio) ge-
nere, in mu-
cronem dera
fi, in manubri
um ligneum
inferto.

L. Lateres
è luto finguntur & coquunt, ad ædi-
ficiorum parietes, pauimenta, cami-
nos: item ad furnos, aliosǫ vfus.

Lithoftrota dicuntur loca lapidibus ftrata: vt apud Varronem pauimenta nobilia lithoftrota. fiebant au-
tem è cruftis paruis, marmoreis præ-
cipuè, quibus folum pauiméti incru-
ftabatur. Vide Agricolam libro 7. de
nat. fofsilium.

M. Menfæ fiunt nó folùm è ligno:
fed etiam lapidibus & marmore, fiue
folidæ: fiue marmore aut lapide fifsili
incruftatæ duntaxat.

Molaris lapidis icon pofita eft Ca-
pite

*Translation: "The stylus ... is made ... from a sort of lead
(which I have heard some call English antimony), shaved to
a point and inserted in a wooden handle." From* De rerum
fossilium lapidum et gemmarum maxime, figures et
similitudinibus liber, *a book on the shapes and images of
fossils, esp. those in stone and rock. Gesner wrote a Greek-
Latin dictionary, was a doctor, lectured on physics, and,
obviously, was a rock hound.*

best pencil graphite (or plumbago, as it was often called), came from Borrowdale, in England. There were other graphite deposits around the world, but
their ore was not particularly pure. Impure ore crumbled or produced a
scratchy line. In the later eighteenth century, the Borrowdale deposits began
to run low, and exports were curtailed. After the French Revolution, with his
supply of English graphite permanently embargoed, the French pencil-maker

Nicholas-Jacques Conté learned to produce a workable writing medium by grinding the local graphite, mixing it with clay and water, and forcing the mixture into wooden casings.

This process allowed the French to produce their own pencils, and it also permitted manufacturers to control the hardness of the lead, which in turn controlled the darkness of the mark made by the pencil. (The more clay, the harder the lead, and the lighter and crisper the mark; less clay gives a darker, grainier mark). So successful was Conté's process that Conté became synonymous with pencil, and Conté crayons are still valued by artists. In Nuremberg, Staedtler learned to mix ground graphite with sulfur. He and his rival, Faber, founded German pencil dynasties that also survive to this day.

The superiority of Borrowdale English graphite was evident to American consumers as well, and they regularly preferred imports to domestic brands. American pencil manufacturers had a hard time convincing the public that they could make a good native pencil. In 1821 Charles Dunbar discovered a deposit of plumbago in Bristol, New Hampshire, and he and his brother-in-law, John Thoreau, went into the pencil business. By 1824 Thoreau pencils were winning recognition. Their graphite, however, was not as pure as Borrowdale, and since the Conté process was unknown in the United States, American pencils, though cheaper than imports, remained inferior.

Henry Thoreau set about to improve his father's pencil. According to Petroski, Thoreau began his research in the Harvard Library. But then, as now, there was little written on pencil manufacture. Somehow, Thoreau learned to grind graphite more finely than had been done before and to mix it with clay in just the right proportion, for his improvements on the pencil-making process, combined with the high import duty imposed on British pencils after the War of 1812, led to great demand for Thoreau pencils.

Thoreau did not ascribe transcendent value to pencils. As Petroski sees it, Thoreau's purpose was simply to make money. Once he developed the best pencil of the day, Thoreau saw no sense in trying to improve on his design. His pencils sold for seventy-five cents a dozen, higher than other brands, a fact which Emerson remarked on, though he still recommended Thoreau pencils to his friends. It is easy for us to think of Thoreau only as a romantic who lived deliberately, disobeyed civil authority, and turned Walden Pond into a national historic site. But to do these things, he was also an engineer and marketing expert. When pencil competition grew, shaving his profit margin, Thoreau stopped pushing pencils and sold his graphite wholesale to electrotypers because this proved more lucrative (Petroski 122).

Perhaps, then, Thoreau, despite his technological expertise, opposed Morse's telegraph just to protect the family business. It is more likely, though, from the absence of references to pencil-making in any of his writings, that Thoreau honestly thought pencils were better for writing than electrical impulses, and he simply kept his business life and his intellectual life in separate compartments. In any case, Thoreau's resistance to the telegraph didn't stop the project.

THE TELEPHONE

The introduction of the telephone shows us once again how the pattern of communications technology takes shape. The telephone was initially received as an interesting but impractical device for communicating across distance. Although as Thoreau feared, the telegraph eventually did permit Maine and Texas and just about everywhere else to say nothing to one another, Samuel F. B. Morse, who patented the telegraph and invented its code, saw no use for Alexander Graham Bell's even newer device, the telephone. Morse refused Bell's offer to sell him the rights to the telephone patent. He was convinced that no one would want the telephone because it was unable to provide any permanent record of a conversation.

Indeed, although we now consider it indispensable, like writing, the uses of the telephone were not immediately apparent to many people. Telephone communication combined aspects of speaking and writing situations in new ways, and it took a while to figure out what the telephone could and couldn't do. Once they became established, telephones were sometimes viewed as replacements for earlier technologies. In some cities, news and sports broadcasts were delivered over the telephone, competing with the radio (Marvin 1988). Futurologists predicted that the telephone would replace the school or library as a transmitter of knowledge and information, that medical therapy (including hypnosis) could be delivered and criminals punished over the phone through the use of electrical impulses. The telephone even competed with the clock and the thermometer: when I was growing up in New York in the 1950s, my family regularly called MEridian 7–1212 to find out the time, and WEather 6–1212 for the temperature and forecast.

Of course the telephone was not only a source of information. It also threatened our privacy. One early fear of putting telephones in people's homes was that strangers could call up uninvited; people could talk to us on the phone whom we would never wish to converse with in person—and no one predicted then that people selling useless products would invariably call at dinner time. Today, as our email addresses circulate through the ether, we find in our electronic mailboxes not just surprise communications from long-lost acquaintances who have tracked us down using Gopher and other Web browsers, but also unwelcome communiqués from intruders offering get-rich-quick schemes, questionable deals, and shoddy merchandise. Even unsolicited religious messages are now circulating freely on net news groups.

The introduction of the telephone for social communication also required considerable adaptation of the ways we talk, a fact we tend to forget because we think of the modern telephone as a reliable and flexible instrument. People had to learn how to converse on the telephone: its sound reproduction was poor; callers had to speak loudly and repeat themselves to be understood, a situation hardly conducive to natural conversation. Telephones were located centrally and publicly in houses, which meant that conversations were never private. Telephones emulated face-to-face communication, but they could not transmit the visible cues and physical gestures that allow face-to-face conversation to proceed smoothly, and this deficiency had to be overcome. Many people still accompany phone conversations with hand and facial gestures; very young children often nod into phone instead of saying "Yes" or "No," as if their interlocutor could see them.

Initially, people were unsure of the appropriate ways to begin or end phone conversations, and lively debates ensued. The terms "hello" and "good-bye" quickly became standard, despite objections from purists who maintained that "hello" was not a greeting but an expression of surprise, and that "good-bye" coming from "God be with you," was too high-toned and serious a phrase to be used for something so trivial as telephone talk. As people discovered that telephones could further romantic liaisons, guardians of the public morality voiced concern or disgust that sweethearts were actually making kissing noises over the phone. Appropriate language during conversation was also an issue, and phone companies would cut off customers for swearing (like today's computer Systems Operators, or Sysops, the telephone operators, or "hello girls" as they were called in the early days, frequently listened in on conversations and had the authority to interrupt or disconnect calls).

While the telephone company routinely monitored the contents of telephone calls, when transcripts of telephone conversations were first introduced as evidence in trials, phone companies argued that these communications were just as private and privileged as doctor-patient exchanges (Marvin 68). Phone companies also tried to limit telephone access solely to the subscriber, threatening hotels and other businesses with loss of phone service if they allowed guests or customers to make calls. Telephone companies backed down from their demand that phones only be used by their registered owners once another technological development, the pay telephone, was introduced, and their continued profits were assured (this situation is analogous to the discussions of copy protection and site licensing for computer software today).

THE COMPUTER AND THE PATTERN OF LITERACY TECHNOLOGY

Writing was not initially speech transcription, and pencils were first made for woodworkers, not writers. Similarly, the mainframe computer when it was introduced was intended to perform numerical calculations too tedious or complex to do by hand. Personal computers were not initially meant for word processing either, though that has since become one of their primary functions.

Mainframe line editors were so cumbersome that even computer programmers preferred to write their code with pencil and paper. Computer operators actually scorned the thought of using their powerful number-crunchers to process mere words. Those who braved the clumsy technology to type text were condemned to using a system that seemed diabolically designed to slow a writer down well below anything that could be done on an IBM Selectric, or even with a pencil. (Interestingly, when the typewriter was developed, the keyboard was designed to slow down writers, whose typing was faster than the machine could handle; initially computers too were slow to respond to keystrokes, and until type-ahead capability was developed, typists were frustrated by loud beeps indicating they had exceeded the machine's capacity to remember what to do.)

Early word-processing software for personal computers did little to improve the situation. At last, in the early 1980s, programs like Wordstar began to produce text that looked more like the typing that many writers had become used to. Even so, writers had to put up with screens cluttered with formatting characters. Word wrap was not automatic, so paragraphs had to be reformatted every time they were revised. Furthermore, printed versions of text seldom matched what was on the computer screen, turning page design into a laborious trial-and-error session. Adding to the writer's problems was the fact that the screen itself looked nothing like the piece of paper the text would ultimately be printed on. The first PC screens were grayish-black with green phosphor letters, displaying considerably less than a full page of text. When it came along, the amber screen offered what was seen as a major improvement, reducing eye strain for many people. Today we expect displays not only with black on white, just like real paper, and high resolution text characters, but also with color, which takes us a step beyond what we could do with ordinary typing paper.

If the initial technical obstacles to word processing on a PC weren't enough to keep writers away from the new technology, they still had to come up with the requisite $5,000 or more in start-up funds for an entry-level personal computer. Only die-hards and visionaries considered computer word processing worth pursuing, and even they held on to their Selectrics and their Bics just in case.

The next generation of word-processing computers gave us WYSIWYG: "what you see is what you get," and that helped less-adventurous writers make the jump to computers. Only when Macintosh and Windows operating

---

FIGURE 7.4   Instructions from a Wordstar Manual

If you type this:

^BCombining Special Effects^B. To combine special effects, simply insert one control character after another. For example, your ^BWordstar^B^VTM^V cursor may look like this: H^HI^HN^HZ.

|^Ba^B| = /(a^Vx^V^T2^T+a^Vy^V^T2^T+a^Vz^V^T2^T)

You (might) get this:

Combining Special Effects.   To combine special effects, simply insert one control character after another. For example, your **Wordstar**™ cursor may look like this: ■.

$|\mathbf{a}| = /(a_x{}^2 + a_y{}^2 + a_z{}^2)$

---

systems allowed users to create on-screen documents that looked and felt like the old, familiar documents they were used to creating on electric typewriters did word processing really become popular. At the same time, start-up costs decreased significantly and with new, affordable hardware, computer writing technology quickly moved from the imitation of typing to the inclusion of graphics.

Of course that, too, was not an innovation in text production. We'd been pasting up text and graphics for ages. The decorated medieval charters of eleventh-century England are a perfect parallel to our computerized graphics a millennium later. But just as writing in the Middle Ages was able to move beyond earlier limitations, computer word processing has now moved beyond the texts made possible by earlier technologies by adding not just graphics, but animation, video, and sound to documents. In addition, Hypertext and HTML allow us to create links between documents or paths within them, both of which offer restructured alternatives to linear reading.

The new technology also raises the specter of digital fraud, and the latest literacy technology is now faced with the task of developing new methods of authentication to ensure confidence and trust in its audience (see figure 7.5).

Over the years, we have developed a number of safeguards for preventing or detecting fraud in conventionally produced texts. The fact that counterfeit currency still gets passed, and that document forgeries such as the *Hitler Diaries* or hoaxes like the physicist Alan Sokal's spoof of deconstruction, "Transgressing the Boundaries: Toward a Transformational Hermeneutics of Quantum Gravity," come to light from time to time shows that the safeguards, while strong, are not necessarily foolproof. The average reader is not equipped to detect many kinds of document falsification, and a lot of text is still accepted on trust. A writer's reputation, or that of a publisher, predisposes readers to accept certain texts as authoritative, and to reject others. Provenance, in the world of conventional documents, is everything. We have learned to trust writing that leaves a paper trail.

Things are not so black and white in the world of digital text. Of course, as more and more people do business on the Internet, the security of transactions, of passwords, credit card numbers, and bank accounts becomes vital. But the security and authenticity of "ordinary" texts is a major concern as well. Anyone with a computer and a modem can put information into cyberspace. As we see from figure 7.5, digitized graphics are easy to alter. Someone intent on committing more serious deception can with not too much trouble alter text, sound, graphics, and video files. Recently several former Columbia University students were arrested for passing fake twenty-dollar bills that they had duplicated on one of Columbia's high-end color printers. The Treasury Department reported that while these counterfeits were easy for a nonexpert to spot, some $8,000 to $9,000 of the bad money had been spent before the counterfeiters attracted any attention. Security experts, well aware of the problems of digital fraud, are developing scramblers, electronic watermarks and invisible tagging devices to protect the integrity of digital files, and hackers are probably working just as hard to defeat the new safeguards. Nonethe-

Figure 7.5   Example of Digital Fraud

From Feb. 1994 Scientific American, *William J. Mitchell, "When is seeing believing?" (68–73). Mitchell explains the process used to create this photograph of Marilyn Monroe and Abraham Lincoln that never existed in the original. The final result can be so seamless that the forgery is undetectable. Examples of the intrusion of such false images include an ABC News broadcast in which correspondent Nina Totenberg was shown on camera with the White House in the background. In actuality, she was miles away in a studio and the montage gave the impression she was reporting from the field. Needless to say, fraudulent computer text is even easier to compose and promulgate across the bandwidth.*

less, once a file has been converted to hard copy, it is not clear how it could be authenticated.

Digitized text is even easier to corrupt accidentally, or to fiddle with on purpose. Errors can be inadvertently introduced when print documents are scanned. With electronic text, it may be difficult to recover other indicators that we expect easy access to when we deal with print: the date of publication, the edition (sometimes critical when dealing with newspaper or literary texts), editorial changes or formatting introduced during the digitization process, changes in accompanying graphics (for example, online versions of the *Washington Post* and the *New York Times* use color illustrations not found in the paper editions). And of course digital text can be corrupted on purpose in ways that will not be apparent to unsuspecting readers.

Electronic texts also present some challenges to the ways we attribute expertise to authors. When I read newsgroups and electronic discussion lists, I must develop new means for establishing the expertise or authority of a poster. I recently tried following a technical discussion on a bicycle newsgroup about the relative advantages of butyl and latex innertubes. I can accept the advice of a bicycle mechanic I know, because we have a history, but posters to a newsgroup are all strangers to me. They may be experts, novices, cranks, or some combination of the three, and in the case of the two kinds of tire tubes, I had difficulty evaluating the often conflicting recommendations I received. After reading the newsgroup for a while, becoming familiar with those who post regularly, and getting a sense of the kinds of advice they gave and their attitudes toward the subject, I began to develop a nose for what was credible. My difficulty was compounded, though, because the most authoritative-sounding poster, in the conventional sense of authoritative — someone who evoked principles of physics and engineering to demonstrate that flats were no more common or disastrous with latex than butyl tubes, and who claimed to have written books on bicycle repair — was clearly outshouted by posters attesting the frequency and danger of rupturing latex inner tubes. In the end I chose to stay with butyl, since everyone seemed to agree that, though heavier than latex, it was certainly not the worst thing in the world to ride on.

My example may seem trivial, but as more and more people turn to the World Wide Web for information, and as students begin relying on it for their research papers, verifying the reliability and authenticity of that information becomes increasingly important, as does revisiting it later to check quotations or gather more information. As anyone knows who's lost a file or tried to revisit a website, electronic texts have a greater tendency to disappear than conventional print resources.

CONCLUSION

As the old technologies become automatic and invisible, we find ourselves more concerned with fighting or embracing what's new. Ten years ago, math teachers worried that if students were allowed to use calculators, they wouldn't learn their arithmetic tables. Regardless of the value parents and teachers still place on knowing math facts, calculators are now indispensable in math class. When we began to use computers in university writing classes, instructors didn't tell students about the spell-check programs on their word processors, fearing the students would forget how to spell. The hackers found the spelling checkers anyway, and now teachers complain if their students don't run the spell check before they turn their papers in.

Even the pencil itself didn't escape the wrath of educators. One of the major technological advances in pencil-making occurred in the early twentieth century, when manufacturers learned to attach rubber tips to inexpensive wood pencils by means of a brass clamp. But American schools allowed no crossing out. Teachers preferred pencils without erasers, arguing that students would do better, more premeditated work if they didn't have the option of revising. The students won this one, too: eraserless pencils are now extremely rare. Artists use them, because artists need special erasers in their work; golfers too use pencils without erasers, perhaps to keep themselves honest. As for the no-crossing-out rule, writing teachers now routinely warn students that writers never get it right the first time, and we expect them to revise their work endlessly until it is polished to perfection.

The computer has indeed changed the ways some of us do things with words, and the rapid changes in technological development suggest that it will continue to do so in ways we cannot yet foresee. Whether this will result in a massive change in world literacy rates and practices is a question even more difficult to answer. Although the cost of computers has come down significantly enough for them to have made strong inroads into the American office and education environment, as well as in the American middle class home, it is still the case that not every office or every school can afford to computerize, let alone connect to the World Wide Web. And it is likely that many newly-computerized environments will not have sufficient control over the technology to do more than use it to replicate the old ways.

After more than a decade of study, we will know relatively little about how people are using computers to read and write, and the number of people online, when viewed in the perspective of the total population of the United States, or of the world — the majority of whose residents are still illiterate — is still quite small. Literacy has always functioned to divide haves from have nots, and the problem of access to computers will not be easy to solve. . . .

In addition, researchers tend to look at the cutting edge when they examine how technology affects literacy. But technology has a trailing edge as well as a down side, and studying how computers are put to use raises serious issues in the politics of work and mechanisms of social control. Andrew Sledd (1988) pessimistically views the computer as actually reducing the amount of literacy needed for the low end of the workplace: "As for ordinary kids, they will get jobs at Jewel, dragging computerized Cheerios boxes across computerized check-out counters."

Despite Sledd's legitimate fear that in the information age computers will increase the gap between active text production and routine, alienating, assembly-line text processing, in the United States we live in an environment that is increasingly surrounded by text. Our cereal boxes and our soft drink cans are covered with the printed word. Our televisions, films, and computer screens also abound with text. We wear clothing designed to be read. The new computer communications technology does have ability to increase text exposure even more than it already has in positive, productive ways. The simplest one-word Web search returns pages of documents which themselves link to the expanding universe of text in cyberspace.

Computer communications are not going to go away. How the computer will eventually alter literacy practices remains to be seen. The effects of writing took thousands of years to spread; the printing press took several hundred years to change how we do things with words. Although the rate of

In the brave new world virtual text, if you chain an infinite number of monkeys to an infinite number of computers, you will eventually get, not Hamlet, but Hamlet BASIC.

change of computer development is significantly faster, it is still too early to do significant speculating.

We have a way of getting so used to writing technologies that we come to think of them as natural rather than technological. We assume that pencils are a natural way to write because they are old — or at least because we have come to think of them as being old. We form Lead Pencil Clubs and romanticize do-it-yourselfers who make their own writing equipment, because homemade has come to mean "superior to store-bought."

But pencil technology has advanced to the point where the ubiquitous no. 2 wood-cased pencil can be manufactured for a unit cost of a few pennies. One pencil historian has estimated that a pencil made at home in 1950 by a hobbyist or an eccentric would have cost about $50. It would cost significantly more nowadays. There's clearly no percentage in home pencil-making. Whether the computer will one day be as taken-for-granted as the pencil is an intriguing question. One thing is clear: were Thoreau alive today he would not be writing with a pencil of his own manufacture. He had better business sense than that. More likely, he would be keyboarding his complaints about the information superhighway on a personal computer that he assembled from spare parts in his garage.

WORKS CITED

Clanchy, Michael T. 1993. *From Memory to Written Record: England 1066–1307.* 2nd ed. Oxford: Blackwell.

Crystal, David. 1987. *The Cambridge Encyclopedia of Language.* Cambridge: Cambridge Univ. Press, p. 196.

Eisenstein, Elizabeth L. 1979. *The Printing Press as an Agent of Change.* Cambridge: Cambridge Univ. Press.

Harris, William V. 1989. *Ancient Literacy.* Cambridge: Harvard Univ. Press.

Henderson, Bill. 1994. No E-Mail from Walden. *New York Times* (March 16), p. A15. *New York Times.*

Marvin, Carolyn. 1988. *When Old Technologies Were New: Thinking about electric communication in the late nineteenth century.* New York: Oxford Univ. Press.

Petroski, Henry. 1990. *The Pencil: A History of Design and Circumstance.* New York: Alfred A. Knopf.

Sledd, Andrew. 1988. Readin' not Riotin': The Politics of Literacy. *College English* 50: 495–507.

Street, Brian V. 1984. *Literacy in Theory and Practice.* Cambridge: Cambridge Univ. Press.

Unabomber. 1996. Letter to the *San Francisco Chronicle* (April 25).

8

Champing at the Bits: Computers, Copyright, and the Composition Classroom

JOHN LOGIE

Whenever composition instructors use computer technology within their classrooms, they raise exponentially the likelihood that the work completed within their classes will run afoul of current intellectual property laws. Even low-powered, free-standing personal computers provide students with extremely powerful tools for circulation, appropriation, and alteration of texts and images. And, each of these practices, under certain circumstances, might violate current copyright laws. Moreover, if a class uses computers, linked to one another or to the Internet, this use will almost inevitably result in violations of the letter, if not the spirit of America's copyright laws. At present, standard Internet practices, such as quoting others' electronic correspondence to provide context and "tweaking" appropriated HTML to generate a World Wide Web page, fall into a legal limbo strewn with obsolete laws, contradictory rulings, failed legislation, and muddled policies.

In 1976, when United States Copyright laws were last revised, the personal computer was still a prototype in a California garage, and the Internet was an emergency military communications network tailored to cold war fears. E-mail, the World Wide Web, and multimedia were almost wholly unanticipated and, thus, wholly unaddressed by the 1976 revision. Because U.S. Copyright laws do not directly address many common computer practices, a motivated copyright holder might well be able to successfully persuade a sympathetic judge that one or more of these practices constitutes a copyright violation. While it is unlikely that a "first offense" by teachers or students able to document a good-faith effort at compliance with copyright laws would result in harsh penalties, it is also the case that a criminal copyright conviction is a felony, carrying potential penalties of up to five years in prison, and that monetary damages for copyright infringements can swell as high as $250,000 per infringement. With stakes this high, it obviously behooves composition instructors to familiarize themselves with the law and to make sure uses of intellectual property within their classrooms are both sensi-

From *Computers and Composition* 15 (1998): 201–14.

ble and strategic. To these ends, this article first provides a brief history of American intellectual property laws with a special emphasis on the relationship between copyright and communicative technologies. In addition, recent developments which may influence future legislation will be surveyed. Finally, an annotated list of online resources for teachers seeking more in-depth information is provided.

The history of American intellectual property laws is fraught with confusion and complexity. Specialists in intellectual property law routinely acknowledge the vagueness and imprecision of the laws and decisions at the center of their practice. For example, in his 1996 book, *Shamans, Software and Spleens,* law professor James Boyle argued that copyright law is among the most difficult branches of the law because

> in copyright law—to a greater extent than in most other fields of legal doctrine—there is a routine *and acknowledged* breakdown of the simplifying assumptions of the discourse, so that mundane issues force lawyers, judges and policy-makers to return to first principles. It is as if the building of every bridge required us to derive Newtonian physics from the ground up, as if every breakfast demanded a Cartesian refutation of solipsism before it could be consumed. (p. 18)

And, the precise meaning of the "first principles" of U.S. Copyright law remains a site of continuing contentiousness. In United States law, both copyrights and patents are rooted in Article I, Section 8 of the Constitution, which stated that Congress shall have the power "to promote the progress of science and useful arts, by securing for limited times to authors and inventors the exclusive right to their respective writings and discoveries." The Constitution's emphasis on a public good (the promotion of "progress") arising from limited grants of rights represented a decisive break with most European approaches to copyright, in which the primary concern was (and is) the grant of "moral rights" or "natural rights" to intellectual property creators. Although subsequent revisions to the Copyright and Patent Acts have shifted the balance point between public rights of access and creators' rights of ownership, many jurists still point to the Constitution's language to frame arguments that public rights should take precedence over creators' rights. In the 1991 case of *Feist v. Rural Telephone Service,* Justice Sandra Day O'Connor made just such an appeal in an opinion supporting the Supreme Court's determination that a telephone book's alphabetical arrangement of names within its "white pages" was not subject to copyright protection:

> The primary objective of copyright is not to reward the labor of authors, but "to promote the Progress of Science and useful Arts." To this end, copyright assures authors the right to their original expression, but encourages others to build freely upon the ideas and information conveyed by a work. (*Feist v. Rural Telephone Service*)

But O'Connor's clear articulation of the Constitutional bias towards public access is not representative of the discourse which circulated throughout the two centuries between the Copyright Act of 1790 and the *Feist* decision. Nor is it representative of much of the discourse in the 6 years since *Feist*. More commonly, arguments for expansions in both the range and duration of copyright carry the day.

In part, the continuing expansion of copyright can be understood as a response to the development of novel communicative technologies. At the time of copyright's inception, the law's scope and duration were sharply delimited. In the Copyright Act of 1790, the first Congress set the term of copyright for any "book, map or chart"[1] at 14 years (with the possibility of renewal if the creator survived this initial term, but an absolute maximum term of 28 years). The 14-year term closely paralleled the protection granted to inventors in the Patent Act of 1790. Twelve years later, Congress amended the act to cover printed works of art such as engravings and etchings. In 1831, a major revision of the Copyright Act added original musical compositions to the list of protected works and extended the term of copyright to 42 years. Thus, the first half-century of American copyright law is characterized by a close link to written and printed media. During this period a *copy* was generally understood as a page of mechanically reproduced art, whether literary or visual.

In 1865, Congress for the first time addressed a communicative technology, which had not existed at the time of the drafting of the Constitution—photography. In photography, the role of the mechanical in the creative process is foregrounded, and the creator's role is arguably more diffuse and dependent than in drawing or writing. For these reasons, Congress was slow to recognize the products of the then-new medium as worthy of protection. An 1865 amendment extending copyright protection to photographic prints and negatives occurred only after Matthew Henson Brady's photographs of the American Civil War began reaching wide audiences, though negative photography had been invented 3 decades earlier. The 1865 revision of the Copyright Act represents the point at which United States copyright law adopted a reactive posture with respect to novel technologies, establishing a precedent for the expansion of copyright as a direct response to the development of a novel communicative media.

In the twentieth century, the relationship between copyright and new communicative media has become even more closely intertwined. The 1909 Copyright Act is considered by most scholars to be a direct response to the development of mechanical methods for the reproduction of sound. According to Jane M. Gaines (1991), the popularity of the newly-invented player piano and the phonograph drove the Supreme Court, in the 1908 case of *White-Smith Co. v. Apollo Co.,* to determine that player piano rolls (and, by extension, phonographic recordings) did not constitute "copies" of the underlying musical compositions but "performances" (p. 133). The Court's decision was a fair application of the existing copyright laws, but Congress swiftly moved to correct the Court and expand copyright's reach. The 1909 Copyright Act effectively rewrote the Supreme Court's decision in *White-Smith,* protecting the mechanical reproduction of sound in records and piano rolls and extending the term of renewed copyrights to 56 years.

Although the 1909 Congress dramatically expanded both the scope and duration of copyright protection, legislators nevertheless asserted that their revision was in keeping with the Constitutional bias towards the public's use of and access to intellectual property. The legislative report on the Copyright Act of 1909 stated that copyrights should be given "not primarily for the benefit of the author, but primarily for the benefit of the public," and further that "in enacting a Copyright law Congress must consider . . . two questions: First, how much will the legislation stimulate the producer and so benefit the public, and second, how much will the monopoly granted be detrimental to the public?" But the 1909 Congress' references to a single author or producer were already becoming anachronistic, with phonographs necessarily involving the combined efforts of musicians and recording engineers. And, when in 1912, Congress added motion pictures to the list of works eligible for copyright protection, the legislators were shoehorning an expressly collaborative electronic medium into a legal construct designed around the model of a print text produced by a single author.

Between 1912 and 1976, copyright law remained largely stable, despite dramatic developments in the forms, uses, and availability of communicative technologies. Minor revisions partially subsumed both radio and television within the existing copyright architecture, despite the dramatic differences between broadcast programming and printed works. In the early 1970s, after years of Congressional silence, a wave of court cases raised pointed questions about the use of new technologies for the recording and duplication of copyrighted materials and forced Congress to revisit copyright. Chief among these technologies was the photocopier, which was the subject of a 1975 Supreme Court case *(Williams and Wilkins Co. v. National Library of Medicine)* in which an evenly divided Court (with Justice Blackmun abstaining) refused to characterize the photocopying of medical journal articles as an infringement of copyright.[2] Much as the 1909 Congress overturned the Supreme Court's holding in *White-Smith* in order to protect materials which might be reproduced via the recently developed technologies of pianola and gramophone, so, too, did the 1976 Congress overturn *Wilkins*, extending protection to materials reproduced by the newly popular photocopier.

The 1976 revision of the Copyright Act testified to a profound sense of discomfort with the ready reproducibility of print texts through photocopiers and the possibility of parallel reproducibility in other electronic media. By 1976, the Supreme Court had heard cases involving the use of audiotape to record musical performances and the prospect of home audio and videotaping loomed on the horizon (though few American households had audio tape decks, and videotape recorders were rarely seen outside television production facilities). Although home-taping technologies had not yet arrived, the photocopier had, and the 1976 revision attempts to both circumscribe the uses already being made of the photocopier while preempting future uses of tape technology and other electronic media. The 1976 revision characterizes its subject matter as "original works of authorship fixed in any tangible medium of expression, *now known or later developed,* from which they can be perceived, reproduced, or otherwise communicated, either directly or with the aid of a machine or device."[3] And the broad reach of works of authorship is testified to by a list enumerating the tangible mediums of expression now known which specifies:

1. literary works;

2. musical works, including any accompanying words;

3. dramatic works, including any accompanying music;

4. pantomimes and choreographic works;

5. pictorial, graphic, and sculptural works;

6. motion pictures and other audiovisual works;

7. sound recordings; and

8. architectural works.

The expanded scope of works protected by copyright was complemented by the extension of the term of copyright to the current "life of the author plus fifty years,"[4] and the creation of a new, separate category for intellectual property created by employees. This term—75 years from publication or 100 years from creation (whichever is shorter)—insures that the public will pay for the products of corporate collaboration for at least three generations. In addition, registration requirements, which until 1976 had resulted in the expedient entry of abandoned works into the public domain, were eliminated, as were notice requirements. Since 1976, the sole requirement for the establishment of a copyright has been *fixity,* a degree of finality or wholeness, which might be determined by the creator's whim. On the whole, the 1976 revision constitutes the most dramatic expansion of copyright protection in this nation's history.

For teachers of composition, however, the most important element in the 1976 Copyright Act revision is the codification of "fair use" exemptions to copyright. The Fair Use doctrine is rooted in the 1841 Supreme Court case of *Folsom v. Marsh* in which a biographer of George Washington used some of Washington's private letters without securing permission from the letters' owner. Justice Storey, writing for the majority, outlines the standards for fair use:

> In short, we must often, in deciding questions of this sort, look to the nature and objects of the selections made, the quantity and value of the materials used, and the degree in which the use may prejudice the sale or diminish the profits, or supersede the objects, of the original work. (Association of Research Libraries, 1995)

The 1976 Copyright Act substantially revises Storey, adding layers of complexity and confusion to the questions of when and how noncommercial public and scholarly use of copyrighted materials should be allowed:

> The fair use of a copyrighted work, including such use by reproduction in copies or phonorecords or by any other means specified by that section, for purposes such as criticism, comment, news reporting, teaching

(including multiple copies for classroom use), scholarship, or research, is not an infringement of copyright. In determining whether the use made of a work in any particular case is a fair use the factors to be considered shall include—

1. the purpose and character of the use, including whether such use is of a commercial nature or is for nonprofit educational purposes;

2. the nature of the copyrighted work;

3. the amount and substantiality of the portion used in relation to the copyrighted work as a whole; and

4. the effect of the use upon the potential market for or value of the copyrighted work.[5]

Although the 1976 Copyright Act would appear to protect much of the scholarly activity which transpires in and around college campuses, this language has been narrowly interpreted by the courts. Two recent Federal cases, *Basic Books v. Kinko's* and *Princeton University Press v. Michigan Document Services* have established that, at least for the time being, coursepacks prepared by campus copyshops do not constitute "nonprofit educational purposes." In a third case, *Salinger v. Random House,* the Supreme Court appears to have overturned the *Folsom* precedent, ruling in favor of J. D. Salinger's assertion of copyright to block the publication of a largely critical biography, which depended upon the use of letters written by Salinger and donated (by the letters' recipients) to various university libraries.

In light of these cases, teachers of composition are wise to tread carefully in their use of copyrighted materials within the classroom. The coursepack cases seem to turn on the involvement of a nonuniversity-based third party. Both cases contain suggestions that if individual students were to go to libraries and independently make copies of individual articles for their own use, that such use would be fair. The fact that copyshops are able to make copies at low prices, and to generate copies much more efficiently, did not bar findings of infringement. The *Salinger* case, by contrast, points up the degree to which a creator maintains the right to blockade use (especially *critical* use) of his or her particular creative expressions even after the creator has renounced all rights to the physical creations. Salinger does not own the letters, but he nevertheless owns their contents, and will for many years. The case's implications for the classroom are clear. In the wake of *Salinger,* no student-authored text should *ever* be used for illustration or critique without the express permission of the student author, and this permission should probably be in writing, to protect the teacher. Simply obscuring the student's name and then critiquing the paper would leave the teacher open to charges that the student's copyright had been infringed upon. Although the damages in such a case would probably be so minimal as to preclude the case's ever reaching trial, the negotiations surrounding the use of the student's work would likely be enormously time-consuming and disruptive. Securing written permission can be accomplished quickly with a blanket form distributed on the first day of class. Such a cautious approach to classroom practice may well seem burdensome and may violate some instructors' sense of propriety. However, in the absence of clear guidelines within the law and without a clear sense of how existing laws will be interpreted, securing permission may well provide welcome protection for teachers of writing who wish to make use of student writing.

Those seeking a "bright line," which might serve to protect them in the event of a charge of infringement, might turn to guidelines developed but never formally adopted during the drafting of the 1976 Copyright Act. In hopes of remedying the Act's vagueness, a broad coalition of authors, publishers, and scholars drafted specific guidelines for the scholarly use of copyrighted materials, but these guidelines survive only in the transcripts of the debates leading to the adoption of the current law.

The Ad Hoc Committee on Copyright Law Revision's guidelines (1976) neatly balance the interests of copyright holders and educators by first providing fairly generous allowances of single copies of various kinds of works for teachers to use for purposes of "scholarly research, teaching, or class preparation." But it is the section addressing the making of multiple copies of copyrighted texts for classroom use, which presents a reasonably well-balanced—albeit awkwardly expressed—standard, that nevertheless could serve as the basis for a simple, efficient, and fair set of guidelines for use of copyrighted materials. The guidelines propose allowing spontaneous uses of "(a) either a complete article, story or essay of less than 2,500 words, or (b) an excerpt from any prose work of not more than 1,000 words or 10% of the work, whichever is less, but in any event a minimum of 500 words." In operation, this means educators would have free access to whole works of less than 2,500 words, that is, works of approximately ten typescript pages or less. For works of more than 2,500 words, educators would generally be entitled to freely use 10% of the work, with a more generous maximum of 500 words (roughly two pages) adhering to smaller works of 2,500 to 4,999 words (10 to 20 pages) and an absolute across-the-board maximum of 1,000 words (roughly four typescript pages) even for works of more than 40 pages. These guidelines were specifically designed for prose works: Poetry and illustrated children's books are covered under a separate rule which also allows roughly 10% of the work to be freely used.

In many respects, the coalition's guidelines were ahead of their time. The guidelines predate the wide availability of word processors, precisely the tool needed to facilitate the otherwise overwhelming process of establishing an accurate word count for a large document. Moreover, the guidelines put forward a carefully balanced economy of scale, with smaller works circulating relatively freely, while larger works, in which the creator's investment is presumed to be more substantial, receiving roughly 90% protection. In operation, the guidelines allow for more ephemeral print texts, such as newspaper and short magazine articles, to be used and consumed within the classroom, while insuring that longer articles, essays, and books still participate in the economy of incentives and protections, which is presumed by the Constitution to prompt their creation. Although never written into law, the core principles of the guidelines continue to be endorsed by many consumers of copyrighted materials. Many users of electronic media have been using the 1976 guidelines as the basis for a 10% rule, which is applied not only to textual information but to the use of sounds and images as well. Although scrupulous adherence to these guidelines might well serve as the basis of defense that a use of copyrighted materials was understood to be a fair use, it is important to recognize that the law itself does not put forward specific guidelines for fair use. Indeed, the Secretary of Patents and Trademarks, Bruce Lehman, has expressly rejected the suggestion that specific guidelines ought to supplant the 1976 Act's fluid four-point standard.

Since 1993, Secretary Lehman has been chair of the Working Group on Intellectual Property Rights. The group was charged by President Clinton with the responsibility of examining the points of tension between current intellectual property laws and uses made of the Internet, redubbed the "National Information Infrastructure" or "NII." These questions were complicated by the United States' 1989 signing of the Berne Convention, an 1884 international treaty which binds its adherents to a copyright model drawn from European moral and natural rights traditions. In response to international- and internet-based challenges to the traditional operation of United States patents and copyrights, Lehman's group produced a "White Paper" entitled "Intellectual Property and the National Information Infrastructure" (1994). In the "White Paper," the Working Group argued that:

> It is reasonable to expect that courts would approach claims of fair use in the context of the NII just as they do in "traditional" environments. Commercial uses that involve no "transformation" by users and harm actual or potential markets will likely always be infringing, while nonprofit educational transformative uses will likely often be fair. Between these extremes, courts will have to engage in the same type of fact-intensive analysis that typifies fair use litigation and frustrates those who seek "bright lines" clearly separating the lawful from the unlawful.

Educators should be especially troubled by the Working Group's apparent addition of transformation as a requirement for fair use. Indeed, the value of fair use hinges precisely upon the ability to, under certain circumstances, make *non*transformative use of a copyrighted work. Moreover, the Lehman Group's express endorsement of a case-by-case analysis of fair use leaves educators to assume substantial exposure whenever they wish to incorporate materials composed after 1921 (when the 75 year copyright term was operative) within their pedagogies. The "White Paper" has since served as the model for a series of bills proposing revisions to the Copyright Act, and though these bills have since stalled, educators whose use of electronic media within their classrooms draws them near the cutting edge should both monitor the legislative process and attempt to positively influence it.

The monitoring process is difficult, as the legislative process often moves in fits and starts. The Conference on Fair Use (CONFU) is a particularly illustrative example. CONFU was a 1994 spin-off of the Working

Group on Intellectual Property Rights. Working under Secretary Lehman, CONFU has evolved into a broad assemblage of groups representing copyright holders and users working to draft guidelines for the fair use of digital works. In December of 1996, CONFU published an interim report, which seemed to acknowledge the Conference's failure to achieve its stated goal of formulating guidelines acceptable to the bulk of the Conference's member organizations. Reading between the lines, it seemed clear that CONFU's members were deadlocked — unable to find balancing points between public needs and creator's rights — and CONFU appeared to be on the verge of disintegrating. But in September of 1997, CONFU triumphantly announced the completion of its "first phase" and published a report which, while acknowledging dissensus among Conference members, nevertheless proposed a series of fair use guidelines addressing digital images, distance learning, educational multimedia, and the use of computer software by libraries. Throughout the report, it is repeatedly suggested that CONFU's publication of these guidelines is intended to prompt a period of voluntary adherence by learning institutions, to evaluate the guidelines' viability. Although CONFU initially sought consensus, the Conference is now forwarding guidelines in the absence of consensus.

In general, the current CONFU guidelines serve to sharply limit fair use of copyrighted materials to scholarly work conducted under the auspices of educational institutions. The 1976 Act's specification of "criticism, comment, [and] news reporting," as activities which might be subject to the fair use exemption, appears to have given way to a much narrower interpretation. For example, the CONFU report's section on "Educational Multimedia" is alarmingly specific in its definition of possible fair uses:

> The Guidelines apply to the fair use portions of lawfully acquired copyrighted works in educational multimedia projects which are created by educators or students as part of a systematic learning activity at nonprofit educational institutions. Such institutions are defined as nonprofit organizations whose primary focus is supporting research and instructional activities of educators and students for noncommercial purposes.

Although teachers who conduct systematic learning activities within nonprofit educational institutions that support (for noncommercial purposes) research and instructional activities of educators *and* students might still be able to depend upon the fair use exemption, many educators will not be able to meet such a rigorous standard. Elsewhere, the CONFU report seems to endorse the "10% rule," which has been adopted by many creators of multimedia, but if this protection is ultimately extended to only a narrow class of educators, the result will be a dramatic erosion of the fair use exemption. The CONFU Report is a self-contradictory document, both tentative and summative, and at times, maddeningly convoluted.

Recent international initiatives are further complicating the intellectual property landscape. In December of 1996, the United Nations' World Intellectual Property Organization (WIPO), an organization made up of over

160 nations which adhere to the Berne Convention, effectively revised Berne with two new treaties, the WIPO Copyright Treaty and the WIPO Performances and Phonograms Treaty. On the whole, these treaties appear to represent a positive development for educators. The member nations wisely eliminated a draft proposal, which would have treated even ephemeral copies of electronic information as though they were print copies, recognizing that these copies are necessary for the bulk of communication occurring over the Internet. Another positive development occurred within the preamble to the Copyright Treaty which states that WIPO's member states recognize, "the need to maintain a balance between the rights of authors, and the larger public interest, particularly education, research, and access to information as reflected in the Berne Convention." But the treaty's tacit endorsement of Berne having effectively balanced public and authorial rights is highly questionable.

In his 1994 book *Copyright's Highway,* Stanford Law Professor, Paul Goldstein pointed out that the Berne has been challenged both within and outside the United States as heavily biased in favor of copyright holders. The United States' century-long refusal to sign Berne was grounded, in part, in a rejection of Berne's elimination of notice requirements, which effectively renders any work a copyrighted work the moment it can be described as having reached finished form. The United States, by contrast, for many years required creators and their heirs and assigns to actively assert and register their copyright claims, effectively engendering a circumstance wherein works of little economic value fell into the public domain well before their potential protection had expired. From an international standpoint, Berne's bias against notice requirements was the subject of a 1960's challenge by a broad coalition of African and Asian nations, many of them former colonies, who argued that "international copyright conventions are designed, in their present form, to meet the needs of countries which are exporters of intellectual works" (as cited in Goldstein, p. 188). But the result of this challenge, a reduction in the minimum copyright term required for nations wishing to sign on to Berne to twenty-five years, has since been swept away in a return to the generally protectionist agenda, which is characteristic of Berne.

In a July 1, 1997 policy paper, President Clinton expressly endorsed the WIPO treaties and suggested that the treaties provide adequate fair use protection for consumers of intellectual property. Clinton wrote:

> Both treaties also contain provisions that permit nations to provide for exceptions to rights in certain cases that do not conflict with a normal exploitation of the work and do not unreasonably prejudice the legitimate interests of the author (e.g., "fair use"). These provisions permit members to carry forward and appropriately extend into the digital environment limitations and exceptions in their national laws which have been considered acceptable under the Berne Convention. These provisions permit members to devise new exceptions and limitations that are appropriate in the digital network environment, but neither reduce nor extend the scope of applicability of the limitations and exceptions permitted by the Berne Convention.

But Clinton's emphasis on uses, which are "permissible" or "acceptable" under Berne, pointed up the degree the United States is gradually relinquishing its status as a leader in the protection of public access to creative works. Indeed, Clinton's endorsement of the WIPO treaties and, by extension, Berne, directly threatened the United States' fair use exceptions. The 1996 WIPO Copyright Treaty states that "authors of literary and artistic works shall enjoy the exclusive right of authorizing the making available to the public of the original and copies of their works through sale or other transfer of ownership," casting the public as passive recipient rather than the grantor of authorial rights. The Copyright Treaty also states that member nations are free to "determine the conditions, if any, under which the exhaustion of the [author's exclusive right] applies after the first sale or other transfer of ownership of the original or a copy of the work with the authorization of the author." The implicit suggestion is that for many nations there will be *no* conditions under which the author's exclusive rights are exhausted. A similar lack of attentiveness to public access is found in the Performances and Phonograms Treaty, suggesting that movement towards what is "permissible" or "acceptable" under Berne will cost American consumers of intellectual property many of their rights of fair use and much of the public domain. Clearly, this language does not constitute a ringing endorsement of either fair use or the public domain.

In the past, educators could have relied, to a degree, upon the preeminence of United States law within United States classrooms. This may no longer be the case. Thus, instructors need to be especially conscious of the degree their use of Internet-capable computers necessarily places work completed within their classrooms in an international context. A web site housed on a server in Kalamazoo is accessible from Adis Abeba, and vice versa. Almost all material on a web page can be appropriated easily with a click or two of a computer mouse. Further, most sophisticated web browsers provide easy access to the source code web page creators use to shape their arrangements of texts and images. For the moment, United States law does not specifically address the appropriate practices common in a networked environment. But United States laws might not be the only laws composition instructors need to consider.

Even if educators manage to avoid violations of international copyright laws, the general international tendency towards longer and more comprehensive protection of intellectual property is nevertheless threatening to shrink the public domain within the United States. Two years ago, the House and Senate failed to pass identical drafts of "The Copyright Extension Act of 1995," which would have extended the term of most copyrights 20 years. The ostensible purpose for the bills was a supposed need to "harmonize" American laws with those of the Berne signatories, but the proposed term, in most cases, of the life of the author plus an additional 70 years is by no means an international standard. This expansion of the United States copyright term would only "harmonize" with a fraction of the Berne signatories, with most signatories adjudicating systems as convoluted and varied as our own. Despite their 1995 failure, the bills recently resurfaced as Senate Bill 505 and House Resolution 604, both entitled "The Copyright Extension Act of 1997."

Although these bills would generally benefit copyright holders immeasurably at the expense of public access, some recording industry concerns have pressed for still greater protection, and their influence prompted Representative Sonny Bono to introduce a revised version of the House Bill, H.R. 1621. If passed, H.R. 1621 will insure that royalty checks from "I Got You Babe" will continue to flow to Bono or his heirs or assigns until at least the year 2069, and that any attempts to make a fair use of Mr. Bono's oeuvre for educational purposes (however unlikely this might be) could be effectively blocked by an assertion of a continuing copyright.

Even before the computer became an important part of academic practice, educators were already chafing against restrictive assertions of copyright whenever they attempted to assemble coursepacks or place copyrighted materials on reserve within campus libraries. David Stone's 1995 *Lingua Franca* piece, "Just do it," spoke for many within academia when Stone advocated a "principled exercise of fair use" in which educators would, in most cases, refuse to seek permission for the works they use (p. 42). But this is not a posture which reasonably risk-averse instructors, especially those without tenure, might be comfortable making. The increasing presence of computers in the composition classroom provides teachers with both a challenge to the standard approaches to text preparation and a resource for examining the issues that arise when students become aggressive consumers of intellectual property.

The teaching of composition has always obliged instructors to pay particular attention to the techniques writers use to appropriate material from their surroundings and the ways writers incorporate this material into works, which are, if not original, nevertheless something they can claim as their own. With so much of the law surrounding these practices in a state of flux, this is an extremely exciting time to teach and study the composing process. This may also be a time in which composition instructors are able to acknowledge that there is much still to be learned about strategies of appropriation, reconfiguration, and recontextualization, and how these strategies might come to be regarded as every bit as important as canonical strategies of invention.

As we move into an increasingly networked, increasingly collaborative creative context, the challenge is to make sure the composing strategies we teach to students balance our sense of what is right against the developing global definitions of what is legal—and to insure that when the gap between the two is too large, we take action and use our close proximity to the composing process to inform the development of future policies.

The following selective list of websites is designed as a springboard for instructors and students who wish to research intellectual property issues. By investigating these sites and pursuing some of the links contained within them, educators and students will be exposed to much of the current work on intellectual property both within and outside composition studies. Although these sites do not provide "bright lines," which will absolutely protect well-meaning scholars or educators from charges of infringement, these sites *can* help to prepare teachers and students for the task of drawing their own lines and thereby insuring their uses of others' work are as fair as they ought to be.

NOTES

1. See 1 Stat. 124.
2. This holding has been effectively reversed by the decisions in *Basic Books v. Kinko's* and *Princeton University Press v. Michigan Document Services.*
3. See U.S.C. 102(a) (1976).
4. See U.S.C. 102(a) (1976).
5. See U.S.C. 107 (1976).

REFERENCES

Ad Hoc Committee on Copyright Law Revision. (1976, March 19). *Agreement on guidelines for classroom copying in not-for-profit educational institutions with respect to books and periodicals.* [Online]. Available: <http://www.music.indiana.edu/tech_s/mla/legcom/guidebks.htm> [1997, July 10].

Association of Research Libraries. (1996, November 15). *Timeline: A history of copyright in the U.S.* [Online]. Available: <http://arl.cni.org/info/frn/copy/timeline.html> [July 10, 1997].

Basic Books v. Kinko's, 758 F. Supp. 1522 (1991).

Boyle, James. (1996). *Shamans, software and spleens: Law and the construction of the information society.* Cambridge, MA: Harvard University Press.

Clinton, William J. (1997, July 1). *A framework for global electric commerce.* [Online]. Available: <http://www.whitehouse.gov/WH/New/Commerce/read.html> [1997, July 10].

Conference on Fair Use. (1997, September 30). *Report to the commissioner on the conclusion of the first phase of the conference on fair use.* [Online]. Available: <http://www.uspto.gov/web/offices/dcom/olia/confu/conclutoc.html> [1997, October 10].

Feist v. Rural Telephone Service. (1991). The copyright & fair use pages at Stanford University Library. [Online]. Stanford University Library Available: <http://www.findlaw.com/cgi-bin/getcase.pl?court=US&vol=499&invol==340> [1997, July 10].

Gaines, Jane M. (1991). *Contested culture: The image, the voice and the law.* Chapel Hill, NC: University of North Carolina Press.

Goldstein, Paul. (1994). *Copyright's highway: The law and lore of copyright from Gutenberg to the Celestial Jukebox.* New York: Hill and Wang.

Princeton University Press v. Michigan Document Services, Inc., 74 F. 3D 1512 (1996).

Salinger v. Random House, 811 F2d 90 (2d Cir.), cert. Denied, 108 S. Ct. 213, 98 L. Ed. 2D 177 (1987).

Stone, David W. (1995). Just do it: How to beat the copyright racket. *Lingua Franca, 6,* 32–42.

Working Group on Intellectual Property Rights. (1994). *Intellectual property and the national information infrastructure (The "White Paper").* [Online]. Available: <http://www.uspto.gov/web/offices/com/doc/ipnii/ipnii.txt> [1998, March 14].

White-Smith Co. v. Apollo Co. 209 U.S. 1 (1908).

Williams and Wilkins Co. v. United States, 487 F. 2d 1345, aff'd by an equally divided court, 420 U.S. 376, 97 S. Ct. 1344 (1975).

World Intellectual Property Organization. (1996, December 2–20). *Diplomatic conference on certain copyright and neighboring rights questions.* [Online]. Available: <http://www.wipo.org/eng/diplconf/distrib/94dc.htm> [1997, July 10].

APPENDIX

10 Web Sites Which Can Help Composition Instructors and Students Determine Their Own Approaches to Using Intellectual Property within the Classroom

The Copyright & Fair Use Pages at Stanford University Library

Available: <http://fairuse.stanford.edu/>

This outstanding website contains the full texts of virtually all major intellectual property cases in United States history. The site also features: a timeline of

U.S. copyright history; links to the Copyright Act and many pertinent treaties and regulations; and special guides to websites addressing coursepack cases, multimedia, and the NII legislation. Better yet, the site contains a search engine, which allows researchers to move directly to more narrow topics of interest. This is a terrific, albeit somewhat overwhelming, starting point.

The Digital Future Coalition

Available: <http://www.dfc.org/>
The DFC represents a broad coalition of business, education, and public organizations "committed to international copyright law and policy that rewards and promotes creativity." The DFC site contains links to many of the coalition's 38 member organizations (including NCTE and the MLA) as well as pithy analyses of intellectual property legislation and treaties.

Rebecca Moore Howard's Home Page

Available: <http://wrt-howard.syr.edu>
Dr. Howard's home page features an extensive bibliography of intellectual property resources, as well as a comprehensive chronology of authorship throughout the ages and links to syllabi for her classes, many of which model ways intellectual property issues can be made a part of pedagogy within English departments. In addition, Dr. Howard has placed editions of several of her papers addressing plagiarism and related issues on the site, making this a rich and varied resource for scholars interested in intellectual property issues.

The Intellectual Property Caucus of the Conference on College Composition and Communication (CCCC-IP)

Available: <http://www.ncte.org/cccc/gov/committees/ip>
This site tracks the Intellectual Property Caucus' continuing efforts to lobby against copyright legislation, which is at odds with the needs and interests of composition instructors. In addition, the site provides a list of links to additional resources and instructions for joining the Caucus's electronic mailing list, which addresses intellectual property issues with a particular focus on how these issues intersect with the teaching of composition.

Dennis Karjala's Home Page

Available: <http://homepages.law.asu.edu/%7Edkarjala>
Arizona State Law Professor Dennis Karjala's site debunks many of the specious arguments put forward in defense of the proposed 20-year extension to the current terms of copyright. The site also features links to pertinent legislation, the Berne Convention, and the names and addresses of legislators actively addressing intellectual property issues. Karjala's site is concise, opinionated, and entertaining.

Thomas — U.S. Congress on the Internet

Available: <http://Thomas.loc.gov/>
This online version of the Congressional Record provides search capabilities and indices that allow scholars to monitor the progress of intellectual property legislation (or any other legislation) through the legislative branch. It also provides a quick search engine for addresses, phone numbers, and fax numbers of legislators, all of which are handy whenever one wishes to lobby against legislation.

The United States Patent and Trademark Office

Available: <http://www.uspto.gov/>
This site houses the official government documents addressing the NII (recently redubbed the GII for "Global Information Infrastructure"), CONFU, WIPO, and other ungainly acronyms, as well as the "White Paper" and its predecessor the "Green Paper," in which the Clinton Administration first outlined its plans for retooling intellectual property law to meet the challenges of the Internet.

The UT System Crash Course in Copyright

Available:
<http://www.utsystem.edu/OGC/intellectualproperty/cprtindx.htm>
For composition instructors, librarians, or anyone else who wishes to learn a whole lot about copyright from within an engaging, artfully presented, and, yes, entertaining website, this is the place to start. Georgia Harper and her cohorts at the University of Texas have crafted a wonderful resource, which is especially welcome for its willingness to advocate specific approaches to dealing with intellectual property on college campuses. The only thing disappointing about the site is that some of its better features, for example, "Ask a lawyer," are limited to UT employees. The site could function well as assigned reading for a composition class, interrogating intellectual property issues or designing its own websites.

The World Intellectual Property Organization (WIPO)

Available: <http://www.wipo.int>
The United Nations' intellectual property arm maintains a well-organized site, tracking the many treaties and iterations of the Berne Convention, which currently dominates the international intellectual property landscape. It does not provide significant links to organizations outside WIPO, but what's here *is* available in English, French, or Spanish.

The Yahoo Guide to Intellectual Property

Available: <http://www.yahoo.com/Government/Law/Intellectual_Property>
This is not a content-rich site, but an extremely extensive catalog of the wealth

of information on intellectual property available throughout the World Wide Web, indexed in a reasonably intuitive fashion. The Yahoo site also contains a comprehensive search engine that might well lead researchers to their particular areas of interest.

EDITORS' ADDENDUM

The Digital Millennium Copyright Act in its entirety, enacted in 1998, may be found at: http://www.copyright.gov/legislation/dmca.pdf.

The UCLA Online Institute for Cyberspace Law and Policy, found at www. gseis.ucla.edu/iclp/dmca1.htm, provides a summary of the major provisions of The Digital Millennium Copyright Act.

Of particular interest for computers and composition teachers is that the Digital Millennium Copyright Act:

- "Outlaws the manufacture, sale, or distribution of code-cracking devices used to illegally copy software."
- "Provides exemptions from anti-circumvention provisions for nonprofit libraries, archives, and educational institutions under certain circumstances."
- "In general, limits Internet service providers from copyright infringement liability for simply transmitting information over the Internet."
- States explicitly that "[n]othing in this section shall affect rights, remedies, limitations, or defenses to copyright infringement, including fair use. . . ."

9

"It wasn't me, was it?":
Plagiarism and the Web

DÀNIELLE DeVOSS AND ANNETTE C. ROSATI

1. SHARING OUR STORIES

1.1. It wasn't me, was it?

Having experienced plagiarism in her classes, Annette has adopted a twofold approach to avoiding it: First, early in a class, she engages students in discussions of plagiarism, talking with them about what plagiarism is, why it's wrong, and how they can avoid it. Secondly, she designs assignments that deter students from plagiarizing by encouraging original ideas, a focus on process, and multiple drafts.

In a recent introduction-to-literature course she taught, students read *King Lear.* After reading the first papers that students in her class submitted, out of curiosity, she went to an online paper mill[1] just to see what sort of papers were available on the topic of *King Lear.* As she skimmed the papers available for download, she realized that several seemed quite familiar. Without intentionally looking for any one student's paper, she inadvertently found that three students in her class had plagiarized—had downloaded papers from the Web and turned them in as their own. In class the next day, she castigated the act and invited all of the students to visit her during her office hours, but noted that if the three people who plagiarized (she didn't point them out publicly) didn't come to speak with her, they would fail the class.

At her office hours the following week, a student shuffled in. She was surprised to see him, as he wasn't one of the plagiarists. He was nervous and asked, "It wasn't me, was it?" Annette asked why he felt he had plagiarized, and he admitted that he used a Cliff's Notes version of *King Lear* to better understand the text and write his paper. Annette explained why this wasn't plagiarism and sent him on his way. The same story played out with three more students, all worried that they had plagiarized. Finally, when Annette looked in the hallway, was shocked to see a line of students still waiting to see her. A total of 14 students visited her office. The three plagiarists were among the

From *Computers and Composition* 19 (2002): 191–203.

fourteen, but the remaining eleven students weren't sure if they had plagiarized or not.

1.2. You have to do all that?

Dànielle always arranges for a library tour with students in her first-year composition courses. Last fall, one of the students in her course didn't show up for the tour. He was an older student with a bit more academic experience, and she was willing to give him the benefit of the doubt. When she looked over the first draft of his paper, however, it was evident he would have benefited from the tour. All of his sources were web sites, and a few of them were really shaky—not credible at all.

Dànielle met with the student at the library and she provided a quick run through of their services, then together they headed to a computer to search the library databases for material. They did a search on a service called Infoseek and he found a couple of articles he wanted. Dànielle explained the steps to receive them: You copy or print the author's name, title, magazine name, volume, and issue. Then you go to the library holdings area of the library web site. You look to see if the library carries the magazine, and, if so, you copy the library code you need to find the magazine on the stacks. Then you go look up the volume you're looking for, find the article, and photocopy it. He balked. He stared at Dànielle, mouth open, and asked, "You mean I have to do ALL THAT?" Research, to him, was going to YAHOO! (a commonly used search engine on the Web), doing a simple search, and using the first 10 to 20 hits.

1.3. No . . . I didn't write the paper

The first paper that an international student submitted in a first-year composition course Dànielle recently taught was engaging and smart—he was a good writer and had incredibly interesting ideas. The paper had quite a few of the problems typical of students who learn and speak English as a second language, and, during Dànielle's office hours, they walked through these and talked about them, about American style conventions, and about how he could read for and identify these differences. The second paper he turned in was flawless but flat—it was lacking the spark of imagination in the first paper. Dànielle knew right away that he hadn't written the paper. She asked him to stop by her office to talk about the paper, and she asked him about the research he had done preparing for the paper and also asked to see his earlier drafts of the paper.

During their meeting, the student was clearly uncomfortable, and his answers were short. Finally, she asked if he had plagiarized the paper. He said, "No." She asked if he wrote the paper himself. He said, "Yes." She paused for a moment, while he stared at the floor, and asked again if he had written the paper. He said "No . . . I didn't write the paper." He admitted that he had found it on the Internet and decided to turn it in. This was a tough moment— he had wanted to please Dànielle, he was shy about his writing, and he knew he had done something wrong. They talked about typical writing practices taught in schools in his country, and he explained that it was more acceptable in his country to quote extensively from other sources and that giving credit wasn't as formal as in American schools. But he did admit that he understood that—both in his home country and the United States—it was unacceptable for students to copy another person's paper in its entirety and turn it in as their own.

1.4. What These Stories Tell Us

These stories remind us that issues of research and issues of plagiarism are complex and often interconnected. Stories about papers stored in the basements of fraternity houses and available for students to plagiarize have circulated among composition teachers for quite some time, but the virtual space of the Web and the download and cutting-and-pasting techniques available pose new questions related to issues of plagiarism, questions that we, as composition instructors, must address to be best equipped to better understand plagiarism, deter students from plagiarism, and encourage students to be thoughtful and critical researchers.

Two beliefs scaffold this article: First, we are witnessing students adapting their literacy, research, reading, and writing skills and processes to the virtual space—and complexity—of the World Wide Web. Second, first-year composition teachers have a key role in helping students adapt to this space, and encouraging students' critical research and writing skills in this space. Although students enter our classrooms well versed in writing-related values and ideas relayed to them in their past school experiences, often this instruction does not address—or does not go far enough in addressing—issues of online research and writing. First-year composition seems, to us, to be the ideal place to initiate discussions related to such issues; first-year composition courses tackle (among many other functions) the task of acculturating students into academic writing. Because academic writing now relies so heavily on the reading, writing, and research accessed via virtual spaces, it is necessary for first-year composition courses to address research and writing in electronic realms and to help students develop techniques that will aid them to best use these systems. From this perspective, we address the intersections of online research and plagiarism, discuss how we can best handle plagiarism in our first-year classrooms, and how we can best equip students with the tools necessary to do appropriate research—both online and offline.

2. WHY PLAGIARISM? DISCIPLINARY FUNCTIONS AND RETHINKING PLAGIARISM

A. E. Malloch (1976) asked a question in 1976 that is still relevant today: "Why plagiarism?" (p. 165). Why do we penalize and punish, discipline and drill where plagiarism is concerned, especially when, as Malloch noted, there are other worthy vices in academia (for example, laziness, carelessness)? Malloch argued that part of the reason we punish plagiarism is that, frankly, plagiarism makes us look—and feel—bad. We preach process, we teach approaches, and we scour student work, commenting, suggesting, and exclaiming—to find that some of the students in our classes have downloaded their papers from the Internet.

It is not surprising that plagiarism is still a common subject of discussion and research as plagiarism is a fairly contemporary notion—individualistic authorship is a relatively new idea. Prior to our Modernist notions of author and authorship, most work was collaborative in a larger sense (Barthes, 1985; Foucault, 1984; Howard, 1995). Roland Barthes and Michel Foucault both noted that the author figure came into being as we know it today when the value of the individual became prestigious and our notions of subjectivity shifted.

Many of us are well read in contemporary composition theory and have adopted a process approach—and even an approach that both addresses and somewhat dismisses the romantic, modernist notion of Author (writing in isolation, suffering, the tortured artist at *his* craft)—most of us at the same time still focus on a polished, final product by an author whose name appears (alone) at the top of the first page. And our institutions hold these same values.

Most academic institutions offer definitions of academic honesty for students and recommended actions for teachers to deal with situations of academic dishonesty. Embedded within these policies are language and attitudes toward plagiarism typical of the rhetoric of crime and punishment regarding plagiarism. Generally, instructors are expected to report, in writing, all students who break or even bend policy. Reported students face punishment ranging from failing a class, being put on academic probation, and/or facing suspension or expulsion from the university. Malloch (1976) compellingly argued, however, that policies such as these have little or no impact until and unless we convince students that their written work is valuable *and* valued— a small, but potent gesture (Selfe, 1999) toward encouraging students' writing, thinking, and development.

Although institutional policies are broad and totalizing, alternative approaches to understanding plagiarism have been proposed. Rebecca Moore Howard (1993), for example, noted that most policies define plagiarism only in negative terms. Howard suggested that students engaging in the sort of work often attacked as plagiarism are often engaging in a positive activity she called *patchwriting,* which allows students a place to borrow from text, manipulate it, and work through new concepts by piecing their writing with the original work. Malloch (1976) characterized plagiarism as *kidnapping,*[2] rather than theft, and referred to this type of borrowing, weaving writing as *impersonation*— writing as experimentation, as mimic. This sort of writing—clearly a *stage* in writing development—allows students to test new approaches, process new ideas, and learn new writing strategies. These patchwriters, rather than "being unethical plagiarists, often strive to observe proper academic conventions" (Howard, 1993; p. 236).

3. WHY STUDENTS PLAGIARIZE

Equally as interesting as how teachers and their institutions define plagiarism is *why* students plagiarize. Reasons for plagiarizing are as diverse and complex as definitions of plagiarism. Students may plagiarize because they feel that assembling sources, citations, and quotes is the primary goal of writing a paper—and that their original ideas are secondary (Whitaker, 1993). Students may stumble toward plagiarism when they fail to cite properly because they don't entirely understand the point or argument of a primary work, or in a struggle to define what "common knowledge" means, they struggle to identify which information merits a citation (Whitaker, 1993). Plagiarism might emerge because students have a poor understanding of an assignment or of the rhetorical aspects of an assignment—that is, a weak understanding of situation, audience, and their purpose in completing an assignment (1990). Students may plagiarize because they feel pressured to privilege a project or paper for another course or to free up time to put in more hours at work. Students may plagiarize to get the work done; as Augustus Kolich (1983) noted, "the stolen essay serves a practical purpose; it is a finished product that fits into a specific slot and that completes an assignment" (p. 146). Finally, students may plagiarize because of the often-appearing-unconscious cultural principles of written work. Cultures vary in how writing, authorship, identity, individualism, ownership rights, and personal relationships are perceived, and these variances in values and approaches to text affect student writing (Fox, 1994).

Although we regularly tell students that plagiarism is wrong, a variety of factors and temptations beyond those listed above complicate this generic warning. American academic writing is full of often conflicting complications, the most obvious of which is expecting students to come up with and develop an original idea, while requiring them to find plenty of material to back up their supposedly new and original idea or perspective on a subject. Those of us indoctrinated into academic writing traverse this complication quite easily—that is, we can explain new ideas and complement them with existing research and theory—but it should still be clear to most of us that this complication poses a challenge to students in our classes.

Further complicating students' negotiations of both comfortable and new ideas is the fact that although many seasoned academic writers can often negotiate the original ideas/supporting work paradox a bit more easily, this seemingly contradictory task leaves many high school and college-level composition students in an intellectual lurch. Common questions may include: Where does one person's work leave off and another's begin? What can be considered "common knowledge?" Does *everything* have to be cited? Is it cheating or plagiarizing to use resources like Web sites offering summaries or Cliff's Notes, as the nervous students in Annette's class did?

We can tell students that plagiarism is an academic crime, but we often assume they understand what that means and that they hold academic honesty policies in as high esteem as we do. Asking a student to create original ideas encourages plagiarism in the sense that students often feel the need to consult sources for help. How many new insights are readily available for readers of *King Lear,* for example? We ask students not just for their insights, but for their original ideas, ideas that must also—in some instances—be "correct." For example, it would not be correct for a student to write an essay describing how King Lear loved Goneril more than he loved Cordelia. Such ideas are certainly original, but not correct within acceptable, intellectual, shared discourse on *Lear.* This need to be correct motivated the students in Annette's class to seek additional sources for originality. They searched to meet the demand imposed upon them—to conjure up their own perspectives on *King Lear.* In other classes, however, the line defining what is "correct" is quite blurry. Courses that focus with a broad cultural lens or ask students to consider social issues, for example, may have a body of related work suggesting "correct" stances, but many of us may, in fact, discourage students from a final, fixed belief about an issue. Students often have classes that encourage them to learn a fixed, correct approach to an idea or theory, *and* classes that encourage them to retain a broad, critical, "gray-area" approach to a subject.

Online plagiarism is just as, if not more, complicated as any other form of plagiarism, and these same—and different—complications apply to research and writing in online realms. Students may plagiarize from online research spaces because it's easy to do so; cutting and pasting is a common virtual text manipulation trick. Students may plagiarize from online research spaces because there is no review, publication, and catalogue process for most Web pages, and, on top of that, authors aren't always privileged the way they are in print texts. Students may plagiarize from virtual realms because they lack sophistication in searching and evaluating sources within this realm and, frustrated, resort to stealing texts. Students may plagiarize from web pages because they are refocusing their literacy, research, and writing skills to online spaces, and they are adapting to the rhetorically and technologically complicated demands of the web.

One of these complicated demands is the evolving idea of what a *text* is. What we consider to be texts have shifted due to online realms (see, for example, Bolter, 1991; Joyce, 1995; Landow, 1992; Lanham, 1993). Texts now include sound and integrate visuals in ways that allow for more complex and fragmented presentations of connections, topics, and representations within richly layered systems. Thus, the tools that we and the students in our classes need to write, read, and understand new variations of composing have also changed. One such tool is understanding the complicated interfaces of machines—what is seen on the screen. The virtual–visual interface of the operating system (for example, WINDOWS 95, *Macintosh O/S 8.5*) is sophisticated and complex. The other software installed on the machine presents an equally complex literacy challenge, with sophisticated error messages, complex toolbars, elaborate menu bars, and incredibly detailed and embedded help features. Users have to negotiate both a textual ("File," "Edit," and so on) and a graphical (icons that represent "open file" or "paintbrush") interface.

Through these interfaces and with this software, students go online, and face yet another layer of complexity. On the Web, students must learn to navigate complex and layered hypertexts, texts that often have embedded and complex graphical content, audio, and rich visual textures. For students who have typically been asked to negotiate traditional texts, navigating and interacting within these new realms is a strange and often quite difficult, frustrating task.

4. Addressing Plagiarism in Changing Research Spaces

4.1. Finding a Foothold

A variety of scholars have offered grounded, practical approaches to addressing issues of plagiarism, ranging from the suggestion that writing teachers develop a stronger understanding of students' approaches to tasks and the invitation that we trust students' understandings of responsibility and authorship (Kolich, 1983). Likewise, we should share with students definitions of academic honesty and cases of plagiarism to enable students to read, analyze, and understand institutional approaches to academic dishonesty (Hawley, 1984; Whitaker, 1993; Wilhoit, 1994). In our classrooms and curricula, building strong rhetorical purpose into our assignments allows students to have a much more clear focus when they begin their work, and as they work through a writing activity (Kantz, 1990). Focusing on microtasks and task management is another approach to encouraging students to better understand and manage a complex assignment and to deter them from plagiarism (Kantz, 1990; Kloss, 1996).

All of these suggestions are helpful for dealing with issues of plagiarism and provide a crucial foundation for better understanding plagiarism, online or offline. None of them, however, directly addresses issues of Internet plagiarism. In the rest of this article, we explore available remedies for us and for the students in our classrooms as we attempt to bolster our approaches to reading, writing, and research in new realms.

4.2. Negotiating Online Spaces

The Web offers a current, vast, and rapidly expanding research and information-delivery system. The Web, however, exacerbates existing problems that we don't often enough address in writing-intensive classrooms, including the issue of plagiarism. In a realm where anyone with a computer, Internet access, and a basic knowledge of HTML and web publishing can be an electronically published "expert," information changes shape, as do our approaches to it. Information is also much easier to plagiarize from the Web. We might even go so far as to say that cutting and pasting is almost natural in this realm, as the Web is typically accessed through an interface where cutting and pasting are basic and often-used techniques.

There are few checks and balances in the electronic realm—no librarians, no one thoroughly checking the validity of information posted, and no one checking the validity of source material. In addition, savvy students are copying or downloading entire papers and industrious web designers are copying not only code, but also content from web sites. In this realm, it's almost surprising to imagine students *not* being tempted to follow suit.

Of course, most students buying a paper from a paper mill (online or physical) or borrowing a paper from the filing cabinet in the basement of their fraternity or sorority house probably know that they are doing something wrong. And, we would probably not rely on postmodern theories of authorship and shifting subjectivity to excuse their behavior. However, the vast majority of students who plagiarize might not even realize that they are plagiarizing, and others may even harbor a somewhat constant fear that they are possibly plagiarizing. We want to believe that many students aren't necessarily evil or unthinking, but instead they're learning to negotiate and do research in new spaces, in spaces that can offer fresh and exciting research possibilities, but also offer technical tricks like cutting and pasting and rhetorical complications like "eye candy," distracting gimmicks, and advertisements.

5. Recommendations for Research and Writing in Online Spaces

Although a variety of articles in the popular press have addressed online plagiarism (see, e.g., Chidley, 1997; Hickman, 1998; Innerst, 1998; Jones, 1997; Kleiner & Lord, 1999; Mooney, 1999; Plotz, 1999; Sanchez, 1998; Witherspoon, 1995), few scholarly resources offer specific advice to teachers of writing. Vicki Tolar Burton and Scott Chadwick (2000) analyzed the Internet-oriented advice offered in a variety of handbooks for composition students and concluded that most handbooks that supposedly offer advice related to Internet research are merely supplemented by Internet source citation styles. Burton and Chadwick argued that

> even among the burgeoning supply of Internet how-to guides marketed for writing students, a number of authors who minutely document every move involved in an Internet search tend to gloss over the critical thinking processes involved in evaluating research sources on the Internet and assume students will intuitively know how to assess the sources they find. (p. 312)

Burton and Chadwick provide an excellent analysis of Internet research, but, like many other authors addressing issues of Internet research, do not discuss issues of plagiarism.

Here we offer two approaches[3] that apply to both offline and online research and writing—supplements crucial to our first-year composition classes if we are to successfully integrate web work into our curricula, a choice not up to us to make as more and more students rely on the Web as a research space and as more and more institutions adopt web-based teaching interfaces (like WebCT, Blackboard, and Daedalus Online).

5.1. Intellectual Property as a Lens

Karla Kitalong (1998) shared a cut-and-paste story, noting the ease with which one of students admitted to plagiarizing the design of a web page. The student—after the original web author contacted the student and his professor—admitted "I really didn't think I had done anything wrong," but later admitted to being "hasty and impulsive" (p. 254). The question Kitalong asked is the same we are still faced with: Did this student plagiarize? How does electronic publishing complicate our print-based assumptions about what plagiarism is and isn't? What is common practice on the Web? How do we separate code from design in online space? Design from content?

The student whose site was plagiarized in the instance Kitalong (1998) shared added a warning on his site after the incident. In doing so, he accepted some responsibility in deterring anyone from plagiarizing his online work. This is also a possible remedy to plagiarism, but a warning on one site might mean that an absence of a warning on another site is an invitation to plagiarize. Calling attention to copyright and authorship issues generally and on web sites specifically serves as one activity composition teachers can use for leverage in discussing issues of plagiarism.

At Michigan Technological University, the majority of students are engineers and are highly industry oriented (in fact, more and more majors at the university are requiring earlier co-operative experience, internships, and industry-led courses). A useful tactic to "sell" the notion of plagiarism to students is to introduce the topic of plagiarism embedded within a discussion of intellectual property. Students understand plagiarism as relating to school work, which often comes secondary to their industry focus. Intellectual property, however, allows for a broader discussion of ethics and responsibility. (Clearly, however, plagiarism as school related and intellectual property as industry related is a false dichotomy; in everyday academic work students come into contact with a variety of copyrighted works, such as textbooks, lab materials, equipment, and so on.)

The primary reason that we suggest focusing on issues of plagiarism through the lens of intellectual property is we sometimes find ourselves having to convince students why plagiarism is wrong. It is, as we argued earlier, not enough for us to just say, "Don't do it"; it is important to tell students why plagiarism is important and *why* and *how* it should be avoided. It's one thing to tell students that it is wrong to steal a few sentences of someone's work, but it's another thing entirely to demonstrate the importance of respecting another's work by using a "real-world" legal example of an intellectual property issue. An example Dànielle has used with her classes is the Vanilla Ice "Ice Ice, Baby" case. In the early 1990s, the rapper Vanilla Ice sampled an identifiable riff from an earlier Queen/David Bowie collaboration.

Vanilla Ice did so without the explicit permission of the original artist, and a lawsuit ensued. Eventually, the case was dropped, but only after Vanilla Ice's label had invested tens (if not hundreds) of thousands of dollars in their legal defense. Likewise, another band—The Verve—slightly altered and reproduced a copy of a Rolling Stones' song ("Bittersweet Symphony") without the permission of the Rolling Stones or their corporate representation. The further reproduction and distribution of the album, after an initial run, was halted by the legal team representing the Rolling Stones, providing a grand set-back to The Verve and costing their recording company a good deal of money. And Napster is, obviously, an excellent example of intellectual property changing shape online, and a great topic to use to encourage discussion of the ownership of texts, ideas, and recordings.

Examples like these—embedded in a larger discussion of issues of copyright, fair use, and plagiarism—help solidify the importance of respecting the work of others. These discussions are particularly rich when focused on the shifting legal and ethical landscape of the Web and what intellectual property means in virtual space.

5.2. Encouraging Critical Online Research

Believing that issues of research and plagiarism are often closely connected and believing that first-year writing instructors should support students as they negotiate new research spaces, we also suggest equipping students with the skills to be critical thinkers and critical researchers in all of the realms in which they do research, especially within online spaces. The first step is to help them be effective searchers of the Web and evaluators of the information they find. Doing online research, for many students, means connecting to the search engine they're used to; doing a basic, unnarrowed search; and then looking at the first hits that come up and using the material from those sites.

Madeleine Sorapure, Pamela Inglesby, and George Yatchisin (1998) also argued that the assessment and evaluation of online sources be taught in composition courses. These authors pointed out three of the challenges the Web poses: First, no universal cataloging or categorizing takes place on the Web (although at this point in time, search engines have become more and more sophisticated, changing at a fast pace in the years since the 1998 article by Sorapure, Inglesby, and Yatchisin. Second, the Web is rhetorically complex—web sites sell products, offer information, give data and statistics, and so on. And, finally, the design of web sites doesn't often reflect their purpose, and the interface of the Web is incredibly rich with text, images, animated images, video clips, and audio files. Discerning how the multimedia pieces of a web site come together to serve a specific purpose can be a daunting task. Sorapure, Inglesby, and Yatchisin draw upon resources offered by university library sites and by web design and publication sites for guidance on evaluation.

To scaffold the activities listed below, we also adopted a web-page evaluation approach and generated the following categories of questions:

- *author/credibility* (for example, "What is the authority or expertise of the author of the page?" "With what organization or larger site is the web page connected/affiliated?")

- *reliability of information* (for example, "Who do you think is the expected audience?" "What is the primary purpose of the age?" "Does the information support or contradict what you know or what you already have learned from another source?")

- *interface design* (for example, "Is the site conceptually exciting? Does it do more than can be done with print?" "Do the graphics serve a rhetorical purpose, or are they decorative?")

- *navigation* (for example, "Can you find your way around the page to find the information you want?" "Do all of the links work?")

Clearly, most of these are questions we should encourage students to ask of all media and all texts, not just those gathered within online realms. However, although we—and the students in our classrooms—may be comfortable evaluating the credibility of paper texts, evaluating the credibility of online texts is a task that often feels foreign, mainly because of the lack of clear catalogue processes and the complicated nature of online, multimedia texts.

There are a variety of practical, critical, writing-rich ways to engage students in web-based research and evaluation. A few suggestions include:

- Have students write a short self-reflective paper analyzing their research methods and how they approach different types of sources.

- Have students bring to class a print source and a web source and analyze and critique each, then practice summarizing, paraphrasing, and quoting from each.

- Have students create a handout for the class to use including recommendations for citing web sources in their papers.

- Have students search for information on evaluating sites on the Web. Have groups of students evaluate the information on evaluation, then have students present their findings and collaboratively create guidelines for evaluating online sources handout for the class.

- Have students choose a web page to revamp, drawing upon the evaluation criteria (how would they improve this page? What is this page missing? What new information is needed to make the page more effective?).

- Have students perform the same search—using the same key words and search criteria—on several different search engines and write a paper explaining the differences (and, if applicable, similarities) in the results and why they think such differences exist.

- Have students do a Web versus the library search—provide the students with five questions. Have half the students look up the answers in the library, and have half look up the answers on the Web. Then have them switch roles. Ask students to write a paper evaluating the strengths and limitations of each research space.

- Have students research and come up with their own definitions for and examples of plagiarism. Have students present their findings and collaboratively create a plagiarism guidelines handout for the class.

- Have students research the different approaches or guidelines different institutions or colleges suggest and enforce about plagiarism and intellectual property.

- Have students research the process for getting something copyrighted or trademarked and also research what copyright or trademark protection allows. Require that students include examples and, if possible, legal cases.

- Have students find something with a trademark or copyright symbol on it and research what the symbol means (using the object itself, information on intellectual property, the company's web page, and so on) and also research what the symbol allows or protects.

Each of these activities offers several rhetorically smart possibilities: Students hone their research skills; students write documents for a real audience (the other students in the class); students work collaboratively and engage in discussions about what plagiarism is and what it means; and students explore plagiarism and intellectual property issues, hopefully leading to a stronger realization that the rules of academia aren't entirely divorced from the "real-world" issues of industry.

6. CONCLUSION

To make the Web a better research space—a space where students will be doing critical, thoughtful, thorough research instead of searching for papers to plagiarize—we must engage students in tasks appropriate to the complexity of online space. At the same time, we should engage students in a complex understanding of what plagiarism is and why it's penalized in our institutions. We also have to reconcile our understanding of plagiarism, the author function, and what a text actually is and what purpose a textual product serves, especially in light of online text. This approach should enable students in our classes to be thoughtful online researchers and careful, critical writers.

Rather than approach plagiarism as an affront to our values and authority as teachers, issues of plagiarism can provide a scaffolding for discussions relating to appropriate research, good writing, similarities and differences in research spaces, intellectual property rights, and the pitfalls and potentials of electronic media. With broader and more intense information dispersion, teachers will have to help prepare students to do research in online spaces. This is incredibly exciting work because many of us are on the verge of a turning point in our teaching: We're currently moving from a more how-to approach (how to get on the Web, how to use a search engine, and so on) to a rhetorically savvy, complex, and critical approach to Internet research. This is also important work because of the function first-year writing serves.

Admittedly, most first-year writing courses and curricula are already packed, perhaps overloaded—testament to the importance of first-year writing.

But as we work toward acculturating students into the processes and function of academic writing *and* engaging them in appropriate academic processes, we must make room for addressing new research and writing spaces. This does not mean we have to entirely shift our focus or replace much of our curricula. What this means is that we need to shift and adapt our curricula to include new research spaces and the promises and perils they pose. This sort of approach is what we need to further develop if we are going to better understand the temptations students face in online realms, and the complications they face in adapting their literacy, research, and writing skills and processes to the virtual space—and complexity—of the Web.

NOTES

1. An online paper mill is a site on the Web that allows—and encourages—students to download research papers to turn in as their own.

2. Kidnapping almost feels like a generous analogy in comparison to other authors' labels of plagiarism; for example, "abduction," "literary piracy" (Hawley, 1984, p. 35) and "virulent . . . disease" (Drum, 1986, p. 241).

3. One obvious route often suggested in much literature is a proof-of-process approach; that is, to require front matter from students—notes, drafts, sources, and so on. A proof-of-process approach can be integrated easily into the writing classroom, and obviously offers benefits that extend beyond the avoidance of plagiarism. Valuing students' ongoing deliberations and the construction of their written work helps to create an environment for writing that discourages some of the reasons for defaulting to plagiarizing. A proof-of-process approach can complement the approaches we suggest here.

REFERENCES

Barthes, Roland. (1985). The death of the author. In *Image/music/text* (Trans. Stephen Heath) (pp. 142–148). New York: Hill and Wang.

Bolter, Jay David. (1991). *Writing space: The computer, hypertext, and the history of writing.* Hillsdale, NJ: Lawrence Erlbaum.

Burton, Vicki Tolar, & Chadwick, Scott A. (2000). Investigating the practices of student researchers: Patterns of use and criteria for use of Internet and library sources. *Computers and Composition, 17,* 309–328.

Chidley, Joe. (1997, November 24). Tales out of school: Cheating has long been a great temptation, and the Internet makes it easier than ever. *Maclean's,* pp. 76–80.

Drum, Alice, (1986). Responding to plagiarism. *College Composition and Communication, 37,* 241–243.

Foucault, Michel. (1984). What is an author? In Paul Rabinow (Ed.), *The Foucault reader* (pp. 101–120). New York: Pantheon Books.

Fox, Helen. (1994). *Listening to the world: Cultural issues in academic writing.* Urbana, IL: National Council of Teachers of English.

Hawley, Christopher S. (1984). The thieves of academe: Plagiarism in the university system. *Improving College and University Teaching, 32,* 35–39.

Hickman, John N. (1998, March 23). Cybercheats: Term-paper shopping online. *The New Republic,* pp. 14–16.

Howard, Rebecca. (1993). A plagiarism pentimento. *Journal of Teaching Writing, 11,* 233–245.

Howard, Rebecca. (1995). Plagiarisms, authorships, and the academic death penalty. *College English, 57,* 788–806.

Innerst, Carol. (1998, March 9). Students are pulling off the big cheat. *Insight on the News,* p. 41.

Jones, Patrice M. (1997, December 8). Internet term papers write new chapter on plagiarism. *Chicago Tribune,* p. 1.

Joyce, Michael. (1995). *Of two minds: Hypertext pedagogy and poetics.* Ann Arbor: University of Michigan Press.

Kantz, Margaret. (1990). Helping students use textual sources persuasively. *College English, 52,* 74–91.

Kitalong, Karla. (1998). A web of symbolic violence. *Computers and Composition, 15,* 253–264.

Kleiner, Carolyn, & Lord, Mary. (1999, November 22). The cheating game. *U.S. News and World Report*, pp. 54–66.

Kloss, Robert J. (1996, Winter). Writing things down vs. writing things up. *College Teaching, 44*, 3–7.

Kolich, Augustus M. (1983). Plagiarism: The worm of reason. *College English, 45*, 141–148.

Landow, George P. (1992). *Hypertext: The convergence of contemporary critical theory and technology.* Baltimore: Johns Hopkins University Press.

Lanham, Richard A. (1993). *The electronic word: Democracy, technology, and the arts.* Chicago: University of Chicago Press.

Malloch, A. E. (1976). A dialogue on plagiarism. *College English, 38*, 65–74.

Mooney, John. (1999, February 11). Universities battling sale of term papers. *Sun News*, p. 6A.

Plotz, David. (1999, October 14). New frontiers in cheating. *Rolling Stone*, p. 107.

Sanchez, Roberto. (1998, December 21). College, cheaters, computers coincide. *The Seattle Times*, p. B1.

Sorapure, Madeleine, Inglesby, Pamela, & Yatchisin, George. (1998). Web literacy: Challenges and opportunities for research in a new medium. *Computers and Composition, 15*, 409–424.

Whitaker, Elaine E. (1993). A pedagogy to address plagiarism. *College Composition and Communication, 44*, 509–514.

Wilhoit, Stephen. (1994). Helping students avoid plagiarism. *College Teaching, 42*, 161–164.

Witherspoon, Abigail. (1995, June). This pen for hire: On grinding out papers for college students. *Harper's Magazine*, pp. 49–58.

10 Reading Hypertext: Order and Coherence in a New Medium

JOHN M. SLATIN

The basic point I have to make is almost embarrassingly simple: Hypertext is very different from more traditional forms of text. The differences are a function of technology and are so various, at once so minute and so vast, as to make hypertext a new medium for thought and expression—the first verbal medium, after programming languages, to emerge from the computer revolution. (The computer has spawned new media in the visual arts and music as well.) As a new medium, hypertext is also very different from both word processing and desktop publishing, two other computer technologies which have had an enormous impact on the production of texts. Both word processing and desktop publishing have as their goal the production of conventional printed documents, whereas hypertext exists and can exist only online, only in the computer. A new medium involves both a new practice and a new rhetoric, a new body of theory. I hope this essay will serve as a step in that direction.

The first requirement for a rhetoric of hypertext is that it must take the computer actively into account as a medium for composition and thought—not just as a presentational device and not simply as an extension of the typewriter. This means different things, depending on the level of abstraction at which one stands. At some levels, for example, one has to deal with data structures, with the construction of knowledge (if the term even applies) within and to the hard- and software of the computer as well as the construction of knowledge by and for humans. It means, also, that the rhetoric itself must be abstract, like Wallace Stevens's supreme fiction, in order to permit movement up and down the ladder of abstraction and to permit the articulation of principles that will enable practice. By the same token, the rhetoric of hypertext will have to be capable of change, for it is tied to a still immature (perhaps perpetually immature) technology which is itself changing at an exponential rate.

On the assumption, then, that description is the first step toward theory (see Bateson), I will contrast hypertext with more traditional text. I will focus

From *College English* 52.8 (1990): 870–83.

on the assumptions each makes about what readers do and the ways in which those assumptions about reading affect the author's understanding of composition. For the purposes of this discussion, taking the computer into account means that we have to find ways of talking about documents that have multiple points of entry, multiple exit points, and multiple pathways between points of entry and exit points. Moreover, we must find ways to talk about the still more exciting kinds of activity fostered by this proliferation of possibilities: I mean interactive reading and its more or less inevitable concomitant, interactive writing, or co-authorship.

Widespread literacy is a comparatively recent phenomenon—that is to say that in Western societies such as those of England, Europe, and North America, general literacy is at best a couple of hundred years old. But Western culture was a print culture long before the coming of general literacy, and the text environment we are all familiar with is the product of fully mature, highly stable manuscript and print technologies which have been in place for many centuries. Principles and strategies for effective written communication are therefore based on assumptions about readers and reading. It will be helpful to consider these assumptions briefly before going on to discuss the different assumptions embedded in the design of hypertext and hypermedia systems.

The assumption that reading is a sequential and continuous process is the foundation on which everything else rests (see, for instance, Stanley Fish). The reader is expected to begin at a clearly marked point whose appropriateness has been determined by the author—usually with considerable effort: one of the hardest moments in any writing project is to figure out where to start—and to proceed from that beginning to an ending which is just as clearly marked and which has also been determined by the author in accordance with his or her understanding of the subject matter and the reader. The reader's progress from the beginning to the end of the text follows a route which has been carefully laid out for the sole purpose of ensuring that the reader does indeed get from the beginning to the end in the way the writer wants him or her to get there.

All but the most naïve and inexperienced writers recognize that all but the most naïve and inexperienced readers inevitably and rightly make inferences about what's going to happen next, on the basis of what they have already read—not only in the current text, but in other texts resembling it. The reader's perception of the predictability of a given text is an important factor in his or her qualitative evaluation of the text.

Prediction operates on a number of different levels and is determined by different things at different levels of abstraction. The predictability of a given text is a function of the relationships among phenomena at microscopic, macroscopic, and metatextual levels of abstraction. At the microscopic levels, the reader's ability to predict the course of the text from moment to moment is a function of such factors as paragraphing, sentence length, complexity of phrasing, vocabulary, and so on—that is, the factors that are evaluated in producing a so-called "readability index." Indeed, one might descend even further down the ladder of abstraction and argue that prediction takes place at the graphemic or phonemic levels as well (see Fry). At the macroscopic levels, the reader is aware of such things as general subject matter, topics and subtopics, and the structural devices organizing the text as a whole—sections, chapters, and subchapters, and so forth. At this level the reader is also at least subliminally aware of such things as how much more material there is to read. On what we might call the metatextual level, the reader makes inferences about the text as a whole, based on his or her understanding of the larger context to which he or she regards the text as belonging. These inferences are often implicit, or else they may take the form of mental or marginal annotations. In any case, they are outside the text and separate from it; they are integral to hypertext, as I shall explain later on.

The end product of the writing process is a text written or printed on paper, and then, often, sewn or glued or otherwise bound between covers. This is obvious, I know, and yet it needs to be said. Every writer has had the awful experience of opening a book or article hot off the press, only to stare in horror at a glaring error in a crucial passage that somehow escaped the most agonizing scrutiny. The fixity of the printed text as an object in physical space makes the text as an object in mental space seem equally stable and fixed. Or at least that's how we tend to want it. As Richard Lanham has said, "It was establishing the original text that the Renaissance scholars thought their main task, and generations of textual editors since have renewed their labors. The aim of all this was to fix the text forever" ("Convergent Pressures" 4). The continuing controversy over Hans-Walter Gabler's edition of Joyce's *Ulysses* (1984; see Rossman) makes abundantly clear just how intense the desire "to fix the text forever" can be. Gabler's re-conception of the editing process may have occurred independently of his decision to use the computer (Groden 29), but the controversy over his "synoptic" version of *Ulysses* offers a clear illustration of the way computers will revolutionize our understanding of text. Every word in Gabler's synoptic text was written by Joyce himself—and yet the final "reading text" is a text no one ever wrote—it had never existed prior to its publication. (In this sense, Gabler's *Ulysses* resembles Benoit Mandelbrot's fractals, in which recursive mathematical formulae are graphically plotted to produce visual structures that, while in some cases resembling phenomena in the day-to-day world, have no counterpart in that world.) Gabler's is a simulated *Ulysses*, like the *Don Quixote* that would be produced by Borges' Pierre Menard if Menard were real and if he had a computer. This is what becomes of the work of art in an age of electronic reproduction. Text is always mutable, always subject to inadvertent error and deliberate change, and it has to be coerced into standing still. That's why publishers charge you money if you make too many changes in a text after it's been typeset.

For all these reasons—because a text looks like a permanent thing, because readers expect to begin at the beginning and end at the end and to know which is which (that's why students so often begin the last paragraph with "in conclusion"), because readers expect to get from beginning to end via a clearly-marked route—sequence is of paramount concern to a writer. Much of his or her effort goes into figuring out the correct sequence for the material that's going to be presented. The writer's job in this context is to contrive a sequence that will not only determine the reader's experience and understanding of the material but will also seem to the reader to have been the only possible sequence for that material; you want it to seem to have been somehow inevitable.

Of course this inevitability has a good deal to do with the issue of predictability I raised earlier. Readers have to be able to predict what will come next, at least up to a point, or they start to feel lost, which makes them start to feel nervous, which makes them want to put down what they're reading and go watch a football game or something—at which point the writer has failed miserably. But the flip side is just as bad, and the end result is going to be the same.

Writing that's too predictable is governed by a presupposition succinctly expressed by a certain hotel chain's ad campaigns. The presupposition that there should be "no surprises" may be fine for hotels. But it becomes a fundamental conceptual error where writing is concerned. The informational value of a given document is not simply a function of the quantity of data it presents or the facts it contains. At one level of abstraction, what we call information may indeed consist in numbers, dates, and other data, other facts. But as Gregory Bateson says, "All receipt of information is necessarily receipt of the news of *difference*" (32). At a somewhat higher level of abstraction, therefore, none of these data can be considered information until they have been contextualized, arranged in such a way that both the significant differences and the significant relationships among them may become apparent to the intended reader. In Christopher Dede's terms, this is when information becomes knowledge. In other words, as literary artists and their readers have always known, there can be no information without surprise.

Rhetoric typically has little to say about the physical processes by which a text is brought into being. Or I could put it even more strongly and say that rhetoric has traditionally been indifferent to the technology of communication. One reason for this indifference is that the technology is so mature that it's simply taken for granted, that it is essentially invisible *as* technology. There was a point in history, of course, when writing itself was a radically innovative technology and was regarded as such, as Eric A. Havelock, Father Walter J. Ong, and Richard Lanham have shown us. The computerization of writing has similarly made the technology itself highly visible, especially in the cases of desktop publishing and hypertext/hypermedia. By contrast with traditional text, hypertext and hypermedia depend upon an emergent technology which is still immature and still subject to radical transformation; indeed, all indications are that accelerating change is an inherent characteristic of this technology. It may *never* stabilize. Thus rhetoric for hypertext cannot afford to disregard the technological substrate upon which composition and reading depend.

There are many continuities between conventional text and hypertext. Anyone involved in creating a hyperdocument will still have to worry about the problems I've outlined so far. But hypertext is a very different kind of beast than a conventional text, and creating a hyperdocument poses some very different problems as well. The remainder of this paper will concentrate on those differences and their implications.

First of all, the hyperdocument may well contain material from different media such as text, graphics, video, and sound. While this is an important factor, I don't think it's decisive. After all, printed books often contain text, line drawings, tables of data, reproductions of visual images, and so forth— though of course they cannot manage full motion video or sound. Besides containing different types of materials than those to be found in printed text, the hyperdocument is likely to contain considerably more material than a printed book. Again, this is not a decisive difference in itself: encyclopedias also contain an enormous quantity of material. The quantity of material in a hyperdocument does pose problems, and it does make for complexity. But the greatest difference between text and hypertext is not in the relative quantity of material each form handles: it's in the technology that handles the material.

What makes all the difference in the world is the fact that hypertext exists and can exist only in an online environment. This is crucial, not just because it substitutes monitors, keyboards, and mice for the customary physical apparatus associated with text—paper, books, pencils, and so forth. The fact that hypertext exists only in the online environment is crucial because, as Douglas Hofstadter says, "It is the organization of memory that defines what concepts are" (528). Hypertext uses machine memory in a way that has no analogue in the traditional text environment, where composition relies on the organization of human memory. It is the organization of memory in the computer and in the mind that defines hypertext and makes it fundamentally different from conventional text.

In such an environment, the problem is not simply to develop effective strategies for implementing well known and long established principles of effective communication. On the contrary, one of the chief functions of rhetoric in the hypertext environment is to discover the principles of effective communication and then develop ways of implementing those principles through the available technology.

The rapidly evolving technological environment makes hypertext possible by permitting the embodiment of a very different set of assumptions about readers and reading—and about thinking. These assumptions in turn form the basis for decisions made in the process of creating a hyperdocument.

Reading, in hypertext, is understood as a discontinuous or non-linear process which, like thinking, is associative in nature, as opposed to the sequential process envisioned by conventional text. Associative thinking is more difficult to follow than linear thinking. Linear thinking specifies the steps it has taken; associative thinking is discontinuous—a series of jumps like the movement of electrons or the movements of the mind in creating metaphor. This discontinuity is not fortuitous; rather, as Stewart Brand points out, it is a basic aspect of the digital encoding of information. Brand offers the illuminating contrast between the surface of a traditional phonograph album, with its continuous grooves, and the surface of a compact disc, with its distinct, discontinuous pits (18).

Reading in this sense has little to do with traditional notions of being at the beginning and going through to the end. Instead, the reader begins at a point of his or her own choosing—a point chosen from a potentially very large number of possible starting points. The reader proceeds from there by following a series of links connecting documents to one another, exiting not at a point defined by the author as "The End" but rather when he or she has had enough. Accordingly, the most common metaphors in discussions of hypertext equate reading with the navigation or traversal of large, open (and usually poorly-charted) spaces. As Jeff Conklin has pointed out, because the hyperdocument contains so much material, and because relations between the components of the hyperdocument are not always spelled out, there is a significant danger that the reader will get lost or become badly disoriented.

The difficulty is compounded because hypertext systems tend to envision three different types of readers: the reader as browser, as user, or as co-author. The relationship between these three classes can be fuzzy and therefore difficult to manage. One function a rhetoric for hypertext will have to serve will be to provide ways of negotiating it.

The browser is someone who wanders rather aimlessly (but not carelessly) through an area, picking things up and putting them down as curiosity or momentary interest dictates. In this respect the browser is someone who reads for pleasure, with this important difference: there is no expectation that the browser will go through all of the available material; often the expectation is just the reverse. It is difficult to predict the browser's pathway through the material—and in fact it is less important to predict the pathway the browser will take than it is to provide a backtracking mechanism, what Mark Bernstein calls a Hansel-&-Gretel trail of breadcrumbs to allow the browser to re-trace his or her steps at will. (Of course this same mechanism is essential for readers in the two remaining categories as well.)

By contrast with the browser, the user is a reader with a clear—and often clearly limited—purpose. He or she enters the hyperdocument in search, usually, of specific information and leaves it again after locating that information. The user's path is relatively predictable, provided those who have created the hyperdocument have a sufficient understanding of the task domain. In these respects, then, the user resembles a typical student doing the assigned reading for a course. But there is also an important difference between the user and the student, which is most clearly recognized from the vantage-point of the author rather than the reader. The author(s) of a hypertext documentation system (e.g., a software product like Microsoft QuickBASIC 4.5™) will have met their goal when the user finds the information he or she needs and returns to the work in progress. However, the instructor designing a set of hypertext course materials may well not be satisfied with such an outcome. The instructor aims at a dynamic process, in which the student moves among three different states: from a user the student becomes a browser (and may then become a user once again); ultimately, he or she becomes fully involved as co-author. Thus what looks like a hierarchy of readers collapses.

One of the most important differences between conventional text and hypertext is that most hypertext systems, though not all, allow readers to interact with the system to such an extent that some readers may become actively involved in the creation of an evolving hyperdocument. Co-authorship may take a number of different forms—from relatively simple, brief annotations of or comments on existing material, to the creation of new links connecting material not previously linked, to the modification of existing material or the creation of new materials, or both. Both literary theorists (e.g., Wolfgang Iser, Paul Ricoeur, Stanley Fish) and cognitive scientists like Jerome Bruner have talked for years about the reader's involvement in the construction of textual meaning. But hypertext's capacity for literally interactive reading and co-authorship represents a radical departure from traditional relationships between readers and texts. The implications of this departure from traditional relationships between readers and texts are enormous, both for the creative arts (see, for instance, Moulthrop; Ziegfeld) and for education: as many theorists now agree, understanding comes about when the mind acts upon the material. Marshall McLuhan's distinction between hot and cool media is relevant here—a cool medium being one that invites active participation, a hot one being one before which one sits passively. McLuhan was thinking, of course, about the difference between print and television, but one might argue that hypertext combines the heat and visual excitement of film, video, and television with text's cool invitation to participate (also Lanham, "The Electronic Word").

"Writing," in the hypertext environment, becomes the more comprehensive activity called "authoring." Authoring may involve not only the composition of text but also screen layout and other things that fall under the general rubric of interface design; it may also involve a certain amount of programming (as in Apple's HyperCard, where complex navigational and other processes are scripted by the stack's author). Perhaps most importantly, authoring involves the creation and management of links between nodes.

Ted Nelson, who coined the term "hypertext," defines hypertext as "nonsequential writing" (117). This means writing in which the logical connections between elements are primarily associative rather than syllogistic, as in conventional text. One implication of this is that the hyperdocument "grows" by a process of accretion, whereas the conventional document tends to have been winnowed out of a larger mass of material. That is, in preparing to write a conventional document, you almost inevitably assemble more material than you can possibly use; the closer you come to final copy, the more you find yourself excluding material that "doesn't fit" the subject as you've finally defined it. Hypertext, by contrast, is an inclusive medium. Thanks to the capability of creating nodes and links, material not linearly related to the point being discussed at the moment but still associated with that point may be placed in a node of its own and linked to other nodes as appropriate; the material need not be thrown away (see also Howard). In much the same way, no individual point of view need be excluded.

This inclusiveness makes it unlikely that any one individual will see all the elements making up the system. It also means that the hyperdocument is in fact a collection of possible documents, any one of which may be actualized by readers pursuing or creating links between elements of the system (Slatin, "Hypertext and the Teaching of Writing" 113).

The end product of the authoring process, the hyperdocument, is not a closed system, like a book; it is rather an open and dynamic system. The hyperdocument is an online system or network whose constituents are of two basic types, nodes and links. Nodes may consist of documents, images, or other materials electronically connected—linked—to one or more other documents or images. Very likely, the different nodes will represent the work of quite a few individuals, who may have been working at different times and in different locations. Indeed, one impetus for the development of hypertext systems has been in the need to address exactly this issue among members of development teams (see Conklin; see also Trigg, Suchman, and Halasz; Suchman and Trigg). The development of protocols and procedures for co-authorship thus becomes an important issue. So does the development of procedures for moving through the system.

The reader's progress through a conventional text is governed by the arrangement of the material; the burden of prediction falls more heavily upon the reader than on the writer. This situation becomes considerably more complicated in hypertext. Given a system of discrete and interconnected nodes, the reader/user must decide which links to follow; in order to make that decision intelligently, he or she must be able to make reliable predictions about the consequences of particular choices. But the freedom of movement and action available to the reader—a freedom including the possibility of co-authorship—means that the hypertext author has to make predictions as well: for the author, the difficulty at any given moment is to provide freedom of movement and interaction, while at the same time remaining able to predict where the reader/user will go next. The most effective solution here, I think, will be to treat each node as if it were certain to be the reader's next destination. This is time-consuming in the short run, but in the long run probably saves time by creating a more readily usable system.

This brings us to the issue of linkage, the mechanism that creates the hyperdocument and allows the reader to move through it. Douglas Hofstadter has suggested that the perception of relatedness is a defining characteristic— perhaps *the* defining characteristic—of intelligent behavior. Hypertext embodies this idea, for everything in hypertext depends upon linkage, upon connectivity between and among the various elements in the system. Linkage, in hypertext, plays a role corresponding to that of sequence in conventional text. A hypertext link is the electronic representation of a perceived relationship between two pieces of material, which become nodes once the relationship has been instantiated electronically. That is, the link *simulates* the connections in the mind of the author or reader; and it is precisely because the electronic link is only a simulation that problems will arise.

The interdependency of links and nodes is such that it is impossible to talk about one without talking about the other. Thus the question of how to define a node leads to additional questions about linkage. These lead in turn to questions about structure (Slatin, "Hypertext and the Teaching of Writing") and coherence, and so back again to the issue of prediction.

A node is any object which is linked to another object. It may be as large as an entire book or as small as a single character; theoretically, it could be as small as a single pixel (picture element) on a display, though such extremes seem hardly practical. It may consist of a document or a block of text within a larger document; it may be a drawing, a digitized photograph, a (digitized) detail of a painting, a sound recording, a motion picture, or a scene—even a frame—from a motion picture.

There is no set answer to the question, how big should a node be? just as there is no set answer to the question, how long is a paragraph? Like the paragraph, the hypertext node is a way of structuring attention, and its boundaries, like those of the paragraph, are somewhat arbitrary. A node may contain a single paragraph; it may contain many; it may contain something else entirely. Jeff Conklin offers criteria for guidance in determining node size. To what extent, he asks, is the information in question so tightly bound together that (a) you always want to view it together; (b) you never want to take it apart; and (c) you rarely even want to reference parts of it outside of the context of the rest (38–40). In other words, a node is an integrated and self-sufficient unit; its size will be a function of the complexity of the integration. This in turn is contingent upon the author's perception of the nature of the material it contains and the relation of that material to other things in the hyperdocument.

The individual node, then, behaves in certain respects like a more conventional text. But the node is not just a self-contained unit. A node cannot, by definition, be entirely free of links—a node is a knot, is always embedded in a system—and that connectedness in turn gives the node its definition: "A node is something through which other things pass, and which is created by their passage" (Slatin, "Hypertext and the Teaching of Writing" 126).

A text becomes a node when it is electronically placed in relation to other materials (documentary or otherwise), which may (or may not) already contain links to other elements within the system. The difficulty here, of course, is that what are self-evident associations to me may not be even faintly apparent to you, and vice versa. This imposes an obligation on the author(s) of a hyperdocument which has no exact parallel for the writer of conventional text: the nodes must seem complete in themselves, yet at the same time their relations to other nodes must be intelligible. The problem of relationality here, as I argue elsewhere, is analogous to the problems of intertexuality confronting readers of, say twentieth-century poetry. This problem becomes increasingly challenging as the hyperdocument expands. Links exist for many different reasons—that is, to represent many different kinds of relationships between objects. The more links there are between the current node and other elements of the hyperdocument, then, the greater the necessity of identifying the attached material clearly—especially when the reader is allowed considerable freedom in choosing among the available links. (See Landow, "Relationally Encoded Links" and "Hypertext in Literary Education" for several pertinent rules of thumb.)

These identifiers carry an enormous burden. Indeed they are often asked to do the kind of explanatory work that ordinarily takes several sentences or paragraphs. Not surprisingly, there are several different methods of identifying link or node types. Some hypertext systems, such as MCC's gIBIS, use "typed nodes" (Conklin), while others—Xerox PARC's NoteCards, for example—employ "link types" (Trigg, Suchman, and Halasz). These systems allow the co-author creating a new node to choose from a list of pre-defined relationship categories, whose names then become part of the node or link.

HyperTIES, developed by Ben Shneiderman at the University of Maryland and distributed by Cognetics Corporation, offers a variation on this approach by encouraging the author to compose a brief (two-line) description of the linked node. In HyperTIES, where reading is defined primarily as browsing and where browsing is completely separate from authoring, activating a link is a two-step process. The first step, clicking on a highlighted word or phrase, brings up the description of the attached node; the second step either brings up the attached node or returns the browser to the current screen.

The developers of Intermedia at Brown University have chosen a third alternative. Links belong to "webs" rather than to documents; webs are displayed onscreen as visual maps. An Intermedia document is first displayed as if it were freestanding; then, when the user opens a web, the links belonging to that web are displayed (Garrett, Smith, and Meyrowitz 1986). This approach allows an individual node to be placed within multiple frames of reference, or "webs," while avoiding both the screen clutter and the mental clutter that can accrue so easily when multiple links radiate to and from a node. Which links the user sees will depend upon which web he or she has elected to open.

As the Intermedia approach suggests, one way to address the question of how many links a node should have is by turning it into the question of how many links should be displayed at any moment. Research on memory suggests that we can hang on to between five and seven "chunks" of information at a time and that creating links between these chunks is a way to increase the effective size of the chunk. However, the number of chunks that can be retained decreases in inverse proportion to their size (see Kozma).

Probably no single method of identifying nodes and their relationships to other nodes is adequate to all needs; some combination will be needed. Choosing from a list of predefined relationships has certain advantages, since there is a strong likelihood that a newly created node will fall within an existing classification. However, the list must offer real choices without becoming so big as to make choice impossible. And co-authors may also wish to give a fuller description of the attached node than the list approach permits; something like the HyperTIES strategy becomes appropriate here. And when a given node has multiple links to and from other nodes, it may be advisable to use an Intermedia-style mapping strategy.

The approach you choose to the problem of identifying links and nodes will depend on several factors: your understanding of the ways in which the material is related; your sense of who your readers are (are they primarily browsers? users? co-authors?). Your sense of what you want those readers to do is especially important.

You don't have to worry about interactive readers when you write a conventional text—the only thing you want the reader to do is to go on to the next sentence. But in hypertext, where there are a number of possible "next sentences" or nodes for the reader to go on to, you do have to make some decisions about what ought to happen next. That is, do you care whether the reader (a) opens a specific node or sequence of nodes; (b) chooses more or less randomly from the available links; (c) creates a new node, linking it not only to the current node but also to such other nodes as the reader—now a co-author—deems appropriate?

If you want the reader to open a specific node or sequence of nodes, you can either try to influence the reader's course of action, for example by highlighting a "preferred pathway" through the material, or you can simply preempt the reader's choice by automating the sequence or hiding links you don't want the reader to pursue. (Though if you take that route you give up many of the advantages of hypertext, it seems to me.) Or if you don't have a preference about the sequence the reader follows, you may opt not to give directions, leaving the choice of which links to activate—or whether to activate any link at all—entirely up to the reader. If you want to encourage response—that is, if you want the reader actually to get involved as a co-author—you should say so somewhere on the screen and make it as easy as possible for the reader to change roles. In HyperCard, for instance, you can script a button to open up a text field with a date/time stamp and the name of the new co-author; you can even let the co-author enter keywords to make later searches faster.

I've already said that the author of a hyperdocument has a hard time trying to predict where the reader will go from any given point. The reader who activates a link often has a hard time, too, because it can be so difficult to predict what the result will be. The more cryptic the link or node identifiers are, the harder it is for the reader to predict the results of activating a particular link. The harder it is to make such predictions, the greater the likelihood that the reader will simply opt out of the process in frustration. And even if the reader does go ahead there is no guarantee that he or she will know the place when he or she gets there.

The reader has to make several different kinds of predictions. First, he or she has to predict the kind of material he or she will encounter upon activating a link. It would be quite distressing, for example, to activate a link in the expectation of moving to a narrative explanation of some issue, if in fact the associated node contains only raw data in tabular form. Second, he or she makes some predictions about the content of the node: at the most general level, the reader makes some kind of assumption about the closeness of the relationship between the current node and the material linked to it.

The questions of link and node labeling which are obviously of such central importance here impinge on the issue of predictability at what I have been calling the macroscopic level. At the microscopic level, predictability revolves around such things as screen-design: typography, visual effects, layout of information on the screen, and so forth, all have an impact on the reader's ability to organize the material in his or her own mind, and thus on his or her ability to operate effectively within the hypertext environment. Typographical conventions are such that the reader of a conventional text has a pretty good idea what kind of object will appear next. The period at the end of a sentence leads one to expect a capital letter and the beginning of a new object belonging to the same class—a new sentence; the blank space at the end of a paragraph signals the beginning of a new paragraph; and so on. The signals in hypertext systems aren't nearly so clear.

Because the technology isn't mature enough yet to support a single set of conventions, each hypertext system has to develop its own conventions. For that reason, it is probably necessary to incorporate procedural discussions about these conventions into the hyperdocument itself; thus one element of the hyperdocument will be an ongoing critique of its own procedures. Participants might consider, for example, whether to assign specific fonts to individual co-authors (see Trigg, Suchman, and Halasz) so that their contributions can be readily identified; text styles might be assigned to specific node or link types; a question might always be italicized, for instance, while an explanation might be underlined; and so on. Color can be used for similar purposes in systems where color is available. So can visual effects such as wipes, dissolves, and zooms, which are available in HyperCard. These and other special effects can easily become distracting or even annoying, but if particular devices are consistently and intelligently used in association with particular node types, they can also function as more or less subliminal aids to prediction, helping the reader to perceive the hyperdocument as coherent.

We regard a conventional text as coherent to the extent that all the material it contains strikes us as being related in an appropriately direct way to the subject and to the author's thesis and arranged in the appropriate sequence. The perception of coherence in hypertext seems to me much more problematic, however, though I don't have time to do more than suggest what might be involved. Nor do I know enough to do more than that.

I think of hypertext coherence as appearing at the metatextual level—that is, at the level where the reader perceives what Bateson calls "the pattern which connects" (12). The pattern which connects is the organizing notion around which all the disparate elements of the hyperdocument revolve. (An author's feel for the pattern which connects plays a significant part in decisions about node size and linkage as well.) This can be a relatively straightforward thing—a given hyperdocument might contain all the materials generated during a particular design project, for instance. This metatextual level is perhaps best represented by a visual map of some kind, whose nodes would open up to map subordinate patterns. This map ought to be readily accessible from any point in the hyperdocument, which suggests that it might be "iconized" and placed at a consistent screen location. This sounds simple enough, perhaps; but it becomes problematic again when we remember that we're dealing with a fluid system and multiple participants, and we start to ask whose understanding such maps represent. Maybe there needs to be a facility to allow any user to create such a map, whether for private consideration only or for public use might be up to the reader/co-author.

Conceptually, hypertext has a place, I think, in any environment where it's necessary or desirable to bring together large, complex, highly diversified bodies of information in such a way as to emphasize their interconnectedness—especially if physical space is at a premium, as of course it is on board a space station or an orbital device, or in a control room—or, for that matter, in a classroom (see Slatin, "Text and Context"; Slatin, "Hypertext and the Teaching of Writing"; see also Jaffe and Lynch; Bourne et al.).

Perhaps the greatest value of hypertext is its ability to link enormous quantities of material that, in a conventional text environment, would be kept separate, perhaps even in different buildings, so that things which someone perceives as being related do in fact become related. Hypertext is weakest when it comes to spelling out what these relationships entail. It is important to say this because the techniques for explanation are quite highly developed within traditional rhetoric, and it would be a mistake to abandon them as outmoded.

Hypertext places different demands on both readers and authors than demands facing readers and authors of conventional text. The principal reason for this, in my view, is that hypertext is truly a new medium. Employing the full resources of technology to represent and correlate information, hypertext grants both readers and authors an unprecedented degree of freedom to arrange materials as they deem best, and it permits interaction between readers and authors to an unprecedented degree. In so transforming the methods of organization which have served traditional text for millennia, hypertext requires authors and system designers to find new methods of indicating relationships, representing and constructing knowledge, and achieving coherence.

WORKS CITED

Bateson, Gregory, *Mind and Nature: A Necessary Unity*. New York: Bantam, 1980.
Bernstein, Mark. "The Bookmark and the Compass: Orientation Tools for Hypertext Users." *ACM SIGOIS Bulletin* 9.4 (1988): 34–45.
Bourne, John R., et al. "Intelligent Hypertutoring in Engineering." *Academic Computing* 4.1 (1989): 18–20, 36–48.
Brand, Stewart. *The Media Lab: Inventing the Future at MIT*. New York: Viking, 1987.
Conklin, Jeff. *A Survey of Hypertext*. MCC Technical Report Number STP-356-86. Austin, TX: MCC, 1986.
Dede, Christopher. "The Role of Hypertext in Transforming Information into Knowledge." NECC. Dallas, 15–17 June 1988.
Fish, Stanley. *Self-Consuming Artifacts: The Experience of Seventeenth-Century Literature*. Berkeley: U of California P, 1972.
Fry, Dennis. *Homo Loquens: Man as a Talking Animal*. Cambridge: Cambridge UP, 1977.
Garrett, L. Nancy, Karen Smith, and Norman Meyrowitz. "Intermedia: Issues, Strategies, and Tactics in the Design of a Hypermedia Document System." Conference on Computer-Supported Cooperative Work. Austin, TX, 3–5 December 1986.

Groden, Michael. "Editing Joyce's *Ulysses:* An International Effort." *Scholarly Publishing in an Era of Change: Proceedings of the Second Annual Meeting, Society for Scholarly Publishing, Minneapolis, Minnesota June 2–4, 1980.* Ed. Ethel C. Langlois. Washington, D.C.: Society for Scholarly Publishing, 1981. 27–34.

Havelock, Eric A. *The Literate Revolution in Greece and Its Cultural Consequences.* Princeton: Princeton UP, 1982.

Hofstadter, Douglas R. *Metamagical Themas: Questing for the Essence of Mind and Pattern.* New York: Bantam, 1986.

Howard, Alan. "Hypermedia and the Future of Ethnography." *Cultural Anthropology* 3.3 (1988): 304–15.

Jaffe, Conrade C., and Patrick J. Lynch. "Hypermedia for Education in the Life Sciences." *Academic Computing* 4.1 (1989): 10–13, 52–57.

Kozma, Robert. "Designing Cognitive Tools for Computers." Hypertext Workshop. Intelligent Systems Branch, Air Force Human Resources Laboratory, Brooks AFB, TX, 23 February 1988.

Landow, George P. "Hypertext in Literary Education, Criticism, and Scholarship." *Computers and the Humanities* 23.3 (1989): 173–98.

_____. "Relationally Encoded Links and the Rhetoric of Hypertext." *Hypertext '87 Papers.* Chapel Hill, 13–15 November 1987.

Lanham, Richard A. "Convergent Pressures: Social, Technological, Theoretical." Conference on the Future of Doctoral Studies in English. Wayzata, MN, April 1987.

_____. "The Electronic Word: Literary Study and the Digital Revolution." *New Literary History* 20.2 (1989): 265–90.

McLuhan, Marshall. *Understanding Media: The Extensions of Man.* New York: New American Library, 1964.

Moulthrop, Stuart. "Containing Multitudes: The Problem of Closure in Interactive Fiction." *ACH Newsletter* 10 (1988): 1, 7.

Nelson, Theodor Holm. *Literary Machines.* San Antonio, TX: Theodor Holm Nelson, 1987.

Ong, Walter J., S. J. *Orality and Literacy: The Technologizing of the Word.* London: Methuen, 1982.

Rossman, Charles. "The New *Ulysses:* The Hidden Controversy." *New York Review of Books* 25.19 (1988): 53–58.

Slatin, John M. "Hypertext and the Teaching of Writing." *Text, Context, and Hypertext.* Ed. Edward Barrett. Cambridge, MA: MITP, 1988. 111–29.

_____. "Text and Context: Reflections on the Role of the Computer in Teaching Modern American Poetry." *Humanities and the Computer: New Directions.* Ed. David S. Miall. Oxford: Oxford UP, 1990. 123–35.

Suchman, Lucy A., and Randall H. Trigg. "A Framework for Studying Research Collaboration." Conference on Computer-Supported Cooperative Work. Austin, TX, 3–5 December 1986.

Trigg, Randall H., Lucy A. Suchman, and Frank G. Halasz. "Supporting Collaboration in Note-Cards." Conference on Computer-Supported Cooperative Work. Austin, TX, 3–5 December 1986.

Ziegfeld, Richard. "Interactive Fiction: A New Literary Genre?" *New Literary History* 20.2 (1989): 340–72.

PART THREE

Writers and Identity

Introduction to Part Three

I t is no exaggeration that, while women and other marginalized groups have participated in the rise of the digital age, the Internet revolution has largely been the domain of straight, white, able-bodied, middle-class males. One only needs to glance over a Who's Who of high-tech billionaires to see the predominance of this group. The epistemology of the digital age has been constructed in the image of its creators, so it is not surprising that digital technology and those first involved in it have a tendency to exclude minorities and others who do not fit the physical, mental, and emotional categories established by this group. Nonetheless, minorities have not been deterred from moving into, appropriating, and making this technology their own. This has not always been an easy task. As the essays by Dennis Baron (116–134) and Cynthia Selfe (93–115) emphasized, in the last section, access and literacy are very much tied to cultural markers, and minorities have found that they must either learn to accept the culture and conditions of digital access and literacy or risk being left out.

Consequently, when minority students come into our computer-netted composition classrooms, they may well bring along the baggage of the culturally dispossessed. It is important for teachers to understand what such students face and what teachers can do to make the digital environment welcoming and productive for them. The readings in this section begin to examine these issues: the cultural gap between diverse groups; the hopes teachers have for using technology as a solution for social problems; and the limits of technology for social, economic, and political empowerment.

We admit that choosing articles for this section was particularly difficult, and that many specific minorities and their issues may seem left out here; we hope it is clear that exclusion and marginalization are not our agenda. Given the restraints of space as well as the focus of this collection, we have chosen articles that we feel raise issues and begin to generate conversations that are relevant to many who live and work in and from the margins. The field of computers and composition has a great body of research in this area—

but there is a lot of research yet to be done. It is our hope that someone will someday assemble a collection wholly dedicated to computers and composition and teaching and learning from the margins.

First published in 1999, Lisa Gerrard's essay "Feminist Research in Computers and Composition" grapples with many of the issues of gender that teachers need to consider as they prepare to work in digital composition classrooms. And while we acknowledge that some of the statistics Gerrard presents from the early to mid-90s have changed—for example, more women are buying computers and using the Internet now, and more women are gaming—most of the issues and concerns Gerrard foregrounds are still with us. Setting out four areas of examination, Gerrard first looks at "the broader context in which computer-based writing takes place" (185) and finds that computer culture has largely been "an exclusive boys club" (186). Noting that prior access to computers affects our students' performance, Gerrard calls upon researchers to "find out what our male and female students know about computers when they enter our classes" (189) so that we can begin to help those who feel like outsiders more readily integrate into academic culture. Gerrard next examines ways to facilitate a feminist pedagogy. She encourages teachers to use computers and Internet exchanges in ways that allow women to connect their personal experiences with political awareness, thus equalizing power among students and democratizing the classroom. In her third section, Gerrard calls for compositionists to study and test feminist theories of learning, language, and discourse in order to begin to understand the patterns of gender in electronic communication. Finally, in her fourth section, she calls for feminist researchers to "extend the discussion of ways of seeing beyond gender to ethnic, cultural, and socioeconomic groups, with the goal of challenging the idea that a single way of thinking is superior to all others" (200).

In "Out of the Closet and into the Network: Sexual Orientation and the Computerized Classroom," Jonathan Alexander recognizes how the Internet has helped traditionally marginalized lesbian, bisexual, and gay students by providing information, giving them voice and community, allowing them to create bonds, and letting them find communal support and understanding. But Alexander acknowledges that raising the issue of homosexuality in the computerized composition classroom—in an era of American history in which homophobia is particularly vocal and organized—may result in polarization, contentious debate, and the possibility of misunderstanding and danger, especially for lesbian, bisexual, and gay students. Drawing upon his own classroom experience, Alexander argues that implementing carefully facilitated exercises in a computerized classroom—particularly, anonymous role playing—can successfully create a positive learning environment for addressing issues of sexual orientation that not only lesbian, bisexual, and gay students but also straight students may profit from. Alexander notes that by helping even straight students realize and think about the "social constructedness of all sexual orientations," they may come to understand that "straight lives, largely condoned and thus naturalized by society, are also part of a complex interweaving of social pressures and forces" (210). In such an environment, marginalized voices, and particularly lesbian, bisexual, and gay students, may finally be able to speak, but also speak freely and safely.

Observing that early research offered hope that computer-netted classrooms could promote equality, tolerance, and inclusion, Todd Taylor's "The Persistence of Difference in Networked Classrooms: *Non-negotiable Difference* and the African American Student Body" notes that more recent research has "tempered this enthusiasm by pointing out that the ideological forces that lead to oppression do not, in fact, suddenly disappear in on-line exchanges" (218). Working from insights by Mina Shaughnessy and J. Elspeth Stuckey that "academic discourse exacts a violence of assimilation on students from outside dominant culture whereby difference is not negotiated but obliterated to the detriment of those on the margins" (220). Taylor attacks the concept of *negotiating difference*, which he describes as a "Disney-esque success story in which the lowly and alienated inevitably fight for justice and prevail . . ." (219). Taylor contends that "difference is too rarely successfully negotiated" and offers the concept of *non-negotiable difference*, a term that "is meant to emphasize that profound, deep-seated difference is, by definition, non-negotiable" (220). Consequently, Taylor asserts that we can know only two points about our African American students: that they have experienced racism and that we need to "consider more fine-grained and customized approaches to identity and difference (222)." One solution Taylor proposes is that we turn to extra-linguistic cues, reading faces, postures, tone, and gestures—to get beyond the essentialized notions of what we may think "black" is, as well as the academic "game face" African American students may present to us in computer-netted classrooms.

Finally in this section, we present an abstract, a Web address, and the first page of an online article by Patricia A. Dunn and Kathleen Dunn De Mers, "Reversing Notions of Disability and Accommodation: Embracing Universal Design in Writing Pedagogy and Web Space," first posted in *Kairos* 7.1, 2002. In examining the issues of access to computer-web spaces for people with disabilities, Dunn and De Mers ask, how can we design classroom and Web pages to make them more accessible to more people? Their answer is universal design, which is defined as "The design of products and environments to be usable by all people, to the greatest extent possible, without the need for adaptation or specialized design." Applying this concept to the computer composition classroom, the authors propose that as with the interiors and exteriors of architecture, we must not think of retrofitting our classrooms or hardware and software, but instead imagine, design, and build them as accessable from the beginning. Also advocating a universal design writing pedagogy that incorporates "a variety of visual, aural, spatial, and kinesthetic approaches," Dunn and De Mer contend that designing a writing pedagogy based on these concepts would offer more flexible, multimodal choices not just for students with disabilities but all students. The authors provide many wonderful links that further define and elaborate universal design concepts, lead to discussion groups, and offer practical, concrete strategies and approaches to implementing universal design in the computer-netted and composition classroom.

11 *Feminist Research in Computers and Composition*

LISA GERRARD

Feminist research would do for computers and composition what Elizabeth Flynn (1991) says a feminist critique of composition studies should do for composition generally: 1) identify androcentrism, which she defines as "ignorance of women's different epistemological perspective and of women's subordinate position in society" (p. 143); and 2) introduce a female epistemological perspective. With these goals in mind, I have identified four areas within computers and writing that offer feminist researchers substantial opportunities for study. Ultimately, such studies might show us how our male and female students are learning in the computer-based writing course and teach us how to make our classrooms friendlier and more productive places for everyone. They might also clarify our professional practice outside the classroom.

The first section of this chapter begins by looking at the broader context in which computer-based writing takes place—the world of computers, which, despite a vigorous community of "net chicks" ("It's about being a grrrl with a capital R-I-O-T"; Sinclair, 1996, p. 6), is still very much a man's world. It suggests that researchers consider how students may be influenced by this association of computers with masculinity and raises questions for investigating this influence. The second section describes some of the ways computers might be fostering or undermining a feminist pedagogy—defined as a pedagogy that connects personal experience with political knowledge, reduces hierarchical relationships in the classroom, promotes collaboration, validates women's experiences, and offers a forum for women's voices. This section suggests ways researchers might study different computer-based practices and tools to determine which ones support feminist goals and which may not. The third section outlines some of the theories advanced by feminist linguists and psychologists about how men and women learn, think, write, and converse. It argues that the computerized writing classroom provides unique

From *Feminist Cyberscapes: Mapping Gendered Academic Spaces.* Eds. Kristine Blair and Pamela Takayoshi. (Stamford: Ablex, 1999), 377–400.

opportunities to test these theories, and poses questions for further study. The last section moves away from the classroom and toward the broader profession of computers and composition studies, describing how some of our scholarly interests and ways of interacting with colleagues appear to be gender-linked, and identifying issues for future research into gendered practice in the computers and writing community. In all four sections, I discuss past studies that feminist researchers might want to build on, challenge, or incorporate into their own work. As is inevitable in such a multidisciplinary field as computers and writing, these studies cover a range of interests, from boys' and girls' preferences in software design to academics' interactions on professional listservs. Feminist research in computers and writing thus offers substantial opportunities for discovery.

COMPUTER CULTURE: THE SOCIAL CONTEXT FOR OUR TEACHING

The Male Image of Computers

Computers have long been perceived as male machines, and computer culture as an exclusive boys club. This perception is not surprising, given the modern computer's origins—the largely male enterprise of warfare. The first modern computer, the British Colossus, was designed in 1943 to decode German radio transmissions; in the 1940s, the first computer in the United States, the ENIAC, calculated ballistic tables for bombing targets; and the Internet, launched by the Department of Defense in 1969, was meant to save information that would be lost if the military's computers were destroyed. In recent decades, the civilian image of the computer user has remained that of the adolescent male hacker, despite the existence of a small, but feisty, female hacker underground (Romero, 1993).[1] Since the early 1980s, studies of computers and gender have indicated that computer culture is still seen as a male preserve. An analysis of computer advertisements found images of confident male executives interpreting computer output and women as typists, computer phobics, and bimbos (Marshall & Bannon, 1988). Studies of the computer industry have portrayed a workplace hostile to female computer professionals, who, as in other technical fields, receive less pay, less responsibility, fewer opportunities to advance, and overt harassment (Frenkel, 1990; Hornig, 1984). In the computer industry, women have occupied the bottom of the hierarchy; according to a 1990 study by the U.S. Department of Labor, 91 percent of the data entry operators—the least-skilled workers in the industry—were women, whereas only 32 percent of the programmers and 30 percent of the systems analysts were women (Goff, 1990).[2] For the most part, men have designed the new technologies; women have simply "push[ed] buttons" ("Technology Jobs," 1993). In cyberspace, men outnumber women about 3 to 1 (Maier, 1995); Nancy Tamosaitis's 1995 survey, run by CompuServe, found that 92 percent of the Internet population consisted of men; a 1996 study by the Georgia

Institute of Technology found that males constituted 69 percent of the users of the World Wide Web (see "On Line," 1996). Sexist jokes, pornography, stories of "cybercads," sexual harassment, stalking, torture and rape fantasies, and even an online rape send the message that virtual reality is a male reality.

In practice, women have always been important in the computer industry—in the 1840s, Augusta Ada Lovelace invented the algorithm and became the first programmer; in the 20th century, the "ENIAC girls" programmed the first modern computer, Admiral Grace Hopper invented COBOL, and Roberta Williams wrote the first adventure games. Women have long been computer users, a fact computer marketers have finally begun to notice. In 1992, Apple began to advertise in *Parenting, House Beautiful,* and *Sunset* magazines; in 1993, Compaq advertised in *Mirabella, Self,* and *Working Woman.* Market researchers are discovering that women have considerable buying power: In 1995, women constituted 37 percent of the buyers of computer equipment for business and made 47 percent of the buying decisions for the home market—percentages that have been growing each year (Kondo, 1995).[3] Counting on the increasing number of women buying personal computers and modems, magazines such as *Self, Woman's Day, Elle,* and *New Woman* have made themselves available in online versions. Hundreds of websites, newsgroups, and listservs cater specifically to girls and women of all tastes, interests, and attitudes—to name a handful, Women's Studies, Parent Soup, Feminist Majority, Nancy Drew, GeekGirl, Heartless Bitches International. Nevertheless, the dominant *image* of computing is masculine: "Computers are power, and power, in our world, must be the realm of men" (Coyle, 1996, p. 43).

What matters for us here is that this perception pervades the social context in which we teach. As compositionists, we might study how this cultural schema affects our students' work. Does the image of the computer as a male technology make men initially more comfortable and women less so in a computer-dominated classroom? Or does the neutral—possibly feminized—ground of composition neuter this image? Many compositionists have described composition as a feminized field. Elizabeth Flynn (1988) notes the preponderance of female researchers in the development of the discipline, as well as the image of the composition teacher as a nurturing mother, "concerned about the growth and maturity of her students, who provides feedback on ungraded drafts, reads journals, and attempts to tease out meaning from the seeming incoherence of student language" (p. 424). Similarly, Cynthia Tuell (1993) compares her job as compositionist to the midwife's, "to provide a generative atmosphere in which to assist and encourage [students] as they give birth to themselves as authors" (pp. 134–135). Susan Miller (1991) sees the image of composition instructor not only as mother and nurse, but also as a sadomasochistic disciplinarian, with "enormous capacities for untheorized attention to detail" (p. 46). When a masculinist icon like the computer (*Time* magazine's 1982 "Man of the Year") is joined with a feminist and feminized pedagogy, does it lose its masculine associations? What preconceptions of computers do students have when they enter our courses, and do these conceptions change over the academic term?

Students' Past Computer Experience

Another issue that may affect our students' performance in computer-based writing classes is prior access. Students' first sustained encounter with computers is likely to be games — games designed for boys. A game like *Night Trap* — described on the package as "five beautiful coeds . . . being stalked on an eerie estate" — is not going to appeal to girls. The subject of most games is not so much violence against women, but violence in general — shoot-'em-ups of one kind or another. But it's not just the violence that repels girls, it's the design of these games. The very characteristics that attract boys repel girls, the focus on rules and winning, for example. According to game theorists, boys like rules and are energized by competition, whereas girls prefer to bend rules and generally avoid competitive games. In addition, boys find the quick, reflexive action exciting; girls like to take their time; boys like the rigid structure (if you lose, you "die"); girls find it constraining; boys are challenged by the redundancy of these games (if you fall off a cliff, you start over); girls get bored and quit (Jacobs, 1994). Not surprisingly, 75 percent of all video games are purchased for boys. One researcher argues that video games develop depth perception and spatial reasoning skills, which prepare boys to use other computer applications. Thus, video games are helping boys to become adept with computers, while girls are being left behind (Pereira, 1994).

Some game manufacturers, however, have tried to appeal to girls. Some games reinforce female stereotypes, such as *Barbie Super Model* (High Tech Entertainment), in which the user puts makeup on Barbie, follows her to the mall for a date with Ken, and walks her on a fashion show runway; or *Girls' Club* (Philips), where the user chooses her "dream date" from a set of boys' heads that pop up on a slot machine (Jacobs, 1994). Others are less stereotypical: the CD-ROM adventure *Hawaii High: Mystery of the Tiki* has two girls working together to solve a mystery (Colker, 1994); *My Computer Diary for Windows* (Stone and Associates) has players create a diary and a password to protect it; *Hello Kitty Big Fun Storymaking* (Big Top Productions) helps children tell stories (Perenson, Ehrenman, & Brown, 1994); the *Berenstain Bears* (Sega) allows the player to choose between male and female characters; and *Chop Suey* and *Smartypants* (Theresa Duncan) follow young girls on an adventure in a small town, where they explore a root cellar, watch 1930s cartoons, make jewelry, and act in the school play. But because boys won't play girls games, historically the market for these products has been small. According to Nancy Chodorow (1978), boys learn to define masculinity negatively, as that which is not feminine, and thus avoid activities noticeably earmarked for girls. Some of the earliest feminist games — *Jenny of the Prairie, Cave Girl Clair, Kristen and her Family,* and *Sara and her Friends* — were history games, intended to teach history and map-reading and note-taking skills. Developed in the mid-1980s, these products were intended as an alternative to the alien attack and war games, but they did not stay in print long. As I write, however, the market for girls' games is gaining new life. Sega of America has a Girls Task Force to develop products for girls; e-Girl Interactive is designing software with the kind of reward system they believe will appeal to girls, games in which girls play socially rather than competitively. In 1995, software developer Laura Groppe studied girls' computer use and found that girls use computers for briefer periods than boys do and prefer to do something useful as well as entertaining. She started the company Girl Games and developed the CD-ROM *Let's Talk About Me* for 8- to 14-year-olds, which departed from industry practice by having girls give their input throughout development of the product rather than testing it when completed. Let's Talk About Me allows players to keep a scrapbook, meet others from around the world, and hear successful women (for example, author Maya Angelou, Senator Dianne Feinstein, designer Kate Spade) talk about their teenage years (Becklund, 1996). In its first eight months on the market, Let's Talk About Me sold half a million copies (Corley, 1997). Believing that girls games can make a significant dent in the software market, the companies Purple Moon, Her Interactive, and Girl Tech, all founded in 1997, are developing computer adventures that focus on sharing information, resolving problems, building relationships, and competing in a friendly way—strategies they believe will appeal to girls.

Games matter because they are teaching a whole generation of children about computers. If girls don't play games, they may come into our classrooms with little prior computer experience. Several studies have shown that fewer young girls than boys use computers: parents are more likely to buy computers for their sons than their daughters, and send three times as many boys as girls to computer camp (Hess & Miura, 1985). In school, girls get less hands-on experience, less attention, and easier assignments than boys do (Levin & Gordon, 1989; Lewis, 1985). Furthermore, before fourth grade, girls and boys are equally excited about computers, but with every year after that, girls develop an increasing aversion to the technology. By high school, they are seldom found in the advanced math courses, where most computer instruction takes place (Abtan, 1993). Few women major in technological fields in college, and those who do find a cold reception (Dain, 1991; Frenkel, 1990).

Given this social context, researchers might find out what our male and female students know about computers when they enter our classes. They might survey high school and college students to find out if they have a computer at home, and, if so, if they use it; if they've had any formal computer training and if so, where and what kind; whether they play computer games; what attitudes they hold toward computers and what their experiences with the technology have been like. The research from the late 1980s and early 1990s suggested that our female students come to us with an experience deficit; is this still the case? Few female college students take the advanced math and engineering courses that require extensive computer work, so we might ask graduating students if their computer-based writing classes offered them hands-on experience they might not have had otherwise.

If the computer-based writing class is a student's first extended encounter with computers, developing control over the machine can give her confidence and a sense of belonging in a potentially alien place. When students enter a computer-equipped classroom, they confront a world that is doubly male: 1) the masculinist computer world, and 2) academia, a patriarchal institution dominated by a male professoriate and infused with competitive and hierarchical values. M. K. Cayton (1990) points out that men entering college are likely to think of themselves as apprentices "mastering a process that will allow them to contribute to a generalized body of knowledge," whereas women are more likely to perceive themselves as outsiders "with misgivings about entering the circle of the elect" (p. 333). If women are already predisposed to feel like outsiders in academia, does the computer-based writing class make them feel even more alienated? Or does it help integrate them into academic culture?

FACILITATING A FEMINIST PEDAGOGY

Connecting Personal Experience with Political Awareness

Another area to research is how we might use computers to support a feminist pedagogy and to what extent we are already doing so. Feminist pedagogy guides students to reflect on their lives and to connect personal experience with ideology and social issues. Early consciousness-raising groups emphasized the sharing of personal experience as a starting point for social analysis and action. In feminist methodology, "feeling is looked to as a guide to a deeper truth than that of abstract rationality" (Weiler, 1991, p. 463). Given that electronic discussions are by nature opportunities for sharing, might an electronic classroom encourage students to discuss personal issues? Several instructors have reported that e-mail (especially when students use pseudonyms) invites less inhibited conversation (Cooper & Selfe, 1990; Faigley, 1990; Spitzer, 1986). At the same time, one study found that anonymity does not necessarily lead to free expression. In a study of e-mail use in women's studies classes, students in an all-female class were more likely to discuss personal experiences online than students in a gender-mixed class, even though both classes posted their messages anonymously (Newton, 1995). Anonymity did not free these students from their reticence in front of member of the other sex. Thus, we might investigate how freely our students express their personal feelings on the net. Does e-mail personalize intellectual activity and thus facilitate feminist pedagogy? How can students use networks in ways that connect the ideas, language, and literature they are studying with their own and others' lived experience?

Another goal of feminist pedagogy is to make students aware that not all women are oppressed in the same way, that in addition to being female, women may be oppressed because they are lesbian, black, or poor, and that they may—by virtue of being white, heterosexual, or middle-class—be members of groups that oppress other women (Weiler, 1991). As a potential agent of consciousness-raising, can the Internet facilitate this goal? Several writing classes are conversing with their counterparts across the globe. It would seem that such cross-cultural conversations would enable students to examine their status as members of a race, ethnic group, or economic class. Does a pedagogy that uses the Internet this way help students not only understand their own experience, but also see their relationship to that of others?

Democratizing the Classroom

Compositionists might also study whether e-mail promotes another goal of feminist pedagogy: to diminish hierarchical relationships within the classroom. Feminist teachers seek to equalize power among students and, as much as possible, between the instructor and students (Weiler, 1991). While the Internet is sometimes described as a democratizing force "resist[ing] control of governments or any central authority" (Perry & Adam, 1992, p. 22), its ability to democratize the composition classroom has been contested: some instructors have argued that e-mail minimizes power inequalities based on characteristics such as race, age, or gender (Selfe, 1990), whereas others have argued that networks cannot prevent such imbalances of power (Castner, 1997). If instructors hid behind a pseudonym, do they divest their voices of greater authority? Are there ways we can use networks to democratize the classroom?

If the computer-based classroom increases collaboration among students, does it simultaneously increase interdependence among students and thus minimize the instructor's authority? Collaborative activity, a strategy of feminist pedagogy, has become routine in composition classes, and computers, in making it easy to share and send files, seem to make group work inevitable even in non-networked classrooms. Is group work more frequent in the computer-based writing classroom? Does the frequency or degree of collaboration depend on whether the classroom is a computer facility, as opposed to one with a computer or two, or a course where students meet in a traditional class, but make occasional trips to the lab?

So much collaborative activity takes place in computer-based writing classrooms that we might also investigate the nature of these collaborations. What kinds of collaborative interactions equalize power among students? Evelyn Ashton-Jones (1995) has argued that writing groups do not necessarily bring about equality in the classroom; often, they merely perpetuate conversational practices that silence women—conversations in which women's contributions are interrupted, devalued, or ignored. In a similar vein, a study of 10- and 11-year-olds doing computer-based assignments in pairs found that collaborative computer projects didn't automatically produce a feminist pedagogy. Single-sex pairs working at a computer solved problems by negotiation, but in mixed-sex pairs, the boys made the decisions and the girls typed (Underwood, McCaffrey, & Underwood, 1990).

Students come to class aware of their status relative to their classmates— status conferred not only by gender, but also by such markers as membership in campus groups, athletic skill, academic achievement, ethnicity, race, wealth, physical attractiveness, and "coolness." While no classroom activity is likely to erase this consciousness of hierarchy, computers make it especially easy to bring together students who might otherwise dismiss one another. In the same way, as long as the instructor grades students' performance and has expertise students lack, a truly democratic relationship between instructor and student is impossible; but networked discussions can give students a much more active and authoritative position than they typically hold. Instructors have debated how much the computer diminishes inequalities of power (Romano, 1993), and it is clear that considerable research remains to be done here. Researchers might observe (directly or through videotape) students working together, noting such behavior as who initiates projects, who organizes the group's work, who encourages other group members, whose opinions are taken seriously, and who speaks loudest or most often. They might require students to write narratives, describing their experiences in these groups. They could experiment with different group structures and assignments and compare students' relationships from one project to another. They might study the number and nature of contributions students make in networked discussions, compare online discussions conducted with and without pseudonyms, or compare online talk that occurs with and without the instructor's participation.

Using the Internet

One of the earliest goals of feminist pedagogy was to validate women's experiences and voices: to create a learning environment where women students would be taken seriously (Rich, 1979). Given the widespread belief that the Internet is "blind to race, age, gender, or handicap" (Perry & Adam, 1992, p. 22), does e-mail provide a forum for marginalized perspectives, as some computers and writing practitioners have claimed, and do women using e-mail feel any freer to voice their distinct concerns? Dale Spender (1980) argues that men are generally more comfortable with public discourse and the chance to exercise leadership through persuasion, while women are more comfortable with personal conversation. Given the fact that the Net is a public space, do our students use e-mail as personal conversation or as display or oratory, and does their practice vary by gender? Are women developing a public voice in response to this new form of expression? Or does the Net simply replicate the power relations that dominate other areas of their lives?

Some classes have students participating in listservs and newsgroups on the Internet, a valuable learning activity in many ways. But the Internet is not always a welcome place for women. "Online lotharios" (Shade, 1993) harass women, pornography is widely distributed over the Net, as are sexist jokes (for example, the responses to one newsgroup's query, "Why is the Internet like a vagina?"). Uninvited sexual invitations on the net have become so commonplace that in 1994, *Glamour* magazine published guidelines for fending them off (Broadhurst, 1994).[4] In 1993, a virtual rape was reported on a MOO, a form of virtual reality. The rapist impersonated another participant and had her commit degrading sexual acts (Dibbell, 1993).[5] On one campus, a student was arrested for stalking a woman after she and the police repeatedly told him to stop; on another campus, a student was arrested for posting a fantasy about torturing, raping, and murdering a female classmate (DeLoughry, 1995).

Though hostility toward women is widespread on the Net, it should not be overstated, given that there are thousands of listservs, newsgroups, MUDs (multiuser dungeons),[6] and other sites of electronic interaction, with millions of conversations taking place everyday. But where harassment is not a problem, women may still feel uncomfortable with the aggressive discourse they find online. As Lori Kendall (1996) points out, on the Net, "women encounter a social environment and behavioral norms formed largely by men" (p. 211). Researchers have argued that women are not used to the competitive and boastful language that are common in conversations between men, whereas among male users, adversarial behavior is regarded as friendly. Netiquette guides approve of "flaming," describing it as part of the game of online conversation, "part of the fun" (Sutton, 1996, p. 181).

Thus, we might study whether males in fact generate more aggression by boasting and flaming on the Net, and whether such behavior is more frequent in certain sites that others. For example, some users have found that the participants in pay services like CompuServe and America Online are more hostile to women than those on the Internet and Usenet; and that sites frequented by the hacker underground are a feminist nightmare, as are—more predictably—such sites as alt.fan.howard-stern and any of the alt.sex series (Clerc, 1996; Gilboa, 1996; Sutton, 1996). We might also consider the extent to which such behavior deters women from participating in online discussions. Finally, researchers might compare female students' experiences on mixed-sex listservs with those on the many women-only lists and services, such as WELL, ECHO, Women's Wire, Systers, and Macwomen.[7] These lists were specifically set up as alternatives to the other services, all of which—including those devoted to women's issues—are dominated by men.[8] Some, such as U.S. News Women's Forum on CompuServe, include visits from such well-known participants as Patricia Ireland, president of the National Organization of Women, and journalists Susan Faludi and Barbara Walters. Others engage in political action: In 1993, when Mattel introduced its Talking Barbie, whose mindless utterances included "Math is hard," Systers organized a protest that pressured Mattel into revising Barbie's script (Camp, 1996).

Feminist Software

Composition researchers might also consider what kinds of software might support a feminist pedagogy. Are some interfaces more appealing to students of one sex than the other?[9] One study found that educators developing a program to teach the use of the comma designed differently for male than female students. When the user's gender was not specified, the designers assumed a male user. They designed software for male students more as a game than a learning tool; it used less sound and required more aggressiveness, hand-eye coordination, and quick reflexes than the program they designed for girls. The girls' program required more typing skill, more sound, and was more like a tool than a game (Huff & Cooper, 1987). This design accords with the observations of others in the software industry: girls and women prefer software that is practical. According to Robin Abrams, general manager of Apple Asia,

> men are seduced by the technology itself and fall into the faster-race-car syndrome, bragging about the size of their "disks" and the speed of their microprocessors. [But] if the computer industry wants to put more and more machines in the hands of the masses, that means appealing to women with practical, accessible technology tools. (qtd. in Wilkinson, 1995, p. 22)

The word "tool" recurs in analyses of girls' and women's uses of software, even when the program is a game. Whereas men like to tinker and explore, women want to accomplish something: "[Women] are looking to save time, which makes them less tolerant of . . . messing with endless variations of modern strings or system configurations" (Wylie, 1995, p. 3).

We might also look closely at the metaphors implicit in software design, and see if they appeal principally to men or women. Karen Coyle (1996) observes that the macho image of network software is embedded in the information highway metaphor:

> The highway metaphor lends itself well to masculine images. [A] *New York Times* article that talked of computers in hot rod lingo showed a cool dude with a souped-up computer leaving tire tracks over his slower rivals. . . . An advertisement for software that allows a direct Internet hookup from a personal computer shows a man on a motorcycle and the caption "Pop a wheelie on the Information Highway." On closer inspection you see a pair of high heels flying off the back of the bike: His wheelie has just dumped a woman on the road. Not a friendly image for women but the guy is portrayed as having the time of his life. (p. 52)

Richard and Cynthia Selfe (1994) have suggested that we imagine a Macintosh interface with a different metaphor from that of the office—such as that of a kitchen. A change in metaphor would disrupt the masculine mythology associated with computers. What might feminist software look like? What metaphors would it use?

TESTING FEMINIST THEORIES ABOUT GENDERED LEARNING AND LANGUAGE

Learning Styles

The computer-based writing classroom offers opportunities to reconsider current theories about how men and women learn, write, and converse. Compositionists might use their observations of students writing with computers to reexamine research into gendered learning styles. Does the way students use computers in the writing classroom confirm or challenge claims that researchers have made about these patterns? Gilligan, Ward, Taylor, and Bardige

(1988) argue that men are solitary and competitive learners, whereas women learn better through collaboration. Studies of children working with computers partly support their view: Girls are more attracted to technology when they work in groups rather than alone (Kantrowitz, 1994). Even before composition pedagogy began to embrace theories of socially constructed knowledge, instructors noticed that the computer itself, even a standalone machine, socialized the classroom (Payne, 1987). Now that local- and wide-area networks make sharing of drafts and long-distance discussion commonplace in the classroom, we might study what effect these collaborative practices are having on our male and female students. Classes that require students to post on e-mail or exchange work online demand considerable interdependence among class members and a sense of duty toward other students—traits that Gilligan (1982) sees as singularly suited to women. Do female students have an advantage in such classes? Does such a pedagogy conflict with the learning styles of solitary, silent students—who, according to Gilligan, are more likely to be male than female? Does it change the learning style of such students? We might use the computer-based classroom to test whether these two distinct ways of learning follow gender lines.

Gilligan (1982) also suggests that female students prefer to explore connections among disparate bits of information, whereas men are more likely to appreciate the efficient acquisition of facts. E-mail discussions in the writing classroom can be chaotic. Unlike a face-to-face discussion, the comments usually appear on the screen out of order, and the discovery of "truth," if such a discovery takes place, is likely to be messy and inefficient. Do some students find such e-mail conversations irritating, a waste of time? Are such reactions gender-linked?

The computer-based classroom can also provide an opportunity to test the claim that men tend toward linear, and women toward associational thinking. Gilligan (1982) has found that women are more likely than men to think in nonlinear ways. Sherry Turkle and Seymour Papert (1990) found a similar pattern in female computer programming students, who rejected the hierarchical algorithms of traditional programming in favor of "bricolage," a process of constructing computer programs by moving around the elements of the program as if they were tangible objects. One way to study male and female preferences for linear or associational thinking might be to look at students' uses of hypertext. Unlike the linear, argumentative essay, which rhetorical theorists have argued is a "masculine" form—hierarchical, contentious, and competitive (Sanborn, 1992)—hypertext is a nonlinear and nonhierarchical way of accessing information. Instructors who assign students to write hypertexts rather than essays or to construct home pages on the World Wide Web might consider whether women are more comfortable with these modes of exploring and presenting ideas than men are[10] and whether men are more at ease writing a thesis-directed, single-line argument.

Hypertext can be used not just as a writing tool, a way of presenting knowledge, but also as a tool for exploring others' ideas. Madeleine Grumet

(1988) defines a male epistemology as one that values either/or constructions of truth, predictability, distinct boundaries, and certainties, and devalues ambiguity, flexibility, and interconnectedness, values she ascribes to women. Such a way of thinking, gendered or not, would seem to be incompatible with hypertext. Given the way hypertext supports nonlinear exploration of ideas and nonhierarchical thinking, do men and women respond differently to hypertext documents? In addition, Kathleen McCormick (1994) argues against a writing pedagogy that pressures students to reconcile conflicting ideas in order to present a unified stance, and suggests instead that students learn to explore contradictions in an issue they are researching. Does hypertext encourage students to interrogate contradictory positions rather than rush toward reconciliation? If so, do male and female students react differently to this challenge?

If our students' responses don't follow the male/female epistemologies Gilligan and other researchers have identified, can the experience of men and women in the computer classroom help us reconsider these formulations of how men and women think? In other words, how does our students' experience contradict or support the research done in noncomputer environments?

Gendered Writing Styles

The computer classroom may also provide opportunities to test theories of gendered writing styles. Pamela Annas (1985) identifies female language as "sensual, contextual, and committed" and male language as "abstract, logical, and impersonal" (p. 360). Do these differences hold true when students write in nontraditional contexts—constructing web pages and other hypertexts or chatting on networks? These tools provide opportunities for students to play with language and to use styles and content (such as personal writing) not usually validated in academia, but that Annas sees as essential to students' gaining power there. Does the writing produced under these circumstances follow the gendered distinctions Annas defines? Furthermore, those who find, as M. K. Cayton does (1990), that women students do not see themselves as sufficiently authoritative to engage in academic discourse or even to use its "privileged language" might explore whether computerized writing tools give female students a chance to be heard.

Are women more comfortable with private writing and men, with public writing, as Cinthia Gannett (1992) has argued? If so, does the computer-based writing class, which publicizes an individual's writing in many ways, affect men and women differently? Individual work is not completely private, because in a computer lab, the monitor exposes an individual's writing to anyone walking by. And computers facilitate the public sharing of writing, so that students routinely see their words exposed to others: their instructors require them to send files to one another, co-author papers by merging files, project their work onto a large screen in front of the class, and conduct e-mail discussions with other class members or with classes across the world.

Gendered Discourse

Composition instructors using electronic mail might study online discourse for what it reveals about male and female rhetorical styles. How well does our students' conversational behavior accord with research on gendered discourse? Linguist Deborah Tannen (1990) finds that women's talk is more cooperative and intimate than men's, whereas men are more likely to report information and debate opinions. Tannen has also observed that in conversation, women try to minimize or avoid conflict, while men are more likely to be confrontational. Roxanne Missingham's 1994 survey of librarians on two library lists, FEMINIST and PACS-L, found a similar pattern in online conversation: Women used the Internet to seek information, participate in general discussion, and support others, while men posted reports about resources, gave opinions, and presented criticism. Susan Herring's 1992 study of the listserv LINGUIST came to similar conclusions and also found that the different rhetorical styles caused conflict: While women were more tolerant of newcomers who didn't know what they were doing, they also tended to ask basic questions, which annoyed men.

Sociologists Candace West and Don H. Zimmerman (1975) found that in face-to-face communication, men interrupt women three times as often as they do other men. Do women have a better chance of being heard in *online* conversations? So far, studies of academics on two listservs suggest that they don't. One study found that even open networks focusing on women's issues were dominated by men, and that topics of special concern to women were not taken seriously (Kramarae & Taylor, 1993). In their 1991 study of the computers and writing list Megabyte University, Cynthia Selfe and Paul Meyer found that men wrote twice as many messages and 40 percent more words than women. When Susan Herring analyzed Megabyte University and LINGUIST in 1993, she reported similar results: Women contributed only 30 percent of the messages and their posts were shorter than men's. Herring also found that women's messages were more likely to be ignored than men's.[11] A small male minority dominated the discussion, both in length and frequency of posts and psychologically, through self–promotion and combativeness. Men either ignored women's posts or attempted to delegitimize them. As researchers studying face-to-face conversation have found, Herring (1993) also noted that when women's participation approached 50 percent, they were perceived as dominating the discussion: During three such occasions,

> a handful of men wrote in to decry the discussion, and several threatened to cancel their subscription to the list. . . . At no other time during the period of observation did women participate as much as men, and at no other time did any subscriber, male or female, threaten publicly to unsubscribe from the list. (n.p.)

Herring concludes that academic lists are power-based and hierarchical, continuing the pattern of male dominance in academia and in society as a whole.[12]

Do these patterns hold true when we study *student* discourse on the Net? We need additional studies of rhetorical behavior on the Net, asking such questions as who initiates topics of discussion, and changes topics? Whose messages are ignored, who responds to requests for help? Who expresses personal feelings, who asks questions, who displays knowledge? Who agrees, argues, boasts, gives support, apologizes? Who lurks and why? Which topics interest women, which interest men, which interest both? What uses do men and women make of the Net?

If there is a gendered pattern to online talk, we might also ask if synchronous conversations show the same patterns as asynchronous ones. And if there are gender-based differences, do they correlate with other personal characteristics, such as students' ages, ethnic or economic backgrounds, or success in school? And finally, we might compare the discourse on mixed-gender lists with male-only and female-only lists.

THE PROFESSION OF COMPUTERS AND COMPOSITION STUDIES

Both men and women have been active in computers and composition from the outset, and women have been especially influential in shaping and organizing the discipline. In the early years of the field (1977–1984), roughly equal numbers of male and female compositionists developed software: Among the female software developers were Mimi Schwartz (Prewrite), Kate Kiefer (adaptation of Writer's Workbench), Helen Schwartz (SEEN), Ruth Von Blum and Lisa Gerrard (WANDAH), Christine Neuwirth (DRAFT), Lillian Bridwell-Bowles (ACCESS), Dawn Rodrigues (Creative Problem-Solving), Deborah Holdstein (Writewell), Cynthia Selfe and Billie Wahlstrom (Wordsworth II), and Nancy Kaplan (PROSE).[13] Women have been the principal organizers of all but 2 of the 13 computers and writing conferences (1982–1997). They have edited the earliest journals in the field: Kathleen Kiefer and Cynthia Selfe edited *Computers and Composition* from 1983 to 1988, and Cynthia Selfe and Gail Hawisher have edited it from 1989 to the present; the editors of *Computer-Assisted Composition Journal* were Lynn Veach Sadler and Wendy Tibbetts Greene from 1986 to 1987, and Lynn Veach Sadler from 1988 to the final issue in 1996. Nearly all the editors of anthologies on computers and writing have been female, as are approximately half of the authors of the articles within these texts.[14] Roughly equal numbers of men and women have instituted composition listservs, though men pioneered the two original ones, Participate, organized by Michael Spitzer in the mid-1980s, and shortly afterwards, Megabyte University, founded by Fred Kemp.

Those who research the work of men and women in the discipline might investigate not only the degree, but also the *nature* of men's and women's influence, both in the past and present. How do men and women conceptualize computers and composition studies? What do they write about? In a review of 17 panels at the 1989 Conference on College Composition and Communication, Emily Jessup noted that men talking about computers and writing tended to emphasize technology. They discussed hypertext, computers and text analysis, the technology of networking, and a national project on computers and writing. By contrast, the women speakers emphasized the social implications of computers in writing instruction: computers and basic writers and the "social rhetoric of empowerment in computer-supported writing communities" (qtd. in Jessup, 1991, p. 340). Is this difference in intellectual interest a recurrent pattern? Does it appear elsewhere in the profession—in publications on computer-based composition, in conversations on MOOs and listservs, or at the annual computers and writing conference? Are there other gendered patterns of inquiry?

We might also consider the relative status of men and women in computers and writing. Are men's and women's contributions equally valued? Is there such a thing as men's and women's work in computers and writing? Traditionally, academia has valued theory over classroom practice; does the subdiscipline of computers and composition replicate this value? How egalitarian are we as a community? Susan Herring's (1993) study of Megabyte University found that we are not a democratic group: Men and women recognized as experts in the list's topic posted more often, posted longer comments, and were responded to more often than nonexperts were—expertise transcended gender. But where expertise was not an issue, men still dominated women in all these ways. In short, e-mail replicated the pre-existing power relationships in academia. We need to do additional studies on male and female interactions on professional listservs. What kind of Net behavior is rewarded by others on the listserv, what is censured, and does any of it follow gender lines? In addition to analyzing transcripts of online conversations, researchers might query colleagues who have quit a listserv or ask listserv members their reactions to specific discussions. They might ask journal editors which approaches to computers and writing are regarded as publishable and which aren't and ask committees that give awards what kind of work most deserves recognition; and consider who determines the value system underlying both cases. In analyzing whether the work of the profession follows a gendered pattern, researchers could also explore the making of a computers and writing conference; who does the intellectual work (reads proposals, determines the program) and who administers (plans the budget, delegates clerical work)? We might query colleagues whose work in computers has contributed to their tenure or promotion, find out what kinds of work matters, and determine if such work is gender-linked.

FEMINIST METHODOLOGY

Counting posts on a bulletin board, interruptions in a conversation, and female software developers can reveal a great deal about male and female behavior in computers and composition. But to get fully at how men and women are using technology and responding to its culture, researchers need to go beyond statistics and look at context. If women participate less often in electronic discussions, is it because they find the topics uninteresting, they've been alienated by the prevailing netiquette, they're less technologically adept than men, or do they simply have less time? Contextualized research, such as interviews, surveys, and case studies—methods that have become staples of feminist research—help answer questions like this and provide a rich analysis of how men and women use—or why they don't use—technology. Observing students in class, considering the material and social conditions in which they work, and listening to their narratives are important ways of collecting information. In addition, these methods give researchers a chance to consider how their own expectations shade what they ask and what they see. Influenced by Sandra Harding (1986) and Evelyn Fox Keller (1984), who have shown the masculine bias in traditional scientific methodology, feminist researchers strive to consider how their own personal perspectives—their ethnicity, sex, or economic class—affect the validity of their research.[15]

Feminist scholars have focused on gender differences because traditionally, male experience has been regarded as human experience. In the social sciences as elsewhere, male behavior has been the standard against which women have been judged. Thus, it has been important for feminist scholars to address male biases in research methods, in the questions researchers consider worth posing, and in the conclusions they draw. Nancy Chodorow's work (1978) on the development of gender identification, Carol Gilligan's work (1982) on the moral development of girls and boys, and Belenky, Clinchy, Goldberger, and Tarule's (1986) research on intellectual development all emphasize gender differences in order to challenge the assumption that male behavior is the norm.

At the same time, human behavior—whether it be our colleagues' e-mail habits or our students' learning styles—is too complex and contradictory to fall consistently into categories of male or female. Not all men flame on the Net, not all women nurture, and while men may lean toward hierarchical thinking, most of us probably think in webs sometimes, and in hierarchies other times, regardless of our gender. What feminist theory gives us is an ability to recognize a multiplicity of learning styles and ways of interacting and to reconsider their usefulness. Rather than polarizing male and female experience, feminist research has the potential to extend the discussion of ways of seeing beyond gender to ethnic, cultural, and socioeconomic groups, with the goal of challenging the idea that a single way of thinking is superior to all others. Thus, we will need to go beyond gender to investigate this question: If there are differences in the way men and women learn, work with computers, talk to one another on e-mail, and interact as computers and writing professionals, how do these differences intersect with other differences—those of class, race, age, computer background, writing ability (our students), and status in the profession (us)?

POSTSCRIPT: COMPUTERS, GENDER, AND SOCIAL CLASS

The computer world is still male turf, from the video arcades crammed with adolescent boys to the over 40,000 bulletin boards on the Internet, populated mainly by men. But technology is not only a gender issue; it is a class issue as well: two factors that consistently correlate with computer use are education and income. A 1995 study of 1,000 men and women found that of those who considered themselves noncomputer users or technophobes, 42 percent had a high school education or less, whereas 9 percent had graduated college; this study concluded that it was "education, not gender, that correlated with fear or hostility toward computers" ("It's the Education, Stupid," 1995, p. 8). A 1996 study of 1,200 Southern California households connected computer ownership with both a college education and a high income; it found personal computers in only 22 percent of households with annual incomes under $25,000, compared to 69 percent of those with incomes over $50,000 (Harmon, 1996).[16]

Women with minimal education and low-paying jobs are thus at a particular disadvantage; both their gender and their social class are likely to keep them from being computer users. Women who work outside the home frequently use computers, but do so in the least interesting ways: word processing and data entry.[17] Women who work chiefly as homemakers are unlikely to have even that much exposure. If there is a computer in their home, they don't use it; a third of American families own a computer, but most of these are purchased and used by males (Kantrowitz, 1994).[18] Neither these women nor their daughters are likely to see themselves as computer users.

A 1994 survey, however, found that the more familiar women became with computers, the more likely they were to use them, and that women were especially attracted to electronic mail and online services (men preferred games or educational software) (Dholakia, Dholakia, & Pedersen, 1994). Given the vast resources and attractions of the net, will e-mail be the tool that makes computers as routine a part of women's lives as the telephone? The history of the telephone offers an analogy. Just as the computer was originally developed for the military (rather than for education or entertainment), so the telephone's original purpose was serious: it was strictly a business tool. The people who developed and marketed telephone systems came primarily from the telegraph industry and expected the telephone to be used as the telegraph was. Men used the telephone in the office, and though they often had a phone connection from home, they saw phoning one's friends for "trivial gossip" as an abuse of the technology. By the 1920s, however, their wives began using this phone connection from home to office to talk to their family and friends; confined to the home with small children, they discovered that the telephone gave them access to the outside world. In so doing, they simultaneously made the telephone a gender-inclusive tool and redefined its function (Wajcman, 1995).

Most of the female users of the Net work in the professions; others are in management, technical fields, or are students. Few are homemakers. A study of over 4,000 female subscribers by Women's Wire found that 2 percent were homemakers; similarly, homemakers made up only 1 percent of the 60,000 users surveyed by Yahoo!/Jupiter (DeBow, 1996). But will the movement of computing from the office to the home increase the participation of homemakers (and their daughters) in this technology? Like telephone users in the

1920s, a large proportion of home network users receive their network connection through their business or university, and 85 percent of them, according to the Yahoo!/Jupiter survey, have connections from home. It remains to be seen, then, as access to the Net becomes a household staple, whether it also becomes the entrée into the computer world for girls and women.

Whether logging in from home or office, women constitute the fastest-growing group of network users (Pine, 1996). Since I began researching this article, women have not only increased their participation online, but also set up hundreds of websites, listservs, and user groups of special interest to them as women. With this increased visibility of women and women's concerns on the Net, the context in which we practice computers and writing will change, and so, too, will the questions we ask.

NOTES

1. According to Irony, "an all-around Swiss Army hacker," capable of breaking into bank accounts and police radio frequencies, women not only know their hardware, but they also have a "knack for social engineering": "If there's someone who doesn't trust anyone, and doesn't give out information, I could get it in a week, without fail. Guys could try for years and never get it" (Romero, 1995, p. E1).

2. Another study, which broke down patterns of employment according to ethnicity as well as gender, found that white males received the highest salaries and the highest level positions, followed by black men, white women, Hispanic men, black women, and Hispanic women (Banks & Ackerman, 1990).

3. In 1996, one analyst identified women as "the fastest growing segment of the online market," a judgment based on such statistics as this: Between 1994 and 1996, female subscribers to CompuServe more than doubled, increasing from 12 percent to 25 percent (Pine, 1996).

4. The guidelines included these caveats: don't flirt unless you want someone to flirt back, be aware of any unintended nuances in what you post, don't post your home phone number or address, and, if someone harasses you, notify the online staff. A few months earlier, the February 1994 *Glamour* had reported the experience of a male University of Kansas student who used a female pseudonym on the Internet. He was surprised to find that male users assumed he wanted sexual come-ons ("Can I kiss you? Can I hug you? Will you kiss me back?"), that he needed the most elementary computer advice, and that he would want to hear them confess their personal problems (see Dominus, 1994).

5. In an MOO, participants adopt a persona that interacts with other personae in the same virtual community. The perpetrator used a "voodoo doll," a subprogram that allows users to attribute actions to other participants' personae. The victim suffered considerable emotional upset in real life, and the entire community was outraged and eventually had the rapist "toaded," removed from the MOO.

6. An MUD is also translated as multi-user "dimension" or "domain." "Multi-user dungeon" is its original name, reflecting the origins of MUDs in such role-playing games as Dungeons and Dragons.

7. Women's Wire is an Internet service based in San Francisco; ECHO (East Coast Hang-Out) is a service directed toward women, based in New York; Systers is a mailing list for women in the technical professions; and Mac-women is a Help forum for female Macintosh users. ECHO offers three bulletin boards for female subscribers only, and one for men only. Its managers make phone checks of potential subscribers to ensure that men don't subscribe to the women's forum (Rigdon, 1994). The founders of Women's Wire believe their service to be far more supportive (they describe it as a "small town") than male-dominated services, such as America Online and CompuServe (which are 10–15 percent female, as opposed to Women's Wire, 90 percent of whose 700 participants are female). They make a special effort to reach women who are intimidated by their lack of computer experience, and their participants avoid the flame wars and one-upmanship characteristic of other services (see Ness, 1994).

8. For example, in the Usenet newsgroup soc.women, specifically started as a place to discuss women's issues, men's posts outnumber women's (Camp, 1996). A 1993 study of the newsgroup alt.feminism found that men contributed at least 74 percent of the postings (Wylie, 1995).

9. In 1984, in a critique of computer literacy programs, Margaret Lowe Benston, professor of computer science and women's studies at Simon Fraser University, argued that feminists needed to develop their own computerized educational tools. Only then could men and women gain some control over the technology and understand the social context in which technology is produced and consumed—her definition of computer literacy.

10. Gilligan (1982) as well as Turkle and Papert (1990) described their female subjects' way of thinking as a "web."

11. The direction of responses was as follows: men to men 33.4 percent, women to men 21.3 percent, men to women 15.8 percent, women to women 11.2 percent.

12. In her essay in Chapter 5 of this volume, Shannon Wilson also notes the difficulty of erasing hierarchy in online discussion when hierarchy is already inscribed in the participants' relationship.

13. Among the men developing writing software during this period were Hugh Burns and George Culp (Topoi), Michael Cohen (Homer and WANDAH), James Strickland (FREE), William Wresch (Writer's Helper), Michael Southwell (COMP-LAB), Stephen Marcus (Compupoem), Raymond Rodrigues (Creative Problem-Solving), Donald Ross (ACCESS), Charles Smith (adaptation of Writer's Workbench), and Stuart Davis and Joseph Martin (PROSE).

14. For example, female authors are represented in the following percentages:

The Computer in Composition Instruction (Wresch, 1984)	47%
Writing On-Line (Collins & Sommers, 1985)	56%
Writing at Century's End (Gerrard, 1987)	46%
Critical Perspectives on Computers and Composition (Hawisher & Selfe, 1989)	67%
Computers and Writing (Holdstein & Selfe, 1990)	70%
Computers and Community (Handa, 1990)	54%
Evolving Perspectives on Computers and Composition Studies (Hawisher & Selfe, 1991)	71%
Re-Imagining Computers and Composition (Hawisher & LeBlanc, 1992)	47%
Literacy and Technology (Selfe & Hilligoss, 1994)	58%

15. In analyzing research on gender and communication, Daniel J. Canary and Kimberley S. Hause (1993) fault researchers for such bias. Though they believe there are sex differences in communication, Canary and Hause argue that the researchers' tendency to stereotype and polarize men and women clouded their studies.

16. According to the Southern California survey, of those who used computers at home, 22 percent had a high school education or less, while 57 percent had graduated college. The study also found computer use divided by ethnicity; twice as many non-Latino whites as Latinos reported owning a personal computer (Harmon, 1996).

17. Carol Hildebrand, in a 1992 study, found that among 301 computer users in administrative and clerical positions, two-thirds were women. Among women computer professionals, Latina and African-American women occupy a higher percentage of low-paying positions (Banks & Ackerman, 1990).

18. According to one survey, most home computers are purchased for children's education or for keeping track of personal finances, but are actually used for entertainment ("At Play on Home PCs," 1994).

REFERENCES

Abtan, P. (1993). The gender gap. *Computing Canada, 19*(5), 9.

Annas, P. J. (1985). Style as politics: A feminist approach to the teaching of writing. *College English, 47*(4), 360–371.

Ashton-Jones, E. (1995). Collaboration, conversation, and the politics of gender. In L. W. Phelps & J. Emig (Eds.), *Feminine principles and women's experience in American composition and rhetoric.* (pp. 5–26). Pittsburgh, PA: University of Pittsburgh Press.

At play on home PCs. (1994, November, 15). *Wall Street Journal,* p. B1.

Banks, M. E., & Ackerman, R. J. (1990). Ethnic and gender computer employment status. *Social Science Computer Review, 8*(1), 75–82.

Becklund, L. (1996, May 27). Let's talk about a market niche worth billions. *Los Angeles Times,* pp. D1, D4.

Belenky, M. F., Clinchy, B. M., Goldberger, N. R., & Tarule, J. R. (1986). *Women's ways of knowing: The development of self, voice, and mind.* New York: Basic Books.

Benston, M. L. (1984). The myth of computer literacy. *Canadian Women's Studies, 5*(4), 20–22.

Broadhurst, J. (1994, October). On-line sexual advances: How to fend them off. *Glamour,* 101.

Camp, L. J. (1996). We are geeks, and we are not guys: The Systers mailing list. In L. Cherny & E. R. Weise (Eds.), *Wired women: Gender and new realities in cyberspace* (pp. 114–125). Seattle, WA: Seal Press.

Canary, D. J., & Hause, K. S. (1993). Is there any reason to research sex differences in communication? *Communication Quarterly, 41*(2), 129–144.

Castner, J. A. (1997). The clash of social categories: What egalitarianism in networked writing classrooms? *Computers and Composition, 14,* 257–268.

Cayton, M. K. (1990). What happens when things go wrong: Women and writing blocks. *Journal of Advanced Composition, 10,* 322–337.

Chodorow, N. (1978). *The reproduction of mothering: Psychoanalysis and the sociology of gender.* Berkeley, CA: University of California Press.

Clerc, S. (1996). Estrogen brigades and "bit tits" threads: Media fandom online and off. In L. Cherny & E. R. Weise (Eds.), *Wired women: Gender and new realities in cyberspace* (pp. 73–87). Seattle, WA: Seal Press.

Colker, D. (1994, June 14). Everything a girl wants in a game—and less. *Los Angeles Times,* pp. E3, E4.

Collins, J. L., & Sommers, E. A. (Eds.). (1985). *Writing on-line: Using computers in the teaching of writing.* Upper Montclair, NJ: Boynton/Cook.

Cooper, M. M., & Selfe, C. L. (1990). Computer conferences and learning: Authority, resistance, and internally persuasive discourse. *College English, 52*(8), 847–869.

Corley, T. (1997, June 9). Her turn. *Los Angeles Times,* pp. D1, D6.

Coyle, K. (1996). How hard can it be? In L. Cherny & E. R> Weise (Eds.), *Wired women: Gender and new realities in cyberspace* (pp. 42–55). Seattle, WA: Seal Press.

Dain, J. (1991). Women and computing: Some responses to falling numbers in higher education. *Women's Studies International Forum, 14*(3), 217–225.

DeBow, Y. (1996). Women's Wire profiles wired women. *Interactive Content, 2*(21), 11.

DeLoughry, T. (1995, February 24). Online. *Chronicle of Higher Education, XLI,* A27.

Dholakia, R., Dholakia, N., & Pedersen, B. (1994, December). Putting a byte in the gender gap. *American Demographics, 16*(2), 20–21.

Dibbell, J. (1993, December 21). A rape in cyberspace. *The Village Voice, 38*(51), 36–42.

Dominus, S. (1994, February). One man's life as a woman. *Glamour, 72.*

Faigley, L. (1990). Subverting the electronic network: Teaching writing using networked computers. In D. A. Daiker & M. Morenberg (Eds.), *The writing teacher as researcher: Essays in the theory and practice of class-based research* (pp. 290–311). Portsmouth, NH: Boynton/Cook.

Flynn, E. A. (1988). Composing as a woman. *College Composition and Communication, 39*(4), 423–435.

Flynn, E. A. (1991). Composition studies from a feminist perspective. In R. Bullock & J. Trimbur (Eds.), *The politics of writing instruction: Postsecondary* (pp. 137–154). Portsmouth, NH: Heinemann.

Frenkel, K. (1990). Women and computing. *Communications of the ACM, 33*(11), 35–46.

Gannett, C. (1992). *Gender and the journal: Diaries and academic discourse.* Albany, NY: State University of New York Press.

Gerrard, L. (Ed.). (1987). *Writing at century's end: Essays on computer-assisted composition.* New York: Random House.

Gilboa, N. (1996). Elites, lamers, narcs and whores: Exploring the computer underground. In L. Cherny & E. R. Weise (Eds.), *Wired women: Gender and new realities in cyberspace* (pp. 98–113). Seattle, WA: Seal Press.

Gilligan, C. (1982). *In a different voice: Psychological theory and women's development.* Cambridge, MA: Harvard University Press.

Gilligan, C., Ward, J., Taylor, J., & Bardige, B. (1988). *Mapping the moral domain: The contributions of women's thinking to psychological theory and education.* Cambridge, MA: Harvard University Press.

Goff, L. (1990). Is there a computer gender gap? *MIS Week, 11*(14), 29.

Grumet, M. R. (1988). *Bitter milk: Women and teaching.* Amherst, MA: University of Massachusetts Press.

Handa, C. (Ed.). (1990). *Computers and community: Teaching composition in the twenty-first century.* Portsmouth, NH: Boynton/Cook.

Harding, S. (1986). *The science question in feminism.* Ithaca, NY: Cornell University Press.

Harmon, A. (1996, October 7). Computing in the '90's: The great divide. *Los Angeles Times,* pp. D1, D4.

Hawisher, G., & LeBlanc, P. (Eds.). (1992). *Re-imagining computers and composition: Teaching and research in the virtual age.* Portsmouth, NH: Boynton/Cook.

Hawisher, G., & Selfe, C. L. (Eds.). (1989). *Critical perspectives on computers and composition.* New York: Teacher's College Press.

Hawisher, G., & Selfe, C. L. (Eds.). (1991). *Evolving perspectives on computers and composition instruction studies: Questions for the 1990s.* Urbana, IL: National Council of Teachers of English.

Herring, S. (1992). *Gender and participation in computer-mediated linguistics discourse.* Washington, DC: ERIC Clearinghouse on Languages and Linguistics. (ERIC Document Reproduction Service No. ED345552)

Herring, S. (1993). Gender and democracy in computer-mediated communication. *Electronic Journal of Communication* [Online], *3*(2). Available: http://www.cios.org/www/ejc/v3n293.htm

Hess, R. D., & Miura, I. T. (1985). Gender differences in enrollment in computer camps and classes. *Sex Roles, 13,* 193–203.

Hildebrand, C. (1992). Desktop division: Study finds gender roles differ. *Computerworld, 26,* 37.

Holdstein, D. H., & Selfe, C. L. (Eds.). (1990). *Computers and writing: Theory, research, practice.* New York: Modern Language Association.

Hornig, L. S. (1984). Women in science and engineering: Why so few? *Technology Review, 31*–41.

Huff, C., & Cooper, J. (1987). Sex bias in educational software: The effect of designers' stereotypes on the software they design. *Journal of Applied Social Psychology, 17*(6), 519–532.

It's the education, stupid; forget the gender gap: Schooling drives the market. (1995, April). *Marketing Computers, 15*(4), 8.

Jacobs, K. (1994, May/June). RoboBabes: Why girls don't play videogames. *I. D.: The International Design Magazine, 41*(3), 38–45.

Jessup, E. (1991). Feminism and computers in composition instruction. In G. E. Hawisher & C. L. Selfe (Eds.), *Evolving perspectives on computers and composition studies: Questions for the 1990s* (pp. 336–355). Urbana, IL: National Council of Teachers of English.

Kantrowitz, B. (1994, May 16). Men, women, and computers. *Newsweek,* 48–55.

Keller, E. F. (1984). *Reflections on gender and science.* New Haven, CT: Yale University Press.

Kendall, L. (1996). MUDder? I hardly know'er! Adventures of a feminist MUDder. In L. Cherny & E. R. Weise (Eds.), *Wired women: Gender and new realities in cyberspace* (pp. 207–223). Seattle, WA: Seal Press.

Kondo, A. (1995). The gender trap. *Marketing Computers, 15*(4), 37–42.

Kramarae, C., & Taylor, H. J. (1993). Women and men on electronic networks: A conversation or a monologue? In H. J. Taylor, C. Kramarae, & M. Ebben (Eds.), *Women information technology and scholarship* (pp. 52–61). Urbana, IL: Center for Advanced Study, University of Illinois.

Levin, T., & Gordon, C. (1989). Effect of gender and computer experience on attitudes toward computers. *Journal of Educational Computing Research, 5,* 69–88.

Lewis, L. H. (1985). New technologies, old patterns: Changing the paradigm. *Educational Horizons,* 129–132.

Maier, F. (1995, February 19). Cyberspace: Where the women aren't. *San Francisco Examiner,* pp. B5–B6.

Marshall, J. C. & Bannon, S. (1988). Race and sex equity in computer advertising. *Journal of Research on Computing in Education, 2,* 115–127.

McCormick, K. (1994). "On a topic of your own choosing. . . ." In J. Clifford & J. Schilb (Eds.), *Writing theory and critical theory* (pp. 33–52). New York: Modern Language Association.

Miller, S. (1991). The feminization of composition. In R. Bullock & J. Trimbur (Eds.), *The politics of writing instruction: Postsecondary* (pp. 39–53). Portsmouth, NH: Heinemann.

Missingham, R. (1994). *Cyberspace: No women need apply; librarians and the Internet.* Unpublished manuscript.

Ness, C. (1994, November 27). Computer network puts women online. *San Francisco Examiner,* p. A4.

Newton, J. (1995). What is feminist pedagogy anyway?: Distinctions in content and process. In B. Bradbury (Ed.), *Teaching women's history: Challenges and solutions* (pp. 135–145). Athabasca, Alberta, Canada: Athabasca Press.

On line, (1996, June 21). *Chronicle of Higher Education, SLII,* A17.

Payne, D. (1987). Computer-extended audiences for student writers: Some theoretical and practical implications. In L. Gerrard (Ed.), *Writing at century's end: Essays on computer-assisted instruction* (pp. 21–26). New York: Random House.

Pereira, J. (March 16, 1994). A toy for men: Video games help boys get a head start. *Wall Street Journal,* p. B1.

Perenson, J. J., Ehrenman, G. C., & Brown, E. (1994, November 8). What do women want? Software for women and girls. *PC Magazine, 13*(19), 437.

Perry, T. S. & Adam, J. A. (1992). E-mail: Pervasive and persuasive. *IEEE Spectrum, 29*(10), 22–23.

Pine, D. (1996). A chat room of one's own: Women in cyberspace. *Home PC, 3*(5), 143–146.

Rich, A. (1979). *On lies, secrets, and silences: Selected prose, 1966–1978.* New York: W. W. Norton.

Rigdon, J. E. (1994, March 18). Now women in cyberspace can be themselves. *Wall Street Journal,* p. B1.

Romano, S. (1993). The egalitarianism narrative: Whose story? Which yardstick? *Computers and Composition, 10*(3), 5–28.

Romero, D. (1995, December 1). A new force lurks amid the cyber shadows. *Los Angeles Times,* pp. E1, E6.

Sanborn, J. (1992). The academic essay: A feminist view in student voices. In N. M. McCracken & B. Appleby (Eds.), *Gender issues in the teaching of English* (pp. 142–160). Portsmouth, NH: Boynton/Cook-Heinemann.

Selfe, C. L. (1990). Technology in the English classroom: Computers through the lens of feminist theory. In C. Handa (Ed.), *Computers and community: Teaching composition in the twenty-first century* (pp. 118–139). Portsmouth, NH: Boynton.

Selfe, C. L., & Hilligoss, S. (Eds.). (1994). *Literacy and technology: The complications of teaching and learning with technology.* New York: Modern Language Association.

Selfe, C. L., & Meyer, P. (1991). Testing claims for on-line conferences. *Written Communication, 8*(2), 162–192.

Selfe, C. L., & Selfe, R. L., Jr. (1994). The politics of the interface: Power and its exercise in electronic contact zones. *College Composition and Communication, 45*(4), 480–504.

Shade, L. (1993, August 17). *Gender issues in computer networking.* Paper presented at Community Networking: The International Free-net Conference, Ottawa, ON, Canada.

Sinclair, C. (1996). *Net chick: A smart-girl guide to the wired world.* New York: Henry Holt.

Spender, D. (1980). *Man made language.* London: Routledge and Kegan Paul.

Spitzer, M. (1986). Writing style in computer conferences. *IEEE Transactions on Professional Communications, 29,* 19–22.

Sutton, L. A. (1996). Cocktails and thumbtacks in the old west: What would Emily Post say? In L. Cherny & E. R. Weise (Eds.), *Wired women: Gender and new realities in cyberspace* (pp. 169–187). Seattle, WA: Seal Press.

Tamosaitis, N. (1995). Why don't women log on? Cyberspace shouldn't be just where the boys are. *Computer Life, 2*(2), 139–140.

Tannen, D. (1990). *You just don't understand.* New York: Ballantine Books.

Technology jobs fail to end gender gap: Study finds occupational segregation. (1993, February 7). *San Jose Mercury News,* p. 2PC.

Tuell, C. (1993). Composition teaching as "women's work": Daughters, handmaids, whores, and mothers. In S. I. Fontaine & S. Hunter (Eds.), *Writing ourselves into the story: Unheard voices from composition studies,* (pp. 123–139). Carbondale, IL: Southern Illinois University Press.

Turkle, S., & Papert, S. (1990). Epistemological pluralism: Styles and voices within the computer culture. *Signs, 16,* 128–157.

Underwood, G., McCaffrey, M., & Underwood, J. (1990). Gender differences in a cooperative computer-based language task. *Educational Research, 32*(1), 44–49.

Wajcman, J. (1995). Feminist theories of technology. In S. Jasanoff, G. E. Markle, J. C. Petersen, & T. Pinch (Eds.), *Handbook of science and technology studies* (pp. 189–204). London: Sage.

Weiler, K. (1991). Freire and a feminist pedagogy of difference. *Harvard Educational Review, 61*(4), 449–474.

West, C., & Zimmerman, D. H. (1975). Sex roles, interruption and silences in conversation. In B. Thorne & N. Henley (Eds.), *Language and sex: Difference and dominance* (pp. 102–117). Rowley, MA: Newberry House.

Wilkinson, S. (1995, November 6). What's a fast car to some is just a tool for others. *PC Week, 12,* 22.

Wresch, W. (Ed.). (1984). *The computer in composition instruction: A writer's tool.* Urbana, IL: National Council of Teachers of English.

Wylie, M. (1995). No place for women: Internet is flawed model for the infobahn. *Digital Media, 4*(8), 3.

12

Out of the Closet and into the Network: Sexual Orientation and the Computerized Classroom

JONATHAN ALEXANDER

When I began teaching composition at the University of Southern Colorado in 1994, the state was embroiled in controversy over Amendment Two. The amendment to the Colorado state constitution, which was overturned by the United States Supreme Court in May 1996, would have deprived gays, lesbians, and bisexuals of the right to claim discrimination based on sexual orientation in housing and employment disputes. The topic, continuously reported by all the state's media forces, was on the minds of many of my students, and I had only to say the words "Amendment Two" to plunge the class into a maelstrom of heated debate. In many ways, this was a composition teacher's dream; especially in my rhetoric and argumentation classes, we never failed to come up with some aspect of the debate worth analyzing for rhetorical consistency, logical clarity, consideration of audience, emotional appeal, and "objective" reporting of opposing viewpoints. Although the furor over the amendment has passed, issues surrounding sexual orientation remain "hot" topics in composition classrooms, and they are likely to remain so for some time as they are debated at the national level; one need only say "gay marriage" or "gays in the military" to polarize a classroom and inaugurate debate.

In addition to its contemporary socio-political relevance and its ability to excite class discussion, sexual orientation is a subject that engages many students' interest at more personal levels. After all, we live in a culture in which, as Michel Foucault (1975) pointed out, sexuality is configured as identity—so much so that the probing of one's sexual orientation is supposed to unlock the hidden "truth" about oneself. Joseph Litvak (1995), an openly gay professor and queer theorist, described the social significance of what has traditionally been thought of as *private*. "It was becoming clear to me," he said, that

> acquiring cultural literacy—as one is supposed to do in school—meant, to no small degree, acquiring sexual literacy, not learning how to exclude the private from the public but learning how to read the private as it is everywhere obliged to manifest itself in public. (p. 20)

From *Computers and Composition* 14 (1997): 207–16.

But, as most teachers who have introduced or entertained the issue of homosexuality in their classrooms know, the polarization and often contentious debate that results from discussion of sexual orientation is not unproblematic. Dealing with material so close to the core of the way we think about ourselves can produce tension-filled exchanges laden with the possibility of misunderstanding and danger, especially for gay, lesbian, and bisexual students (and teachers who may justifiably fear being outed, or at least completely misconstrued, during open discussions of homosexuality). Furthermore, straight students will often wonder at the relevancy of issues of sexual orientation for their own lives, preferring instead to think of homosexuality as something completely *other,* something strange and alien and, thus, they fail to realize the social implications of their heterosexuality as well as the social nature of all sexual orientation. The search for sophisticated pedagogical methods of grappling with this subject continues in work such as Harriet Malinowitz's (1995) *Textual Orientations: Lesbian and Gay Students and the Making of Discourse Communities.* Such work should particularly hold the attention of compositionists, as our classes offer some of our students the most concentrated analysis of how the social medium of language shapes our conception of our selves and determines our social interactions. Thus, considering the cultural weight given to sexuality, composition classes are excellent forums for discussion of the ways in which talking and writing about sexual orientation is tantamount to talking and writing about our selves. This is not an easy discussion, however; it requires finesse and care.

Such discussions can, nonetheless, be successfully facilitated in computerized classrooms, and my contention for the remainder of this essay is that networked classrooms offer an unparalleled opportunity for students and teachers to address issues of sexual orientation in powerful and unprecedented ways. The Internet, the World Wide Web, and software that permits synchronous conferencing—staple features of many networked classrooms—provide tools through which students can learn more about these issues and probe the relevance of sexual orientation to *all* students' lives, whether they are lesbian, bisexual, gay, or straight.

One of the most obvious advantages of dealing with sexual orientation in the computerized classroom is the tremendous amount of information available to any student interested in pursuing research on homosexuality. The amount of information currently circulating through various computer networks is stunning, and quick Net searchers will deluge the interested "surfer" with a variety of sources and viewpoints. But particularly for the young homosexual student, the advantages of Internet access are undeniable; traditionally marginalized gay, lesbian, and bisexual individuals can find information, voice, and community, allowing them to create bonds with others to reinforce their gay subject position and contribute to each others' sense of identity through communal support and understanding.

Furthermore, networked discussion that allows for the use of pseudonyms or anonymous contributions can play a particularly important role in helping homosexual students safely explore the possibility of speaking as gays and lesbians. This opportunity is crucially important because the dangers of speaking from a gay subject position are very real. Judith Butler has pointed out how each of us "performs" various subject positions, as well as the ways in which those subject positions involve performances that are potentially risky. Use of the term *performativity* should not mislead anyone into thinking that our subject positions are always chosen; as Butler (1993) maintained, "These are for the most part compulsory performances, ones which none of us choose, but which each of us is forced to negotiate" (p. 237). This is especially true for gay students who, although they may have the opportunity to "cloak" their homosexuality, are nonetheless caught in the midst of various forces that, on one hand, ask them to be honest about themselves, and on the other, disapprove of what they have to reveal. Negotiating this position is fraught with danger because individuals may make statements that open them to the possibility of physical attack or identity crisis, as their subject positions are questioned for social and cultural legitimacy. Additionally, students—or teachers for that matter—who identify as gay or lesbian may become targets of a wide array of attacks, from physical and verbal violence to damaging insinuations about credibility and ethicality.

As an openly gay teacher, I know from experience the potential dangers and pedagogical pitfalls of addressing issues of sexual orientation in my classes. Just this past week, one of my rhetoric students accused me of "promoting homosexuality" because I had the class read articles about homosexuality but did not also direct the class to read anti-gay propaganda. The whole notion of "promoting homosexuality," in the student's phrase, is laden with the homophobic fear of gays "recruiting" straights, a fear exacerbated in this case because my students know that I am gay. For teachers who are closeted, dealing with such issues may be discomfiting because such teachers open themselves to the possibility of being outed or accused of biased interest in having the discussion in the first place.

Perhaps more dramatic are the dangers confronting our gay and lesbian students, for whom peer pressure and approval are forces still powerfully shaping their lives. Many are coming to an awareness of their tenuous social positions, and they rightfully fear the vulnerability of coming out. For these students, my presence as openly gay is both helpful and potentially harmful. On one hand, they appreciate my presence and often come to me for advice and consultation; on the other hand, I am threatening to them because the wrong word or any sign of special in-group treatment might out them to their peers, who, like them, are often just coming to an awareness of the public space they occupy and who often use difference, especially sexual difference, to gain a clearer, more definitive, and sometimes harsher and more exclusionary sense of their own identities.

None of this is to suggest that issues of sexual orientation should be avoided in class discussion, particularly in rhetoric and composition classes. It is to suggest, however, that such discussion is potentially fraught with peril. It is at exactly this perilous point that computerized classrooms offer the possibility of discussions of homosexuality that will (a) allow gays and lesbians the opportunity to speak and (b) allow them the opportunity to speak safely. Most theorists and educators are quick to acknowledge that computerized learning spaces both increase levels of student participation and allow traditionally marginalized voices and personal histories to find the voice in forums, such as the classroom, that have not always been welcoming or tolerant of polyvocal questioning of traditional norms. By 1994, Ann Hill Duin and Craig Hansen (1994), on the basis of their observation and analysis of actual classroom practices, could echo an oft-heard sentiment: "The [networked] system improved accessibility—that is, it appeared to liberate minorities, to restore voices to all students regardless of their sex, race, class, or age. Students who might be dominated by others in a traditional class discussion expressed their views openly via the [networked] system" (p. 100). This is true not just for students from traditionally marginalized sexual, racial, class, or age groups, but for the homosexual student as well—particularly if the student is allowed to contribute anonymously or under a pseudonym.

Indeed, pseudonymous participation ensures that the widest variety of voices will be able to speak in a public forum. Furthermore, the use of pseudonyms allows curious students to perform subject positions different from the ones they deploy and are subject to outside the classroom. As with gender-hiding exercises, for instance, it is important that a student be allowed to experience a different subject position initiated by choosing a pseudonym, and participate without censure or the threat of retribution. Especially in discussions of sexual orientation, which many students on small campuses find threatening, it is important to allow students to feel that they can contribute without the fear that people will make assumptions about them based on their comments or interests. Face-to-face discussions do not always allow for the kinds of "safety" measures, such as pseudonymous contributions, that are required to generate discussion on the sensitive topics of sexual orientation and homosexuality. This is one reason why networked discussions are vital: They offer the opportunity of increased participation from students, especially those who might not take part in oral discussions.

Although the advantages to gay and lesbian students are clear, it is important to keep in mind that they are not the only ones who can benefit from grappling with sexual orientation issues in computerized classrooms. Networked discussions of sexual orientation allow all students the opportunity to question and understand the social constructedness of all sexual orientations. In other words, students can begin to understand that sexual orientation is not just something that "happens" to gays and lesbians, but is the complex intersection of a variety of social and personal forces that come together and shape how all of us—gay and straight—think of ourselves and our sexual identities. In a cultural climate that encourages the policy of "don't ask, don't tell," it is easy for students to see how gay lives are heavily inflected with and impacted by societal norms and pressures; it is less obvious to them that straight lives, largely condoned and thus naturalized by society, are also part of a complex interweaving of social pressures and forces. It is just where we think our personal lives are most natural and untouched by outside forces that we are most blind to the ways in which our society has conditioned us to think about ourselves and understand our identities. This is particularly true of sexual orientation, which most students, indeed most people, understand as innate and inherent—and, thus, fail to see the ways in which society actively contributes to and constructs meaning for various sexual feelings and practices, condoning and regulating some while completely proscribing others. As social historian Jeffrey Weeks (1985) eloquently put it,

> Struggles around sexuality are . . . struggles over meanings—over what is appropriate and not appropriate—meanings which call on the resources of the body and the flux of desire, but are not dictated by them. This approach fundamentally challenges any idea of a simple dichotomy between "sex" and "society." Sex and sexuality are social phenomena shaped in a particular history. (p. 178)

The question now is, of course, how do computers help students realize and think about the "social phenomena shap[ing this] . . . particularly history?" At one level, the sheer amount of material about homosexuality on the Internet queries hetero-normativity and the cultural dominance of the heterosexual. But even in classrooms that are locally networked without Internet access, the questioning of the master narrative of hetero-normativity can powerfully continue, demonstrating Cynthia Selfe and Susan Hilligoss's (1994) assertion that "computers change the ways in which we read, construct, and interpret tests. In doing so, technology forces us to rethink what it means to be human" (p. 1).

Indeed, the questioning of what it "means to be human" is at the heart of contemporary debates about the pedagogical possibilities of computerized learning spaces. As early as 1992, Lester Faigley optimistically announced in *Fragments of Rationality: Postmodernity and the Subject of Composition* that

> in [the] aftermath of the overthrow of what Lyotard refers to as "magisterial" discourses—discourses that claim the status of a body of truth—a proliferation of suppressed discourses arises, as we have seen an enormous literary and artistic productivity recently from men and women of a multitude of racial and ethnic groups and from different *sexual orientations*. (p. 217, emphasis added)

As we have begun to question notions of "received" truth, expressed through metanarratives that organize and name our experiences and, thus, condition what is culturally expected and societally permissible, we have simultaneously recovered and allowed for the creation of voices, such as gay and lesbian voices, which have been hitherto marginalized and ignored. The dominant culture's monologic voice has steadily been challenged by a heteroglossia of voices that argue with our society's controlling structures and that combine, break down, and recombine to form stories and narratives that challenge cultural and societal wisdom. Faigley saw the college-level composition courses as ideal settings for students to explore and analyze the "discourses that have shaped them and confront . . . the discourses they have struggled against" (p. 218). These comments and ideas appeared in a chapter following one of the first theoretical discussions of computerized educational spaces and networked classrooms, in which Faigley maintained that local computer networks allow students and teachers to question the hierarchial power structures, such as hetero-normativity, that adhere in most classrooms. Perhaps more significantly for Faigley's postmodern argument, networked environments, which allow all students to contribute to and collaborate on one polyvocal text, create heteroglossic text-experiences in which "most students come to acknowledge that the terms in which we understand experience are not fixed but vary according to our personal histories and are always open to new possibilities for creating meaning" (p. 184).

Although the creation of such texts is exciting, it is not that radically different from other attempts to get students to accept or at least tolerate difference. But, particularly in terms of difference in sexual orientation, teachers are tempted to treat the subject gingerly, attempting to instill, at most, tolerance for homosexuality and an awareness of the unacceptability of homophobia. Janet Wright (1993), in a moving essay, "Lesbian Instructor Comes Out: The Personal is Pedagogy," wrote of the impact of openly gay and lesbian teachers on reducing "societal hatred, fear, and misunderstanding" (p. 31). Such aims are admirable, whether in a computerized composition class or not, but teachers trying to achieve them lack some of the more sophisticated means of analysis available only in computerized learning spaces. Specifically, anonymous networked discussions enable various role-playing exercises that not only prompt the questioning of a monologic cultural voice in order to allow for the inclusion of marginalized voices but also open up the possibility for all students to understand how social norms and pressures condition the ways everyone speaks—whether gay or straight.

To explain, networked classrooms, especially those with synchronous conferencing software, have allowed teachers to develop role-playing exercises that are pedagogically important in two specific ways. First, role-playing is the quickest way for one individual to experience another's social positioning, especially a position that the student may never have had the opportunity of experiencing before; and second, it ensures that such experiences are conducted in fairly safe and controllable contexts. In *Texts and Contexts,* Judith Summerfield and Geoffrey Summerfield (1986) noted that

> Impersonation [i.e. role-playing] ... we prefer to construe as "in-personation": as a retrieval of, an entry into, the psyche and the voice of an other, or as the other's entering into one's own voice—the process invariably strikes us as inseparably two-way, reciprocal. (p. 197)

Such "in-personation" is useful in allowing students to experience situations, dynamics, and difficulties that their usual daily experience may never show them. In terms of allowing students to gain insight into the experiences of marginalized or oppressed peoples, role-playing serves a valuable function, even as it allows the traditionally marginalized the opportunity to speak with new power and voice. Utilizing the pseudonym capabilities of Daedalus INTERCHANGE, for instance, students and teachers can write from different subject positions and take on identities that are not their own and experiment with different subject positions' discourses.

Much has already been written (Wahlstrom, 1994) about the pedagogical bonuses of gender-hiding exercises, in which students have the opportunity to "play" at being another gender and experience various and shifting positions of empowerment, subordination, gender expectation, and the prevalence of gender stereotyping (pp. 171–185). Students express surprise in metawriting about these interchanges, and upon examining the transcripts of these discussions, at how readily they stereotype and categorize each other along gender lines. It is my contention, based on my classroom experience, that such stereotyping and categorization vis-à-vis sexual orientation can become just as obvious and that students can become aware of how all our sexual identities are heavily inflected by social and cultural forces.

At this point the individual teacher's creativity must guide him or her, and experimentation is encouraged. The exercises I have tried and will describe here briefly illustrate, however, that a little role-playing can go a long way in getting students to think more critically about how all identity, and particularly identity related to sexual orientation, is socially construed, constructed, and controlled. These exercises work particularly well in rhetoric classes when definitional arguments are examined, and students have the opportunity to reflect on the polyvocal and dialogic nature of any defining label or category. In one exercise, for instance, I have students log into a Daedalus INTERCHANGE, choose a pseudonym, and begin a discussion about waking up in a world in which homosexuality is the norm and heterosexuality is demonized or considered "not the norm"[1] (see note for the full text of a prompt). You think of several choices available to you. Will you try to turn gay? Will you stay straight and pretend to be gay? Will you allow others to know that you are straight and risk the consequences? What might they be? How do you decide to deal with the situation? Why? Examination of the exchange transcripts suggests to me that this forty-minute role-playing exercise gives students the opportunity to problematize deep-seated beliefs about the stability of identity and the primacy, especially as it is held to be separate from public and social concerns and forces. In examining the transcripts, one can observe that three stages of thought crystalize as the students move toward an understanding of the social forces shaping sexual orientation identity. First, there is a strong defense of essentialist notions of identity; second, there is a growing recognition of how gay and lesbian lives are socially monitored and proscribed; and, finally, there is a tentative consideration of how all identities may be socially constructed.

A closer analysis of sample transcripts will reveal the force of these currents of thought, especially as they change direction and re-route themselves. To start, most students begin by writing about how they would never change and about how they would remain "true" to their individual notions of an essential identity. Typical comments include the following:[2]

> I believe the moral standards I hold now are universally true. They are not influenced by society nor what most people think. I would choose to stick to what I believe in. I would not be violent about my stand nor would I even defend myself if attacked.

> Just feel comfortable with yourself and as long as you are not hurting anyone then don't worry.

> I would definitely try to deal with the situation as smoothly as possible. I would not turn gay just to make it easier. I guess I would just live my life as I usually did and just have to live with the consequences, even if they were really hard.

> I would not become a homosexual if my life depended on it.

These comments, and there are many similar to them, reveal an essentialist notion of sexual orientation and identity; you are what you are and that's that.

The comment about "moral standards" being "universally true" is typical of the initial response, but students soon begin to realize that there is an inherent contradiction in their many claims that they would not "turn gay," even if their "li[ves] depended on it." Specifically, they begin to talk about feeling "outcast," "isolated," "alone," and "weird." They write of being labeled a "pervert" and of having to deal with "a lot of adversity" — so much so that many of them begin to realize how it is possible for gays to want to "turn" straight:

> Reading this has made me realize what homosexuals wake up to every morning.

> I think that if this gay society was extremely strong and very defensive towards their preferences in their partners and their way of life it would probably be hard to make a stand on your opinions and your preferences. Especially when the whole society is against you, you would probably feel powerless and weak when it came to what you feel is right.

> HAY EVERYONE, all of these responses seem to be how the gay's feel about straight people. That kind of pisses me off because no one seems to understand a homosexuals point of view. You don't even realize that you are thinking like them right now.

One of the most important realizations these students made is how heavily inflected gay lives are by social pressures and forces. The last comment is particularly revealing because it suggests, even in assuming that everyone in the class is straight, that feelings of isolation and abjection are socially conditioned and not inherently part of a gay identity; this student astutely points out how a "homosexual point of view" is transferable to straights when the social context is changed, ultimately suggesting a bit more fluidity between the categories of "straight" and "gay" than most students are accustomed to considering.

Although many gays and lesbians would contend that it is not possible for someone who has been straight to comprehend what living life as a gay person is like, it is undeniable that students, up to this point in the exercise, are on the verge of appreciating the ways in which social pressures toward normalization affect individual lives. This recognition allows some students to double back and reconsider how all lives are complex junctures of the individual and the social, the personal, and the political. Comments such as the following become increasingly frequent toward the end of the hour:

> What does the word "normal" mean?

> How do you know you were born heterosexual? A lot of gay people feel they were born something hetero, but they realized they were homo or bi. Remember you were never born feeling a certin way you were always taught what to believe in by your family.

> I have been brought up to do what I am suppose to do. I have been told to get good grades and a good education and I financially benefit in the future. I have been taught that I should look, dress, and behave like my gender. My parents have not taught me these things I have learned them from the people around me.

> I am not saying that everyone follows the norms of society. I am saying that those who don't have a very big disadvantage. If following the norms of society was not important to the majority than why is it so hard for people to accept gay people? People can't except it because it was taught to be abnormal behavior, with some exceptions.

The increasing emphasis in these comments on learned attitudes and behaviors suggests a growing awareness of how "normalcy" is a construct and not a given. Even in their generalizations, these students have begun to consider that the ways in which a culture thinks of itself and interprets behaviors and feelings are important in understanding how we *know* some things to be acceptable and others not. Behaviors and identities do not exist in vacuums, but rather in cultures that actively interpret them and ascribe meaning to them and, thus, determine what is considered legitimate and natural on one hand and diseased and abnormal on the other. It may be through such realizations that students come closest to understanding that homosexuality is not *inherently* morally and ethically suspect but that fear of homosexuality is culturally conditioned and, thus, culturally reversible. Such work, made possible through anonymous role-playing, may do much more to encourage tolerance of difference than anything we have yet attempted in our classrooms.

It is important to note that the development of this kind of thinking became obvious only once we discussed and analyzed the transcripts, a procedure that should be *de rigueur* as it allows everyone to become aware of assumptions made during a conversation. Even I, at the beginning of the hour, did not know what direction the discussions would take and was as surprised as my students to see the progression of ideas that I could not have controlled in the writing of the discussions even if I had wanted to. It is this lack of control that some teachers will have a hard time allowing, and they are correct in intuiting that there are risks involved in this type of open and anonymous discussion. Some students will engage in flaming, and, unfortunately, some of my students have taken advantage of their anonymity to give voice to homophobic positions. But it is only when the teacher is willing to take such a risk that there is an opportunity for students' deep-seated ideas to come forth and for students to make profound realizations on their own. Most students, in fact, simply ignored such homophobic comments and moved on with the discussion.

Of course, there are some who would question the legitimacy of using such an exercise and claim that it is an artificial manipulation of students into thinking about social construction. I cannot deny that role-playing is "artificial," but it is equally arguable that all "performative sites" are artificial, are products of historical, material, and social interactions that only seem natural because we have been occupying them for years on end. Others, especially those outside the academic community, may wonder about the legitimacy of espousing tolerance for homosexuality in our classrooms; by what right, some ask, do we claim to speak about personal matters best left to individual choice?

More theoretically complex but nonetheless real is the threat of identity confusion that Diana Fuss (1991) addressed in her introduction to *Inside/Out:* "The fear of the homo, which continually rubs up against the hetero, . . . concentrates and codifies the very real possibility and ever-present threat of a collapse of boundaries, an effacing of limits, and a radical confusion of identities" (p. 5–6). Asking students to think about the social construction and relational relativity of sexual orientation may produce a cognitive uncertainty in those who thought they knew themselves. But if such exercises are used in content-emphasis courses, such as rhetoric classes with a gender studies component, then they will be part of a well-thought-out examination of the intersection between society and identity. Ultimately, I am reminded of the student who accused me of "promoting homosexuality." I can only respond by saying that I encourage all students—both gay and straight—to think of ways each identity is shaped by the stories and narratives that surround and permeate us through the social clusters of family, friends, colleagues, city, state, country, and culture. As compositionists—and as analysts and teachers of language and story—we can have no greater calling.

Acknowledgment: I am grateful to my colleague, Margaret Barber, for the fruitful conversations we have had about teaching gender issues in networked classrooms.

NOTES

1. The prompt for the conferences held on March 13, 1996, and October 2, 1996, is as follows:

> This morning when you awoke from a night's sleep, you became aware that society was no longer as you remembered it. In fact, it had universally made a 180 degree turn in sexual orientation, and the world you remember as being a comfortable environment for heterosexuals like yourself no longer accepts people like you. You don't want to return to isolation, so you must deal with this situation, and do it right now.

But now you don't fit in. Homo-erotic love is the required standard. Heterosexuals are moral outcasts. They are widely thought to molest children, and the marriage to your fiancé(e) that you have looked forward to for several years will not be legally recognized. Procreation takes place in test tubes and hired wombs according to accepted procedures, and couples like you and your fiance(e) are considered hazardous to population growth.

You turn on the TV news, only to see a demonstration on the court house steps by anti-heterosexual activists shouting "heterosex is sin" and "ban the straights." A sense of doom envelops you as the truth sinks in. You have a cup of coffee and sit down to think about how you will deal with the situation. What do you think? How will your life change? What will happen to your relationship with your family and friends, now all gay? What will you tell your mother or father, sisters, brothers? What will happen when you get back to work? Will you attend the office dinner party? Will you take your fiance(e) with you?

You think of several choices available to you. Will you try to turn gay? Will you stay straight and pretend to be gay? Will you allow others to know that you are straight and risk the consequences? What might they be? How do you decide to deal with the situation? Why?

2. All quotations of conference transcripts have students' names removed but retain mechanical inaccuracies of the texts.

REFERENCES

Butler, Judith. (1993). *Bodies that matter: On the discursive limits of "sex."* New York. Routledge.

Duin, Ann Hill, & Hansen, Craig. (1994). Reading and writing on computer networks as social construction and social interaction. In Cynthia L. Selfe & Susan Hilligoss (Eds.), *Literacy and computers: The complications of teaching and learning with technology* (pp. 89–112). New York: MLA.

Faigley, Lester. (1992). *Fragments of rationality: Postmodernity and the subject of composition.* Pittsburgh: University of Pittsburgh Press.

Foucault, Michel. (1978). *The history of sexuality: An introduction.* New York: Vintage Books.

Fuss, Diana. (1991). *Inside/out: Lesbian theories, gay theories.* New York: Routledge.

Litvak, Joseph. (1995). Pedagogy and sexuality. In George E. Haggerty & Bonnie Zimmerman (Eds.), *Professions of desire: Lesbian and gay studies in literature* (pp. 19–30). New York: MLA.

Malinowitz, Harriet. (1995). *Textual orientations: Lesbian and gay students and the making of discourse communities.* Portsmouth, NH: Boynton/Cook.

Selfe, Cynthia L., & Hilligoss, Susan. (1994). *Literacy and computers: The complications of teaching and learning with technology.* New York: MLA.

Summerfield, Judith, & Summerfield, Geoffrey. (1986). *Texts and contexts: A contribution to the theory and practice of teaching composition.* New York: Random House.

Wahlstrom, Billie. (1994). Communication and technology: Defining a feminist presence in research and practice. In Cynthia L. Selfe & Susan Hilligoss (Eds.), *Literacy and computers: The complications of teaching and learning with technology* (pp. 171–185). New York: MLA.

Weeks, Jeffrey. (1985). *Sexuality and its discontents: Meanings, myths, and modern sexualities.* London: Routledge.

Wright, Janet. (1993). Lesbian instructor comes out: The personal is the pedagogy. *Feminist Teacher, 7*(2), 26–33.

13

The Persistence of Difference in Networked Classrooms: Non-negotiable Difference and the African American Student Body

TODD TAYLOR

> African American students do not usually leave school because they fail to master an academic discourse. Instead, as the research of John Ogbu suggests, schools have failed to make good on the promise that literacy instruction in the schools will reward African American students socially and economically. Equally serious is the fact that schools have failed to change the perception (and reality in most cases) that for African American students literacy instruction entails "deculturation without true assimilation" (p. 151).
>
> – THOMAS FOX, "REPOSITIONING THE PROFESSION" (1994, P. 104)

This essay examines issues of diversity and literacy education primarily in terms of the concept of *difference*. In *Computers and the Teaching of Writing in American Higher Education, 1979–1994: A History,* Gail Hawisher, Paul LeBlanc, Charles Moran, and Cynthia Selfe (1996) characterized the development of the field, in part, as a movement from "growth and enthusiasm" to a "consideration of difference" (p. vii). Indeed, a pervasive sense of enthusiasm and optimism influenced early landmark scholarship such as Marilyn Cooper and Cynthia Selfe's (1990) "Computer Conferences and Learning" and Lester Faigley's (1992) "The Achieved Utopia of the Networked Classroom." This early work was encouraged by the prospect that networked conversations might help overcome or mask cultural markers that have typically led to oppression based upon class, gender, and race. However, more recent scholarship, such as Cynthia Selfe and Richard Selfe's (1994) "The Politics of the Interface" and Faigley's 1996 CCCC address, *Literacy After the Revolution,* tempered this enthusiasm by pointing out that the ideological forces that lead to oppression do not, in fact, suddenly disappear in online exchanges.

Thus, the most current scholarship in the field is not merely about a "consideration of difference" but about the persistence of issues of difference in every aspect of culture, even online. To date, a significant amount of work has examined the persistence of difference online in terms of gender, particularly from a feminist perspective. For example, Gail Hawisher (1996) and Patricia

From *Computers and Composition* 14 (1997): 169–78.

Sullivan (1996) have reported on continuing research that analyzes women's online writing practices, and Cynthia Selfe (1996) has researched cultural constructions of women and technology. Others have considered sexual orientation online: Alison Regan (1993) and Susan Warshauer (1995) have discussed homophobic flaming in writing classes. Too little of our work in computers and writing, however, has considered the persistence of racial difference in electronic environments. Consequently, this essay examines networked classrooms and African American students. Because *difference* has become such a widely used term, I first discuss various connotations of the concept and introduce the term *non-negotiable difference.* Next, I critique some research to date on students of color, particularly in regard to the problem of tokenism and the tendency to essentialize black student experience. This essay's primary thesis, however, is that networked classrooms provide writing instructors with unique extralinguistic cues, or body language, that can help teachers and students become more responsive to racial difference. As such, I hope to point out that electronic and networked learning environments can generate crucial and unique insights into the teaching of writing in general, insights that may be difficult or impossible to uncover in conventional classrooms.

PROBLEMS DEFINING *DIFFERENCE:* THE CONCEPT OF *NON-NEGOTIABLE DIFFERENCE*

In "What Does 'Negotiating Difference' Mean?" Patricia Bizzell and Bruce Herzberg (1996) wrote that part of the struggle of immigrants, African slaves, and Native Americans

> has been to communicate across cultural boundaries, and not only to communicate but to argue for rights, to capture cultural territory, to change the way America was imagined so that it would include those who were newer or less powerful or spoken about but not listened to—in short, to negotiate the differences of culture, race, gender, class, ideology. (p. v)

The problem here is that Bizzell and Herzberg's definition is monodirectional: It describes *negotiating difference* as a Disney-esque success story in which the lowly and alienated inevitably fight for justice and prevail in the sense that they eventually secure *communicative power, rights,* and *cultural territory.* What Bizzell and Herzberg actually described in this definition is not the present act of *negotiating difference* but the result of *difference negotiated* successfully. The distinction between the two is that difference is too rarely successfully negotiated, whereas *negotiating difference* is an ongoing and typically unsuccessful struggle. In other words, the sunny, liberal, will-to-overcome-difference is pleasant but not realistic.

At the heart of the disparity between rarely negotiated difference and the ostensible drive among many educators to do so anyway lies the age-old debate over assimilation versus reverse acculturation. As Reginald Martin (1990) pointed out in his guest editorial in a special issue of *College English* on literature and African Americans, African American scholars express passionate disagreement over whether to pursue *separatism* to preserve and validate black culture or to endorse *syncretism* in order to assimilate black culture into the dominant culture and improve both from within. Similarly, in rhetoric and composition there are those who seek to counter the assimilation perpetuated by institutionalized literacy instruction. Theorists such as Mina Shaughnessy (1977) and J. Elspeth Stuckey (1991) were concerned that academic discourse exacts a violence of assimilation on students from outside dominant culture whereby difference is not negotiated but obliterated to the detriment of those on the margins. On the other hand, Bizzell (Dobrin & Taylor, 1994, p. 68) and Min-Zhan Lu (1992) had more faith in the power of reverse acculturation. They argued that students from the margins can effectively operate, or negotiate, within both dominant and home culture and that the effect of such border crossings can be the subversive and productive reverse acculturation of the dominant group by the marginalized.

Precise definitions of *difference* are, therefore, implicated in the debate over assimilation versus reverse acculturation. For those who believe in the possibility that the *university* can, in David Bartholomae's (1985) terms, be *invented* from within by the Other, *difference* is a malleable obstacle, something defined, in fact, by its ability to be *negotiated.* This is a more transient concept of difference. However, other critics configure *difference* as the profound and non-negotiable qualities and characteristics that define one's position in contrast to others. While positions and cultures can and do shift so that they appear either no longer at odds or suddenly at odds (as is now the case in the former Yugoslavia), we need to question whether or not difference, in the nontransient sense, can ever be resolved or *negotiated.*

The term *non-negotiable difference,* therefore, is meant to emphasize that profound, deep-seated difference is, by definition, non-negotiable. An example of non-negotiable difference would be the widely debated assertion that a white person in America cannot ever genuinely understand the experience of being black in this country and that as progressive as a white person may be, he or she can never get beyond at least subconscious racist thought and action. In other words, because many critics define *difference* as that which determines one's cultural position in contrast to another, it must be admitted that such determinations establish at least some borders that are impermeable, even online. In short, we can never really understand what it is like to stand in someone else's shoes. This is not to say that because we are different we should not try to resolve our differences or that we can never get along. On the contrary, the concept of non-negotiable difference should be used to address radical subjectivity frankly and to suggest that we foreground the realities of our vastly different cultural perspectives instead of placating ourselves with talk of negotiating difference.

PROBLEMS RESEARCHING DIFFERENCE: GRIDLOCK, ESSENTIALISM, AND TOKENISM

As a white, male teacher who attended integrated public elementary and secondary schools in Florida and Georgia, I recognize that I have, at best, only a fragmented understanding of the perspectives of the African American students who now attend my classes. Like Fox (1994) in the epigraph to this essay, I am frustrated by education's as well as by my own "continuing inability to meet the needs of African American students" (p. 105), despite my intention to do so. And, I am frustrated by the lack of insight our scholarship provides on this issue. Many white scholars feel tremendous, often unarticulated, tension about addressing this subject because they believe they have little authority on the subject of black student experience, and they fear being thought politically incorrect. African American researchers may also want to avoid the subject because they do not want to be typecast as *black scholars* rather than as *scholars* like everyone else. And, as previously stated, there is widespread and passionate disagreement over whether to pursue separatism or syncretism. The result, unfortunately, is that these crucial but potentially explosive issues do not get covered in our scholarly conversations often enough. We can too easily become gridlocked on the very problems that most desperately need solutions.

Furthermore, our scholarship on this subject is often weak and does not give us effective ways to talk about difference or to address it in our classrooms. For example, Fox (1994) argued that Afro-American literary theory can help writing teachers appreciate the unique literate practices of black student writers, but his argument leads to essentialized statements about black student experience. He discussed the practice of *authentication,* whereby published narratives written by former slaves contained prefaces by white *guarantors* attesting to a text's integrity. After a discussion of the practice of authentication, he then wrote that "African American writers have an intensified need to authenticate their texts by stressing or 'marking' their own literacy ... they seek to authenticate their place in the university" (pp. 108–109). To be sure, many students feel such pressures and undertake such strategies as authentication in a contemporary sense, but it can be dangerous to assume that all black writers feel this "intensified need" and to make palpable links between this need and slave narratives. What about those students who have already embraced the idea currently promoted by so many: that the university belongs to African American students as much as anyone and that by actively "authenticating" one's status, one reinforces the negative construct that, unlike other students, African American students still must earn their place in the academy? What about African American students who might not want to be associated with humiliating, racist practices such as authentication as it was practiced a hundred years ago? Does it help to embrace Fox's insights regarding student writers if one of the likely responses is to define all African American student experience in terms of a characteristic (authentication) with ugly antecedents in slavery?

There are also other problems with our scholarship, such as *tokenism.* Although racial tokenism comes in many varieties, in contemporary scholarship, one common form occurs when a researcher brings up issues of difference or suggests that he or she is attempting to consider the circumstances of people of color but then fails to address either difference or color in substantial ways. For instance, in "The Achieved Utopia of the Networked Classroom," Faigley (1992) prefaced a transcript of an electronic exchange with this information about three of his students: "Since I am going to raise is-sues of difference, I should note that Samuel McCray is African-American, Richie Kwan is Chinese-American, and Delores Garza is Mexican-American" (p. 186). But Faigley neglected to analyze specifically how these three ethnic backgrounds influenced the exchange other than to suggest that the online hostility he witnessed in this class might be attributed to gender, race, and ethnic diversity. Why point out that Samuel is African American, Richie is Chinese American, and Delores is Mexican American, only to conclude that flaming may be attributed to diversity without examining how these specific cultural positions contributed to the phenomenon observed? It's almost as if tagging the ethnic and racial origins of students has become a chic convention in some scholarship about pedagogy, a convention that is superficial if it does not interrogate the meaning of these tags.

This brings us to additional gridlock: As we cannot talk universally about black student experience, and as we are apparently aware of race, but, like Faigley, have difficulty making sense of it, what *exactly* can we say about black experience? I would argue that, in general, there are only two points we can make with confidence:

1. African American students do, universally, experience firsthand the effects of racism in our culture today, although this experience, as well as response to it, will be varied in degree and kind.

2. If we seek to help specific African American students in our classes, we should consider more fine-grained and customized approaches to identity and difference.

Maureen Hourigan (1994) pointed out that too much of our research has considered race, gender, culture, and class as isolated and essentialized de-terminants of difference. She argued that we need to interrogate more closely the intersections of these issues instead of considering them sepa-rately. For example, an African American male from the northeast with ex-tensive computer experience who is a first-generation college student will have a vastly different standpoint from a Latin American female from Florida with no computer experience whose parents attended college. Clearly, individual configurations of difference are likely to be so varied and complex that if writing instructors seek to effectively negotiate such differ-ences, they must find ways to understand and to appreciate each student as an individual—a thorny task by any estimation. What strategies might help students communicate their differences to instructors and to other students without forcing them to reveal too much of their private lives? Autobio-graphical essays are one approach. However, such assignments run the risk of prying into students' lives as well as encouraging misleading and melo-dramatic narratives designed to make for interesting reading rather than to relay accurate information. I suggest that body language can be a highly in-formative source of such information and that the unique configurations of networked classrooms present opportunities to learn from our students' extra-linguistic cues.

PROBLEMS NEGOTIATING DIFFERENCE IN NETWORKED CLASSROOMS: EXTRA-LINGUISTIC CUES AS ONE SOLUTION

One example of how we sometimes pacify ourselves with hopes of negotiating difference is the abundance of talk about how networked interchanges can help negotiate difference because they obscure some culturally marked, extra-linguistic cues such as body language, tone of voice, and oral dialect that tend to favor those in dominant groups. But even if we believe networked interchanges can be used in these ways despite the increasing doubt that this can be done, how useful are such momentary suspensions of difference if once the interchanges have concluded, difference immediately re-emerges because it is non-negotiable? The *telos* of attempting to eradicate extra-linguistic cues that strongly communicate difference is also suspect because, in the absence of the Other, dominant culture re-emerges transparently as the "natural" default. In other words, difference cannot be addressed by attempting to level it, for it is by definition *non-negotiable.* Thus, I am interested in embracing the reality of extra-linguistic cues in networked classrooms instead of hoping to get beyond them, as many others have to date. I think we have much to learn by considering carefully the body language of students in networked environments. To demonstrate my point, later I describe the extra-linguistic characteristics of three African American students.

Like Foucault in *Discipline and Punish* and the French feminist philosophers and critics Cixous and Irigaray, Susan Miller (1996) encourages us to think about the body—in this case, about student bodies. A number of scholars have already re-examined the nature of the body in cyberspace. Both Raul Sanchez (1996) and Beth Kolko (1996) presented papers at the 1996 Computers and Writing Conference that argued that the virtual world is an *embodied* place, not only because of the expanding impact of virtual chat spaces whose metaphors strive toward the re-creation of a physical presence but also because our notions of *body* are largely constructed rhetorically, and rhetoric is clearly present in cyberspace. Although theorizing the body in cyberspace is a compelling topic, too little of our research has examined the nature of the morphing physical spaces that interface with the virtual world, namely, important spaces such as networked classrooms.

Thus, I would argue that we should also consider the actual, physical bodies of students as they work online. Tom Willard (1995) said that "the personal computer has given us two things: bad metaphors and bad posture" (p. 443). On one level, Willard's observation might make us chuckle; on another, he has touched upon an important point: Physical interactions with computers generate body language that can be informative. In a published transcript of a MUD conference, N. Katherine Hayles wrote:

> I understand lots of people say the Internet is disembodied—but in another sense it isn't at all. What difference does it make, for example, that one types the keys and sees responses flicker on the screen? I think one of the areas of investigation it proposes is the relation of embodied practices of reading and writing—the kinesthetic, tactile, visual—and how these

affect the messages and experience of the medium, (quoted by Taylor & Erben, 1995, p. 110)

In computer classrooms, considerations of the "kinesthetic" and the "tactile" reveal that because technology asks and in many ways *coerces* students to do things with their bodies (often on cue), writing instructors receive unique and highly informative feedback in the form of students' body language. One of the pronounced differences between teaching in conventional versus networked classrooms is the level of such feedback. Because a teacher cannot read minds and because students are more often silent than vocal when there is a problem, the ability to read faces, postures, tones, and gestures can help one teach effectively. For example, students in conventional classes are often adept at *appearing* as though they are fully engaged in listening to a discussion, reading a text, or writing, when their thoughts may be miles away. By the time they leave high school, they have often perfected an academic "game face." As a teacher, I have noticed that because networked classrooms can be especially active environments, game faces are often betrayed when students are asked to do something physically with a computer.

Probably the most familiar examples of this phenomenon are what I refer to as *monitor hypnosis, menu miscue,* and *spontaneous collaboration.* Monitor hypnosis occurs when the focus of a class meeting has shifted away from the terminals, but students remain glued to their screens—often in large numbers. The Web appears to intensify this phenomenon; it seems that Web sessions are like adventurous expeditions that, once begun, explores do not want to abandon. Menu miscue happens almost every time students are asked to complete one activity and begin another on their computers. Inevitably, two or three students will sit motionless as their classmates sail from menu to menu until arriving at the proper screen. These miscues may be exacerbated because students are reluctant to admit that they were not paying attention when instruction on navigating the menus began. Both monitor hypnosis and menu miscue are examples of how networked classrooms can provide unique and valuable kinds of feedback, feedback that convinces me that I probably lose contact with students in conventional classrooms more often than I realize, because there I do not have such information. I wonder if students have begun to develop "virtual game faces" for online class activities. For example, I imagine some students have learned how to make timely, periodic responses in synchronous exchanges so that they appear fully engaged while they are not participating genuinely. Of course, not all body language indicates a problem; some of it is positive. Teachers in computer-assisted classrooms are also probably familiar with students spontaneously moving chairs and sharing keyboards and screens, physically demonstrating engagement in collaborative learning and, possibly, when one student is helping another with a technical problem, an ethic of care.

Monitor hypnosis, menu miscue, and spontaneous collaboration, then, are three examples of student body language that might be used to uncover similar phenomena and to help identify difference. I would like to use those as well as other extra-linguistic cues as ways to describe experiences of African American students in a recent technical writing course. At the University of South Florida, basic technical writing is a popular sophomore- or junior-level course that helps students fulfill core writing requirements. Evenly populated by students from across the curriculum, it includes significant numbers from engineering departments and from the technical writing program. Of the 25 students in my Fall 1995 technical writing course, three were African American. Earlier in this essay I argued against essentializing or universalizing "black student experience," and the individual characteristics—largely communicated through extra-linguistic cues—of the three African American students in this class are good examples of this principle.

Stephanie is business major who dresses and acts the part; her clothes, posture, and demeanor suggest a professional attitude. One who sees her walking down the sidewalk could easily mistake her for someone on the way to the office, not class. Headed for law school and serious about her education, she politely conveys the idea that she expects to leave the course with something that will help her in a career. Her body language and the confident tone of her voice suggest that she is comfortable speaking in class. She uses primarily a standard, professional (white) dialect. On the first day of class she boldly raises her hand and admits that she is concerned about her lack of computer experience; she has never even used a mouse before. I then assure the class that no computer skills are required and that students who initially lack experience seem inevitably to gain the most ground during the semester.

In contrast to Stephanie, Chris has much more computer experience. Extremely shy, he typically sits on the edge of his seat, head lowered with his elbows on his knees, his eyes and face hovering over his keyboard even during class discussion. He is less comfortable speaking in class than is Stephanie, perhaps due to self-consciousness about his predominantly black spoken dialect. His computer background, however, provides a way for him to participate in class; he assumes the role of technical tutor to students in one corner of the room. He gives most of his attention to a third African American student, Felicia, who sits next to him, directly in front of the door.

Felicia seems frightened. She sits rigidly upright in her chair, facing her monitor even when it is turned off, apparently afraid to move much from this posture. Occasionally, she glances toward others in the class, but only after allowing her eyes to carefully trail up from the floor; her lips are tightly closed. Like Chris, she mostly uses black dialect in whispers, usually among just the three of us, but, unlike Chris, she never finds a way to join in. Like Stephanie, she lacks computer skills, but, unlike Stephanie, she does not try to bring this to my attention. Only after noticing a continuing pattern of menu miscues do I recognize her unfamiliarity with this technology. Chris quickly picks up on Felicia's awkwardness and assigns himself a role as her tutor throughout the semester. Huddled together on the opposite side of the room from Stephanie, Chris and Felicia appear emotionally close, as well. Observing their body

TABLE 13.1   Characteristics of Difference

Student	Computer Skills	Spoken Dialect	Class Participation
Stephanie	low	professional	active
Chris	high	black	selectively active
Felicia	low	black	silent

language, one might assume that they are brother and sister or lifelong friends. Toward the end of the semester, Chris tells me that he does not know Felicia outside class, which surprises me.

For the most part, the body language of these three remains constant throughout the semester. Stephanie seems independent and confident; both Chris and Felicia are shy and seem to use their relationship as support to make themselves feel less out of place. Suddenly, however, in a small, collaborative peer group at the end of the semester, Chris emerges as a leader. Each group selects a managing editor to coordinate a project, and Chris is chosen in his group. Their final project is second best of five done by the class.

Table 13.1 summarizes important characteristics that define various configurations of *difference* for each of these three African American students. Each of these configurations was made accessible to me primarily through extra-linguistic cues.

Although more thorough and detailed descriptions of these and other students would be certain to uncover more complicated and useful information, my brief look at Stephanie, Chris, and Felicia suggests (a) how powerful and informative student body language can be in a networked classroom, (b) that one must avoid universalizing so-called black experience, and (c) that to successfully negotiate difference, we must attend to more complex, fine-grained notions of difference, as Hourigan (1994) suggested. This idea here is to move away from demographic- and consumer-oriented perspectives that look at and treat individuals as if their identities are largely determined by artificial and inexact sociological groupings that facilitate marketing to consumers more than treating them equitably in educational institutions. This means that although we may want to be aware that, statistically, African American students are more likely to be first-generation college students and that phenomena such as authentication may influence the way they write, we are likely to do as much damage as good if such presumptions dominate our perspectives as teachers. We need to consider individuals as individuals who defy tight demographic or cultural grouping. The unique perspectives of computer-networked classrooms can facilitate such re-examinations and considerations.

REFERENCES

Bartholomae, David. (1985). Inventing the university. In Mike Rose (Ed.), *When a writer can't write: Studies in writer's block and other composing process problems* (pp. 134–165). New York: Guilford Press.

Bizzell, Patricia, & Herzberg, Bruce. (1996). *Negotiating difference: Cultural case studies for composition.* Boston: Bedford.

Cooper, Marilyn M., & Selfe, Cynthia L. (1990). Computer conferences and learning: Authority, resistance, and internally persuasive discourse. *College English, 52,* 847–869.

Dobrin, Sidney I., & Taylor, Todd. (1994). Radical pedagogy: An interview with Patricia Bizzell. *Writing on the Edge, 5*(2), 57–68.

Faigley, Lester. (1992). The achieved utopia of the networked classroom. In *Fragments of rationality: Postmodernity and the subject of composition.* Pittsburgh, PA: University of Pittsburgh Press.

Faigley, Lester. (1996, March). *Literacy after the revolution.* Address presented at the conference on College Composition and Communication, Milwaukee, WI.

Fox, Thomas. (1994). Repositioning the profession: Teaching writing to African American students. In Gary A. Olson & Sidney I. Dobrin (Eds.), *Composition theory for the postmodern classroom* (pp. 105–117). Albany: SUNY Press.

Hawisher, Gail E. (1996, March). *Women on the net: Constructing gender in electronic discourses.* Paper presented at the conference on college Composition and Communication, Milwaukee, WI.

Hawisher, Gail E., LeBlanc, Paul, Moran, Charles, & Selfe, Cynthia L. (1996). *Computers and the teaching of writing in American higher education, 1979–1994: A history.* Norwood, NJ: Ablex.

Hourigan, Maureen M. (1994). *Literacy as social exchange: Intersections of class, gender, and culture.* Albany: SUNY Press.

Kolko, Beth. (1996, June). *Sex and the student body: Feminist pedagogy and teachable moments in the electronic classroom.* Paper presented at the twelfth annual conference on Computers and Writing, Logan, UT.

Lu, Min-Zhan. (1992). Conflict and struggle: The enemies or preconditions of basic writing? *College English, 54,* 887–913.

Martin, Reginald. (1990). Current thought in African American literary criticism: An introduction. *College English, 52,* 727–731.

Miller, Susan. (1996, December). *Addressing the class: Power and gendered teaching.* Paper presented at the convention of the Modern Language Association, Chicago, IL.

Regan, Alison. (1993). Type normal like the rest of us: Writing, power, and homophobia in the networked composition classroom. *Computers and Composition, 10,* 11–23.

Sanchez, Raul. (1996, June). *My body, my self(s): Teaching the drama of virtual reality.* Paper presented at the twelfth annual conference on Computers and Writing, Logan, UT.

Selfe, Cynthia L. (1996, March). *The gendering of technology: Images of women, men, and computers.* Paper presented at the conference on College Composition and Communication, Milwaukee, WI.

Selfe, Cynthia L., & Selfe, Richard J., Jr. (1994). The politics of the interface: Power and its exercise in electronic contact zones. *College Composition and Communication, 45,* 480–504.

Shaughnessy, Mina P. (1977). *Errors and expectations.* New York: Oxford University Press.

Stuckey, J. Elspeth. (1991). *The violence of literacy.* Portsmouth, NH: Boynton/Cook.

Sullivan, Patricia. (1996, March). *The changing faces of discourse: Women, e-spaces, and the World Wide Web.* Paper presented at the conference on College Composition and Communication, Milwaukee, WI.

Taylor, Todd, & Erben, David. (1995). Prototypes: New forums for scholarship in "the late age of print." In Joseph M. Moxley & Lagretta T. Lencker (Eds.), *The politics and processes of scholarship* (pp. 105–113). Westport, CT: Greenwood.

Warshauer, Susan C. (1995). Rethinking teacher authority to counteract homophobic prejudice in the networked classroom: A model of teacher response and overview of classroom methods. *Computers and Composition, 12,* 97–111.

Willard, Tom. (1995). Review of the book *The electronic word: Democracy, technology, and the arts. Rhetoric Review, 13,* 440–443.

14 Reversing Notions of Disability and Accommodation: Embracing Universal Design in Writing Pedagogy and Web Space

PATRICIA A. DUNN AND
KATHLEEN DUNN DE MERS

Patricia A. Dunn and Kathleen Dunn De Mers' webtext article in the Spring 2002 issue of *Kairos*, an online journal of rhetoric, technology, and pedagogy, introduces the concept of universal design and its importance for assuring accessibility to the disabled in computer environments. The authors argue that we should see composition pedagogies as spaces of design and be conscious of the ways in which we can accommodate all students through good design principles and ADA guidelines. The authors provide an overview of these issues as well as helpful resources to new teachers such as assignments and hyperlinks to further information.

We have captured the opening screen and abstract (the piece has a total of six screens) to give you an overview of the content of the article. We encourage you to go online and read the article in its entirety. The web address is

<http://kairos.technorhetoric.net/7.1/binder2.html?coverweb/dunn_demers/index.html>.

From *Kairos* 7.1. (2002): <http://kairos.technorhetoric.net/7.1/binder2.html?coverweb/dunn_demers/index.html>

FIGURE 14.1   Title and Table of Contents.

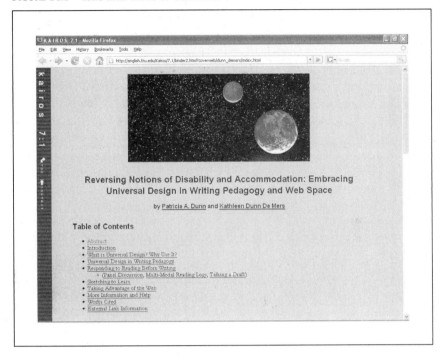

Source: Kairos 7.1 (2002): <http://kairos.technorhetoric.net/7.1/binder2.html?coverweb/dunn_demers/index.html>.

FIGURE 14.2   Abstract.

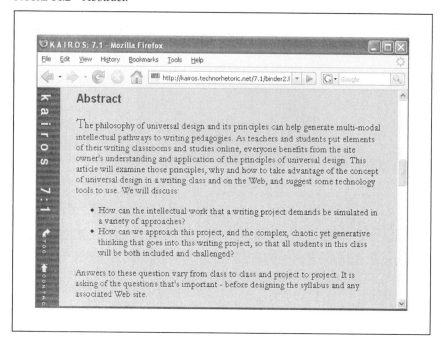

Abstract

The philosophy of universal design and its principles can help generate multi-modal intellectual pathways to writing pedagogies. As teachers and students put elements of their writing classrooms and studies online, everyone benefits from the site owner's understanding and application of the principles of universal design. This article will examine those principles, why and how to take advantage of the concept of universal design in a writing class and on the Web, and suggest some technology tools to use. We will discuss:

- How can the intellectual work that a writing project demands be simulated in a variety of approaches?
- How can we approach this project, and the complex, chaotic yet generative thinking that goes into this writing project, so that all students in this class will be both included and challenged?

Answers to these question vary from class to class and project to project. It is asking of the questions that's important - before designing the syllabus and any associated Web site.

Source: Kairos 7.1 (2002): <http://kairos.technorhetoric.net/7.1/binder2.html?coverweb/dunn_demers/index.html>.

PART FOUR

Writers and Composing

Introduction to Part Four

Computers have evolved into composing environments that influence thinking, writing, visuals, and revision. Software programs and the Internet have changed the context in which learning and communication take place, enhancing and complicating writing in ways unimaginable a few decades ago. Word processing programs, probably the most common software used in writing classes, change all stages for the composing process: brainstorming is enhanced with outlining and drawing tools; early drafts can be saved in multiple ways and manipulated with editing functions; later drafts can be exchanged and responded to with electronic comments; and proofreading can include grammar and spelling checks as well as marginal commenting. This list of possibilities barely scratches the surface of word processing capabilities, and of course, other software programs and technologies offer many additional innovative tools for writing and learning.

Along with altering the composing process through word processors—software generally used to create written documents eventually intended for print—computers have facilitated many forms of oral and visual communication. PowerPoint, for example, enables students to create presentations with color and images, making oral and visual literacy even more prevalent in composition classes. Moreover, as sound and moving pictures become easier to integrate in presentation software, students can also enhance their multimedia literacy, an issue explored in Part Six of this volume. These technologies, along with speech recognition software, may signal a return of composition to its classical roots in orality.

The Internet and the Web have also expanded composing strategies for composition students, not the least of which is the research process. Increasingly, students rely on online research for academic writing, visiting virtual college libraries far more frequently than their brick and mortar counterparts. The Web allows for immediate access to materials from all types of sources, including Web pages, blogs, wikis, digital newspapers and magazines, online journals, electronic books, and subject-specific databases. These sources are both more diverse and more confusing than sources previously encountered in writing classes; consequently, the teaching of research encourages exploration and yet becomes a daunting task.

The eight readings in this section offer guidelines for planning the transition from teaching in a traditional classroom to teaching in a computerized writing space, and they present practical suggestions for implementing technology. Although some pieces discuss computer technologies no longer in use—and some articles were even written before the widespread use of the Web—the suggestions they give apply equally well to 21st century technologies and composition pedagogy because they offer broad guidelines for using appropriate writing technologies in our classes, including appealing to audience, working collaboratively, and revising effectively. Moreover, like composition in a traditional classroom, teaching and learning in computerized classrooms involves a recursive, situated, and purpose-driven approach to writing.

In the first essay, "Pedagogy in the Computer-networked Classroom," Janet M. Eldred reminds us that "our classroom dilemmas do not disappear with a computer network; they change" (245). The change—a potentially more social, collaborative environment for composing—requires teachers to integrate the text-sharing features and forums of technology into the composing process. Teachers must make sure the students have access to the technology and understand how to use it, but, more importantly, teachers must coordinate the interaction and encourage "genuine dialog" as well as "reflective monolog" (246). Eldred argues that because technology has the potential for educational harm as well as good, teachers and administrators must plan ahead as they implement computerization. She outlines four pedagogical responsibilities in particular that must be attended to: choice of technology, ease of use, participation, and audience awareness. Though her examples in this discussion are often dated (for instance, when discussing technology choices, she mentions bulletin boards, an Internet feature that is now seldom used), her general guides are still very relevant and offer starting points for new teachers as they adapt their teaching to computer-netted classrooms.

The next article, a chapter from *Transitions: Teaching Writing in Computer-supported and Traditional Classrooms* by Mike Palmquist, Kate Kiefer, James Hartvigsen, and Barbara Goodlew, draws on a large research study about new teachers in computer classrooms and echoes many of Eldred's concerns. We have included the chapter, "Contrasts: Teaching and Learning about Writing in Traditional and Computer Classrooms" (Chapter 3) in this collection because it provides research-based findings that lend support to the anecdotal, site-specific accounts in many reports of computers in the writing classroom. The authors focus on seven issues that differed between traditional and computer classroom environments: curriculum, teacher roles, classroom interaction, classroom atmosphere, transference of activities between traditional classrooms and computer classrooms, the introduction and use of technology, and student attitudes and performance. Like other researchers, they did not find a significant difference in the students' essays between traditional classrooms and computer classrooms; however, they found "significantly higher numbers of contacts with classmates and teachers" in the computer classroom (258). It is this interaction—

and more writing by students (also noted by others)—that make the networked classrooms beneficial. In the last section of the essay, the authors report briefly on student attitudes and performance, noting that issues such as computer anxiety, writing competence, teacher feedback, and writing performance also influence students' writing experiences. In general, Palmquist et al. conclude that though instructional differences exist between traditional classrooms and computer classrooms, these differences are not always black-and-white and tend to "represent a *continuum of change*" (emphasis theirs, p. 270) as teachers and students adapt to the new computerized environment.

Diane Penrod describes the adjustments needed to assess writing in the networked environment in "Rethinking Validity and Reliability in the Age of Convergence," chapter 4 of her book *Composition in Convergence: The Impact of New Media on Writing Assessment.* The convergence of composition and the networked environment, a "blending of several technologies into a single source" (*Composition in Convergence,* xvii), requires multiple genres of writing and communication from students. In addition to the traditional academic essay, students communicate through e-mail, online discussions, drafts, peer critiques, and much of the routine communication (mundane writing) that often does not get attention when student writing is assessed. The sources students use and the documents they produce incorporate visuals and multimedia features that must also be included in assessment. Penrod proposes broader definitions of *validity* and *reliability* for developing a "deep assessment" (279) of students' writing.

Kathleen Blake Yancey also supplies an heuristic for deep assessment of student writing in "Looking for Sources of Coherence in a Fragmented World: Notes toward a New Assessment Design." Yancey begins her discussion by arguing that digital texts and print texts are alike in at least three ways: Coherence is a requirement for both types of documents, both types are compositions, and the heart of both types is rhetoric (294). To help navigate the complexities of digital compositions, Yancey offers an "assessment heuristic" that proceeds by asking several broad questions:

1. What arrangements are possible?
2. Who arranges?
3. What is the intent?
4. What is the fit between the intent and the effect?" (301).

Yancey applies the heuristic to an e-mail and a digital portfolio and illustrates the heuristic by focusing on patterns of interactivity among digital texts and the coherence that results. This heuristic, she argues, both guides assessment of student works and offers an opportunity for the rater, as reader, to find new meaning in, and connection with, the digital text. Yancey sees digital texts "as compositions . . . that create their own unity through patterning, that are located in a kind of coherence like print and yet different from print, too—more visual, more dynamic, ultimately more contextual— that weave together. . . . fragments of a postmodern world" (304–5).

The network environment requires us to review and negotiate our evaluation process for writing; as we teach in computer classrooms, we must also evaluate and negotiate the environment itself. In "The Politics of the Program: MS Word as the Invisible Grammarian," Tim McGee and Patricia Ericsson urge us to "interrogate technology" (322). They encourage teachers, with their students, to look beyond the surface and critically evaluate the technologies used in the classroom—and, when necessary, to make changes to the environment to meet the needs of the writers and readers. The authors suggest that we teach students how to change the default settings for MS Word's grammar checker and review options available in the software. Most importantly, writers should be aware that the suggestions made by the software are just that—suggestions. McGee and Ericsson focus on MS Word's grammar checker, but their cautions apply to any software or technology, and the authors remind us to be aware of the way such pervasive software mediates and influences student writing in our classes. First, "Microsoft gets more 'teachable moments' than the English teachers do" (310). As they point out, Word (and other word processing software with similar grammar checkers) is on millions of desks—vastly outnumbering grammar teachers. Second, the grammar guidelines used by the MS Word grammar checker are often different from the handbooks used in our English classes. Grammar checkers and other textual analysis aids are designed not for student writers who are still learning the nuances of word choice and rhetorical situations but for advanced writers who learn to negotiate and even ignore advice from the software, so we must teach students to view the technology as an aid, not the ultimate arbiter of proper grammar.

Getting students to revise for meaning beyond the word or sentence has been a challenge for English teachers; word processors complicate—and potentially enhance—that dilemma as well. Christine A. Hult in "The Computer and the Inexperienced Writer" suggests that the software may actually "inhibit" (327) the revision strategies of student writers if students are not taught how to use the computer environment to create multiple drafts, reorganize using cut and paste features, and incorporate suggestions from peers and other readers into their text. Hult argues that we need to help students see word processing as part of the writing process (not simply a tool), to use the network environment to expand the interaction with readers, and to provide time (and access) for students to do more than type and submit their work. Our goal should be to get substantive revisions from the students that use many of the tools available in word processors. And, like McGee and Ericsson, Hult stresses the importance of teaching students to negotiate grammar and spelling checkers and to understand word processors' roles in enacting "principles of effective revision" (332).

Just as word processors affect composing, the Internet and the World Wide Web mediate much of students' research and change the nature of information gathering, so any overview of students' composing practices is incomplete without a discussion of the Internet, and particularly the influence of the World Wide Web, on research and composition. Madeleine Sorapure, Pamela

Inglesby, and George Yatchisin introduce the concept of "Web literacy" in their article, "Web Literacy: Challenges and Opportunities for Research in a New Medium." Web literacy requires students to evaluate and manage the information gathered from the Web in the form of text, hypertext, visuals, and multimedia along with the different degrees of interactivity with communication devices as small and powerful as their cell phones. Students' literacy must encompass more aspects of information and flex with the changing environment. Sorapure, Inglesby, and Yatchisin focus as much on the *context* as the *content* of the information students encounter, arguing that even the links on a site—or the placement of a site—affect its credibility. The authors balance practical advice with examples while describing a framework that can be adapted with each change of the Web environment. They identify three Web site features to which students should attend when performing research: images, links, and interactivity. These features help determine the value of information found online and also offer a new way to teach students about rhetoric and discourse. Most importantly, engaging students with technology helps them become more Web literate as they not only research online, but communicate in virtual spaces as well.

As students conduct research on the Web, they will encounter large, complex databases, and Michelle Sidler describes this challenge in the next article, "Web Research and Genres in Online Databases: When the Glossy Page Disappears." Sidler focuses on sources commonly used by students—search engines, databases, directories, and other means of accessing information on the Web—even when they do not know much about these technologies. Like Sorapure, Inglesby, and Yatchisin, Sidler argues that students must develop awareness and evaluate not just the content but the context of the information. A frequent problem with information gathered from online databases is that the context of the online source is limited to "only simple graphic design and little interactivity . . . words on a page with few obvious visual markers" (351–2). Some of this confusion has changed because more and more articles from databases are presented in full text, PDF format; however, students often select the first source that appears and, as Sidler points out, do not pay attention to the Web space in which they find it (the Web or source address and the sponsor). Sidler encourages mapping the "geographies of online research" (357) to help students develop strategies for online searches. She provides questions student-researchers might use to map sites they visit and gives examples of the geographical metaphors that she has found helpful for students.

The articles in Part 4 of this collection introduce the issues of composing and researching in the network environment. Two of the essays in this section are from larger works. We encourage readers interested in assessment to read Penrod's *Composition in Convergence: The Impact of New Media on Writing Assessment*. In addition to Chapter 4, included here, we found Chapter 2, "Transforming Texts, Transforming Assessment," useful. The chapter provides more background in assessment and suggestions for coordinating assessment in the computer environment with learning outcomes. The Palmquist et al. essay in this section introduces issues that come out of research studies reported in *Transitions: Teaching Writing in Computer-Supported and Traditional Classrooms.* We encourage interested readers to pursue the more detailed discussion of these issues in the subsequent chapters: classroom dynamics, teacher-centered and student-centered classrooms, authority, curriculum design and class planning, technology, and teacher training.

15 Pedagogy in the Computer-networked Classroom

JANET M. ELDRED

If we plot the narrative of computers in the writing classroom, we see events in two areas that have influenced the direction computer technology has taken: one, of course, is the rapidly developing technology itself; the second is composition pedagogy. As I have argued elsewhere, the technology used in our classrooms has reflected changing ideas about teaching writing. With traditional, product-centered teaching came an emphasis on editors, spell-checking features, and the like. Those classrooms that stressed process looked to word processing, to heuristic programs, and to the promise of an artificially intelligent machine that could help students think or "pre-write" more critically. In the past decade, with the introduction of critical theories and with the resurgence of classical rhetoric, we have seen the growth of social pedagogies, pedagogies that stress writing as a dialogic, dialectic act which should at its best "empower" writers.[1] Given that writing classrooms are now stressing composing as a *public* act, instructors or administrators who want to integrate computer technology into their classrooms should begin with two basics: word-processing packages and networking. Because networking is relatively new to composition classrooms,[2] I will devote this space to a discussion of networking. *Networking can work* in a writing classroom because it can be used to stress composing as a social, collaborative act, as an act of synthesizing and negotiating knowledge. But networking will work for us *only if* we plan carefully how we will use it in our classrooms, how we will take advantage of its strengths and downplay its weaknesses.

My purpose here is to stress the importance of planning, of carefully integrating networking technology into class plans. When word-processing packages became widely available, teachers who felt their benefits for their own writing eagerly embraced it as part of their classrooms, believing that students would instantly revise more. But after many students,[3] researchers discovered that this premise was simply wrong: students did not revise any more than they had in the past. What these studies didn't measure was *pedagogy;* they focused, as Hawisher (1989) points out, on computers rather than

From *Computers and Composition* 8.2 (1991): 47–61.

on how students use them. When students were encouraged to revise, when revision was made part of the classroom plan, they revised more on paper as well as on diskette. However, the word-processing packages did make students feel that the task was easier. Teachers using word-processing packages thus discovered the necessity of emphasizing process, of making revisions an integral part of their class plans.

Likewise with networking. Discussing computer communication in business settings, Hiltz (1984) observes that

> computer-mediated communication systems are not a technological magic wand that can be waved over an organization to achieve instantaneous transformations. . . . It takes some time for new users to become comfortable with the medium and realize the potential that it offers. It also takes the right social implementation, from the initial choice of an application that will supply a critical mass for the on-line community, through constant attention to facilitating or managing the group's work on-line. (p. 197)

Though we might balk at the words "social implementation" and claim that, unlike a business, we have no political or economical agenda, some careful reflection might prove the wisdom in Orwell's aphorism, "All issues are political issues." As Trent Batson (1989b) reminds us, "in schools we have different populations, purposes, and economics" (p. 247). Technology is not neutral: as soon as we implement it, we slant it in a certain direction. To hope for it just to "fall in place" is to play Russian roulette with the effectiveness of our classrooms. Management is thus a crucial issue.

When integrating networking into a writing or literature classroom, it's simply not enough to say to students, "you can now send messages and papers to me and to other members of your class any time you want." Given only this introduction, students will see the system as busy work. Networking must be an integral part of the class—this usually means requiring students to use the network, making it part of their assignments. For like any technology, although networking has the possibility to be a fruitful addition to any classroom, it also carries the potential for doing more harm than good. For this reason, I want to stress four areas that must be attended to if the full potential of networking is to be reached: (1) Choice of Technology, (2) Ease of Use, (3) Participation, and (4) Audience Awareness.

CHOICE OF TECHNOLOGY

First, one must decide which of the available technologies—electronic mail, file-sharing, bulletin boards, synchronous conferencing or a combination—to incorporate into class plans. *Electronic mail* can be used to apprise students of daily assignments and class plans, to send them individual comments, and to "chat" with them, making time outside class even more personal than face-to-face contact in the classroom. Although computers have been blamed for their dehumanizing effects, for their reducing of human personalities to numeric codes, many instructors and students alike comment on just the opposite phenomenon, on the computer's ability to make the writing classroom a much more personal space. With mail, writing becomes a way of communicating with others between class sessions; students receive and send personalized letters to both instructors and peers. Instead of an academic exercise, writing in the electronic classroom can become a project which networks individuals into a larger group.[4]

As one might guess, *file-sharing* is useful to the composition classroom because it facilitates peer editing. Instead of Xeroxing and distributing essays to campus mailboxes, students simply send their papers back and forth to each other. In addition, peer editing is enriched by the distinct nature of on-line communication. On-line conversations are usually much more forthright than face-to-face encounters; people of equal status and rank in an organization or classroom tend to do away with the niceties and to offer their opinions more readily. Even when there is a clear hierarchical structure, such as teacher-student or manager-employee, people seem willing to take more "risks" on-line, to express themselves more freely (Sproull & Kiesler, 1986). Electronic mail might encourage the reticent editor, the student a bit uncomfortable with the idea of "criticizing" a peer's work. File-sharing also takes the place of Xeroxing or mimeographing in the classroom. Rather than reproduce paper assignment, exercises, syllabi, or other materials, one simply sends the appropriate files to the class or to individuals. Students can then choose whether to print the information and keep paper copy or to save the information on-line. This is one area in which the computer saves time when needed: a file can be created just before class, even in class, and be immediately available to all students. All the steps necessary for reproducing materials via photocopying or mimeographing have been eliminated.

Electronic bulletin boards prove useful in a slightly different way. Students and faculty can use the bulletin boards recreationally to buy and sell books, spread news, discuss the merits and drawbacks of programs, share poems and lyrics, or practice their Spanish or French composition. Instead of sending mail to just one person on the network, bulletin boards provide a forum for groups of users: all members of a group can read the posted messages. The bulletin board also fosters a sense of community, gives individuals a stronger sense of their place in a group. Again, the sense of writing as a social, communal act is heightened. In literature and writing classes, bulletin boards can be used to supplement in-class discussions. For example, in one unit for our first-year writing sequence, students produce a paper in which they synthesize different viewpoints. Our particular topic was "Defense," specifically issues surrounding nuclear weapons. After reading several articles, I posted a question for students on the bulletin board: "Do or should governments abide by the same ethical code as individuals when it comes to issues of war? (i.e., Do governments need to think of war in terms of murder? Is it more justifiable to kill many people out of state's interest than to kill one person out of self-interest?)" Students in the class were required to respond before the next class session; some of them did so more than once. Students from outside the class also joined our "discussion," thus bringing in perspectives that had not been covered in the reading or introduced by the instructor and class members. Once the forum was strongly under way, students were quick to play devil's advocate with one another, thus relieving me of most—though not all—of the job. I've also used bulletin boards for literature classes in much the same way. In a novels course, for example, each week I would post a question concerning the work we were reading. When we read *Billy Budd,* I posted the question, "Did Captain Vere make the right decision?" Students answered these questions and posted their responses well in advance of class meetings. Before class meetings, students were expected to read all the responses.

I would like to add here a caveat about using bulletin boards in this way. It has been several years since Toby Fulwiler taught us how useful it could be to begin class discussions with brief five-minute journal entries. When I incorporated on-line assignments, I assumed that these bulletin board responses would work in the same way. I soon discovered that they do not. I could begin class, in fact, by asking the exact question that I had posed on-line, only to receive no response (this after each student had written well over the 250-word minimum). Dawn Rodrigues noticed the same problem, and suggested in her 1989 CCCC presentation that perhaps students considered discussions outside class and those inside class quite separate. I did find that class discussion could be rescued when I played "moderator," reviewing their responses, taking class time to read parts aloud or to outline the positions that emerged from their collective entries. Still, I often found that this moderating worked just as well in encouraging discussion outside of class time. In other words, moderating was an essential part of on-line discussions,[5] but on-line conversations were not the best means of encouraging in-class discussions. Journal entries at the beginning of class, entries based on a question completely different from that which formed the basis of our on-line, out-of-class talks, still produced the best in-class discussions.

The bulletin board served a purpose other than the one I intended, but an important one nonetheless. The students judged the on-line responses an important part of the class. They liked seeing how their peers responded; and though they complained at times about the reading load (they were responsible for reading what turned out to be the equivalent of 20 printed pages before class each week), they did like being able to save the entries and refer to them when studying for the final exam. The responses also seemed to join them as a class, to increase their sense of identity as part of a group, and to reinforce the idea that they could hold an opinion about the novel that differed from mine. As Sproull and Kiesler (1985) suggest, the "real value" of electronic mail "could be increased sociability and organizational attachment" (p. 1511). The bulletin board thus enhanced our collective understanding of texts, it made available in text form differing ideas and analyses, and it allowed for full and rich critical discussions outside of class time. Though people often fear that new technologies will make the old obsolete, here is an example of how these new technologies exist alongside of and complement our tried and true practices.

In addition to electronic mail, file-sharing, and bulletin boards (asynchronous conferencing), *synchronous conferencing* (conferencing between individuals all logged on at once) is a promising technology for the writing classroom. Writing classes which use this "real-time" conferencing are often referred to as ENFI classrooms. The project received its name from a pilot program at Gallaudet University with deaf students and was quickly put to use with hearing students. During class sessions or in a networked lab, students work at computer screens with two windows: a "composing" window and a "dialog" window. Students compose in the lower half of their screen while reading incoming comments in the top half.[6] All of the class discussion thus takes place on-line and the result is a written record, what Fred Kemp often refers to as a "polylog."[7]

EASE OF USE

Because local area networks are sophisticated pieces of software and hardware and because mainframes are machines so complex that they are maintained by system analysts and people with other such titles, they can be intimidating to use—even for those of us who use word-processing packages and other software regularly. In order for networking to be truly effective in our class, we must be able to make the technology as transparent and as easy to use as possible. First and foremost, this means writing clear instructions that students can follow. But this kind of preparation does take *time*, time that may not be rewarded in tenure or merit decisions.

Perhaps more challengingly, ease of use means choosing software programs that work well together—a task easier said than done—or it means writing programs, or having programs written, that make the whole system more user-friendly. Let me offer a specific example. We use a mainframe system because it can be maintained centrally, because terminals were already in place around campus so that new equipment did not have to be purchased, because it could support many users at once (something our microlab could not do), because technical support—programmers and analysts—were already in place, and because it is accessible at almost all times of the day and night. But mainframes are notoriously user UN-friendly. In order for our computer-mediated classes to work, we had to find a way of surmounting this problem. Our solution was to work together with the Computing Center, which monitors the mainframe. A programmer, who works specifically in instructional computing, wrote menus that I designed. Students now log on and see the following screen:

English Menu

1. Word Process

2. Mail

3. Bulletin Boards

4. Print

5. Quit and Log Out Your Choice: #

If the student chooses 2 *Mail,* he or she see another menu

Mail Sub-Menu

1. Read Your Mail

2. Send Mail to Someone

3. Send a Paper to Someone

Your Choice: #

This is not the most sophisticated menu ever produced; because of the constraints of our system, it has no graphics and can be displayed only in black and white. But it does allow students to work without having to memorize several commands, commands that would change with each new system they had to learn. Moreover, students can use the system without having to know the ins and outs of it; they don't need to know, for example, that to send a paper to someone they must first access the mail program, then the word-processing package in order to save the file in ASCII format, and then the mail program again. They simply have to indicate that they want to send a paper with a specific title to a person who has a specific electronic address. The idea is to stress composition functions—collaborative brainstorming, composing texts, mailing texts for review and evaluation—rather than specific hardware or software. It probably goes without saying that the easier the system appears, the likelier students are to use it.

PARTICIPATION

Almost everyone who has worked with the technology notes that networking's main advantage is the egalitarian quality of the participants' discourse, the dissolving of certain inequities—produced by gender, class, ethnicity, and personality differences—that exist in normal classroom discussions. And to a great extent, networks do meet this expectation.[8] But this approach works only as well as we encourage it to work. For the idea of electronic egalitarian discourse depends largely on the absence of visual cues such as the person's age, sex, appearances, on a kind of "white-washing" of the traits which define us visually and aurally and which also, unfortunately, prompt discriminatory responses in others. But this anonymity is not complete and perhaps not even desirable. Even in a system that allows for complete anonymity, verbal cues still exist along with visual cues. As language theorists remind us, language carries with it the places it has been. Language, like technology, is never neutral, always socially charged. And while it is possible that students will practice and try on different voices, I was surprised to discover how many of the students carried their classroom "roles" with them on-line. For example, at least one 19-year-old woman in my class started her entries with phrases like "I don't know very much about that, but I guess . . ." In other words, given a situation where she could assume herself to be the intellectual equal of any other user on that network, she chose to recreate herself in or fell into a language that recreates her as someone young, naïve, and unreflective. This kind of example is not uncommon and raises questions. Does this mean then that we, as Lester Faigley (1988) suggests, judge that self inappropriate for our academic purposes? And if so, what does that tell us about the extent to which we are willing to accept this "egalitarian effect" of electronic networks?

Computer networks do not automatically solve the empowering/co-opting dilemma described by scholars such as Patricia Bizzel.[9] Though users on an electronic network are more equally situated, this is not the promised land: social inequities still exist. It is not by accident that highly stratified and hierarchical groups, like large corporations or the military, have found computer networks an effective managerial tool. On networks we can see new hierarchies forming: computer users pull rank over novices, tossing out computer jargon as easily as writing teachers pronounce words like "heuristics" or "dialogism"; aggressive personalities overshadow shyer ones. One might argue that the shift from a classroom that depends on speech to one in which students are required to communicate primarily on-line, in writing, privileges the instructor's domain, the arena of the technologically produced word. Moreover, some of the same social relationships that exist in a classroom continue over the network. Many students who are simply more accustomed to listening than to speaking will participate quietly, reading rather than writing. Our classroom dilemmas do not disappear with a computer network; they change. But there may be ways that we as instructors can foster egalitarian discourse. Our task over the next few years will be to discover appropriate pedagogy and to train teachers to use the technology effectively. The following pedagogies may help foster participation in asynchronous, networked dialog.

- Use the system as much as possible. Send memos through electronic mail for each class session and urge students to check their mail daily. If possible, log on at least once, or better yet, twice a day. As Spitzer (1989) observes, new users can become apprehensive or discouraged if they send mail that goes unanswered.

- Require all students to participate, even if this means giving them grades for doing so. Build participation on the computer network into your grading plan.

- Set minimum lengths for responses, so that everyone participates fully. In other words, integrate networked discourse into the syllabus as another writing assignment.[10]

- Talk to students about the goal of classroom discussions and talk to them about disclaimers or "tags" (e.g., "I don't know much," "I'm not really sure but I think maybe that," "you're crazy if you think that," "that's a pretty dumb statement").

- Ask them to sign their responses. While some of the freedom of anonymity might be lost, the responses will benefit from the sense of responsibility that comes when one signs her or his name or a penname.

AUDIENCE

Audience is perhaps the most complicated issue facing teachers who are integrating networks into their classrooms. At first glance, it seems that a technology that links single users with others, that provides easy access to knowledge available through libraries or peers, that makes letter-writing almost assume once again the prominent place it had in the 19th-century—that a technology that delivers all of this must by logical extension develop in the user a keen sense of audience.

But some research in the social sciences suggests otherwise. Hiltz together with Turoff (1978) and Kiesler with her colleagues (1984) find that users on electronic conferencing systems become more self-absorbed, producing more writer-based prose than even those of us who are used to reading piles of first-year student papers are accustomed to encountering. Sproull and Kiesler (1986) note that people "focus relatively strongly on themselves and on what they want to say and less strongly on their audience" (p. 1000). In an experiment comparing face-to-face and on-line conversations, the observers note that computer users tend to "talk in parallel with the partner, rather than in response to the partner" (Kiesler, Zubrow, Moser, & Geller, 1985, p. 96). It is perhaps, somewhat ironically, a tendency toward self-expression or self-disclosure that makes users feel themselves a coherent part of a group, a group that permits them to speak their views. All for the good, one might say, but we as teachers of writing have a commitment to the idea of audience awareness and to meaningful, engaging dialog, to help students turn writer-based prose into reader-based prose. As Dawn Rodrigues (1989) continues to point out, this dialog does not happen automatically:

> Many students do not know how to discuss ideas with one another. They have had almost no experience in their lives interacting with others in a continual oral discussion—thus attempting to track others [sic] ideas, to synthesize what others have said and to attempt to find their own voice.[11]

And indeed, this dialog does not emerge automatically. In fact, the longer the students' responses, the more self-absorbed they may become; sometimes students admit to becoming so self-absorbed that they forget the question with which they started. True dialog emerges with the presence of an effective moderator (in a classroom, usually the teacher, though this by habit rather than necessity perhaps), who negotiates and weds the various voices and perspectives. Again, it is our pedagogy that will determine whether reflective monolog or genuine dialog will occur. Both, it seems, might be the goals of a writing course. But again, we must use our pedagogy to shape the technology, not vice versa. The following tips may prove helpful when dialog and an acute sense of audience are the goals.

- Remind students that asynchronous bulletin board discussions are public, not private. The idea initially takes some getting accustomed to; after all, when they sit down to the screen, no one else is present.

- When students are first learning to use the network, introduce members of the group to one another. Begin by introducing yourself. Then instruct each person to introduce him- or herself and end the introductions by asking a question about the person whose entry precedes theirs. The person to whom the question is addressed should, of course, answer it. This game will soon get chaotic. But it will teach students to read and respond to entries rather than to think of them as a linear series of reports. It will also show them how fluid and how public the medium is.

- Require students to respond not just to the question you, as the instructor, ask, but to the entries others using the system have made. Teach them to be specific about these references. A response like "I agree with this idea . . ." is bound to get lost or passed over in the myriad messages and topics that are a part of electronic discourse. Again, newcomers to electronic discourse are often apprehensive and become more so if their messages do not prompt responses. Specific references to other messages also work against tendencies toward self-absorption; they remind the writer of an obligation towards others on the network.

- Moderate the discussions. Once students are accustomed to the system, have students or groups of students take over the role of moderator. When they moderate a discussion, students should summarize the various entries, pointing out similarities and differences between them. They should also pose questions that arise from their synthesis. Elizabeth Sommers suggests that when students act as moderators, they practice the critical act of synthesis. And when they see the wealth and diversity of text generated by electronic networks, they understand clearly the need to summarize, focus, and synthesize information, to sharpen their critical thinking skills.

Networking in all its forms is a powerful new technology, one that can work to complement social writing pedagogy. And for this reason, those of us introducing it in our classrooms have been optimistic. But if a fear of technology has blinded many to its promises, an overenthusiasm for technology can blind us to the serious problems that might emerge. Networking is not, as Hiltz (1990) reminds us, an electronic magic wand that once having been waved instantly produces benefits such as democratization, audience awareness, and dialog. We cannot expect to put students in classrooms that dabble with networking, that teach computers "on the side," and have them emerge as writers believing in the value of collaboration, the importance of making knowledge together with other people. I have tried to be forthright about problems that arise when integrating computer technology into writing classes, but I hope that I have not stressed the pitfalls over the benefit: the benefits are clearly there. Networking is an exciting and powerful new technology that has much to offer teachers of writing. In order for networking to work for us, we have much work to do.

NOTES

1. I realize that the term "empower" is highly problematic and often discussed in literature surrounding social theories of teaching writing, most notably by Patricia Bizzell. For literature that discusses social theories of writing and computer networks, see articles by Batson (1988a, 1988b),

Eldred (1989), Kinkead (1987, 1988), Peyton and Mackinson-Smith (1989), Peyton and Miller (1989), Schriner and Rice (1989), Selfe (1987, 1988), Selfe and Wahlstrom (1986), Spitzer (1989), and Thompson (1988a, 1988b, 1987). An excellent overview of networking and its potential and realized social effects is presented in the book by Hiltz, S. R., and Turoff, M., (1978) *The network nation: Human communication via computer.* Reading, MA: Addison-Wesley.

2. Though network technology has existed for over a decade (see Hiltz S. R., & Turoff M., 1978, *The network nation: Human communication via computer.* Reading, MA: Addison-Wesley), only recently has its promise for the composition classroom become an issue. At the 1987 CCCC in Atlanta, 2 of the 20 computer sessions mentioned networking; at both the 1988 CCCC in St. Louis and the 1989 CCCC in Seattle, roughly 8 of 18 presentations concerned themselves with networking; in the 1990 meeting in Chicago, 5 of the 15 computer sessions used networking in the title—even more talks assumed a networked classroom.

3. See Hawisher, G. E. (1989) Computers and Writing: Where's the Research? *English Journal, 78,* 89–91 and Hawisher, G. E. (1989) Research and Recommendations for Computers and Composition, in G. E. Hawisher and C. L. Selfe (eds.), *Critical Perspectives on Computers and Composition Instruction* (pp. 44–69) New York: Teachers College Press.

4. See Rodrigues (1989) and Kinkead (1987) for descriptions of college writing courses that make use of electronic mail. Schwartz's 1990 article (Using an electronic network to play the scales of discourse. *English Journal, 79,* 16–24) details a distance learning project that electronically links students from Pennsylvania, Montana, and South Dakota.

5. Moderators facilitate conversation, summarizing what has previously been written, raising new questions when discussion lags, recasting old questions, etc. As Hiltz (1984) argues, the success of on-line conferences is determined in part by the interest and importance of the topic, but also by the "effort and skill of the group leader" (p. 80) or leaders. Moderators may be formally appointed or they may arise naturally; they may shift and share responsibility. A conference in which the moderator is ineffective or in which a moderator is not appointed and does not emerge is most often an inactive one (p. 80). Thus, the question for a successful, active computer network is not "will there be a moderator," but as Arms (1988) suggests, "what will be the moderator's role; how will the moderator be chosen, what authority does the moderator have?" (p. 45).

6. For a description of how ENFI works, see Thompson, D. P. (1987) Teaching Writing on a Local Area Network. *T.H.E. Journal, 15,* 92–97. Thompson describes five different teaching methods that can be used in an ENFI networked classroom. *The Teacher's Guide to Using Computer Networks for Written Interaction,* (1989), D. Beil, (ed.), a compilation of articles for ENFI teachers, is an excellent source for those looking to implement synchronous conferencing systems in writing and literature classrooms. A special issue of *Computers and Composition,* (1984), also a collection of articles by scholars and teachers working with synchronous conferencing, is a must for those using or planning to use computer networks.

7. Kemp has used the term "polylog" in conversations on Megabyte University, an on-line discussion that he (YKMBU@TTACS) moderates.

8. See work by Batson (1989a, 1989b), Ehrmann (1988), Eldred (1989), Hiltz and Turoff (1978), Peyton (1989a, 1989b), Schriner and Rice (1989), Selfe (1987, 1988), and Thompson (1987, 1988a, 1988b).

9. For a discussion of the problem of empowering vs. coopting, see Bartholomae, D. (1986). Inventing the University, *Journal of Basic Writing, 5,* 4–23; Bizzell, P. (1982). College Composition: Initiation into the Academic Discourse Community, *Curriculum Inquiry, 12,* 197–207; Bizzell, P. (1986). Foundationalism and Anti-Foundationalism in Composition Studies, *Pre/Text, 7,* 37–56; and Bizzell, P. (1988). 'Resistance' and Writing Instruction, paper presented at CCCC. Bizzell, in particular, has struggled with the issues of empowerment, assimilation, resistance, and co-optation.

10. In a draft, " 'I Prefer Not to': Lurkers, Speakers, and Writers," I argue that metaphors for speaking and writing create policies for participation in our classrooms. Networked discourse, as Thompson, Peyton, Batson and others have suggested, is somewhere between speech and writing and poses special problems. Thompson's (1988) article, Interactive Networking: Creating Bridges Between Speech, Writing, and Composition. *Computers and Composition, 5,* 17–27, makes a fine argument for using computer networks to close the gap between what a student can say and what he or she might write. But this approach still doesn't solve the speech/writing puzzle. For those who see networked discourse primarily in terms of speech, requiring students to participate in network "conversation" might prove disturbing. As a group, writing teachers are generally not comfortable with the idea of forcing participation in oral discussions. We would, however, respond differently if we assigned a written composition and a student responded "I prefer not to." If we conceive of networked discourse as writing, then we can build assignments that involve electronic networks into our syllabi.

11. These comments are part of a conversation on Megabyte University. Conversations from this loop are reproduced in the electronic journal, *Composition Digest,* moderator Robert Royar (COMPO1@ULKYVX).

REFERENCES

Arms, V. (1988, March) Computer conferencing: Models and proposals. *Educational Technology,* 43–45.

Bartholomae, D. (1986). Inventing the university. *Journal of Basic Writing, 5,* 4–23.

Batson, T. (1988, Feb.) The ENFI project: A networked classroom approach to writing instruction. *Academic Computing,* 32–33, 55–56.

Batson, T. (1989). Overview and philosophy—the ENFI project. *Teacher's Guide to Using Computer Networks for Written Interaction.* D. Beil, (Ed.).

Batson, T. (1989). Teaching in networked classrooms. In C. L. Selfe, D. Rodrigues, and W. R. Oates (Eds.), *Computers and the language arts: The challenge of teacher education* (pp. 247–255). Urbana, IL: NCTE.

Bizzell, P. (1988). Arguing about literacy. *College English, 50,* 141–153.

Bizzell, P. (1982). College composition: Initiation into the academic discourse community. *Curriculum Inquiry, 12,* 197–207.

Bizzell, P. (1986). Foundationalism and anti-foundationalism. *Pre/Text, 7,* 37–56.

Ehrmann, S. C. (1988, May/June). Assessing the open end of learning: Roles for new technologies. *Liberal Education, 74,* 5–11.

Eldred, J. M. (1989). Computers, composition pedagogy, and the social view. In G. E. Hawisher and C. L. Selfe (Eds.), *Critical Perspectives on Computers and Composition Instruction* (pp. 201–218). New York: Teachers College Press.

Faigley, L. (1988). Judging writing, judging selves. *College Composition and Communication, 40,* 395–412.

Hawisher, G. E. (1989). Computers and writing: Where's the research? *English Journal, 78,* 89–91.

Hawisher, G. E. (1989). Research and recommendations for computers and composition. In G. E. Hawisher and C. L. Selfe (Eds.), *Critical Perspectives on Computers and Composition Instruction* (pp. 44–69). New York: Teachers College Press.

Hiltz, S. R. (1990). Collaborative learning: The virtual classroom approach. *T.H.E. Journal, 17,* 10, 59–65.

Hiltz, S. R. (1984). *On-line communities: A case study of the office of the future.* Norwood, NJ: Ablex.

Hiltz, S. R., & Turoff, M. (1978). *The network nation: Human communication via computer.* Reading, MA: Addision-Wesley.

Kiesler, S., Siegle, J., & McGuire, T. (1984). Social psychological aspects of computer-mediated communication. *American Psychologist, 39,* 1123–1134.

Kiesler, S., Sproull, L., & Eccles. J. (1985). Pool halls, chips, and war games: Women in the culture of computing. *Psychology of Women Quarterly, 9,* 451–462.

Kiesler, S., Zubrow, D., Moser, A. M., & Geller, V. (1985). Affect in Computer-to-Terminal Discussion. *Human Computer Interaction, 1,* 77–104.

Kinkead, J. (1987). Computer conversations: E-Mail and writing instruction. *College Composition and Communication, 38,* 337–341.

Kinkead, J. (1988). Wired: Computer networks in the English classroom. *English Journal, 77,* 39–41.

Kremers, M. (1988). Adams Sherman Hill meets ENFI: An inquiry and a retrospective. *Computers and Composition, 5,* 70–77.

Peyton, J. K., & Mackinson-Smith, J. (1989). Writing and talking about writing: Computer networking with elementary students. In D. M. Johnson and D. H. Roen (Eds.), *Richness in Writing: Empowering ESL Students* (pp. 40–57). New York: Longman.

Peyton, J. K., & Miller, J. D. (1989). Dramatic interaction on a computer network: Creating worlds with words and ideas. In *Teacher's Guide to Using Computer Networks for Written Interaction.* D. Beil, (Ed.).

Rodrigues, D. (1989, March). *Electronic mail in English classes.* Paper presented at the Conference on College Composition and Communication, Seattle, WA.

Sayers, D. (1989). Bilingual sister classes in computer writing networks. In D. M. Johnson and D. H. Roen, (Eds.), *Richness in writing: Empowering ESL students* (pp. 105–125). New York: Longman.

Schriner, D. K., & Rice, W. C. (1989). Computer conferencing and collaborative learning: A discourse community at work. *College Composition and Communication, 40,* 472–478.

Schwartz, J. (1990). Using an electronic network to play the scales of discourse. *English Journal, 79,* 16–24.

Selfe, C. L. (1987). Creating a computer lab that composition teachers can live with. *Collegiate Microcomputer, 5,* 149–158.

Selfe, C. L. (1988). The humanization of computers. Forget technology, remember literacy. *English Journal, 77,* 69–71.

Selfe, C. L., & Wahlstrom, B. J. (1986). An emerging rhetoric of collaboration: Computers, collaboration, and the composing process. *Collegiate Microcomputer, 4,* 289–296.

Spitzer, M. (1989). Computer conferencing: An emerging technology. In G. E. Hawisher and C. L. Selfe (Eds.), *Critical Perspectives on Computers and Composition Instruction* (pp. 187–200). New York: Teachers College Press.

Sproull, L. & Kiesler, S. (1985). Reducing social context cues: Electronic mail in organization and communication. *Management Science, 32,* 1492–1512.

Teacher's Guide to Using Computer Networks for Written Interaction. (1989). Beil, D. (ed.).

Thompson, D. (1988, August). Conversational networking: Why the teacher gets most of the lines. *Collegiate Microcomputer, 6,* 193–201.

Thompson, D. (1988). Interactive networking: Creating bridges between speech, writing, and composition. *Computers and Composition, 5,* 17–27.

Thompson, D. (1987). Teaching writing on a local area network. *T.H.E. Journal, 15.2,* 92–97.

16

Contrasts: Teaching and Learning about Writing in Traditional and Computer Classrooms

MIKE PALMQUIST, KATE KIEFER,
JAMES HARTVIGSEN, AND
BARBARA GOODLEW

[We have] sketched the context of our studies of traditional and computer-supported writing classrooms [and then] sharpened the focus somewhat as we detailed the two studies that constitute the research focus of this text. In this chapter, we highlight the results of both the Transitions Study and the New Teachers Study and break out key issues that deserve fuller treatment in a text designed to help teachers accept the challenge of crossing the boundaries between traditional and computer-supported writing classrooms.

When we planned the two studies, our research questions focused directly on the concerns of teachers and students. We assumed that the goals of teachers would not change as they moved from one setting to another, but that teachers would use different teaching strategies to achieve them. We expected that differences between the two settings might lead students to act differently, and perhaps even to learn different things about writing. We also believed that the core of what they learned—about considering audience and purpose, about developing and supporting ideas, about planning, drafting and revising, about collaborating with each other—would be similar. Moreover, we assumed that differences in the two classroom settings might lead students to develop different attitudes about writing and possibly even different behaviors as writers and collaborators. In sum, we expected that the central goals of a writing course would be met in both settings, but with differences in the teaching and learning in traditional and computer classrooms.

With these thoughts in mind, we set out to explore in as much detail as possible the kinds of teaching and learning that occurred in the traditional and computer-supported writing classrooms in our institution. We chose not to focus on specific technologies, reasoning that the technologies would change long before the results of our studies could be shared with others.

From Palmquist, Mike, Kate Kiefer, James Hartvigsen, and Barbara Goodlew. *Transitions: Teaching Writing in Computer-supported and Traditional Classrooms.* (Greenwich: Ablex, 1998), 31–51.

Instead, we explored how teachers made the transitions between the two settings, how students and teachers interacted with each other in the two settings, and how students and teachers thought about and engaged in writing in the two settings.

As you'll see, this book is less about the impact of particular technologies on teaching and learning than it is about the impact of shifting the context for teaching and learning. Whether teachers find themselves in classrooms that rely heavily on network-supported real-time interaction or in classrooms with stand-alone computers that are used primarily for word processing, we hope that teachers will recognize and transfer results of our studies to their contexts. We do not aim to set up a model with universal application to all computer-supported writing classrooms or to define all the challenges faced by teachers moving between traditional and computer-supported writing classrooms. Instead, we provide a detailed discussion of the contexts we observed so that teachers can apply our findings to their teaching.

The questions we asked as we designed our studies focus on:

- teaching strategies and class preparation;
- teacher attitudes about teaching in the two classroom settings;
- interactions among students and between teachers and students;
- student attitudes about writing, and
- student writing performance.

In the rest of this chapter, we sketch broad outlines of our findings. In subsequent chapters [of *Transitions*], we take up in greater detail the issues raised here.

CHARACTERIZING DIFFERENCES BETWEEN TRADITIONAL AND COMPUTER-SUPPORTED WRITING CLASSROOMS

The Transitions Study and the New Teachers Study provide us with a great deal of information about teaching and learning in traditional and computer-supported writing classrooms. Our exploration of that information reveals several themes:

- Differences between classroom settings had a clear impact on daily planning, both in the kinds and the number of activities that teachers asked students to carry out.

- Teachers adopted different roles in the two classroom settings. Teachers reported that they felt the need to take charge in the traditional classrooms, leading them to conduct more front-of-the-classroom activities (large-group discussions, lectures) in the traditional classrooms than in the computer classrooms. In contrast, they indicated that they expected students to take more responsibility for their learning in the computer classrooms. They described their role in the computer classrooms as facilitator rather than leader and typically asked their students to work in small groups or to write during class rather than to engage in large-group discussions or listen to lectures.

- Students in the computer classrooms talked with their classmates and with their teachers much more frequently during class than did students in the traditional classrooms. Moreover, conversations among students in the computer classrooms tended to focus on writing, while those in the traditional classrooms tended to focus on issues unrelated to the class.

- The computer classroom functioned primarily as a work site, where students and teachers talked about writing in progress. In their interviews, teachers and students called attention to the benefits of talking about student writing as it was being written, among them the impact on revising and student improvement during the course. In contrast, teachers remarked — and students confirmed in their interviews — that students resisted writing in the traditional classrooms.

- As the semester progressed, teachers transferred successful activities from the computer classroom into the traditional classroom. In particular, they asked their students in the traditional classrooms to engage in more writing during class, and they explored ways to foster more interaction during class sessions.

- Teachers and students addressed the need to introduce new technologies to students early in the course and to link technology clearly to the goals and content of the course. However, the teachers that we observed tended to resist adopting technologies with which they were unfamiliar even when they believed the technology could help their students become better writers.

- Students in the two classroom settings differed in their attitudes about writing and in the relationships among attitudes about writing, writing performance, previous writing instruction, and interaction with classmates and teachers. Among other findings, students in the computer classrooms ended the course with higher levels of confidence in their writing ability and showed greater enthusiasm about writing than students in the traditional classrooms. Previous writing instruction also correlated with student writing performance in the computer classrooms. Students who reported that their writing instruction had focused heavily on grammar and mechanics tended to receive lower grades on their writing assignments.

In the rest of this chapter, we take up each of these themes in greater detail. Before we turn to those discussions, however, we address an issue critical to any study based on comparison — the similarities and differences between the two groups of students we studied.

Differences between Students at the Beginning of the Study

We based our study largely on comparison. In general, we looked for differences between classroom settings and changes in student behaviors and attitudes over time. To make valid comparisons, we needed to ensure — before we analyzed the data — that the groups of students we compared were similar.

To accomplish this goal, we compared scores on standardized tests and on our University's composition placement examination, and on our measures of writing anxiety, writing confidence, computer anxiety, and experience in previous writing classes. We based our comparisons on information drawn from student's academic records and from surveys administered at the beginning of the semester.

We did not find significant differences in students' test results on the English portion of the ACT or in the verbal scores on the SAT. We also found no significant differences in students' grade-point average earned in high school or in their CSU composition placement exam scores. For those students who had accumulated credits at CSU prior to taking first-year composition in our study, there were no significant differences between groups in grade point average earned at CSU or in the number of credits passed at CSU.

We saw no significant differences between the two groups of students on our measures of writing anxiety or confidence in their writing ability. We did, however, find differences in their reported levels of anxiety about using computers. In their responses to our survey at the beginning of the semester, students in the computer classrooms reported significantly lower levels of anxiety about using computers than did students in the traditional classrooms. On a one-to-five scale, with one indicating the lowest level of anxiety and five indicating the highest, students in the computer-supported classrooms had an average score of 1.76, while their peers in traditional classrooms had an average score of 1.99.

When we asked students about their experiences in previous writing courses, we found no significant differences between classroom settings in students' responses about grammar instruction. However, we found significant differences between students in the computer and traditional classrooms on our measure of process-based writing instruction. Students in the traditional classrooms indicated that they engaged in activities such as composing multiple-draft assignments and participating in peer-review workshops more frequently than did their peers in the computer classrooms. Previous process-based writing instruction was measured on a one-to-five scale, with one indicating little such instruction and five indicating high levels of process-based instruction. Students in the traditional classrooms reported an average score of 4.02 in process-based instruction, while students in the computer classrooms reported an average score of 3.74.

In general, the key differences between students in the two classroom settings were computer anxiety and process-oriented instruction in previous writing courses. The latter difference surprised us, but not the former. We believe that the difference in computer anxiety reflects students' decisions to enroll in a computer-supported or traditional class. In a traditional experimental study, students are randomly assigned to teacher and classroom setting. However, our study was conducted using a "quasi-experimental" design, that is, one in which "naturally occurring" classrooms were studied. In our case, students knew whether the course was taught in a computer-supported or a traditional classroom because a note to that effect appeared in the course catalog. The lower level of computer anxiety among students in the computer-supported classrooms may reflect a conscious decision on the part of some students to avoid the computer-supported sections or, alternatively, to seek them out. The students indicated that they "agreed" or "strongly agreed" that they weren't particularly anxious about using computers.

The difference between classroom settings in reported process-oriented instruction is more difficult to explain. We initially thought that the difference might reflect students' decision to choose a computer or traditional classroom setting, but we found only a minimal correlation ($-.060$) between computer anxiety and reported process-oriented instruction. Similarly, we saw no significant correlations between reported process-oriented instruction and standardized test scores, high school or university grade-point averages, or scores on the composition placement exam. We suspect that attempting to explain this difference would result in little more than speculation, so we leave you with the straightforward observation that a difference existed which we find difficult to explain.

We turn now to the seven themes that we identified above:

- curricular issues;
- teacher roles;
- interaction among classmates and between students and teachers;
- the classroom context;
- transfer of activities from the computer to the traditional classrooms;
- the introduction and use of technology in the computer classrooms, and;
- student attitudes and writing performance.

Curricular Issues: Relationships between Classroom Context and Class Plans

When we asked about planning, the four teachers in the Transitions Study called attention to three key differences between the classroom settings: students seemed much more interested in writing during class in the computer classrooms, the presence of computers in the computer classroom greatly expanded the range of activities that could be carried out, and the complications of using computers reduced time for activities. When students in the computer classrooms began writing, they wanted to continue writing, regardless of whether they were working on a draft of a major assignment or on an in-class exercise. Recognizing this, the teachers searched for other ways technology could support student writing—for instance, using the Internet to locate sources for writing assignments or using electronic mail to comment on drafts. As Candace told us:

> I can't see one [teaching technique] at this point, that I can't do in my computer classroom that I could do in a traditional classroom, and there's a million things that I can do in the computer classroom that I can't do in the traditional classroom.

Perhaps because in-class drafting and revising took up a significant part of class sessions in their computer-supported classrooms, the teachers told us that they felt greater flexibility in scheduling activities in the traditional classrooms. Reflecting on her experiences teaching in computer and traditional classrooms over a period of nearly 10 years, Anita observed:

In the regular classroom, there's more room for activities. I hesitate to plan tons of activities for the computer classroom because we have these wonderful tools that help the students write. And you know, you like to put them on the machines. You like to get them writing. I think in the regular classroom, I'm more apt to group them up and make them talk about a study question and so on.

In addition to concerns about the activities they wanted to use in each classroom, the four teachers told us that they struggled with questions of how similar they wanted their daily plans to be. Although their goals as teachers remained the same regardless of classroom setting, they discovered that techniques which worked successfully in one classroom did not work as well—or even at all—in the other. Caitlin learned, for instance, that whole-class discussion—a technique at which she was adept in the traditional classroom—did not succeed in the computer classroom:

When I was trying to do the same lesson plan in the traditional classroom and the computer classroom, whole-class discussion was just not working in the computer classroom. My students weren't focused in on it, they weren't getting the main points that I wanted them to get out of the discussion. They weren't thinking. I knew they could think that way and they just weren't doing it. And so, you know, I'd come back and think, "My gosh! My morning class, they came up with this and this and this and this." And so, I stopped and thought, "Am I doing something wrong because I'm in the computer classroom? Do I need to structure this differently?" And so, I moved away from whole-class discussion and we don't have very much. . . . I try to make everything tie back very directly with what the students are writing. But even more specifically, that seems to need to happen in the computer classroom and I wasn't doing that as well as I should have in the beginning.

Caitlin adds that she initially thought the problem with full-class discussions stemmed from her students. "When I started thinking about the differences, my thought process was 'What are the differences between my traditional classroom and my computer classroom? Well, my traditional classroom is going well. My computer classroom, my students are just dumb.'" When she stepped back from that line of thought, she says, she began to consider seriously the differences in classroom contexts, which led to class plans containing different mixes of front-of-the-classroom instruction, group work, and in-class drafting.

Adapting Teaching Roles to Classroom Context

In addition to differences in the minds and number of activities that the teachers used in each setting, they called attention to differences in the roles that they adopted in each classroom. Each of the four teachers in the Transitions Study commented that they differed in the way they related to their students and in what they expected from their students. In general, the four teachers believed in a student-centered approach to teaching composition. Yet they found themselves relying on activities that were more teacher-centered in the traditional classroom, such as lecture and whole-class discussion, and on activities that were more student-centered in the computer classroom, such as in-class drafting and mini-conferences. At least in part, these differences stemmed from what they expected from students in each classroom. Caitlin indicated that she expected students in the computer classroom to take more responsibility for their own learning:

> I would say I do a better job of making my students more personally responsible for figuring things out on their own in the computer classroom . . . I give them a chance to write, to discuss a little bit, with their peers around them and then I ask, "Do you have any questions? Is there anything you feel like we need to talk about?" And then we'll move on. And so they're more responsible, I would say, for saying, "This is a problem, I don't understand this." Or "I don't know what's going on." Where, because I think I have whole-class discussion in the traditional classroom, I feed them more information."

Similarly, Anita said that she expected more from the students in her computer classrooms:

> Teaching in the regular classroom, I feel the need to orchestrate much more. "Okay, we're going to do this, this, this, and this. Students, okay, get prepared to do this, blah, blah, blah. Okay, now we're going to do this." In the computer classroom, we always have a mission. . . . I literally could go in there and say, "Okay, pre-write." And they would know how to do it . . . I could say, "Okay, read this story and write a paragraph on whatever." And that would be perfectly okay. It wouldn't seem lazy; it wouldn't seem like I wasn't doing my job.

These differences in expectations affected the degree to which the teachers saw themselves as leaders or facilitators and the extent to which they adopted a formal or informal stance in the classroom. For Anita, this meant that she took on different teaching roles in each classroom:

> I'm more of an organizer in the regular classroom. I'm more of a facilitator in the computer classroom . . . When I facilitate, I'll let the student determine how they need me. In the regular classroom, I have to predetermine how the students need me and then I have to make that work. In the computer classroom, I let them determine what they need from me more so. If you're a good instructor, you'll make sure you're moving the thought processes toward the end goal—more effective writing. But I find it much more unstructured in the computer classroom.

The other teachers echoed Anita's comments, describing the different roles they adopted in terms of formality, teacher-centered versus student-centered teaching, and coaching metaphors. In each case, the teachers felt that they adopted the role of leader in the traditional classroom and of supporter in the computer classroom.

Interaction Among Classmates and between Students and Teachers

One of the most striking differences between the two classroom settings was interaction during class sessions. Our observations of the classrooms, along with student and teacher reports of their interactions, indicate that students in the computer classrooms had significantly higher numbers of contacts with classmates and teachers than did students in the traditional classrooms. Moreover, our observations and our interviews with students suggest that the interactions among students in the computer classrooms focused on writing, rather than social issues, while the opposite was true of interactions among students in the traditional classrooms. Commenting on the differences in her interactions with students in the two classrooms, Jen observed:

> I think it's different just because you get to walk around while they're drafting, and you can interact with them very much during the drafting phase . . . I try to do that in the traditional classroom when they're in workshop, but I think it's harder because they do less up-front drafting and revising in the classroom.

The other teachers echoed Jen's observation that the workshop atmosphere of the computer classroom contributed to their higher level of interaction with students. In addition, they noted that the majority of their interactions with students in the computer classroom were initiated by students and focused directly on their writing. Caitlin explained:

> The contact that I have with students is more closely related to the writing project that they're working on. And a lot of it is more student solicited.

> They're the ones that determine when they want me to help them with their writing, rather than me saying in the traditional classroom, "Okay, on Tuesday and Wednesday, we're going to have conferences." I have conferences with my students continuously in the computer classroom.

In contrast, noted Caitlin, the traditional classroom typically fostered different kinds of interactions between teachers and students:

> I think that a student in the traditional classroom has access to me the whole 50 minutes that we're in that classroom too, but so often things are large-group oriented that a student has to break out of that large group and ask an independent question that might be related very specifically to something on his or her draft and may not feel as free to do that as in the computer classroom where people are working very independently with input all of the time from the people around them. [In the computer classroom,] it's not such a break maybe in the flow of the class for an individual student to say, "Hey, Caitlin. Come over here and look at this."

In only one category of interaction—student contact with teachers outside of class—did the traditional classrooms have higher levels of contact than the computer classrooms. Yet this may stem less from reluctance on the part of students in the computer classrooms to seek out their teachers outside of class than from the sense that they didn't need to do so. A student in Anita's class said during an interview at the end of the semester:

> She leaves herself very open to just going up to her and ask her if she thought this was a good person to interview or if this resource would help or questions like that. I never went and made an appointment with her to discuss a paper outside of class, but that was mainly because during class I usually got a lot of her attention, and she would come around and make sure that she answered everyone's questions. Or did her best to. And she was very helpful. Very, very helpful.

A further factor that complicates direct comparison of out-of-class contacts is electronic interaction. If we include out-of-class interactions via electronic mail between teachers and students in our measure of out-of-class contact, then the computer classroom has a higher average level of student-teacher contact outside the classroom. Yet we must ask ourselves whether an electronic mail message is equivalent to a face-to-face meeting between a student and teacher. Counting electronic mail as a replacement for face-to-face contact is probably appropriate if the subject of the message is something that can be dealt with quickly and without the need for subsequent elaboration, as might be the case when a student asks about a homework assignment. When the subject of an electronic mail message concerns something as complex as the overall direction of a revision plan or a student's behavior during class, however, we suspect that teachers might prefer to discuss the issue with a student face-to-face.

Keeping these complications in mind, our analysis of the interaction data suggests that significantly more discussions of student writing occurred among classmates and between students and teachers in the computer classroom. In Chapter Four [of *Transitions*], we discuss in greater detail the types of interaction and the conditions that appear to have fostered them in the computer classroom.

The Classroom Context: Workshop Atmosphere Versus Traditional Atmosphere

A major reason for the higher levels of interaction in the computer classroom is a difference in the kind of work that took place in each classroom. We can describe the traditional classroom as a place where *writing was discussed*—during, for instance, lecture, whole-class discussion, group activities, or peer-review sessions. In contrast, we can describe the computer classroom as a place where *writing was done*—either during writing activities designed to prepare students for major writing assignments or during drafting or revising sessions for those major assignments. Each of the four teachers remarked on the extent to which the computer classroom immersed students in their writing and on the extent to which it fostered a workshop atmosphere with ongoing dialogue about students' writing. As Anita remarked:

> The computer classroom is much more writing oriented. You can say, "We're going to draft today." And you can't do that in a regular classroom. That time is so wonderful because students don't just sit and draft. They talk to their neighbor about their draft. They ask you questions. You filter around the room, it becomes a giant workshop. And yet, students are producing, so it's a workshop with some production going on. It's really pretty marvelous.

In contrast, the teachers felt that their students in the traditional classrooms resisted writing during class. In some cases, students felt that the writing they were asked to do in class was a waste of time, since they simply retyped it when they worked on their computers or word processors outside of class. In other cases, students apparently resisted because the notion of writing in a writing class was outside their experience and expectations. As Candace said:

> It's almost impossible to get people to draft with a pen and piece of paper in the traditional classroom . . . If I have students sitting around in a circle doing freewriting by hand, I find that they're resistant. They're lethargic. They roll their eyes. They often don't want to do it.

One of the students in a traditional classroom clearly voiced his resistance to writing during class. When asked how the class might be improved, he responded:

> I would say like don't have too much free time in class where you expect the students to write, you know . . . I didn't find it as helpful for me to try to write in class there . . . It was just difficult to try to write in that setting. . . .

Transferring Activities from the Computer Classroom to the Traditional Classroom

As the semester progressed, the teachers commented in their interviews and teaching logs that they were beginning to transfer teaching strategies and classroom activities from the computer to the traditional classrooms. They attempted to create a workshop atmosphere in the traditional classrooms by requiring more in-class drafting, by encouraging more interaction during class, and occasionally by moving class sessions out of the classroom. They attempted to shift the focus of class sessions from the teacher to the students. And they attempted to adapt technology-based activities for use in the traditional classroom. Although these attempts met with varying degrees of success, they clearly indicate that the transfer of teaching skills between traditional and computer classrooms moves in both directions.

The attempt to create a workshop atmosphere in the traditional classroom was a clear response to what the teachers valued in their teaching in the computer classrooms. The teachers indicated in their interviews and teaching logs that they were optimistic about transferring to the traditional classroom some of the energy and enthusiasm exhibited by their students in the computer classroom. All the teachers indicated that they asked their traditional students to write more during class. Caitlin pointed out that she began to ask students in her traditional classrooms to use the DAILY activity that was used extensively in the computer classrooms. Adapting DAILY for the traditional classroom was fairly simple, according to Caitlin:

> I start a lot of my classes with "write-to-learn" type of activity. In the traditional classroom, it's just on the board and they begin class by coming in and sitting down and writing. In the computer classroom, it's in the DAILY. They come in and they access the DAILY and they get going. And so, I see that's something I didn't do as much in the traditional classroom before I taught in the computer classroom and that's something I think I've carried over.

In addition to incorporating more writing into their traditional classroom sessions, the teachers also made an effort to encourage more interaction in their traditional classrooms. Jen, the only one of the four teachers who consistently arranged the desks in her traditional classroom in rows rather than a circle, explained that she had initially viewed the rows as a barrier between her and her students. As the semester progressed, she worked to break down that barrier:

> I mean, I'm not scared of the rows. I used to be terrified of them, but now it doesn't make much difference. I'll walk down. I'll sit with students. I'll mingle because I think that's how I teach best, and I think that's how they learn best. They get lots of one on one help, and . . . a lot of that carries over from the computer room . . . Working in a computer lab may have helped me get to that point where I'm not scared to go into the middle of them and say "hey" and sit with them.

Caitlin adopted a different technique to encourage interaction between herself and her students. Taking a cue from the willingness of students in her computer classroom to discuss their writing with her, she actively encouraged her students in her traditional classroom to seek her out:

> What I ended up doing, kind of I think as an adjustment . . . I would write notes to them on their paper about things that were going on. But then, I would also say, "Why don't you come up and talk to me about this during class?" Then I could reinforce what I had written on their paper with some verbal conversation about it too. Because I saw how effective that was in the computer classroom.

A third strategy that the teachers used to make the traditional classroom more like a workshop was to change the location of class. Some class sessions were held in the library, where students worked one-on-one with their teacher while they looked for sources. Sometimes class sessions were canceled so that students could meet for extended conferences with their teachers. On still other occasions, classes were held in a location, such as an art gallery, where students wrote about what they saw around them.

In addition to creating a workshop atmosphere in the traditional classroom, the teachers also shifted the focus of the traditional classroom from the teacher to the students. Their desire to create a more student-centered environment in the traditional classroom may have resulted from the different levels of enthusiasm they saw among the two groups of students. It may have resulted from a desire to make students in the traditional classrooms more responsible for their own learning. Or it may have resulted from a strong belief that a student-centered approach to teaching writing is more effective than a teacher-centered approach. In their interviews, the teachers touched on one or more of these reasons. Caitlin realized that she wanted to move away from her initial training as a front-of-the-classroom teacher:

> I was trained by an education department to be a teacher. And what that means for many education departments is that you are THE teacher. And you do THE teaching. And it's taken me time to be able to give up that power in a sense . . . I knew I wanted to go in that direction with my teaching, but it was expedited by the computer classroom. Because it doesn't work to be the center of attention and to be ringleader in the computer classroom. There are a lot more interesting things in there—computers—than the teacher . . . So when I returned, then, to the traditional classroom, I didn't feel the need to be in that position again.

Teachers also adapted activities that relied on various technologies, such as commenting on a series of messages on a class bulletin board, for use in the traditional classroom. The DAILY exercises exemplify this transfer, but the teachers also explored how activities designed for electronic mail and electronic bulletin boards might fit into traditional classrooms. In her interview at the middle of the semester, Caitlin talked about her plans to adapt one of these activities:

> I thought about what I wanted my students to do in the computer classroom as far as discussion of e-mail and responding to each other's e-mail messages and things. So then I thought, "How can I have the same kind of discussion in the traditional classroom," so, I'm going to try and do it on paper. They each have a piece of paper and they write some ideas or thoughts or opinions and we kind of do the round robin thing where they pass it around the room and try to figure out, you know, in the end it'll come back to them. And hopefully then they'll be doing some responding to the responses that people put on their paper. . . .

Introducing and Using Technologies

One of the most important questions we addressed in the Transitions and New Teachers Studies concerned the use and introduction of technologies in the computer classrooms. In interviews, teachers and students addressed the need to introduce new technologies to students early in the course and to link that introduction clearly to the goals and content of the course. However, the teachers resisted adopting technologies with which they were unfamiliar even when they believed the technology could help their students become better writers.

In the Transitions Study, the teachers were particularly interested in how they might more effectively introduce students to the technology available in the computer classrooms, particularly word processing, electronic mail, and Internet tools. The techniques they discussed ranged from providing detailed handouts to students to demonstrating the programs using LCD displays to providing almost no guidance and allowing the students to figure it out on their own. In all cases, the teachers indicated that computer use should begin on the first day and should directly support writing activities. One key concern the teachers voiced was the danger of separating the technology from the goals of the class. Ellen, who participated in the New Teachers Study, reflected on the changes she had made from her first semester in the computer classroom to the second:

> This semester I was much better in implementing the technology into the actual goals of what I wanted for the class. And of having the technology become part of that instead of thinking of the technology as something separate that I had to teach. I basically taught the technology in terms of what I thought was important for the writing class.

Like Ellen, Jen was concerned about the dangers of separating the technology from the course goals. In her final interview, she called attention to the downfall of using the technology simply because it was there, rather than because it met a specific course goal:

> I think it might be easy to be lulled into feeling that the technology is just so great, but you could end up taking up class time that they really need for all the things that we're trying to teach them. [Interviewer: So you can get lost in the technology?] Yeah, waste a lot of time setting up stuff for them to do which really—what did it teach them? It might have been fun. It might have been novel, but did it really help them become better writers?

As we worked with the teachers in both studies, we noted that all of them resisted using some technologies even when they felt that effective use of the technologies would benefit their students. The common thread running through the teachers' resistance to using certain technologies was a concern that, if the teachers did not feel confident using a particular program, then it couldn't be used effectively. For some teachers, this resistance was based on experience in the classroom. Candace explained in her mid-semester interview:

> There is a point where it really slowed me down and we didn't get much done for about two weeks while we were trying to figure [electronic mail] out. And now I've sort of had to find a balance between using it and not using it. I'm using it a lot more than I was last semester, but probably not as much as Mike would like to see me using it. I've had to find a workable balance, because we were spending so much time figuring it out. It really started to get in the way, and that's the point where I just pulled back and

said, "OK, we're gonna use this and this," but, for example, we haven't used attachments very much. I'd like to use it again at least once more and they do send each other mail. And I encourage them to send me mail.

One of the teachers simply refused to move beyond her comfort zone in the computer classroom. By the middle of the semester, Anita, who had the most experience teaching in computer classrooms of all the teachers in the two studies, used the computers in an extremely limited fashion:

I've gone back, even though I have WordPerfect with Windows and SharkMail and all of that, I've really gone back to using the computer the way I did before, as a real helpful tool for word processing. . . .

Student Attitudes about Writing, Student Writing Performance, and Relationships among Attitudes, Performance, and Interaction with Classmates and Teachers

In this section, we provide additional results of the transition study. The issues we cover in these sections have important implications for understanding the context of the two classroom settings. As topics in and of themselves, however, they do not lend themselves to detailed discussions. Because we want you to have access to as much information about the study as possible, however, we provide summaries of key findings in six areas:

1. computer anxiety;
2. writing confidence;
3. student perceptions of the helpfulness of feedback from teachers;
4. students' willingness to talk with their teachers;
5. student writing performance; and
6. the relationships between writing performance, attitudes about writing, and interaction with classmates and teachers.

Computer Anxiety

We used surveys to track differences in student attitudes about writing and computers. As it did at the beginning of the semester, our end-of-the-semester survey indicated significant differences in computer anxiety between students in the traditional and computer-supported classrooms. On a one-to-five scale, with one indicating the lowest level of anxiety and five indicating the highest, students in the computer-supported classrooms averaged a score of 1.68 while students in the traditional classrooms averaged a score of 1.88. These scores decreased in both settings from the beginning of the semester.

Writing Confidence

At the end of the semester, students in the computer classrooms reported higher levels of writing confidence than did their peers in the traditional classrooms. Writing confidence was measured on a one-to-five scale, with one indicating low confidence in writing ability and five indicating high confidence. At the end of the semester, students in the computer classrooms had an average score on the writing confidence scale of 3.54, while students in the traditional classrooms had a mean score of 3.33. Students in the computer classrooms also showed a significant increase in writing confidence over the course of the semester, with the average score rising from 3.43 at the beginning of the semester to 3.54 at the end. Students in the traditional classrooms showed no parallel increase.

The actual difference between the two classrooms, although statistically significant, is not large in a practical sense. We can't say, for instance, that students in the computer classrooms completed the semester feeling twice as confident as students in the traditional classrooms. However, the pattern is one that we believe is important. Not only was there a significant difference at the end of the semester, but there was a significant increase (when each student's scores at the beginning and end of the semester are compared) over the course of the semester in the computer classrooms but not in the traditional classroom. Students left the computer classrooms with more confidence in their writing ability than they had when they started the semester and were, on average, more confident in their writing ability at the end of the semester than were students in the traditional classrooms.

Student Perceptions of the Helpfulness of Feedback from Teachers and of Their Willingness to Talk with Teachers

Students in the traditional classrooms reported significantly higher perceptions of the helpfulness of comments received from teachers and willingness to talk to teachers about their writing than did students in the computer classrooms (see Figure 16.1). We rated each of the measures on one-to-five scales,

FIGURE 16.1   Perceived Helpfulness of Student and Teacher Comments and Willingness to Talk with Teachers (From End-of-Semester Survey).

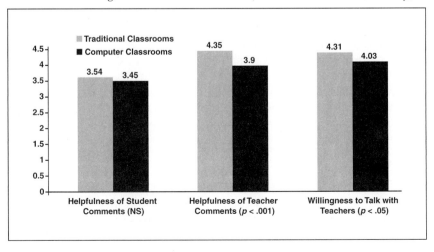

with a score of one indicating low levels of perceived helpfulness or willingness to talk with teachers and a score of five indicating high levels of perceived helpfulness or willingness to talk with teachers. Students in the traditional classrooms averaged 4.35 for helpfulness of teacher comments, while students in the computer classroom averaged 3.90. Students in the traditional classrooms also averaged 4.31 on willingness to talk with teachers, while students in the computer classrooms averaged 4.03.

These differences in perceived helpfulness of teacher comments and reported willingness to talk with teachers surprised us. We had assumed that the higher overall levels of interaction between teachers and students in the computer classrooms that we observed and that students reported in their weekly interaction reports would translate into higher levels of perceived willingness to talk with teachers and perceived helpfulness of teacher comments.

We suspect that these perceived differences might reflect the kinds of comments that students in the two classrooms received from their teachers. The majority of feedback that students in the traditional classrooms received came in the form of written responses to graded assignments. In the computer classrooms, however, students received a great deal of additional feedback on their writing, not only after they had turned it in for a grade but also *as they were writing*. It seems possible that the atmosphere in the computer classroom, in which interactions between students and teachers were fairly casual and relatively frequent (compared to those in the traditional classrooms), contributed to students seeing their teacher's feedback on their papers as simply one more voice offering suggestions. In both classroom settings, students rated their teachers' comments as more helpful than their classmates' comments. But the rating for perceived helpfulness of teachers' comments was significantly higher in the traditional classrooms than in the computer classrooms. The average difference in perceived helpfulness was twice as large, in fact, in the traditional classrooms as it was in the computer classrooms.

Perhaps students in the computer classroom become more comfortable with feedback from their teachers than did students in the traditional classroom. In the computer classrooms, feedback from teachers became commonplace while, in the traditional classrooms, feedback was something out of the ordinary. In making this argument, we do not want to suggest that it's simply a case of familiarity breeding contempt so much as we want to suggest that frequent feedback on writing afforded by the computer classroom may have altered students' perceptions of the overall value of that feedback. It may be, of course, that the teachers were doing a better job of providing feedback to their traditional classroom students, but our classroom observations and our analysis of the written feedback that students received do not support this explanation.

Student Writing Performance

We did not find any differences in student writing performance between the two settings. Students received comparable grades on their written assignments and had comparable levels of quality in their writing. Students in the computer classrooms, however, both wrote more and appeared more willing to write during class than were their peers in the traditional classrooms. They also revised more frequently than did their peers in the traditional classrooms.

Relationships among Writing Performance, Attitudes about Writing, and Interaction with Classmates and Teachers

We observed a number of differences between classroom settings in the relationships between writing performance, attitudes about writing, and interaction with classmates and teachers. Those differences include relationships between writing anxiety and interaction, student confidence in their writing ability and interaction, grades and interaction, and grades and previous writing instruction.

We found, in the computer classrooms but not in the traditional classrooms, that students with higher levels of writing anxiety were less likely to talk with their teachers before or after class and less likely to indicate a willingness to seek out their teachers of classmates outside of class. These students, however, were more likely than their classmates to communicate with their teachers by electronic mail (see Table 16.1). In the future, we hope to pursue questions about students' writing anxiety and out-of-class contact with teachers because these preliminary findings suggest that computer technologies may provide a specific benefit for these students.

We also saw, in the traditional classrooms but not the computer classrooms, that students with higher levels of confidence in their writing ability were less likely to interact with classmates outside of the classroom—and, conversely, that students with lower levels of confidence in their writing ability were more likely to interact with classmates outside of class (see Table 16.1). Again, we hope to follow up on the research reported here with additional study. We are particularly interested in identifying teaching strategies that encourage increased interaction during and outside of class.

Our third key finding concerning interaction applied to the traditional classrooms but not to the computer classrooms. In the traditional classrooms, grades for the course and for the second portfolio were negatively correlated with student/teacher contact outside of class and immediately before and after class (see Table 16.1). Similarly, in the traditional classrooms but not in the computer classrooms, scores on standardized tests (the ACT English score) were negatively correlated with frequency of out-of-class contact between students and teachers (see Table 16.1). We understand why students who feel more successful in class feel less need to seek out teachers, but the difference between the level of contact and setting surprised us. We look at these data in much more detail in Chapter Four [of *Transitions*] when we examine specific levels of contact and grades.

Finally, in the computer classrooms but not in the traditional classrooms, students who reported higher levels of prior instruction that focused on grammar and mechanics had lower grades for the first portfolio, the second portfolio, and the course (see Table 16.1). Recall that at the beginning of the

TABLE 16.1 Selected Correlations Across Classroom Settings

Measure 1	Measure 2	Traditional Classrooms			Computer Classrooms		
		r	n	p	r	n	p
Writing Anxiety (beginning of semester)	Contacts Reported by Teachers that Occurred Immediately Before and After Class	.052	86	.634	-.231	78	.042
Writing Anxiety (end of semester)	Reported Willingness to Seek Feedback from Teachers or Classmates Outside of Class	-.194	84	.076	-.334	77	.003
Writing Anxiety (end of semester)	Total E-mail Between Student and Teacher	—	—	—	.263	77	.021
Confidence in Writing Ability (beginning of semester)	Reported Out-of-Class Contacts with Classmates	-.353	85	.001	.005	78	.963
Confidence in Writing Ability (end of semester)	Reported Out-of-Class Contacts with Classmates	-.245	84	.024	.050	78	.665
Grade for Course	Student Reported Contact with Teachers Outside of Class	-.232	90	.027	.070	83	.530
Grade for Course	Teacher Reported Contact with Students Immediately Before or After Class, Total	-.257	90	.014	.072	83	.517

Measure 1	Measure 2	Traditional Classrooms			Computer Classrooms		
		r	n	p	r	n	p
Grade for Course	Teacher Reported Contact with Students Immediately Before or After Class, Teacher Initiated	−.271	90	.001	−.082	83	.460
Grade on Second Portfolio	Student Reported Contact with Teachers Outside of Class	−.261	90	.013	.266	83	.015
Grade on First Portfolio	Previous Writing Instruction that Focused on Grammar	−.037	64	.771	−.257	59	.049
Grade on Second Portfolio	Previous Writing Instructions that Focused on Grammar	−.013	85	.905	−.258	79	.022
Grade for Course	Previous Writing Instruction that Focused on Grammar	−.068	85	.535	−.260	79	.021
ACT English Score	Student Reported Contact with Teachers Outside of Class	−.301	66	.014	.033	63	.797
ACT English Score	Teacher Reported Contact with Students Outside of Class	−.402	66	.001	−.175	63	.171

semester, we found no significant overall difference between classroom settings in the amount of prior instruction focusing on grammar. This suggests to us that the dynamic of the computer classroom builds on skills that receive less attention in courses that focus heavily on grammar and mechanics. We suspect that the difference between the two groups reflects the greater emphasis on a workshop environment in the computer classrooms. Students who reported higher levels of previous writing instruction that focused on grammar and mechanics may have entered the computer classrooms at a disadvantage. Because their prior instruction focused more heavily on the product of writing, they may have been unprepared for a classroom environment that emphasized the process of writing. Clearly, writing teachers should consider this issue should they choose to teach in a computer-supported writing classroom. Teachers may find it helpful to determine if some of the students in their classes need additional help adapting to a classroom in which writing, revising, and interaction are so strongly emphasized.

CONTRASTS OR CONTINUUM

This chapter has focused on contrasts between the students in our traditional and computer classrooms, but we hesitate to conclude this chapter on that note. Although we pursue the differences between classroom settings in the next several chapters, remember that these differences represent a *continuum of change*. The differences are not black and white; the teachers in our studies do not throw out everything they know about teaching just because they move from one setting to the other. Rather, as they move between settings they adapt—to the setting and to their students.

17 Rethinking Validity and Reliability in the Age of Convergence

DIANE PENROD

The commonsense notion in Composition Studies is to create assessment strategies that correspond to our pedagogical practices. When writing teachers use the traditional quantitative understandings of validity and reliability to evaluate their students' e-texts, instructors are doing the opposite of what past wisdom suggests. New methods and processes in technology, similar to new methods and processes in the teaching of writing, requires users to reexamine older practices that measure how far, how fast, or how accurate is the recent change. Often this reweighing of earlier ways comes from inaccuracies discovered during an evaluation, from a shift in perspective that allows a different view to emerge, or from more information learned over time. For writing assessment in an age of convergence, all three possibilities contribute to the importance of rethinking the old standby concepts of validity and reliability to address students' written competence because computers have provided a (r)evolutionary movement in the teaching of writing.

Validity and reliability are the two epistemiological cornerstones of assessment, this much writing teachers know. Because reliability is easier to define, left me start there. Simply put, *reliability* refers to the ability to consistently give the same answer at different points in time. Reliability depends on three factors: the stability of a result to withstand time, the internal consistency of performance along a scale, and the ability of two parallel forms to measure the same concept (Wimmer & Dominick, 1997, pp. 54–55).[1]

Validity frequently is defined as whether a test measures what it is supposed to measure. There are many, many other forms of validity that can affect an assessment, however. Evaluators look to see whether a test has face validity, predictive validity, concurrent validity, and construct validity to determine whether a test's questions gauge the information fairly for what the question asks of the respondent (Wimmer & Dominick, 1997, pp. 55–56). More

From Penrod, Diane. *Composition in Convergence: The Impact of New Media on Writing Assessment.* Mahwah: Erlbaum, 2005. 87–115.

precisely in performance situations, such as a writing exam, validity addresses the significance of test scores. Samuel Messick, of ETS, following education research L. J. Cronbach's view of test validation, stated that

> these scores are a function not only of the items or stimulus conditions but also of the persons responding as well as the context of the assessment. In particular, what needs to be valid is the meaning or interpretation of the scores as well as any implications for action that this meaning entails. (1989, p. 15)

Generally speaking, for most genuine writing evaluation circumstances, validity is not a totalizing situation; validity depends on the evaluators' skill in judging whether an item measures what it is supposed to. Even Messick (1989) supported this position. For Messick, validity, like reliability, involves "social values that have meaning and force whenever evaluative judgments and decisions are made" (1989, p. 17). So to some degree, validity is a subjective interpretative process. Because of the social value and subjective aspects of validity, there is an inherently political side to validating a student writer's ability.

What makes Composition's use of validity and reliability particularly problematic is etymology. The terms *validity* and *reliability* are historically grounded in the scientific approach to knowledge and knowledge making, as well as the psychometric approach to test measurement, which assumes several conditions for the composing process:

- *Writing is orderly and can be regulated.* In the scientific method, all actions and events happen in a regular, orderly manner. Even when an environment is under great change and rapid fluctuation, scientists presume there is still a degree of order that can be observed under any condition.

- *Writing is a knowable object.* The assumption that anyone can "know" writing is without proof. However, test and measurement practitioners who follow the scientific method argue that writers, like other natural objects that exist in the world and have unique characteristics, can be understood and their actions explained by the same methods used to study other natural phenomena.

- *All writing has natural causes. Natural* in the scientific sense means not rooted in fundamentally religious, supernatural, or magical forces. Once an object is determined to be natural, then a cause-and-effect relation can be discerned. Depending on one's personal or cultural philosophy, this statement can be debated.

- *Writing is drawn from the acquisition of experiences.* In the scientific approach, writing is empirical because it relies on perceptions, experience, and observations. Individuals' perceptions arise from sensory and abstract situations. Moreover, experiences give rise to a knowledge base, as interactions with the physical and social world affect one's perceptions. Observations allow persons to make generalizations, speculations, and inferences based on earlier perceptions and experiences.

Therefore, the epistemic principles of validity and reliability in writing assessment will create a sense of understanding about writing using a methodology based on an arrangement of clear, normed rules and procedures. These rules and procedures construct a system of evaluation that permits ordered observations, inferences, generalizations, predictions, and analyses. Yet, as Messick and educational researcher M. T. Kane have indicated, the resultant scores that emerge from these evaluation systems supposedly connect to "relevant content and operative processes" that are "presumed to be reflected in scores that concatenate responses in domain-appropriate ways and are generalizable across a range of tasks, settings and occasions" (Nachmias & Nachmias, 1981, p. 145). However, what happens far more often is that the interpretations and actions derived from the scores are "typically extrapolated beyond the test context on the basis of documented or presumed relationships with nontest behaviors and anticipated outcomes or consequences" (Nachmias & Nachmias, 1981, p. 146).

As with most things, in practice, ideas such as validity and reliability are more complex than they are simple—particularly when the concepts are applied to something with as many variables and issues as writing. Writing specialists need to understand that an assessment tool has to be evaluated against other characteristics to conclude its worth as a measurement instrument. Assessment instruments are only useful when they are both reliable and valid, and far too often in something like the evaluation of real writing outside of highly constrained test conditions, the chance for attaining solid confidence levels for validity and reliability is nearly impossible.

Now, I'll concede that some assessment proponents might differ with my observations. These individuals will argue that holistic essay scoring and portfolio reading have depended on behaviorism's recognition of validity and reliability for decades to offer credibility. If real validity and reliability exist in these situations, though, it is usually because the students' test conditions provide a veneer on the process that tricks teachers, departments, and institutions into thinking and believing that their exam is reliable and valid. Let me argue here that most writing assessment instruments are unreliable for several reasons, from students misunderstanding the prompt's wording or its expectations to instability in students' responses (which could be a sign of growth or cheating instead of an error, but only in clearcut cases is one ever quite sure) to a lack of internal consistency to a problem with intercoder reliability (commonly called "splits" in holistic readings). In the language of tests and measurements, these lapses are called *variable errors* because the "error varies from one observation to the next and also because the error is different each time it is measured" (Lauer & Asher, 1988, p. 140). Rarely will a writing assessment tool give a consistent, stable, equivalent result, which is what evaluators look for in a reliable measurement instrument because too many variable errors have the potential to exist each time an evaluation opportunity occurs. Composition researchers Janice Lauer and William Asher (1988) noted that the precision of the criteria, the amount and quality of the procedures used in evaluator training, the continual monitoring of readers during an evaluation session, the speed of rating, and the readers' background and attitudes all affect reliability. To that list, in the age of convergence, writing teachers can now add the medium used to produce the text.

Writing programs that depend on stability in their assessment instrument scores may not be accurately evaluating their student writers. Usually, group stability in a writing assessment is virtually nil, as I have tried to show, which is what writing instructors should expect. After all, if stability occurs in a student's assessment over time, then growth has not occurred. For this reason, writing specialists should tread carefully if they are basing their assessment instrument's reliability on its stability in an exam environment. This is even more concern for caution if the student is working with new technological media to write the exam. Student writers' abilities can and do change over time, especially with their facility in using computer programs. Assess students' skills too soon or too long a period after introducing new material or software, and false results can occur. If faculty are expecting stability to happen with the test, a student's higher score on a second round may not necessarily indicate a flaw in the testing tool. Other variables, such as greater or lesser comfort levels with composing on screen or the students' familiarity with the software program, can make a difference in student scores.

Given the difficulties regarding variable errors, consistency of results is also difficult to maintain in a writing assessment. In the psychometric model, consistency in assessment should not turn up any conflicting elements. For instance, a consistent reader is expected to read in accordance with other readers. Or a writer is expected to make consistent errors or possess a consistent style on the task. Of course, writing instructors know that consistency in assessment is also subject to error. Any change in genre can expose different writing errors or a shift in voice, tone, or word choice. Certain types of assignments—such as argumentative writing—create more errors in students' writing because of the increased demands the activity places on the thinking and information-gathering processes and because ecological or individualistic fallacies that teachers have about writing interfere with readers' abilities to make decisions on many of these pieces.[2]

Equivalence frequently causes problems in writing assessment, which affects an assessment's reliability. As Lauer and Asher (1988) described equivalency reliability, two sets of test scores given simultaneously to a sampling of people are correlated to each other. All aspects of the data must be the same (equivalent) such as the averages, standard deviations, and average intercorrelations among items before running a correlation of the data. Although equivalence works well with a standardized, indirect writing test, the problem arises with holistic readings of essays and portfolios, because the data across two assessment settings may not be equivalent based on variable error. It is entirely possible to have differing averages, standard deviations, and average intercorrelations among items that can skew correlations.

Validity is also a problem for writing mechanism because of errors caused by the lack of face validity. This is simple error in that the test does not measure what it appears to measure on the surface of the test. But other problems for validity exist as well. The inability of a testing instrument—whether testing indirect or direct writing—to predict a student's future success in writing can also affect some forms of validity. So can unstated criteria used to pretest the assessment mechanism affect some aspects of validity. Moreover, validity can also be affected by the lack of connecting an essay, portfolio, or multiple-choice exam to any departmental or pedagogical framework.

Too often writing faculty and their departments go for the easy form of validity, face validity, as their defense against other problems in the assessment mechanism. The difficulty with this practice is that an evaluation tool can have face validity and be completely invalid in the more important areas of tests and measurements. Of course, when many compositionists realize this point—generally when they are in some administrative or other across-the-campus meeting—the results are sometimes less than amiable. Writing faculty need to be aware that problems of validity frequently occur in assessment because writing is an indirect process, and, if educational researchers are truthful about the subject, no one is totally certain that what is being measured in a piece of writing is precisely what is intended to be measured. This is not a flaw with the teaching faculty or the students' achievements in the class; this is a condition of trying to evaluate the unknowable—that is, how each person creates a written product. After all, there are significant connections to craft and to aesthetics in writing, and those variables cannot be measured objectively and quantified.

How validity and reliability have been presented in writing assessment, especially in writing assessment that is post-indirect method, reflects the language of an earlier, psychometric understanding of writing. For psychometricians, writing can be reduced to discrete variables addressed by multiple choice quantifiers. So, it makes sense that terms applicable to quantifiable research be used to describe evaluation. Composition, writing instructors should hope, has moved beyond this point. In the last 25 years, the field of Composition Studies has progressed in the direction of qualitative and action research methodology in both its scholarship and assessment philosophies. The advent of poststructuralism and postmodernism ushered in social constructivism, ethnography, content analysis, and discourse analysis—none of which paralleled the quantitative processes. Consequently, changes have occurred in the ways in which writing assessment is conducted. Holistic scoring, in principle, corresponds to the qualitative researcher's belief that writing cannot be divided into subparts and the entire work must be looked at as a whole unit. However, to mollify the psychometricians, holistic scoring in writing has numerous subsets and criteria that do indeed divide the students' work into pieces. These subsets and criteria form the rubrics that teachers use regularly in evaluating writing.

Similarly, portfolios also correspond to the qualitative position that writing can be assessed only after students engage in an intensive, lengthy involvement working with a series of texts. Instructors can only evaluate students' writing after the instructors observe the changes that are noted through teacher and peer comments, student reflection, or other types of documented evidence. The reporting of results during an assessment includes detailed explanations, commentary, and more layers of reflection. Yet usually, portfolios are read holistically based on some sort of rubric that segments writing. Moreover, portfolios are increasingly subjected to the breaking out of criteria in a barrier exam format. Therefore, what instructors find is that even a more qualitative form of assessment like portfolios can be transformed into the language and actions associated with the psychometric model.

Because most composition specialists now try to create a very different reality concerning writing assessment compared with the psychometricians' methods, one has to ask, why is Composition still using the definitions from an antiquated approach to describe and explain the changes that occur in student writing? As Brian Huot (2002) noted, because Composition never truly claimed writing assessment as part of its domain, there is no reason for the field to attempt to reclaim or rearticulate the psychometricians' discourse. With the great influx of computer-enhanced writing classes, this question is particularly salient, and it clearly affects what happens in the college writing curriculum. Not only does the blending of assessment technology and computer technology reconfigure classroom space and instructional techniques, students' perceptions of their authorial rights, and the characteristics of the text; it also affects how compositionists study their students' finished work. These older rubrics and concepts are a poor fit for the multiple layers of composing that happen in networked assignments because they have accounted for neither visual rhetoric nor the development of the types of content and the variations of style that exist in electronic texts.

Writing instructors must realize that quantitative and qualitative methodologies ask faculty to view the individual writer in distinct ways; the quantifier sees the student writer as one of many, and she places the writer in categories that correspond to general observations about behaviors, attitudes, and expectations. The qualifier looks at students as independent beings, each one possessing very different sets of abilities, and assessment cannot group these abilities into nice, neatly separated categories. This separate worldview toward assessment leads to the quantifier needing large numbers of students to satisfy an explanation of what is happening in the writing classroom and the qualifier to prefer smaller numbers of students to provide a general pattern of activities in a composition class. What is significant about this point is that writing departments are now filled with readers from both camps and each side reads student papers. Although assessment indeed drives instruction, recognizing that assessment can be defined through two opposite theoretical approaches illustrates the fissures that can occur in departments regarding written evaluation as well as the rifts that emerge in pedagogy.

The schism that seems to exist in writing assessment practices from program to program, perhaps even from instructor to instructor, mirrors Composition's mistrust of assessment. Few practitioners and scholars understand tests and measurements, as Brian Huot (2002) rightly noted. Even fewer recognize that Composition is not bound to quantitative definitions of concepts like validity and reliability to describe what occurs in the classroom. It is possible to reconfigure these terms to accommodate the flexibility necessary to discuss the writing process in networked writing classes and to do so without causing great conflict with social constructivist pedagogical models. The way to realign validity and reliability in writing assessment in these computer-enhanced contexts is to think even more qualitatively about evaluation.

University of Michigan education professor Pamela A. Moss, in her research on accountable assessment with portfolios (1992), indicated that frequently a student writer's growth is made evident by examining the qualitative aspects of the writing. For instance, having instructors look at the increasing levels of complexity in student problem solving often reveals that there is a loss of control in mechanics or organization as student writers develop richer interpretations of a text. According to Moss (1992), there are other subtle indicators of growth like quality of voice and elaboration. These characteristics tend to be understated in psychometric approaches and subsumed under broader criteria, which causes faculty to miss or to misinterpret critical moments of a writer's development.

In thinking qualitatively about writing assessment in networked environments, instructors are asked to consider depth instead of comprehensiveness in evaluation. This means that instead of collecting webfolios or electronically generated assignments from everyone in the class, teachers work with smaller representative samples of each assignment to examine what happens in the course over time. In the process, a theory of instruction that is situated to the course and to the institution develops. Not only is approaching writing assessment from this perspective more in line with Composition's interest in cooperative writing, ethnography, protocols, and discourse analysis, but the inductive method of inquiry common to qualitative research also parallels more closely a writer's composing activities. From a practical standpoint when working in internetworked spaces, qualitative assessment helps faculty construct categories of incidents or events that happen in students' online writing processes that then can be refined and examined for patterns or themes to describe various relations among the multiple literacies and activities in the class. Once the preliminary connections are made, instructors can integrate the information into a coherent explanation of what transpires in the computer-enhanced classroom using a theoretical framework that corresponds with their teaching philosophies.

Even in the more quantitative instructional design and development circles, qualitative methods are now thought of as having some validity and reliability compared with a decade or so ago. This is particularly so when qualitative approaches are used to triangulate student test scores or to discuss specific student populations. This suggests that there is enough of a precedent set in research design for qualitative assessment to be valid in all writing classes. To have qualitative writing assessment data stand alone and maintain validity and reliability without statistical support, however, a level of confidence must be created for quantitative folks to respond favorably to the data put before them.

For those who teach in computer-enhanced classrooms, this point is especially important. I don't mean to scare writing instructors, but new electronic essay-reading software programs that imitate variations of the ETS holistic scoring process or the predicate analysis method found in the Intelligent Essay Assessor are gaining publicity. These programs can easily become the type of representation quantitative researchers recognize as acceptable writing assessment mechanisms for networked writing classes. The administrative appeal for these systems is understandable; low-cost, high-volume production that speaks in statistically accurate language. To counter such a regressive approach to writing evaluation, though, compositionists and their program heads need to consider what qualitative techniques offer writing assessment that is better and more dependable for their institution's needs.

Currently, electronic portfolios are the first foray into qualitative methods applied to writing assessment procedures for online classes. This move is based on the success that the common papertext portfolio has had. Over the last 25 years, the traditional paper portfolio has gained value as a valid and reliable application for assessing student writing. Therefore, it makes sense to import the idea into networked classrooms. However, as noted earlier, the same difficulties that exist with paper portfolios also exist with electronic portfolios. Selective pieces may be overwritten by faculty or outsiders; only individual teachers or a team of teachers completes the evaluation process; fictionalizing—or maybe overextending—the writer's abilities occurs because of clever reflective texts, or in the case of e-texts, because of stronger visual literacy skills or pixel manipulation; and the focus of evaluation still rests primarily on product instead of process. All this becomes apparent in many current computer-based writing assessment plans like the one W. Dees Stallings presented to new teachers in his monograph *Distance Education* (1997). Although Stallings is correct in suggesting that subjective and objective criteria are critical for providing effective writing assessment in computer-enhanced composition classes, his model is based on traditional primary trait analysis combined with an analytic scoring guide (1997, pp. 26–27). Although rubrics like these work for standard academic writing assignments, and will work for the standard writing assignment submitted to an instructor as an electronic file or in a webfolio, they fall far short of addressing the qualities of interactivity, usability, and visuality that are the hallmarks of e-texts. Instead, Stallings' use of assessment checklists and scoring guides reinforces current–traditional approaches to electronic writing instruction—and the students' products still remain at the forefront of evaluation.

Authentic assessment in the networked classroom space must account for more than finished work that can be accessed online. It should also include the public e-mails and chat exchanges, student commentary from drafts composed in software programs like WebCT or BlackBoard, or other non-finished communication among the class participants. Generally speaking, e-portfolios do not contain this material, although they should. As Douglas Hesse recently noted, these informal, conversational pieces when threaded together in an archive form an "essayistic artifact" (1999, p. 38)—a local narrative that presents a history of the course work that does not appear in the portfolio. An essayistic artifact like a class's listserv archive becomes important in evaluation to examine how student writers develop a consciousness about their assignments and how students' various rhetorical and structural movements toward writing a longer e-text unfold over the course of an assignment. It makes sense for writing teachers to include a document like a listserv archive in an electronic assessment to account for change and growth in students' writing, yet how many compositionists do this? Not many—if any at all. From the various e-portfolio samples I've seen as online representatives for conducting an evaluation of networked writing, no links exist to a list archive. In fact, most student webfolios look like digitized versions of the common paper portfolio—something that Batson (2002) encouraged. This suggests that writing faculty may be missing rich sources of qualitative data to support assessment decisions.

Evaluation discussions must also extend to design and content concerns in more formal web documents. There are clear differences between writing online and writing on paper, as outlined in chapter 2 [of *Composition in Convergence*]. Authentic assessment for internetworked writing has to account for the changes in style that occur when students create mundane e-texts. There can no longer be face validity connected to e-texts because writing instructors can no longer rely on assessing only the surface structures of their students' online assignments. More comprehensive feedback mechanisms need to be created to explain to students and to skeptical faculty members and administrators that real writing happens in electronic classroom spaces.

DEVELOPING "DEEP ASSESSMENT"

Because technological convergence brings changes to the text and to the students' writing processes, it becomes critical for writing instructors who are interested in pursuing computer-enhanced composition classes to contemplate alternative assessment strategies beyond those that already exist. These newer strategies have to build on the flexibility found in portfolios, be manageable enough to incorporate into an active writing classroom, be able to address a full range of formal and informal networked writing contexts, and be concise enough to appease administrators and other officials who typically understand quantitative data. Although this idea sounds utopian, it is not. Instead of examining the dilemma of evaluation from its traditional tests and measurement roots, writing instructors can look to a more congruent area for communication convergence—the media. Compositionists can find innovative avenues of critique and commentary in media research that can transform older notions of writing assessment without sacrificing validity and reliability.

One new way to think about writing assessment in networked environments is what I call "deep assessment." Deep assessment arises from the work of two different compositionists writing almost a decade apart, Margaret Himley (1991) and Ann Watts Pailliotet (1999). The concept underlying deep assessment emerges from Himley's "deep viewing" techniques (1991) that were applied to children's writing. In 1999, Pailliotet adapted deep viewing to accommodate critique of visual and electronic texts. In the deep assessment approach, I modify Pailliotet's (1999) and Himley's (1991) ideas to initiate a postmodern turn in the evaluation of writing.

As with deep viewing, deep assessment reflects a three-tiered approach. Together, teachers and students, as participant observers, amass multiple data sources and artifacts that lead to describing elements of the texts. These descriptions form the basis for responses and interpretations of what is found in the texts. Whether in teams that divide the responsibilities of deep evaluation or as single evaluators, the instructors write comments, notations, or sketches about the material in front of them as talk begins about each selection. This talk unfolds into interconnected discussion, and the written comments emerge as the artifacts that concretize the evaluators' exchanges.

Two Strategies for Implementing Deep Assessment

Using qualitative research to invert the traditional meanings of validity and reliability in assessment is important for documenting the evolution of writing and writing instruction that takes place when extensive computer use is introduced to the composition classroom experience. Because computer-enhanced writing instruction is frequently a fluid series of exchanges among writers and because the products that arise from networked classes are frequently seamless and without closure, the deep assessment mechanisms used to study these students' work must have great flexibility. In addition, any assessment strategies for these contexts need to have some common ground with the historical understanding of validity and reliability to gain the respect of the quantitative folks who generally sit in decision-making capacities on campus and who frequently deride any measurement system that does not look like a numeric study.

One method for building credibility in deep assessment is to develop what is called in media research an *analytic induction strategy* (Wimmer & Dominick, 1997). In this technique, the evaluator forms a hybrid between quantitative and qualitative research methods. The first step in this strategy is for the assessment team or the instructor to state clearly the criteria to be investigated and to construct a hypothesis to guide the evaluation procedure. Next, the instructor pulls a representative sample from the entire group of students using a commonly recognized random sampling formula like "1 in X." For an instructor who teaches four sections of composition (approximately 100 students), she can use her class lists to select a 1 in 10 sample to pull 10 students' electronic assignments at random to study further. Then she can examine a single case from the representative sample to test the hypothesis. If problems occur in the evaluation, she reworks the hypothesis or the criteria and tests again. Otherwise, she judges the remaining cases from the representative sample, looking for patterns and themes that refine her hypothesis. When finished, the teacher returns to the 10 sample assignments to study any negative cases that could disprove her hypothesis. If problems occur, the instructor again reworks the hypothesis and continues testing. Although this is a time-consuming activity, the teacher should develop a very strong argument that maintains elements of quantitative and qualitative assessment. Moreover, this inductive and recursive evaluation method has credence in other academic communities; numerous educational researchers, for instance, find this form of naturalistic inquiry to be a valid form of accountability (Hopkins, 1998). This becomes important if a faculty member or a program must present harder data to administrators or faculty senates to support curriculum matters.

A second, somewhat less labor-intensive, way of building a deep assessment context that is credible without relying on historical understandings of validity and reliability also comes from media research. Maykut and Morehouse (1994) proposed four conditions for establishing trustworthiness in reporting qualitative data. Here I have adapted Maykut and Morehouse's 1994 model for use in a writing assessment situation:

1. *Collect Data from Numerous Sources.* Student e-texts, protocols, e-mail exchanges, listserv archives, and other classroom artifacts show others that the evaluator studied the students' work from many perspectives. This content does not necessarily have to be in an electronic portfolio; in fact, a polished e-portfolio may hinder the study. An electronic portfolio does not provide the raw information needed for the evaluator to truly measure growth and change in the student writers' processes. A few "finished" pieces might be useful, but instructors should have a mix of work in various stages, genres, and contexts for more believability in the evaluation.

2. *Develop an Audit Trail.* Whether in a LAN space, or on a disk, CD, or keychain hard drive, teachers need to create a safe, permanent record of the class's original data, comments about the data, and any analytical methods used to conduct the assessment. This permanent record is called an "audit trail." Audit trails are the easiest way to demonstrate the possibility of replication in qualitative research. Audit trails are especially important when arguing the validity of an assessment procedure, as anyone can retrace an instructor's steps and check the results for accuracy. An audit trail for 10 students may take up to several kilobytes in a single assessment, though, so instructors might want to consider putting this information on some removable, easily stored, permanent system (rewriteable CD-ROM or DVD, for instance) if they do not have access to their campus network or if the bandwidth exceeds campus allocations.

3. *Conduct Member Checks.* As teachers make notes and develop conclusions about what they read, those on the assessment team review their findings with each other and with the students to ensure accuracy in reporting the material. This step is very important if instructors use protocol interviews with students, because teachers will want to be certain that they precisely capture the students' words and intentions.

4. *Develop an Assessment Team to Avoid Epoche.* In research speak, *epoche* means researcher bias or prejudice. Establishing a team of evaluators to keep everyone focused on the criteria when describing or interpreting the student samples helps reduce the potential for bias. Sometimes it is helpful to bring in an evaluator from outside the composition classes to serve as an external reader whose primary function is to keep everyone honest in her assessment of the work. For instance, in a networked writing class that has hypertexts or web sites as part of the class work, the assessment team might include a willing faculty member from the computer science or art departments who would

lend his or her expertise if needed. This person could observe the process and raise questions of possible bias or misinterpretation of the work should the situation arise.

    5. *Apply Deep Viewing Approach to the Data.*

These two methods are workable for instructors and are fairly nonintrusive for students. Students can and should be involved with the data collection beyond the gathering of completed student assignments, particularly in the deep viewing sections of the evaluation. Protocol interviews, reflective statements, video or audiotapes of sessions, comments from students about the stages of their work, and their reactions to instructor responses are all necessary components of qualitative assessment and are common data-collection techniques in composition studies. Including student participation in the assessment activities acknowledges students' authority as writers in a legitimate way that respects their interests and stakes in the writing and evaluating processes. This move is an especially important one when assignments are cooperatively written, because students have already invested a high level of ownership in the formation of their work. Furthermore, to exclude a range of student responses or critiques (or only to include student reflections) in online assessment contexts seems to me to be antithetical to the democratizing rhetoric underlying computer-enhanced composition pedagogy. It suggests that the teacher still holds the only authoritative position in the classroom, and the student writers' voices carry little weight. Without student input, the assessment would not be considered deep nor would it be as democratic as many in Composition hope writing assessment could be.

THREE MOVES TOWARD DEEP ASSESSMENT: THE ONLINE LEARNING RECORD, TOPIC/ICON, AND DYNAMIC CRITERIA MAPPING

The Online Learning Record at the University of Texas at Austin is an excellent bridge between using conventional writing assessment plans and deeply evaluating students' writing in electronic contexts. Recently, Margaret Syverson and John Slatin created the Online Learning Record (OLR), the first public inroad toward deep assessment that moves beyond the electronic portfolio (see www.crwl.utexas.edu/~syverson/olr/contents.html for an overview of the system). Although the OLR has been designed primarily for the K–12 writing teacher, it can be adapted for the college or university writing instructor. The OLR contains many principles expressed in this chapter; it fosters student participation in the evaluation process, draws evaluation artifacts from several different sources, accounts for the range of multiple literacies needed to write in networked spaces, and traces students' progress graphically instead of numerically or alphabetically. Moreover, the OLR allows instructors to construct narratives or visual tracks regarding student work that reflect teacher accountability and respect for the students' efforts in the classroom. Syverson and Slatin's OLR model (1999) points to the positive effects that technological convergence brings to writing assessment by illustrating how humane and democratic evaluation can be in a composition course.

The OLR's greatest benefit is that instructors now can follow student progress rather than focus on the product. Through various forms of graphical plotting, writing specialists can track students' perceptions of growth and change without the stigma of grades. This is a critical step in realizing an authentic assessment program for computer-enhanced writing classes, because many students still come to these courses with the fear of technology. By reducing much of the grading to a series of sliding bar scales and scattergrams, the instructor can observe how various students rise and fall in relation to certain challenges in writing for electronic environments. Final grades still exist, as do individual assignment grades, but the numeric or alphabetic distinction given to students now carries an observable history, a context for understanding why students receive the grades they do in a course.

What is also impressive about the OLRs is that, although retaining some of the usual quantitative representations for data like sliding bar scales and scatterplots, the information gathered is highly qualitative. Because data are gathered from numerous sources, including archived files, current projects, and student observations and reflections of their growth as writers, an audit trail can be easily built with graphical dimensions to discuss writing development in a systematic manner. Thus, a teacher can reach the most quantitative and qualitative members of a campus-wide study group, instructional design team, or administrative committee interested in how writing is affected by technological convergence. Over time, these audit trails establish a rich, generalizable body of knowledge about a particular student population (or, for large-scale assessment, an entire class of students).

As a way to deeply assess the writing activities and abilities of students in interactive settings while retaining student ownership of the written product, the OLR addresses five important stages: (a) building writers' confidence and independence, (b) acquiring skills and strategies, (c) monitoring levels of prior and emerging experience, (d) using writing and inquiry as ways of knowing and understanding, (e) developing critical reflection (Syverson, 1999). For these reasons, in OLR the evaluation better situates itself in the shifting contexts of the computer-enhanced writing classroom because it depends far less on the one-dimensional approach to measurement found in skill-and-drill work or the two-dimensional procedures like "competence and confidence" grounded in much of the current holistic essay and portfolio reading models that form the basis of other computer-driven assessment tools.

The OLR is still in its infancy, and it is used in a limited manner at the K–12 level in California and at the university level at the University of Texas at Austin. Despite its newness, the OLR's early phases indicate that Composition's convergence with competing technologies can lead to developing a transformative assessment practice that combines independent inquiry, ability, student ownership, limited teacher intervention, and critical knowledge about situated discourse. As the OLR concept spreads and evolves, more compositionists and administrators should see firsthand the effect that deep assessment and convergence have for the teaching of writing at the K–college level.

In fall 2002, Fred Kemp at Texas Tech University (TTU) instituted the TOPIC/ICON program to handle the writing evaluation for TTU's 2,250 students in first-year composition. Given the size of TTU's program, the sheer volume of information collected in TOPIC/ICON's database would have to be enormous. According to the TOPIC/ICON web site (www.english.ttu.edu: 5555/manual), the database holds more than 180,000 student documents. Clearly, in one semester, TTU has built a massive foundation from which to mine information about students' online writing activities and behaviors.

However, it is not the mammoth database that makes TOPIC/ICON worthy of recognition in the blending of networked writing and assessment. Rather, the openness with which TTU conducts this deep assessment procedure is estimable. All stakeholders involved in the assessment process are able to obtain critical information when it is needed. Students have access, both public and password-protected, to a variety of class-generated information. Instructors have access to various classroom management tools and archives, all fairly automated for ease of use. Program administrators have access to important section statistics at their fingertips when statistics are needed to answer questions or to solve problems. The accessibility to data that all participants have in the TOPIC/ICON system demonstrates that it is possible to create a writing assessment plan that merges two technologies and provides responsibilities to everyone involved in the learning process.

One might think the TOPIC/ICON system would be cumbersome given its size, but it is a model for efficiency. The TTU faculty involved in building TOPIC/ICON have redesigned the roles of instructor, dividing the work load into two separate activities: classroom management and document evaluation. Consequently, there are classroom instructors and document instructors. Classroom instructors direct classroom learning. Document instructors maintain responsibility for evaluation and commentary on student work. The division of labor here is important, because it becomes incredibly grueling for instructors to act as classroom manager, motivator, writing coach, and final arbiter of student work while teaching in networked space. Separating the practices allows instructors to gravitate to their strengths. For universities with large graduate teaching staffs or adjunct faculty, this option offers better programmatic control over the quality of instruction in that writing specialists who have a better presence in the classroom or who are more experienced with students can have the burden of grading removed. Those who are exceptional readers of student texts but who may falter in the classroom because of their lack of graduate or teaching experience can do their best as well as gain a stronger background in working with student texts. With this system, it is easy to set up a rotating teaching schedule so all instructors eventually spend time either in the classroom or on evaluation. Therefore, the work load is shared by everyone, and a coordination of best practices in the teaching and assessing of writing can emerge.

The planning of the TOPIC/ICON program reflects the deep assessment model presented earlier in this chapter in several significant ways. First, the program collects data from numerous sources and places the information in databases or archives that allow stakeholders easy access. Second, the databases and archives establish a strong audit trail for administrators and instructors. Third, the writing program administrator is able to conduct member checks through the program administrator's functions. Fourth, the TOPIC/ICON planners attempt to avoid epoche through the establishment of working groups that read student papers. Additionally, TOPIC/ICON values not only the pedagogical needs of students in a computer-enhanced writing class but also the instrumental and affective needs of both students and instructors in the assessment process.

This last point is evidenced most clearly when one reviews the criticisms posted to the public. From the students' perspective, their concerns were similar to those in any first-year writing class: papers too long for instructors to grade, classes that did not seem rigorous enough, and instructors not prepared enough in using the technology (www.english.ttu.edu: 5555/manual). The instructors' issues were the same as many humanities professors who are teaching elsewhere. Technology dehumanizes the class experience. Students seem ill-prepared to work with the TOPIC system. Grading papers takes forever. If the reader did not realize she was reading about a course that is a hybrid of computer and F2F contexts, she would have thought the end-of-term comments came from a completely classroom-centered situation with some computer component attached. Therefore, it seems that in the TOPIC/ICON system, merging these two technologies does not drastically alter students' or instructors' perceptions of the work load attached to first-year composition. What the comments do suggest strongly, though, is that students and faculty need time to familiarize themselves with any new technology if the system is to be truly successful.

Like the OLR, the TOPIC/ICON approach is the next wave in large-scale university writing assessment that does not rely on either a one-shot electronically scored essay or an e-portfolio for deep assessment. Both the OLR and TOPIC/ICON programs put forward an exciting next step in the development of deep assessment strategies that recognize shared responsibilities in the networked writing classroom. Furthermore, TOPIC/ICON constructs a prototype for what larger writing programs can do to be more efficient in delivering course content in an age of technological convergence. At the K–12 level, OLR demonstrates a similar effectiveness in working with younger students' writing. What the OLR and TOPIC/ICON systems show compositionists is that deep assessment of networked writing can occur in very different forms to meet various institutional needs. Composition does not have to be dependent on older understandings of writing assessment to offer legitimate evaluation methods for electronic texts. It is possible for writing specialists to construct new assessment models that draw on the two technologies and still acknowledge validity and reliability, albeit in ways that break away from Composition's past.

Bob Broad proposed a fresh idea with regard to writing assessment that shows potential for working with electronic texts. In his book *What We Really*

Value (2003), Broad detailed the Dynamic Criteria Map (DCM). The DCM is a series of circular regions, some linked, others not, that address varying textual qualities. Two regions, Change in Student/Author and Rhetorical, are linked through Broad's "epistemic spectrum" (2003, p. 40). Changes in Student/Author are marked by growth in learning and in revision, whereas the Rhetorical region is defined by audience awareness and persuasive abilities.

Broad ranked the epistemic spectrum as the "most substantial criterion" in the model, because it positions affective and moral thinking, epistemic knowledge, and intellectual analysis along a continuum that bisects the Change in Student/Author and Rhetorical constellations (2003, p. 40). An offshoot constellation, Aesthetics, that reflects criteria dependent upon the writer's craft (texture, creativity, humor, etc.), links to both the Change cluster and the epistemic knowledge range of the continuum.

The DCM also includes assessment criteria clusters regarding Agency/Power (author as writer) that intersects with Ethos (author as person) and a discrete area defined as "part to whole," which houses the structural elements of writing such as focus, pace, relevance, clarity, flow, and so on (Broad, 2003, p. 40). Two smaller compartments, "mystery criterion" and "general writing ability," are set apart from the larger domains.

The appeal of the DCM for e-texts is in how the model addresses a full complement of writing needs. Regardless of whether the electronic text is a blog, a MOO, a web site, or hypertext, the work can be evaluated on a full range of technical, mechanical, aesthetic, affective, rhetorical, intellectual, and social criteria defined by the instructor, the program, or the department. Broad's DCM system depends on the deep assessment approach put forward earlier in this chapter in order to collect and discuss student networked writing in a thoughtful manner. Through an instructor's use of the DCM, students can chart their progress in various areas and note where growth and slippage occur across assignments or over time. For a program or a department, the adoption of a model like the DCM provides the context in which to discuss the evaluation of students' electronic texts to enact curricular or instructional changes that improve writing instruction for networked environments. As I propose in the next section, the DCM approach leads Composition Studies to redefine validity and reliability in ways that mesh with the growing use of e-texts in the writing classroom.

DEVELOPING A "NEW" VALIDITY AND RELIABILITY

The notion of deep assessment and the development of deep assessment programs like the OLR, TOPIC/ICON, and DCM is that they replace the flat, objectivist descriptions of validity and reliability with an enriched overview of the students' real processes and contexts for writing. One critical effect of technological convergence on assessment is the destabilization of the scientific method used to ground writing assessment by the computer's ability to emphasize the social values and subjectivity present in evaluation. This destabilizing of established understandings inherent in the scientific method surely changes how writing undergoes evaluation.

A start in this new direction for assessment begins with a revised set of assumptions concerning writing, validity, and reliability. In place of the older principles that guide assessment and were outlined earlier in this chapter, a new collection of components drives evaluations in computer-enhanced writing courses:

- *Writing is multidimensional.* The convergence of these two technologies has displaced the earlier concept that writing is an orderly and regular activity. Hypertext, MOOs, Daedalus Integrated Writing Environment (DIWE), and archives of synchronous and asynchronous e-mails indicate that writing runs across different geographical spaces and time zones; accommodates multiple topics, users, and sources; and fragments into short bursts with the addition of graphical images and hyperlinks. What has happened to writing with the cross-impact of technological convergence is a process of deterritorializing words from their preestablished orders. Electronic forms of writing now mirror what theorists Gilles Deleuze and Felix Guattari (1987) called a rhizomatic linguistic structure. That is, writing no longer maintains a distinct, three-part split among the world, the text, and the author. Instead, different aspects of perception allow different connections to be made; however, there is no genuine start or finish to the writing. In Composition's technological convergence, writing is multidimensional because it is always placed in the middle of things, positioned between visual images and sound or between the actions of the writer and the reader.

- *Writing is an observable process.* What specifically triggers writing is unknowable; also, explaining how a student writer achieved a particular outcome from examining a single sample or a series of written products outside of the classroom context is equally unknowable. However, technological convergence makes a student author's processes observable even though the product is seamless. Therefore, instructors in computer-enhanced courses can conduct nonintrusive evaluation beginning with the students' first forays in networked writing. The assessment becomes increasingly more authentic, because students are expected to contribute to the evaluation process through a series of analytical activities based on their own work. Thus, teachers' online archives become a rich, longitudinal source of metacognition and metawriting as well as a database for students' technical competence and writing effectiveness. Although specialists are still unable to know what exactly initiates the sequence a writer takes in the composing process, through a rich archival database, instructors can observe the stages that online composition takes once the spark occurs.

- *Writing is one form of many situated discourses.* Instead of privileging alphabetic literacy and papertexts, technological convergence provides strong evidence that writing is just one discursive activity and knowledge maker among others. Albeit writing is still a central communication method in e-texts, writing now includes graphical interfaces, hybridized oral and written language patterns, sound and video applets, and a range of reader-writer interactivity. Internetworked writing exists in a very different format compared with the historical pen-and-paper forms that many instructors have come to recognize. Although writers and readers still have to manage the meaning, intent, structure, and effect with e-texts, the volume of associations, connections, and evidence that needs to be constructed for the prior experiences and literacy levels of a global audience is expanded at least a hundredfold. So, although writing is a central activity, it emerges as one of many discourses available to a writer in online environments.

- *Writing reflects social exchanges influenced by numerous causes.* Convergence in Composition reinforces Kenneth Bruffee's claim that "knowledge is a consensus" and "people construct independently by talking together" (1993, p. 113). In networked classroom environments, there are several sources for affecting the outcomes of the types of social exchanges that exist among writers (adapted from Bruffee, 1993, pp. 116–117):

    Levels of technical knowledge or interest

    Levels of shared expertise or common information base

    Patterns of argument and approval (e.g., ad hominem, flames, use of narration vs. citation, "dittos," short supportive slogans, etc.)

    Patterns of reward ("cool site awards" or other markers of web site excellence, permission to publish list comments, friendly emoticons in posts)

    Acts of competition (verbal sparring, one-upping, leveling, and the like)

    Levels of trust and comfort (e.g., lurking vs. regular contributions to lists)

    The writing done in networked situations, then, serves in some way to embody all those who are connected, that is, to act as a medium to express private thoughts publicly with those who are of similar minds. This is an important aspect of what technological convergence brings to the writing process; it makes visible the social relationships that writers attempt to establish with their audiences. In these contexts, just as Bruffee (1993) noted happens in all collaborative contexts, writers validate their beliefs through each other. Therefore, online assessment that is collaborative will have a deeper effect on students because they will measure the worth of their writing based on the types of response received.

- *Writing depends on experiences, values, and technological access.* Those who were alive during earlier periods of technological convergence in writing cannot tell today's writing specialists of the massive changes in experience that occurred when letters pushed aside speech or when the printing press revolutionized hand-lettered texts. From reading rhetoricians, historians, and scholars across the ages, one can only imagine or try to envision the transformations each moment in convergence had for society then and how those instances altered people's experiences, literacy levels, values, and access to technology.

We are, however, living in the most current wave of technological convergence. With our own eyes, many writing specialists see firsthand the triumphs and challenges that this critical moment in convergence brings to literacy. As more writing tasks shift from pen and paper to electronic type, students' experiences with composing the written word evolve. Most compositionists can recall one student (or possibly several students) or one class that had advanced cases of technophobia on the first day of class in a computer lab. Through trial and error, questioning, and a mix of confusion and confidence, these students arrive at a point where hypertextual or HTML composing, e-mail or ICQ ("I seek you") correspondence, PowerPoint presentations, MOO writing, or producing other electronically based assignments becomes second nature. What we discover is that writing in networked environments, like other forms of writing experiences, depends on students encountering the opportunity to practice on a regular basis.

With these newer assumptions about writing and the writing process in the culture of Composition, modifications must occur regarding the concepts of validity and reliability. Currently, as educational theorist William L. Smith noted, standard assessment methods assume too much both of the rater's ability for consensus on rating points and of the accuracy of the rating scales' intervals (in Huot & Williamson, 1993). Smith proposed a turn to *adequacy*, particularly in placement situations, to evaluate student work. Assessing for adequacy does not depend on extensive rater training or calibration of sample essays or texts; rather, the function of assessing for adequacy parallels the tasks of manuscript reviewers. The reviewers, chosen from members of a community, depend on their experiences with the material in front of them (in this instance, sets of student data archived online), to "accept, reject, or revise and submit (substantial revision or minor revision needed before decision reached)" (in Huot & Williamson, 1993, p. 198). In assessing for adequacy, students may learn to be more rigorous in showing competency compared with more traditional assessment settings. This is because assessing for adequacy looks at students' real writing abilities instead of measuring them against a generalized, idealized norm of written competence. Broad's DCM model (2003) points us toward a highly workable manner of assessing for adequacy in that the criteria are localized for a series of courses, a set program, or an institution based on the shared beliefs of the stakeholders involved with the evaluation.

Because archived data can be included in this type of evaluation, assessing for adequacy also allows for multidimensional plotting of student progress, takes responding to a student's work out of the linear numerical order that often substitutes for a grade, and presents responses in narrative (qualitative) forms that make better sense to students, faculty committees, and program administrators who may be unskilled or uncomfortable with quantitative research methods and statistical evidence. The ability to measure writing in this manner puts forward the position that the evaluators know the community in which the writer writes and that they can be fairer in their judgments about the material based on the evaluators' prior experience with teaching similar courses and students' prior experiences with writing in similar courses. Moreover, assessing for adequacy respects the local conditions of the institution where a student produces her assignments.

Smith's adequacy model is a reliable form of assessment for use with e-texts because the categories (variables) from which an evaluator selects a decision are limited enough to produce clear, consistent decisions. In assessing for adequacy, writing specialists simply measure whether the writing is acceptable for the situation. If the student's writing is not acceptable, the distinction becomes whether more revision is needed or whether the problems are severe enough to reject the piece completely. For networked writing composed of many components, literacies, and rhetorical strategies, assessing for adequacy is ideal. Instructors familiar with electronic communication can distinguish acceptable work in ways that break from the linear holistic scoring guides, yet still retain the sense of reliability that many test-and-measurement people want to see in outcomes assessment.

This "new" reliability does not depend on the consistency of writing specialists guessing the same score to keep consensus and interrater reliability or to ensure the reliability of test instrument, two situations that frequently lead to a Panopticon of sorts in assessment settings. Instead, this new reliability insists on faculty reviewers who are experienced with the currency of technological convergence and student e-texts to make decisions about the adequacy of students' writing in these genres.

Assessing for adequacy moves deep assessment closer to validity because the evaluators have the opportunity to examine a fuller scope of the students' writing activities and contexts. Not only will the archived data contain numerous examples of writing produced under various conditions and for various audiences, the students' own analytical examinations of their work and the instructors' points of intervention; the data should also reflect the teacher's comments. All these elements provide the breadth needed to make a valid writing assessment. Deciding whether a student's archived writing is acceptable depending on local criteria should pass the test for face validity because the data are evaluated by local experts using familiar criteria to measure the writing. Additionally, when a panel or team of teachers who are experienced in electronic communication evaluates the students' adequacy as writers of online material, there is also predictive validity. That suggests that evaluators acknowledge the students are reasonably able to do the work again later based on examining the archived materials. Concurrent validity can be included in this type of evaluation if the assessment team wants to measure the students' electronic writing against students' F2F writing; this approach might be an especially useful step in writing programs where there are computer-only sections (and, conversely, F2F-only sections). Testing for concurrent validity will be useful only if the criteria used to measure the writing remain identical for both sections. If is also important to note that in programs where computer-enhanced composition is under fire or where there is great skepticism, testing for concurrent validity may answer administrators' or faculty members' concerns about the benefits of using computer technology in the writing classroom.

Last, deeply assessing writing for adequacy meets the demands for establishing construct validity. Because evaluators can link a theoretical framework to the assessment mechanism—in this instance, the body of information existing about writing in networked space, the growing collections in visual rhetoric, or the work done in media literacy describing the effect of media convergence on alphabetic literacy—the results become even more valid. The assessment team can explain the relations between what happens in the students' e-texts and other variables that exist in the theories being applied to study the writing. Providing construct validity in deep assessment reflects a more authentic assessment experience because not only are instructors evaluating what they value in an e-text, but the assignments and activities also demonstrate to students and observers what is valued in a text or a course. Applying construct validity in deep assessment respects both the students' development of multiple literacies through the writing process and the writing instructors' judgment that students can perform a cluster of writing tasks in cyberspace.

Technological convergence has transformed the text. Of that, most have no doubt. Writing instructors who work in computer-enhanced classes recognize that there is a range of modifications that occur in the writing process when students shift their composing practices from pen, paper, and an implied audience to keyboard, screen, and an actual audience. To make others across departments, campus, and society realize that these changes happen in students' assessment as well, compositionists familiar with these two technologies must transform assessment, because that is the language of administrators, university boards of trustees, and state legislatures. Collectively, compositionists who have expertise in computers and writing assessment must argue that deep assessment of students' online writing reflects the ultimate performance-based assessment for the following reasons:

- Instructors can examine complex learning outcomes and student abilities in writing beyond traditional pen-and-paper assignments.

- The focus of assessment is placed on process, which is critical for students' finished projects to function properly (e.g., graphics appearing correctly in web sites, Java applets that run and do not crash a user's machine, MOO sites that carry out an activity, simple discussion lists that run most of the time without failure, etc.).

- The emphasis on process and deep assessment offers a more plausible, direct, and complete study of the types of literacies, reasoning, and techniques writers use to communicate online with real audiences.

- Infusing the composition course with computer-enhanced writing activities motivates students to write, because genuine readers exist for their work.

- Online writing is "real world" writing even though it takes place in virtual spaces.

- Like other forms of authentic performance assessment, deep assessment demands greater instructor time, involvement, and effort to collect, code, and analyze the data.

Outcomes assessment is possible, and maybe even desirable, in writing classrooms where convergence has taken place. However, fair outcomes assessment of networked writing cannot happen as long as older notions of validity and reliability are used to measure a nonquantifiable, nonstandard writing experience. These new intellectual projects come with the demand for developing suitable assessment criteria and models that address the range of students' processes, knowledges, and motivations when composing e-texts. Without writing instructors rethinking the psychometric concepts of validity and reliability in the age of convergence, Composition Studies will become severely constrained and this will lead to an even greater gap between classroom practices and evaluation. If the commonsense beliefs about assessment and instruction still hold true, then it is time that Composition redefines such central terms to reflect the broader aims of literacy in the electronic classroom and the changing shapes of the electronic text. We are on the cusp of changing the nature of writing assessment in the age of technological convergence; however, more work needs to be done. To do nothing further limits innovative pedagogical practices, the possibility of new scholarship, and the social values inherent in multiple literacies to the political whims of administrators, pundits, philanthropists, and policymakers.

NOTES

1. Briefly, following Wimmer and Dominick's explanations (1997, pp. 55–56), *face validity* describes whether on the face of an exam or an assignment the question measures what it is supported to measure. *Predictive validity* examines an assessment instrument against a future outcome. In writing assessment, if a multiple-choice exam on grammar can predict the success of students in a first-year composition (FYC) course because the exam correlated positively with passing scores in FYC, then faculty can say that the exam has high predictive validity even though the face validity is extremely low. This is because the multiple-choice exam is not testing the student writing, only a subset of skills. *Concurrent validity* evaluates how a measurement tool performs against an established criterion. For instance, if writing teachers wanted to gauge the validity of an editing exam, they could administer the exam to a group of professional copyeditors and a group of students. As Wimmer and Dominick noted, if the exam shows a clear discrimination between the two groups (and, of course, it should based on predictive ability), then faculty can claim that the editing exam has concurrent validity. *Construct validity* connects the measurement tool to a theoretical structure to show a connection related to other items in the structure. Linking this idea to composition classes, an assessment instrument needs to relate to the program's or the instructor's pedagogical practices to indicate there is some relation between what is being measured and other variables in the course. The converse here is also possible: An assessment method can have construct validity if it does not relate to other variables in the course or if there is no theoretical or pedagogical reason for a relationship to exist. *System validity* describes the process that the exam or evaluation has to a larger structure, such as a writing curriculum or institution, to ensure that what is being assessed bears a relation to the stated goals outlined by a program, department, or institution.

2. In empirical research, an *ecological fallacy* refers to using aggregate data that help to analyze a group to make inferences on the behavior or properties of an individual or individuals. For example, in a holistic reading (portfolio or essay structure), applying gender or racial statistical data for the campus or the region to assess an individual student's work would be using an ecological fallacy. The opposite of an ecological fallacy is the *individualistic fallacy*. In this situation, a reader makes inferences about an entire group of students or an educational system in general on the basis of a single student's work. An example of this would be condemning all high school writing instruction on the basis of one student's writing sample. See Nachmias and Nachmias (1981, p. 57) for a social scientist's perspective on these two fallacies.

18 Looking for Sources of Coherence in a Fragmented World: Notes toward a New Assessment Design

KATHLEEN BLAKE YANCEY

1. INTRODUCTION

That we live in a fragmented world is not news. That textuality has pluralized is, likewise, not news. What we make of these observations pedagogically is news—and is still, as they say, under construction. *Computers and Composition* is prescient in this regard in that, even in its title, there is the claim that in writing, medium indeed matters. In the journal title is also the promise that the combination of computers and composition would signal a profound shift in the ways we write. The ways we write aren't quite shifting, however; we *aren't* abandoning one medium for another. Rather, the layered literacies Cynthia Selfe (1989) described have become textured in interesting ways: Print and digital overlap, intersect, become *intertextual*.

And key to these new ways of writing, these new literacies, these new textures, I'll argue, is *composition*, a composition made whole by a new kind of coherence. If we are to value this new composition—text that is created on the screen and that in "finished" form is also mediated by the screen[1]—we will need to invent a language that allows us to speak to these new values. Without a new language, we will be held hostage to the values informing print, values worth preserving for that medium, to be sure, but values incongruent with those informing the digital. This, then, is one foray into a new assessment breach: How might/do we value the digital composition? How might those values lead to an assessment?

2. SOURCES OF COHERENCE IN A FRAGMENTED WORLD

That we need a new language is evident almost everywhere we look. Pedagogically, for instance, we seem comfortable with intertextual composing, even with the composed products. But we seem decidedly discomforted when it comes time to assess such processes and products—regardless of

From *Computers and Composition* 21 (2004): 89–102.

whether by assess we mean responding to student texts or putting a grade to them; articulating the values demonstrated in the work of colleagues who help students create these texts; or even attempting to ascertain the value of our own digital compositions. A larger question here is: Do we assess writing in virtual space and writing embodied in a physical document differently?[2]

Although many scholars have addressed issues of intertextuality and digital composing in more theoretical ways (e.g., Bolter & Grusin, 2000), what seems to happen in practice is that we use the frameworks and processes of one medium to assign value and to interpret work in a different medium. Beginning with a comparison of print and digital can provide ways of understanding what we value in both textualities, especially as we see how the virtues of one diverge from the virtues of the other, particularly in terms of coherence. Coherence is at the heart of print texts, of course, bringing into relationship arrangement and development, form and content, author and reader. Moreover, there is a considerable body of research and theory on coherence in print, providing us with a framework through which we might think about the coherence of digital texts. Before I begin to discuss this framework, some assumptions:

- First, I am assuming that coherence is a defining feature of composition.
- Second, I am assuming that digital texts are compositions, or can be.
- Third, I am assuming rhetoric is at the heart of our worlds—be they fragmented, print, digital—and that the point of rhetoric is to bring people together. From this perspective, then, coherence is all about relationships.

The distinction between print and digital textualities rides a fine line. Print seems unable to offer the seemingly infinite opportunity to arrange and rearrange text: That is, to compose it, and (then) to (re)compose it again—even now, in the age of word-processing software (or beyond it), when, admittedly, print is somewhat hybrid. Often composed in the digital environment, text loses fluidity when it becomes fixed as *the page*. And the reverse is true: The fact that something is created for and delivered on the screen doesn't make it *unlike* print. In other words, even though a text is produced in a digital environment and appears on the screen, it can remediate print (Bolter & Grusin, 2000). Such texts, when school-produced, are the academic analogue to the print catalogue—a genre written for the page, not the screen, where digitality serves one of two purposes: easier storage or quicker dissemination (or "print uploaded"; Wickliff & Yancey, 2001). Regardless of the fact that they are housed in the digital environment, these texts do not participate in it, but instead are represented in the composition of print. As I have explained elsewhere, the text embodies the values we associated with print: a claim; a single arrangement; support, typically developed in an explicit and linear style; a conclusion (Yancey, 2001). Digital texts, in other words, come in two general flavors: print uploaded or digitally designed. The coherence of print uploaded, not surprisingly, is that of print, and because it sets the stage for coherence in digital compositions, understanding how it is achieved is my next task.

3. COHERENCE IN PRINT TEXTS

Print texts achieve coherence in two ways: through words and through context. Conventional advice focuses on the relationship between words, as we see in the advice offered by Daniel Kies (2003):

> Coherence is product of many different factors, which combine to make every paragraph, every sentence, and every phrase contribute to the meaning of the whole piece. Coherence in writing is much more difficult to sustain than coherent speech simply because writers have no nonverbal clues to inform them if their message is clear or not. Therefore, writers must make their patterns of coherence much more explicit and much more carefully planned. Coherence itself is the product of two factors — paragraph unity and sentence cohension. (n.p.)

This handbook advice, however, as Richard Haswell (1989) argued, reminds us of the disjunction between what we advocate and what we do. We advocate — to students particularly — that text is bound one word to the next, one sentence to the next. And these "bindings" — or ties as Michael K. Halliday and Ruqaiya Hasan (1976) would have it — do point to the connections between words that, yes, in part compose coherence. At the same time, the words are often linked not one-to-one, but one-to-many, dispersed across fields of words and fields of contexts invoked by those words: A substitution for one word, occurring three sentences after the original reference, can provide the tie that binds. Relations between words as a source of coherence in print texts? Yes, to be sure. And, as important, relations between words and context. Coherence in print, then, seems a two-dimensional relationship: A coherent composition is created through the relationship of words to words, and words to context.

From an assessment perspective, coherence is important in a couple of ways. As we have seen, coherence shows up in handbooks: The student audience of writing handbooks produced in the United States is advised to write a coherent text, to write a text that *connects*. Coherence also brings with it its own handbook vocabulary and devices. Handbooks advise, for instance, that to create coherence, we repeat key words and we add transitions. Perhaps most important to standard North American academic prose, coherence itself is seen as one criterion for good writing. By definition, organized writing is coherent, and good writing is organized, and in print, it is organized in a single way: front to back. The construction of coherence in U.S. culture, then, tells us much about what we value in writing and, accordingly, much about what we assess.

Halliday and Hasan's (1976) work on coherence focused on non-fictional texts. But obviously texts fit into other genres as well — fiction, poetry, and mixed genres like creative non-fiction and alt.writing, the latter a text that displays characteristics of a discourse other than academic discourse and whose purpose may in fact be to disrupt those conventions intentionally (Dobrin, 2001).[3] These genres also aspire to coherence, although they achieve it by somewhat different mechanisms. Words connect, for instance, but the relationships holding between them tend to be associative and juxtapositional rather than literal and explicit. When words provide such connections, words—which are always metaphorical—seem doubly so.

When we look at language poetry and some alt.texts in particular, we see a shift to a third source of coherence: the page itself. As Richard Lanham (1993) remarked of electronic texts, such texts—because of their special relationship to the page (or in Lanham's discussion, to the screen)—offer a canvas on which and through which text is composed. In other words, writers of poetry and alt use the page as a partner to create meaning; in this sense, the context of the page becomes an explicit part of the text, thus providing another source of coherence. Another less-determined relationship is offered to the reader: one created by word to (metaphorical) word, by word to context, and by word to its position on the page and to its position to the other words. Lanham also spoke to the coherence possible on the screen when he noted that "the textual surface is now a malleable and self-conscious one," enabling the author to work in a medium that is "bi-stable" (p. 5). The author can create text we look both at and through. The overall effect, Lanham said, is a kind of "rehearsed spontaneity" (p. 6), itself located within other kinds of coherence as well, as we shall see.

r-p-o-p-h-e-s-s-a-g-r
by E. E. Cummings

r-p-o-p-h-e-s-s-a-g-r
who
a)s w(e loo)k
upnowgath
PPEGORHRASS
eringint(o-
aThe):l
eA
!p: . . . .

In one last digression before drafting notes toward assessment of digital texts, I need to point out the obvious. My notes toward such an assessment are already a day late and a dollar short. As Carl Whithaus (2002) eloquently explained, the texts that all of us—students and faculty members alike—are producing in the simplest word-processing programs are *already assessed* in some key ways:

> Are our systems of reading, responding to, and evaluating student work in electronic portfolios doomed to reproduce current-traditionalist mod-els of writing instruction when students are already receiving detailed feedback on their sentences from their word-processing software? Turn-

ing Microsoft WORD's grammar checker off is one option; customizing the grammar checker is another. But neither one of these solutions addresses the underlying problem: Advances in word-processing software have already internalized a vision of writing effectiveness as writing "correctly." In the near future, writing teachers will inherit a generation of students who already know how to fix the "menial" problems with their language—simply look for the green squiggly line and right click. (n.p.)

As Whithaus rightly pointed out, what might seem to be an advance—that is, who wants to argue in favor of invented spelling rather than a standard form, at least in the abstract?—can morph into a decided difficulty, especially when many of us are hoping to teach discourses other than the academic. As Whithaus asked: "How do we teach what Pat Bizzell has called hybrid discourses when students are being corrected as their language spills out onto the screen? When and where will students be given a chance to write like Victor Villanueva in *Bootstraps?*" (n.p.)

We can only assess what is produced, and what is produced is increasingly something not only assisted by technology, but, as Whithaus showed, created by technology and in ways that can be at odds with a desired effect. Technology isn't the villain; but as a tool, technology is not innocent. It is both shaping and assessing the writers whose work we want to assess—and not only in word-processing software—as Teddi Fishman reminded me when she noted in a personal email that her "last email may have sounded negative which was not what I intended (especially since spell-check changed my 'Aaaah' at the beginning to 'ha'"). This is also so in email applications like QualComm's EUDORA, in which chili peppers automatically mark an email that contains potentially offensive text, and in spam detectors that break links within email messages. Online, assessment is ubiquitous, and yet we do not often observe its effects.

In addition, even when we become aware of the assessment embedded in the tools we use and even when we pay attention to the effects of such assessment, it's frequently after the fact. Take, for instance, our responding practices and students' reading of our notes to them, and our responding practices to each other. What we create is not always what's received. In still other cases, we do see but are seduced by the technology, as Cheryl Forbes' (1996) narrative about responding practice suggested: Excited about the power of technology to enhance her assistance to students, Forbes inadvertently took over student texts and her comments *became* the texts. Only in retrospect did she find that the ease of the technology was too easy: Responding became rewriting, a rewriting she did not engage in when responding to student work with the technology of the pencil. As Forbes concluded, technology is a partner and we are its often-unwitting accomplices.

So, assessment is already in play. A first condition for assessment of digital compositions, then, is awareness of the condition. A second condition is that we specify what the digital makes possible and what we intend for it—or an assessment informed by intent, effect, awareness, and design.

4. DIGITAL COMPOSITIONS AND COHERENCE

In thinking about digital textuality, digital compositions, and ways coherence is achieved in them, we could simply list possibilities. The possibilities include those of print because verbal text is included, even if sometimes morphed, other times deployed visually, and still other times included almost as an afterthought. Regardless of the kind of digital text, we have the ties of print text, the semantic associations and juxtapositions of poetic text, and the play of text on the page or screen as partners. But this of course begs a question: How many kinds of digital texts are there? Rather than try to account for all of them, because they seem to proliferate more quickly than we can list them, we might find it useful to begin to construct some notes toward digital assessment by reviewing a couple common types of digital text.

We have email, where coherence is created, in part, through repetition as responders copy text to provide a context for reply. That repetition creates a kind of Halliday and Hasan tie from one email to the next, creating a meta-text. Is this meta-text a (collaborative) composition? Equally interesting is the Sort function of email programs, which allows users to arrange and re-arrange email materials by date, by sender, by header, and so on, thus allowing the email reader to control the context in which an individual email is sorted and read. This ability to arrange and re-arrange (and re-arrange again) is a central feature of many if not all digital texts. Arrangement is key—or put more accurately, multiple arrangements are key.

> Generally, excellent web portfolios will be characterized by the extent of the web, the creativity of the links, the meaningful coherence of the whole, the quality of the individual sites, the clarity of the overall design . . . and the overall aesthetic quality of the portfolio ("Web Portfolios," 2003, n.p.).

Another electronic text is the digital portfolio, and here I mean more and other than an online assessment system, which tends to be a drag-and-drop templated set of responses. Rather, by digital portfolio I mean a set of materials gathered for a particular purpose and audience, and narrated or introduced by means of a reflective text. Typically, digital portfolios rely on links to show connections, and these links provide the structure we associate with coherence. As the evaluative guidelines for the St. Olaf portfolio criteria suggest, *the meaningful coherence of the whole* is directly related to *the creativity of the links* and to its *design* ("Web Portfolios," 2003). Links, like an email sorter, provide an arrangement linked to coherence.

Another common text is provided through presentation software, the most popular of which is Microsoft POWERPOINT. Like digital portfolios, POWERPOINT can achieve coherence though templates. As a 2001 *New Yorker* article suggested, the templates in POWERPOINT are so powerful that the software literally templates thought—and not to good effects (Parker, 2001). When templates are not used, coherence is achieved in several interacting ways. One case study I conducted (Yancey, 2001), for instance, demonstrated that as

students revised POWERPOINT presentations, using them for print compositions, they relied on a refrain created through the repeated visual canvas of
the slide; repeated words and phrases; repeated images; the relationship of
words and images; and the placement of words and images both on individual screens and throughout the set of screens/slides. In other words, the patterning of information—putting the verbal and the visual in dialogue with
each other—created coherence.

Two other digital texts are MUDs (multi-user domains) and MOOs (multi-
user object-oriented domains), and hypertext. According to Peg Syverson
(1998), the basic source of coherence in MUD/MOO texts is pattern:

> The concept of pattern languages composing relationships which form
> structures to resolve dynamic tensions is a powerful way to look at vari-
> ations in patterns of human reasoning, particularly as they are mani-
> fested in electronic environments such as MOOs and MUDs. Some of the
> patterns I've observed include stars, spirals, collectivities, stories, net-
> works, spatial architectures, and fractals. These patterns are not confined
> to MOOs and MUDs, but the environment of MOOs and MUDs affords
> us unique opportunities for observing them. (n.p.)

Others have also commented on the digital textuality of MUD/MOO texts
(see, e.g., Haas & Gardner, 1999; "Pedagogies in Virtual Spaces," 1996; Rouzie,
2000). And we have hypertexts, those compositions that open many doors
plotted by an author but activated by a reader—compositions whose logic
makes more than monological sense, but whose arrangement is a collaborative effort. Others have written much about the design/logic/space of hypertext (see, for example, Amato, 1992a, 1992b; Carter, 2003; Cullen & Balkema,
1995; DeWitt, 1996; DiPardo & DiPardo, 1990; Fischer, 1996; Golson, 1995;
Gruber, 2002; Johnson-Eilola, 1997).

In sum, coherence in digital compositions seems to be a function of a pattern that is created through the relationships between and among context,
screen, image, the visual, and aural, the verbal, and with repetition and multiplicity as the common features.

5. CONNECTIONS: PATTERNS, WEAVING, THREADS, AND GAPS

In creating digital texts, then, composers can create coherence in a number
of ways:

- with/in a text/by a reader/contextually
- directly/associatively/spatially
- reiteratively
- verbally/visually.

Through un/mediated ties and links, digital texts permit and require attention to space and canvas, context (and context as part of textual meaning), and
sorting potential and linking. New relationships are pluralized within a new

space. The space itself provides a background and simultaneously represents a culture against which the screen is plotted. And that screen may itself be linked to another, may be re-sorted, may even be copied onto paper. Its design is plural by definition: It is composed by more than one element, and its arrangement tends to come in at least two forms.

Patterns are one way to talk about coherence in digital texts. Another way to think about this patterning and how the pieces within a pattern connect, not only to themselves but also to other pieces outside of the immediate reference, is to think in terms of weaving. The word weave

> derives from the Latin *texere,* meaning "to weave," which was used also to refer to that which is woven (textile) and the feel of the weave (texture). But it also refers to a "weave" of an organized arrangement of words or other intangible things (context). A textile is created by bringing together many threads and, as such, represents ordered complexity. Language, too, is ordered complexity, and when we understand a word by its context we are discerning a pattern and filling in a gap, sewing together what is torn, extracting meaning not only from what is said but from the relationships this act of saying sets up with other statements, conditions, events, and situations. (Adams, Hoelscher, & Till, 2001)

Digital compositions *weave* words and context and images: They are exercises in *ordered complexity*—and complex in some different ways than print precisely because they include more kinds of *threads*. As important, because the context for digital compositions is still so new and ever emerging, these texts tend to live inside the *gaps,* such that the reader/reviewer/responder is a more active weaver, creating arrangement and meaning both, and, I think, participating in a Bakhtinian creation of textual prototypes. In other words, we don't have a final definition of many of these texts—and perhaps we never will. But as a genre, or even as separate genres, they aren't stable yet, in the way that a novel or a poem is.

6. A Heuristic for Assessment

To assess these texts, then, we might consider the use of a heuristic. The value of a heuristic is that it is inquiry-based: It opens up a reading and an assessment by asking a consistent set of questions. In so doing, a heuristic helps provide information that can be used in evaluation. In addition, a heuristic used consistently—across a set of texts, in this case digital texts—can help us think more systematically about these texts. And not least, a heuristic leads to inquiry, which means that as readers of texts, we are encouraged by the technology of the assessment itself—(i.e., the heuristic) to respond as someone who inquires, who thinks to know, who thinks through inquiry (Yancey & Huot, 1997).

To create this heuristic, we will need another language, and we will—as Whithaus (2002) suggested—need to move our assessment to a higher level of abstraction, what he called making "communicative- and context-based evaluations on the macro-level" (n.p.). What this means is that we need to think in terms of pattern/arrangement as functioning in both design and reception. Patterns can be static, as in the case of some POWERPOINT presentations: The slides are not hyperlinked, and they follow the same pattern throughout, with each slide having identical backgrounds and following a linear path. Patterns can also be dynamic, as in the case of digital portfolios that branch to the right and left through linking. When both static and dynamic patterns are used, they tend to have some relationship to each other: The static opening page of a hypertext sets up expectations for the dynamic pages that follow — they are in relationship to each other. One email can be static or dynamic, but it is patterned in relationship to future emails or emails past. How a reader or a writer or a composer establishes these relationships is through patterning.

We tend to know — or think we know — how a text functions in reception (i.e., how we receive it), which is why we have less trouble responding to a text; we respond based on our reception. Whether that reception is informed by print or digital values can change the evaluation. For instance, the criteria for a print portfolio may include connections between a student's coursework and other experiences, but it is unlikely to include links to those experiences. A digital portfolio, on the other hand, is likely to include and privilege those links: They will help form the structure of the text. The text has a design to it, a pattern, and to assess that pattern, we need assistance from the designer, much as we solicit information about the logic of a painting from an artist or about the interpretation of a novel from a novelist. In asking for such an explanation, we encourage attention to the patterning that is a primary source of coherence in digital texts.

A heuristic, then:

1. What arrangements are possible?
2. Who arranges?
3. What is the intent?
4. What is the fit between the intent and the effect?

6.1. Email Coherence and the Heuristic

How might we use such a heuristic? To take a simple example, let's think about email. On the one hand, there are suggestions one might follow to write an effective email. However, the way we process the email has everything to do with what we read, given that what we read is, in part, a function of context; through the ability to arrange and re-arrange, we shape the context. I can read my daughter's email in the context of my daily emails (about 150 or so). I can read it in the context of the email that my daughter has sent me over the last few months, in which case it's more personal, more like a part of a series of letters. I can read it in the context of emails that I have to answer immediately. So:

- What arrangements are possible? Many, from the routine delivery of email into my email-box, to writer-only, to task-based, to attachment, and so on.
- Who arranges? The email software I use has arranged what is possible, and provides for multi-arrangements. I have default settings, which I can change. I control the arrangements, and they are plural.
- What is the intent? The intent is to talk to me in writing that is not speech, in a manner that provides for a quick response.
- What is the fit between the intent and the effect? In part, this depends on how cleverly my daughter has written her email.

And regarding this last point, there seems to be a new arrangement as well, as William Condon (2001) noted in talking about email discussion lists:

> Lists operate cumulatively. What I say, I develop over several shorter messages, and it's interleaved with what others say . . . we have quite an extended, varied, detailed, deep, and rich conversation . . . We do have long and probing conversations . . . and those conversations often morph into other long and probing conversations. . . . SOMEone needs to teach people how to interact in these environments. We are talking about literacy, certainly, and it does matter. (n.p.)

Discussing interlayering for classroom email purposes, I suggested that there were three specific ways of effective layering:

- Connecting with earlier posts by providing sufficient context and synthesizing;
- Responding specifically to issues already raised; and
- Taking issues already raised and extending or complicating them (Yancey, 2002, pp. 114–115).

In a classroom situation, we can always ask for a reflection that speaks to the intent, which we can then use as a canvas against which to plot effect. Outside of a classroom situation, email writers and email readers likewise need to be more reflective in their own processing. A classroom reflection encourages this habit of communication.

6.2. Digital Portfolio Coherence and the Heuristic

I want to think, just briefly, about another digital composition: a digital portfolio. In 2003 I taught a general education literature course where students composed digital portfolios of their writing. For this discussion, I will focus on the portfolio of one student, Mimi Dial (2003). Mimi's portfolio is organized in two ways: First through a listing of work samples, which we see in Figure 18.1, and then through a reflective letter, which we see in Figure 18.2. The order of the work samples in each genre—the list and the letter—varies. Neither order is chronological. In the case of the list, it's not clear what the

FIGURE 18.1   Mimi's Portfolio List.

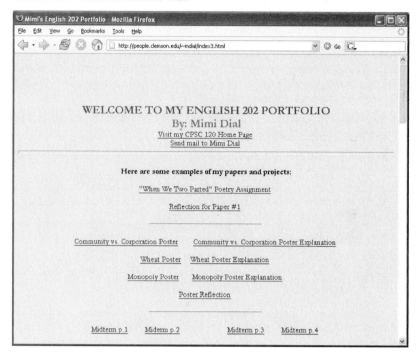

FIGURE 18.2   Mimi's Portfolio Reflective Letter.

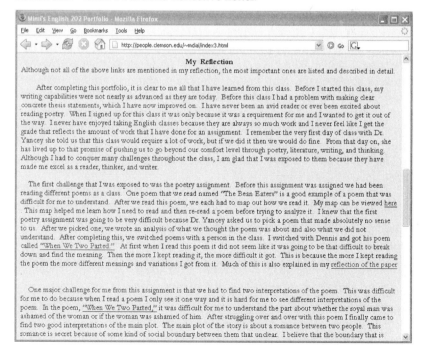

logic is, and no explanation is provided, nor is any context. The second set of links emerges from the context of the letter, so the reader can literally see the relationship between the initial links and the claims made in the letter. How a reader proceeds is up to him or her. To return to the heuristic, then:

- What arrangements are possible? Two, at least: I can link to items through the list, and that takes me through one path or I can link as I choose through the letter. I can also go back and forth.

- Who arranges? Both of us: Mimi set up some navigational structures, and I make them work as I choose.

- What is the intent? To provide a window into Mimi's development and accomplishments over the term.

- What is the fit between the intent and the effect? It works—in fact, I used both arrangements and saw through both lenses. And, of course, I had the reflection in the letter to guide me, which helped.

The relationship between the two arrangements in Mimi's portfolio parallels a point about scoring made by Brian Huot and Judy Pula (1993), who conducted a study in which readers were trained to be raters. What they found was that once trained as a rater, readers could read more fully:

> In fact, the holistic scoring training, rating sessions, and other attendant socialization actually work as a type of enculturation where raters create an immediate discourse community within the larger community to which they already belong. The smaller community permits raters to work as a group, achieving consensus, but at the same time retaining the individual and personal nature of their reading. (p. 261)

Another way to think about what happens to raters here is that through work with a scoring system, they develop a schema that provides a framework for the reading. Because they have a scoring system in place, they don't have to be anxious about how to arrive at an evaluation, and they are freed to read as they might. Multiple arrangements in digital portfolios provide the same schemata: We use one as a default and thus are able to exploit fully the other because we trust that default. Thus, the logic of the hypertext, which provides multiple arrangements through searches, site maps, navigation bars, and the like. One of these provides a default schema, the others a chance to rearrange, inventing each time we do.

7. Composing Digitally, Writing Coherence, Expressing Relationships

> Composition (noun): an essay (especially one written as an assignment): "He got an A on his composition." (One Look, 2003)

I have thought of digital texts as compositions that live inside digital gaps, that create their own unity through patterning, that are located in a kind of coherence like print and yet different from print, too—more visual, more dynamic, ultimately more contextual—that weave together, if only temporarily, fragments of a postmodern world.

And in their own design, digital compositions may unintentionally offer us new opportunities for invention, for the making of meaning. Earlier, for instance, following Forbes (1996) and Whithaus (2002), I suggested that assessment is either overly seductive as a consequence of the computer or already built into much computer-generated discourse. Like the other topics under discussion, however, assessment is also a construction, and we can exert some influence over assessment. For instance, software programs flag problems, but we do not have to agree that they are, indeed, problems. Thus, Brenda Kremer (2001) noted that when her word-processing software electronically signaled that "por" (underlined by a squiggly red line as I write this onscreen) doesn't match a word in the software's dictionary, it also provides a composer with a list of possibilities—pore, poor, pour—that themselves open up new avenues for meaning. As Kremer noted, let "the spell check por . . . [and it will] *pop up* what else might have been, and you might laugh, you might have a new idea. You might become aware of language" (p. 97). As in the case of found poetry and found images, the found words point to potential meanings.

Just because the word-processing application paints a word in red—an example of print uploaded; will red as error ever change?—doesn't necessarily make the word an error or wrong. We decide. The software can initiate a search for the correct; it can provide a new opportunity for invention; it can make the computer a co-composer.

> Composition *(noun):* the spatial property resulting from the arrangement of parts in relation to each other and to the whole: "Harmonious composition is essential in a serious work of art"; *composition (noun):* something that is created by arranging several things to form a unified whole: "He envied the composition of their faculty." (One Look, 2003)

The ultimate sources of coherence are always in relationship: A composition is an expression of relationships—between parts and parts, between parts and whole, between the visual and the verbal, between text and context, between reader and composer, between what is intended and what is unpacked, between hope and realization. And, ultimately, between human beings.

Digital compositions, then, bring us together in new ways and provide us with an opportunity to form new relationships—through multiple constituents of meaning and arrangement with each other—and perhaps to be more intentional in so doing. The language and heuristic provided here constitute one effort to assure that these new ways are acknowledged and valued appropriately. And, perhaps, the heuristic—together with new digital texts—will provide us, as they have for me here, with new questions about the relationships between and among composers, readers and texts. In that way, such compositions may indeed constitute a new site of inquiry about how we invent, how we read, and how we create texts that invite us to do both.

NOTES

1. One way to think about composition in the last 50 years is to see it occurring in stages or waves: First, print composition; second, digitally produced composition and processed composition. How multi-modal such a text might be is an open question, as is the set of skills we need to teach and learn such compositions.

2. This question was the topic of a TechRhet Thursday Night MOO on May 22, 2002; the week's topic was "C&W 2002: Reflections on Teaching and Learning in Virtual Spaces" (Walter, 2002).

3. For a discussion of the differences between and among alt, hybrid, and mixed texts, see Pat Bizzel, Helen Fox, and Pat Schroeder (2001).

REFERENCES

Adams, Paul C., Hoelscher, Steven, & Till, Karen. (Eds.). (2001). *Textures of place.* Minneapolis, MN: University of Minnesota Press.

Amato, Joe. (1992a). Science–literature inquiry as pedagogical practice: Technical writing, hypertext, and a few theories, Part I. *Computers and Composition, 9*(2), 41–54.

Amato, Joe. (1992b). Science–literature inquiry as pedagogical practice: Technical writing, hypertext, and a few theories, Part II. *Computers and Composition, 9*(2), 55–69.

Bizzell, Pat, Fox, Helen, & Schroeder, Chris. (2001). *AltDiscourse.* Portsmouth, NJ: Heinemann.

Bolter, Jay David, & Grusin, Richard. (2000). *Remediation: Understanding new media.* Cambridge, MA: MIT Press.

Carter, Locke. (2003). Argument in hypertext: Writing strategies and the problem of order in a non-sequential world. *Computers and Composition, 20,* 3–22.

Condon, William. (2001). *Chatting away. Writing Program Administrators Listserv (WPA-L).* Retrieved November 21, 2001, from <http://lists.asu.edu/cgi-bin/wa?A2=ind0111&L=wpa-l&D=1&O=A&P=16736>.

Cullen, Roxanne, & Balkema, Sandra. (1995). Generating a professional portfolio in the writing center: A hypertext tutor. *Computers and Composition, 12,* 195–201.

DeWitt, Scott Lloyd. (1996). The current nature of hypertext research in computers and composition studies: An historical perspective. *Computers and Composition, 13,* 69–84.

Dial, Mimi. (2003). *English 202 portfolio.* Retrieved February 15, 2003, from <http://people.clemson.edu/~mdial/index3.html>.

DiPardo, Anne, & DiPardo, Mike. (1990). Towards the metapersonal essay: Exploring the potential of hypertext in the composition class. *Computers and Composition, 7*(3), 7–22.

Dobrin, Sid. (2001). A problem about writing "alternative discourses." In Pat Bizzell, Helen Fox, & Chris Schroeder (Eds.), *AltDiscourse* (pp. 57–68). Portsmouth, NJ: Heinemann.

Fischer, Katherine M. (1996). Down the yellow chip road: Hypertext portfolios in Oz. *Computers and Composition, 13,* 169–183.

Forbes, Cheryl. (1996). Cowriting, overwriting, and overriding in portfolio land online. *Computers and Composition, 13,* 195–206.

Golson, Emily. (1995). Student hypertexts: The perils and promises of paths not taken. *Computers and Composition, 12,* 295–308.

Gruber, Sibylle. (2002). Power and the World Wide Web [special issue]. *Computers and Composition, 19*(3).

Haas, Mark, & Gardner, Clinton. (1999). MOO in your face. Researching, designing, and programming a user-friendly interface. *Computers and Composition, 16,* 341–358.

Halliday, Michael K., & Hasan, Ruqaiya. (1976). *Cohension in English.* London: Longman.

Haswell, Richard. (189). Textual research and coherence: Findings, intuition, application. *College English, 51,* 305–319.

Huot, Brian, & Pula, Judy. (1993). A model of background influences on holistic raters. In Brian Huot, Michael Williamson, & Marcia Farr (Eds.), *Validating holistic scoring for writing assessment: Theoretical and empirical foundations* (pp. 237–266). Cresskill, NJ: Hampton Press.

Johnson-Eilola, Johndan. (1997). *Nostalgic angels: Rearticulating hypertext writing.* Norwood, NJ: Ablex.

Kies, Daniel. (2003). *Coherence in writing. The HyperTextBooks.* Retrieved February 15, 2003, from <http://papyr.com/hypertextbooks/engl_101/coherent.htm>.

Kremer, Brenda. (2001). So it was this beautiful night. In Pat Bizzell, Helen Fox, & Chris Schroeder (Eds.), *AltDiscourse* (pp. 127–139). Portsmouth, NJ: Heinemann.

Lanham, Richard. (1993). *The electronic word: Democracy, technology, and the arts.* Chicago: University of Chicago.

One Look Dictionary Search. (2003). *Entry for composition.* Retrieved August 10, 2003, from <http://www.onelook.com/?loc=lemma2&w=composition>.

Parker, Ian. (2001, May 28). Absolute PowerPoint. *New Yorker,* pp. 76–87.

Pedagogies in virtual spaces: Writing classes in the MOO. (1996). *Kairos.* Retrieved February 15, 2003, from <http://English.ttu.edu/kairos/1.2/index.html>.

Rouzie, Albert. (2000). The composition of dramatic experience: The play element in student electronic projects. *Computers and Composition, 17,* 139–160.

Selfe, Cynthia L. (1989). Redefining literacy: The multi-layered grammar of computers. In Gail E. Hawisher & Cynthia L. Selfe (Eds.), *Critical perspectives on computers and composition studies* (pp. 3–15). New York: Teachers College Press.

Syverson, Peg. (1998). Patterns and process of reasoning in virtual worlds. In Christopher Landauer & Kirstie Bellman (Eds.), *Proceedings of the Virtual Worlds and Simulation Conference* (pp. 107–112). San Diego, CA: Society for Computer Simulation International. Retrieved June 6, 2003, from <http://www.cwrl.utexas.edu/~syverson/papers/vwsim98.html>.

Walter, John. (2002, May 22). C&W 2002: Reflections on teaching and learning in virtual spaces [Announcement]. Message posted to <techrhet@interversity.org>.

Web Portfolios. (2003). *Web portfolios: Enhancing the coherence of students' careers.* St. Olaf College Center for Integrative Studies. Retrieved February 15, 2003, from <http://www.stolaf.edu/depts./cis/web_portfolios.htm>.

Whithaus, Carl. (2002). Green squiggly lines: Evaluating student writing in computer-mediated environments. *Academic Writing, 3.* Retrieved February 15, 2003, from <http://wac.colostate.edu/aw/articles/whithaus2002/>.

Wickliff, Greg, & Yancey, Kathleen Black. (2001). The perils of creating a class website: It was the best of times, it was the. . . . *Computers and Composition, 18,* 177–186.

Yancey, Kathleen Blake. (2001). *A matter of design: The uses of writing, speech, and the visual in learning across the curriculum.* Paper presented at the Fifth National Writing across the Curriculum Conference, Bloomington, IN.

Yancey, Kathleen Blake. (2002). The pleasures of digital discussions: Lessons, challenges, recommendations, and reflections. In Pamela Takayoshi & Brian Huot (Eds.), *Teaching writing with computers* (pp. 105–118). Boston: Houghton Mifflin.

Yancey, Kathleen Blake, & Huot, Brian. (Eds.). (1997). *Assessing writing across the curriculum: Diverse methods and practices.* Greenwich, CT: Ablex.

19   *The Politics of the Program: MS Word as the Invisible Grammarian*

TIM McGEE AND PATRICIA ERICSSON

The most profound technologies are those that disappear. They weave themselves into the fabric of everyday life until they are indistinguishable from it.

—MARK WEISER (1991)

1. INTRODUCTION

The idea for this article was conceived accidentally. As we exchanged drafts for a conference presentation, we were entertained by some of the inane recommendations that our word processor's grammar and style checker suggested. Soon, casual entertainment led to questions: Who programs these checkers? What approach to language does this automated system represent? What might this ever-present corrective force be teaching students? Does a grammar and style checker support or undermine what composition teachers are trying to accomplish? As our list of questions grew longer, we realized that we had, serendipitously, found a topic for another conference presentation and for this article.

As our discussions progressed, Cynthia L. Selfe and Richard Selfe's (1994) enjoinder from "The Politics of the Interface" echoed regularly: Composition teachers need to be more than users of technology; they need to "think carefully about the implications of its use within their own classrooms" (p. 496). The Selfes encouraged us "to teach students and ourselves to recognize computer interfaces as noninnocent physical borders . . . cultural borders . . . and linguistic borders" (p. 495).

Joel Haefner's (1999) "Politics of the Code" recommended an initial focus. Haefner quoted Theodor Nelson's claim that "a computer language is a system for casting spell[s]," and concluded his article by asserting that if Nelson is right, "then English instructors in computer-supported classrooms need to know something about the context and the necromancers of the code" (p. 338).

From *Computers and Composition* 19 (2002): 453–70.

Because we have concerns about the uses of technology, particularly word processing software in the composition classroom, we focused on the style and grammar checking tool in MS WORD, the most widely used word processing software in the world. Its ubiquity is unquestionable. And its Grammar Checker (MSGC)[1] is now the product of an increasingly sophisticated branch of Microsoft's research efforts, the National Language Processing Group, whose particular linguistic approach exerts an undeniable, though largely invisible, influence upon writers. The specifics of that approach and the philosophies of language that it embodies begged some investigation.

We also became intrigued by how machine-checking of grammar and style alters the very concept of teaching grammar.[2] Its default status ("Check grammar as you type") makes grammar a primary concern by foregrounding correctness even while writers are in the drafting stage. It gives grammar and style (both narrowly defined by this digital program) a precedence, at least temporally, over content, mode of discourse, or other rhetorical concerns.[3] This precedence could well have a negative effect on the development of writing ability. Although the field of composition and rhetoric enjoys some diversity of opinion as to what constitutes "best practice," there is considerable agreement about some classroom activities that do *not* improve student writing, first among which would have to be grammar instruction (Braddock, Lloyd-Jones, & Schoer, 1963; Hartwell, 1985).[4] The stronger indictments assert that formal grammar instruction is not just ineffective, but positively harmful if it consumes limited instructional time that could be dedicated to activities that actually help students become better writers. Where, however, does an artificially intelligent checker fit into that understanding of the place of grammar instruction in the composition curriculum? Does the checker provide instruction? Take up time? A related question is when, within a writing process, is the best time for a student to attend to those issues to which Grammar Checkers do attend? Mike Rose (1984) listed editing "too early in the composing process" as a primary cause of writer's block.[5] And, significantly, among the five distinct meanings of grammar that Patrick Hartwell identified, to which does the MSGC attend?

Finally, we considered the strategies that users and teachers might employ to maximize the help (or minimize the harm) that the Grammar Checker in WORD could actually cause in (or around) a composition classroom. Various authors have recognized the opportunities for customizing the programs we use (Haefner, 1999; Haist, 1999; Selfe & Selfe, 1994). Caroline Haist concluded her thorough analysis of Grammar Checker in WORD 97 with a list of recommendations, the first of which is to "have students proofread their work to eliminate as many errors as possible before using the Grammar Checker," a wise suggestion given her finding that "the more errors there are in a sentence, the more likely that Grammar Checker is to provide incorrect suggestions" ("Recommendations" section, 1999, par. 2). However, because the default setting in recent versions of WORD is "Check grammar as you type," most users will do just the opposite of what Haist recommends. Furthermore, as Haefner noted, "customization assumes a single user for the software, not a lab or classroom environment where many students use the same software copy, the same workstation, many times a day" (p. 334). Finally, there is a limit to how much customizing any program will accept. As Fred Kemp (1992) wrote, "Computer software . . . no matter what flexibility it may claim or what ability to accept 'user definition' or modifying parameters, can never escape the instructional attitudes and even the ideology of its programmers and designers" (p. 9–10).

Our argument, then, is that the Grammar Checker in MS WORD represents an especially important piece of software for composition teachers to use critically for several reasons: its ubiquity, its near invisibility, its increasing power, its theoretical mismatch, and, in most cases, its actual conflict with and possible undermining of pedagogies that are now considered most effective for improving student writing.

2. Ubiquity of Microsoft's Grammar Checker

In a purely numbers game, Microsoft wins the software war hands down. In the early 1990s, Microsoft claimed to have 35 million users of its operating system and software; however, since the monopoly controversy of the late 1990s, specific numbers are difficult, it not impossible, to find. Industry experts estimate Microsoft's current share of the word processing software market at somewhere between 80 and 90%,[6] and in 1997 Microsoft was aiming to become a major force in the educational software market, reversing their position earlier in that decade (Microsoft makes, 1997). The ever-expanding "Microsoft in Education" branch of its web site illustrates the corporation's desire to promote its presence in the educational market. Simply by virtue of its ubiquity, Microsoft gets more "teachable moments" than the English teachers do. There are now just over 500,000 English teachers in the United States. Because WORD is on millions of desktops and Grammar Checker is turned on by default, it has many more, practically invisible, "over the shoulder"[7] opportunities to be a grammar teacher than the typical English teacher—formerly one of the only purveyors of grammar instruction in a student's writing experience.

3. Whose Grammar Is It?

This change in instructional personnel is no small matter. It reminded us of the Selfes' warning that unless "those who are familiar with language and learning theory, who understand issues raised by technology studies and cultural studies" pay close attention to the design of programs, "interface design will continue to be dominated primarily by computer scientists and will lack perspectives that could be contributed by humanist scholars" (1994, p. 498). However, the issue here goes deeper than interface design to become not only a matter of who is teaching grammar and how they are teaching it, but a matter of what they mean by "grammar" in the first place.

Some users may assert that the Grammar Checker in WORD is nothing but a mechanical delivery system for the grammar found in handbooks, and, therefore, represents no cause for alarm. Others, however, while accepting the view of MSGC as a mechanical handbook, would consider that to be an indictable offense, as handbook grammar is sometimes a dumb-downed version of "real" grammar,[8] and simply tossing it at a struggling writer is far from effective pedagogy. We, however, contend that the content of MSGC is, in fact, quite different from a traditional handbook. And although it might be comforting if we could demonstrate that the grammar those computational linguists poured into MSGC represents an impoverished or debased form of what English teachers (wise humanists, they) have been dispensing for years, the reality is not so simple.

Yes, some MSGC content comes straight out of handbooks, and is therefore every bit as beneficial or useless as what can be found in some "school grammars." And some points of careful usage that better grammar handbooks try to preserve get flattened by the binary Grammar Checker, thereby depriving users of a subtle marker of formal tone. For example, several recent handbooks insist upon "which" for nonrestrictive relative clauses and recommend "that" for restrictive clauses, but will allow "which" for restrictive clauses, noting that such usage indicates a more informal tone. The MSGC, however, takes a strictly binary approach. It flags any "which" that is not bracketed by commas, thereby suggesting that restrictive clauses ought to use a "that." It is difficult to determine whether the MSGC does this because it's easier for the program to handle a simple binary or because the computational linguists had loaded in the more restrictive prescriptions of Strunk and White, rather than the more accurate description of more recent handbooks.

Nevertheless, the Grammar Checker in WORD embodies a far more sophisticated approach to grammar than most users have noticed (sophisticated in terms of computational linguistics (CL), yet increasingly mongrelized in terms of grammars). Paradoxically, however, its increased sophistication may make it more dangerous than ever before. And although it may seem ironic if the wise humanists were suddenly to be trumped by those with less enlightened views of language, the history of English grammar would simply be repeating itself. Writing about the rise of prescriptive grammar in the eighteenth century, Albert C. Baugh and Thomas Cable (1993) reported that Joseph Priestley's linguistic "tolerance, and good sense" lost out in the marketplace to Robert Lowth who was "much more conservative in his stand, a typical representative of the normative and prescriptive school of grammarians" (p. 269). About the flurry of grammars published in the late eighteenth century, Baugh and Cable remarked that "most of these books were the work of men with no special qualification for the thing they attempted to do" (p. 270). Two centuries later, a similar event may be occurring as those who are highly qualified to do CL start assuming functions that had traditionally been the bailiwick of English teachers.

4. Critical Use

Heeding Haefner's call to examine "the context and necromancers of the code" behind the Grammar Checker requires looking into Microsoft's Research Group, first established in 1991. The establishment of these research labs indicated Microsoft's interest in "speech recognition, futuristic user interfaces and 3-D graphics-cutting-edge technologies" (Buderi, 1999, p. 45). The branch of Microsoft's Research Group that produced the MSGC is the Natural Language Processing Group, consisting of about 50 researchers—almost all of whom are computational linguists. Although some consider the field of CL synonymous with Natural Language Processing (NLP), the editors of *The Handbook of Natural Language Processing* assert "a clear demarcation between domain-specific theory on the one hand and practical development of computational language processing systems on the other." It is the latter, purely utilitarian approach that they put at the center of NLP, calling it the "least ambitious" of those fields that link computational ideas and human cognitive functions, limiting itself largely to producing "practical tools for the design of input–output modules" (Dale, Moisl, & Somers, 2000, pp. vi–vii). An epitome of such practicality would be a tool to check that aspect of written discourse that so many writers have some insecurity about—their grammar.

The Natural Language Processing Group hit paydirt when they produced a grammar and style checker better than the one that Miscrosoft had been licensing from Inso.[9] When Microsoft installed its own checker in WORD 97, they not only improved their product and saved some money, but, according to Dan Ling (former Research Director at Microsoft and now the Vice-President of Microsoft Research), the sentence parsing program now built into every copy of WORD was "the foundation for building lots of different natural language tools" (qtd. in Buderi, 1999, p. 47). This foundation has much to do with Microsoft's long range goals regarding usability and office automation, but very little to do with the teaching of writing. George E. Heidorn, a researcher in Microsoft's NLP group, described the "product orientation" in the NLP research group as an "enormous benefit." Instead of being interested only in theoretical ideas and "interesting linguistic examples," researchers now pay attention to "real text as written by real people" (Heidorn, 2000, p. 205) due to the requirements of such a practical project. Their attention, however, is still that of linguists, and the linguist's interest in language is far different from that of the rhetorician and the composition teacher,[10] and even farther still from that of the typical student writer. As Eric Johnson (1997) concluded, some "checkers have the ability to use sophisticated means to identify some grammatical blunders . . . but because they sometimes propose embarrassingly bad changes, the user must exercise great care in accepting suggestions" (par. 8). The "typical student writer" often has neither the grammatical expertise nor the patience to take the "great care" Johnson deemed necessary. In a similar vein, Caroline Haist found "most of the explanations Grammar Checker provides . . . helpful," but judged that "some are confusing and, in at least a couple of cases, just plain wrong" (1999, Introduction section, par. 6).

To become critical users of a program designed not by teachers of writing but by computational linguists, and made not for students of writing, but for workers in Microsoft's generic "Office," we must look closely at the approaches to language used by the NLP Group and then consider the points of contact and conflict with the approaches to language used by composition teachers.

5. CODE UPON CODE

Haefner warned that "how programmers go about writing code structures the way we (can) use computers" and Structured Programming's "grounding in the American corporate environment [has] profound implications for the kinds of writing students do in computer-supported classrooms and the ways we teach writing" (1999, p. 337). The tenor of those implications are captured in Haefner's earlier assertion that "the cultural imperative catalyzing SP has always been corporate productivity and profitability" (p. 330). Sociolinguist Lesley Milroy (1998) reminded us that English prescriptive grammar results from the fact that "by the eighteenth century Britain needed a standardized language to meet the needs of geographically scattered colonial government servants and to facilitate mass education" (p. 96) and that "since the goal of codification is to define a particular form as standard, this process entailed intolerance of a range of choices which speakers and writers had hitherto taken for granted" (p. 95). So, a computerized Grammar Checker, even one that was well designed with student writers in mind, would be likely to include two different kinds of codification constraining the choices of the novice writer.[11] And, as we will show, the Grammar Checker in WORD, because of its peculiar history, is anything but a program well designed for student writers.

6. MORE REAL THAN IDEAL

Building on Seymour Papert's idea that computers are "naturally heuristic," Fred Kemp claimed that we cannot "computerize any activity without having to (1) completely rethink the activity, including all the assumed behaviors that have become virtually invisible, and (2) discover in the new perspectives afforded by such rethinking, possibilities for actions that were never possible through the old perspectives" (qtd. in Rickly, 2001, p. 10). Unfortunately, the NLP Group has not followed this "naturally heuristic" path in programming what users get in the MSGC. The real goal of the NLP Group is natural language processing: a user being able to employ natural language (actual speech) to interface with a computer. The implementation of the MSGC was just a happy coincidence for the Group.

To be responsible scholars and teachers, however, we must take note that no matter how theoretically sound and linguistically appropriate an approach the Group takes to natural language processing, its currently marketable byproduct (the MSGC) does not take a theoretically sound, rhetorically appropriate, pedagogically suitable approach to an ideal grammar and style checker. As Eric Johnson (1992) concluded:

> The ideal grammar and style checker will be produced by a team consisting of linguists, computer programmers, and writing teachers. Linguists are obviously needed to develop the algorithms of word identification and sentence parsing. Programmers create the computer code to implement the algorithms. No less important are the writing teachers. They know the kind of advice that is likely to produce better writing. (par. 19)

A team composed of the members that Johnson suggested, aided by rhetoricians and compositionists, a team setting out to computerize an ideal grammar and style checker would, no doubt, aspire to what Papert and Kemp proposed: They would "rethink the activity, [investigate] assumed behaviors . . . discover new perspectives," and come up with an approach that truly would give them "a new lens through which to view the whole picture," a lens that would show them "new ways of conceiving the very mission itself and supporting it" (qtd. in Rickly, 2001, p. 10).

It is unfortunate for all users that the current MGSC is not "ideal" or even close to it. There is no "new lens," no "new ways of conceiving" grammar or style in the MSGC. Although the programming might be complicated and the interface slick, users get recycled, often confusing advice about grammar and a mixed bag of style suggestions that don't take into account current thinking on the grammar itself, good rhetorical theory, or pedagogical considerations. As we illustrate further, the problems of the MGSC are numerous, often dangerous, and largely invisible.

7. MORE POWER THAN INTELLIGENCE

The Grammar Checker in MS WORD 97 and WORD 2000 (MSGC) is, indeed, a very different beast from the checkers found in previous versions of Microsoft's word processing software. Although the casual user may have noticed little change, one reviewer claimed the WORD 97 was "the first word processor available that comes with a Grammar Checker worth using" (Lowe, 1997, p. 36). The new checker was considerably more sophisticated than its predecessors, at least in terms of CL—a kind of sophistication, however, that may only exacerbate the problem caused by the software's rhetorical naivete (a naivete that is understandable given that the Grammar Checker was not designed by composition teachers for student writers, and that the ultimate goal of its designers was not Standard Written English, but speech recognition).

According to Heidorn, "the NLP system that is behind the Microsoft GRAMMAR CHECKER [but not yet fully implemented] is a full-fledged natural language processing system that is also intended to be used for many other applications. It consists of a programming language and a runtime environment that are both specifically tailored to the needs of an NLP system" (2000, p. 182). One part of that processing system is described as a "bottom-up, multipath, chart-parsing algorithm [that] also makes use of both probabilistic information and a heuristic-scoring scheme to guide the process to a quicker and better termination point" (p. 184).

Although such power and sophistication have caused scholars to grant that the MSGC and other recent checkers demonstrate "undeniable gains in functionality over their predecessors," critics still concluded that "their reliability and accuracy . . . have improved only minimally" (Vernon, 2000, p. 331).

An example of increased functionality with questionable reliability can be seen in the Grammer Checker's newfound ability to revise—not just

FIGURE 19.1   Diagram of NLP Analysis Components.

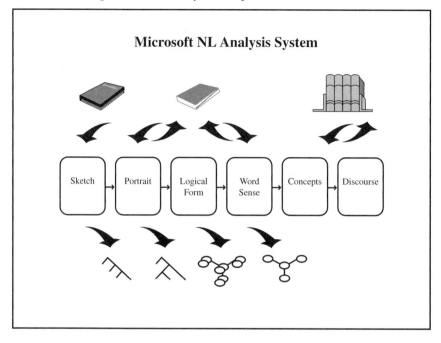

Source: Microsoft Research: Current Research at <http://research.microsoft.com/nlp/analysis..asp>.

flag—passive constructions. For example, when MSGC flags "Bill was left by Mary," it suggests revising it to "Mary left Bill." Unfortunately, however, when the current checker encounters the sentence "Bill was left by the side of the road," it suggests "The side of the road left Bill."

Due to gaffes like that,[12] many remain unimpressed with how the program handles language analysis, despite recognizing that the ability to revise passive sentences into active ones is quite a feat of artificial intelligence. Also, few users suspect that revising passive to active constructions is just the tip of an iceberg of potential functions hidden within Microsoft's Natural Language Analysis System, only a fraction of which are enabled in the MSGC currently on the market. Figure 19.1 depicts all six of the stages that Microsoft's full-fledged NL analysis system can perform upon text in their research lab.

At the top of the diagram three different kinds of texts are depicted: the input text to be analyzed, a dictionary (with input and output arrows occurring twice), and a shelf of books, the large knowledge base they call "Mind-Net" (also showing both input and output arrows). Below the texts are the six stages of analysis, representing the progression from lexical, through syntactic, then semantic, and culminating in discourse analysis.

The MSGC in currently available versions of WORD is limited largely to lexical and syntactic processing, whereas the NLP system behind the checker is well equipped to handle some kinds of semantic processing as well. Semantic processing occurs in the third stage of the Microsoft NLP analysis system, the syntactic portrait. In that stage, the NL analysis system attempts to "produce more reasonable attachments for some modifiers." Heidorn explained how semantic reattachment "makes use of semantic relations that are produced automatically by analyzing the text of definitions and example sentences in an online dictionary. These semantic relations are stored in a rather large knowledge base that is now known as MindNet." That is how Microsoft NLP system knows "that it is more likely that a telescope is an instrument for seeing a bird, rather than a part of the bird in the sentence 'I saw a bird with a telescope'" (p. 185).[13]

However, such a complex system cannot yet be packed in its entirety into the commercial word processor. "Fortunately," according to Heidorn, "some applications of the Microsoft NLP system, such as the current Grammar Checker, can do an adequate job without doing semantic reattachment and, therefore, can be spared the added cost of that processing" (2000, p. 185)—adequate, perhaps, for the mature writer who wants help spotting the occasional slip in grammar or usage, but far from adequate for students with a tenuous grasp on Standard Written English.

If the system behind the MSGC is, in fact, so linguistically sophisticated, why would such a system mistake "the side of the road" for the unnamed agent who had abandoned Bill? This is partly due to gaps in the system's collection of "factoids" and "multiword entries" (MWEs), bits of information that the currently installed system does possess about certain individual words or word groups. Thanks to a factoid, the very program that suggests revising "Bill was left by Mary" to "Mary left Bill" does not suggest that "Bill was left by April" be revised to "April left Bill." Why? Because the software knows that "April" can represent a month. However, "by the side of" would not be a factoid but a multiword preposition stored as its own "MWE" in the dictionary. That is how MSGC knows to suggest "behind" as a replacement for "in back of." Apparently, however, the system does not yet possess "by the side of" as an MWE for "beside," because it never suggests that revision.

In addition to the increased powers of syntactic analysis, another improvement, first added in WORD 2000, is the software's ability to flag successive nouns in groups of more than three. Listed under the "Style" options, this feature allows the user to guard against "Strings of several nouns that may be unclear, as in 'The income tax office business practices remained the same'" (Microsoft, 2000). This feature is one of five new checking options that Alex Vernon said are "likely inspired by WORDPERFECT" (2000, p. 331). Whatever the inspiration, the added proscription against noun + noun + noun represents a new level of style (or grammar)[14] checking of the sort addressed by Joseph Williams, who warns against the long compound noun phrase as a source of ambiguity (Williams, 2000, p. 91). This new addition to the MSGC could represent a slight tonic to its overall rhetorical naivete because linguistic expertise of the sort that Hartwell describes as "developed by psycholinguistic studies of comprehension" appears to be finding its way into the Grammar Checker. This is the sort of perspective that William J. Vande Kopple (1998) felt linguists could offer to compositionists because "research in linguistics and discourse analysis can provide powerful generalizations about how readers will respond to characteristics of sentences and texts," generalizations about which "students deserve to know" (p. 6). So some of the added functionality in WORD 2000 appears to be getting rhetorically smart. Again, however, just how well suited this sort of instruction is for student writers is debatable. Vernon noted that "the target market for these products [is] business and the adult professional," (p. 331) a remark similar to the response some instructors have had toward Joseph Williams's *Style: Ten Lessons in Clarity and Grace;* namely, it represents a style manual particularly well suited to the mature writer of the impenetrable prose sometimes known as bureaucratese or sociologese, but it is a style manual not particularly well suited to the novice writer whose difficulties have more to do with invention and fluency than with turgidity. So much for the visible influences in the most recent version of the MSGC. We now turn to some of its unseen influences.

8. DISAPPEARING POWERS OF MSGC

Two ways that the MSGC exerts its influence are the corporate cache of Microsoft itself and the interface of WORD—powers that are all the more influential as they have become unnoticed norms. Although tarnished by the monopoly trials that began in the late 1990s, the corporate image of Microsoft still shines as the standard bearer of the operating system and software world. Industry watchers keep a close eye on Microsoft's every move, its stock serving as a bellwether for the entire technology sector. Its brand name alone gives the Microsoft Grammar Checker a kind of influence that is difficult (perhaps impossible) to calculate.

WORD's interface is another visible factor with almost invisible power, as its polished surface has become so familiar that it has disappeared below the threshold of our notice. Granted, occasional new additions catch some attention, not all of which is positive. (Why the animated paper clip seems to arouse such antipathy in some users is hard to say; is it the simple intrusiveness or the bizarre coquetry of its eye movements?) In any event, the overall slickness of WORD's interface is something now so familiar we no longer notice it as an incredibly polished product constantly persuading us of its quality and dependability.

Other aspects of the program's influence are encoded into its default settings. Because so many users remain unaware of the options available in the Grammar Checker, millions have grown as accustomed to the squiggly green lines as they had become to the red ones signaling spelling errors. Grammar and style are constantly being checked in real time except for those users savvy enough to have turned off that option. And even the savvy user gets grammar and style advice automatically when choosing to spellcheck a document.

Some might argue that the green squiggles do render the checker visible, especially for those accustomed to word processing before the arrival of WORD 97. Many users may simply learn to ignore the green line or, more accurately, think that they have learned to ignore the green line. However, not acting on the line's recommendation or not bothering to inquire into its meaning is not the same as being uninfluenced by it. Some users have reported switching "which" to "that" whenever a "which" is flagged, but learning to ignore the full-sentence underlines (as they usually indicate "long-sentence," and those users don't mind writing long ones).

Although some users may have doubts about artificial intelligence after seeing the Spielberg/Kubrick film *AI*, the intelligence built into the MSGC isn't nearly as ominous as that in the movie, but does lend another invisible force to the program. The invisible intelligence of a supposedly smart machine has a definite appeal. Fred Kemp commented that to many, the "computer . . . projects the universal ethos of science itself" (1992, p. 10). When this ethos and a trust in artificial intelligence are combined with the supposition that the smart people at Microsoft know more about grammar and style than the typical user, the Grammar Checker gains considerable power. More significant, however, may be the issue of consistency. Unlike teachers who may occasionally contradict themselves and who frequently contradict each other (making "Can I use 'I'?" one of the most frequently asked questions in every composition class), MSGC is as consistent as only a machine can be. In every situation, the Grammar Checker will respond identically to the same grammar and style issues. Students, more so than the general population, have a near desperate need for certainties and "right" answers; a computer program gives them those certainties more readily than all-too-human English teachers.

Of particular interest to us and to others who are interested in the politics of the interface, code, and software is the entire politics of standardized language. This issue is invisible to most users, especially to student writers. Given that their school-based language instruction is largely prescriptive and that few, if any, precollege students have been let in on the secret that the prescriptions of Standard English are neither natural, nor logical, nor productive of language that is "better" (in any meaningful sense of the word) than nonstandard Englishes, most simply accept the authority of this smart machine to police their grammar, just as they have heretofore accepted the authority of their smart teachers. Although many might smart from this power relationship, for most, it has operated invisibly, as just one of the many givens of the school environment. For them, the situation simply could not be otherwise. It is just what is. "Good grammar" is a fact of school life, and the MSGC is licensed to check their grammar by the same invisible authority that licenses the rest of the adult world they are being socialized into.

Although all previous issues are vitally important to us as composition teachers and scholars, perhaps none is as significant as the possible misfit the

MSGC might have with our objectives as teachers of writing. Not surprisingly, our conclusions on that question are as discouraging as the majority of our findings.

9. THE MSGC CONTRADICTS GOOD PEDAGOGY

Throughout the recent history of composition (as well as the entire history of rhetoric), various approaches to teaching writing have existed simultaneously. No one theory or pedagogy has ever taken hold as "gospel." This variety, according to James Berlin (1996), tends to proliferate "in proportion to the freedom tolerated in the society involved" (p. 138). Despite this multiplicity, we can look at current composition theory and pedagogy to get a sense of what is now considered best practice—an important notion to consider if we are going to judge whether the MSGC might support or undermine those attempting to enact such practice.

Best practice is characterized by a concern for the social nature of writing and an eye to the total ecology in which writing is incubated, produced, and consumed. Current best practice acknowledges that writing—whether it be invention, process, production or consumption—is a multilayered, collaborative, often digitally enacted, postmodern ecology. Marilyn Cooper (1989), one of the first scholars to posit an ecological model of writing, explained that this kind of a system "postulates dynamic interlocking systems that structure the social activity of writing" (p. 7). These ecological systems are continually in flux, steadily being created and recreated by readers, writers, and teachers in a complex web of interacting possibilities that those involved encounter. No matter which subtle flavor it takes on, best practice in the new millennium is decidedly social.

The nearly polar opposite of a social/ecological approach to teaching composition is the pedagogy commonly known as *current traditional rhetoric.* This method of teaching is characterized by an overwhelming concern with forms and obsessive attention to precise, correct language. Although scholars as notable as Robert Connors (1997) objected to the term *current traditional* (pp. 4–7), Debra Hawhee (1999) claimed that current traditional rhetoric forms "a discipline in both senses of the word" because current traditional rhetoric has the ingredients of a discipline: "a subject, a 'body of knowledge,' a body of precepts for students to learn and follow"; in addition, it disciplines students by "constructing them as aberrant individuals" (p. 521). The discipline of current traditional rhetoric is passed down from teacher to student and then is replicated in the students who become the next generation of teachers. The precepts of current traditional rhetoric are encoded in handbooks and workbooks that were considered ineffective for the teaching of writing as early as the 1880s (Connors, 1997, p. 117).

Contemporary critics of Grammar Checkers have commented that "style and grammar packages are generally based on an overly narrow—and erroneous—vision of 'correct' language use" (Selfe & Selfe, 1994, p. 489) or have claimed that simply tossing a handbook at a struggling writer represents some pretty bad pedagogy. Kemp posited that "computers can process text in only the most superficial of senses; computers cannot grasp the meaning in the text" (1992, p. 14).[15] The least effective, empirically dismissed approach to the improvement of writing is the approach presented by the MSGC. It is concerned primarily with prescriptive issues of usage and surface concerns of style. Even in its screen appearance, it harkens back to the red pencil of the obsessive English teacher who bled over "mistakes" and paid little or no attention to the quality of thinking. The Grammar Checker in WORD 97, according to one reviewer, "attempts to be a full-fledged writing coach" (Campbell, 1997, p. 109), but the bulk of its comments are based on a digital, right/wrong, binary paradigm that make writing seem to be exactly what it is not: "Writing is not a mistake to be corrected, something broken to be fixed, a gap to be filled, or a wrong to be righted" (Kemp, 1992, p. 23). Sadly, MSGC is primarily a current traditional machine—a machine that looks dangerously smart, especially to users insecure about grammar and usage.

Even though materials on the Microsoft web site tout WORD 2000 as having "new features [that] also make it an excellent tool for collaboration" (Word 2000, 2001, par. 1) and explain how WORD can be used to enhance the writing process, making WORD a useful teaching tool requires that both students and teachers overlook the most obvious critique that WORD makes—red and green highlighted commentary on correctness. In addition, the ability to change styles may seem like a computer-smart guarantee that the writer is going to "get it right" for her particular audience simply by setting a level of formality that the computer verifies. This surface consideration of language that is audience appropriate is almost laughably simplistic.

10. DISARMING THE MICROSOFT NECROMANCER

At the end of our efforts to "pay attention" to this particular software, we are tempted to encourage all writing teachers to throw away their copies of MS WORD and to ban it from their schools. However, if we actually had the power to instigate such a revolution, the most prevalent grammar and style checker on our computer desktops would already be different. Despite this inability, we believe composition teachers are not powerless, even in the face of the Microsoft giant; we believe we can play David to this Goliath. Slaying the giant probably isn't possible (and perhaps now that we know so much more about the software, it might not even be desirable), so how can composition teachers minimize the harms it could cause?

Carolyn Haist provided several suggestions to minimize the harm of the MSGC at the end of her 1999 article, and others have provided similar suggestions (Spinks, Wells, & Meche, 1997; Vernon, 2000). In giving our presentation on this topic at the Computers and Writing Conference in 2000, we still felt quite confident in providing a list of things that a composition teacher could do to ameliorate problems MSGC might present. And we still believe that a list of steps can help a composition teacher—to some degree. However, because of what our critique has uncovered, we find using practical, how-to, or step-by-step guides too insignificant—rather like just throwing rocks at Goliath instead of aiming a slingshot at him.

What can we provide as a metaphorical slingshot? What can we employ to make our aim more accurate and our impacts more substantive? We believe the answer lies in knowledge. To begin with, leaving decisions about grammar up to Microsoft is simply unacceptable. All English teachers need more than a basic understanding of prescriptive grammar; we need a rich understanding, informed by scholarship like that of Patrick Hartwell (1985) and others who have considered grammar in a more complex way. We need to understand that "grammar" can be used politically to limit access to position, power, and wealth. We need to understand the subtleties of grammar far better than most of us do.

We need to spend time digging around in software before using it. When a new grammar-and-style checker appears, we need to take time to dig into it, rummage around in its "options"[16] and "defaults" to see what kind of a beast it is. (Most of us need to do this immediately with the checkers that are currently on our desktops and in our labs—even if they aren't new.) We need to be confident enough with the technology to "play" with it, to open it up for inspection, and to think about what we see and what it means for us and for students in our classes. Mindlessly accepting a piece of software is irresponsible—even if everyone in the world is using it, even if we can't really change it, even if we're afraid of breaking it. We are in complete accord with what Selfe told us in her 1998 CCCC address: *"As composition teachers, deciding whether or not to use technology in our classes is simply not the point—we have to pay attention to technology"* (Selfe, 1999, p. 415, original emphasis).

In this same address, Selfe also told us that we need to get students involved in critiques of technology:

> Composition teachers, language arts teachers, and other literacy specialists need to recognize that the relevance of technology in the English studies disciplines is not simply a matter of helping student work effectively with communication software and hardware, but, rather, also a matter of helping them to understand and be able to assess—to pay attention to—the social, economic, and pedagogical implications of new communication technologies and technological initiatives that affect their lives. (p. 432)

This might appear to be difficult, but we believe that it doesn't have to be. If teachers are confident that the software can't really be broken (and it can't—Microsoft has made sure of that), then we can feel free to ask students to help us investigate it. Whatever age students we teach, many know more about playing with computers than we do, and they are usually more eager to do it. We can ask them to look at the options that the MSGC offers. Once they are inside the software, we can encourage questions about the various grammar, usage, and style choices that Microsoft offers. We think that more than a few students will notice that under the "Formal" option in WORD 97, the checker has all but three possibilities turned on—and one possibility that is *not on* is to check for gender-specific words. If we ask them to check into the explanations of the grammar and style options, they can check to see if their notions of "Commonly confused words" match up with the ones Microsoft provides.[17]

The opportunities that this kind of investigation can provide us are practically unlimited. It gives us a chance not only to talk about grammar in context, but also to think about and talk with students about the politics of Microsoft, how the checker was constructed, and what it might mean for different kinds of students from differing backgrounds.

Finally, those of us in positions to influence teacher education programs must insist that the courses in these programs include up-to-date composition theory, broad-based and complex instruction in grammar, investigations of the ideological underpinnings of technology, and enough hands-on work with computers and software that teachers are eager to go below the primary interface. Those of us in positions to influence hiring practices need to make sure that the people we hire can interrogate technology.

In the end what we need is quite revolutionary, even though the revolution might not include slaying Goliath. Our revolution must go to the heart of how we think about and interact with technology; this revolution is about knowledge, education, and action. We need a revolt in the ranks—people currently teaching with these technologies need to take a critical interest. And we need to include our students in this uprising.

But none of this is really new—those in-the-know have been calling for these kinds of changes for at least a decade. What is new, we believe, is our call for these changes following a thorough critique of a piece of software that can powerfully affect our teaching. We are confident that our critique, one that uncovers a largely invisible influence in our teaching lives, will spur some to action. We hope that what we have uncovered makes the invisible grammarian of MSGC less mysterious, less able to cast spells. We hope we have wrested some power from the Microsoft necromancers and put it back into more capable hands—yours.

NOTES

1. Although its full and most accurate name might be Microsoft's Grammar and Style Checker, for the sake of simplicity we will refer to the tool that appears in MS WORD 97 and WORD 2000 as the Grammar Checker or MSGC for short.

2. In addition to altering the concept of teaching grammar, machine-checking of grammar could, to some extent, alter the concept of writing itself. As Anne Herrington and Charles Moran (2001) concluded their critique of the machines now being used to score student essays, "Writing *to* the machine . . . creates what is for now an unprecedented and unnatural rhetorical situation. . . . Writing to the machine desensitizes us as writers" (pp. 496–97).

3. Proponents of the Grammar Checker might argue that because users can first choose one of five "styles," the Grammar Checker actually gives priority to the notions of audience and occasion; however, many users remain unaware that there are five styles from which to choose or that each of those can be customized—few of the participants in two workshops we have conducted even knew about these options.

4. Hartwell admitted that the grammar issue was still controversial in 1985 and listed papers defending the teaching of formal grammar as well as those attacking it. A 1995 *Composition Chronicle* article with the title "Grammar Making a Comeback in Composition Teaching" (McCleary,

1995), attests to grammar's perseverance. The controversy continues to this day, but, thanks in part to Hartwell's work, the complex notion of grammar has been unpacked to the point of including five distinctly different meanings, a few of which we will employ later in this article.

5. In his attempt to identify the "cognitive variables involved in writer's block," Rose (1984) listed six reasons that some writers block, four of which could well be exacerbated by using MSGC in its default mode. In addition to editing too early, three other causes are these: "(1) the rules by which they guide their composing processes are rigid, inappropriately invoked, or incorrect . . . , (5) they invoke conflicting rules, assumptions, plans, and strategies; and (6) they evaluate their writing with inappropriate criteria or criteria that are inadequately understood" (p. 4).

6. Estimates vary widely depending on how the data are sampled; for example, Microsoft's dominance appears smaller when law offices figure heavily in the sample as WORD PERFECT still commands a large share of the legal word processing market, holding 82% of that market as recently as 1998 (Phelps, 1998, par. 2.).

7. An online *Product Enhancements Guide* for WORD once proudly asserted that WORD can "act as the reader over your shoulder as you type." That document, previously available at <http://www.microsoft.com/TechNet/Word/prodfact/wd97peg.asp>, has been removed.

8. Hartwell (1985), expanding on "The Three Meanings of Grammar" that W. Nelson Francis offered in 1954, provided five distinct meanings, including grammar 1, "The Grammar in Our Heads," and grammar 2, "The Scientific Grammar of Linguists." The third, which Francis referred to as "Linguistic Etiquette," according to Hartwell, "is, of course, not grammar at all, but usage" (p. 110). Grammar 4 is school grammar, a user friendly but slightly inaccurate version of scientific grammar that teachers use with students, is found in most handbooks. Hartwell described the "rules" of "common school grammars" as "inadequate to the facts of written language" (1985, p. 119).

9. That product had first been available for PCs in 1989 as CORRECTTEXT GRAMMAR CORRECTION SYSTEM from Houghton–Mifflin, later from Inso Corporation. No slouch of an application, it was one of two commercial systems identified by Robert Dale (1996) as "the first products to use anything related to the parsing technologies developed in the research field." He went on to predict, accurately, that "as machines become more powerful, and as broad-coverage grammars become more feasible, we can expect to see more of the CPU-hungry techniques developed in research labs finding their way into products" (section 7.5.1, par. 4).

10. The gulf between linguists and compositionists is perhaps greatest around the grammar issue. Discussing what he calls the "romantic" position that "stylistic grammar . . . have little place in the teaching of composition," Hartwell (1985) asserted that "this position rests on a theory of language ultimately philosophical rather than linguistic" and suggested that we "witness, for example, the contempt for linguists in Ann Berthoff's *The Making of Meaning: Metaphors, Models, and Maxims for Writing Teachers*" (p. 124). William J. Vande Kopple (1998) argued that "In the last twenty or fifty years, research on language has gone from an area that specialists in composition and rhetoric took quite seriously to one that specialists now pay little attention to" (p. 4).

11. Some will argue that constraint, especially in the area of standard English and preferred usage, is exactly what novice writers need; however, most compositionists will agree that such constraint is best applied late in the composing process, not "as you type."

12. The Grammar Checker also duly flags "Me and my friends went to the store," but suggests that the writer should have written "My friends and me went to the store."

13. This "rather large knowledge base" represents the solution to the persistent shortcoming of the artificial intelligence use of computers that Kemp (1992) explained as follows: "Despite more than 30 years of effort, artificial intelligence has foundered on the problem of implanting the kinds of experience into computers which provides a linguistic context capable of handling the extraordinary contextualism of natural language" (p. 16).

14. Hartwell's grammar 5 is "Stylistic Grammar," which he says enjoys "two fully articulated positions" that he labels the "romantic" and the "classic," offering Joseph Williams's *Style: Ten Lessons in Clarity and Grace* as an example of the latter position.

15. Interestingly, Kemp (1992) attributed the ultimate failure of "artificial intelligence use of the computer" to the fact that "the problem lay in the computer's inability to employ natural language" (p. 13). The MSGC represents the best commercial effort, so far, to address that part of the problem, but, as its gaffes indicate, its ability to employ (and analyze) natural language is still quite limited.

16. Getting into the innards of the MGSC is as easy as clicking on the "Options" tab when the grammar and spelling checker is running. From there, clicking on "Settings" will open a range of possible choices. To see even more of the workings, clicking on "Help" and typing "grammar and style options" in the search field will give the user a moderately informative explanation of each possible grammar and style option.

17. We are still amused and amazed that "augur/auger" appears in this list of commonly confused words but that "affect/effect" does not. (Perhaps the computational linguists developed their list in collaboration with a school of Mining and Divination.) We assume students will also experience some incredulity.

REFERENCES

Baugh, Albert C., & Cable, Thomas. (1993). *A history of the English language* (4th ed.). Englewood Cliffs: Prentice Hall.

Berlin, James. (1996). *Rhetorics, poetics and cultures: Refiguring college English studies.* Urbana, IL: National Council of Teachers of English.

Braddock, Richard, Lloyd-Jones, Richard, & Schoer, Lowell. (1963). *Research in written composition.* Urbana, IL: National Council of Teachers of English.

Buderi, Robert. (1999). Software's ultimate sandbox. *Technology Review, 102*(1), 44–51.

Campbell, George. (1997). WORD 97. *PC World, 15*(2), 109–110.

Connors, Robert. (1997). *Composition-rhetoric: Backgrounds, theory, pedagogy.* Pittsburgh: University of Pittsburgh Press.

Cooper, Marilyn. (1989). The ecology of writing. In Marilyn Cooper & Michael Holzman (Eds.), *Writing as social action* (pp. 1–13). Portsmouth, NJ: Boynton/Cook.

Dale, Robert. (1996). Computer assistance in text creation and editing. In Ronald A. Cole, Joseph Mariani, Hans Uszkoreit, Annie Zaenen, & Victor Zue (Eds.), *Survey of the state of the art in human language technology.* Retrieved March 21, 2001, from <http://cslu.cse.ogi.edu/HLTsurvey/ch7node7.html#SECTION75>.

Dale, Robert, Moist, Herman, & Somers, H. L. (2000). Handbook of natural language processing. New York: Marcel Dekker.

Haefner, Joel. (1999). The politics of the code. *Computers and Composition, 16,* 325–339.

Haist, Caroline, (1999, November). An evaluation of Microsoft WORD 97's Grammar Checker. *Syntax in the schools, 16*(2). Retrieved July 1, 2001, from <http://www2.pct.edu/courses/evavra/ATEG/Mono/Haist/GCHECK.htm>.

Hartwell, Patrick. (1985). Grammar, grammars, and the teaching of grammar. *College English, 47,* 105–127.

Hawhee, Debra. (1999). Composition history and the Harbrace College Handbook. *College Composition and Communication, 50*(3), 504–523.

Heidorn, George E. (2000). Intelligent writing assistance. In Robert Dale, Hermann Moisl, & Harold Sommers (Eds.), *Handbook of natural language processing* (pp. 181–207). New York: Marcel Dekker.

Herrington, Anne, & Moran, Charles. (2001). What happens when machines read our students writing? *College English, 63,* 480–499.

Johnson, Eric. (1992). The ideal grammar and style checker. *Text Technology, 2*(4). Retrieved July 1, 2001, from <http://www.dsu.edu/~johnsone/ideal.html>.

Johnson, Eric. (1997). The current state of grammar and style checkers. *Text Technology, 7*(1). Retrieved July 1, 2001, from <http://www.dsu.edu/~johnsone/grammar.html>.

Kemp, Fred. (1992). Who programmed this? Examining the instructional attitudes of writing-support software. *Computers and Composition, 10,* 9–24.

Lowe, Doug. (1997). *More WORD 97 for WINDOWS for dummies.* Foster City, CA: IDG Books.

McCleary, Bill. (1995). Grammar making a comeback in composition teaching. *Composition Chronicle: Newsletter for Writing Teachers, 8*(6), 1–4.

Microsoft. (2000). Microsoft WORD 2000 [Computer Software] online help files. Redmond, WA: Microsoft Corporation.

Microsoft makes more into educational software. (1997, September 24). *Lubbock-Avalanche Journal.* Retrieved July 1, 2001, from <http://lubbockonline.com/news/092597/microsof.htm>.

Milroy, Lesley. (1998). Myth 12: Bad grammar is slovenly. In Laurie Bauer & Peter Trudgill (Eds.), *Language myths.* London: Penguin Books.

Phelps, Alan. (1998). Why not Word? Competitors still challenge Microsoft's word processor dominance. In *Smart computing in plain English.* Retrieved July 12, 2001, from <http://www.smartcomputing.com/editorial/article>.

Rickly, Rebecca. (2001, May). Technology, institutional assessment, and big brother. *Council of Writing Program Administrators President's Newsletter,* 8–10.

Rose, Mike. (1984). *Writer's block: The cognitive dimension.* Carbondale, IL: Southern Illinois University Press.

Selfe, Cynthia L. (1999). Technology and literacy: A story about the perils of not paying attention. *College Composition and Communication, 50*(3), 411–436.

Selfe, Cynthia L., & Selfe, Richard, Jr. (1994). The politics of the interface: Power and its exercise in electronic contact zones. *College Composition and Communication, 45*(4), 480–504.

Spinks, Nelda H., Wells, Barron W., & Meche, Melanie. (1997, October). Customizing grammar checking. *Business Education Forum,* 24–26.

Vande Kopple, William J. (1998, April 1–4). Current research on language and its status with composition teachers. Paper presented at the annual meeting of the conference on college composition and communication (ERIC ED418408).

Vernon, Alex. (2000). Computerized Grammar Checkers 2000: Capabilities, limitations, and pedagogical possibilities. *Computers and Composition, 17,* 329–350.

Weiser, Mark. (1991, September). The computer for the twenty-first century. *Scientific American,* 94–104.

Williams, Joseph. (2000). *Style: Ten lessons in clarity and grace* (6th ed.). New York: Longman.

Word 2000. (2001). Microsoft in education. Retrieved July 1, 2001, from <http://www.microsoft.com/education/tutorial/classroom/o2k/word.asp>.

20　The Computer and the Inexperienced Writer

CHRISTINE A. HULT

In a recent Shoe cartoon, the "perfesser" attempts to use word processing for revision. The first frame shows Muffy bringing the professor a bottle of white-out: "Thanks, Muffy. I hope this stuff works better than the last batch. . . ." The second frame shows the professor painting the white-out all over the computer screen: "I don't think he'll ever adjust to the word processor," laments Muffy with a forlorn expression.

Computers are a part of our lives as writers and are increasingly more common in English departments and writing classrooms. But, like MacNelly's professor, we don't always know how to use computers to our best advantage. Which students can benefit from using computers for writing and which educational methods should be used to teach word processing? How can students be taught to adapt their writing habits to take advantage of the possibilities offered by the new technology? These are typical of the questions being asked in the profession.

Certainly unleashing students in the computer lab, with or without elaborate text editors or style-analysis programs, does little to improve the quality of their writing, as a body of research in word processing and writing instruction is beginning to reveal. No studies to date have shown an improvement in writing quality by students using computers as compared to those not using computers (Clark, 1985; Collier, 1983; Kiefer & Smith, 1983; Pfaffenberger, in press). Furthermore, Collier hypothesized that word processing would encourage revision in student writing, but he was not able to confirm that hypothesis in his research (1983). Harris' study (1985) suggests that word processing does not, by itself, encourage revision, and Hult's study (1985) shows that word processing does not make student writing more correct. In the book *Writing On-Line,* several of the contributors caution teachers not to expect computers to effect changes in their students' writing habits and procedures (Selfe, 1985; N. Sommers, 1985). Other authors cited in the bibliography point to similar concerns.

I wish to suggest that using computers in writing classes, in the absence of appropriate instruction, may even reinforce the unproductive composing

From *Computers and Composition* 5 (1988): 29–38.

strategies characteristic of inexperienced writers. Like the professor, our students do not always make the transition from writing on paper to writing on screen very well; they too often simply transfer current writing habits wholesale. I will focus my discussion on revision strategies, since it has been hypothesized that word processing encourages revising; even if word processing does encourage revising (which is still questionable), what kind of revising does it encourage?

Elizabeth Sommers' seminal article "Revision Strategies of Student Writers and Experienced Adult Writers" (1980) identified two main ways in which the revision strategies of student and experienced writers differ: (1) student writers saw their compositions in discrete parts and considered revision to be a rewording activity; experienced writers saw their compositions as a complete unit and considered revision to be a communication activity, and (2) student writers viewed their texts as the embodiment of predefined meaning; experienced writers used writing and rewriting to discover meaning. I would like to explore more closely how word-processing and text-analysis programs may potentially inhibit the very revision strategies we attempt to teach our inexperienced student writers.

Elizabeth Sommers pointed out that students "understand the revision process as a rewording activity. They do so because they perceive words as the unit of written discourse" (p. 381). In contrast, experienced writers saw revising as a way of finding shape for their arguments; they saw their writing as a whole, taking on a reader's perspective and attending to communication in the broadest sense.

The second and related major difference between the two groups studied by Elizabeth Sommers centered on predefined meaning vs. discovery of meaning. While the student writers felt there was a predefined meaning that they need only find the right words to express, the experienced writers sought to discover or create meaning through the act of composing, and particularly through revising. The students' inordinate preoccupation with repetition of words or phrases, which they listed as something they worried about most, illustrates their perspective: eliminating repetition involves lexical (wording) rather than semantic (meaning) changes.

The only evidence that the students modified ideas while revising came when they tried different introductory paragraphs. They stopped revising when they felt that they had corrected any "rule violations," such as "never begin a sentence with a conjunction" or "never end a sentence with a preposition." Any changes made were changes to accommodate such sets of rules. The students failed to use reordering and addition when revising, but rather concentrated primarily on substitution and somewhat on deletion.

On the other hand, experienced writers defrayed concern about vocabulary and style to the end of the writing process. They made changes on all discourse levels and used all revision operations because they saw their composition both as a whole and as a way of discovering meaning. The predominant revision operations used by the experienced writers, in contrast to the students, were addition and deletion. The experienced writers stopped revising when they felt they had met their communication objectives and had come closer to an understanding of their own meaning. Through successive cycles of revision, experienced writers first focused their attention primarily on finding form for their argument, then on matters of expression and style.

How might using computers for writing contribute to students' ineffectual revising processes as described above? Perhaps the already poor strategies of inexperienced writers may be reinforced by computers unless teachers consciously work to integrate the teaching of word processing with the teaching of the writing process. For example, the predilection to see text as parts (words) rather than as a whole (communication) can be reinforced by writing with computers. Only a small amount of text fits on the screen, and the entire text is relatively inaccessible until a printout is made. Thus reading the text on a screen may reinforce an inexperienced writer's "parts" approach to revising. In addition, active reading (so essential for revising) may be hampered by the small screen and the relative inaccessibility of the entire text. In fact, Haas and Hayes point to reading problems observed when students use computers for writing (1986). Many writers who use word processing have learned to compensate for their difficulties reading on-screen by relying on frequent printouts. We need to encourage our students to adjust their own writing processes to the changed writing environment.

The predilection of inexperienced writers to substitute and delete rather than add and rearrange may also be reinforced by word processors. For instance, the rewording functions on most word processors, allowing the writer to substitute and delete, are simple to use and easy to learn. Thus some students spend most of their computer writing time backing up with the backspace key, constantly erasing and rewording rather than getting on with composing. In contrast, the reordering function of word-processing program is usually more complicated than some of the other editing functions. Teachers need to look for word-processing programs that make the "cut and paste" functions—which allow rearranging of text—easy to use. But teachers also must realize that, no matter how sophisticated the capabilities of the word-processing program, students must be taught to see why text reorganization is important and how best to accomplish it, given their own rhetorical purposes.

If we are not careful, inexperienced revising strategies may be heightened when students use text-analysis programs, such as HOMER, HBJ WRITER, GRAMMATIK, or WRITER'S WORKBENCH. Analysis programs concentrate on words and rewording (for example, vague words or sexist language), thus potentially reinforcing the inexperienced writer's emphasis on words rather than whole text. Analysis programs often point out repetition of words and phrases—something students already worry about unnecessarily. Lexical, rather than semantic, changes are encouraged by analysis programs; thus, a student who is told to choose another word for the vague word "most" may change it to an equally vague "many." The inexperienced writer's concern about rule violations may be reinforced by spelling checkers and analysis programs since these programs typically point out usage rules (distinguishing between who or whom and that or which, for example). Furthermore, these programs may be misleading because they identify such a limited set of errors, yet students too often feel that their "grammar" has been "checked" by the computer.

Lastly, students using analysis programs are often encouraged to bring finished drafts to the computer lab and type their drafts into the computer for analysis. This procedure, if not preceded by extensive revision for content, may reinforce the misconception that meaning is already defined and the text just needs to be cleaned up.

The following excerpt from a student's text, in draft and revised form, illustrates the concerns I have outlined:

DRAFT

There is an aspect of college life ~~that~~ *which* is rarely discussed, yet often

considered ~~more~~ *of greater* importan~~t~~ *ce* than the actual college one will be attending.

eatible? edible? good?
For most, it even surpasses the concern of how ~~hood~~ the food will be in

the dorm cafeteria. What could this vital life of death issue be? FINDING

A ROOMMATE! Inevitably one's roommate will become the center and

in
most important part ~~of~~ your college career. For without one there would

throughout
be no one to accompany you on those midnight snack raids(catered cour-

tesy of Pizza Express) no one to engage in those necessary gossip sessions

concerning who saw who with who and where, and no one with to plan

that annual
that Spring Break(journey to Padre.)

REVISED COPY

There is an aspect of college life rarely discussed, yet often considered of greater importance than the actual college one will attend. For many, it even surpasses the concern of how edible the food is in the dorm cafeteria. What could this vital life or death issue be? FINDING A ROOMMATE! Inevitably your roommate will become the center of importance throughout your college career. For without one there would be no one to accompany you on those midnight snack raids (catered courtesy of Pizza Express), no one to engage in those necessary gossip sessions (concerning who saw who with who and where), and no one with to plan Spring Break (that annual journey to Padre).

From this excerpt, you can clearly see the ineffectual revising strategies outlined by Elizabeth Sommers. The student sees revising as a rewording activity, never considering the communicative effectiveness of the whole text. Though the student used word processing (DEC Rainbow/SELECT) to produce the text and a text-editing program (GRAMMATIK) to analyze it, the changes evidence little real revision. The word-processing and style-analysis programs may even have reinforced her misapprehensions. Notice that the student has changed only those words flagged by the analysis program as vague or possibly incorrect ("most, very, good, and nice;" prepositions, and that/which).

Some of the changes are improvements, others just make matters worse (e.g., changing "more important" into the prepositional phrase "of greater importance" when the analysis program had already suggested to the student that she used too many prepositional phrases throughout her entire paper). Although I have only included the introductory paragraph, throughout the entire text the student discovers little new meaning through revising, but rather sees the text as virtually complete, just needing a little cleaning up. Comparing the two versions, one is struck by how little has really changed. There has been little attempt to engage the audience in the opening; there are no global changes—no block moves have been used to reorder parts, no substitutions other than words occur, and there are no additions whatsoever. This pattern of revision continues throughout the entire piece, which is (not surprisingly) five paragraphs long.

As Elizabeth Sommers so aptly put it, "The evidence from my research suggests that it is not that students are unwilling to revise, but rather that they do what they have been taught to do in a consistently narrow and predictable way. . . . The students do not have strategies for handling the whole essay" (p. 383). In the absence of appropriate instruction, computers may just exacerbate the problem. Students in writing classes often find word-processing instruction is largely divorced from the other classwork, as they did (unfortunately) in my own class. In computer labs, students may work independently at computers, with little or no peer or teacher interaction or encouragement to make use of the important capabilities word processing offers to writers. Too often, students do not have enough lab time available to them to actually draft at the computer. Consequently, students bring texts which they type into the computer for revision and analysis—thus reinforcing their habit of seeing first drafts as essentially finished products.

Yet those of us who use word processing to teach writing see the potential for real benefits and are unlikely to lose faith in that potential despite our mistakes and failures of the past. Besides, with or without our help, students are increasingly using word processing on their own, and the number of college word-processing microlabs continues to grow apace—doubling in 1985 alone (Barker, 1985). But if we are to use computers judiciously, we must design instructional settings and curricula that provide for an interactive computer classroom, using what Hillocks calls an "environmental teaching mode" (1984). Entire writing classes can work together to solve writing problems in collaboration with each other and with the teacher. Group problem-solving can be accomplished by projectors interfaced with computers, thus displaying text from one screen onto a large screen for everyone in class to view and discuss. Such projection set-ups allow teachers to demonstrate effective composition strategies in process. Also, networking systems can provide students access to each other's papers for comments and suggestions while work is in progress. Adequate facilities are essential—comfortable work stations, sufficient hardware and software, clear documentation, and immediate assistance for both technical problems and writing questions. Ideally, when working with a class in a lab, the teacher should have a lab assistant available to answer technical questions, thus freeing the teacher's time for writing instruction.

Once a congenial writing atmosphere has been established, students should first be exposed to potentially beneficial uses of computers and then be encouraged to experiment with them at every stage of the writing process, rather than simply to use computers as super-typewriters. Prewriting software and exercises may encourage reluctant writers to use the power of word processing to explore ideas, discover new ideas, make connections between these new ideas and related experiences and knowledge, and perhaps gather or retrieve relevant materials. Word processing may help students experiment and explore, through freewriting and brainstorming, for example. It can also help students gather and retrieve materials, serving as a repository of ideas and sources. Furthermore, word processing can help students plan and organize their writing in a fluid, flexible form that is easily manipulated during drafting.

Often prewriting can provide students with a rich source of ideas and information on disk from which to draw as they compose. Using word processing can facilitate a building-block approach to composition, filling in and expanding an outline stored on disk, for example, or writing from a predesigned frame. As they compose, students should obtain frequent printouts for easier reading of their drafts, and as they revise, they should gain feedback several times from peers and from the teacher. Collaboration (between peers and with the teacher) can be encouraged so that students gain experience from writing with others at the computer.

Revising, editing, and proofreading can all be facilitated by word-processing programs, provided students are instructed in effective revision strategies. Students need instruction in word processing functions that allow them to add and rearrange as well as to substitute and delete. Class time should be spent on rearranging text using block move commands. Analysis programs should not be run until the whole-essay concerns have been addressed through conferencing and repeated revising sessions. Once run, analysis printouts should be brought to class for discussion and for comparison among students. The appropriateness of the advice, in the rhetorical context of the piece being written, can be analyzed by the class. As did the experienced writers, students need to wait until very late in the process to attend to matters of expression and style.

Finally, students must understand the limitations of analysis programs and recognize that careful proofreading is as necessary with computer-printed papers as it is with typewritten or handwritten papers. Even when using a spelling checker, words will be missed, particularly homophones (to, too, and two) which the computer will not flag as misspellings. Furthermore, analysis programs cannot check grammar or usage in any real sense, so careful proof-reading for correctness is still essential.

Although word processors cannot teach writing, I am convinced that word processing can be an important tool for writers. In order to use word processing effectively, however, students must understand the principles of effective revision and apply those principles to writing with a word processor. Writing courses that include word processing must do a great deal more than simply introduce students to the machines. Essentially, instruction in writing with word processing should encourage a process approach to composition that reinforces the difference between the substantive revision of content exemplified by experienced writers and the ineffectual rewording of finished texts too often exemplified by our students.

REFERENCES

Barker, Thomas T. (1985). The English department microlab: An endangered species? *Research in Word Processing, 3,* 2.

Clark, Richard E. (1985). Confounding in educational computing research. *Journal of Educational Computing Research, 1,* 137–148.

Collier, Richard M. (1983). The word processor and revision strategies. *College Composition and Communication, 34,* 149–155.

Haas, Christina, & Hayes, John R. (1986). What did I just say? Reading problems in writing with the machine. *Research in the Teaching of English, 20,* 22–35.

Harris, Jeanette. (1985). Student writers and word processing: A preliminary evaluation. *College Composition and Communication, 36,* 323–330.

Hillocks, George, Jr. (1984). What works in teaching composition: A meta-analysis of experimental treatment studies. *American Journal of Education,* 133–170.

Hult, Christine. The effects of word processing on the correctness of student writing. *Research in Word Processing Newsletter, 3,* 1–4.

Kiefer, Kathleen E. & Smith, Charles R. (1983). Textual analysis with computers: Tests of Bell Laboratories' computer software. *Research in the Teaching of English, 17,* 210–214.

Pfaffenberger, Bryan. (in press). Word processing technology and composition instruction: Toward the environmental mode. *Journal of Educational Computing Research.*

Selfe, Cynthia L. (1985). The electronic pen: Computers and the composing process. In James L. Collins & Elizabeth A. Sommers (Eds.), *Writing On-Line* (pp. 55–66). Upper Montclair, NJ: Boynton/Cook.

Sommers, Elizabeth A. (1985). Integrating composing and computing. In James L. Collins & Elizabeth A. Sommers (Eds.), *Writing On-Line* (pp. 3–10). Upper Montclair, NJ: Boynton/Cook.

Sommers, Nancy. Revision strategies of student writers and experienced adult writers. *College Composition and Communication, 31,* 378–388.

21 Web Literacy: Challenges and Opportunities for Research in a New Medium

MADELEINE SORAPURE, PAMELA INGLESBY, AND GEORGE YATCHISIN

INTRODUCTION

At this point in the age of the computer, it is nearly impossible to teach a writing class without having students ask, "Can we use the World Wide Web as a source for our papers?" There is no easy answer to this question because Web sites vary wildly in reliability and usefulness. To allow students to use the Web as a resource without helping them judge the merits of the information they find there is to invite trouble. But, a different trouble lurks if we prohibit students from drawing on Web sources. Indeed, they might be turning to the Web for entirely valid and well-informed reasons, for instance to find up-to-date and otherwise unpublished information from government agencies, corporations, journalists, scholars, and others. Denying students access to such sources might prevent them from doing the best research possible. Research, broadly conceived, involves not only finding relevant information but also assessing its quality and value for a specific project, and then determining how to integrate that information, together with other sources, into one's own writing. At all stages of the research process, but especially at the assessment stage, the Web poses challenges that students may not recognize and that writing teachers should, we argue, explicitly address. These challenges, in fact, are real opportunities for us to enrich the curricula of writing courses, enhance the research and writing skills of students, and expand our conception of literacy.

Two challenges in particular are posed by the Web as an information resource. The first arises from the fact that the Web offers many modes of writing, many rhetorical situations for students to assess. Web sites advocate causes, sell products, entertain visitors, express opinions, present scholarly research; indeed, some sites try to do all of the above. The Web in itself provides little classification or categorization of these different modes, nor does it reject any offerings; in this sense it is like a vast, open, and uncatalogued library,

From *Computers and Composition* 15 (1998): 409–24.

and one in which reference librarians are nowhere to be found. Employing criteria developed for evaluating print sources (currency, bias, author's credentials, publisher, intended audience, and so on) is useful in sifting and assessing the information one finds on the Web, but it is important that these criteria be applied flexibly to the Web's broad range of rhetorical situations. While library materials are organized and "filtered" (by publishing houses, peer reviewers, faculty, and librarians, for example), the Web presents mostly "unfiltered" material in an uncontextualized manner. Thus, it challenges students to do the kind of primary evaluative activity more often done by advanced researchers.

Web sites not only provide a range of rhetorical situations for students to assess but also do so in a multimedia, hypertextual, interactive format. The second challenge for student researchers, then, is to determine the effects of the medium on the message. For instance, what information do images and graphic design convey? How does the associative logic of a hypertextual Web site affect its content? How does interactivity affect the site's credibility and the audience's response? Answering these questions can help students determine the purpose of a Web site, its reliability, and its ultimate value for their projects; these features can be read as nontextual clues that facilitate evaluation of the text, just as the glossy pages, advertisements, and images in a popular magazine are one mark of its difference from an academic journal. But, what vocabulary do students have for discussing features such as images, links, and interactive technologies? As we suggest, these elements of Web sites have parallels in print documents—particularly, in aspects of print documents most often overlooked in their assessment—and so paying close attention to Web sites should return students to library sources with a keener eye and a wider range of questions. In addition, and no less importantly, reading, understanding, and evaluating the hypertextual and multimedia components of Web sites offer the opportunity to extend literacy skills—such as associative logic, visual rhetoric, and interactivity. This expanded conception of literacy is crucial in an increasingly technological and multimedia world, one in which the library is no longer the primary source of useful and reliable information for student researchers.

Web literacy, then, involves an ability to recognize and assess a wide range of rhetorical situations and an attentiveness to the information conveyed in a source's nontextual features. Teaching students this literacy means supplementing the evaluative criteria traditionally applied to print sources with new strategies necessary for making sense of diverse kinds of texts presented in hypertextual and multimedia formats.

WEB LITERACY AND COMPOSITION

Many scholars in our field believe that the viability of composition depends on such an expanded definition of literacy. Aside from benefiting students by expanding their repertoire of skills in evaluating different modes and media of communication, a broader conception of literacy invites us as scholars to make connections to other disciplines: film and art, graphic design, human-computer interface theories developed in computer science, and literary studies done in hypertext. Thus, it allows us to introduce rhetorical theory into an existing body of work focused on evaluating the content and form of Web sites.

Given these advantages to integrating the Web more fully into writing courses, and given the increasing importance of Web literacy for business, academic, and personal enterprises, there is surprisingly little research by composition specialists on the topic. Instead, the focus of research and of teaching practice has been on those computer and Internet uses that have more direct parallels than the Web to what instructors do in writing classrooms without computers: class discussions take place over local-area networks; drafts of papers are shared on electronic bulletin boards; grammar and revision exercises are done with Computer-Aided Instruction (CAI) programs; portfolios of student writing are compiled, stored, and evaluated electronically; and office hours are conducted via e-mail. In these instances, the computer facilitates new and (perhaps) improved ways of accomplishing familiar tasks. But, the Web is, in many respects, unfamiliar territory for us, bringing into the mix knowledge and experience we may or may not possess. Most writing teachers have notoriously little time and meager institutional support to become experts in this area, and the rewards of such expertise are as yet uncertain. Economic and logistical considerations come into play as well in causing skepticism about integrating the Web more fully into writing courses. Access to the Web is difficult at some institutions and for some students. Moreover, students enter our classes with different degrees of facility and experience with computers and with the Web, and we are rightly hesitant to penalize inadvertently those students already part of the "technological underclass."[1] We may also have ethical concerns about allowing into our classrooms the commercial and offensive material that seem an ineradicable part of the Web. Most broadly, writers such as Sven Birkerts (1994) and Neil Postman (1995) called our attention to the potentially detrimental effects of using the Internet and the Web, arguing that it promotes reduced attention span, poorer writing and communication skills, alienation from print documents, and isolation from human interaction.

These are valid concerns and are, with increasing regularity, topics of discussion at conferences and in journals both on the Web and in print. But, we need to recognize that the Web has already entered our classrooms even as we debate its value and its effects. Students access the Web not only to do research but also to be entertained, to shop, to be informed about current events, and in some cases to compose their own home pages. The activity of reading and creating Web sites will only increase as the software and hardware for it become more accessible. Therefore, it is important to defuse an uncritical acceptance of the Web and rather to guide students in becoming discerning, skillful readers of Web sites, particularly when they are drawing information from those sites for use in their own writing. The two major challenges posed by the Web as an information resource—its diverse and unfiltered content and its hypermedia format—are thus also opportunities for students to develop their critical thinking and research skills.

EXISTING CRITERIA FOR WEB EVALUATION

Resources currently exist on the Web itself and in print that can help students organize their search for information and evaluate both the content and the formal and nontextual elements of Web sites. On the Web, these guidelines fall into two broad categories: university library sites that focus on evaluating the content of Web sites, drawing on analogies to print documents and addressed to people using the Web as a research tool, and Web-authoring and human-computer interface guidelines that focus primarily on the design and technical elements of Web sites, drawing on analogies to graphic arts and broadcast media and addressed to people creating sites. We draw on both categories in the discussion that follows, suggesting that a rhetorical approach can bridge the content-form divide they represent. However, it is unlikely that students doing research on the Web would find either of these types of guidelines easily, or indeed, would even look for such guidance to help them assess Web sites. The evaluative guidelines students encounter most frequently on the Web are also, unfortunately, the least useful to them.

The least helpful but most pervasive evaluative term on the Web about the Web is *cool*. Web sites abound that index "cool sites of the day" or "Joe's top twenty cool sites," where *cool* is most often left undefined or only briefly explained.[2] Without clarification, the term "cool" is meaningless, and the complementary designation of *hot*—applied to frequently visited Web sites— tells us nothing except that for some reason the site is popular. Knowing that a site is both cool and hot is not particularly helpful in assessing the quality of information it offers, merely making the Web seem like a weather map full of fronts about to clash. The other frequently encountered evaluation schema on the Web comes from search engines such as *Lycos, Infoseek,* and *Yahoo,* which provide ratings of certain sites, deeming some as excellent and others as unworthy of a visit. This evaluation process would seem quite helpful for student researchers because they could, in theory, confine their Web searches to only excellent sites, and thus gather only highly reliable information. In actuality, though, the criteria by which these sites are judged, as well as the qualifications of the reviewers making the judgments, are often left unspecified. When they are articulated, as in *Lycos'* Top 5% site (see <http://www.lycos.com/help/top5-help2.html>), the evaluative categories are quite broad (content, design, and overall). Minimal information is given about the specific criteria in each category: for instance, what would it mean to deem the content of a site "interesting" or to say that its images are "well-chosen"? The categories are too vague and uncontextualized to be of much use to serious student researchers, and the reviews of individual sites are similarly superficial, intended primarily to be entertaining and catchy.

In short, the evaluation guidelines on the Web most accessible to and most frequently encountered by students are fundamentally flawed and only minimally helpful. In print, students might find that standard research writing textbooks give them good general advice for assessing sources, although these texts don't deal with the particular challenges posed by the Web; even the more recent composition textbooks that focus on electronic writing offer remarkably little guidance in this regard. For instance, Dawn Rodrigues' (1997) *The Research Paper and the World Wide Web* followed the lead of library Web sites in briefly covering the "internet applicability" of traditional print-oriented criteria for evaluation (pp. 13–15). Jeanette Woodward's (1997) *Writing Research Papers: Investigating Resources in Cyberspace* presented a similar list of print-oriented criteria but with no reference at all to the ways these criteria need to be adapted to address the different rhetorical situations of Web sites (pp. 130–133). In addition, neither of these textbooks, and neither of the Internet-oriented handbooks that have been published recently (Hairston, Ruszkiewicz, & Seward, 1997; Miler & Knowles, 1997), direct students' attention to the quite evident challenges that the Web's hypermedia format poses to an assessment of its offerings.[3]

The following sections propose a more thorough approach to evaluating Web sites and developing Web literacy, taking into account both the similarities of Web and print sources and their significant differences. Focusing first on the wide-ranging content of the Web, we suggest how two of its seemingly unreliable genres—the personal home page and the "infomercial" site—might be used productively by student researchers. In evaluating these sites and determining their value for a particular research project, students confront in an immediate way issues of authorial expertise, reliability, and bias, issues also crucial in assessing print sources. We turn next to several nontextual elements of Web sites—images, links, and interactivity—and suggest that assessing these features can also cultivate key critical thinking skills in students. Incorporating these new features into a rhetorically based analysis of a site's purpose and strategies can yield a more complete understanding of the site, as well as a broader and more sophisticated approach to assessing the value of information found within and beyond the confines of the library.

FROM THE LIBRARY TO THE WEB

The Web evaluation criteria most likely familiar to composition teachers have been developed by instructors and librarians engaged in helping students use the Internet as a research tool. These criteria tend to value Web sites similar in content and authorship to sources found in a typical academic library and treat the Web in general as an extension of the library, thus ignoring or denigrating new types of research sources the Web offers. The temptation to apply print-oriented evaluative criteria to Web sites is manifested by a site published by the library at Cornell University, a guide on "How to critically analyze information sources," which (the library suggests) can be applied to both print and Web texts (Ormondroyd, Engle, & Cosgrave, 1996). The guide posits two levels of evaluation: an "initial appraisal," which involves assessing the author's credentials and publisher's reputation, and a "content analysis," which involves assessing the text's intended audience, objectivity, coverage, writing style, and external evaluation. This approach draws directly from traditional print-oriented research writing textbooks such as Stephen Weidenborner and Domenick Caruso's (1996), which asked students to consider a source's depth of coverage, author's viewpoint, and currency of information, and Nancy Sommers and Linda Simon's (1993), which focused on the status of the source's author and the strength of the evidence presented.

These traditional criteria are useful to some extent when evaluating Web sites for research purposes. For example, a student writing a paper on the critical reception of a movie for a popular culture class might turn to the Web rather than the library because of sites such as *The Internet Movie Database* (see <http://imdb.com>), which offers background information about thousands of movies and offers links to "commentary or reviews" for each one. The site fails to categorize or contextualize the reviews, however, which means students will need to draw on traditional print-oriented criteria to decide which ones represent serious critical commentary. For the movie *The Godfather,* for example, the Database offers a list of 18 reviews credited to sources as diverse as Roger Ebert, "Mr. Showbiz," *Box Office Magazine,* "Matt's Movie Reviews," and *The San Francisco Chronicle.* Using traditional evaluative criteria, the student would identify the author of each review, assess that author's credentials, and consider the nature of the publication and its target audience. Such an evaluation would likely lead the student to favor the kind of reviews typically found in a library (those written by professional critics and published in well-respected periodicals) and reject those with unclear authorship or sponsorship.

Although such an approach would not be problematic for that particular assignment, there are other situations in which dismissing Web sources just because of unclear or unusual authorship, sponsorship, currency, or other attributes might lead to an unwarranted rejection of useful information. In other words, there are potentially valuable Web sites available to student researchers that should not be dismissed just because they are dissimilar to sources found in the library. Because of this difference between the library and the Web, some research-oriented evaluative schemes have moved beyond positing the Web as equivalent to print, and instead, ask readers to become aware of special problems posed by the Web regarding content evaluation. A Web site composed by Jan Alexander and Marsha Tate (1996), reference librarians at Widener University, stated that although "traditional print techniques" are still appropriate for evaluating Web text, new techniques are also needed because of (among other things) the difficulty in identifying authors, the lack of gatekeeping or peer review, and the unclear use of dates. The librarians also call attention to the fact that the Web includes new genres of research sources not found in traditional print; two such genres, ubiquitous on the Web and worthy of particular attention, are personal home pages and infomercial Web sites.

The problem—and opportunity—posed by personal home pages is that almost anyone can create and maintain one on the Web. Indeed, many online services offer free space on the Web for members' home pages, and other Web-based organizations, such as Geocities, offer free Web space to anyone with access to a computer and a modem. This democratization of public communication poses a problem for a student who has been instructed to pay attention to an author's expertise and reputation because many people who create personal Web pages do so precisely because they do not have the cultural capital necessary to be published elsewhere. One way a student can solve this problem is by ignoring personal sites altogether or by extracting from them what seems the safest and most reliable information. For example, a student researching the current peacekeeping mission in Bosnia might encounter the *Bosnia Buddah Home Page* (see <http://members.aol.com/apstyle/bosnia.html>), created by Cesar Soriano, an American Online member who served for nine months in Bosnia-Herzegovina with the Maryland Army National Guard. Directing a student to see if there is "anything useful there," using traditional evaluative criteria, would lead the student to focus on the authoritative sources included or referenced in the site (a bibliography, wire service stories, and so on).

Such an approach, however, would neglect important resources that the Web—and in particular, personal home pages—have to offer, which in this case is the perspective and experiences of the individual constructing the site. At the *Bosnia Buddah Home Page*, the author provided a diary of his military experiences in Bosnia, a photograph album, and a Frequently Asked Questions (FAQ) section in which he gives his opinion on what the war is about, describes what it is like to live in Bosnia, explains the day-to-day dangers faced by peacekeeping troops there, and offers advice for partners of soldiers in Bosnia. This type of information could be used to enrich a research paper on Bosnia by providing an insider's perspective; the student could also use the site to contact other potential primary sources as it explains how to obtain a military pen-pal. Allowing students to use such Web sites as primary sources forces us to rethink what is meant by authorial expertise and reputation. Although we might legitimately demand certain educational or professional credentials of a secondary source, primary sources are often valued because of the author's unique experience and insight. The new availability of such sources on the Web can thus be regarded as an opportunity for student researchers, one which challenges them to distinguish between primary and secondary sources and to determine how they can be incorporated differently in a paper.

Although personal home pages may be difficult to assess in terms of authorial expertise, infomercial sites are problematic because their purpose is multiple—conflating educational and commercial goals—and therefore often unclear. An example of an unusual yet useful infomercial Web site is *SolarDome* (see <http://www.solardome.com>), "a solar theme park on the Web, designed for entertainment and education, along with complete solar components catalog and direct connection to hundreds of local renewable energy installation specialists around the globe." The site was found during a broad Web search using the search term *electric cars*. Librarians often caution students away from commercial sites because, it is argued, they are inherently persuasive and thus biased. We argue, however, that all texts are biased in one way or another; the wide range of texts available on the Web simply highlights this fact. Therefore, sites should be evaluated on a case-by-case basis, by asking relevant questions about a particular site's purpose, authors, and target audience; by conducting follow-up research as necessary; and by balancing the information found in the site with information from other sites as well as from print sources with different rhetorical contexts.

The authors of the *SolarDome* site—Chris Jensen and Steve Lowe—are, respectively, an entrepreneur (an MBA-holding music store owner, who hopes to build a solar-vehicle theme park) and a "solar educator with twenty years of solar industrial experience." The site's sponsorship, purpose, and audience are unclear and difficult to categorize, as it is technically a commercial venture, offering products for sale, yet it appears predominantly educational and advocatory in tone. It would be a shame if a student researcher working on the topic of electric cars allowed this ambiguity to dissuade her from using the site, however, because it contains an informative article on electric and hybrid vehicles by Robert Q. Riley in which an argument advocating the use of electric cars is supported by a great deal of specific factual evidence. Unfortunately, the site contains no information about who Riley is, nor does Riley provide sources for most of his data; these are both common problems encountered on the Web. Students, however, need not decide at this point to accept or reject the source on its own ambiguous merits, because further research can answer some of the questions posed previously. For example, a new Web search on Riley himself reveals that he is a transportation design consultant located in Scottsdale, Arizona, with a great deal of experience in electric cars and provides his e-mail address and phone number if the student wanted to contact Riley. Additionally, students could conduct further Web or library research on electric cars, and compare the information found in other sources with different rhetorical missions to that of Riley's. The point here is that if Riley's article had been published in a reputable periodical such as *Technology Review* or *Automotive Engineering*, a student would not think twice about citing it in a paper. By encountering it on the Web, however, in an ambiguous context, a student is forced to evaluate the piece on its own merits, conduct further research into the credentials of the author, look to other elements on the Web site itself for clues as to its mode and value, seek sources that make an opposing argument to balance her information sources, and present an argument to the teacher as to that source's value. In other words, the challenging nature of Web sources creates new kinds of work for researchers but, as a result, highlights the fundamental critical and intellectual skills necessary for good research writing.

Invoking a set of Web evaluation criteria for students that is broader, more flexible, and more context-oriented than traditional print criteria can thus serve several functions in the research-oriented writing classroom. We can use it to call attention to the fact that there is no single set of criteria that can be used to evaluate all Web sites or indeed all print texts; instead, it is more useful to invoke a broad set of questions and ask questions as they become relevant. As Pixie Ferris (1997) pointed out, the only universal judgment that can be applied to any source of information is that, for a particular individual, it has value. Research exercises such as the one described previously have the immediate utility of helping students locate and evaluate Web information sources in a manner appropriate for the particular research they are conducting; in the long term, forcing students to decide on a case-by-case basis what contains value develops their ability to ask appropriate critical questions regarding the source, content, and presentation of information in any context, academic or not.

INTO THE WEB . . . AND BEYOND

Analyzing and evaluating textual information from sources with diverse purposes and authors is not the only challenge faced by students using the Web. The medium through which this information is presented—specifically, the images, links, and interactivity on the Web—pose perhaps more obvious and more daunting challenges to student researchers and, correspondingly, opportunities for composition teachers. Images, links, and interactivity are not, strictly speaking, *new* elements in the reading and research experience; they have parallels in scholarly print texts and so compel us to revisit and give new emphasis to certain issues that have not previously played a large role in the evaluation of sources. Moreover, attention to the Web's hypermedia and interactive nature extends the horizon of rhetorical analysis in productive and intriguing ways.

Visual Literacy and the Web

Because of the ease with which high-quality images as well as text can be displayed, and because of its frequent use by entertainment and commercial organizations, the Web is a more visually-oriented place than the traditional library. Most Web sites incorporate images—photographs, charts, maps, original designs—as well as colors and other graphic elements (not to mention animation, video, and sound). The danger, of course, is that students get caught up in the coolness of a Web site's visual presentation; it is not too reductive to compare the Web to a con artist dangling shiny objects in front of a mark's eyes. But, although impressive, high-quality images may enhance the credibility of a Web site, conveying the impression that its author has the ability, interest, and resources to make a strong aesthetic appeal to readers, excellent images alone don't guarantee reliability or validity. Visual elements need to be read in two ways: as conveying information in themselves—information that may complement, complicate, or contradict the message conveyed by the text—and as providing clues to the overall rhetorical situation of the site. In both cases, visual elements are incorporated into a researcher's overall assessment of a site, yielding an analysis that acknowledges that the image as well as the text convey pertinent information.

A good starting point is to consider the relation between image and text. Although images themselves are rarely neutral, they become even less so when paired with words that can limit or alter their possible interpretations. A valuable example comes from John Berger's (1972) *Ways of Seeing*. Early in the book, Berger reprints a painting and asks readers to consider it. He then asks us to turn the page, and beneath the painting is written: "This is the last picture that Van Gogh painted before he killed himself" (pp. 27–28). Suddenly, the birds in the picture look more ominous, the wheat field more disturbed. Has the picture changed? Yes and no. What has become clear, though, is that seeing isn't just a physical process. In *The Language of Visual Art: Perception as a Basis for Design*, Jack Frederick Myers (1989) claimed that "perceptions are derived from: (1) biological structure; (2) experience; and (3) knowledge" (p. 9), and as teachers we must help students see how experience and knowledge shape the ways they read images. This experience and knowledge isn't limited to what we had before booting up our computers, either. Web sites teach us how they want to be read, in large part through visual, graphic, and layout elements, and we must be aware of that teaching process as we read.

Berger's (1972) example has particular relevance for the Web, where images are used in abundance and in widely varying ways. For example, students could easily find numerous Web versions of Edvard Munch's *The Scream*. Some are connected to personal home pages ("here are some paintings I like"), some are art reproduction companies selling posters or T-shirts, one is a site that matches Bob Dylan lyrics to famous paintings, one is the Ben and Jerry's site featuring the "Red Nose Day Museum" (touched-up famous images wearing red clown noses done in conjunction with *Comic Relief* (see <http://www.benjerry.com/rednose/6.html>), and one is a medical site that discusses Munch's clinical problems in light of his art. These sites present the painting cropped and full-sized, in both black-and-white and color, with and without title, artist, date, and museum information. If a student was working on an art history paper about Munch, she would have to be prepared to find the image in many different contexts and to consider what each of those contexts then does to the painting. A simple *Webcrawler* search and link to the Ben and Jerry's site could lead to disastrous conclusions ("Munch was a joyful painter who put clown noses on what might otherwise be startling images . . ."). The meaning of the image, in short, is dependent on the context in which it is presented.

Students must also be cognizant of the possible dissonance between image and text on a Web site. In an effort to discover a unified meaning of a site, students might miss the clues that make it easier to determine the site's validity. "The 'convention of unity' is a powerful ideological weapon," Mieke Bal (1990) theorized, "because of the pressure it exerts on the reader to choose one interpretation over another rather than to read through the conflict of interpretations" (p. 507). The conflict between seemingly dispassionate words and a quite emotionally charged visual, for instance, might be the key to determining the purposes of a Web site, and students must be encouraged to find and read such discontinuities.

Apart from their connection to the text, images themselves convey not only information but also possible bias. Michael Rock (1994) represented the concerns of graphic designers when he wrote that "images and charts seem to not imply an inherent point-of-view. They radiate a false objectivity because the concept of the image-as-opinion is difficult for most people to grasp" (p. 148). Students need, at the least, to be made aware of the possible ways visual information can be manipulated. Charts and graphs are not just neutral presentations of facts. Pictographs can "lie" if the base image doesn't equal a standard unit; bar graphs can "lie" if the y-axis has no zero point. Drawings and photographs can manipulate the eye through tricks of perspective and visual illusions. All these issues, obviously, also pertain to print documents. In an age when news magazines crop Saddam Hussein's mustache to make him look more like Hitler or darken O. J. Simpson's skin to heighten racial tensions, questioning where the truth meets the image is always worth doing, whether on the Web or off. Because the Web highlights these issues, it encourages us to reinvigorate our teaching about the graphic and visual components of print texts. Although the combination of graphics and text is far from new (illustrated manuscripts go back hundreds of years), the field of visual literacy is still relatively in its infancy, particularly in writing courses. The Web compels us to attend to it.

Links: Intertextuality and Structure on the Web

As with visual images, both Web sites and print documents incorporate intertextuality—implicit or explicit references to other sources—although a Web site's intertextuality, operating largely through its links, poses challenges for students in evaluating the source. In a print document, the references or bibliography section indicates the sources an author cited explicitly, and these resources can be tracked down and evaluated by student researchers to determine the credibility, comprehensiveness, and possible biases of the original source. Links in Web sites operate similarly to give readers clues about the value of the information the site presents. Although the mere existence of links in a Web site seems to imply that research has informed the site and that it is connected to a broader context of related and relevant information, links are only worth the information on the other side of the mouse click, just as an extensive bibliography doesn't necessarily indicate that the author has drawn on reliable, valid, or current information. In short, a necessary component of evaluation is assessing the sources to which an author refers.

Links pose certain challenges to students in making that assessment, some which stem from the Web's wide array of material; one is likely to find sites linked to other sites that have different purposes and different degrees of reliability. Although a status bar at the bottom of a Web browser generally will provide an URL (Universal Resource Locator) of a link when a Web-user puts the cursor over that link's name, URLs are rarely as descriptive and helpful as the publishing information of a reference page. Even the seemingly more trustworthy "edu" domain doesn't always mean that material has been sponsored by a university (let alone approved through some sort of peer review) because students and professors can display personal home pages through their university's server. In general, determining the value of a linked site is difficult without actually checking that site, and with the number of links on the Web, student researchers may find that their search for relevant information can become time-consuming and unfocused.

Students must also resist simplistically thinking that the number of links on a Web site correlates with the quality of the site. Obviously, a lack of links could signal that a source is not situated within its own particular research context; it could mean a source is lacking the equivalent of a literature review. However, students must also be aware that sites produced by academics frequently contain few links yet offer a reference page. Just because a source is not taking full advantage of being a Web document by using hypertextual links doesn't mean it presents unworthy information. Its value must be evaluated separately from its value as hypertext. On the other hand, a site could suffer from too many links. A technical writer and consultant, William Horton (1990) suggested that a writer link sparingly, citing Schneiderman's advice to link two to eight times per page (p. 310); an over-use of links can confuse researchers attempting to ascertain the priority and relevance of linked information. A Web site with too many links suggests an author's inability to discriminate: How can one trust an author who cannot seem to distinguish the valuable from the not valuable?

Links also present in a more forceful way a problem that exists in print material as well: Where does a source's borders exist? This question has troubled theorists writing on influence and intertextuality in print texts, but it is even more troubling in hypertext documents. Students can at least tell where articles begin and end in journals, but determining when a link merely goes to another page within a site as opposed to when it leaps to another Web document by different authors on a server far, far away is a trickier matter, and one at the heart of evaluating sources on the Web.

In the "Rhetoric of Hypermedia: Some Rules for Authors," George Landow (1991) provided nineteen rules for creating useful links, and one can read through his list to consider how sites should properly treat their readers. Landow prefaced his rules with three reader-centered reasons rules are necessary: 1) readers must be oriented as to their position in hyperspace, so they may "read efficiently and with pleasure;" 2) readers must be informed where links lead (a site must provide departure information); and 3) readers must be made to feel at home in a document after using a link (a site must provide entrance information) (p. 82). Clearly, any site that cannot bother to do all three things is less trustworthy, given that consideration is one element of ethos.

Landow (1991) also stressed the active nature of hypertext, what most often gets called interactivity, particularly with rule four: "The author of hypermedia materials must provide devices that stimulate the reader to think and explore" (p. 86). He sees links as the way to encourage such thought and exploration, and so his rules offer ways to make links most helpful by creating context and relationships, by mapping links visually, and by leaning on existing metaphors of navigation (navigation itself is a metaphor he deconstructs in a footnote). Landow's work on hypertextual linking reveals that its significance extends beyond intertextuality into more broadly relevant rhetorical issues; links can become a means for stimulating and engaging readers, a Web-specific rhetorical strategy students should be encouraged to understand.

Links also compel students to attend to structure and organization. Through its capacity to link, a hypertext elicits associational, not linear thinking, a move that could seem a call for sloppiness of thought. However, linear thinking is just as much a construct as associational thinking can be; indeed, it has been suggested that the nonlinear, recursive way hypertext presents information is actually closer to the way certain non-Western cultures organize and process ideas. It has also been argued that hypertext is a more appropriate and effective way to structure certain kinds of information. Horton (1990) suggested the following as the best use for links: teaching concepts, writing highly annotated documents, creating problem-solving systems, providing loose collections of interrelated documents, and modeling and teaching organization itself (pp. 307–308). As they assess the way a site uses links, student researchers can consider the effectiveness of the structure of links within the context of the entire Web site as well as the effectiveness of individual links in providing related and reliable information. Hypertext links enable readers to create their own reading experience, and this in itself is a powerful tool for teachers. Discussing how and why links link can help us understand not only the value of a Web site, but also how ideas can connect, coordinate, and subordinate in any writing.

Interactivity on the Web

Although images and links on Web sites have some clear parallels to what we find in print texts, a feature such as interactivity, which is an essential element of the Web, would seem to manifest itself infrequently in print and so present a particular challenge to students as they evaluate Web sites during the research process. Some of the more popular, mass-market magazines and books occasionally include interactive elements such as quizzes, opinion polls, mail-in response forms, or membership applications. Scholarly writing, on the other hand, almost never requests such interaction from the reader, and indeed, is notable for the one-way direction of its communication. Of course, all critical readers do interact with scholarly writing in a variety of ways, ranging from intellectual engagement and response to material activities such as scribbling in the margins, writing letters to the author or editor, or publishing articles responding to other articles or calls for papers. The authors may not solicit this interaction, as they do on the Web, but it takes place nonetheless and is an important part of the process of understanding texts, an assumption that underlies the use of journal-writing exercises in conjunction with reading assignments. We might say, then, that the Web makes explicit and public the author-reader interaction that occurs with print sources and so draws students' attention to this component of evaluation, causing them to reflect on the kinds of interaction allowed or encouraged by a text. As students reflect on Web sources and determine how the interactive features of a site help indicate the quality, accuracy, bias, and overall value of the information it presents, they learn to give more consideration to the response of the reader in the overall rhetorical situation.

Simply browsing the Web makes one aware of the variety of interactive modes available there. As the discussion of links in the previous section made clear, the Web's hypertextual structure in and of itself enables a degree of interactivity. Readers can choose different paths through a Web site by making choices to follow certain links, thus personalizing their use of the site. An evaluation of a Web site's links necessarily includes an evaluation of the range and quality of choices the site offers for the reading experience. However, hypertextuality in itself is a relatively low order of interactivity, allowing the reader only to customize his or her own experience—an opportunity also offered in printed texts—and not to contribute to or affect the site in any way.[4] A higher order of interactivity is found in several other fairly common features of Web sites: It has become a rule of *netiquette,* for instance, to include an e-mail address or a "mail-to" at the bottom of a home page, allowing readers to contact authors with comments or questions. This possibility can lead students to do more primary research, and in so doing chip away at the notion of the unquestioned authority of the author. Advances in Web programming, driven largely by the development of commercial activities on the Web, also enable more complex types of interactivity: local search engines, questionnaires, application and purchasing forms, guest books, bulletin boards, chat rooms, question-and-answer forums. In each case, a different kind of information is solicited from the reader, and for a different purpose. In assessing interactive features, then, student researchers need to consider why the site is soliciting interaction, from whom, and toward what end. In short, they need to read interactive elements as clues in determining a Web site's rhetorical mode and purpose.

For instance, membership applications at nonprofit and advocacy organization sites, such as the NRA and Planned Parenthood, remind readers that the information offered there is, to some extent, intended as an advertisement for the organization, helping it to solicit members. Thus, the response sought from readers indicates that the information presented throughout the site should be regarded warily and should perhaps be double-checked for accuracy. The same is true for marketing and sales on the Web; interactive questionnaires and purchasing forms at these sites remind readers that the other information there is, at least in part, promotional. Chat rooms and discussion forums might also be used at a commercial site to generate increased customer contact and improve customer satisfaction; entertainment-oriented sites regularly provide this feature to increase the number of visitors and thus increase the Web sites' advertising revenue. The genre, purpose, audience, and persuasive strategies of the Web site, in other words, can be discerned through the interactive choices it offers.

However, not all interactivity on the Web has a promotional or commercial orientation, and indeed in some instances opportunities for reader input indicate that the site is produced and visited by experts in the field. In "Wired Science," Herb Brody (1996) noted that there are a number of Web sites where scientists, engineers, medical researchers, and technical professionals regularly post drafts of papers to solicit feedback from peers. Brody described the Internet as a virtual chalkboard for scientists, on which "theories, experimental results, shoot-from-the-hip notions are all shared, electronically, with the geographically dispersed community of people who find this information important" (p. 43). Similarly, the *Journal of Computer-Mediated Communication* . . . , an electronic publication affiliated with the Annenberg School of the University of Southern California and the Hebrew University of Jerusalem, includes in a recent issue several means to draw on the expertise of its readers and editors of the journal, a list to which readers can submit addresses of important resources on the Web, and a newsletter that solicits submissions. In these examples of academically-oriented sites, the opportunities for reader interaction might be seen as enhancing the reliability, comprehensiveness, and authority of the information found therein. Through their interactive options we see that these sites are attempting to become loci for communities of experts and for the compilation and advancement of knowledge in certain fields, and therefore, they are dynamic and potentially rich sources of information for student researchers.

Authors of Web sites have a range of interactive possibilities from which to choose, and their choices both affect the experience of reading a Web site and afford insight into the site's overall purpose. Because interactive features directly address and solicit information from readers, assessing these features gives students quite direct experience in assessing audience. Indeed, the Web makes visible and legible the role of the reader in any rhetorical situation by making authors more accessible and readers' responses more public.

CONCLUSION

Clearly, the question "Can we use Web sources for this assignment?" opens up a series of teaching opportunities, particularly when our goal is to help students assess information and incorporate it into their own writing. Drawing the Web into the classroom enables us to teach more about rhetorical modes and strategies and to expand upon notions of literacy in general. We see it as a compelling and effective way to help students develop stronger research, reading, and writing skills, while enhancing their ability to perform useful primary and secondary research.

This is not to say, however, that we see the Web as some Panglossian answer to all of composition's ills. Indeed, any attempt to increase the presence of networked computing in writing classes brings to the fore certain very real material constraints affecting our field and academia generally; foremost among them is the unequal and inadequate distribution of resources, technological and otherwise. Within and across educational institutions, students do not have equal access to computers or to the Internet, nor do most composition teachers have the equipment or the time for professional development in this area. Even if all departments and universities could rise above previous limitations of funding, providing computer and Internet access to every student and providing teachers the wherewithal to stay at least a step ahead of their students, it is still the case that the Web is not an ideologically neutral territory. It is inextricably bound to its time and place and to the ideologies of that time and place. The Web is unfortunately like the typical academic library, and like most of academia, in that it reflects and perpetuates inequalities of language, nationality, ethnicity, gender, and class. To these biases, the Web adds a heavy dose of capitalist values and consumerism.

However, it is unwise, we believe, to reject the Web for these reasons. We have outlined here how a close and careful reading of Web sites can enhance students' research and writing skills; it is also an important step in educating students to be critical users of the Web and the Internet. Assessing the value of information offered at individual Web sites leads naturally to a critical approach to the Web as a whole and invites students to enter important debates about the social, cultural, political, and economic implications of this new medium of communication. The Web has the potential to be shaped in some degree by its users; indeed, the Web users of this morning are the Web authors of this afternoon. Therefore, harnessing students' initial and perhaps uncritical enthusiasm for the Web, and cultivating in its place an attentive, thorough, and discerning approach, may ultimately lead to improvements in the Web itself.

NOTES

1. Cynthia Selfe and Richard Selfe (1994) pursued a related issue in their examination of computer technology's inscription in and complicity with dominant cultural and ideological constructions. They interpret computer interfaces in particular as promoting the grand cultural narratives that "foreground a value on middle-class, corporate culture; capitalism and the commodification of information; Standard English; and rationalistic ways of representing knowledge" (p. 494). Although Selfe and Selfe don't address the Web in their critique, a study of the cultural and ideological maps represented in the Web's interface(s) is clearly important. Moreover, we agree with their assertion that teachers and students should be encouraged to become "technology critics as well as technology users" (p. 484).

2. Alan Liu (1998), in his *Voice of the Shuttle* website (<http://humanitas.ucsb.edu>), remarked that cool is "one of the most single-minded and totalitarian aesthetics ever created. Why are there 'cool sites of the day' but no beautiful, sublime, or tragic sites?" In an attempt to clarify "cool," Liu's *Laws of Cool* page offers improvised categorizations such as "Ultra Graphical," "The Experience of the Arbitrary" (e.g., sites with random URL generators). "'Ordinary' Cool" (pages recording someone's grocery list or daily journal), "Corporate and Government Cool," "Technologically Advanced Pages," and "Cool Personal Home Pages." As these categories imply, "cool" allows for a wide range of interpretations dependent in large part on the purpose, audience, and content of the site.

3. Mass-market paperbacks, such as *The Internet for Dummies* and *The World Wide Web Unleashed*, are available to guide students through the process of searching for information on the Web and on the Internet more broadly (FTP sites, Gophers, mailing lists, MUDs, and MOOs, etc). But, because they are not specifically addressed to academic researchers, these books generally don't concern themselves with how to evaluate the reliability of quality of information once it is found. A similar orientation guides Paul Gilster's (1997) *Digital Literacy*. Although Gilster stated that "critical thinking" is the most important "core competency" demanded of Internet users, and although he advised checking an author's credentials and reading the address of a Web site for clues as to its

reliability, Gilster mainly endorsed various Internet search tools and strategies as the primary solution to evaluating information. For instance, he advised that "you need to learn how to assemble this knowledge; that is, build a reliable information horde from diverse sources. You must choose an environment within which to work and customize it with Internet tools" (p. 3).

4. More interactive are those hypertexts that enable readers to make some contribution—for example, by adding plot elements or characters to a story. This is not yet a common feature of web sites, however, and is mostly found in CD-ROMs or special software programs.

REFERENCES

Alexander, Jan, & Tate, Marsha. (1996, October). The web as a research tool: Evaluation techniques. [Online]. Available: <http://www.science.widener.edu/~withers/evalout.htm> [1998, March 9].

Bal, Mieke. (1990). De-disciplining the eye. *Critical Inquiry, 16,* 506–531.

Berger, John. (1972). *Ways of seeing.* London: Penguin.

Birkerts, Sven. (1994). *The Gutenberg elegies.* Boston: Faber and Faber.

Brody, Herb. (1996). Wired science. *Technology Review, 99,* 42–52.

Ferris, Pixie. (1997). Writing in cyberspace. *CMC Magazine.* [Online]. Available: <http://www.december.com/cmc/mag/1997/jun/ferris.html> [1998, March 9].

Gilster, Paul. (1997). *Digital literacy.* New York: John Wiley & Sons.

Hairston, Maxine; Ruszkiewicz, John J.; & Seward, Daniel E. (1997). *CoreText: A handbook for writers.* New York: Longman.

Horton, William K. (1990). *Designing and writing online documentation.* New York: John Wiley & Sons.

Landow, George P. (1991). *Hypermedia and literary studies.* Cambridge, MA: MIT Press.

Liu, Alan. (1998, March). *The voice of the shuttle.* [Online]. Available: <http://humanitas.ucsb.edu> [1998, March 9].

Miller, Susan, & Knowles, Kyle. (1997). *New ways of writing: A handbook for writing with computers.* Upper Saddle River, NJ: Prentice Hall.

Myers, Jack Frederick. (1989). *The language of visual art: Perception as a basis for design.* Fort Worth, TX: Holt, Rinehart, and Winston.

Ormondroyd, Joan; Engle, Michael; & Cosgrave, Tony. (1996, October). *How to critically analyze information sources.* [Online]. Available: <http://www.library.cornell.edu/okuref/research/skill26.htm> [1998, March 9].

Postman, Neil. (1995, October 9). Virtual students, digital classroom. *The Nation, 261,* 377–382.

Rock, Michael. (1994). Since when did *USA Today* become the national design idea? In Michael Bierut, William Drenttel, Steven Heller & D. K. Holland (Eds.), *Looking closer: Critical writings on graphic design* (pp. 146–149). New York: Allworth Press.

Rodrigues, Dawn. (1997). *The research paper and the World Wide Web.* Upper Saddle River, NJ: Prentice Hall.

Selfe, Cynthia L., & Selfe, Richard, J., Jr. (1994). The politics of interface: Power and its exercise in electronic contact zones. *College Composition and Communication, 45,* 480–504.

Sommers, Nancy I., & Simon, Linda. (1993). *The HarperCollins guide to writing.* New York: Harper-Collins College Publishers.

Weidenborner, Stephen, & Caruso, Domenick. (1996). Writing research papers: A guide to the process (4th ed.). New York: St. Martin's Press.

Woodward, Jeanette A. (1997). *Writing research papers: Investigating resources in cyberspace.* Lincolnwood, IL: NTC Publishing Group.

22 Web Research and Genres in Online Databases: When the Glossy Page Disappears

MICHELLE SIDLER

1. INTRODUCTION

In 1991, Jay David Bolter forecasted revolutionary changes in the process of writing that came about because of computer technologies: "Electronic writing will therefore be felt across the whole economy and history of writing: this new technology is a thorough rewriting of the electronic space" (p. 40). Indeed, electronic space continues to shift beneath our virtual feet, constantly changing the ways we write and perceive texts. The World Wide Web, in particular, expands the spaces that writing can inhabit as well as the forms it can take. On the Web, textual distribution and virtual circulation create new genres of writing through combinations of words, visuals, and immediate links to outside texts (Heba, 1997; Reynolds, 1998). Network technologies have the potential to reach large audiences instantaneously and support a variety of publication sources. At times, this immediate exchange of texts overwhelms our ability to discern the credibility and usefulness of information sources (Gilbert, 1997; Sorapure, Inglesby, & Yatchsin, 1998). Nowhere is this struggle more evident than in the increasing dependence on Internet research in composition classes; often, the speed of change in the information age presents new challenges before even we (the "experts" of such literacy) are prepared to engage them.

This article addresses one of those challenges. Teachers can help extend students' analyses of online texts by encouraging them to consider the place of source materials within the larger structure of the Web in addition to examining the structural features of a given site. I detail the impact of online databases, the PROQUEST database in particular, on composition students' research and explain new evaluative methods for online documents that utilize knowledge of online genres, information retrieval processes, and metaphorical imagery. Further, I suggest that students' difficulties indicate larger issues of virtual literacy emerging from the current transitional age of electronic and print cultures. As students research, they are not equipped with adequate

From *Computers and Composition* 19 (2002): 57–70.

knowledge about Web genres and need a metaphorical framework with which they can understand the ways different texts operate in different virtual spaces.

2. ONLINE DOCUMENTS: CHANGING THE (S)PACE OF RESEARCH AND EVALUATION

Previously localized research databases such as Periodical Abstracts, OVID, ERIC, and PROQUEST allow student researchers to find traditional source information online, providing large databases of magazine, newspaper, and journal articles along with conference papers and other documents from the last couple of decades, all collected in one space. This information can be found on the Web, the same virtual space within which they access a multitude of other search tools like library card catalogs and search engines. PROQUEST and similar databases provide students with many advantageous services during the complex and busy process of research. However, with these technical advantages come disadvantages. Online databases complicate research because traditional and (usually) credible sources like *Time, Newsweek,* and *The New York Times* reside within the wider circulatory space of the Web itself which, of course, houses a variety of information sources, some less traditional and credible than others. Articles from online databases are different from other Web sources because they are decontextualized, text-heavy reproductions of print sources and because they are retrieved through specialized retrieval programs, not through search engines and other familiar Web search mechanisms. Indeed, online reproductions of print articles are just one of many different types of genres available on the Web, including emails, newsgroups, chat rooms, PDF files, and, of course, various types of Web sites. Current pedagogies of Web source evaluation are just beginning to address the incredible differences among all online texts, and my discussion here extends previous work by presenting a broad framework for addressing some of the multiple genres and contexts increasingly emerging on the Web.

In "Web Literacy: Challenges and Opportunities for Research in a New Medium," Madeleine Sorapure, Pamela Inglesby, and George Yatchsin (1998) detail several ways students might evaluate Web sources, but their discussion is limited to what are now conventional Web sources—Web pages with colors, graphics, and many other contextual cues. The authors identify two main challenges presented by the Web as an information source: "its diverse and unfiltered content and its hypermedia format," (p. 412) which lead to questions of accuracy and credibility. They present evaluation strategies that concentrate on the visual design, intertextuality, and interactivity of Web pages. These strategies help students differentiate between various genres of Web discourse and evaluate their viability as academic sources (pp. 417–22).

However, some texts online—including those in online databases of print texts—require even more methods of critical analysis. These online texts present only simple graphic design and little interactivity, relying primarily on what I call "disembodied text," words on a page with few obvious visual markers. Such pages include online journal articles, single page-text-only-sites, and online periodical databases and single-page, text-only sites. Helping students determine the different genres of these Web sources becomes even more difficult because students lump all the texts together; the formal similarities of documents with disembodied text lead students to believe that they are all of the same information quality. Articles in the PROQUEST database, for example, lose many familiar attributes of popular periodicals: the colorful charts and photographs, the smudgy ink of the newspaper, and the glossy sheen of magazine paper. These physical markers are replaced with computer screens, browser interfaces, laser printer paper, and ink jet toner. Although some periodical entries supply scanned images of the print originals, such clues are easily overlooked. An essay on a personal Web site about the rise of global warming often resembles a *Newsweek* article about the same topic, complicating researchers' attempts to evaluate texts and even recognize appropriate MLA or APA citation format.[1]

When we teach traditional library research, students already struggle to learn the motivations and purposes of print media, and these problems can be further exacerbated in online research. Performing Web research requires us to teach students about new expectations for written texts, including the relationship between form and genre in online documents because visual design plays a major role in determining the genre of Webbed documents. The "disembodied text" of documents such as those in PROQUEST present an ironic challenge to the analysis of form and genre in electronic spaces—that of formlessness. The *lack* of form among Web genres creates generic ambiguity. While different print genres often appear similar in form (in news magazines, for example, editorial articles might look similar to informative articles), online technologies further mask generic similarities, obscuring rhetorical issues like context, purpose, and audience. Periodical articles such as those on PROQUEST are presented in a new digital context; such sources resemble other Web documents but retain many of the generic features of their originating print texts, a hybridization of information sources. In short, the visual, physical, and material experience of texts constitutes, at least to some extent, the form of texts.

As genre theories evolve in the age of electronic texts, we need to be aware of the power that visual, physical, and material experiences have over readers. This power comes from the use of space, and even the power "to control textual space" (Reynolds, 1998, p. 15), changing the contexts within which documents are reproduced and as such, the possibilities such texts may have (Miller, 1984, p. 165). The impact of space in Web research presents new evidence to support and extend Catherine Schryer's (1999) recent theory of genre and textual analysis. She wrote that when we:

> address the issue of genre and power, we also need to explore a genre's relationship to time and space, not just in terms of its relationship to the past, present, or future, but most importantly in terms of a genre's attempt to control time/space by defining what categories of time/space are at work within specific genres and accepted as just common sense. (p. 84)

Documents on the Web create challenging categories of time/space because they exist in immediate time (available almost instantaneously) while residing in virtual space (present online but not in the physical realm). As these print and electronic media merge in many ways, it is easy to assume databased PROQUEST documents have the same credibility, context, and audience as other Web documents because online discourse seems to reside in a time/space that is immediate and without origins. It is "common sense" to view even PROQUEST documents solely as electronic texts with no print predecessors. Because information technology increasingly reproduces and alters traditional print sources, we teachers of composition research must constantly note the textual ambiguities (in arrangement, form, genre, and time/space) that can impede the ability to evaluate texts.

Textual ambiguities also develop from power of the Web environment itself. Gary Heba (1997) explained that multimedia environments create fluid processes of change that can disorient readers accustomed to print:

> The distinction between rhetorical, printed "texts" and HyperRhetorical multimedia "environments" is important conceptually because a text is a static, physical object, whereas an environment is a fluid, electronic place, composed of numerous objects, thus each represents a different discursive form and context. (p. 23)

Heba's distinction applies to the alteration of print articles on PROQUEST and other online databases. Original printed periodicals are found in the actual space of the library, requiring physical processes of retrieval—finding the magazine on the shelf, photocopying the article, and so on. However, time and space are compressed on the Web, creating a more immediate retrieval environment and promoting the assumption that because a text is online, it fits only one generic category—that of a prototypical "Web page." Successful researchers must understand that various types of documents can be found online, including reproductions of print texts as well as multiple "Web page" genres. The following discussion presents a few basic tools and strategies that employ Web addresses analysis, mental maps, and heuristic metaphors to help students become more literate about online texts and Web source evaluation.

3. ANALYZING WEB ADDRESSES

A primary tool researchers must have when recognizing the source of an online document is a working knowledge of different Web addresses, particularly those that indicate retrieval programs. Because both stable addresses and addresses employing retrieval programs appear in the location field at the top of a Web browser screen, students often assume that all information in that field is a traditional URL address. However, retrieval programs, most notably CGI scripts, are not stable URL addresses but something much more complicated: a programming function that a database uses to locate information. The National Computational Science Alliance (1998) explains CGI programming this way: "A plain HTML document that the Web daemon *retrieves* is *static,* which means it exists in a constant state: a text file that doesn't change. A CGI program, on the other hand, is *executed* in real time, so that it can output *dynamic* information" (original emphasis). Although we often consider conventional Web pages to be fluid and tenuous—even temporary—in their online existences, databased documents offer even less stability and consistency. The Web addresses of many databased texts float, changing from space to space as new retrieval requests are made and the information in databases change. PROQUEST, in fact, uses a scripting mechanism that will not return users to the site of an article if they input the original CGI-scripted "address" information at a later time (Kevin Kuiper, email to author, March 1, 1999). Further, many online databases require licensed access for use. Readers who do not have subscriptions to these databases are forbidden from accessing the information, further complicating the retrieval process. Such access issues create an exclusionary dimension to databases not found in other retrieval mechanisms like search engines.

Along with their print origins, the differences in Web addresses indicate that databased sources constitute a new genre of online documentation, different from that of other Web pages with stable URLs.[2] As such, we need a variety of methods to determine the genre of a particular online source; we must analyze its retrieval mechanism in addition to examining the visual components on the screen. An immediate way to help students determine the retrieval process used in a given search is to teach the differences between URL addresses and other retrieval markers like CGI scripting. Teachers could then explain how CGI-scripted search mechanisms are used in databases that house certain types of information, including digitally reproduced versions of print texts.

Although this lesson in virtual addresses is a useful step, it may not solve all online research confusions. Students' struggles with online databases also indicate difficulties in negotiating the current paradigmatic transitions between print and online information. In particular, students experience two major difficulties when they make the paradigmatic leap from the physical world of glossy print pages to the virtual world of digitized online texts: a need for more Web space knowledge when they research online and a need to better understand origins, sponsors, and distinctions among ambiguous Web genres. As such, students need evaluative strategies different from those of print texts, including a way to analyze Web spaces, a working knowledge of current information retrieval processes, and a metaphorical method for recognizing different Web genres.

4. Spatial Orientation and Cognitive Mapping

A primary step in evaluating online information is students' ability to locate themselves within the vast virtual space of the Web, a process I call *spatial orientation.* Spatial orientation is necessary for research and literacy in the current print-digital paradigm because the Web provides information from a variety of sources, including digital texts that are reproductions of print media and those documents written exclusively for online consumption. In addition, research requires complex literacies that entail both the virtual space of the Web and the physical space of libraries. We can help students understand the origins and sponsors of online sources by providing strategies for understanding where and why they access information in different spaces.

Online databases like PROQUEST provide an illuminating example of the need for spatial orientation when analyzing online genres. Johndan Johnson-Eilola (1997) recognized the tendency for online databases to confuse and disrupt students' abilities to find themselves in virtual space. He argued that systems like PROQUEST present "immense, dynamic spaces through which users move" (p. 103). Such spaces must be navigated and mapped by "consumers of information" in order to understand their power and significance (p. 103). The navigation process of online research is in many ways different from traditional library research because access to information is more immediate and includes different generic features that distinguish texts. Becoming successful researchers in both print and digital paradigms requires two different, though equally difficult, types of retrieval processes. One involves the physical space of the library and the other involves engagement with virtual texts. While print media and traditional libraries require researchers to learn significant visual cues such as tables of content, directional signs, card catalogs, and the organization of bookshelves, online databases require users to mentally map the places where they find information. Online databases often have few clues to help orient readers, requiring students to map their retrieval process in highly cognitive and technical ways.

This experience with mapping is what students sometimes lack; many cannot recognize defining characteristics among different online information spaces. As researchers and writers, they find it difficult to distinguish between material found "outside" the space of PROQUEST and information housed within it. As consumers of information, they browse several types of textual stores, retrieving documents at will, gleaning information from less traditional or credible sources in the same way they rely on more established sources. Ironically, some students' textual confusion also indicates that they approach information from traditional, credible sources (like those in PROQUEST) with inadequate scrutiny, just as they often do with texts from less reliable personal Web pages.

When performing online research, students may be confused as a result of the ubiquitous digital form Web texts usually take. Because they are not viewing a material object and undergoing the sensory experience of magazines, books, and newspapers on library shelves, students lose some of the physical grounding that has traditionally helped researchers to distinguish one media from another. This shift in emphasis from physical to mental perception is analogous to the technological challenges described by Shoshana Zuboff (1998) when a pulp plant computerized its bleaching process. Workers previously checked all gauges manually and experienced cognitive difficulties when they began reading the gauges in the computerized control room, a shift she calls "informating":

> The intrinsic power of [technology's] informating capacity can change the basis upon which knowledge is developed and applied in the industrial production process by lifting knowledge entirely out of the body's domain. The new technology signals the transposition of work activities to the abstract domain of information. (p. 23)

Online technologies de-emphasize the role of material space in the process of information retrieval. By informating the research process, we take away much of the body' sensory experience of texts, requiring abstract reasoning processes with which students may not be familiar. As students enter the PROQUEST database and procure texts, they often have difficulty distinguishing the sources of texts because the material conditions of their research are obscure; most notably, the "feel" of the page and the position on the shelf are no longer available. Currently, successful researchers must have the ability to analyze and evaluate information using both the physical experience of print documents and the mental design of digital texts.

Along with learning the organization and cues of traditional libraries, students must have the ability to create mental maps of line spaces, a skill different from that of traditional methods of information retrieval. Zuboff (1998) called this skill "refinement" and argued that it "may imply the reconstruction of knowledge of a different sort" (p. 23). Indeed, Web research requires us to reconstruct the ways we perceive certain aspects of textual space, creating mental maps of the sites we visit and the retrieval routes we take. Frederic Jameson (1991) called these maps "cognitive maps" and argued that as our relationships to physical space and multinational structures become increasingly complicated, individuals need sophisticated ways to orient themselves in daily life (p. 44). He noted that cognitive maps "enable a situational representation on the part of the individual subject to that vaster and properly unrepresentable totality which is the ensemble of society's structure as a whole" (p. 51). The Web, a social structure too large in its totality to be comprehended, can be broken down into symbolic bits and connected through cognitive mapping, creating what Nedra Reynolds (1998) called "imagined geographies," virtual metaphors of space (p. 13). Researchers can use metaphorical representations of online spaces, and the mechanisms used to locate those spaces, to describe, analyze, evaluate, and compare information found within different areas of the Web.

Mapping online geographies necessitates a sort of virtual memory, a pre-existing knowledge of Web landscapes. Reynolds (1998) likened electronic space to "city life" with anxiety-inducing bustle and confusing, crowded streets (p. 29). To extend this metaphor, we can compare online sites to the "neighborhoods" [3] of a city—suburbs, downtown, and even neglected, impoverished slums that make up a virtual city landscape. As teachers of Web research, we need to help students become oriented to different online neighborhoods and discuss how one online neighborhood might lead to information that is qualitatively different from information in another area. When students research online, they are interacting with multiple sites and addressing rhetorical issues beyond just the immediate space and time occupied by any one Web page on the computer screen. Cognitive mapping of imagined geographies can help student researchers understand the metaphorical relationships among these different online sites.

Along with the concept of "neighborhoods," other metaphors present different perspectives about the function and makeup of online communication. Those metaphors include: enormous virtual libraries (Bolter, 1991; Bush, 1945), extended online communities (Doheny-Farina, 1996; Rheingold, 1993; Turkle, 1995), and living entities such as a central nervous system (Viglizzo, 1996).[4] These perspectives require different levels of understanding and so-phistication about networked discourse; some metaphors more appropriately describe the experience of advanced online users while others work well as introductory representations for less sophisticated users. As teachers, we can help student researchers by introducing practical metaphors that are closely associated with textuality and knowledge such as the notion of the library. In addition, we can help them by working from their experience learning new neighborhoods and cities, creating maps of streets and landscapes as they enter new communities (including, for example, learning the landscape of a new college campus and town).

When applying metaphor to human–computer interaction, Benyon and Imaz (1999) argued, "There are no universal metaphors to be applied; instead they are related to the community that will use the implemented system" (p. 184). By emphasizing a researcher's activities in both physical and virtual libraries, we work from students' experience and the library's connection to a larger textual marketplace. In this context, students are not just researchers but also citizens, consumers, and workers—familiar roles in their physical lives that correlate to cityscape and mapping metaphors. These practical metaphors facilitate students' abilities to locate themselves online, and eventually, they can lead to an understanding of more complex metaphors that reveal the esoteric plasticity of the Web and its fluid, enormous size. By understanding geographies of online research, students learn strategies for completing immediate research goals and initiate a process for understanding of the Web's larger function, evolution, and structure.

5. ARRANGEMENT ON/OF THE WEB: IMAGINED WEB GEOGRAPHIES

Equipped with basic metaphors about neighborhoods and libraries, students can use their knowledge of Web spaces to determine the genre (and as such, the generic conventions) of a particular text. Knowing the generic conventions of a particular online source will help students ascertain its credibility, particularly those in a database like PROQUEST, where magazine and newspaper articles ultimately share the Web with less reliable types of information like ill-informed editorials on personal Web pages and grossly biased reports published by corporations or political groups. Without strategies appropriate for evaluating digital texts—strategies that differ from the physical experience of print texts—students may equate the credibility of these documents. Collin Gifford Brooke (1999) noted that such textual disorientation arises from our assumptions about arrangement, assumptions based on print technologies. He argued: "the confusion that readers of hypertext experience is due to our inability to invent an alternate discursive space more appropriate to the medium" (p. 260). As teachers and "experts" of writing and technology, we can create metaphors to help students understand virtual space, starting with the recognition that online texts are part of a large Web of linked discourse.

Recognizing the many connections among online discourses, Brooke (1999) pointed to the need for notions of arrangement that go beyond the image of a container, a solitary box into which we place discourse, and instead move closer to the idea of a pattern, an "evolving multidimensional structure" (p. 264). Teachers might help students to distinguish Web pages more effectively if we begin by showing them that the Web itself creates a pattern of discourse, a large "docuverse"[5] of multiple texts and origins. We can help students map this pattern in ways that address both the confusing anonymity of a single, text-only Web page and the overwhelming enormity of the entire Web.

My students' Web research struggles seem to underscore Brooke's (1999) assertion that patterning will make "arrangement a self-conscious part of our discursive spatial practice" (p. 265) because evaluating online documents requires students to understand both the arrangement of single Web pages and the pattern of at least some areas on the Web. Although it is impossible at this point to visualize and comprehend the pattern of the entire Web (and, of course, it is always changing anyway), students can begin to understand the process by which they access certain online spaces. This process, at least in part, establishes the context, structure, and even audience for each online text. We can help our students identify similarities among certain online genres (and the textual stores in which they are housed) by mapping the ways they reach individual texts. As students explore various virtual neighborhoods and use cognitive mapping to record their findings, they may begin to recognize the recurrence of certain retrieval processes within different sites. They can then take note of their mutual characteristics and the types of texts they reveal.

Creating imagined geographies and performing cognitive mapping of the Web can be enacted in at least two distinct ways. First, students can learn how a certain retrieval process works, record their findings, and apply that knowledge when they visit a new site containing the same process. Second, students can apply their own experience of learning the layouts of real cities to learning metaphorical communities on the Web. They can connect individual sites by creating mental images of city neighborhoods and by applying metaphors of actual buildings and stores to those sites.

5.1. Recording Retrieval Processes

Similar retrieval mechanisms often yield similar types of information, so noting the ways materials are accessed provides one method of source evaluation.

However, students must first determine the type of retrieval mechanism used in a given search. Three main categories of retrieval processes available online currently are search engines, databases, and directories. Search engines include Boolean mechanisms on public, commercial sites such as Alta Vista and YAHOO! Database searches retrieve what the National Computational Science Alliance Web page calls "dynamic information," documents collected and stored within textual stores such as PROQUEST, ERIC, and LEXIS-NEXIS. Directories are listing mechanisms found on a wide variety of sites, including corporate and organizational resource pages, university site listings, and even within search engines like that of YAHOO! Students can begin examining retrieval mechanisms by asking questions such as: who sponsors the directory? How is information prioritized? They might also make assumptions about the credibility of texts found, given the sponsoring retrieval mechanism and its general contents. Knowing that a given text comes from PROQUEST or LEXIS-NEXIS, for example, indicates that it probably comes from a current news or media source, implying at least some level of reliability. Presumably, a magazine article in PROQUEST is more likely to be unbiased than a self-published article found through a public search engine or the directory of a corporate Web site. While these methods are not absolute evaluative parameters, they at least yield some sense of a text's purpose, background, and level of credibility. Web address indicators like the presence of CGI scripting tell how information is stored and retrieved—cues about the type of sponsoring site. Along with Web addresses, the sponsor and type of a retrieval process can be examined in at least two more ways: directory listings and gateway indicators.

Directory listings: Directory listings help researchers understand the ways a given search mechanism prioritizes and categorizes information, indicating the quality and type of documents retrieved. Different types of search mechanisms supply different lists of links to retrieved sources, but search results are usually ordered in some hierarchical way. Unlike a library card catalog, the results are not necessarily listed by an author's name or a work's title. They may be listed in order of the relevance of the results—the percentage of content that matches the search parameters. Or, they may be ordered by the date of publication. All of these factors can indicate the type of retrieval mechanism used. To evaluate the search mechanism and reliability of its results—whether those results are derived from a search engine, textual database, or an organization's Web site—researchers might ask the following questions:

- What type of directory develops when I create a search? What type of information is provided in the directory's listings?
- Do the listings offer the title of the work? What about the author or journal/magazine? Do they provide a summary? Or, do they only provide the first few words?
- In what order are the results listed? Is it by the percentage of relevance? Date? Author's name? Title?

If a directory includes the full citation of texts, such as its author, title, and place of publication, most likely, the directory will contain the full text or abstracts of some articles, either reproduced from print publications or gleaned from online journals. The students can then examine the type of journal or magazine that publishes the work to help determine credibility, purpose, and audience. If the directory gives a title, followed by the first few words, phrases, or sentences of a text, most likely the search has been performed by an engine that retrieves Web pages of a variety of types. The Web pages could be from the Web in its entirety, or if students search within an organization's page, they will probably retrieve Web pages created by that sponsoring organization. At this point, students must ascertain who created the page, why, and how, whether it be a sponsoring organization or individual writer. By questioning the methods of retrieval used by the search mechanisms, students can determine the author(s), organizations, and publishers behind a given text, leading them to question the credibility and motives of the text's origins as they would print texts like magazines, business reports, and books.

Gateways: Along with result listings, careful consideration of a gateway's purpose and makeup will help in the evaluation process. At times, Web research requires students to enter into, register with, or log on to certain sites and pages—or gateways—in order to access search mechanisms. Types of search gateways might include: college library Web sites, public search engines, online media outlets, and corporate or organizational Web sites. Like directories, gateways can indicate a wide variety of informational stores, from academic resource materials to general news sources to indiscriminate Web pages. While academic resource materials and public news sources usually offer some level of credibility and reliability, Web pages retrieved by public search engines require a more diligent level of scrutiny. Furthermore, gateways sponsored by corporations or other interested organizations pose a particular challenge because they will most likely reflect the biases and motivations of that sponsor.

Evaluative methods based on retrieval mechanisms appear to be local in their application because they only address one process at a time. However, as students perform these searches, they can begin to recognize the similarities between listings and gateways and between similar URL addresses. Connecting these processes together requires a second level of cognitive mapping: using imagined geographies to describe the learning process online and to familiarize oneself with the different types of sites online. Because evaluative methods for online research require complex mental perceptions, students can benefit from connections between these virtual spaces and the familiar space of actual city buildings, streets, and landscapes.

5.2. Geographical Metaphors

Geographic metaphors, the second phase of cognitive mapping, help students connect their own experience of learning the layouts of cities to the process of learning the Web. Students can map small spaces of the Web, then connect those smaller maps together as part of the overall Web pattern, much like we learn the streets of a new city. When we drive in a new city, we come to recognize particular roads and neighborhoods, then as we learn more about the city, we come to understand where some of those routes connect. Students will not learn the complete Web pattern, just as we do not always learn all routes in a city, but they can make connections between the different spaces they use often during research. When students understand the differences between the PROQUEST "neighborhood" of texts and that of a corporate Web site or a personal home page, they can then begin to tailor their expectations for credibility and evaluation according to each type of source.

Along with mapping and connecting areas, students can connect types of sites to real world buildings and stores, like businesses, schools, and charitable organizations. Just as different buildings in a community can house different categories of information with different levels of credibility, bias, and usefulness, so could online sites sponsored by those types of organizations. We can use metaphor to describe these sites. For example, the L.L. Bean home page (<http://www.llbean.com>) is an online storefront. It includes store merchandise, sales signs, and purchasing services. Storefronts on the Web should be browsed the same way we browse at shopping centers, viewing them as sites containing information, certainly, but more importantly, as places of commerce whose main goal is to sell merchandise. Students must take the sponsors' motivations into account as they glean information from such sites. The information found on the corporate home page of L.L. Bean should be viewed with the same scrutiny that information found in an actual L.L. Bean store or catalog would. In fact, I often extend this commerce metaphor, reminding my students that they are consumers in a textual marketplace and part of the research process entails evaluating the quality of the merchandise provided.

These community metaphors carry over to other types of public sites as well; library home pages online can be viewed as metaphorical extensions of real world libraries. University libraries often include different information than community or high school libraries, and the same kinds of assumptions can be made about their corresponding Web sites. Even pornographic sites online have community counterparts; they represent the "red light" districts within many communities that are considered less reputable—taboo, scandalous, and threatening. Various types of sites on the Web can be categorized, at least partially, through metaphor. Table 22.1 includes the site categories that students often encounter when doing research.

Many online sites can be explained through their real world correlatives, but these site categories are not intended to be exhaustive and definitive. Just as any community has a variety of different services, companies, libraries, and other organizations that perform several tasks, online site categories cannot represent all possibilities. Indeed, the categories are incomplete, fuzzy, and exclude some places. However, they do provide a broad framework for understanding many Web texts.

In addition, the metaphorical framework provides a context for recognizing and discussing sites, services, and information that are unique to the Web.

TABLE 22.1 Web Metaphor Categories

Type	Function	Selected Examples
Personal residences	Provide information on different topics (including personal information) for a variety of purposes; found on single-author pages	Michelle Sidler (auburn.edu/~sidlema)
Retail stores	Sell merchandise directly	Amazon (amazon.com) Etoys (etoys.com)
Corporate headquarters	Primarily advertise the products and services of a company, including annual reports and corporate descriptions; may also sell merchandise like a retail store	Coca-Cola (coca-cola.com) Toyota (Toyota.com) EDS (eds.com)
Service sites	Include information about (and sell) commercial services like finance and travel	The Street (thestreet.com) AAA (aaa.com)
Entertainment centers	Promote entertainment, just as arcades, movies houses, and clubs do in the real world	MTV (mtv.com) Napster (napster.com) Major League Baseball (majorleaguebaseball.com)
Newsstands	Provide current event news and advertising; includes both print-based media and online magazines	*New York Times* (nyt.com) *Time magazine* (time.com/time) *Slate* (Slate.msn.com)
Libraries	Represent and extend real world libraries, including community, school, and university libraries; provide access to licensed information databases	Penn State Library (libraries.psu.edu) NY Public Library (nypl.org) Library of Congress (loc.gov)
Not-for-profit organizations	Provide information and public awareness of charitable organizations	Boy Scouts of America (bsa.scouting.org) American Cancer Society (cancer.org)
Auction houses	Solicit consumer bids on merchandise	eBay (ebay.com) Priceline (priceline.com)
Government agencies (town halls)	Provide information, policies, and statistics regarding legislation, acts, and other public policy issues	Environmental Protection Agency (www.epa.gov/) U.S. Senate (www.senate.gov/)

Most notably, no clear "storefront" metaphor exists that correlates with search engines. Although search engines are gateways to a variety of information just like virtual libraries, they have no real world counterpart. Rather than places with communities, search engines might be seen as directories like the Yellow Pages, television viewing guides, and, of course, card catalogs. By employing metaphors, students have tools to describe abstract geographies of the Web, imagining and sorting spaces online just as they translate the streets and buildings in a city. Because search engines do not have a real world city equivalent, students can then devise new ways of evaluating those spaces with the recognition that they cannot depend on more traditional assumptions of resource credibility.

6. WEB GENRES AND THE PRINT/ELECTRONIC PARADIGM SHIFT

Spatial metaphors—imagined geographies—might help students make the transition from print-based libraries to electronic libraries. Before we overwhelm students with the grand landscape of a city, teachers might begin with a single building, using Bolter's (1991) description of a future electronic library where a graphic video screen "could even display the spines of books on shelves and allow the reader to reach in and open the books" (p. 100). Although such technical advancements are futuristic at this point, the metaphor for an online electronic library might help students understand the differences between what they find in ProQuest and what they find on other Web sites. By using this metaphor, we can "place" documents in an imagined library geography, with popular magazines on the periodical shelves and online encyclopedias in the reference section. As students become familiar with researching in traditional libraries, they can begin to examine their online counterparts.

However, students will soon find that the Web houses a more diverse range of texts, necessitating metaphors and maps different from those of a traditional library. Many Web documents cannot be found in the library, such as corporate home pages, online auctions, and tabloid news sites. The metaphor of a city or neighborhood would apply to these sites; after they comprehend metaphors for the more traditional and credible sources available online, students can eventually begin to venture out of the metaphoric library. Teachers can discuss why certain online texts are not generally found in a traditional library, and where in the community that material might be found. Students will begin to connect online documents with their places in an imagined city, recognizing their print counterparts, "real-world" audiences, and the motivations of their producers.

Many factors play a role in our perception of a print document's credibility: where a text is found in the physical word, the material conditions of its making, and the methods we use to find it. Documents on the Web should be no different, but the evaluative tools our students must use are still foreign because information technology continues to meld print and electronic paradigms. However, students can substitute imagined spaces, texts, and processes from the physical world to conceive of our place in the electronic realm. As students research online in a database like PROQUEST, they need to begin with a metaphor for that space and the documents it holds, one that will connect the disembodied text of a digitized magazine article to the pictures, fonts, and glossy pages of a physical magazine on a bookshelf. Until our long-term cognitive abilities catch up with the immediate paradigm shifts underway between print and electronic sources, perhaps we can rely on imagined geographies from the physical world to describe and comprehend complex discursive spaces.

NOTES

1. The Modern Language Association and The American Psychological Association do not specifically designate a method for citing previous print, databased documents. However, PROQUEST has devised standard citation methods based on their recommendations. For further information, see the Help section of the PROQUEST database or access the Web site directly at <proquest.umi.com/help/citing.htm>.

2. Students can examine the URL of an online source to determine its sponsor. The suffix of a Web page will indicate the type of sponsor for the site: *.com* for commercial sites, *.gov* for government sites, *.edu* for educational sites, and so on.

3. Steven Doheny-Farina (1996) introduced the metaphor of neighborhoods to describe online spaces in his book, *The Wired Neighborhood*.

4. For a broad discussion of Internet metaphors, see Mark Stefik's (1996) collection, *Internet Dreams: Archetypes, Myths, and Metaphors*.

5. I borrow this term from Theodor Nelson (1982) and George Landow (1992).

REFERENCES

Benyon, David, & Imaz, Manuel. (1999). Metaphors and models: Conceptual foundations of representations in interactive systems development. *Human-Computer Interaction, 14,* 159–189.

Bolter, David J. (1991). *Writing space: The computer, hypertext, and the history of writing.* Hillsdale: Lawrence Erlbaum.

Brooke, Collin G. (1999). Making room, writing hypertext. *JAC: A Journal of Composition Theory, 19,* 253–268.

Bush, Vannevar. (1945). As we may think. *The Atlantic Monthly, 176,* 101–108.

Doheny-Farina, Steven. (1996). *The Wired Neighborhood.* New Haven: Yale University Press.

Gilbert, Pamela. (1997). Meditations upon hypertext: A rhetorethics for cyborgs. *JAC: A Journal of Composition Theory, 17,* 23–38.

Heba, Gary. (1997). HyperRhetoric: Multimedia literacy and the future of composition. *Computers and Composition, 14,* 19–44.

Jameson, Frederic. (1991). *Postmodernism, or the cultural logic of late capitalism.* Durham: Duke University Press.

Johnson-Eilola, Johndan. (1997). *Nostalgic angels: Rearticulating hypertext writing.* Norwood: Ablex.

Landow, George P. (1992). *Hypertext: The convergence of contemporary critical theory and technology.* Baltimore: Johns Hopkins University Press.

Miller, Carolyn. (1984). Genre as social action. *Quarterly Journal of Speech, 70,* 151–167.

National Computational Science Alliance. (1998). Common gateway interface: Overview. The NCSA HTTPd Home Page. Retrieved October 22, 1999 from <http://hoohoo.ncsa.uiuc.edu/cgi/intro.html>.

Nelson, Theodor H. (1982). A new home for the mind. *Datamation, 28,* 168–180.

Reynolds, Nedra. (1998). Composition's imagined geographies: The politics of space in the frontier, city, and cyberspace. *College Composition and Communication, 50,* 12–35.

Rheingold, Howard. (1993). *The virtual community: Homesteading on the electronic frontier.* Reading, MA: Addison Wesley.

Schryer, Catherine F. (1999). Chronotopic strategies in the experimental article. *JAC: A Journal of Composition Theory, 19,* 81–89.

Sorapure, Madeleine, Inglesby, Pamela, & Yatchsin, George. (1998). Web literacy: Challenges and opportunities for research in a new medium. *Computers and Composition, 15,* 409–424.

Stefik, Mark. (Ed.). (1996). *Internet dreams: Archetypes, myths, and metaphors.* Cambridge, MA: MIT Press.

Turkle, Sherry. (1995). *Life on the screen: Identity in the age of the internet.* New York: Simon and Schuster.

Viglizzo, Barbara. (1996). Internet dreams: First encounters of an online dream group. In Stefik Mark (Ed.), *Internet dreams: Archetypes, myths, and metaphors* (pp. 353–387). Cambridge, MA: MIT Press.

Zuboff, Shoshana. (1998). *In the age of the smart machine: The future of work and power.* New York: Basic Books.

PART FIVE

Institutional Programs

Introduction to Part Five

Because writing is an inherently communicative enterprise, composition pedagogy has always worked at an intersection of several disciplinary and institutional discourses; different institutions offer different courses and services that all fall under the category of writing instruction. Many of these programs have been deeply impacted by the rise of computer technology, including distance learning, writing centers, developmental writing, second language instruction (ESL), and writing across the curriculum (WAC). And often, institutional forces such as administrators and external funding have married the success of many programs with the implementation of networked writing instruction.

Computer technology allows programs such as distance learning and writing centers the opportunity to reach a broader student base, one that is often nonresidential and nontraditional. Moreover, like other literacy programs, computers have been touted as potentially empowering for less prepared students like those in developmental or ESL courses. Indeed, computers expand the communication options for institutional writing programs, as they do with composition instruction, but each individual program faces a new range of possibilities and challenges.

The readings in this section offer an introduction to challenges faced by institutional programs, surveying arguments for and against computer implementation and offering practical advice for program administrators who consider going online. The writers caution that computer technology sometimes impedes classroom community, creates barriers for at-risk writers, and presents an ongoing project that must always be updated with the development of new technologies. But the writers also stress that with proper planning, technologies both enhance writing instruction and reflect the real-world composing practices of all writers, making them a valuable addition to programs that often serve diverse populations of students.

The five essays in Part Five address issues of the online environment for distance learning, writing centers, basic writers, ESL, and WAC. Each article expands on the possibilities and complexities of implementing instructional technology, surveying recent trends and reflecting on potential challenges.

Patricia Webb Peterson opens this section with "The Debate about Online Learning: Key Issues for Writing Teachers." Peterson describes a "map" that highlights three issues particularly pertinent to online composition instruction: teachers' roles, goals of the program, and student learning. She emphasizes that, in this new environment, changes to the traditional image of college instruction can bring positive results, including further decentering of classrooms and more active student engagement. Throughout her essay, Peterson echoes a caution found in other readings in this collection: Writing teachers must be actively involved in the changes to writing courses. If teachers choose to ignore the trend toward online education, they will not halt its progression; outside forces such as classroom space and budget constraints continue to power the rise of online instruction. Moreover, if teachers do not take a proactive stance, less pedagogically experienced forces, such as for-profit universities, developers of course management software, and financially motivated administrators, will determine the content and delivery of online instruction. Rather than view online education through a binary of good teaching and technology vs. bad teaching and technology, Peterson suggests that teachers should oversee the student learning outcomes and move beyond the two-sided debate to look for "the most effective and ethically responsible ways to incorporate these technologies" (382).

Like online educational programs, writing centers have incorporated technologies into their settings/mission to become a very visible part of most universities and colleges. They no longer serve only the basic writers and first-year composition students. Their role has expanded to include tutoring on subjects other than writing and to serve the university community as a whole, not just students in the English department. OWLs (the online writing lab component) have played a major role in increasing this visibility and the service. Stuart Blythe provides an overview of OWLs in "Why OWLs? Value, Risk, and Evolution," an article found online in the electronic journal *Kairos.* Blythe discusses the "assets" and "liabilities" surrounding OWLs. He also presents many of the important questions and concerns facing writing centers as they implement an online component. In particular, he emphasizes that OWLs enhance the credibility of the writing center on campus, offering an online presence that both highlights the physical writing center and offers some immediate services for students unable to visit the actual center. In addition, he discusses the advantages and disadvantages of investing money and resources into OWLs.

Like Peterson and Blythe, Linda Stine, in "The Best of Both Worlds: Teaching Basic Writers in Class and Online," identifies problems that developmental writers and their teachers encounter as they integrate instructional technology into classroom instruction. She then describes potential issues and the reasons they should be addressed and overcome to bring the online environment to basic writers. Reasons include "Time Management," the argument that online coursework allows for more flexibility with time and location, and the "Nike argument" which states that "the most effective learning occurs, experts agree, when students follow Nike's advice and 'just do it'" (395). Although Stine recognizes the validity of arguments for online learning, she also emphasizes the importance of good teaching practice. Reviewing the Seven Principles for Good Practice in Undergraduate Education published by the *AAHE Bulletin* (Chickering and Ehrmann), she then gives a framework for working with basic writers in online environments. Good teaching and learning practice can be pursued online if the student and teacher are actively involved in the learning environment, but to achieve this good practice, Stine recommends a hybrid approach to teaching developmental writers with technology wherein students meet face to face sometimes and online at other times. Such a blend helps to foster nontraditional students' participation and cooperation while recognizing their need for personal guidance.

Stine's illumination of how the seven good practice principles can benefit basic writers in a hybrid classroom can easily serve as a frame for Martha C. Pennington's discussion of teaching ESL students, "The Impact of the Computer in Second Language Writing," the fourth article in this section. Pennington offers a thorough review of research on second language writing in three digital environments: word processing, networking, and the Internet and World Wide Web. Carefully foregrounding computers' advantages and disadvantages, Pennington concludes that they increase students' efficiency, motivation, interaction, and collaboration, among other benefits. However, she also cautions that issues of equal access, assessment, and plagiarism have the potential to complicate classroom dynamics. Arguing that second language writers, like all students, increasingly engage multiple forms of technology, she asserts: "No ESL teacher can afford to remain on the sidelines of these developments, which have transformed and are continuing to transform literacy, language, and all communication in very significant ways" (422). Although a few of Pennington's references to technologies are somewhat dated, her conclusions about word processing, networking, and the Internet apply equally well to current (and most likely future) technologies.

In "WAC Wired: Electronic Communication across the Curriculum," Donna Reiss and Art Young provide a brief history of WAC and the development of ECAC (electronic communication across the curriculum). They present a helpful continuum that makes distinctions among personal, classroom, and public discourses, showing how many of the mainstream approaches to composition study are reflected in ECAC as well. Because of technology's increasing importance to written communication in many academic fields, e-portfolios, multimedia résumés, and student Web sites will become even more prevalent in writing instructions, so Reiss and Young suggest that WAC teachers must integrate writing-to-learn strategies with computer-intensive instruction. Such instruction will include "the computer-supported activity designed and guided by an instructor whose 'prompts' lead students to fruitful inquiry, research, synthesis, and collaborative writing" (444). To ensure proper integration of WAC and good teaching practices, the writers also urge the continued use of the workshops for teachers that have been so much a part of the development of WAC programs.

The articles in this section offer valuable insight about the most appropriate uses of technology in diverse composition-related programs. Perhaps the most important lesson is that technologies should serve the needs of students and the contexts within which we teach them; computer-assisted writing instruction is not a one-size-fits-all endeavor. For program coordinators, the authors provide research and resources to support thoughtful and responsible program planning. Their experiences may prove useful as you develop your curriculum and experience institutional pressures (budget, classroom space, class size, and so on) and scrutiny (if not attack) by administrators, colleagues, and students.

REFERENCES

Chickering, Arthur W., and Stephen C. Ehrmann. Implementing the Seven Principles: Technology as Lever. *AAHE Bulletin Teaching and Learning, 50* (1996): 3–6.

23 The Debate about Online Learning: Key Issues for Writing Teachers

PATRICIA WEBB PETERSON

1. INTRODUCTION

Many university professors are fearful of distance learning's impact on the traditional university learning. They predict that online learning will lessen academic rigor and will separate students from teachers. Arguably, the academic experience of a distance learner changes dramatically because the physical space of the classroom is displaced and the primary mode of interaction is computer mediated. Whether or not this experience is necessarily — or even overwhelmingly — negative is still up for debate.

The time has come in which university professors can no longer simply ignore the issues, even if they fear where the path will lead. Writing teachers in particular need to pay attention to the onslaught of rhetoric about the benefits of and problems with distance learning for two reasons: First of all, because the primary interface of a distance-learning course is the written word[1], writing teachers' expertise will be increasingly needed as courses are written and delivered in online environments. Second, the only course universally required at almost all colleges and universities is the first-year writing course. Almost every student has to take at least one writing course during college. It makes sense, then, that this ubiquitous course has found its way into the online curriculum and may continue to be a major player in the online learning curriculum. The nature of the post-process writing course[2] has shifted to an interactive, collaboratively constructed space of engagement. Unlike typical lecture classes, first-year composition is typically (or so we hope) a small, interactive group of students working together to investigate and write about current, key issues. When these kinds of courses are moved online, what is lost and what is gained? These questions are yet to be discussed fully by scholars within Composition Studies.

Writing teachers need to be prominent voices in distance-learning debates for both of these reasons, but interestingly enough, most of the books

From *Computers and Composition* 18 (2001): 359–70.

and articles written about distance learning come from fields other than composition (e.g., Education, Computer Programming). This article is an attempt to map out[3] and clarify the key issues in the debate about distance learning—both the enthusiasm and the fear—in an attempt to delineate what is at stake in these debates, specifically for composition teachers. The key coordinates of this map—teachers, students, learning—are familiar, yet they are made strange by the new electronic environments in which we now find writing classes. My intent is for this map to invite more writing teachers into the ongoing conversation about *if* and *how* distance learning should be integrated into higher education.[4]

2. First Key Issue: Teachers' Roles

Rhetoric about both the promise and peril of distance learning is felt acutely in the changing role of the teacher. What will the job of a teacher look like in virtual learning environments? James Perley and Denise Marie Tanguay (1999) offered one image:

> The fundamental difficulty with institutions that rely heavily, or exclusively, on distance education is that they are characterized by a practice called "unbundling." In that practice, course materials are prepared by a "content expert" and delivered by a "faculty facilitator," in a uniform manner, producing predictable and measurable "outcomes" that fit uniform assessment tools. Such a process of turning education into modular units represents a basic change in an essential characteristic of higher education. (p. B4)

This process of unbundling means that the faculty member who writes the course is not the one who will teach the course; hence, the student and the content expert are further separated, not brought closer together by the technology. Perley and Tanguay expressed the fears that many faculty members have about distance learning and its effects on their role. They warned that the quality of education will suffer because, in traditional capitalist fashion, workers (in this case, teachers) and products (the class material) are divided. What may result, they argued, is an assembly-line delivery of courses by people who are not content experts.

Some teachers who fear distance-learning courses, however, assert that distance-learning technologies change the role of the professor into a deliverer of corporate values and goals, instead of a deliverer of traditional, liberal humanist goals. With the imagined and real collaboration between corporations and academia through distance-learning initiatives, faculty members fear that they will be forced to reshape themselves into the image of corporate trainers. Those who share this fear link distance learning to for-profit, online universities whose goals are controlled by big business and not by a progressive view of education. Lester Faigley (1999) pointed out that institutions such as Western Governors University are premier examples of what academics fear when it comes to virtual learning: "Western Governors University is designed from an employers' perspective. Degrees from WGU are certifications of particular skills, thus in theory guaranteeing the employer that a trained worker is being hired" (p. 137).

The image that Faigley (1999) presented is threatening because, first of all, academic freedom is a key component of the traditional perception of the university professor. Academic freedom is the heart of tenure guarantees, including freedoms in both scholarship and teaching. The drive to distance learning has been represented as a threat to this because corporate interests, rather than faculty members, determine the curriculum. With the increasing influx of corporate sponsors and for-profit institutions of higher learning, the fundamental goals of distance-learning classes appear to be driven by corporate visions rather than by academic standards.

The other side of this seemingly two-sided debate is expressed in an article by Steven Crow (1999) who argued that

> nothing inherent in an online institution demands radical redefinition of those traditional roles. At many institutions that use the Internet as a vehicle for instruction, the design, delivery, and evaluation of each course remain in the hands of a single faculty person, often full time. Faculty members control the learning environment; they use e-mail to lecture and encourage discussion on line, and to read, comment on, and grade papers. (p. B6)

In this vision of distance learning, online education appears to be very similar to traditional, face-to-face teaching except students and professors meet in virtual spaces instead of in the same physical space. Students and content experts (called *professors* in the traditional vision of the university) are still very much in contact with one another, and the quality of the course is not lessened.

These two disparate stances on teaching with distance-learning technologies clearly show that one of the stickiest issues in the debate is the role of the teacher in the technological age, which is not a new issue in the field of rhetoric and composition. In fact, for over a decade now, computers and composition specialists have been claiming that one of the benefits of using computers in the writing classroom is that the teacher is decentered, thus inviting students to become co-constructors of knowledge in the classroom. For example, Nancy Kaplan (1991) argued that the newness of computer technologies in the classroom allowed us to challenge the existing assumptions that were guiding our teaching. We could, Kaplan argued, become aware of many of our print-based assumptions and the problems they posed. Having this awareness, we could then adjust our role as teachers to create and encourage a more collaborative working relationship between students and teachers. Thus, in other areas of study, we have transcended the binary of good technology/bad technology and have begun to explore opportunities that information technologies may offer writing teachers.

With the widespread adoption of distance learning, the challenges to traditional teaching roles are heightened. The spatial changes introduced by distance learning have highlighted the assumptions we have about what it means to be an English professor. As Zane L. Berge (2000) pointed out, the traditional role of the professor of English was driven by the characteristics of traditional, specifically located, university education:

> a residential student body; a recognized geographic service area from which the majority of the students are drawn (a local community, a region, a state, or a nation); full-time faculty members who organize curricula and degrees, teach in face-to-face settings, engage in scholarship, often conduct public service, and share in institutional governance; a central library and physical plants: nonprofit financial status; and evaluation strategies of organizational effectiveness based upon measurement of inputs to instruction, such as funding, library holdings, faculty, faculty/student ratios, faculty qualifications, and student qualifications. (p. 209)

Berge effectively paints a picture of the university life with which most faculty members are familiar and stresses that the subjectivity of "professor" has historically been grounded in a particular physical relationship between students and teachers.

With online teaching, the physical distancing of student and teacher raises questions about what makes a good teacher. Online teaching also reminds us that technology alone cannot cause changes; it is the teacher's use of technology and the designers' construction of the technology that shapes its impact. Thus, we stand at a moment of opportunity for change, but we must transcend the seemingly two-sided approach (pro or con) to this issue. Lorraine Sherry (1996) points out that while traditional forms of teaching (that is, lecturing) can be replicated in online environments, inquiry-based learning can also be fostered by the new and innovative space. The introduction of new technologies opens up opportunities for multiple kinds of training for teachers—both technological and pedagogical—and with this training can come the exposure to innovative teaching strategies. Sherry wrote:

> Inquiry learning is a new technique to many teachers. No longer is the teacher "the sage on stage"—the deliverer of a fixed body of knowledge; she becomes the facilitator of discovery learning for her students, through progressive discourse. Thus, even if a teacher is well-practiced and at ease with the equipment in the classroom, she still requires training in order to integrate new teaching strategies with the technology. (p. 9)

Advocates of distance learning like Sherry point out the ways in which distance-learning technologies can help us challenge traditional patterns of learning that no longer (if ever) work well and suggest that these changes are not automatic or guaranteed. Sherry's perspective offers us a third alternative: Distance-learning technology is neither inherently good nor bad, but presents a moment of opportunity to question our usual standards of teaching. Such positions encourage us to ask the crucial question: What role should the teacher of writing adopt? Our old answers no longer fit.

Writing teachers who fearfully or stubbornly resist examining the possibilities for online writing courses do not avoid the issues I have mapped out here. Instead, they abdicate their responsibility to actively participate in the shaping of new roles for instructors. By turning away from these issues, university, college, and community college writing teachers allow other institutions (online, for-profit institutions) to decide what online writing courses will look like.

If we jumped into the debate, we could positively influence the roles of both online and traditional writing teachers. If we do not enter this debate, however, we may find online writing courses are no longer capped at a manageable number of students, writing assignments are no longer inquiry-based, and that the pay that online teachers receive to teach a course is substandard and exploitative. If those of us who do work at institutions of higher learning have a say in the construction of online writing courses, these potential pitfalls could certainly be addressed and alleviated. Our national organizations could create additional documents that lay out recommendations for online classes that specify the role of the teacher and her relationship to students. Clearly, we are not faced with *either* choosing distance learning and selling out on our belief systems *or* holding true to our belief systems and resisting distance learning. Corporatization is not the only path we can take if we choose to pursue online writing courses.

3. SECOND KEY ISSUE: EDUCATIONAL GOALS

In addition to fears about the effects of distance learning on teachers' roles, faculty members are also currently debating the effects that these new information technologies will have on what gets taught and how that content gets produced. *Lifelong learning* has become the buzz phrase of the newly re-engineered higher-education system. Although the traditional liberal arts vision of learning and teaching is still prevalent in higher-education institutions, much of the marketing to those outside the university (e.g., prospective students, alumni, legislators, parents) has begun to focus on teaching re-tooling skills. This shift to lifelong learning suggests that what gets taught and how it gets taught should be adjusted to suit a diverse population of students and a variety of learning modes, a somewhat novel idea in the traditional university. Much of the literature on distance learning suggests that accommodation of this newly diverse population of learners is the primary benefit of online courses. For example, Lynnette R. Porter (1997) argued that

> because educational programs are becoming available at reasonable costs, through a variety of media and institutions, and with flexibility in scheduling to meet many different learners' needs, lifelong learning is not only possible, but becoming accepted as a requirement for actively participating in the modern world. Distance learning helps make lifelong learning possible and attractive to more people. (p. 12)

From this perspective, distance learning is touted as a technological solution to the problem of making lifelong learning more accessible to people who traditionally have been excluded from higher education.

Others, however, find the focus on using online technologies to further the goal of lifelong learning problematic. The problematic points are who will get to define what counts as education in this new lifelong-learning framework and what will the primary goals be? Critics of distance learning state that completely online institutions are frequently for-profit enterprises whose academic integrity is in question. Although many pedagogical reasons are given for adopting distance learning at traditional institutions (and also for constructing other virtual institutions), these critics claim that financial gain is an overdetermining drive behind the move toward distance learning. As Faigley (1999) argued,

> the primary motive driving Western Governors University is providing higher education on the cheap. The logic is economy of scale. What can be taught to 10 can be taught to 100. What can be taught to 100 can be taught to 1,000. What can be taught to 1,000 can be taught to an infinite number. (p. 137)

Critics claim that this large-scale delivery of courses strips the learning experience of any of the social and cultural effects that traditional face-to-face learning offers.

These critics assert that higher education has involved more than just book learning; instead, higher education has offered a crucial affective experience. As Marcy Bauman (1997) pointed out,

> Students have a variety of needs when they come to a college classroom, many of which have little or nothing to do with the content of the subjects they are studying. We know, for example, that students' academic success is in some way dependent on their being able to become integrated into the academic community, at least to the degree that they understand its expectations and the ways in which it operates. We know that students have social needs when they come to college: they need to be able to find a group of like-minded people with whom they can form friendships . . . And yet, comparatively little attention has been paid to how to create and foster the sort of social climate online that will contribute to student success. When we think of planning online classes or programs, we think primarily about the intellectual content of the course or program, and we tend to forget that the other factors are important. (p. 2)

I quote Bauman at length to illustrate the complexities of the argument about distance learning and its effect on students. Bauman argued that the affective factors of face-to-face teaching are not easily (if at all) replicated in distance-learning courses. Without considering what students need in order to learn, our adoption of distance-learning technologies will not serve our educational goals.

Creating a space for more diversity in higher learning is an important goal. The best way to accomplish this goal, however, is tricky. Sharon Crowley (1998) pointed out that any time a new population has been admitted to higher education, a learning crisis has been identified (or constructed) due to the challenges posed by the outsiders to the traditional structure of the university. Nontraditional students are demanding entrance to higher education because the link between literacy and technology that has been constructed carefully by multiple institutions in our country (see Selfe, 1999) requires workers to have a higher level of technological expertise. Further, as the state and federal governments continue to underfund universities, administrators are searching for ways to make the university more profitable. At Arizona State University, for example, this involves increasing admissions (while nearly freezing the hiring of tenure-track faculty). Both of these factors mean that a population of students who have not had access to higher education will now have access.

The crisis posed by this new population, then, is actually a crisis generated by decisions made *within* the university and by an influx of new people *into* the university. The crisis within the university is based in the realization that the administrative methods of running a university don't work in the current conservative economic and political climate. The fear of corporatization, then, is not necessarily generated by distance-learning technologies, but by budgetary constraints and administrators' responses to them. For example, at Arizona State University, the English department has undertaken an experiment with hybrid undergraduate writing courses in which students meet face-to-face one day per week and asynchronously online the other day. The motivation for this experiment was the shortage of classroom space. In the hybrid model, two classes can be scheduled in the same classroom, a model that saves the university money but may not necessarily meet the needs of students.

The problem for composition teachers, then, is promoting diversity in higher education without selling out to a corporate model or allowing state budgets to guide pedagogical choices. The debate over distance learning highlights already existing problems, but can offer a site for visibly changing institutional choices that influence the writing classroom and challenging those current financial decisions impinging on our pedagogical choices. To use this moment productively, though, we must get beyond the dualistic response to distance-learning technologies. Once again, the critical use of technology that Gail E. Hawisher and Cynthia L. Selfe (1991) called for nearly a decade ago remains our goal.

4. THIRD KEY ISSUE: STUDENT LEARNING

The last key issue I address is, perhaps, one of the most crucial questions in the distance-learning debate: How is student learning changed, bettered, or damaged by distance-learning courses? This issue encompasses the other two key areas discussed here because both teachers' perceptions of their roles and schools' assertions about academic goals influence the experience that students have in courses. At the heart of a teacher's role is (or should be) a desire to affect certain kinds of learning outcomes for students; at the heart of the educational goals outlined by universities and colleges lies a similar desire. This key issue is, like the others, often presented as a two-sided debate. On one side are those who argue that because distance learning provides access to some students who could not go to the "actual" college or university, it benefits students and promotes lifelong learning. These scholars also suggest that the experience of an online course can be as rich and fulfilling as the experience of a traditional course. They look at how collaboration is encouraged online (Alexander, Lefrere, & Matheson, 1994; Cern, 1994; Nyce & Bader, 1995; Porter, 1997), how the teacher and student become partners in learning (Hart, 2000; Peters, 2000; Sherry, 1995), and how students engaged with experts through online discussions (Selinger, 2000). On the other side are those who identify the difficulties that students have with online courses. These theorists argue that we need to study how students actually interact with the courses to evaluate the courses' effectiveness (Hara & Kling, 2000).

The first stance taken on this issue is that students benefit from distance-learning technologies in various ways. Different populations of learners can find a place within distance-learning curricula. As Lorraine Sherry (1995) pointed out,

> adult learners have a wide variety of reasons for pursuing learning at a distance: constraints of time, distance, and finances, the opportunity to take courses or hear outside speakers who would otherwise be unavailable, and the ability to come in contact with other students from different social, cultural, economic, and experiential backgrounds (Willis, 193). As a result, they gain not only new knowledge, but also new social skills, including the ability to communicate and collaborate with widely dispersed colleagues and peers whom they may never have seen. (p. 10)

Proponents also claim that distance learning allows teachers and students to embrace and work with different learning styles, ones not necessarily accepted in traditional classrooms. Sherry (1995) suggested the "if a teacher recognizes the existence of these alternate learning styles, and if he attempts to make a match between these modes and the content to be learned, then he can develop a local instructional theory" (p. 10) that works for different populations of students. Sherry is not alone in this positive appraisal of the potentials that distance learning offers students and is certainly representative of the kinds of arguments made in favor of it. The teachers, administrators, and researchers who embrace the benefits of this kind of learning acknowledge the fear that the learning experience will be diminished, but conclude—as Australia's Review of Higher Education Financing and Policy Committee did— that "face-to-face teaching does not always live up to its ideal image" (Blight, Davis, & Olsen, 1999, p. 25) and that distance-learning courses could actually create better learning environments.

Others, however, are less enthusiastic about the effects of distance learning on learning. Michelle Selinger (2000) claimed that although distance learning supposedly accommodates various forms of learning, "the focus of the debate . . . is largely on teachers; how they match teaching to learning, and seldom about enabling the learners to make their *own* choices about where, when, and how they learn" (p. 86–87). Thus, the flexibility touted as a strength of distance learning is not necessarily present in distance-learning courses. In fact, distance-learning courses can be more inflexible, opponents claim, than traditional classes. Dan Carnevale (2000) pointed out that spontaneity

> falls by the wayside in an online course. In a conventional course, a professor can change lesson plans as necessary, perhaps grabbing a VCR and showing a video instead of sticking to a lecture. But online education requires any movie or film that is played to have copyright requests taken care of in advance. (p. A37)

Further, members of the populations that distance learning supposedly supports (e.g., nontraditional students) do not always have the technological capabilities to participate in the courses. Access to computer technology and the Internet required for distance learning is not as widely available as some may believe.

In addition to not solving the problems that many of the proponents claim it does, distance-learning technology, opponents argue, actually introduces new difficulties into the learning process. Noriko Hara and Rob Kling (2000) showed that much of the literature about distance education presents it positively, but few studies have actually examined students' responses to taking an online course. In their study, they observed and interviewed students taking a master's level educational-technology course and found that students' frustrations went beyond feelings of isolation. In addition to difficulties posed by being physically separated from their teacher and peers, students could also not determine what the instructor thought of their ideas or their progress in the online course. One student wrote: "I haven't gotten any feedback about my contribution [to the class]. I cannot tell from the email. You can tell from the classroom what the professor thinks about you from the body language and the way they talk. So, I am not feeling that I'm getting enough assessment" (p. 14). Another issue that students in the study raised was difficulty understanding the written instructions given to them by their instructor: "I think the biggest problem is the instruction of our assignments. I usually don't understand what she wants, either in email or from the website" (p. 18). If students are having difficulty understanding the teacher's written communication in a face-to-face course, they can simply ask the teacher to clarify; in an online course, that option is not available. These problems are not only frustrations, opponents argued; they are also blocks to learning.

As with the other two key issues addressed in this article, the debate about the effects of distance learning on students should not be considered only in these divisive pro/con terms. Even the students who expressed frustration in Hara and Kling's (2000) article still rated the class highly, suggesting that despite problems, they still value the learning experience. Writing teachers should certainly pay attention to possible problems online learning presents to students, but they should also keep an eye on the potential benefits that some students may reap from online courses. Instead of a knee-jerk reaction to technology that leads us to either rush to use it or hide from it, this debate over student learning should raise a concern about the best ways for us to teach diverse populations of students and the roles that technologies such as distance-learning products can play. If the debate about distance learning reminds us that students learn in various ways and that we should set up our classrooms to allow them choices in their own learning, then we have gained from the debate, whether or not we choose to teach an online course.

Further, writing teachers should consider ways to incorporate student feedback into their courses more thoroughly. Hara and Kling (2000) pointed out that many researchers were not focusing on students' responses to various technologies. The introduction of distance-learning technologies has reminded us of the importance of this kind of feedback, and online technologies can offer new ways of gathering that information from students. The debate about student learning also leads researchers of writing to reconsider their projects. Patricia Sullivan and Jim Porter's (1997) *Opening Spaces* recommended that our research should benefit those being researched and not simply the researchers. When we establish a research study, they argue, benefiting the researched should be a core part of our agenda. We can explore what courses work well online, what teaching strategies are effective in that environment, and how to adapt what we currently know to a changing world. Students are facing different challenges in the workplace and are not necessarily coming to college straight from high school. Instead of simply dismissing online courses because they do not look like the classes we are used to, we need to discuss the most effective and ethically responsible ways to incorporate these technologies. If we can get beyond the binaries of the debate, then our conversations about distance learning can help us critically examine our assumptions about teaching and research—a useful project indeed.

5. CONCLUDING REMARKS

Writing teachers have long been concerned with the process and product of written communication. The Internet has introduced a new world filled with new forms of written and visual communication—a world that students must become critical consumers and users. As Cynthia Selfe (1999) argued, we can no longer afford to deny the carefully constructed link between literacy and technology in our culture. If we respond to technology with either uncritical enthusiasm or fear, we are missing the point. More than ever, we need to adopt a critical perspective of technologies influencing and shaping the learning environments we are creating. Because writing is a part of this new technological world, it makes perfect sense for writing teachers to be at the heart of the debate about if, how, and when to use distance-learning technologies in higher education.

I have mapped out three key issues at the core of the debates in an attempt to show the ways in which the divisive positions taken about those issues actually simplify complex issues about teaching and learning. Understanding basic tenets of the debates and complexity of the issues can better prepare writing teachers to take an informed, critical stand in the debate. Hopefully, this map will help teachers work toward a critically informed assessment of the opportunities and drawbacks that distance learning presents. I invite you into the discussion.

NOTES

1. Currently, this is the case, but with the increasing availability of video and audio capabilities on the Internet, the written word may not be the only feature of online courses; however, because video and audio capabilities require that students have powerful machines, many online institutions are not using them. For example, as of November 2000, Harcourt Higher Education (HHE), the accredited online institution funded by the created through Harcourt Brace Publishing, required its content experts (those who create the course) to not use video or audio components in their courses. HHE is not alone, either. So the written word will continue to be a primary force in an online course, at least for awhile.

2. I understand that this is not the only kind of, or even the predominant, theory guiding first-year composition courses. In fact, as Sharon Crowley (1998) argued, the current-traditional paradigm is still the dominant force in first-year composition. The current theory in rhetoric and composition books and journals, however, values the kind of classroom I am describing here, and thus this theory holds sway in our community, even if every classroom does not resemble it.

3. Patricia Sullivan and James Porter (1997) argued for mapping as one way to understand the complexities of the research scene. They contended that maps allow researchers to "situate themselves in relation to their own sites of study and reflect on their potential positionings within those sites" (p. 96). Maps can be used to describe the research scene as well as the methodological frameworks inherent in a study. As Sullivan and Porter urged, "mapping is a way to identify preferences, tendencies, and of course blind spots. Such a mapping exercise can serve to critique fields' interests and locations . . . It can also serve to suggest places for new researchers to locate" (p. 99). Postmodern theorist Edward Soja (1996) suggested using mapping to understand the ways in which the physical, imaginary, and political aspects of a physical and psychological space influence and shape each other. Alice Jardine (1985) argued that maps are powerful constructions that tell one story by making other stories invisible. The way I'm using mapping in my article is a combination of all three approaches.

4. In *Technology and Literacy in the Twenty-first Century,* Cynthia Selfe (1999) makes a similar call. The subtitle of the book, *The Importance of Paying Attention,* summarizes her key argument. We can no longer be satisfied with ignoring technology or with focusing solely on technology in the classroom. Larger institutional issues and national literacy projects need our careful scrutiny, or else decisions will (and are) be made about what technology use should look like and who will have access, and we will have no say in how these issues get mapped out.

REFERENCES

Alexander, Gary, Lefrere, Paul, & Matheson, Steve. (1994). Towards collaborative learning at a distance. In Melisa F. Verdejo & Stefano A. Cern, (Eds.) *Collaborative dialogue technologies in distance learning,* (pp. 60–64). Berlin: Springer-Verlag.

Bauman, Marcy. (1997). Online learning communities. Available: http://leahi.kcc.hawaii.edu/orgitcconf97/pres/bauman.html [Accessed: 10 September 2000].

Berge, Zane L. (2000). Why not reengineer traditional higher education? In: L. A. Petrides, *Case studies on information technology in higher education: Implications for policy and practice* (pp. 209-216). Hershey, PA: Idea Group Publishing.

Blight, Denis, Davis, Dorothy, & Olsen, Alan. (1999). The internationalization of higher education. In Keith Harry (Ed.), *Higher education through open and distance learning* (pp. 15–31). New York: Routledge.

Carnevale, Dan (August 4, 2000). Turning traditional courses into distance education. *Chronicle of Higher Education,* A37.

Cern, Stefano A. (1994). Models and systems for collaborative dialogues in distance learning. In Melisa F. Verdejo & Stefano A. Cern (Eds.), *Collaborative dialogue technologies in distance learning* (pp. 119–125). Berlin: Springer-Verlag.

Crow, Steven (October 29, 1999). Virtual universities can meet high standards. *The Chronicle of Higher Education,* B5–B6.

Crowley, Sharon. (1998). *Composition in the university: Historical and polemical essays.* Pittsburgh: University of Pittsburgh Press.

Faigley, Lester. (1999). Beyond imagination: The Internet and global digital literacy. In: Gail E. Hawisher & Cynthia L. Selfe (Eds.), *Passions, pedagogies, and 21st century technologies* (pp. 129–139). Logan, UT: University of Utah Press.

Hara, Noriko, & Kling, Rob. (2000). *Students' distress with a Web-based distance education course.* Available: http://www.slis.indiana.edu/CSI/uflOO-OI.html [Accessed: 30 September 2000].

Hart, Jan K. (2001). The role of computers and technology in health care education. In Lisa A. Petrides (Ed.), *Case studies on information technology in higher education: Implications for policy and practice* (pp. 195–208). Hershey, PA: Idea Group Publishing.

Hawisher, Gail E., & Selfe, Cynthia L. (1991). The rhetoric of technology and the electronic writing classroom. *College Composition and Communication, 42,* 55–65.

Jardine, Alice (1985). *Gynesis: Configurations of women and modernity.* Ithaca: Cornell University Press.

Kaplan, Nancy. (1991). Ideology, technology, and the future of writing instruction. In Gail E. Hawisher & Cynthia L. Selfe (Eds.), *Evolving perspectives on computers and composition studies* (pp. 11–42). Urbana: National Council of Teachers of English.

Nyce, James M., & Bader, Gail. (1995). To move away from meaning: Collaboration, consensus, and work in a hypermedia project. In Mark Shields (Ed.), *Work and technology in higher education: The social construction of academic computing* (pp. 131–140). Hillsdale, NJ: Lawrence Erlbaum.

Perley, James, & Tanguay, Denise Marie. (October 29, 1999). Accrediting online institutions diminishes higher education. *The Chronicle of Higher Education,* B4–B5.

Peters, Otto. (2000). The transformation of the university into an institution of independent learning. In Terry Evans & Daryl Nation (Eds.), *Changing university teaching. Reflections on creating educational technologies* (pp. 10–23). London: Kogan.

Porter, Lynnette R. (1997). *Creating the virtual classroom: Distance learning with the Internet.* New York: Wiley Computer Publications.

Selfe, Cynthia. (1999). *Technology and literacy in the twenty-first century: The importance of paying attention.* Carbondale: Southern Illinois University Press.

Selinger, Michelle. (2000). Opening up new teaching and learning spaces. In Terry Evans & Daryl Nation (Eds.), *Changing university teaching: Reflections on creating educational technologies* (pp. 85–97). London: Kogan.

Sherry, Lorraine. (1996). *Issues in distance learning.* Available: http://www.cudenver.edu/~lsherry/pubs/issues.html [Accessed: 30 September 2000].

Soja, Edward. (1996). *Thirdspace: Journeys to Los Angeles and other real-and-imagined places.* London: Blackwell Press.

Sullivan, Patricia, & Porter, James E. (1997). *Opening spaces: Writing technologies and critical research practices.* Greenwich: Ablex.

24   *Why OWLs? Value, Risk, and Evolution*

STUART BLYTHE

Stuart Blythe's webtext article in the first issue of *Kairos,* an online journal of rhetoric, technology, and pedagogy, provides an overview of the issues raised with online writing labs (OWLs). His experience is with the Purdue University OWL, one of the first to be established. While several of his links no longer connect and some of the technology issues have changed (for example, Blythe describes problems with attaching documents to e-mail), the issues continue to focus on the types of services to provide students and the university community and budget and staffing constraints.

We have captured the opening screen and two (of 25) additional screens to give you an overview of the content of the article. You can find the complete article in the online journal *Kairos.*

We encourage you to go online to read Stuart Blythe's article and visit some of the many useful OWLs available on the web. The Web address is <http://kairos.technorhetoric.net/1.1>.

From *Kairos* 1.1 (1996). <http://kairos.technorhetoric.net/1.1/owls/blythe/owl.html>.

FIGURE 24.1   Title Page.

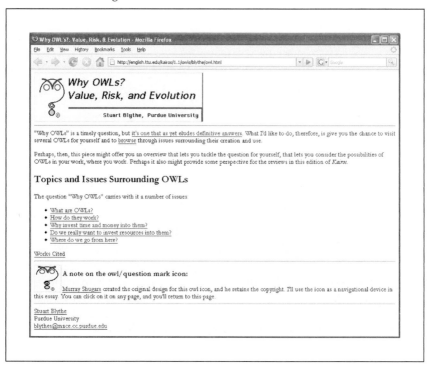

Source: Kairos 1.1 (1996). <http://kairos.technorhetoric.net/1.1/owls/blythe/owl.html>.

FIGURE 24.2   Benefits of OWLs.

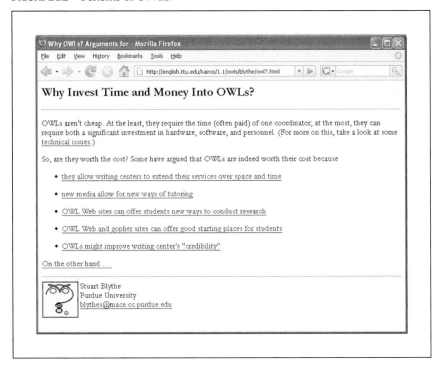

Source: Kairos 1.1 (1996). <http://kairos.technorhetoric.net/1.1/owls/blythe/owl7.html>.

FIGURE 24.3   Possible Limitations of OWLs.

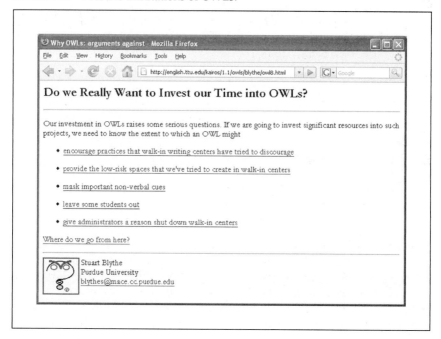

Source: Kairos 1.1 (1996). <http://kairos.technorhetoric.net/1.1/owls/blythe/owl8.html>.

25

The Best of Both Worlds: Teaching Basic Writers in Class and Online

LINDA STINE

COMPUTERS AND BASIC WRITERS: THE ISSUE

In a 1994 ERIC Clearinghouse summary on computer-assisted writing instruction, Marjorie Simic noted, "Writing researchers have long advised that the key to fluent writing is to write as much as possible. The key to exact writing is to revise repeatedly" ("Revising," par. 1). Basic writers, so much in need of increased fluency and exactness, have from the onset seemed ideal candidates for a writing course featuring word processing, precisely because of the computer's promise in these two areas. It is now the rare developmental course that does not, at least minimally, incorporate computer use into its curriculum. In a remarkably short time, the computer has evolved from being a tool with potential to improve student writing to being the tool with which people write, and if Peter Elbow is correct that "the best test of a writing course is whether it makes students more likely to use writing in their lives" (136), then most writing teachers today would have to agree that it is hard to justify a basic writing course that does not explore and exploit the advantages of word processing.

Agreement is harder to find, however, on the question of whether *online* instruction is equally justifiable for basic writers. The following article describes a hybrid option, in which students meet on campus every other week and work online during the off weeks, as one possible means of minimizing problems encountered in fully online writing classes while still allowing students to gain access to learning experiences unique to online instruction. This particular hybrid is, to be sure, only one of many possible variations. Richard Straub, considering how faculty can best comment on student papers, once acknowledged that "different teachers, in different settings, with different students, different kinds of writing, different course goals, and alas! with different time constraints may do different things with their comments, and do them well" (2). The same applies to teaching with technology: one size does not fit all. Nevertheless, the

From *Journal of Basic Writing* 23 (2004): 49–69.

more options we consider, the more likely we are to find the match that best fits our students' needs, our institutional resources, and our own individual teaching strengths. And, if we are lucky, that match may turn out to involve neither expensive equipment nor extensive technology skills on the part of teachers and students. In "From Pencils to Pixels," Denis Baron reminds us, "Researchers tend to look at the cutting edge when they examine how technology affects literacy. But technology has a trailing edge . . ." (32). With so many over-worked and under-supported basic writing teachers feeling fortunate if they can grab hold of even the trailing edge of technology, it is worth noting that a hybrid course like the one described below can double the number of students who can use a school's scarce computer laboratories and, at the same time, halve these students' commuting costs.

BASIC WRITERS ONLINE: THE PROBLEMS

A number of arguments can be made to explain why developmental students and online learning might not, in general, make a good match. One group of arguments raises societal issues. There is, for instance, the obvious problem of accessibility. As Charles Moran has stated, "The issue of access is easily and quickly framed: in America wealth is unequally distributed; money buys technology; therefore technology is inequitably distributed" (207). A 2000 report from the United States Commerce Department of Americans' access to technology tools, *Falling through the Net: Toward Digital Inclusion,* concludes that while people of all ethnic groups and income and educational levels are making gains, noticeable divides still exist between those with different levels of income and education, different racial and ethnic groups, old and young, single and dual-parent families, and those with and without disabilities. Basic writing students, typically older, poorer, less apt to come from stable, highly educated families, and more apt to have learning disabilities, are still less likely than the average student to have easy access to the kind of technology that distance learning requires, both in and out of the classroom. Are we justified in requiring basic writing students to work online, given the hardships that may cause for some?

Also troubling is the homogeneous culture into which our disparate students are asked to fit. As Richard and Cynthia Selfe have warned, "Students who want to use computers are continually confronted with . . . narratives which foreground a value on middle-class, corporate culture: capitalism and the commodification of information; Standard English; and rationalistic ways of representing knowledge" (494). They encourage teachers to recognize, and help their students understand, that the computer interface is "an interested and partial map of our culture and . . . a linguistic contact zone that reveals power differentials" (495). How should our pedagogy reflect this concern? Is it enough just to remind students of the limitations of grammar and spell checkers or do what we can to make sure that the physical layout of our classrooms does not reinforce a hierarchical structure? Or should we, who teach those students most likely to be marginalized, also make technology itself—its potential for liberation as well as oppression—the subject of more discussions and essays? How actively should we be working in our basic writing courses to raise student consciousness about the power of symbols and the politics of the technological contact zone?

A third set of worries for teachers of basic writers is related to technological issues. Distance education requires students to learn writing while often at the same time learning the relatively advanced computer skills required to produce writing online (for a discussion of this problem, see "Issues of Attitude and Access: A Case Study of Basic Writers in a Computer Classroom" by Catherine Matthews Pavia in this issue). Most of the adult students I encounter know how to use their computer for a few clearly defined tasks but have not developed a broad range of technology skills. Stuart Selber argues in a recent *CCC* article that students must be able to *control* a computer—that is, possess what he calls functional literacy, not just computer literacy—in order to work with it effectively (470–503). If students lack this type of functional literacy, how much does it interfere with an acquisition of writing proficiency? A related problem, which Lauren Yena and Zach Waggoner term "muting," occurs as a result of either an *actual* lack of technological literacy on the student's part or the anxiety that he or she experiences about a *perceived* lack of computer expertise ("Student Muting"). Will efforts to offset this problem double the responsibilities of the teacher, who must provide directions not only for what students are expected to say but also for how to navigate through the technology comfortably enough so that they are able to say it? Another technology-related problem, which applies whether students are writing online or off, is the tendency for developmental writers to put too much faith in the computer's authority. Might an online class tempt students even more to obey without question the dictates of those red and green "squiggly lines" produced by the computer's spelling or grammar checker (Whithaus) or to accept the largesse of their brower's search engines blindly, without the type of useful reflection that leads to linguistic and cognitive growth?

Another set of questions focuses on pedagogical issues. Chris Anson writes of "our basic beliefs about the nature of classroom instruction, in all its communal richness and face-to-face complexity" (263). Does the Internet—though undoubtedly rich and undoubtedly complex—provide such an atmosphere? And what might be the effect of the reduced cues environment in which distance learning functions? Haythornthwaite, Kazmer, Robins, and Shoemaker have characterized this environment as "text without voice, voice without body language, class attendance without seating arrangements." They point out that the very same environment that reduces the fear of *negative* feedback—when writers type something silly or inappropriate online, they cannot see the readers rolling their eyes, so they feel free to keep typing—also reduces *positive* feedback. In such a setting, individuals do not know if they are saying the "right" thing. How much might this add to the writing anxiety basic writing students struggle with in the best of situations?

Additional pedagogical issues of concern grow out of changes that the Internet and widespread computer use are bringing about in composing and reading processes. Leslie C. Perelman, director of the writing-across-the-curriculum program at MIT, describes the difference in the way people compose today by explaining that writers normally think out the entire sentence before they start writing it on paper; otherwise, things get too messy because everything is crossed out. "But on a computer," Perelman explains, "people just start a sentence and then go back and move things around. The computer screen is elastic and therefore the composing process has become very elastic" (qtd. in Leibowitz, A67–68). While such elasticity could prove liberating for basic writers, could it not just as easily reinforce bad habits for students who often lack a sense of the shape or boundary of a sentence or are not sure where they are going with an idea when they start?

A related question can be asked about online reading. According to James Sosnoski (161–78) good hyper-readers possess the following "positive" skills:

- Filtering (selecting out only details of the text that they want to read)
- Skimming (reading less text)
- Pecking (not reading in linear sequence)
- Imposing (constructing meaning by one's self more than from the intent of author)
- Filming (paying more attention to graphical than verbal elements to get meaning)
- Trespassing (plagiarizing code, cutting and pasting and reassembling)
- De-authorization (following links, losing sight of the author)
- Fragmenting (preferring fragmented texts because such texts are easier to re-assemble)

Basic writing teachers, who struggle continually with their students' tendency to read selectively and thus miss main arguments, read only parts of a text and not get the underlying meaning, read with a limited range of internalized schema that would help them gather meaning, find only those meanings they want rather than ones that the author presented, and misunderstand the boundary between paraphrasing and plagiarizing, might well question whether requiring basic readers to do much or all of their reading online could inadvertently reinforce poor print reading habits. The hypertext reading "skills" Sosnoski applauds seem remarkably like many reading weaknesses we try to help our students overcome. Similar misgivings emerge because of differences between the writing conventions appropriate to e-mail, chats, and online discussion posting and those conventions that teachers encourage in the classroom. The different rhetorical situations call for different styles; the writing displayed in a chatroom would not be acceptable in an academic writing assignment. Can we be sure that any increased fluency and confidence students gain by participating in a variety of online writing tasks will prevail over the "bad" habits such online writing might foster?

Yet another set of reasons that developmental writers sometimes fare poorly in online courses involves student-related issues. Online courses require self-direction, but basic writers, while often highly motivated, frequently have not developed the structured study habits and time management essential to success in distance education. When family, work, and other personal problems interfere, students can easily — and invisibly — fade away. Another worry is the possibility of overloading, with time spent on developing necessary technology skills getting in the way of a focus on writing skills. K. Patricia Cross has described what she calls the Chain of Response model of learning. One tenet of this model is that higher order needs for achievement and self-actualization cannot be realized until lower order needs for security and safety are met. If students do not feel safe online, secure in their technical abilities, will they be able to move on to the next writing challenge? An additional student-related problem arises because distance learning, unlike the face-to-face classroom, requires a basic writer to function in what is predominantly a text-based environment, even allowing for the multimedia options that the Internet enables. Will that demand play to the weakness rather than the strength of many developmental students? Furthermore, as Collison, Elbaum, Haavind, and Tinker warn, "Participants in net courses, even those who don't consider themselves new to the digital world, seem to lose their usual set of problem-solving strategies in the new environment. . . . [E]ven when instructions are provided, some participants still need help interpreting the directions to the discussion area or a particular thread" (52). No matter how many hours teachers spend creating detailed step-by-step directions — in words and pictures — to show students how to log on and respond to an online discussion list from home or where to post an essay draft for online review, some students will still call in a panic because the directions "aren't working" and they cannot complete their assignment.

Finally, having to anticipate all the potential problems described above and address those that may materialize later adds to the demands placed on faculty members who must find the time to create, maintain, and teach an online class. In one of the modules of Teaching Composition, a faculty listserv run by McGraw-Hill, J. Paul Johnson concludes that online writing courses work "only for faculty with expertise and experience." How do we gain this needed expertise and experience when faculty time and institutional budgets are so limited? Teaching online requires more up-front planning, more detailed course design, and often as many, if not more, contact hours with students than traditional classroom-based courses require. Furthermore, teachers have to keep up with the pace of technological change. In a recent *Computers and Composition Online* article, Evan Davis and Sarah Hardy likened faculty using technology to "travelers on sightseeing boats, hugging the coast while priding [themselves] for venturing into the ocean." Writing teachers in general, basic writing teachers in particular, rarely have the time and institutional support to explore the depths of the ocean of technology. Thus, the result Kristine Blair and Elizabeth Monske note: "In the rush to meet institutional pressures and curricular demands to create effective distance learning environments, as teachers we may be the ones who benefit *least* within these new virtual communities" (449).

Basic writing instructors must, at the least, carefully consider how they will address problematic issues accompanying online instruction, both in their pedagogy and with their students, before jumping on the technology bandwagon.

Basic Writers Online: The Potential

All these legitimate cautions and concerns notwithstanding, however, many features of online learning still seem made to order for basic writing students. Advantages of Web-enhanced courses fall into ten general categories. First comes what I think of as the "Can You Hear Me Now?" argument. Unlike class discussions, in which timid voices may go unheard, online learning—at least when using asynchronous features such as discussion lists—greatly extends possible reflection time: it lets students participate at their rate of speed and skill, think through a question, and polish up a response as long as needed before posting it.

Then there is the "Ken Macrorie" argument. In *Twenty Teachers,* Macrorie's book profiling the kind of teachers who enable students to learn, a basic assumption is that students learn by doing something worth doing. Rightly or wrongly, the Internet is considered "worth doing." Even something as mundane as practicing subject/verb agreement—should you want your students to do that—gains authority simply by being on the Web. Paradoxically, writing done virtually seems more "real."

A third consideration is expressed in the "Only Game in Town" argument. The vast majority of adult basic writers have no option other than online learning if they want to carve a few precious hours out of their busy week to go to school. Many single parents with jobs and families simply cannot get away to attend class, even when classes meet on evenings and weekends. They are also unlikely to be able to spend extended periods of time conducting library research or meeting face to face with other students for group projects, so even if they are able to make it to campus, their participation and, thus, their learning opportunities, are limited.

Related to this issue is the "Time Management" argument. When teaching online, faculty can provide their overworked adult students with a wealth of resources just a mouse click away rather than requiring a long ride to a library or a campus. Using software like *CommonSpace* or Bedford/St. Martin's *Comment,* for instance, teachers can link a problematic phrase in a student draft to a rule and examples in an embedded handbook or enable online peer review. They can provide a list of useful URLs through which students can access the riches of all the OWLs (Online Writing Labs) on the Web, or download helpful tools like *ReadPlease,* a simple and free voice recognition program that helps with proofreading by reading students' essays back to them.

A fifth set of reasons focuses on the "Academic Skill-Building" argument. Davis and Hardy, describing their experience teaching with Blackboard course management software, suggest that such software is useful because "students need the skills that it foregrounds: organizing and tracking documents, participating in a community discussion, sharing work with peers, claiming a voice through writing." Basic writers, it can reasonably be argued, need precisely these skills and thus should be exposed, if at all possible, to a learning environment that fosters them.

Less concrete but no less important is the "Virginia Woolf" argument. Paul Puccio, pointing out that "the setting in which we meet with our students is a factor in the composition of student-teacher relationships," compares his feelings about his computer classroom at the University of Massachusetts with Virginia Woolf's desire for a room of her own. His thesis is that teaching writing in a room set up to teach writing, with all the modern amenities, has a positive effect on his students' intellectual work as well as on their sense of community. "Schools," claims Puccio, quoting nineteenth-century educator F. W. Sanderson, "should be miniature copies of the world we should love to have." I would argue for extending this analogy to the virtual classroom and making even disadvantaged students welcomed guests online, with full run of the house.

Once students have a room of their own, of course, they tend to invite company over. That leads to the "Howard Dean" argument. A February 22, 2004, *New York Times* article about Howard Dean's presidential campaign strategy and the social impact of the Internet quoted Cass Sunstein, author of *Republic.com,* as saying, "If you get like-minded people in constant touch with each other, then they get more energized and more committed, and more outraged and more extreme" ("So What Was *That* All About?" section 4, 3). Though not necessarily wanting outrage and extremism, teachers of basic writers do continually look for ways to energize students and keep them committed to the learning process. Web-based communication has the potential to create some Deaniac-type energy otherwise difficult to engender among socially and geographically isolated basic writing students.

This, in turn, leads to the "John Dewey" argument. Beatrice Quarshy Smith, in a thought-provoking article about what she calls the colonial pattern that permeates our use of technology, points out the fact that her community college students by and large have inadequate access not only to the technologies but also to the literacies of power. Arguing for a *transactional* conception of technologies, Smith writes of John Dewey and Arthur Bentley, "For them knowing was a process of learning though reflection on experience and through the exchange of ideas with others" (5). Developmental writers typically have such sadly limited time and opportunity to participate in person in that sort of reflective conversation that the opportunity the Internet opens for virtual idea exchange, be it through chatrooms, e-mail, blogs, listservs, or simply Googling a concept, is in itself a powerful argument for moving classes online.

For teachers of adult students, the "Nike" argument holds special merit. The most effective learning occurs, experts agree, when students follow Nike's advice and "just do it." Active learning, important for students of all ages, is essential to adults. Arthur Wilson contends that . . . adults no longer learn from experience, they learn in it as they act in situations and are acted upon by situations" (75). Online courses, at least those that are well designed, force students to play an active role in the learning experience—posing questions, voicing opinions, engaging in discussions, spending as much time as necessary on weak areas, and self-testing their knowledge when and as appropriate.

Finally, and perhaps most generally persuasive, is what might be termed the "Can We Talk?" argument. As Sharan Merriam points out, "Critical reflection and awareness of why we attach the meanings we do to reality . . . may be the most significant distinguishing characteristic of adult learning" (9). The "persistence" of online communication enables and encourages this critical reflection. Thomas Erickson, from IBM's T. J. Watson Research Center, describes "persistence" in the context of online communication as follows:

> Persistence expands conversation beyond those within earshot, rendering it accessible to those in other places and at later times. Thus, digital conversation may be synchronous or asynchronous, and its audience intimate or vast. Its persistence means that it may be far more structured, or far more amorphous, than an oral exchange, and that it may have the formality of published text or the informality of chat. The persistence of such conversations also opens the door to a variety of new uses and practices: persistent conversations may be searched, browsed, replayed, annotated, visualized, restructured, and recontextualized, with what are likely to be profound impacts on personal, social, and institutional practices. (par. 3)

Gaining access to the "persistence" of the communication on the Internet— talk going on 24 hours a day, around the world, accessible at least as long as the web site lasts—can be profoundly important in helping basic writers view themselves as writers and participate in the sort of critical reflection Erickson describes.

We need to help our students become part of that persistent conversation, as skilled listeners and as persuasive speakers, if we are indeed going to help them find, and value, their own voices. Last semester, one of my students who works for campus security at a neighboring university, whose essays generally consisted of short, underdeveloped paragraphs, wrote a lengthy, thoughtful, fully developed response to an online discussion topic. Answering my e-mail complimenting her on both the writing and the content, she replied:

> Message no. 713: Thanks, Professor. This is the first time, in a long time, that I get to express my opinions without being accused of being insubordinate. Having a good old time!

Although I try to make all course work relevant, assigning essays that ask my adult students to explore issues they know and care about in their work and personal lives, this student did not feel comfortable expressing ideas and defending her opinions until she left the classroom environment, where she had defined herself, narrowly, as a student, and moved online, where she was free to redefine herself as a writer.

The Best of Both Worlds: Teaching in a Hybrid Environment

Instructors' assessment of the relative pros and cons of an online basic writing class will differ, of course, depending on their own personal and institutional conditions. The students I teach at Lincoln University in Pennsylvania are predominantly African American (Lincoln is a historically black university), range in age from about 25 to 64, and must be employed full time in a human service agency as a condition for admission. The Pre-master's Program, as this developmental writing course is informally called (the official name is the Pre-graduate Semester in Writing and Critical Thinking Skills) was created to help students improve their basic academic skills so as to be eligible to enter Lincoln's non-traditional Master of Human Services (MHS) Program, a graduate program in which applicants may quality for admission based on years of work experience in the human service field without having first earned a bachelor's degree. Most applicants, employed in a field in which talking and listening skills learned from life experience are more important than academic writing proficiency, come to the MHS Program with little or no college training; they tend to be uncomfortable communicating in Standard Written English and inexperienced at meeting the demands of academic writing. Depending on their score on the writing portion of the entrance exam, students may be assigned to the Pre-master's Program before entering the MHS Program for a 15–week semester, an accelerated 8-week semester, or a "stretch version," which extends the one semester's work over two semesters. It is this last option, the two-semester program, which we offer in the hybrid form described in this article.[1]

Students in this program are all commuters, some traveling considerably more than 100 miles to attend once-a-week classes, which are held either in the evening or on Saturdays. These students fit neatly into Mina Shaughnessy's description of basic writers as students who tend to produce "small numbers of words with large numbers of errors . . . restricted as writers but not necessarily as speakers, to a very narrow range of syntactic, semantic and rhetorical options, which forces them into a rudimentary style of discourse that belies their real maturity or a dense and tangled prose with which neither they nor their readers can cope" (179). Hoping to widen the range of options for our adult students as much as possible in as short a time as possible, we chose to design the writing course around computer-mediated teaching and learning. The setting in which classes are taught has evolved steadily since its 1987 beginnings in a basement room equipped with 15 Apple IIs, moving first to faster, stand-alone Windows-based PCs, then to a networked lab, next to a networked lab with Internet access, and finally to a networked lab enhanced with WebCT course management software. In 2002, after weighing the advantages and disadvantages of distance education, we decided to take the next step and add a distance component to the writing program. Students enrolled in the second semester of the two-semester "stretch version" of our basic writing course[2] now have the option of meeting in the campus writing lab only every other week, working from home using WebCT on the off weeks. The class is still evolving, but in general in-class meetings are used to introduce grammar and writing issues and describe assignments; in these sessions students also work in groups for idea generation and take all quizzes and exams. During the online weeks, students practice the grammar and composition issues discussed the previous week, respond to discussion topics, write and revise essays, and participate in online peer review. We initially saw the hybrid version of the course simply as an interim step towards a totally online program, but our experiences with both the difficulties and the success of online learning over the past two years have led us to believe that it is the hybrid experience itself that offers our particular students the best of both pedagogical worlds.

It has been fifteen years since the "Seven Principles for Good Practice in Undergraduate Education" were first published in the *AAHE Bulletin* as a model for best teaching practices (Chickering and Ehrmann). Although articulated well before the Internet had begun to change the way learning and teaching took place, these seven principles still provide a concise overview of effective pedagogy. In the final section of this article, with hopes of stimulating further conversation on models that other instructors have found useful and encouraging more research about the ways technology could or should advance the basic writing curriculum, I group the "value added" aspects that I have begun to experience from my hybrid writing class around these seven principles, describing how a hybrid approach has offered us a means of lessening the negative effects of many of the problems described in the first part of this article while still allowing students to benefit from the advantages listed in the second.

- **Good practice encourages student/faculty contact.** The opportunity for unlimited office hours via e-mail or chatrooms is a clear advantage in online courses, which frequently cater to commuting or geographically distant students. Students get used to sending off an e-mail or setting up an online chatroom meeting when a problem arises rather than letting it go unquestioned. Teachers can provide the needed information promptly, preventing student frustration and lessening the chance for a late or incorrect assignment. A study by Robert Woods and Samuel Ebersole has found instructor immediacy in feedback to be "the strongest predictor of learning—both affective and cognitive learning—among students."

  The benefit that comes from having my online students in my physical classroom as well, on alternate weeks, is that I can follow up on e-mails, deal with new or remaining problems, and give the students a chance to explore their issues in more depth. E-mailed requests and personal conversations seem to be used for different purposes, with e-mails being more task-oriented (asking about assignments, due dates, technical problems, etc.) or else reserved for the kinds of problems students are embarrassed to bring up in person. Face-to-face discussions typically involve working through academic problems thoroughly, as well as following up e-mailed comments on life events as needed. An e-mail can give an answer; a face-to-face meeting can show how the answer was obtained. Students are not forced to rely solely on text-based communication for their questions and answers.

- **Good practice encourages cooperation among students.** Online access to e-mail, discussion lists and chatrooms clearly expands collaborative opportunities exponentially. For one thing, despite the potential harm to our collective egos, writing teachers in this Internet age are, as Gail Hawisher and Cynthia Selfe point out, experiencing Margaret Mead's concept of "prefigurative cultures," that is, cultures in which the adults are trying to prepare children for experiences the adults themselves have never had. In such a world, students have no alternative but to bond with and learn important lessons from each other (4). This benefits both the teacher and the learner.

  What a hybrid class adds is the chance to strengthen the personal ties so important to effective collaboration. Caroline Haythornthwaite, in a paper presented at the Hawai'i International Conference on System Sciences, notes that, because of the "reduced cues" environment, online communication is less appropriate or useful for emotionally laden exchanges, for the delivery of complex information, and for creating a sense of "being there." This presents a problem for classes conducted entirely online, since obviously, these factors are essential to an educational setting. She found, however, that strongly tied pairs, with their higher motivation, eagerness to communicate, and desire to include more intimate and varied communications, manage to modify this "lean" environment to support their needs, while weakly tied communicators do not. Maintaining connectivity among both the strongly and weakly tied members of a group, Haythornthwaite argues, requires a means of communication that reaches all group members, yet requires little effort or extra work from them. A schedule that allows students to meet face to face in class every other week satisfies that criterion. If students do nothing more than show up in class, the weak ties required for basic connectivity after they leave the classroom are established. At the same time, the personal bonds which classroom interactions create should encourage the development of stronger ties and therefore lead to more proactive communication outside of class, resulting in less chance of muting and, ideally, better participation and retention of students

- **Good practice encourages active learning.** Stronger interpersonal ties lead communicators to seek out the means and opportunities for exchanges that support their relationships. This results in a more active learning experience. In online discussion group assignments, for instance, students can satisfy their desire for interaction while at the same time applying the principle of "write to learn/learn to write" (Mayher, Lester, and Pradl).

  I had initially planned for discussion to take place solely online until student evaluations after each of the first two semesters consistently requested more time afterwards to explore the issues in the classroom. When students discuss a topic online one week and carry that discussion over into the face-to-face class the next, the best features of both activities apply. Online, the students have time for thoughtful, reflective response; in class, the follow-up discussion allows for the serendipity that perhaps only occurs in the rapid give and take of face-to-face conversation. Additionally, any meaning missed because of the "reduced cues" environment online can be regained in the oral classroom setting.

- **Good practice gives prompt feedback.** In addition to getting prompter teacher responses, students can take quizzes or do practice exercises online and get immediate feedback. Course management tools like WebCT and Blackboard allow teachers to post their own practice quizzes, adding with relative ease personalized explanations for the correct options as well as explanations of what makes the wrong choices incorrect. I have found that students will work much longer at online exercises than they do on the same exercises in their workbooks. The tasks are more visual and more fun. Working online also strengthens students' on-screen proofreading skills and can be done at the point of need, with slower students being required to do more tasks or allowed a longer time to finish an assigned task.

  When a face-to-face meeting follows an online experience, students get the added benefit of going over things together after the fact and hearing others' questions, thus reinforcing what they had learned on their own. Students take charge of their own learning needs, noting the places when they require additional instruction and profiting from the realization that they can sometimes answer questions raised by others.

- **Good practice promotes time on task.** Course management software like Blackboard or WebCT has several features that enable teachers to model ways to structure time effectively. The calendar tool can remind students each week what is due when. The content module feature allows all the materials needed to write a given essay—preliminary reading, planning tools, essay directions, peer review questions—to be assembled in one place, available wherever the student has access to the Internet, eliminating the "I lost the reading assignment" or "I didn't have the essay directions" excuse. Nevertheless, those features and all others work only insofar as a student is motivated to use them; that is where the face-to-face class comes in, students know that they will have to face their instructor's wrath in person if they are not prepared while enjoying positive reinforcement when they are. They can drift away in the anonymity of cyberspace for no more than a week.

- **Good practice communicates high expectations.** Because of the convenience of the Web, students can reasonably be expected to read more, write more, and do more group projects. Even students with limited time can do research through online academic data bases. The "Dean effect"—the motivation engendered by persistent conversation—can also be counted on to improve performance. Moreover, as Alvan Bregman and Caroline Haythornthwaite explain, "Where we approach persistent conversation, we are faced with communication that inherits genre from both speech and literary practices. The learning environment inherits the speech genres of the traditional classroom, such as how to participate in class, communicate with an instructor, or carry on a discussion with fellow students, as well as the literary practices of academia, such as how to write a term paper, complete a homework assignment, or present a written argument."

  When students have the opportunity to discuss both online and face to face, to submit an assignment in print form or as an online posting, to argue a point in person or via e-mail, many more of the possible communication modes are used, practiced, reinforced, and made visible. This can help to make up for any actual or perceived lack of "richness" in the online environment, and enables us in a sense to teach the students a double lesson: how to function effectively as members of two different and equally important academic discourse communities, the virtual and the actual classroom.

- **Good practice respects diverse talents and ways of learning.** One student told me toward the end of last semester that she really likes and uses all the online resources available to her via WebCT. She can do her homework faithfully, do all assigned practice exercises, view explanations in the PowerPoints I have posted, and study the reading selections. But it is not until she comes to class and participates in a discussion reviewing the concepts that it all comes together for her. For many students, directions, demonstrations, and explanations—at least at some point in the learning process, whether as preview or review—need to take a form other than print. Even Murray Goldberg, the "father" of WebCT, acknowledged in a 2001 column for the *Online Teaching and Learning Newsletter* that variety provides the spice of academic life: "We all know by research or intuition that some people simply learn better when they can see a person's face and converse in real time with a peer or instructor. My own research shows that students perform best when they have access to lectures in addition to a web-based course as opposed to the web-based course alone."

When given the opportunity to learn both online and in class, students, whatever their preferred learning style, are affirmed and stretched. They also find skills other than writing—graphical, technological, organizational, group-building—being evaluated and valued, so more opportunities exist to acknowledge strengths instead of simply identifying weaknesses.

CONCLUSION

It has been my experience that adult basic writers arrive in class with a curious and difficult-to-deal-with mixture of dependence and independence. A number of years ago we tested our students—slightly more than 150 at that time—on the Grasha-Riechmann Student Learning Style Scales, an instrument developed in the 1970s that categorized student preferences with respect to classroom interactions with peers and teachers along six dimensions: cooperation/competition, participation/avoidance, and independence/dependence. We were not surprised to see how our students fit clearly into the expected profile of adult learners: more *cooperative* than *competitive* and much more *participant* than *avoidant*. What did at first surprise us was that they strayed from the adult norm by emerging as more *dependent* than *independent* in their learning preferences. Further research showed us that this conflict was not unusual. Robert Sommer, for instance, points out that adults returning to school "may regress to the conditioning of early education and past roles of dependence and submission to the authority of teachers and institutions" (9). We realized that a vacillation between independent and dependent learning preferences was to be expected from our student population, whose lack of traditional academic experience created a sense of uncertainty that was at war with their adult sense of independence. Given this ongoing conflict, the current structure of this basic writing course, with one week online and one week face to face in a classroom, seems to offer our students the best of both worlds: the infinite freedom of the Internet enhanced and made manageable by regular classroom interactions.

Acknowledgement: Portions of this article were first presented at the March 2004 Conference on College Composition and Communication held in San Antonio, Texas.

NOTES

1. Anyone interested in more specific information about either Lincoln University's Master of Human Services Program or the Pre-master's Program is invited to visit our website at http://www.lincoln.edu/mhs or contact me directly at stine@lu.lincoln.edu.

2. We chose to offer only the second semester in hybrid form, wanting to be sure that all students had a semester of WebCT use in a web-enhanced face-to-face class so that they could become comfortable with the software. We hoped in this way to prevent technological concerns from distracting from or impeding writing instruction when students moved out of the familiar classroom setting.

WORKS CITED

Anson, Chris. "Distant Voices: Teaching and Writing in a Culture of Technology." *College English 61* (1999): 261–80.

Baron, Denis. "From Pencils to Pixels: The Stages of Literacy Technologies." *Passions, Pedagogies, and 21st Century Technologies.* Ed. Gail E. Hawisher and Cynthia L. Selfe. Urbana, IL: NCTE, 1999. 15–34.

Blair, Kristine L., and Elizabeth A. Monske. "Cui Bono?: Revisiting the Promises and Perils of Online Learning." *Computers and Composition 20* (2003): 441–53.

Bregman, Alvan, and Caroline Haythornthwaite. "Radicals of Presentation in Persistent Conversation." *Proceedings of the Jan. 3–6, 2001 Hawai'i International Conference On System Sciences.* 1 Feb. 2004 <csdl.computer.org/comp/proceedings/hicss/2001/0981/04/09814032.pdf>.

Chickering, Arthur W., and Stephen C. Ehrmann. "Implementing the Seven Principles: Technology as Lever." *AAHE Bulletin* (October 1996): 3–6.

Collison, George, Bonnie Elbaum, Sarah Haavind, and Robert Tinker. *Facilitating Online Learning: Effective Strategies for Moderators.* Madison, WI: Atwood, 2000.

Cross, K. Patricia. *Adults as Learners: Increasing Participation and Facilitating Learning.* San Francisco: Jossey-Bass, 1981.

Davis, Evan, and Sarah Hardy. "Teaching Writing in the Space of Blackboard." *Computers & Composition Online* (Spring 2003). 15 Feb. 2004 <http://www.bgsu.edu/cconline/theory.htm>.

Elbow, Peter. "Reflections on Academic Discourse: How It Relates to Freshmen and Colleagues." *College English 53* (1991): 135–55.

Erickson, Thomas. "Editor's Introduction." *Journal of Computer-Mediated Communication 4.4* (1999). 4 Mar. 2004 <http://www.ascusc.org/jcmc/vol4/issue4/>.

Goldberg, Murray. "Synchronous vs. Asynchronous: Some Thoughts." *Online Teaching and Learning.* 11 Sept. 2000. 14 Feb. 2004 <http://www.webct.com/service/viewcontentframe?contentID=2339346>.

Hawisher, Gail E., and Cynthia L. Selfe. "The Passions That Mark Us: Teaching, Texts, and Technologies." *Passions, Pedagogies, and 21st Century Technologies.* Ed. Gail E. Hawisher and Cynthia L. Selfe. Urbana, IL: NCTE, 1999. 1–14.

———, eds. *Passions, Pedagogies, and 21st Century Technologies.* Urbana, IL: NCTE, 1999.

Haythornthwaite, Caroline. "Tie Strength and the Impact of New Media." *Proceedings of the Jan. 3–6, 2001, Hawai'i International Conference on System Sciences.* 1 Feb. 2004 <http://alexia.lis.uiuc.edu/~haythorn/HICSS01_tiestrength.html>.

———, Michelle M. Kazmer, Jennifer Robins, and Susan Shoemaker. "Community Development Among Distance Learners: Temporal and Technological Dimensions." *Journal of Computer-Mediated Communication 6.1* (2000). 12 Feb. 2004 <http://www.ascusc.org/jcmc/vol6/issue1/haythornthwaite.html>.

Johnson, J. Paul. "What Happens When Teaching Writing Online?" 2003. 15 Feb. 2004 <http://www.mhhe.com/socscience/English/tc/Johnson/JPJohnsonModule.htm>.

Leibowitz, Wendy. "Technology Transforms Writing and the Teaching of Writing." *Chronicle of Higher Education* (26 Nov. 1999): A67–68.

Macrorie, Ken. *Twenty Teachers.* New York: Oxford UP, 1984.

Mayher, John S., Nancy Lester, and Gordon Pradl. *Learning to Write/Writing to Learn.* Portsmouth, NH: Boynton/Cook, 1983.

Merriam, Sharan, ed. *An Update on Adult Learning Theory.* San Francisco: Jossey-Bass, 1993.

Moran, Charles. "Access: The 'A' Word in Technology Studies." *Passions, Pedagogies, and 21st Century Technologies.* Ed. Gail E. Hawisher and Cynthia L. Selfe. Urbana, IL: NCTE, 1999. 205–21.

Puccio, Paul M. "The Computer-networked Writing Lab: One Instructor's View." ERIC Clearinghouse on Reading, English, and Communication Digest #80. EDO-CS-93-03. Apr. 1993. 14 Mar. 2004 <http://www.indiana.edu/~reading/ieo/digests/d80.html>.

Selber, Stuart. "Reimagining the Functional Side of Computer Literacy." *College Composition and Communication, 55* (2004): 470–504.

Selfe, Cynthia, and Richard Selfe. "The Politics of the Interface: Power and Its Exercise in Electronic Contact Zones." *College Composition and Communication 45* (1994): 480–504.

Shaughnessy, Mina. "Basic Writing." *Teaching Composition: 10 Bibliographical Essays.* Ed. Gary Tate. Forth Worth, TX: Texas Christian UP, 1976. 177–206.

Simic, Marjorie. "Computer-Assisted Writing Instruction." ERIC Clearinghouse on Reading, English, and Communication Digest #97. EDO-CS-94-10. Jun. 1994. 20 Feb. 2004 <http://www.indiana.edu/~reading/ieo/digests/d97.html>.

Smith, Beatrice Quarshy. "Teaching with Technologies: A Reflexive Autoethnographic Portrait." *Computers and Composition, 21.1* (2004): 49–62.

"So What Was *That* All About?" *New York Times* 22 Feb. 2004: section 4, 3.

Sommer, Robert F. *Teaching Writing to Adults: Strategies and Concepts for Improving Learner Performance.* San Francisco: Jossey-Bass, 1989.

Sosnoski, James. "Hyper-readers and Their Reading Engines." *Passions, Pedagogies, and 21st Century Technologies.* Ed. Gail E. Hawisher and Cynthia L. Selfe. Urbana, IL: NCTE, 1999. 161–78.

Straub, Richard. *A Sourcebook for Responding to Student Writing.* Cresskill, NJ: Hampton, 1999.

United States. Department of Commerce. *Falling through the Net: Toward Digital Inclusion.* Oct. 2000. 13 Aug. 2004 <http://www.ntia.doc.gov/ntiahome/fttn00/Front00.htm#Mineta>.

Whithaus, Carl. "Think Different/Think Differently: A Tale of Green Squiggly Lines, or Evaluating Student Writing in Computer-mediated Environments." *Kairos 7* (2002). Mar. 1 2004 <http://wac.colostate.edu/aw/articles/whithaus2002/>.

Wilson, Arthur. "The Promise of Situated Cognition." *An Update on Adult Learning Theory.* Ed. Sharan Merriam. San Francisco: Jossey-Bass, 1993. 71–81.

Woods, Robert, and Samuel Ebersole. "Becoming a 'Communal Architect' in the Online Classroom: Integrating Cognitive and Affective Learning for Maximum Effect in Web-based Learning." *Online Journal of Distance Learning Administration, VI* (2003). 20 Feb. 2004 <http://www.westga.edu/%7Edistance/ojdla/spring61/spring61.htm>.

Yena, Lauren, and Zach Waggoner. "One Size Fits All?: Student Perspectives on Face-to-Face and Online Writing Pedagogies." *Computers & Composition Online,* Fall (2003). 30 Jan. 2004 <http://www.bgsu.edu/cconline/virtualc.htm>.

26 The Impact of the Computer in Second Language Writing

MARTHA C. PENNINGTON

The computer in its many guises as writing tool and communications medium is changing the way we interact with information and with each other. Whether in the form of a word processor installed on a personal computer (PC), a group of PCs linked in a computer lab or a university network, or the Internet connecting people and electronic information sources around the globe, the computer is having a profound effect on literacy practices in the present age. It is, at the same time, contributing to an ongoing expansion of information and communication resources that has put English in the hands of more and more people around the globe.

These trends have created a great demand for literacy in English as a second language (ESL) as well as for literacy in computer writing tools, issues that are sometimes hard to separate. Many of our literacy practices in education, work, and social life have moved off the page and onto the screen: more and more people are doing the majority of their writing and reading on computer and transmitting messages electronically rather than on paper (Warschauer, 1999).

As the communicator of the present day and especially of the future is inevitably linked to electronic media, those charged with instructing ESL students in writing cannot afford to remain outside these developments, teaching without regard to the communication technologies that are increasingly at the center of their students' world; teachers should be prepared to bring computers into the center of their own pedagogical practice. The modern ESL writing teacher needs to understand the nature of electronic writing media, the kinds of impacts these media have on students' writing, and the ways they can best be employed in the teaching of writing. This chapter aims to raise the awareness of ESL writing teachers regarding electronic writing media, their effects on ESL writers, and their pedagogical applications, beginning with a review of some critical issues in word processing and then

From *Exploring the Dynamics of Second Language Writing*. Ed. Barbara Kroll. New York: Cambridge UP, 2003. 287–310.

moving on to networking, hypermedia, and the use of the Internet as a research tool/assistant for writers.

WORD PROCESSING

The basic writing tool provided by the computer is a word processor, with most word processors including a spellchecker and many including a grammar checker as well. Most people agree that word processors are useful for writing because they facilitate the mechanical processes of putting words on paper; revising text by substitutions, deletions, additions, and block moves; and producing attractive and readable finished copy. The word processor is not only a convenient tool combining an automated typewriter, editor, and printer; it is also a composing medium that with time and practice can significantly change the writer's process and product. Many studies have shown that beyond their facilitating effects, word processors have an impact on student writers' attitudes, the characteristics of their texts, their revising behavior and the attention they pay to form and mechanics, and the order and the type of writing activities in which they engage (for reviews and discussions of research, see Bangert-Drowns, 1993; Cochran-Smith, 1991; Pennington, 1996b, 1996c, 1999a, 1999b; Snyder, 1993).

Student Attitudes

Most students have a good initial reaction to the computer and feel that it can help them in their work, though some users, especially older students, may be uncomfortable with the technology or may even be "computerphobic." Another minority of users may have their enthusiasm dampened if they experience technical problems early on, have difficulty typing or mastering computer commands, or have limited access to computers and to experienced users who can offer assistance when things go wrong. As a result, a few who try word processing will give up in frustration. Typically, however, after a period of weeks or months spent improving their keyboarding skills, most students persist and become regular computer users.

The mechanical capabilities of a word processor are especially valuable in a second language (L2) context, where the physical processes of putting words on paper and revising text to a finished product, and the cognitive processes underlying these, are more effortful and less automatized (Jones & Tetroe, 1987) than when writing in the first language (L1). Not only the actual capabilities of the machine but also the students' view of these as helpful for their writing are significant for L2 writers, who may, even more than inexperienced L1 writers, lack confidence in their writing ability (Betancourt & Phinney, 1988). Word processors can relieve the anxiety some L2 writers feel about writing the L2 script, about producing academic work in their L2, and about writing in general (Pennington, 1999a; Phinney, 1989).

Many studies conducted with L2 writers report positive attitudes associated with word processing (e.g., Neu & Scarcella, 1991; Pennington & Brock,

1992; Phinney, 1991; Phinney & Mathis, 1990). For example, in their comparison of word processing and pen-and-paper composing in English by Turkish
university students, Akyel and Kamisli (1999) report that the use of the computer improved student attitudes toward writing and built up their confidence. In a longitudinal investigation of a group of mature ESL writers in
Hong Kong who were able to use the computer as much or as little as they
wished in their written work for a course (Rusmin, 1999), the majority of the
students were positive toward the computer and adopted it for their writing
from the beginning of the term or increasingly as the course progressed. On
the basis of the different patterns of attitudes and computer use, Rusmin
(1999) classified the 27 students in the class into six categories, which she labeled "devotees," "enthusiasts," "rededicateds," "positives," "converts," and
"skeptics," categories that may be applicable to a host of students in a wide
variety of locales.

Textual Properties

Also related to attitude is self-consciousness. The student writer working in a
computer medium is led to write in a less self-conscious way and with greater
engagement, thus writing with a freer mind and less "rewriting anxiety." As a
result, the student's greater involvement may lead him or her to write for
longer periods of time and produce longer texts. Several studies with L2 writers
(e.g., Brock & Pennington, 1999; Chadwick & Bruce, 1989; Pennington & Brock,
1992) document that longer texts are a general effect of word processing.

In addition to the production of longer texts, the physical easing of the
writing process that results in a less constrained, more relaxed writing process
may produce texts that are in a sense also "more relaxed." Written products
generated on a word processor "are often unconstrained and experimental,
being more likely to be in a non-generic form that sometimes amounts to
what has been called 'train of thought' or 'spaghetti writing'—long strings of
loosely connected strands of ideas" (Pennington, 2000, p. 14). In some cases,
computer-produced text represents an unfinished, intermediate work that
given sufficient time for continued development will result in a high-quality
product (Pennington, 1996b, 1996c). In other cases, it may represent a new
type of work, as when writing in hypertext—for example, for a Web page or
in an e-mail context.

Revision Strategies and Accuracy Concerns

Surface-level editing for spelling and mechanics is encouraged in a word processing environment, where the small size of text visible on one screen may
engender an especially focused type of revision at word, phrase, and sentence
level (Pennington, 1996b, 1999b). At the same time, the ease with which individual words can be searched and whole sections of text deleted, added, or
moved suggests that word processing may have value as a macro-level revision tool. Rather than being a separate activity following the generation of a

draft, revision in a computer context is closely linked to text generation. Pedagogical intervention aimed at increasing students' awareness of and ability to apply revision strategies in their own writing (e.g., Steelman, 1994) has demonstrated the value of the computer medium for helping learners increase the type and depth of their revisions.

In other research, L2 writers have been found to revise more when writing with a computer than when writing by traditional means (e.g., Chadwick & Bruce, 1989; Li & Cumming, 2001; Phinney & Khouri, 1993); to revise more dynamically and continuously (Phinney & Khouri, 1993); and to spend more time revising in a computer context, where they may "continue revising after planned changes [have] been made" (Phinney & Khouri, 1993, p. 271). Writers also make more revisions beyond the surface level. There is some evidence that word processing is more effective in stimulating meaning-level revision when aligned to a process approach to writing (Daiute, 1985; Susser, 1993) than when used without process support or with other computer writing aids such as grammar checkers (Brock & Pennington, 1999; Pennington & Brock, 1992). The research thus supports an approach that teaches the writing process in the context of learning to write and revise using a word processor.

Implications for Planning

In pen-and-paper composing, writers often spend a lot of time in intensive planning before writing to avoid making mistakes or changing their minds about what they want to say and then having to undertake the tedious chore of rewriting or recopying text already written down. Under such conditions, pen-and-paper writers may habitually write a paper without any revision or with only a minimum amount of revision to avoid producing more than one draft. In sharp contrast to this paper-based mode of composing, the automated text-generation and revision tools provided on computer, coupled with the malleability of text on screen or disk, encourage a very different computer-based writing mode (Bernhardt, Edwards, & Wojahn, 1989; Haas, 1989; Williamson & Pence, 1989). In a contrasting "computer writing style," the writer generally begins writing immediately, soon after a topic is decided — or even before it is decided.

Instead of writing to fit a plan, computer writers plan as they are writing (Haas, 1989), an effect also documented for L2 writers (Akyel & Kamisli, 1999; Li & Cumming, 2001). Planning thus becomes more of a middle stage than a beginning stage activity, and the time and intensive cognitive activity that would have been involved in pre-planning is instead involved in writing itself. The sharp division of composing into the three stages of planning, writing, and revising breaks down in a computer context, in which planning as well as revision occurs as part of the writing process. In the computer-engendered approach to writing, cognitive effort is distributed throughout the writing process and writing is developed more on the basis of concrete text already generated when on an abstract plan; this procedure would seem to be especially valuable for L2 writers, who have less cognitive capacity available for writing than do L1 writers.

Weighing the Advantages and Disadvantages

In spite of the obvious advantages of the computer over pen-and-paper writing in terms of automation, flexibility, and cognitive demands, the results of research on the quality of writing produced in a computer context are not all favorable, as only some studies have yielded positive effects for student compositions produced by word processing in contrast to pen and paper (see Pennington, 1996b, 1996c, 1999a, 1999b, for reviews). A mixed pattern of findings can be seen in the L2 literature: in some studies, word processing gave writers an advantage in terms of writing quality (e.g., Lam & Pennington, 1995; McGarrell, 1993), while in others, word processing gave no advantage over pen and paper (e.g., Benesch, 1987; Chadwick & Bruce, 1989).

These mixed results from individual studies have often been used to caution teachers against an easy acceptance of word processing; however, three summative (meta-analytical) reviews of research results comparing word processing to pen-and-paper composing have demonstrated an advantage for computer-produced over pen-produced text in terms of traditional measures of writing quality (Bangert-Drowns, 1993; Roblyer, Castine, & King, 1988; Schramm, 1989). In addition, most studies showing negative results for word processing were carried out from the late 1970s to the mid 1980s, and some of the negative findings may have been related to the characteristics of early word processors, subjects' unfamiliarity with computers, the context of research, or the ways in which effects were measured in these early studies. Teachers are therefore cautioned against placing too much weight on the older studies of word processing; they are advised instead to base their decisions about computer use on more recent findings and the accumulated comparative evidence, which generally show a positive impact of word processing on students' writing. At the same time, teachers should always keep an eye out for the latest trends in computer use and research findings, bearing in mind that the focus and the results of research are likely to change as the context for writing on computers also changes—from word processed compositions to e-mail and Web pages.

As in all other cases in which new technologies or teaching approaches are introduced, teachers' and learners' behavior is dictated by their knowledge and understanding of the innovation. As students learn how to apply their word processing capabilities in their writing, they are likely to develop positive attitudes toward the computer writing medium and the context of writing, which may in the case of L2 writers extend also to their attitudes toward the English language. When the learners' knowledge and attitudes are favorable, that is, when their "cognitive-affective response" to word processing is positive, in the process of learning about the medium they will gradually experience effects on their writing behavior of three types (Pennington, 1996b, 1996c, 1999a, 1999b):

FIGURE 26.1   The Positive Path in Computer Writing Effects

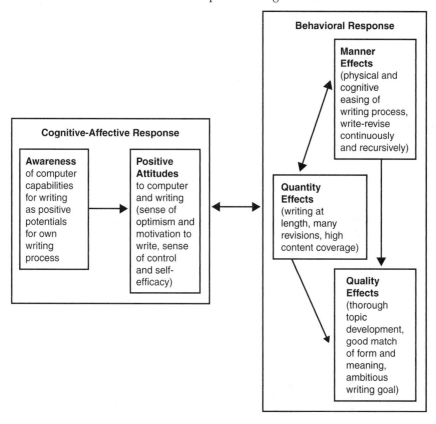

Adapted from Pennington 1999a, p. 283. Used with permission from Swets & Zeitlinger.

Manner Effects. A sense of the ease of writing and revising in a fluid writing process involving continuous and recursive write-revise cycles

Quantity Effects. Writing for extended periods of time, producing long texts with much content and many revisions

Quality Effects. Writing to a high standard in terms of topic development, formal characteristics, and writing goal

Given enough time and favorable circumstances for learning, these three types of effects, represented in Figure 26.1, may ultimately result in high-quality written products.

Under less favorable conditions, learners may not experience a positive cognitive-affective response to word processing if they have low awareness of computer potential that can help them in their writing, if they are intimidated by the computer or find it difficult to use, or if they experience frequent

FIGURE 26.2   The Negative Path in Computer Writing Effects

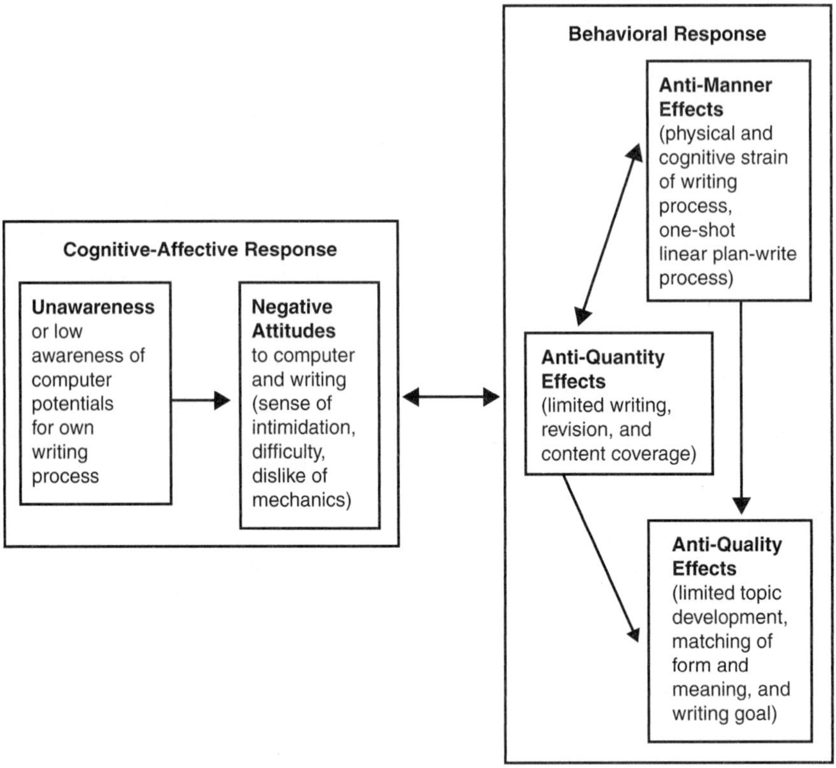

Adapted from Pennington 1999a, p. 285. Used with permission from Swets & Zeitlinger.

mechanical breakdowns. Consequently, under such conditions, their behavioral response is essentially the opposite of the learners' response found in more positive circumstances. This negative response consists of

Anti-Manner Effects. A sense of the difficulty of writing and revising, reinforcing a one-shot linear plan-write process

Anti-Quantity Effects. Limited time spent writing, producing short texts with restricted content and few revisions

Anti-Quality Effects. Writing to a minimal standard in terms of topic development, formal characteristics, and writing goal

These three types of behavioral effects, illustrated in Figure 26.2, represent disfavoring conditions that predict poor written products.

Whatever the research findings, the inevitable presence of word processors in L2 contexts and in the future of most of our students is undeniable, and any teacher who ignores this reality is avoiding a responsibility to teach to student needs.

NETWORKING

Another way in which ESL writing teachers find that computers can play a key role in instruction is when they have the opportunity to teach in or have their students participate in a networked environment. A local area network (LAN or intranet), such as in a computer lab, or a wide area network (WAN), such as the Internet or World Wide Web, makes it possible to extend the computer writing environment by linking student writers to other people with whom they may interact to develop their writing. Through a computer network, students' computers may be linked to those of their teachers as well as other students as a way to develop collaborative work or to gain input on their writing other than by face-to-face interaction (Bruce, Peyton, & Batson, 1993; Bruce & Rubin, 1993; Mabrito, 1991; Palmquist, 1993). All types of network arrangements have the potential for motivating L2 students to write and to revise in response to a real audience, for helping them to gain more input on their writing, for encouraging them to experiment in their writing, and for empowering them to seek out the resources they need for developing their ideas.

Within a computer network, students may participate in such novel activities as online feedback on classmates' work or "team editing" (Kaufer & Neuwirth, 1995) as well as the sending and receiving of e-mail "letters" or other sorts of messages (Howard, 1992). Where the students' computers are linked in a network, the potentials for collaboration and participatory interaction are increased (Warschauer, 1997). Some of this collaboration and interaction takes place around the computer; but increasingly it takes place in cyberspace, with the interactors being physically removed—often at great distances—from one another. As a result, the writer may be encouraged to experiment with ideas and with language because of the risk-free social access afforded by electronic connectivity. At the same time networks bring writers together to increase shared knowledge and produce collaborative work, they also seem to help student writers to create an individual voice. Moran and Hawisher (1998) observe that writers can use online space to create alternative selves and to experiment with roles that they might not assume in face-to-face interaction.

E-mail Exchanges

In a departmental or university-wide network, writing teachers can use e-mail to contact their students, and students can have easy access to their teachers to ask questions about their work and to receive feedback on drafts. As a further advantage, e-mail aids students working together on team projects to fulfill written assignments (Hoffman, 1996). With a university-wide network, L2 students can be linked to L1 partners or more experienced L2 students on campus (Nabors & Swartley, 1999). With Internet access, L2 students can participate in information exchange with sister classes and e-mail partners overseas (Sayers, 1989; Slater & Carpenter, 1999; Woodin, 1997), such as via the International Tandem Network (available at: http://www.slf. ruhr-uni-bochum.de/email/stats-eng.html) or via the Intercultural E-mail Classroom Connections (IECC) service (http://www.teaching.com/iecc/). Woodin (1997) points out that in providing an opportunity for real communication one-on-one with speakers of the target language, e-mail functions "as a bridge between the language classroom and the natural setting. There is the opportunity for contact with a variety of native speakers, but from within the safety of one's own environment" (p. 31). In either type of partnering arrangement, the e-mail contact may allow writers to obtain information or input from a real audience in relation to their written assignments. Or the contact with other communicators over a network may itself function as stimulation for students' writing.

Lists, Newsgroups, and Bulletin Boards

An additional possibility is to join a group that communicates by e-mail through a discussion list. Within each of these lists, many of which are available via Listserv, there is a wide range of topics that subscribers may access or participate in. Lists often serve the purpose of providing specialized information or the answers to questions in a field. For example, students or teachers might request information about language teaching from the ESL list, TESL-L (listserv@cunyvm.cuny.edu); about teaching ESL on a network from NETEACH-L (listserv@raven.cc.ukans.edu); or about linguistics, language acquisition, or a specific language such as English from the applied linguistics list, LINGUIST (listserv@tamvm1.tamu.edu). Such specialized lists can be used to locate experts and other sources of information in a specific field or on a specific topic. They also often serve the purpose of debating issues, generating different points of view, and comparing different (well-known or unknown) people's information or points of view. Windeatt, Hardisty, and Eastment (2000) have activities for introducing students to discussion lists (Activity 1.9, pp. 43–45) and for setting up an electronic list (Activity 1.11, pp. 47–49).

A newsgroup is a group of users networked by e-mail for specialized discussions through a service called Usenet, which has newsgroups of various kinds for different countries, such as in the UK (http://www.usenet.org.uk/) or Norway (http://www.usenet.no/). A bulletin board is like a list except that instead of receiving information via e-mail, the user goes to a specific Web site to read messages posted on the bulletin board. Bulletin boards thus allow for individual access to information and individual choice as to whether and when to participate. Students might visit bulletin boards as part of Internet searches (see Windeatt, Hardisty, & Eastment, 2000, for suggestions). A bulletin board can also be set up for a specific class or group of students (e.g., at a site called BeSeen, http://www.beseen.com/board/index.html), as a way to encourage their independence, full participation, and sharing of information. Bulletin boards are also of value to teachers for sharing resources and expertise and for building a sense of community. For example, in a study of students in a TESOL (Teachers of English to Speakers of Other Languages) methods course interacting on a World Wide Web bulletin board, Kamhi-Stein (2000) found that the electronic medium encouraged participants to take responsibility for learning both collectively and individually, as shown by a high level of student-led interaction, collaborative learning, and equal participation by native and non-native students alike.

Synchronous Communication: Chat, MUDs, and MOOs

In addition to the asynchronous, or saved and time-delayed transmission of messages via e-mail and e-mail lists, networked communication includes several types of synchronous, or nearly immediate, real-time communication. One interactive writing program, *Daedalus Interchange* (Daedalus, Inc.), allows students in a networked class to send a message related to a writing task to other students simultaneously. Teleconferencing and videoconferencing, though not widely used in instruction, are other examples of synchronous communication. An increasingly popular type of program is text-conferencing software, most commonly in the form of Internet relay chat (IRC) programs, such as *Microsoft Chat* (Microsoft Corp.) or *mIRC* (available free at: http://www.mirc.com/), which makes it possible for participants to have an online discussion or "chat" by typing at the computer keyboard while others who are also logged on to the same site can watch the interaction evolve. There are many open IRC "chat rooms," and a closed chat room can also be set up for selected participants.

An advantage is the equality of the interaction, as every participant has the same chance to initiate a topic and/or to respond to another's turn. There is also the possibility of any number of people composing input at the same time. These discussion programs therefore offer possibilities for expanding student writers' ability to gather and refine their ideas in interaction with others. They can also, like e-mail and other forms of networked communication, stimulate creativity and personalization. There are some disadvantages, however, as Windeatt, Hardisty, and Eastment (2000) observe:

> Unfortunately, the more people join in a 'chat', the more disjointed the discussion is. In addition, the contributions to the discussion are often short and people tend to use abbreviations, and make a lot of typing mistakes. Nevertheless . . . IRC can be useful for discussion among a small number of people, especially as the discussion can be 'logged', i.e. a copy can be saved on disk, to look at more carefully later. (p. 113)

Such functions have utility for writing, for example, in interacting about ideas for writing and giving feedback on writing, and in general, for establishing and maintaining contact with a community of writers not only in a networked classroom but also beyond the confines of a classroom. Note, however, that IRC software (unlike, for example, the *Daedalus* package) is not specifically designed for composing-related use and in fact seems to promote a type of spontaneous playfulness that encourages the breaking of conventions.

Two additional types of synchronous communication are MUDs (multi-user domains) and MOOs (multi-user domains, object-oriented). Like text-conferencing, these involve multiple users interacting online by going to a specific Web site and typing information on a keyboard. Rather than chat sites, these are Internet-based specialized environments or virtual worlds where participants can interact with each other or access information. Unlike chat rooms, in which the interaction exists only as long as users remain online, these environments are structured to have continuity of characters, spaces (e.g., "rooms"), and objects from one session to another.

A MOO is similar to a simulation in which participants interact online. Since participants are generally linked from all over the globe, a MOO can be seen as a type of "global village" in which students can be linked with an international group of participants as resources for their ideas and their writing. MOO interactions have the special characteristic that users can assume one or more imaginary identities and keep their real identity hidden, thus encouraging playfulness and experimentation. MOO interactions may therefore have some value in stimulating student writers to develop ideas and "freeing" them to experiment with different authorial voices and writing styles.

An example of a MOO that incorporates properties of other sorts of Web sites is schMOOze University (http://schmooze.hunter.cuny.edu:8888/), which is described on the opening page of the Web site as

> a small, friendly college known for its hospitality and the diversity of the student population . . . established as a place where people studying English as a second or foreign language could practice English while sharing ideas and experiences with other learners and practitioners of English. Students have opportunities for one-on-one and group conversations as well as access to language games, an online dictionary, virtual stockbroker and many language games.

The schMOOze University Web site includes an introduction to the MOO environment and the schMOOze University, a Virtual English Language Center, Internet TESL Journal pages for ESL students, a collaborative MOO project, teacher discussions on NETEACH-L, and a link to Dave's ESL Café (an ESL Web site run by Dave Sperling, and ESL instructor based in the United States).

Expanding Peer Response

Communication in a networked environment can change some of the dynamics of peer feedback sessions as found in traditional classrooms. Sullivan and Pratt (1996) discovered that the communication that occurred as peer feedback over the computer network was of a type that might have been especially valuable for students in improving their writing. They summarize some of the contrasts as follows:

> [Face-to-face peer] discussions were often filled with personal narratives (students focusing on themselves rather than the task at hand) and short interjections of agreement (uh-huh) or repetition . . . [whereas, over the network] . . . the responses followed a pattern that consisted of a positive comment about the essay followed by one or more suggestions for revision. (p. 499)

Moreover, the networked feedback from more than one student tended to reinforce the same points and the same suggestions for revision, thereby perhaps focusing the writer's attention on certain points for revision. However, in a study carried out with EFL writing students in Hong Kong, Braine (2001) reports that the feedback given in a networked environment did not result in better written texts. He found that final draft essays written by students who engaged in traditional face-to-face classroom peer interaction received higher holistic scores and showed greater gains than final drafts written by students who carried out peer discussions via a LAN (Braine, 2001, p. 283). Thus, networking student writers electronically does not guarantee better writing.

Changing Patterns of Communication

There is some evidence that more focused use of language is a general effect of networked communication: "With more opportunities and different opportunities to negotiate input in a computer environment come not only a greater quantity of language, particularly, the second language, but also more focused, explicit, and specific uses of language" (Pennington, 1996a, p. 2). This is probably because the relatively "cueless environment" (Spears & Lea, 1992) of the computer context makes it necessary to invoke the context of the speech event more explicitly than would be required in face-to-face communication. In a study of ESL learners exchanging information by e-mail in Canada, Esling (1991) found that "in the initial exchange of notes, the communication is characterized by revelation of information about local setting which would not normally be exchanged but which would rather be taken for granted and left unsaid in face-to-face conversation" (pp. 126–127). A similar finding is reported by Nabors and Swartley (1999) in a study in which e-mail partners were provided for ESL students on an American university campus. Thus, the relatively cueless environment, coupled with the anonymity and ease of communication in an electronic network, may promote both a more content-rich and a more individual and creative form of writing.

Discourse Implications

Writing over a network can add real audiences, input, and motivation to write; also, the online context changes the writing task to one that has some of the attributes of spoken interaction. Thus, for example, Nabors and Swartley (1999) found that the ESL e-mail penpals in their study used a range of strategies to build a relationship with their partner, many of which, such as giving personal information and sharing feelings, are also common in face-to-face relationships. As Moran (1995) notes: "E-mail is, simultaneously, the most intimate and the most public form of correspondence" (p. 16). In consequence, discourse produced in an e-mail context shares characteristics with both personal and professional letters, as well as with some speech genres, particularly, public interviews (Collot & Belmore, 1996). At the same time, based on its unique contextual attributes, e-mail communication appears to be evolving as a new genre, which Baron (2000) describes as a "creole" that merges some properties of both speech and writing. The e-mail context may therefore contribute to improving the student's fluency and willingness to write even as it contributes to a breakdown of established writing conventions and genres. This breakdown of conventions appears to be even greater in synchronous network communication.

HYPERTEXT/HYPERMEDIA

Another development of import to writers is the possibilities for creating hypertext, a computer tool for building "layered text":

> Like Chinese boxes, text can be nested within text, and huge texts can reside within tiny fragments. With the combination of both hierarchical subordination and lateral links from any point to any point, hypertext offers greatly expanded possibilities for new structures characterized by layering and flexibility. (Bernhardt, 1993, p. 164)

In hypertext, writers create "mosaics of information" (Marcus, 1993) made up of chunks of information arranged on computer "pages." These chunks of information, which may be textual, visual, auditory, or any combination of these, are connected by electronic links in a Web page format. Users are then free to create their own paths to negotiate the information from one part of the screen to another or from one screen to another.

The possibility of linking a chunk of text to another to create "information layers" encourages a new mode of "layered thinking" and "layered composing." Because of its nonlinear properties, "hypertext . . . may help support an enriched network of thoughts and associations that assists writers to explore and develop their ideas, thereby enhancing the cognitive potentials of [the computer]" (Pennington, 1996b, p. 23). The possibility of combining chunks of text with "sound bits," "video bits," and other "media chunks" adds creative potential for illustrating written work while also encouraging the creation of new modes of presentation using text, other visual media, and sound media. When all these potentials are combined with Internet access, the computer offers a distributed set of links and a highly creative, all-purpose hypermedia or multimedia communication tool.

WEB PAGES AND WEB SITES

The World Wide Web (generally referred to as "the Web") is a sector of the Internet made up of linked hypertext sites that can be accessed by mouse clicks. A Web browser such as Internet Explorer or Netscape Navigator is needed to read Web pages. Web searches can be conducted online using search engines such as Google (http://www.google.com/) and Alta Vista (http://www.altavista.com/), which, among other things, allow the user to type in a word or phrase to find Web pages that contain all or some of the desired words or that match these most closely. Web pages can be created using various tools and then put up on a local-area network or placed on a public drive. Software such as Microsoft Inc.'s FrontPage or Macromedia's Dreamweaver will allow a teacher to manage a Web site (and also to author Web pages). In addition, Windeat, Hardisty, and Eastment (2000) have a Web site linked to their book with useful information for teachers regarding Web pages and anything to do with the Internet (available via the Oxford Teachers' Club at http://www.oup.com/elt/global/teachersclub/). Another useful resource is the WebCT (World-Wide-Web Course Tools) program (available at: http://www.webct.com/) used by Kamhi-Stein (2000) in her TESOL teacher education course. It offers Web-based bulletin board systems, group presentation and chat areas, conferencing tools, and e-mail.

Increasingly, hypermedia tools and the Web are defining new domains of communication and literacy, including a new emphasis on visual and combined-media literacy (Kress, 1998), extending to new dimensions some of the more conventional reading and writing connections important to L2 students. An investigation comparing texts written by L2 French students in pen-and-paper, word processing, and hypertext modes (Marcoul & Pennington, 1999) found that the latter medium, when aligned to a student newspaper Web site, sparked students' creativity and drew their attention to visual aspects of design at the same time that it drew their attention away from surface correction of language. Interestingly, although the students in the Marcoul and Pennington (1999) study made fewer surface revisions, they made more content and paragraph-level revisions in hypertext than in the other two modes. This comparative study of writing media suggests that having students write in hypertext for a Web page may encourage them to spend more time refining their texts in terms of content and organization of information at the same time that it encourages them to focus on other aspects of presentation that take time away from the writing process per se.

In the instructional project investigated by Marcoul and Pennington (1999), readers could interact with student creators of Web pages to add comments to their text and to visit the links that writers had created to their Web pages. In this way, readers interacted with writers by collaborating in the ongoing development of texts and by exploring a part of the writer's world. The interactive creation of text, which is greatly facilitated by network and Web-based communication, is a major area of literacy innovation that has value for L2 writers.

In a study that involved Web explorations by junior high school students in Mexico, Romano, Field, and de Huergo (2000) report on the students' engagement with knowledge outside their community, including their engagement with the English language, finding "a strong tendency for Web literacy and literacy in English to converge, becoming nearly one and the same" (p. 204). An investigation by Lam (2000) of the e-mail and text-conferencing chat activities of a Chinese adolescent immigrant to the United States revealed that "the English he controlled on the Internet enabled him to develop a sense of belonging and connectedness to a global English-speaking community" (p. 476). In a discussion of Web communication in Australia, McConaghy and Snyder (2000) stress the interaction of local and global knowledge and perspectives that result from this type of communication. As they conclude: "Perhaps, in the final analysis, the possibilities for engaging the local in the global through the World Wide Web represent the new medium's greatest potential" (McConaghy & Snyder, 2000, p. 89).

THE INTERNET AND WORLD WIDE WEB AS RESOURCES

The Internet and World Wide Web provide students access to electronic resources online that may be helpful for their writing, such as journals, library catalogs, topical databases, search services, and resources on English language. Most journals' Web sites give access to contents and abstracts and in some cases, to articles in past issues. Bibliomania (http://www.bibliomania.com/) is a resource for searching reference materials and works of fiction, drama, poetry, and religious texts. Project Gutenberg Electronic Library (http://promo.net/pg/index.html/) offers free download of a variety of electronic texts, and Kidon Media-Link (http://www.kidon.com/media-link/) provides links to Web editions of thousands of newspapers. Online dictionaries are available for English and other languages at http://www.dictionary.com/, a Web site that includes a language discussion forum, *Roget's Thesaurus,* and writing resources such as grammar, usage, and style guides, including some for writing on the Internet. Many grammar references are also available online, such as Charles Darling's Guide to Grammar and Writing (http://cctc2.commnet.edu/grammar/), and Professional Training Company's Good Grammar, Good Style TM Archive (http://www.protrainco.com/grammar.htm). The text by Windeatt, Hardisty, and Eastment (2000) contains a variety of structured activities for students to learn how to negotiate the Internet and to use different types of resources available on the World Wide Web, such as English language stories, films, and new sources.

The Web is also an excellent resource for teachers, offering quick access to professional organization such as TESOL (http://www.tesol.org/) and IATEFL (the International Association of Teachers of English as a Foreign Language) (http://www.iatefl.org/); teaching materials and articles, such as those through ERIC Educational Resources Information Center (http://www.askeric.org/); online journals, such as the monthly *Internet TESL Journal* (http://www.aitech.ac.jp/~iteslj/), and the quarterly *TESL E-J* (http://www-writing.berkeley.edu/TESL-EJ/); teaching sites, such as the Beaumont Publishers' Virtual Learning Community site for K–12 projects (http://www.cyberjourneys.net/), the English Through the Internet projects of Elaine Hoter (http://web.macam98.ac.il/~elaine/eti/), the Email Projects Home Page by Susan Gaer (http://www.otan.us/webfarm/emailproject/email.htm), and the Linguistic Funland TESL Page (http://www.linguistic-funland.com/tesl.html/), a rich site including everything from listings of job opportunities and graduate programs in TESL to teaching and testing materials and services for students. There are also useful individually-sponsored Web pages with information oriented toward teaching English as a second language, such as those of Dave Sperling (http://www.eslcafe.com/), Ruth Vilmi (http://www.ruthvilmi.net/hut/), or Mark Warschauer (http://www.gse.uci.edu/markw/). In addition, a good annotated compilation called "Internet Projects for Learners and Teachers of English" is available at http://www.wfi.fr/volterre/inetpro.html/.

Other electronic resources include concordancing programs, such as TACT (available at http://tactweb.humanities.mcmaster.ca/) or Athelstan, Inc.'s MonoConc (available at http://www.athel.com/); these allow student writers and their teachers to search their own or others' texts for the occurrence and contexts of specific words or phrases. With Internet access, they can search online corpora such as the British National Corpus Online (available at http://www.hcu.ox.ac.uk/bnc) and find out about others, such as those listed at the University of Lancaster UCREL (University Centre for Computer Corpus Research on Language) Web site (http://www.comp.lancs.ac.uk/computing/research/ucrel/corpora.html). There are also online resources for preventing and detecting plagiarism, such as Plagiarism.org (http://www.plagiarism.org/) and the Indiana University Writing Resources Web page (http://www.indiana.edu/~wts/wts/plargiarism.html).

POTENTIALS AND ISSUES

The computer offers a wide variety of literacy and communication tools that may assist more people to achieve literacy in one or more languages than ever before. At the same time, "the result of writing in an electronic medium may not be the written products of a pen-and-paper age but more ephemeral forms of *think-text* and *talk-text*" (Pennington, 2000, p. 21). In addition, in the contexts of computer-mediated communication, writing is moving in the direction of, on the one hand, a more social construction of the activity and interactivity of writing and, on the other, a more media-saturated construction of text as existing within a rich nexus of other resources.

The value of the computer for the L2 writer is considerable for helping to automate the production and revision of text, to encode ideas, and to spark and energize the writing process. With the additional resources of networking and hypermedia, it offers a veritable banquet of media and communication options. Figure 26.3 summarizes some potentials of the computer to aid L2 student writers.

In addition, as Warschauer (2000b) notes, computer media empower students and give them greater control over their own learning, thus increasing their *agency:*

> Agency is really what makes students so excited about using computers in the classroom: the computer provides them a powerful means to make their stamp on the world. Think, for example, of the difference between authoring a paper (i.e., writing a text for the teacher), and authoring a multimedia document (i.e., creatively bringing together several media to share with a wide international audience), and even helping to author

FIGURE 26.3   Computer Potentials for L2 Writers

Computer assistance in the way of mechanical tools and an

environment to help with writing, revising, and

dissemination of text

Increased writing *efficiency and effectiveness*

Increased *motivation*

Increased *amount of writing*

More *effective use of language*

Creative potential

Interactivity and collaboration

New *modes and genres* of writing

Flexibility of access to tools, texts, helps, and partners

Expanded access to writing resources, information, and the world

the very rules by which multimedia is created. . . . By allowing and help-ing our students to carry out all these types of authoring—toward ful-filling a meaningful purpose for a real audience—we are helping them exercise their agency. The purpose of studying English is thus not just to "know it" as an internal system, but to be able to use it to have a real im-pact on the world. (p. 7)

At the same time the computer offers all of these potentials to student writers, certain issues of literacy on the computer remain to be resolved, as summarized in Figure 26.4.

Those of us involved in teaching L2 writing can help to ensure computer access for all to avoid a division of the world into computer "haves" and "have-nots" that Warschauer (2000a) terms the "digital divide."

At the same time, we need to consider what effective limits might be on students' computer access, so as to keep work on the computer from taking up too much of their time and attention and from replacing human contact. There are also issues we need to address about how to assess the new types of work produced in computer contexts, such as group-produced essays, Web pages, and the illustrated texts and texted illustrations made possible by mul-timedia and hypertext. It is also important to consider what values should be stressed in evaluating students' computer-produced work. For example,

FIGURE 26.4   Issues of Literacy on Computer

Access

   How to ensure computer access for all?

   What (if any) is a reasonable limit to computer access?

Assessment

   How to assess group-produced essays?

   How to assess writing in hypertext/Web pages?

   How to assess illustrated text/texted illustrations?

Control

   How/whether to keep students from "using" the work of others

      available on Internet?

   How/whether to keep students from "surfing" the net to find

      "inappropriate" material?

---

should originality be emphasized over correctness and quality of layout emphasized as much as quality of content and linguistic form? Finally, there are important matters we need to consider about whether and how to control students' use of others' work and "unsuitable information" (e.g., pornography or violent material) available electronically.

Issues of access and control in computer contexts are matters that we in ESL need to be concerned about. As observed by Hawisher and Selfe (2000):

> The Web is a complicated and contested site for postmodern literacy practices. This site is characterized by a strongly influential set of tendential cultural forces, primarily oriented toward the values of the white, western industrialized nations that were responsible for designing and building the network and that continue to exert power within it. Hence, this system of networked computers is far from world-wide; it does not provide a culturally neutral conduit for the transmission of information; it is not a culturally neutral or innocent communication landscape open to the literacy practices and values of all global citizens. But the site is also far from totalizing in its effects . . . , [as] [t]he Web also provides a site for transgressive literacy practices that express and value difference; that cling to historical, cultural, and racial diversity; and that help groups and individuals constitute their own multiple identities through language. (p. 15)

How we make use of computer potentials with our L2 learners and how we resolve the issues surrounding the use of electronic media are matters of great interest and concern. Even more important than how these matters are resolved is that we take an active role in computer-affected outcomes, that we are directly involved in resolving computer issues and deciding the best ways to make use of computer potentials for our own population of students, that is, L2 writers. In the present day, no ESL teacher can afford to remain on the sidelines of these developments, which have transformed and are continuing to transform literacy, language, and all communication in very significant ways.

REFERENCES

Akyel, A., & Kamisli, S. (1999). Word processing in the EFL classroom: Effects on writing strategies, attitudes, and products. In M. C. Pennington (Ed.), *Writing in an electronic medium: Research with language learners* (pp. 27–60). Houston: Athelstan.

Bangert-Drowns, R. L. (1993). The word processor as an instructional tool: A meta-analysis of word processing in writing instruction. *Review of Educational Research, 63,* 69–93.

Baron, N. S. (2000). *Alphabet to email: How written English evolved and where it's heading.* London: Routledge.

Benesch, S. (1987). *Word processing in English as a second language: A case study of three non-native college students.* Paper presented at the conference on College Composition and Communication, Atlanta, GA. (ERIC Document No. ED 281383)

Bernhardt, S. A. (1993). The shape of text to come: The texture of print on screens. *College Composition and Communication, 44,* 151–175.

Bernhardt, S. A., Edwards, P. G., & Wojahn, P. R. (1989). Teaching college composition with computers: A program evaluation study. *Written Communication, 6,* 108–133.

Betancourt, F., & Phinney, M. (1988). Sources of writing block in bilingual writers. *Written Communication, 5,* 461–478.

Braine, G. (2001). A study of English as a foreign language (EFL) writers on a local-area network (LAN) and in traditional classes. *Computers and Composition, 18,* 275–292.

Brock, M. N., & Pennington, M. C. (1999). A comparative study of text analysis and peer tutoring as input to writing on computer in an ESL context. In M. C. Pennington (Ed.), *Writing in an electronic medium: Research with language learners* (pp. 61–94). Houston: Athelstan.

Bruce, B., Peyton, J. K., & Batson, T. (Eds.). (1993). *Networked-based classrooms: Promises and realities.* New York: Cambridge University Press.

Bruce, B. C., & Rubin, A. (1993). *Electronic quills: A situated evaluation of using computers for writing in classrooms.* Hillsdale, NJ: Lawrence Erlbaum.

Chadwick, S., & Bruce, N. (1989). The revision process in academic writing: From pen and paper to word processor. *Hongkong Papers in Linguistics and Language Teaching, 12,* April, 1–27.

Cochran-Smith, M. (1991). Word processing and writing in elementary classrooms: A critical review of related literature. *Review of Educational Research, 61,* 107–155.

Collot, M., & Belmore, N. (1996). Electronic language: A new variety of English. In S. Herring (Ed.), *Computer mediated communication: Linguistic, social, and cross-cultural perspectives* (pp. 13–28). Philadelphia: John Benjamins.

Daiute, C. (1985). *Writing and computers.* Reading, MA: Addison-Wesley.

Esling, J. H. (1991). Researching the effects of networking: Evaluating the spoken and written discourse generated by working with CALL. In P. Dunkel (Ed.), *Computer-assisted language learning and testing: Research issues and practice* (pp. 111'131). New York: Newbury House/Harper Collins.

Haas, C. (1989). How the writing medium shapes the writing process: Effects of word processing on planning. *Research in the Teaching of English, 23,* 181–207.

Hawisher, G. E., & Selfe, C. L. (2000). Introduction: Testing the claims. In G. E. Hawisher & C. L. Selfe (Eds.), *Global literacies and the World-Wide Web* (pp. 1–18). London: Routledge.

Hoffman, R. (1996). Computer networks: Webs of communication for language teaching. In M. C. Pennington (Ed.), *The power of CALL* (pp. 55–78). Houston: Athelstan.

Howard, T. (1992). WANs, connectivity, and computer literacy: An introduction and glossary. *Computers and Composition, 9*(3), 41–57.

Jones, S., & Tetroe, J. (1987). Composing in a second language. In A. Matsuhashi (Ed.), *Writing in real time: Modeling production processes* (pp. 34–57). Norwood, NJ: Ablex.

Kamhi-Stein, L. D. (2000). Looking at the future of TESOL teacher education: Web-based bulletin board discussion in a methods course. *TESOL Quarterly, 34,* 423–455.

Kaufer, D. S., & Neuwirth, C. (1995). Supporting online team editing: Using technology to shape performance and to monitor individual and group action. *Computers and Composition, 12,* 113–124.

Kress, G. (1998). Visual and verbal modes of representation in electronically mediated communication: The potentials of new forms of text. In I. Synder (Ed.), *Page to screen: Taking literacy into the electronic era* (pp. 53–79). London: Routledge.

Lam, F. S., & Pennington, M. C. (1995). The computer vs. the pen: A comparative study of word processing in a Hong Kong secondary classroom. *Computer-Assisted Language Learning, 7,* 75–92.

Lam, W. S. E. (2000). L2 literacy and the design of the self: A case study of a teenager writing on the Internet. *TESOL Quarterly, 34,* 457–482.

Li, J., & Cumming, A. (2001). Word processing and second language writing: A longitudinal case study. *International Journal of English Studies, 1*(2), 127–152.

Mabrito, M. (1991). Electronic mail as a vehicle for peer response. *Written Communication, 8,* 509–532.

Marcoul, I., & Pennington, M. C. (1999). Composing with computer technology: A case study of a group of students in computer studies learning French as a second language. In M. C. Pennington (Ed.), *Writing in an electronic medium: Research with language learners* (pp. 285–318). Houston: Athelstan.

Marcus, S. (1993). Multimedia, hypermedia and the teaching of English. In M. Monteith (Ed.), *Computers and language* (pp. 21–43). Oxford: Intellect Books.

McConaghy, C., & Snyder, I. (2000). Working the Web in postcolonial Australia. In G. E. Hawisher & C. L. Selfe (Eds.), *Global literacies and the World-Wide Web* (pp. 74–92). London: Routledge.

McGarrell, H. M. (1993, August). *Perceived and actual impact of computer use in second language writing classes.* Paper presented at the Congress of the Association de Linguistique Appliquèe (AILA), Frije University, Amsterdam.

Moran, C. (1995). Notes toward a rhetoric of e-mail. *Computers and Composition, 12,* 15–21.

Moran, C., & Hawisher, G. E. (1998). The rhetorics and languages of electronic mail. In I. Snyder (Ed.), *Page to screen: Taking literacy into the electronic era* (pp. 80–101). London: Routledge.

Nabors, L. K., & Swartley, E. C. (1999). Student email letters: Negotiating meaning, gathering information, building relationships. In M. C. Pennington (Ed.), *Writing in an electronic medium: Research with language learners* (pp. 229–266). Houston: Athelstan.

Neu, J., & Scarcella, R. (1991). Word processing in the ESL writing classroom: A survey of student attitudes. In P. Dunkel (Ed.), *Computer-assisted language learning and testing: Research issues and practice* (pp. 169–187). New York: Newbury House/HarperCollins.

Palmquist, M. E. (1993). Network-supported interaction in two writing classrooms. *Computers and Composition, 10,* 25–57.

Pennington, M. C. (1996a). The power of the computer in language education. *The power of CALL* (pp. 1–14). Houston: Athelstan.

Pennington, M. C. (1996b). *The computer and the non-native writer: A natural partnership.* Cresskill, NJ: Hampton Press.

Pennington, M. C. (1996c). Writing the natural way: On computer. *Computer Assisted Language Learning, 9,* 125–142.

Pennington, M. C. (1999a). The missing link in computer-assisted writing. In K. Cameron (Ed.), *CALL: Media, design & applications* (pp. 271–292). Lisse: Swets & Zeitlinger.

Pennington, M. C. (1999b). Word processing and beyond: Writing in an electronic medium. In M. C. Pennington (Ed.), *Writing in an electronic medium: Research with language learners* (pp. 1–26). Houston: Athelstan.

Pennington, M. C. (2000). Writing minds and talking fingers: Doing literacy in an electronic age. In P. Brett (Ed.), *CALL in the 21st century* [CD-ROM]. Whitstable, UK: IATEFL.

Pennington, M. C., & Brock, M. N. (1992). Process and product approaches to computer-assisted composition. In M. C. Pennington & V. Stevens (Eds.), *Computers in applied linguistics: An international perspective* (pp. 79–109). Clevedon, UK: Multilingual Matters.

Phinney, M. (1989). Computers, composition, and second language teaching. In M. C. Pennington (Ed.), *Teaching languages with computers: The state of the art* (pp. 81–96). La Jolla, CA: Athelstan.

Phinney, M. (1991). Word processing and writing apprehension in first and second language writers. *Computers and Composition, 9,* 65–82.

Phinney, M., & Khouri, S. (1993). Computers, revision, and ESL writers: The role of experience. *Journal of Second Language Writing 2,* 257–277.

Phinney, M., & Mathis, C. (1990). ESL student responses to writing with computers. *TESOL Newsletter, 24*(2), 30–31.

Roblyer, M. D., Castine, W. H., & King, F. J. (1988). *Assessing the impact of computer-based instruction: A review of recent research.* New York: Haworth.

Romano, S., Field, B., & Huergo, E. W. de. (2000). Web literacies of the already accessed and technically inclined: Schooling in Monterrey, Mexico. In G. E. Hawisher & C. L. Selfe (Eds.), *Global literacies and the World-Wide Web* (pp. 189–216). London: Routledge.

Rusmin, R. S. (1999). Patterns of adaptation to a new writing environment: The experience of word processing by mature second language writers. In M. C. Pennington (Ed.), *Writing in an electronic medium: Research with language learners* (pp. 183–227). Houston: Athelstan.

Sayers, D. (1989). Bilingual sister classes in computer writing networks. In D. M. Johnson & D. H. Roen (Eds.), *Richness in writing: Empowering ESL students* (pp. 120–133). New York: Longman.

Schramm, R. M. (1989). The effects of using word-processing equipment in writing instruction: A meta-analysis. (Doctoral dissertation, Northern Illinois University, 1990). *Dissertation Abstracts International, 50,* 2463A.

Slater, P., & Carpenter, C. (1999). Introducing e-mail into a course in French as a second language. In M. C. Pennington (Ed.), *Writing in an electronic medium: Research with language learners* (pp. 267–283). Houston: Athelstan.

Snyder, I. (1993). Writing with word processors: A research overview. *Educational Research, 35,* 49–68.

Spears, R., & Lea, M. (1992). Social influence and the influence of the "social" in computer-mediated communication. In R. Spears & M. Lea (Eds.), *Contexts of computer-mediated communication* (pp. 30–65). New York: Harvester Wheatsheaf.

Steelman, J. D. (1994). Revision strategies employed by middle level students using computers. *Journal of Educational Computing Research, 11,* 141–152.

Sullivan, N., & Pratt, E. (1996). A comparative study of two ESL writing environments: A computer-assisted classroom and a traditional oral classroom. *System, 24,* 491–501.

Susser, B. (1993). ESL/EFL process writing with computers. *CAELL Journal, 4*(2), 16–22.

Warschauer, M. (1997). Computer-mediated collaborative learning: Theory and practice. *Modern Language Journal, 81,* 470–481.

Warschauer, M. (1999). *Electronic literacies: Language, culture, and power in online education.* Mahwah, NJ: Lawrence Erlbaum.

Warschauer, M. (2000a). Language, identity, and the internet. In B. Kolko, L. Kakamura, & G. Rodman (Eds.), *Race in cyberspace* (pp. 151–170). London: Routledge.

Warschauer, M. (2000b). The death of cyberspace and the rebirth of CALL. In P. Brett (Ed.), *CALL in the 21st century* [CD-ROM]. Whitstable, UK: IATEFL.

Williamson, M. M., & Pence, P. (1989). Word processing and student writers. In B. Britton & S. M. Glynn (Eds.), *Computer writing environments: Theory, research, and design* (pp. 93–127). Hillsdale, NJ: Lawrence Erlbaum.

Windeatt, S., Hardisty, D., & Eastment, D. (2000). *The internet.* Oxford: Oxford University Press.

Woodin, J. (1997). E-mail tandem learning and the communicative curriculum. *ReCALL, 9*(1), 22–33.

27

WAC Wired: Electronic Communication across the Curriculum

DONNA REISS AND ART YOUNG

As a new century begins, educators are giving special attention to the future of higher education in general and of communication and literacy in particular. New technologies figure significantly in these deliberations either directly or indirectly, as illustrated in this example from faculty at a recent writing-across-the-curriculum workshop at a regional university. Writing in their journals and then brainstorming together, teachers generated a list of expectations from constituencies beyond the campus for universities in the twenty-first century:

- increased emphasis on undergraduate education

- interdisciplinary cooperation and communication

- better integrated levels of education: K–12 and two- and four-year colleges; general education and professional education

- decentralization of project-based education, co-ops, internships, reality-based education: distance learning, videoconferencing, site-based course packaging

- *service* as a good word: outreach to communities, schools, industries, non-profits, government

- transfer of knowledge more quickly from researchers to users

- quick adaptation to rapidly changing contexts

- computers integrated to help students participate fully in the global information age

- total quality management: team-based projects, client service, continuous improvement

- wise resource management: do more with less

- accountability: conduct regular assessment of all activities and all personnel, including tenured faculty

From *WAC for the New Millennium: Strategies for Continuing Writing-across-the-Curriculum Programs.* Ed. Susan McLeod, Eric Miraglia, Margot Soven, and Christopher Thaiss. Urbana: NCTE, 2001. 52–81.

- more curriculum buzzwords: *communication skills, international, multicultural, computers, interdisciplinary, service learning, collaborative learning, learning communities, lifelong learning, critical thinking,* and *creativity*

Workshop participants paused only briefly to point out some of the apparent contradictions in their list and to comment that legislators, businesspeople, alumni, parents, and educational commissions don't always understand the traditional and important role of universities in developing knowledge and passing that knowledge on to newcomers in specialized disciplinary fields. Participants also realized that the charge to create the "university of the future" was a pointed challenge to "higher education as usual," in which individuals and departments are rewarded for disciplinary specialization but not for service to other constituencies. Most faculty at the workshop wanted to embrace this challenge, evidenced by their attendance. Writing across the curriculum (WAC) and communication across the curriculum (CAC) represent one consequential way, in theory and in practice, for college faculty to respond to the broad educational and political issues of the new millennium. Additionally, as society and our definitions of literacy are transformed by information technology, we are reexamining our perceptions of language and learning in relation to electronic media. As McLeod and Miraglia point out, a new acronym, ECAC—electronic communication across the curriculum (Reiss, Selfe, and Young)—can be added to WAC and CAC as another approach to literacy, communication, collaboration, and community outreach for educational programs and institutions.

The literacy spaces we inhabit now are located both in physical space and in cyberspace and more than ever across classrooms, campuses, countries, and continents. Barbara Walvoord invited us in 1996 to explore new media in a WAC context when she wrote that with information technology, "lines blur between writing and other forms of communication and between classrooms and other learning spaces" (72). In fact, this blurring of boundaries has long been characteristic of WAC, even though the name "Writing Across the Curriculum" never sufficiently recognized the broader initiatives that WAC has spearheaded or supported: oral and visual communication, creative and critical thinking, interactive and collaborative learning, and informal and formal communication with audiences within and beyond the classroom. Addressing the 1997 international Writing Across the Curriculum Conference in Charleston, South Carolina, Elaine Maimon reminded us that WAC really means "active learning across the curriculum," encompassing a variety of ways to help faculty and students make connections with each other and to effect curricular reform. A number of WAC programs have changed their names or institutional structures to reflect this wider scope, becoming CAC programs or participating in variously named centers for teaching and learning, and we can comfortably predict further expansion to incorporate ECAC. Although WAC programs will not necessarily change their names, an expanded focus to include information technology as an instructional tool in classrooms and in physical and cyberspaces beyond classrooms is inevitable, as well as opportune for transforming the culture of learning. In a no-longer-surprising reversal, information technology is encouraging disciplines across the university to work with WAC in an interdisciplinary quest for the effective educational use of electronic mail, hypertext, the World Wide Web, and multimedia.[1]

Information technology is transforming almost every area of our culture, especially higher education and the professional workplace. Some educators are adapting comfortably to the changes; others are resisting for reasons financial, pedagogical, and personal. Many administrators, legislators, scholars, and classroom teachers remain cautious about investing in infrastructure, bandwidth, intranets, and Internet 2. Fortunately, WAC/CAC program directors and teachers have an opportunity to take leadership roles in these transitions because communication is fundamental to the new computer technologies and because rethinking teaching and learning has long been the foundation of WAC/CAC. In [*WAC for the New Millennium*], many contributors address the impact of computer-mediated communication on WAC and CAC. Chris Thaiss emphasizes the ways our definitions of writing itself are being challenged by new media as increasingly "the act of writing means choosing among a huge array of images and forms, only some of which are 'words'" (p. 307). Susan McLeod and Eric Miraglia write, "In addition to shaping the integration of new learning technologies within the proximal world of the traditional university classroom, the WAC community must now look to apply its profound transformational strategies to new models of student-teacher and student-student interaction" (p. 8).

And these new models are the strength of electronic communication across the curriculum. ECAC at its best is student centered and supports the development of an individual's academic and communication abilities for both personal and professional objectives. We began this chapter with a list of broad issues facing higher education, but often the personal meets the professional for students in the very singular process of securing employment. And so the broad issues proclaimed by prestigious educational commissions might be compared with the sparse wording in the "Help Wanted" section of Donna's local newspaper:

- Legal secretary: "excellent computer and communication skills"
- Senior accountant: "good computer skills, excellent oral/written communication skills"
- Sales and marketing assistant: "prepare/edit technical proposals and reports. Must be computer literate"

In the twin context of broad national issues and local student-centered issues, this chapter describes some of the ways WAC/CAC has changed and is changing in the digital age. Not included here are the thousands of courses and hundreds of programs that use the Internet for instruction, many of which either accidentally or intentionally provide students with one or more language-rich activities that would win the praise of communication-across-the-curriculum specialists. Instead, we focus on those projects that consciously incorporate a computer-supported WAC/CAC dynamic into their classes and programs. Recognizing that some models of information technology on campuses and some distance learning courses will simply transfer drill-and-practice approaches to computers, the digital age's equivalent to multiple-choice scanning sheets, we believe WAC/CAC people in an ECAC environment will advocate (1) an increase in information technology to support the activities of WAC/CAC programs, (2) an increase in alliances between instructional technology programs and WAC/CAC programs, and (3) additional emphasis on communication-intensive uses of technology, or ECAC, among teachers and institutions that emphasize active learning and the development of communication competence in all their students.

WAC/CAC activities at our campuses are certain to have a direct connection to technology. The nature of that connection will vary considerably, just as our technological infrastructures and organizational structures vary. Use of computer-supported information delivery and collaborative writing tools is sometimes institutional, sometimes programmatic, and sometimes the project of a couple of enthusiasts who set up a few computers or a simple internal network or who take advantage of Internet connections to establish e-mail exchanges among students in their own classes or with other audiences. More elaborate models include Web-based classes and multimedia projects that communicate verbally, visually, aurally, and interactively within and between classes and into the community. Some are funded generously, others meagerly. To place the future of WAC/CAC and communication technology in context, "WAC Wired" presents a short history plus description of a range of approaches to ECAC currently in use even as technologies and our related pedagogies continue to change. And so at the new century's beginning, we revisit, this time online, writing and learning across the curriculum.

A SHORT HISTORY OF ELECTRONIC COMMUNICATION ACROSS THE CURRICULUM (ECAC)

The computers that transmit information within and among organizations are increasingly important on college campuses. In *The Campus Computing Project,* his annual survey of information technology in higher education, Kenneth C. Green of the Center for Educational Studies of the Claremont Graduate University states, "Students of all ages and across all fields come to campus expecting to learn about and also to learn *with* technology" ("1998 National Survey"; emphasis added).[2] His survey reports significant increase in the use of e-mail and of World Wide Web pages "for class materials and resources." Administrators cite faculty development and technological support for faculty as among their most pressing concerns. Clearly, WAC/CAC programs must and in many cases already do respond to the faculty development needs with ECAC workshops and resources for using new media to communicate effectively.

Increased numbers of and upgrades to computer labs in campus buildings and dormitories, along with increased personal computing as the price of equipment goes down and the use of the Internet becomes more prevalent in the home as well as the workplace, suggest opportunities for WAC/CAC programs to expand their activities and audiences to include new technologies. Significantly, because the use of e-mail and most Internet resources still involves primarily text, people using these resources are always writing, always reading. Even when using the World Wide Web, with its increasingly glitzy graphics and growing commercialization, students and others are reading, conducting research, making critical choices, and, if there's a feedback form or a threaded discussion, writing, perhaps even joining an interactive discussion. As a result, students are writing for their classes across the curriculum even when they are not formally enrolled in a writing intensive course. They are also writing to their grandparents and to friends and to cyberpals in chat rooms, corresponding with audiences who take their writing seriously.

Many of the key elements of WAC/CAC in the 1970s and the computers-and-composition movement of the 1980s intersect today as ECAC. WAC encourages all teachers to value their students' writing and to respond to it with guidance for improvement rather than with discouragement or punitive remarks. The incorporation of multiple drafts, peer response, and draft conferences into classes across the curriculum, and the establishment of writing centers that support students from every area of a college, are among the ways WAC/CAC has influenced teachers whose primary interest is generating "better writing" on student tests and papers. In his chapter on research in this volume, David R. Russell reports that by studying writing themselves, faculty "critically reflect on their practice and change that practice" (p. 291), a WAC/CAC outcome that our programs can extend to critical reflection on computer-mediated communication across the curriculum. Teachers across the curriculum are also aware of employers' demands for better writing. Russell has written elsewhere that "one characteristic of our post-industrial society is a recognition that competitive advantages come through more effective communication, often written, among workers in al levels and roles" ("Writing Across the Curriculum" 68).

The business world and writing instruction met comfortably around the computer keyboard in the late 1970s and 1980s as writing teachers discovered the benefits of word processing for editing and revising and, by the end of that decade, for text sharing over computer networks. Writing teachers, already the leaders of communication across the curriculum on many campuses, thus became early promoters of computers across the curriculum through their writing centers, WAC/CAC programs, or informal conversations with colleagues. Nonetheless, as Cynthia L. Selfe writes, most faculty "seemed prone in those early years to want to use computers to address surface-level correctness rather than to encourage writing as a way of thinking." In the 1990s, however, as the personal computer became more widely used and as faculty desktops became connected to college networks and the Internet, "WAC faculty in a range of disciplines began to experiment with writing-intensive learning activities" (Selfe xii–xiii).

Recognizing this trend, Barbara Walvoord emphasizes the need for WAC programs—traditionally strong builders of alliances—to develop partnerships with instructional technology specialists (72). After all, at many colleges around the country, WAC/CAC leaders, writing center directors, and writing teachers have been early users of information technology and have participated in institutional technology initiatives, in some cases administering those initiatives, as Karen Schwalm does at Glendale Community College, as Leslie Harris does at Goucher College, and as Trent Batson did for nearly twenty years at Gallaudet University. The director of one national instructional technology project—Steven W. Gilbert of the Teaching, Learning, and Technology Group (TLT Group) affiliated with the American Association for Higher Education—regularly highlights the pedagogical groundwork of faculty in computers and composition. The TLT program also was allied with the Annenberg-PBS grant-funded Epiphany Project, directed by Trent Batson and Judy Williamson, a national professional development initiative directed primarily at writing teachers but always with an ECAC presence because several of the project leaders also were associated with WAC/CAC at their campuses.

That writing teachers and WAC/CAC program heads have become institutional leaders of ECAC is not surprising, for WAC and computers-and-composition grew up almost side by side at Michigan Technological University, where Toby Fulwiler and Robert Jones of the Department of Humanities (chaired by Art Young) led workshops for faculty beginning in 1977. Also at Michigan Tech, Cynthia L. Selfe and Dickie Selfe began building the Center for Computer-Assisted Language Instruction in the 1980s, now the laboratory for the summer workshop on computers in the writing intensive classroom, as well as the center for writing to support students in engineering and other disciplines. In his chronicle of the early conjunctions of WAC with technology, Mike Palmquist dates the first recorded activity as 1983, when Kate Kiefer and Charles Smith used Writer's Workbench with engineering students, a project expanded by Muriel Harris and Madelon Cheek. According to Harris and Cheek: "This can lead to a stronger interest in writing instruction within their [engineering] classrooms, drawing them into the writing-across-the-curriculum movement via the computer" (qtd. in Palmquist 380; Harris and Cheek 5). A few years later, Nicholas Gordon and Susan Mansfield wrote that "it makes sense to expand a writing-across-the-curriculum project into a computers-across-the-curriculum project" (qtd. in Palmquist 380; Gordon and Mansfield 11).

In her chapter on writing centers in this volume, Joan Mullin describes the impact of technology on writing centers and WAC, where "the connection between instructor, student, and WAC and writing centers provides generative feedback through continual reflective assessment about the learning process" (p. 190). At least two books now connect writing centers with computer-mediated communication. In *Wiring the Writing Center* (Hobson), the chapter "WAC on the Web: Writing Center Outreach to Teachers of Writing Intensive Courses" (Kimball) deals directly with the relationships between writing centers, WAC, and technology, while other chapters do so less directly; after all, the mission of most writing centers includes outreach across the disciplines. According to *Taking Flight with OWLS: Examining Electronic Writing Center Work* (Inman and Sewell), at the end of the 1990s, many teachers across the curriculum were using WAC/CAC online in their individual classes or in collaborations with teachers in their own or other disciplines, and growing numbers of schools and colleges have incorporated technology into their WAC/CAC or writing programs or have included WAC/CAC as partners in their technology professional development programs. In selecting its four Colleges of the Year for 2001, Time Inc. and the Princeton Review focused on writing across the curriculum, naming Sarah Lawrence College, Cornell University, Longview Community College (Lee's Summit, Missouri), and Clemson University. Integration of electronic communication was one of the noteworthy characteristics of Clemson's program, and electronic communication at Tidewater Community College was mentioned as "in the running" ("College of the Year").

THE MIDDLE GROUND: WRITING TO LEARN AND LEARNING TO WRITE ONLINE

WAC encourages the instructional use of various functions of written language for learning and communication in the belief that such practices strengthen students' language and critical thinking abilities. Although perhaps we overgeneralize, we sometimes say that the primary function of writing in classrooms has been for testing, evaluation, and demonstration of skills mastered, content learned, problems solved, or homework completed. WAC asks us to use writing for other not mutually exclusive purposes such as "writing to learn," in which emphasis is placed on using written language to learn new and unfamiliar content or to develop analytical or creative habits of mind, rather than to demonstrate how much has been learned. In other words, in writing to learn, mistakes, false starts, hallelujahs, connections, and misconceptions all are viewed as part of the process by which learners learn. Most WAC proponents believe that these two functions should be integral to all writing intensive courses and often label them informal and formal writing, or writing to learn and writing to communicate, or expressive and transactional writing. These two functions have never been viewed as totally distinct, but rather as existing on a continuum on which some of the writing we do in classrooms falls somewhere in the middle. With the advent of ECAC, this middle ground has gained a more prominent focus. At California State Polytechnic University, Pomona, for instance, where Carol Holder served for many years as director of both faculty development and writing in the disciplines, WAC has been integrating information technology for more than a decade, recently emphasizing "electronic kinds of informal writing for an audience (an interesting hybrid of expressive and transactional modes), and radical changes in the features of 'text' with the possibilities that hypertext/web publishing allows" (Holder).

The chart in Figure 27.1 helps us consider further the "interesting hybrid" of "conversational learning" and ways that electronic communication tools can support active and engaged learning. We view this chart as a starting place and a heuristic; it is not meant to construct a universe of discourse but

FIGURE 27.1   Classroom Discourse and Writing Across the Curriculum

	Personal Discourse	Classroom Discourse	Public Discourse
Function	*Expressive Writing* • Self-discovery • Inner speech	*Interactive Writing* • Conversational • Dialectical	*Transactional Writing* • Informative • Persuasive
Purpose	Explains to Oneself	Explains to Classroom Colleagues	Explains to Distant Others
Audience	*Self and Trusted Others* • Privileges language of learner • Accountability to self	*Classroom Community: Familiar and Known* • Privileges language of classroom community • Accountability to classmates	*Distant and Other: Unknown* • Privileges language of critical audiences • Accountability to public
Genre	• Journals • Diaries • Logs • Notebooks • Freewrites • Braindumps	• Letters • Notes • Questions • Poems • Parodies • E-mail • Dialogue journals	• Essays • Articles • Reports • Proposals • Memos • Multimedia • Web publications
Response Time	Immediate: Shaping at Point of Utterance	Quick: from "Real" Audience—Visible and Tactile	Lengthy: to Publication or Presentation
	Classroom Environment • Social and collaborative • Respects diversity and risk taking • Active learning and interactive teaching • Motivation for reading and writing		
	Developing Knowledge That Is Personally and Professionally Useful		

rather to suggest the fertile ground for the development of an interactive discourse that lies between personal discourse and public discourse. On the left side of the chart, personal discourse exhibits the familiar characteristics of informal, expressive writing. This is the discovery writing that writers do for themselves in places such as journals and notebooks, and that word processing and e-mail preserve in electronic journals or word-processed freewrites. On the right side of the chart, public discourse exhibits the familiar characteristics of transactional, formal writing, often composed in the form of essays and reports written to a distant audience.[3] In college classrooms, public discourse is often referred to as academic discourse, the language of the academy in general, or more specifically, the language of the intended audience—for example, the discourse of physics, or the discourse of political science—and a generally agreed-on goal of most college composition courses is to teach students to write this academic discourse. For students, one challenge is to figure out how to write like an academic or like a physicist or a political scientist before actually becoming an academic or a physicist—that is, before knowing what a physicist knows and before acquiring the habits of mind and discourse conventions of physics that come with knowledge and experience in that discipline. Such a rhetorical situation sometimes leads students to "fake" writing like an academic and thereby produce texts that teachers over the years have referred to as dummy runs, pretend writing, or "Engfish."

Our chart visualizes in the center column the actual and virtual space of the classroom, the "middle ground," where students gain knowledge, develop scholarly habits of mind, and acquire rhetorical and communication competence in a variety of public and academic contexts. It is that interactive social space where writers can combine their existing knowledge of content and inquiry with the new knowledge and experience they are acquiring in a particular course in order to generate texts for a "real" audience of classmates. In the process of such an interchange, knowledge is generated collaboratively, and a discourse, in some ways unique to those participants, is created that we situate in the middle ground. Electronic media have been facilitating such discourse in networked environments where students write to and for each other in a place where it is safe to practice the language of a discipline. E-mail discussion lists (listservs), class or Internet newsgroups, and threaded Web discussion forums promote collaborative writing in the language of the learner and do not require students to be in the same place at the same time to engage in these conversations. This discourse activity of the middle ground combines the writer's existing language and rhetorical practices with those of the academy under the tutelage of the teacher, in most cases the more experienced academic practitioner. The goal becomes not to pretend to know and to communicate but actually to do so within the context of being a novice writing to a known "real" audience of other learners on- or offline within a new course or field of study.

This chart on classroom discourse and writing across the curriculum is speculative and dynamic. The three columns should be imagined as on a continuum; most genres can fall in any column or between columns or in more than one column. E-mail, poems, essays, or letters can be written to fulfill any of the three purposes or a combination of them. All writing, in some sense, is personal, and all writing, when read by others, is public. Further, our chart suggests that ECAC does not create new rhetorical forms nor represent a major paradigm shift, but rather represents a useful way to view written, oral, and visual language in both traditional and computer classrooms. Viewed this way, this visualization assists us in "reading" student writing in the context of "conversational learning"—what many of us are doing for the first time with the advent of the Internet, e-mail, and computer conferencing. And it suggests a powerful pedagogy for the development of students' language and critical thinking abilities. It formulates for teachers and students a recursive and dialectical language process in which the cognitive and social inform each other in the development of writers and thinkers. It helps us understand the learning that occurs as teachers across the nation experiment with ECAC activities in courses within and across disciplines.

Teachers are discovering or rediscovering "middle ground" pedagogies as they implement projects that use new technologies to aid student learning and to improve communication with their students and between students in their classes. For example, WAC/CAC principles informed the use of newsgroups in educational psychology classes when Lawrence Sherman at Miami University designed activities for extending communication and collaboration in response to articles in the journal *Teaching of Psychology*. Finding that students read, reflected on, and responded to each other's electronic postings in ways that led by the end of the term to more complex thinking, Sherman concluded, "While the strategies . . . obviously take up more instructor time in reading, responding and evaluating, . . . the gains in student writing abilities and critical thinking (rhetoric), and the motivating stimulation of the class discussions are worth the efforts."

At the University of North Carolina at Charlotte, Deborah Langsam introduced "biochallenges, . . . questions that asked for applications of the material under study," to her nonmajor biology students, who responded sometimes with applications and sometimes with additional questions, which Langsam considered to be a success in ways that WAC advocates will recognize: "Even for those students who simply had questions—and there were many—the e-mail was instructive; it provided (1) a place to try to articulate them, (2) a person who would respond, and (3) an opportunity to learn just in the putting of the question" (Langsam and Yancey 236).

In her literature classes for engineering students, Paula Gillespie of Marquette University found that e-mail journal exchanges led resistant students (resistant to literature, not computers) to discuss fiction enthusiastically and "not only allowed students to write to learn, but . . . allowed them to see how others wrote to learn" (230). After using a read-write-respond approach for an online southern literature class at Loyola University, Barbara Ewell wrote, "The high quality of student engagement and learning that resulted more than convinced me that this kind of structured electronic discussion certainly can substitute for the classroom discussions that many teachers most fear losing in delivering their courses electronically." Featured in *Learning Literature in an Era of Change: Innovations in Teaching* are chapters on incorporating electronic communication—in particular, multimedia—into the teaching of both undergraduate and graduate literature and literary theory courses (Hickey and Reiss).

Many projects incorporate a variety of informal and formal writing tasks in various combinations of print and electronic media, thus reflecting the reality most professionals encounter in their workday lives. For example, Teresa M. Redd of Howard University taught an all-black composition class of engineering students that was linked with a predominately white graphic design class at Montana State University taught by Stephanie Newman-James. E-mail enabled these two classes, 1,600 miles apart, to produce a print publication about racism, with essays by Howard students, graphics by MSU students, and reprints of e-mail exchanges from both groups. Just as important as the development of students' rhetorical and electronic abilities was the knowledge gained by both groups about the difficult social issue of racism. In her essay describing this project, Redd concludes with the words of an MSU student: "The experiences you and your friends have gone through is something I don't have to think about very often and they are startling and painful to read. . . . I truly hope that being able to work together on this project will result in some new understanding and breaking down of barriers" (Redd 146). Another approach that involves the interplay of the visual and the verbal is June Woest's e-art field trips for her online art appreciation courses at Houston Community College. After their visits to art Web sites, students report to a class bulletin board in one of five designated "writing styles" that include making up a story, describing design elements, and using adjectives. She observes that "the quality of the student's written communication skills improve while understanding and interpretation of the visual arts deepen" as a result of their online work.

Electronic communication also helps establish connections beyond classes, colleges, and countries. For instance, formal debate across international borders links business students from the University of Rhode Island with counterparts in Turkey and Germany for a project called International E-mail Debate, guiding students "to understand the constructed nature of each debate position and to appreciate the differences of perspective rooted in divergent cultural experience" (Shamoon 158).

These examples illustrate the benefits for teachers across the curriculum that communication-rich uses of computers have long brought to writing teachers. They also demonstrate the direction that new technologies can take within WAC/CAC programs that incorporate ECAC. With e-mail at their fingertips, teachers across the curriculum can use writing-to-learn online to encourage participation in the writing-as-thinking process, to build communication confidence and competence, to establish authentic peer audiences, and to provide a printable record of the exchanges that subsequently can be used as study guides and resources for planning formal papers. Students learn to use the discourse of the disciplines informally and to ask questions either privately with e-mail to the professor or more publicly with e-mail to class groups, learning even as they frame the questions of their readers.

COLLABORATIVE LEARNING AND WRITING ONLINE

Nearly a decade has passed since Thomas Barker and Fred Kemp described the still-new concept of the collaborative, networked writing classroom as "enfranchising, open, and egalitarian," and its theory as "an application of postmodern pedagogy to classroom needs" (23). The same year Lisa Ede and Andrea Lunsford wrote:

> Nowhere are the competing and disparate definitions of selfhood and collaboration more apparent than in the technological revolution. . . . [W]e must find ways of describing—and valuing—forms of collective or collaboratively generated and electronically disseminated knowledge, knowledge that will not easily fit into our old forms of individual intellectual property. (viii–ix)

Although they were concerned primarily with writing and the teaching of writing, these two collaborative pairs anticipated with their social constructivist perspectives on technology those concerns that would soon confront teachers from every discipline in what we now call ECAC.

Information technology offers a range of tools that make collaborative learning easier and perhaps inevitable. The sharing of quantities of information across distances at a speed more like a telephone message than a telegraph, and the ease of editing even text-based electronic mail messages—for example, writing in ALL CAPS between the lines to distinguish commentary typographically from the original message—gave writers new ways to collaborate faster and at a detailed interlinear level that soon would be developed further as word processors incorporated comment features and text comparison markings similar to those used by professional editors. Pop-up windows, colored type, and yellow highlight swashes superimposed on drafts in progress could pass back and forth between writers, editors, and collaborators to clarify who had changed what.

Writing teachers were quick to adopt these word-processing enhancements that were developed for the business world. The ability to save and compare multiple drafts was a perfect adjunct to process writing. Copy- or cut-and-paste techniques supported revision well. Writing teachers also were early adopters of the groupware that businesses had been using; early "real time" conferencing tools such as the ENFI project, Real-Time Writer, Daedalus InterChange, Connect, Aspects, and CommonSpace were designed by or in collaboration with educators to take advantage of the writing-to-learn capabilities of these shared writing environments. Internet-based MOOs (multi-user domains, object oriented), chat rooms, forums, and new whiteboard technologies that allow people to write synchronously or asynchronously on the same document are extending this capability even further.

The conversational aspects of synchronous shared writing spaces provide alternative discussion media for any subject, as evidenced by the use of these platforms outside of writing classes. At Virginia Tech, for example, collaborative writing software has been used by teachers in history, biology, and art history. It is not surprising that English-as-a-second-language or foreign-language instructors were early adopters of the tools that encouraged students to write to each other online either in networked writing environments or with Internet connections to students in other countries.

The Internet has expanded opportunities for writing online in elementary, middle, and secondary schools as well. Pamela Childers, director of the Caldwell Writing Center at the McCallie School, Chattanooga, Tennessee, collaborates with faculty across the disciplines not only to use writing for learning but also to use the World Wide Web and e-mail to support instruction. She sees the advantages of using "the visuals of technology to help students learn, think and verbalize their thought," but cautions that "people contact needs to be made at the point where students and faculty should encourage appropriate interaction for intellectual, social, spiritual, and physical growth."

The George School, a private secondary school in Pennsylvania, incorporates computer conferencing in history, science, foreign language, ESL, and English instruction (McBride). And at Pioneer High School in Michigan, history teacher Robin Wax uses synchronous computer conferences to provide

> the multicultural classroom environment my students so desperately need. The use of Writing-to-Learn methods with the history curriculum has pulled together ideas rather than separated them. . . . The format of computerized instruction makes access to ideas and to other learners and to means of expression easy, fun, and permanent.

Efforts to establish links between classes in the same and different disciplines, in the past restricted by complex exchange logistics, have been made easier by Internet chat rooms and MOOs, where students can meet online from computers anywhere on campus, anywhere in the world. Online pals became the pen pals of the 1980s and 1990s. Same-time conversations with the immediacy of telephone calls and the reflective and archival advantage of text were especially appealing in classrooms where a single computer could provide a connection to students on other continents. Many World Wide Web sites now provide gateways for matching classes at every school level.

Learning communities also are well served by computer communication. At the University of South Florida, for example, a FIPSE grant project under the direction of Joseph Moxley is supporting the integration of both WAC and technology into USF's Learning Community Initiative, and its 1999 conference, Creating and Sustaining Learning Communities: Connections, Collaboration, and Crossing Borders, focused on the use of technology to support learning communities ("Learning Communities"). Members of the English department are collaborating with colleagues in social science, history, non-Western perspectives, and art to teach and grade collaboratively, working with the same fifty students over a two-year period. This initiative, says Christian R. Weisser, was a direct response to WAC and to the university's need for "assessment, organization, and integrated assignments." Through listservs, MOOs, and student Web pages that link students and teachers across the curriculum, technology can "facilitate and 'bridge the gaps'" while strengthening writing for thinking and learning as well as writing for academic success. Computer communication also plays an important role in the George Mason New Century College learning community model described in this volume (Zawacki and Williams, Chapter 5 [of *WAC for the New Millennium*]).

PROGRAMS: ECAC AND WAC, WRITING CENTERS, AND CENTERS FOR TEACHING AND LEARNING

At present, few collegewide programs formally identify themselves as Electronic Communication Across the Curriculum or by a similar name. Programs within a wide range of departments and initiatives do exist, however, many of them shared ventures among writing or WAC/CAC programs, writing centers, technology centers, and centers for teaching and learning. The need for such explicit connections has been apparent to many WAC leaders (Walvoord; Thaiss). In her travels to campuses throughout the country, Cynthia L. Selfe reports that one of the most frequent questions from faculty is, "How are other teachers using computers to support writing across the curriculum?" (xiii). Centers for teaching and learning have been in the forefront of recognizing that communication-intensive pedagogies best serve students as their teachers incorporate new technologies into instruction.

At the University of Illinois at Urbana-Champaign, Gail E. Hawisher of the Center for Writing Studies, which houses the WAC program, has been active in the engineering department's asynchronous learning network (ALN) project. "Both WAC and ALN," Hawisher and Pemberton (formerly part of the program) report, "are capable of reshaping the social contexts of classes if we bring to them the necessary kinds of critical thinking and pedagogical values that successful educational innovations require." Reflecting on the electronic messages of an engineering class, they conclude that "in good WAC fashion the students often come upon the answers to the problems they pose after they have been able to articulate the problem and after they write (or talk) it through with classmates" (27–28).

In another WAC-influenced technology program, the Mellon Multimedia Courses project at Spelman College in Atlanta, a division of their Comprehensive Writing Program, has electronic communication as its core (Hocks and Bascelli). Psychology, art, Spanish, and French faculty have been active in Spelman's initial projects to use electronic communication.

Some of the connections between WAC/CAC and information technology are piecemeal, some are still in the form of initial steps, and a few already combine to comprise full-fledged programs. In 1996, Patricia Williams, director of the Across-the-University Writing Program at Sam Houston State University,[4] wrote to the WAC-L listserv that the program's workshops and newsletter have featured writing using technology; "I think we are making progress in learning how technology can enhance both student and faculty writing." Writing centers and WAC/CAC programs around the country have been making similar progress a few classes and workshops at a time. One comprehensive initiative is the University of Missouri–Columbia's Institute for Instructional Technology (MUIIT),[5] a group of faculty and staff organized by the Program for Excellence in Teaching to facilitate use of educational technology to enhance teaching and learning. MUIIT has strong ties to the distinguished campus writing program directed by Martha A. Townsend. With its extensive and clearly organized links to resources under the headings Enhancing Traditional Teaching, Changing Pedagogy, and Changing Content or Epistemology, along with examples of projects at the university and elsewhere, MUIIT hosts institutes that use an online daily journaling form. It also features discussion lists for making learning active. The writing program has its own direct ECAC initiative in "Expressive Media: Composing with Technology," developed by Andy White of the writing program with Peter Campbell and Marsha Lyon. In an e-mail message to WAC-L, Townsend emphasized that "writing to learn" in the disciplines includes the use of multimedia.

The Virginia Tech professional development program[6] designed to train faculty to incorporate technology into their courses in meaningful ways has generated communication-rich approaches that include a history professor using networked synchronous conferencing to stimulate interaction in a classroom; a philosophy professor incorporating threaded discussion forums into Web-enhanced classes; and a professor of veterinary medicine having students author multimedia presentations for their classes. Carol A. Bailey, director of the Virginia Tech University writing program, writes that her office has close ties to both the Center for Excellence in Undergraduate Teaching and Educational Technologies and the online courses at their cyberschool. These programs are visible through their Web site, which includes Peter Shires's reflections on the effort and time involved in retooling his veterinary medicine course, a process that "does focus faculty attention and results in improvements to course content that would not otherwise be accomplished. . . . As our specialties involve considerable visual and audible evaluation of problems, this methodology of teaching is well suited to our needs."

For many faculty who attend workshops to learn how well-chosen technology applications can enhance their teaching, the response is similar to Shires's and familiar to those who conduct WAC/CAC/ECAC workshops: the focus on rethinking their courses and curricula is as important as learning new pedagogical and technological strategies. Intrigued by the possibilities of WAC/CAC/ECAC, educators look for ways in which freewriting, journaling, multiple drafts, and collaborative problem solving might guide their students' learning. In other words, WAC/CAC does indeed drive course and curricular change.

So too does information technology, despite claims that the pedagogy should drive the technology. Influenced by the editing opportunities of word processing, writing teachers sought ways to bring these tools to their students. Before long, their colleagues also wanted their students' papers spell checked and printed in Times Roman. Impressed with the information exchanges facilitated by e-mail, teachers looked for ways this platform could serve students, and thus developed discussion groups and paper exchanges. Encouraged by the universality of HTML and the dynamic communication combination of text, graphics, sound, and video, teachers taught themselves and their students the discourse of Web pages, a precursor to Web portfolios.

Before the widespread availability of e-mail and Internet computer conferencing, internal synchronous environments made possible reflective learning communities within classrooms fortunate enough to have networked computers. WAC/CAC teachers who participated in such communities introduced their colleagues in other fields to the benefits of WAC's write-to-learn emphasis through informal freewriting and other methods of prewriting, collaborative planning and exploration of topics, peer response, and multiple drafts. WAC became wired.

REFLECTIONS ON THE FUTURE OF ELECTRONIC COMMUNICATION ACROSS THE CURRICULUM

We cannot predict the future of WAC/CAC/ECAC in relation to technologies that are changing so rapidly. Not included in this chapter but on the near horizon for expanding ECAC, for example, are desktop videoconferencing and speech-generated text production. We can predict, however, that such changes will continue to bring new energy to WAC/CAC programs as they consider their place in the academy of the twenty-first century. We anticipate increasing alliances between WAC and other departments as pedagogies promoted by communication across the curriculum offer some of the best instructional uses of information technology. When she wrote the following statement in 1996, Reiss was thinking of then-innovative uses of computers in her own college's initial projects: "What is e-mail but the epistolary pedagogy so often used by WAC advocates? Now students use writing-to-learn letter exchanges not only across classes and campuses but across the world. What are newsgroups and chat rooms but tools for the kinds of collaborative conversation and composition WAC has modeled?" (722). Today these approaches are commonplace.

Students whose intellectual lives sometimes seem isolated or fragmented might find that the immediacy of electronic media helps them connect, as did students in Mary Beth Oliver's Introduction to Communication Research course at Virginia Tech. One student responded to an anonymous class evaluation that e-mail "makes a large class seem smaller and the teacher more accessible" and provides a "self-evaluation process of what we understand or don't understand." Such self-assessment online resembles the familiar WAC activities on paper of freewrites, microthemes, question-and-answer pairs, one-minute essays, five-minute responses, and journals. With an optional e-mail listserv, students can get timely feedback from classmates and professors in the "middle ground" of WAC/CAC/ECAC activities that new technologies generate almost automatically. With teacher guidance, such e-mail lists can also support more structured write-to-learn activities such as required daily or weekly messages, small-group problem solving, and posted focused freewrites.

Electronic portfolios are likely to become more widespread, perhaps driven by employer demand. Multimedia résumés can enhance job searches and graduate school applications; they might even become the standard for the future. A first-year writing class, or a general education core course, or a student orientation class might be the first step in creating a Web site that presents selected student projects to represent their work in a variety of courses. Most of these projects are likely to involve substantial writing and other forms of communication, and their public nature on the Web might lead the teachers who "approve" these projects for publication to become more directly involved with WAC/CAC/ECAC. For in some ways, electronic port-folios may lead to a natural but public performance assessment for both stu-dents and teachers. At least one college has initiated such a requirement beginning with the class of 2000, according to a report in the *Chronicle of Higher Education*. The academic use of the Web "is meant to enhance the academic-advising process by helping students to reflect on the whirlwind of their college experiences and to articulate what they're getting out of Kalama-zoo's offerings" (Young, "A New Graduation" A23).

Portfolios are not a new concept in writing classes; electronic portfolios were featured in a 1996 special issue of *Computers and Composition* (Yancey) and constitute one of the four perspectives of *Situating Portfolios: Four Perspec-tives* (Yancey and Weiser). The implications for broad professional use are suggested by Kristine L. Blair and Pamela Takayoshi, one of whose students used Hypercard to build a writing portfolio "not unlike the construction of a prospective employee portfolio. It opens with an introductory welcome to her portfolio, followed with a copy of her resume, and then particular samples of her design work" (362). When such portfolios are posted on the Web for all to read, one of the perceived gaps between personal writing, classroom writing, and public writing will have been bridged, for such writing will serve the purposes of the individual student, of classroom instruction, and of formal public communication.

David R. Russell ends his historical overview of college and university writing with this insight:

> With WAC, the old battles between access and exclusion, excellence and equity, scientific and humanist worldviews, liberal and professional edu-cation, all come down to very specific questions of responsibility for cur-riculum and teaching. WAC ultimately asks: in what ways will graduates of our institutions use language, and how shall we teach them to use it in those ways? (*Writing in the Academic Disciplines* 307)

"WAC Wired" suggests that future graduates increasingly will use computer technology to communicate and to learn, and that educators will increasingly use computer technology to teach students to communicate and to learn. We consider traditional WAC/CAC pedagogy to be among the most effective and available ways to carry out this task. But we are aware of the dangers in doing so and the major hurdles to overcome.

In 1990, before the rise of ECAC, Art Young and Toby Fulwiler delineated what they called "the enemies of WAC," that is, those attitudes and practices that subvert WAC's efforts to transform education: resistance from faculty, resistance from students, resistance from English departments, compart-mentalized academic administration, faculty reward systems, departmental priorities, unstable leadership, and testing mania. This litany is familiar to WAC/CAC practitioners, and we might update it for the electronic age sim-ply by adding computer phobia. But there are at least four areas of concern we should pause to consider further: issues of access, of the faculty reward sys-tem, of copyright and intellectual property, and of academic freedom.

Of particular importance for ECAC are the access and equity concerns incumbent upon such expensive tools as computer networks. One major concern is that the pedagogical benefits of information technology will benefit a new elite with access to powerful computers and networks, thereby creating a new information gap and widening the existing economic gaps between wealthy and poor school districts, poor and middle-class students, and native-language speakers and international users with little or no English-language proficiency. Still, this peril is accompanied by the enormous promise of such technology that leads faculty to advocate for improved general student access in higher education and that leads community members themselves to wire their local public schools, libraries, and community centers on Net Days. At one time, books, televisions, and ballpoint pens were out of the reach of nonwealthy citizens; free libraries, less expensive televisions, and disposable pens have made these technologies widely available. Educators must continue to press for universal access to information and tools for communication at all economic and educational levels.

When Chris Thaiss described "interactive language-rich technology techniques" as the "single biggest influence on ways we define writing and thinking about the curriculum and across the curriculum" ("Reliving"), the word *thinking* clearly paralleled *writing*. Thaiss also acknowledged the impact of distance learning on WAC, asserting that "in on-line curricula there's no escaping writing and no teacher thinks of it as an 'extra responsibility'" ("When WAC" 8). We also should recognize, however, that such time-intensive literacy instruction often does involve "extra" work for teachers, work that deserves appropriate recognition and compensation. Currently, the most interactive distance learning pedagogies are constructed around writing, reading, and responding, the responding element providing the socially constructed dynamic and student-centered learning that WAC/CAC/ECAC promotes. ECAC advocates can and should assume a leadership role in distance education projects to speak for communication-intensive communities of learners rather than a correspondence course model of distance learning.

In response to their members' concerns that teaching innovations in general and experimentation with new technologies in particular will interfere with and even damage promotion and tenure opportunities, professional organizations such as the College Art Association, the Conference on College Composition and Communication, and the Modern Language Association, among others, are drafting policy statements regarding ownership of electronic media, institutional support for the time-intensive training and development teachers need to use new media, and revision of promotion and tenure policies to reflect faculty innovations and contributions with new media. Academic conventions now feature sessions on the impact of technology on the discipline and on teaching the discipline. ECAC, we trust, will play an important role in changing many college cultures that devalue undergraduate teaching in the interest of encouraging research, publications, and grants.

Nobody can deny that information production and distribution has changed radically in the past decade now that most major publications put their archives online. After a little time online, people remember URLs as they do oft-dialed telephone numbers: even if they've never bought a book there, educators know www.amazon.com; even if they've never taken the tour, they know about www.whitehouse.gov; if they're looking for academic jobs, they certainly know www.chronicle.com. And they know how to cut and paste and forward and download and file. Issues on how to cite sources, verify sources, copy sources, revise sources, and republish sources are all in the process of being negotiated for electronic media, and the media itself are changing much more rapidly than our laws and accepted publication practices. For example, the *Chronicle of Higher Education* reported that a "former University of Nebraska student has sued the university and a professor for posting on the Internet a personal essay the student had written in class several years earlier" ("Former U. of Nebraska Student"). What are the legal and ethical implications when a student or faculty member "publishes" a Web page or electronic portfolio on the college's Web site?

New technologies add new issues and exacerbate familiar challenges to WAC/CAC. Among these are the role of the professor—in particular, the talented lecturers in higher education reluctant to relinquish the stage to student collaborative projects, and also the teachers in professional fields obligated to prepare students for mastery of material that will meet the criteria of board certification exams. Not to be overlooked is the uncertain impact on promotion and tenure for faculty who invest time and energy in instructional innovations, nor the administrative mandate for larger classes. In the October 3, 1997, issue of the *Chronicle of Higher Education,* for example, the Information Technology section headlines read, "Rethinking the Role of the Professor in an Age of High-Tech Tools" and "Canadian University Promises It Won't Require Professors to Use Technology." Despite the potential of technology to foster the interaction that stimulates learning and prepares students for the contemporary workplace, Phil Agre, associated professor of communication at the University of California, San Diego, warns that "there will be an economic incentive to reduce the interactive components to reduce the labor cost" (Young, "Rethinking" A26). Thus, the struggle to integrate technology into instruction meets an economic reality: it is expensive. Further, the educational uses of technologies that promote active learning and the interactive development of communication abilities are more expensive than those uses that offer only a one-way transfer of information. While administrators sometimes use technology to increase class sizes, outsource instruction, or increase the use of television, video, and computer packages in order to make institutions more efficient, proponents of quality over quantity continue to advocate for instruction that utilizes and emphasizes the higher-order communication and problem-solving skills that citizens, scholars, and workers need to succeed in this information age. Some chief academic officers clearly appreciate the Internet for its active learning capabilities. Despite reservations that "electronic communication will always lack critical elements of 'real' conversation," Neil L. Rudenstine, former president of Harvard, affirmed the power of "conversational learning" from online discussions and the opportunities for faculty and students to reconsider the teaching-learning process. He could have been an ECAC program director when he wrote that the Internet "calls upon the user to be active and engaged: following leads, distinguishing the substantial from the trivial, synthesizing insights drawn from different sources, formulating new questions. Seated before the computer, a student is challenged to make something happen, to act or pursue, rather than merely react or absorb" (A48). It is not the computer, of course, that challenges the student, but the computer-supported activity designed and guided by an instructor whose "prompts" lead students to fruitful inquiry, research, synthesis, and collaborative writing. Therefore, the professional development workshops that have characterized WAC/CAC for a quarter of a century must broaden to include ECAC as active learning with computer-mediated communication. As we demonstrate to teaching colleagues and administrators the potential for such learning, we provide an enlightened response to challengers such as Sven Birkerts and David Noble.

Thus, issues of access, intellectual property, budget and administration, and academic freedom are interrelated. With the advent of distance learning and online courses, who makes key decisions about whether to include a course in a college's online offerings? Or what the course will include? Or whether a course must be taught online? Or who will be able to enroll? Many teachers fear outside interference with course objectives and instructional methods for nonacademic reasons by enthusiastic proponents of the new media or by administrators looking to cut budgets, or sell products, or win legislative support. They fear a college requirement that all course instructors must maintain a Web page, without first conducting an inquiry into whether all courses will benefit from such a tool. They question whether all students should be required to purchase a particular laptop computer. They fear that distance learning might be set up as skill-and-drill, an exercise in dissemination and regurgitation. They lament the megadollars and time and effort spent on technology that might better serve academic purposes such as smaller class sizes. And for such good reasons, we need to proceed with caution, but proceed nonetheless.

As we write this chapter, another educational commission has issued a national report: the Boyer Commission on Educating Undergraduates in the Research University's *Reinventing Undergraduate Education: A Blueprint for America's Research Universities.*[7] Among its ten recommendations are these four: remove barriers to interdisciplinary education, link communication skills and course work, use information technology creatively, and cultivate a sense of community. Hawisher and Selfe also suggest the way forward: "A major project for English teachers will be to develop a responsible professional vision—a vision grounded in sound composition theory and practice, and tempered by critical, informed, and humanistic perspectives on technology and reading" (312). Indeed, teachers across the curriculum might take on this responsibility through ECAC programs or committees. To accept such a responsibility, to be educational activists, WAC/CAC and ECAC faculty and program administrators can exercise wise and informed leadership for the electronic age on their campuses. And while the vision for each campus should be unique to that campus, we can see an outline for a national vision when we combine the list of faculty concerns with which this chapter began with the ECAC projects described throughout: communication, computers, active learning, collaboration, interdisciplinary, international, multicultural, across education levels, interactive, reading out to the public, reality-based, research into practice, adapting quickly to rapidly changing contexts. These issues are the basis of WAC/CAC/ECAC, key components of the evolving WAC vision since the 1970s, and a strong foundation for significant cultural change in higher education in the twenty-first century.

NOTES

1. The ECAC resources Web site—http://onlinelearning.tc.cc.va.us/faculty/tcreisd/projects/ecac/—lists many of these collaborations as well as WAC classic programs and gateways, WAC programs with an ECAC emphasis, and WAC/CAC programs and resources for computer-mediated communication across the curriculum. WAC now has its own online journal and resource, established in 1999 by Mike Palmquist of Colorado State University. *Academic.writing: Interdisciplinary Perspectives on Communication Across the Curriculum* takes advantage of the many communication options of electronic communication to publish refereed texts and hypertexts, links to WAC programs and publications online, columns about WAC and CAC activities, reviews of conferences of interest to WAC, reissues of out-of-print publications, and a new book first published entirely online.

2. Along with the current survey and report, previous surveys are linked to this site.

3. The terms "expressive" and "transactional" come from the work of James Britton et al., *The Development of Writing Abilities (11–18),* London: Macmillan Education, 1975. We gratefully acknowledge their influence on our thinking, even though we realize they would probably quarrel with aspects of our chart.

4. See http://www.shsu.edu/~edu_paw/.

5. Check out the Educational Technologies at Missouri Web site at http://www.etatmo.missouri.edu/.

6. The Virginia Polytechnic Institute and State University (Virginia Tech) Instructional Development Initiative Web site is http://www.edtech.vt.edu/idi.html.

7. The full text of the Boyer report is online and available in print through the Web site: http://notes.cc.sunysb.edu/Pres/boyer.nsf.

WORKS CITED

Academic.writing: Interdisciplinary Perspectives on Communication Across the Curriculum. <http://aw.colostate.edu/>.

Bailey, Carol A. E-mail to Donna Reiss. 3 Jan. 1998.

Barker, Thomas, and Fred Kemp. "Network Theory: A Post-Modern Pedagogy for the Writing Classroom." *Computers and Community: Teaching Composition in the Twenty-First Century.* Ed. Carolyn Handa. Portsmouth, NH: Boynton/Cook, 1990. 1–29.

Blair, Kristine L., and Pamela Takayoshi. "Reflections on Reading and Evaluating Electronic Portfolios." *Situating Portfolios: Four Perspectives.* Ed. Kathleen Blake Yancey and Irwin Weiser. Logan: Utah State UP, 1997. 357–69.

Boyer Commission on Educating Undergraduates in the Research University. *Reinventing Undergraduate Education: A Blueprint for America's Research Universities.* SUNY Stony Brook for the Carnegie Foundation for the Advancement of Teaching, 1998.

Britton, James N., et al. *The Development of Writing Abilities (11–18).* London: Macmillan, 1975.

Childers, Pamela. E-mail to Donna Reiss. 27 Oct. 1997.

"College of the Year: But Can They Write?" *The Best College for You, 2000.* New York: Time-Princeton Review, 2000. 63–74.

Ede, Lisa, and Andrea Lunsford. *Singular Texts/Plural Authors: Perspectives on Collaborative Writing.* Carbondale: Southern Illinois UP, 1992.

Ewell, Barbara. E-mail to Donna Reiss. 6 Oct. 1997.

"Former U. of Nebraska Student Sues over Posting of Personal Essay." *Chronicle of Higher Education* 20 Feb. 1998. 11 June 1998 <http://chronicle.com>.

Gillespie, Paula. "E-Journals: Writing to Learn in the Literature Classroom." Reiss, Selfe, and Young 207–30.

Gordon, Nicholas, and Susan Mansfield. "Computers Across the Curriculum: A Confluence of Ideas." *Computers and Composition* 6.1 (1988): 9–13.

Green, Kenneth C. *The Campus Computing Project*. Claremont, CA: Claremont Graduate University, 1997.

———. "The 1998 National Survey of Information Technology in Higher Education." *The Campus Computing Project*. 23 June 1999 <http://www.campuscomputing.net/>.

Harris, Muriel, and Madelon Cheek. "Computers Across the Curriculum: Using Writer's Workbench for Supplementary Instruction." *Computers and Composition* 1.2 (1984): 3–5.

Hawisher, Gail E., and Cynthia L. Selfe. "Wedding the Technologies of Writing Portfolios and Computers: The Challenges of Electronic Classrooms." *Situating Portfolios: Four Perspectives*. Ed. Kathleen Blake Yancey and Irwin Weiser. Logan: Utah State UP, 1997. 305–21.

Hawisher, Gail E., and Michael A. Pemberton. "Writing Across the Curriculum Encounters Asynchronous Learning Networks." Reiss, Selfe, and Young 17–39. 4 July 1999 <http://www.english.uiuc.edu/cws and http://w3.scale. uiuc.edu/scale/>.

"Help Wanted." Business News. *Virginian-Pilot* [Norfolk]. 15 Mar. 1998: D17–19.

Hickey, Dona J., and Donna Reiss. *Learning Literature in an Era of Change: Innovations in Teaching*. Sterling, VA: Stylus, 2000.

Hobson, Eric H., ed. *Wiring the Writing Center*. Logan: Utah State UP, 1998.

Hocks, Mary E., and Daniele Bascelli. "Building a Writing-Intensive Multimedia Curriculum." Reiss, Selfe, and Young 40–56. 1 Jan. 1998 <http://www.wcenter.spelman.edu/courses.html>.

Holder, Carol. E-mail to Donna Reiss. 7 Oct. 1997. 4 Jan. 1998 <http://www.faculty.csupomona.edu/center/>.

Inman, James A., and Donna N. Sewell. *Taking Flight with OWLS: Examining Electronic Writing Center Work*. Mahwah, NJ: Erlbaum, 2000.

Kimball, Sara. "WAC on the Web: Writing Center Outreach to Teachers of Writing Intensive Courses." *Wiring the Writing Center*. Ed. Eric H. Hobson. Logan: Utah State UP, 1998. 62–74.

Langsam, Deborah M., and Kathleen Blake Yancey. "E-mailing Biology: Facing the Biochallenge." Reiss, Selfe, and Young 231–41.

"Learning Communities at University of South Florida." 4 July 1999 <http://www.usf.edu/~lc/ and http://www.usf.edu/~lc/conf/>.

Maimon, Elaine. "Time Future Contained in Time Past." Writing Across the Curriculum Third National Conference. Charleston, SC. 5–8 Feb. 1997.

McBride, Stephanie. *Testimonials . . . Instructors Have the Last Word*. 26 Dec. 1997 <http://www.daedalus.com/info/testimony.html>.

Oliver, Mary Beth. "Incorporating Technology in the Classroom: Introduction to Communication Research." 3 Jan. 1998 <http://www.edtech.vt.edu/innovations/oliver.html>.

Palmquist, Mike. "Notes on the Evolution of Network Support for Writing Across the Curriculum." *Inventing a Discipline: Rhetoric Scholarship in Honor of Richard E. Young*. Ed. Maureen Daly Goggin. Urbana, IL: NCTE, 2000. 373–402.

Redd, Teresa M. "Accommodation and Resistance on (the Color) Line: Black Writers Meet White Artists on the Internet." Reiss, Selfe, and Young 139–50.

Reiss, Donna. "A Comment on 'The Future of WAC.'" *College English* 58 (1996): 722–23.

Reiss, Donna, Dickie Selfe, and Art Young. *Electronic Communication Across the Curriculum*. Urbana, IL: NCTE, 1998.

Rudenstine, Neil L. "The Internet and Education: A Close Fit." *Chronicle of Higher Education* 21 Feb. 1997: A48.

Russell, David R. "Writing Across the Curriculum in Historical Perspective: Toward a Social Interpretation." *College English* 52 (1990): 52–73.

———. *Writing in the Academic Disciplines, 1870–1990: A Curricular History*. Carbondale: Southern Illinois UP, 1991.

Selfe, Cynthia L. Foreword. Reiss, Selfe, and Young ix–xiv.

Shamoon, Linda K. "International E-mail Debate." Reiss, Selfe, and Young 151–61.

Sherman, Lawrence W. "A Postmodern, Constructivist Pedagogy for Teaching Educational Psychology, Assisted by Computer Mediated Communications." CSCL95 Conference. Bloomington, IN. 17–20 Oct. 1995. 4 July 1999 <http://www.muohio.edu/~lwsherman/csc195.html>.

Shires, Peter. "Integrating Technology into Veterinary Medicine." 5 July 1999 <http://www.edtech.vt.edu/innovations/shires.html>.

Thaiss, Chris. "Reliving the History of WAC—Every day." Writing Across the Curriculum Third National Conference. Charleston, SC. 5–8 Feb. 1997.

———. "When WAC Becomes WE." *Composition Chronicle* 9.6 (1996): 8–9.

Townsend, Martha A. "Re: reading and . . ." E-mail to WAC-L @postoffice.cso.uiuc.edu. 30 Apr. 1997. 1 Jan. 1998 (Campus Writing Program http://www.missouri.edu/~writcwp/); (Expressive Media www.missouri.edu/~witsml/); (MUIIT http://www.missouri.edu/~muiit).

Walvoord, Barbara E. "The Future of WAC." *College English* 58 (1996): 58–79.

Wax, Robin. "University-High School Collaboration: Writing-to-Learn, Student-Centered Learning, and Computer Technology." *Wings* 2.1 (1994). 26 Dec. 1997 <http://www.daedalus.com/wings/wax.2.1.html>.

Weisser, Christian R. E-mail to Donna Reiss. 12 Oct. 1997. 5 Jan. 1998 <http://chuma.usf.edu/~cweisser>.

Williams, Patricia. "Writing/Technology." E-mail to WAC-L @postoffice.cso.uiuc.edu. 22 May 1997.

Woest, E. June. "Welcome to eArt Field Trips." 1997. 4 July 1999 <http://www.hccs.cc.tx.us/JWoest/jw_trips.htm> and "Using the Internet for Art and Writing" <http://www.hccs.cc.tx.us/JWoest/MyProjects/jw_proj.htm>.

Yancey, Kathleen Blake, ed. *Electronic Portfolios.* Spec. issue of *Computers and Composition* 13.2 (1996).

Yancey, Kathleen Blake, and Irwin Weiser, eds. *Situating Portfolios: Four Perspectives.* Logan: Utah State UP, 1997.

Young, Art, and Toby Fulwiler. "The Enemies of Writing Across the Curriculum." *Programs That Work: Models and Methods for Writing Across the Curriculum.* Ed. Toby Fulwiler and Art Young. Portsmouth NH: Heinemann-Boynton/Cook, 1990. 287–94.

Young, Jeffrey R. "Canadian University Promises It Won't Require Professors to Use Technology." *Chronicle of Higher Education* 3 Oct. 1997: A26–A28.

———. "A New Graduation Requirement at Kalamazoo: Create a Web Page." *Chronicle of Higher Education* 23 May 1997: A23.

———. "Rethinking the Role of the Professor in an Age of High-Tech Tools." *Chronicle of Higher Education* 3 Oct. 1997: A26–A28.

PART SIX

*The Rhetoric of
New Media Writing*

Introduction to Part Six

$\mathbf{A}$s we enter the 21st century, our students have become increasingly connected through digital technologies. Most obviously, cell phones and MP3 players allow students access to conversation, music, and even podcasts of college course materials from almost anywhere in an instant. But hypertext and other multimedia computer technologies have facilitated another form of connectivity: associative, hyperlinked composition. Building on earlier discussions of hypertext and multimedia literacy (such as the article by John M. Slatin on page 165), many of the pieces in this section describe a new rhetoric of connective discourse. The authors argue that composition instruction should introduce students to alternate communication genres that include not just text, but hyperlinks, multimedia, and even new types of argumentation. These pieces have become part of a growing trend toward multimodal composition, or what is often called new media writing: "writing with multiple sign systems within technology-mediated environments" (DeVoss, Cushman, and Grabill 17). New-media writing instructors contest the assumption that composition courses should only teach print, double-spaced academic essays, arguing instead for a composition experience that integrates many forms of literacy and technology. Students use computers for more than just word processing and Internet research: They produce and edit images, sounds, movies, and hypertext. Computers no longer facilitate the eventual printed word: They change the nature of composition altogether. The authors in this section emphasize that multimodal approaches to composition necessitate new associative rhetorics that recognize the connective capabilities of emerging media and the new genres, writing spaces, and forms of argumentation they create.

The tension and challenges brought on by technology's tendency toward associative rhetoric is the focus of the first piece in this section, Johndan Johnson-Eilola's "Negative Spaces: From Production to Connection in Composition." Johnson-Eilola argues that composition practice is still rooted in the assumption that texts are decidedly monolithic entities written by recognizable single authors in fairly discrete spaces. Even though composition instruction usually employs collaborative learning strategies in the classroom, students are expected to produce finalized, original works of their own, a process he calls *production*. However, Johnson-Eilola contends that Internet technologies are increasingly challenging those long-held practices by allowing fragmented, multiauthored pieces to exist in multiple spaces. Calling this view *connection*, he argues that the fragmented texts of postmodern culture arrange and connect multiple discourses and develop communities rather than focus on single individuals. He argues that acknowledging and teaching this approach in composition would encourage social responsibility and communal action among students while recognizing the multiple subjectivities inherent in postmodern discourse.

Although Johnson-Eilola's piece was published in 1998—a time when the World Wide Web was still relatively new and many current multimedia applications were not even available—his concerns are no less valid. Most composition courses still adhere to a fairly rigid view of "the" composition text which involves one student writing one paper in her own words. And, as other writers in this volume emphasize, composition teachers and researchers have become increasingly concerned about plagiarism and textual ownership—reinscribing the view that each piece of writing is disconnected (both physically and economically) from other texts. Johnson-Eilola's article predates the next two pieces in this section, which further problematize our assumptions about discrete, individualized student texts. The first of these two pieces, Sean Williams' "Part 2: Toward an Integrated Pedagogy in Hypertext," addresses Johnson-Eilola's concerns about composition practice by extending process-based pedagogy to include what he calls the design model. Williams argues that composition instruction should include both verbal (written and oral) and visual literacy, using hypertext-based assignments that integrate images, words, and links. Echoing steps of the composing process, he presents four stages of hypertext composition: planning, transformation, evaluation, and revision.

Williams explains that not only does this integrated pedagogy enhance students' visual and verbal skills, it also encourages them to explore multiple viewpoints related to any issue by juxtaposing seemingly different components and fragments, then arguing for the connections between them. In this way, students create new knowledge and new arguments from textual and visual fragments. Moreover, integrated hypertext challenges teachers to take a new position in relation to classroom authority wherein they recognize students' expanding technological literacy as well as the possibilities inherent in students' knowledge-building capabilities.

Williams presents his discussion of integrated hypertext in journal-article form, but the third piece in this section, Anthony Ellertson's "Some Notes on Simulacra Machines, Flash in First-Year Composition, and Tactics in Spaces of Interruption" uses the webbed environment of *Kairos,* an online journal, and the multimodal capabilities of Flash to present his discussion of multimodal composition. His piece includes texts, images, and video to explain the technology, theory, and literacy behind "simulacra machines," tools that help us repackage and remake previously digitized texts while immersing us in a multimodal environment of moving pictures and sound. Flash is one such technology; it allows students to create pieces that are dynamic and moving, quite unlike the more static presentational modes of hypertext and print. Ellertson argues that simulacra machines more closely align with students' literacies, which have been shaped by television and the multimedia culture.

Ellertson also presents a qualitative study of students in his own course who have created Flash-driven projects and includes portions of those projects in his *Kairos* piece. His students composed multimodal projects around a chosen central theme, including written questions and statements, still and moving images, and song. Through interviews with the students, Ellertson determines the project improved students' knowledge of multimedia technologies, increased their awareness of audience, and expanded their range of literacies. Moreover, creating their own Flash projects prompted students to critically examine media techniques in other texts, including television and the Web, combating the tendency of these media to create passive viewers.

Our collection ends with "Re: The Future of Computers and Writing: A Multivocal Textumentary," by Bill Hart-Davidson and Steven Krause, which includes fragments of conversational text from multiple voices within the computers and writing community. Hart-Davidson and Krause link pieces of face-to-face and online conversation through a script, including scene direction and lighting, mimicking the action of video. This multimodal format epitomizes the type of nontraditional, connective rhetoric described by the other writers in this section.

Hart-Davidson and Krause include multiple voices within the computers and writing community, all exploring the present and future relationship between the sub-field of computers and writing and the general field of composition studies. Some of the participants on the discussion question the validity of even maintaining computers and writing as a separate field from composition studies as a whole because so many teachers and students utilize technology in most of their daily composing activities. Other writers in this piece argue that computers and composition (or computers and writing) is now a limiting moniker to describe their work because the field covers all types of literacies, including visual texts, and it engages many technologies other than computers. Labels such as rhetoric and technology are arguably more appropriate to describe the wide range of literate practices enabled by digital communication tools, including those that have emerged at the turn of the millennium. Indeed, as multimedia software, mobile phones, and MP3 players increasingly infiltrate our students' literate lives, and computers in the classroom have become a "traditional" mainstay of education, "computers and writing" is an exciting field of study.

REFERENCES

DeVoss, Dànielle Nicole, Ellen Cushman, and Jeffrey T. Grabill. Infrastructure and Composing: The *When* of New Media Writing. *College Composition and Communication* 57, 2005. 14–44.

28 Negative Spaces: From Production to Connection in Composition

JOHNDAN JOHNSON-EILOLA

Writing has always been about making connections: between writer and readers, across time, and through space (Eisenstein; Ong). At another level, writing connects ideas and people. We have come to understand relations operating through footnoting, repetition, vocabulary, parenthetical citation, paraphrase, and commentary (Porter, "Intertextuality"; Devitt; Hilbert; Berkenkotter, Huckin, and Ackerman). At this second level, it is now common to see such intertextual connections as so pervasive that they question the possibility of necessity for subjects to speak in unified, single voices: we live (and literally are at least partially "composed") at the nexus connecting an apparently infinite number of social and technological forces of varying weights, strengths, and directions.

In many respects, my assertions are nothing new. Composition theorists and practitioners have, for some years, explored the idea of subjectivity as a multiple, dynamic, often contradictory set of forces acting to construct people in their everyday lives, especially in writing and reading texts. Social construction and postmodernism in composition theory and practice go back at least twenty-five years (if not further), although much of these complex and wide-ranging movements remain rooted in outdated notions of what counts as a text in composition practice. Even though theorists regularly apply the term *text* to a variety of cultural artifacts, in the composition classroom *text* remains rooted in relatively concrete, individualist notions of authorship. This often uncriticized viewpoint persists across numerous sites, including classrooms involving collaborative writing or environments such as hypertext. The reasons for this persistence become apparent when we trace the history of social construction and postmodernism, including ideas about authorship, ownership, media, intertextuality, and process theory.

Social construction gained popularity with Kenneth Bruffee's early work in composition. Bruffee argues that writing depends on and contributes to social conversations: "We converse; we internalize conversation as thought;

From *Literacy Theory in the Age of the Internet*. Ed. Todd Taylor and Irene Ward. New York: Columbia, 1998. 17–33.

and then by writing, we re-immerse conversation in its external, social medium" (641). Bruffee characterizes writing as internalized conversation, an activity learned through social interaction. One of the problems of education is that students seek to enter new communities (the workplace or the academy) but do not yet have the knowledge necessary to act as "knowledgeable peers" in the community conversation. Collaboration between students can begin to bridge these gaps because "pooling the resources that a group of peers brings with them to the task may make accessible the normal discourse of the new community they together hope to enter" (644). John Trimbur revises Bruffee's model in order to highlight issues of power and dissensus in society. Traditional models of collaborative learning, Trimbur suggests, perpetuate existing structures of unequal power in classrooms, corporations, and factories because they "bolster morale, promote identification with the corporation, legitimize differential access to knowledge and status, and increase productivity" (611). Trimbur proposes a new emphasis on *dissensus* that does not replace consensus but sees it as one way in which power functions to "provide students with exemplary motives to imagine alternative worlds and transformations of social life and labor" (615).

Writing teachers in computer classrooms have added weight to Trimbur's complications of consensus. Lester Faigley, for example, discusses the ways in which writing in networked classrooms often disintegrates community in significant ways: in electronic discussions, students "are forced to confront different ways of constituting meaning from experience and to negotiate those meanings with other students" (185).

But while we have come to value interconnection and dissensus in composition as it acts to construct texts and subjects, we often fail to reconsider the fundamental concept of what counts as a text. We value connection, but only secondarily. We still think of the text as a relatively coherent body of information with determinable bounds produced by an author of one sort or another. (That author may be a group of individuals acting in concert, more or less.) We teach writing as a process, but primarily as a way to map more clearly a final product: the text, the best draft, produced at the end of the writer's struggle to make meaning. We want to point to some*thing*, written by some*one*. Even when working in hypertext, a medium defined by many as exploding traditional notions of writing and authorship (Bolter; Landow; Slatin), the presence of connections between nodes often acts only to contextualize the positive objects (the text or graphics located within the nodes). Discussing a hypothetical hypertext on Joyce's *Ulysses,* Landow points out that if one possessed a hypertext system in which our putative Joyce article was linked to all the other materials it cited, it would exist as part of a much larger system, in which the totality might count more than the individual document; the article would now be woven more tightly into its context than would a printed counterpart (5). In short, while hypertext suggests new possibilities for connection, most of our current uses apply links to augment our visions of traditional authorship: writing with individual letters and words made up by the *author* of that text.

None of this is to say that we should abandon the notion of text production. But what would happen if we disposed, for the moment, with the text and looked primarily at the relations? What would happen if we wrote with fragments?

In this essay, I begin by briefly tracing some of the reasons for our current definitions of *text* and *writer*. Following this analysis, I highlight some of the opportunities for alternative views of writing based on open hypertexts such as those possible (but still rare) on the World Wide Web. Such spaces, which follow an associational rather than accumulative or circulating economy (Johnson-Eilola), are "written" by the mere act of linking together preexisting materials, something Gregory Ulmer has termed a "heuritics" of multimedia. In his attempts to rethink the concept of invention in a postprint world, Ulmer intends heuritics as part of the transition from print logics (linear/indexical) to hypermedia logics (associational) (*Heuritics* 36). A primary aspect of heuritics is chorography, a rethinking of space. The roots of chorography are numerous, including geography (where it describes a method of historicizing spaces) and Plato via Derrida (where it describes an *inventio* founded on geography). Chorography operates through "function[s] by means of pattern making, pattern recognition, pattern generation. It is not that memory is no longer thought of as 'place,' but that the notion itself of spatiality has changed" (36).

Furthermore, although Ulmer explicitly lays out his work in *Heuritics* as applying to hypermedia, heuristic texts develop toward linear, relatively static works. "Grammatology (in the Stacks of) Hypermedia," for example, is written as a linear string of quotations from sources as diverse as colonialist narratives, hypertext theory, and cinema theory. According to Ulmer, the material comes from a "diverse bibliography of materials relevant to hypermedia" (141). While the text is insightful—and Ulmer's introduction to the text raises a number of important concepts—the text itself is still constructed in the format of a line, although the associational qualities of the text are present in the form of intertextuality and in the actions of the reader linking the material in the text to other, personal responses in the act of reading. The text does not depart physically from book culture and, in essence, remains ineffectual in changing it. It is, in fact, difficult to reconcile Ulmer's linear, print texts with the associational networks of multimedia, except as analogies and examples of the slippages within cultural systems of signs. From Ulmer's work, however, we can borrow a number of useful concepts, especially his emphasis on collage technique, "relying on the remotivation of preexisting fragments in a new context for the production of its own significance" (142).

A Brief History of Product

Writing has historically been viewed as product, something produced as (literally) an afterthought in response either to deeply held and inchoate feelings (expressivism) or to seeing the world truthfully (objectivism). In either case, writing is the result of other activities. The expressivist, subjective paradigm focuses on the activities of feeling truthfully and then expressing those feelings in language. The objectivist paradigm approaches language as a (usually imperfect) lens for describing external reality. In contrast to these product-oriented conceptions of writing, the triumph of the process approach is that it attempts to gain access to the previously ignored (and often hidden) activities of writing and reading texts. According to Donald Murray, "Most of us are trained as English teachers by studying the product: writing. Our critical skills are honed by examining literature, which is finished writing; language as it has been used by authors. And then, fully trained in the autopsy, we go out and are assigned to teach our students to write, to make language live" (89).

The process approach reconfigures the teaching of writing so that, rather than practicing medicine based on autopsy, as Murray put it, we understand (and help our students understand) the processes of living. Maxine Hairston, summarizing the influence of Mina Shaughnessy's research on basic writers, insists that "we cannot teach students to write by looking only at what they have written. We must also understand how that product came into being, and why it assumed the form that it did. We have to try to understand what goes on during the internal act of writing and we have to intervene during the act of writing if we want to affect its outcome" (22).

More recently, process pedagogy has been rethought to focus not only on the production of the text but also the power structures in which that text emerges. Bruce Herzberg, for example, details the experiences of students working as tutors in adult literacy programs at a shelter in Boston. While tutors early on in the project read texts such as Mike Rose's *Lives on the Boundary* and Jonathan Kozol's *Savage Inequalities* and "are indeed distressed by systematic discrimination against poorer people and disenfranchised groups" (312), the same tutors tended to see their own tutees as disadvantaged by personal problems: lack of motivation, alcoholism, mental disease. But over a long period of tutoring, discussing, reading, and writing, Herzberg points out, students learned not only to tutor but also (and perhaps primarily) to "investigate the social and cultural reasons for the existence of illiteracy—the reasons, in other words, that the students needed to perform the valuable service they were engaged in" (316–17). Similarly critical versions of process have been constructed by computer and writing theorists such as Marilyn Cooper and Cynthia L. Selfe, Susan Romano, and Allison Regan, who point out the potential for computer networks to facilitate deeper understanding of process as well as critical social inquiry.

Clearly, our conceptions of writing have shifted dramatically over the last twenty years or so. What is most striking about this shift, however, is that the process paradigm perpetuates the idea that the text is a product, a concrete, relatively bounded object for viewing, even though it develops through a process of critical inquiry and may enact or reflect social changes. Portfolio systems of assessment, for example, perpetuate the idea of text-as-product. Portfolio methods actually refine and strengthen notions of the text as relatively coherent and bounded through a historicization of the concrete activities of writing and revision. Liz Hamp-Lyons and William Condon, for example, describe portfolios as "a more complex, more comprehensive 'snap-shot' of the writer's ability" (181). The portfolio acts as a series of analytical measurements showing how a writer's work has progressed from start to finish. Portfolios are surely an improvement over conventional term-paper assignments, to be graded with red pen for problems in structure, development, transitions, style, grammar, and spelling. But, at the same time, the portfolio points only *implicitly* to other voices, to social and political forces that determine the value of the text in the portfolio.

For years, compositionists have thought that moving from product to process offered a more dynamic, humanistic, social approach to composing. Perhaps it does. But as James Berlin correctly pointed out some time ago, the process approach grows out of a cognitivist view of writing, understanding text production as a dynamic process that occurs in a writer's mind. For these reasons, portfolios are constructed as a way to take time-sequenced slices of the development of product over time, toward some tangible, final goal. Always, the goal relates to what the individual writer is able to produce, in *their own words*. Although in many ways we have moved away from an expressivist approach to writing, in other ways, we have barely departed from that school. But if we examine these assumptions against the evolution of the social construction movement, especially as it has been taken up by cultural studies approaches to composition, the social model would have us focus on the creation and negotiation of contexts rather than the production of an "original" text. Unfortunately, however, while current approaches to research-based writing do begin with the process of locating information, as practiced in most classrooms today, these approaches place primary value not on the collection and arrangement of information but on the text the student produces.

It is not surprising therefore that collaborative writing is so difficult: texts are valued when they speak in a single, authentic voice. The field's recent attempts to place some value on dissensus points to the tension here, the recognition that when groups agree on everything they are merely acting, more or less, like a single mind. They are *de*socializing the text in one way or another because either they work so well together that they no longer act as individuals or (perhaps more frequently) a single person writes everything and the group takes credit. Moving to a notion of composition that values arrangement and connection/disjunction is useful for a number of reasons: the skill is more highly valued than single-authored production of a finished text in our emerging digital society because it focuses on problems easily applicable to rapidly expanding information spaces and because it embraces notions of knowledge "production" in cultural rather than cognitivist-individualist ways.

INTERDISCIPLINARY PARALLELS TO CONNECTION

Composition theory and pedagogy must overcome a reliance on the idea of writing as *production* and look instead at ways for considering the values inherent in *connection* between texts and fragments. We can begin to see more of the cultural tendencies toward connection rather than production in information systems such as the World Wide Web.

The movement to valuing connection or arrangement over production is not limited to composition; as Jean-François Lyotard points out, this shift is characteristic of an increasingly postmodernist society. Indeed, composition is behind the curve on this transition: connection is already as valuable or more valuable than simple production in a number of areas, including such diverse places as information design, architecture, art, and finance. These other fields show that while composition may still be able to think of writing as the production of text, doing so lowers the status of writing and writers. Artists such as Nam June Paik and architects such as Frank Gehry work through the techniques of collage and quoting, bringing together preexisting materials in important ways (see discussions in Jameson; Soja). Similarly, in the contemporary factory, value has shifted over time from crafting concrete products (automobiles, furniture, whatever) toward the management of information flow (Reich; Drucker). Line workers are still crucial, but they are seen as concrete instances of easily replaceable resources (either through worker turnover or by relocating plants to areas where labor is cheaper).

As social theorists including Robert B. Reich and Edward Soja have pointed out, late capitalism thrives on uneven development across states, nations, and the world. In a global economy, corporations feel no qualms about closing a plant in one area of the country or world when wage demands rise too high and opening a new plant in a low-wage area. As wages in that area rise, the cycle begins anew. As wage demands in the first area fall, corporations move back in. Workers who rely on their skills at manipulating fragments of information do not suffer in the same way during these flood/drought cycles for two primary reasons:

1. The skills of symbol manipulation command higher pay.

2. Symbolic-analytic workers can either work remotely or, related to the first reason, afford to move.

The devaluation of routine production skills can be largely attributed to the rise of automation in our culture. One of the hallmarks of automation is the removal of control from the worker (Hirschhorn; Zuboff). As workers are deskilled, it becomes easier to shift them in and out of functional positions with little training: knowledge has become exteriorized and now functions within the machine rather than in the worker.

This process, in our culture, is unavoidable.

Possibilities for negotiating this phenomenon are constructed by drawing on a number of important discourses that have already begun to rethink ideas about production. In business and industry, for example, theorists and consultants from Peter F. Drucker to Robert B. Reich now insist on a postcapitalist or decentered model in which highly paid workers orchestrate information flow in order to bring together profitable arrangements in market, finance, and production.

The shift from production to connection in massive, dynamic fields marks a parallel shift in identity, from internalized to externalized notions of subjectivity. The beginnings of these shifts are evident in composition's attraction to the ideas of process and intertextuality. But these phenomena fail to realize *connection* at a postmodernist level because they continue to focus on the production of texts rather than the connection between text fragments, what I termed above "writing with fragments." This process takes relatively radical and influential social theories in composition such as Patricia Bizzell's "contact zones" or Henry Giroux's "border-crossings" and multiplies them a thousandfold.

Bizzell, Giroux, and others have constructed useful approaches to subjectivity and cultural power, but as with most contemporary composition, such approaches are infrequently carried over adequately into conceptions of what counts as a text. On the one hand, contact and border pedagogies rely on an older model of text in which subjectivities work valiantly (if often unsuccessfully) through personal, internal battles negotiating two opposing worldviews; on the other hand, experts working in massive information contexts negotiate differences and connections on a much vaster scale including sometimes thousands of different factors and cultural forces (and millions of potential intersections). We are closer here to Frederic Jameson's cognitive mapping, the juggling of enormous amounts of information that seem to act through an externalization of at least some portions of identity. Cognitive mapping describes the ways that subjects position themselves provisionally and multiply in relation to the world and history. Cognitive maps "enable a situational representation on the part of the individual subject to that vaster and properly unrepresentable totality which is the ensemble of society's structures as a whole" (51). Jameson describes the process working within the contexts of video art such as Nam June Paik's video screens, through which a viewer "is called upon to do the impossible, namely, to see all the screens at once" (31) and John Portman's architecture, including the Los Angeles Westin Bonaventure Hotel, a "space [that] makes it impossible for us to use the language of volume or volumes any longer ... a constant busyness that gives the feeling that emptiness is here absolutely packed" (43). Subjects no longer battle it out within the recesses of their individual and somewhat fragmented minds, but "out there," in culture.

THE POLITICS OF THE LINK

The problem with this work is that it fails to question late-capitalist assumptions about society. The contradiction within late capitalism is that it values postmodernist fragmentation of identity and localization while still aligning itself with the *grand récit* of individual success stories (e.g., Bill Gates, Marc Andreesen, and even the theorists themselves: Peter Drucker, Tom Peters, etc.). There's no easy escape from this contradiction. As Frederic Jameson points out, postmodernist artists are sometimes respected because they see postmodernist conditions more truthfully, a condition that harkens back to enlightenment; Jameson is himself valued because he sees postmodernist conditions clearly. The lack of debilitating tension in most of these paradoxes is itself a hallmark of postmodernism: the ability to appropriate without shame.

The limitations of this view seem especially dangerous given the other powerful spheres in our culture now valuing the skills of connection as much or more than those of production, from information management and brokering in business, finance, and industry to working on the World Wide Web. Despite suggestions inherent in social construction, postmodernist, and cultural studies movements, we continue to think of writers as people engaged in the production of relatively original texts. A useful but unresolved tension resides in these problems of recognition: areas such as cultural studies are involved in recognizing the ways that individuals negotiate power relationships in social contexts. These investigations often productively affirm the power of individuals to resist social domination (if not to the point of resisting change, but at least by surviving and perhaps retaining a sense of dignity). At the same time, however, the importance granted to individual versus social contexts approaches a return to conservative versions of culture currently used to batter the poor, minorities, and women (and nearly everyone else not already on top): a circular argument in which only the so-called fit survive and those who survive are considered unquestionably more "fit."

This conundrum is not new. It has haunted our work since the onset of social constructionist theory. But the importance of an associational-social viewpoint in composition is critical on at least two fronts. First, it connects individuals with social contexts in ways that can help us recognize tendential forces in society and work to change them in productive ways; for example, improving welfare rather than merely restricting it or abandoning it. On the second front, our own pedagogies have increasingly valued *connection* in theory but not in practice. While we espouse social construction and cultural studies, we continue to position students as lone individuals struggling to bring forth "original" texts. Even in cases where students write papers in peer groups, we set those groups up as little more than hiveminds, the subgroup acting as an enlightenment artist capable of seeing truth better than a single student can.

In addition, framing *connection* as an eminently creative act can help us to reintroduce ethics into spheres that work repressively according to the application of "objective" principles. Take, for example, the ways in which nightly television newscasts arrange their stories. In a first-year composition course I taught in the late 1980s, I asked students to look critically at such shows to examine how each show constructed "the news." Students were almost uniformly unwilling to see newscasts as ideological because, they said, good newscasts merely reported what had happened without the distortions of commentary. Only by stepping back and examining the processes of writing and producing a newscast did it become apparent to them how difficult it is to be objective: each show involved the selection of news topics, events, or commentaries from a nearly infinite number of possibilities; once a topic was selected, each segment's writers and producers had to decide who to interview, what footage to show, and in what sequence to arrange the material; each segment needed to be ordered and edited so that it fit neatly into a half-hour format while leaving time for commercials. Critical processes such as these highlight the importance of selection and arrangement.

Viewing connection as creative act places emphasis on selection and arrangement. Traditional ideas of text, to which we still cling, identify writing with positive objects: this text as distinguished from all others. The relations between texts are taken to indicate both similarity and difference (e.g., in traditional literature reviews authors must both rehearse the similarities between their writing and others but then also prove that their work is different). But in a system of writing based on association or connection, writers are ethically responsible not only for the things they write but also for their selection and arrangement of preexisting things. It is no longer so easy to retreat behind the impartial shield of objectivism, asserting that one was only reporting facts. Reconfiguring writing as social connection requires a corresponding recognition of deep responsibility to communities that extends beyond merely asking students to collaborate on producing a text.

The individualist ethic is supported and perpetuated by institutionalized standards of text that value "original" words over connection. As James Porter points out, "Despite the considerable emphasis on collaboration and social construction, the field's principle orientation is still the individual student writer (and also, 'the text'), and the field still favors an individualist ethic (albeit largely an implicit one) over communitarian and other sorts of ethical positions" (*Rhetorical Ethics* n.p.). Ulmer raises a parallel set of critical and ethical questions concerning the use of databases.

Ulmer's linear texts are explicitly reports on the navigation of information spaces ("Grammatology" 141). The concept of information as spatial is somewhat problematic but has gained currency through numerous cultural forces, including the commodification of information in late-capitalist culture, the historical roots of patent law and intellectual property legislation, and contemporary graphical user interfaces that portray the computer screen as terrain. Ulmer, however, uses the metaphor of terrain to critique colonialist aspects of literacy and writing: "As a politics of writing, chorography rehearses this problematic, polysemous association linking the metaphors of method with a 'frontier' whose diagesis includes colonization and wars of imperialism" (*Heuritics* 166). This perspective makes literacy a condition bound up in gestures that are always potentially colonialist, especially in seeing citation as occupying or taking another's space. This does not automatically make quoting an act of violence (although in some cases quoting does enact violence), but it can help us transform our notions of space from something owned to something that is shared by a community; thus texts become social (ethical) responsibilities. If information must be spatialized (and it seems we are too far gone to avoid that), then we need to push harder toward the realization of information spaces as places where discourse communities can form.

Two Examples: Alliance for Computers and Writing and ERROR 404

In this final section, I describe two examples of works oriented toward the collection and arrangement of previously written information fragments, pointers, summaries, etc.; in other words, texts that are not original in the traditional sense of the term. Both examples reconfigure hypertext in useful ways. Although the WWW has been frequently described as a collaborative hypertext, most sites continue to apply hypertext in fairly conservative ways, as an informal form of public relations (corporate or personal), big databases, global libraries, etc. And most Web sites make only cursory and nonsubstantive use of links by merely connecting to a handful of other sites with related personal interests.

The texts that follow represent attempts to work within and against existing structures while granting importance to the acts of writing. The first text is the World Wide Web home page for the Alliance for Computers and Writing (ACW). The ACW page (Fig. 28.1) acts as a clearinghouse for information on computers and writing designed to be used primarily by composition teachers, students, and scholars who use or study computers. The subdiscipline of computers and writing is, as might be expected, growing rapidly, and the Alliance represents members from a wide variety of specializations and institutions.

FIGURE 28.1   Alliance for Computers and Writing Home Page

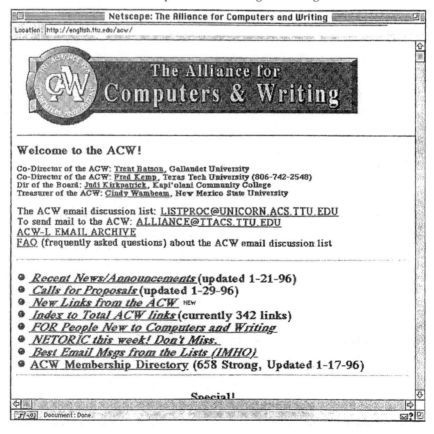

Because of the staggering amount of information on the WWW and the speed with which that information is changed, expanded, and deleted, ACW founders decided that one of the primary functions of the organization would be to disseminate information to a diverse body of users. Although the ACW site does contain a few traditional essays, most of the site is a collection of references organized to be quickly accessed and easily browsed. A small portion of the ACW index is shown in Figure 28.2; it includes a collection of pointers to other sites on the WWW that may be useful to computer and writing teachers and students who are new to the Internet.

The ACW site represents a substantial undertaking in research and revision, primarily on the part of Fred Kemp at Texas Tech University. The site is extremely popular in the field, precisely because it values connection over production. It would be difficult to imagine a single person—or even group of people—writing a traditional essay that could serve the purposes the ACW site does; even if a text could be written that provided an expository overview of the information referenced from the ACW site, it would undoubtedly be more difficult to read and use.

FIGURE 28.2   Index of Connections from the ACW Home Page

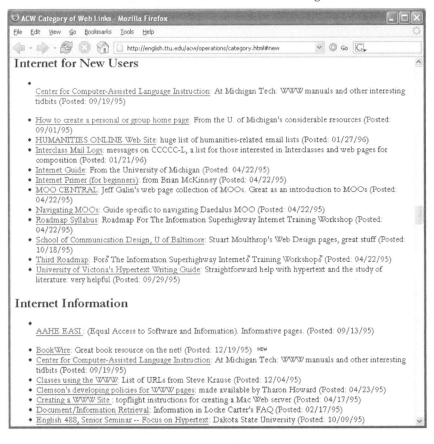

A slightly different approach is taken by a different connection-based site: the ERROR 404 essay. ERROR 404 was collected in the fall of 1995 by a seminar in computers and writing at Purdue University. The seminar, which I facilitated, attempted to address issues of identity, creativity, and argument from a postmodernist perspective—many of the issues developed above—by writing with fragments of other texts.

Consider, for example, the ways that the arrangement of quotes in the thread below, titled "Erotic," critically interrogates the meaning of each of the texts through contrast and complication (node titles are in brackets above node contents):

[Conley.Seductions.180]

Nowhere are the problematic effects of vr clearer than in the realm of the erotic. . . . Bruce Clark has pointed out that the violation or dissolution of body boundaries is inherently erotic; the same observation has been made by writers as diverse as Ovid, St. Teresa, and the Marquis de Sade.

[imag.teler.5]

Teledildonics lend new dimensions to Ma Bell's slogan: "Reach out and touch someone."

[anon.I]

:-o

Anonymous request for a virtual blow job. 9/15/95.

[Flame.Rape]

To participate, therefore, in this disembodied enactment of life's most body-centered activity is to risk the realization that when it comes to sex, perhaps the body in question is not the physical one at all, but its psychic double, the body-like self representation we carry around in our heads.

Julian Dibbell. A Rape in Cyberspace: or, How an Evil Clown, a Haitian Trickster Spirit, Two Wizards, and a Cast of Dozens Turned a Database into a Society. *FlameWars,* Durham: Duke Press 1994.

The texts here were not written by workshop participants, but the configuration of fragments, I argue, is an important form of writing, a Lyotardian act of creativity that is more reflective of postmodernist theories of culture and value than that available in most versions of contemporary composition. Each of the fragments enters into a dialogue with the others in ways not available to the works in their original, relatively isolated form (the book, the essay, the email message). Indeed, the individual fragments retain much different meanings that are read and rewritten as the reader-writer traverses different threads in the text. The anon.I node is the first in another thread in ERROR 404: an "alphabet" thread that rearranges the text according to alphabetical order.

On first reading the "alphabet" thread, I saw the emoticon as a somewhat immature prank written into the text. But, reading along the "Erotic" thread offers a markedly different perspective, juxtaposing the anonymous request for sex with fragments on eroticism and disembodiment, telecommunication, and a response to a figurative rape. None of these readings exhausts the fragments, but each perpetually rewrites its meanings. Each is crossed by numerous other threads, and the text is still open for the addition of either fragment or link.

Neither the ACW nor the Error 404 site succeeds completely in reorganizing "text" in a way that adds enough social importance to the act of linking. (This might always be the case, for if a technology perfectly matches our needs, it is often because our needs have been carefully and complexly orchestrated). The ACW page, for example, like all WWW pages, does not allow readers to become writers (either in the classic sense or in the postmodern sense of reorganizing or connecting). The WWW is, at this writing, still largely tied to individual ownership of pieces of text: individuals point at other individual's or institution's files.

The ERROR 404 text, in its WWW incarnation, suffers from the same difficulties, although the Storyspace version (in which most of the text was linked together by seminar participants) did allow everyone to add connections and new fragments—and even to delete them, although participants avoided this, as far as I can tell. Storyspace, despite its many other benefits, allows individual writers to "sign" nodes that they add but not links, perpetuating once again the idea of the node as primary. Connection and arrangement in ERROR 404 and Storyspace seem more creative than in traditional texts, but these impulses could easily be extended further.

CONCLUSIONS/RENEGOTIATIONS

Over the last twenty-five years we have enriched our work in composition studies by increasing our focus on the social and political roles of writers. We have replaced a concern for static product with a sense of texts as dynamic, social processes. We have introduced discussions of power into our journals and our classrooms, facing head-on the often embittered process of challenging the status quo in order to bring about a more just society. But such renegotiations must also encourage us to think through the implications of those shifts at cultural, disciplinary, and individual levels. On one hand, we insist that writing is social and that texts are not unified, bounded objects; on the other hand, we require our students to write single-voiced texts (even when they write in groups their texts aren't supposed to sound disjointed or as though they were written by committee); we grade those objects by what they contain rather than what they connect. Except for unique circumstances, such as writing annotated bibliographies, we estimate a text's value not according to the information it gathers and arranges but by what the writer *adds*. We need to learn to reverse this approach or at least to correct the imbalance.

None of this is to say composition should abandon the production of text. The dialectical tension between node and link provides us with a way to navigate a path between extremes of enlightenment authorship and postmodernist dispersal of agency and identity into powerless lines of indeterminate intensities. But, like systems of language, positive objects only gain relative values by being related to one another: positive spaces are constituted out of negative ones.

WORKS CITED

Berkenkotter, Carol, Thomas N. Huckin, and John Ackerman. "Conventions, Conversations, and the Writer: Case Study of a Student in a Rhetoric Ph.D. Program." *Research in the Teaching of English* 50 (1988): 9–44.

Berlin, James A. *Rhetoric and Reality: Writing Instruction in American Colleges, 1900–1985.* Carbondale: Southern Illinois University Press, 1987.

Bizzell, Patricia. "'Contact Zones' and English Studies." *College English* 56 (1994): 163–69.

Bolter, Jay David. *Writing Space: The Computer, Hypertext, and the History of Writing.* Hillsdale, NJ: Lawrence Erlbaum Associates, 1991.

Bruffee, Kenneth A. "Collaborative Learning: Some Practical Methods." *College English* 34 (1973): 634–43.

Cooper, Marilyn M., and Cynthia L. Selfe. "Computer Conferences and Learning: Authority, Resistance, and Internally Persuasive Discourse." *College English* 52 (1990): 847–69.

Devitt, Amy J. "Generalizing about Concept: New Conception of an Old Concept." *College Composition and Communication* 44 (1993): 573–86.

Drucker, Peter F. "The Coming of the New Organization." *Harvard Business Review* (Jan.–Feb. 1988): 45–53.

Eisenstein, Elizabeth L. *The Printing Press as an Agent of Change: Communications and Cultural Transformations in Early-Modern Europe.* 2 vols. Cambridge: Cambridge University Press, 1979.

Faigley, Lester. *Fragments of Rationality: Postmodernity and the Subject of Composition.* Pittsburgh: University of Pittsburgh Press, 1992.

Giroux, Henry. *Border Crossing: Cultural Workers and the Politics of Education.* New York: Routledge, 1992.

Hairston, Maxine. "Diversity, Ideology, and the Teaching of Writing." *College Composition and Communication* 43 (1992): 179–93.

Hamp-Lyons, Liz, and William Condon. "Questioning Assumptions About Portfolio-based Assessment." *College Composition and Communication* 44 (1993): 176–90.

Herzberg, Bruce. "Community Service and Critical Teaching." *College Composition and Communication* 45 (1994): 307–19.

Hilbert, Betsy. "Elegy for Excursus: The Descent of the Footnote." *College English* 51 (1989): 400–404.

Hirschhorn, Larry. *Beyond Mechanization: Work and Technology in a Postindustrial Age.* Cambridge: MIT Press, 1984.

Jameson, Frederic. *Postmodernism; or, The Cultural Logic of Late Capitalism.* Durham, NC: Duke University Press, 1991.

Johnson-Eilola, J. "Accumulation, Circulation, Association: Economies of Text in Online Research Spaces." *IEEE Transactions on Professional Communication* 38 (1995): 228–38.

Landow, George P. *Hypertext: The Convergence of Contemporary Critical Theory and Technology.* Baltimore: Johns Hopkins University Press, 1992.

Lyotard, Jean-François. *The Postmodern Condition: A Report on Knowledge.* Trans. Geoff Bennington and Brian Massumi, Minneapolis: University of Minnesota Press, 1984.

Murray, Donald M. "Teach writing as Process, not a Product." In *Rhetoric and Composition: A Sourcebook for Teachers and Writers.* Ed. Richard L. Graves. 2nd ed. Upper Montclair, NJ: Boynton/Cook, 1984. 98–92. Reprinted from *The Leaflet*, Nov. 1972: 11–14.

Ong, Walter J. *Orality and Literacy: The Technologizing of the Word.* London: Methuen, 1982.

Porter, James E. "Intertextuality and the Discourse Community." *Rhetoric Review* 5, no. 1 (1986): 34–47.

Porter, James E. *Rhetorical Ethics and Internetworked Writing.* Norwood, NJ: Ablex, in press.

Pratt, Mary Louise. *Imperial Eyes: Travel Writing and Transculturation.* London: Routledge, 1992.

Regan, A. "Type Normal like the Rest of Us: Writing, Power, and Homophobia in the Networked Classroom." *Computers and Composition* 10, no. 4 (1993): 11–23.

Reich, Robert B. *The Work of Nations.* New York: Vintage, 1992.

Romano, S. "The Egalitarian Narrative. Whose Story? Whose Yardstick?" *Computers and Composition* 10, no. 3 (1994): 5–28.

Slatin, John M. "Reading Hypertext: Order and Coherence in a New Medium." *College English* 52 (1990): 870–83.

Soja, Edward. *Postmodern Geographies: The Reassertion of Space in Critical Social Theory.* London: Verso, 1989.

Trimbur, John. "Consensus and Difference in Collaborative Learning." *College English* 51 (1989): 602–16.

Ulmer, Gregory. "Grammatology (in the Stacks) of Hypermedia: A Simulation." In *Literacy Online: The Promise (and Peril) of Reading and Writing with Computers.* Ed. Myron C. Tuman. Pittsburgh: University of Pittsburgh Press, 1992. 139–58.

———. *Heuritics: The Logic of Invention.* Baltimore: Johns Hopkins University Press, 1994.

———. *Teletheory: Grammatology in the Age of Video.* New York: Routledge, 1989.

Zuboff, Shoshana. *In the Age of the Smart Machine: The Future of Work and Power.* New York: Basic, 1988.

29 Part 2: Toward an Integrated Composition Pedagogy in Hypertext

SEAN D. WILLIAMS

1. INTRODUCTION

In "Beyond the Electronic Book: A Critique of Hypertext Rhetoric," Stuart Moulthrop (1991) asked: "What kind of dialogue do humanists seek with the designers of new media? Do rhetoricians see themselves as advocates of an endangered literacy or as pathfinders for new modes of information exchange?" (p. 292). The question is important because it restates the argument of my previous article "Part 1: Thinking Out of the Pro-verbal Box" (published in Volume 18, Number 1 of *Computers and Composition*). Specifically, I argued in this earlier article that composition instruction currently favors verbal forms but needs to be renovated in terms of emerging literacies, and especially visual literacy because digital technology has rendered visual texts so pervasive. In short, I argued that we need to be pathfinders for new modes of information exchange.

I also suggested that abandoning verbal rhetoric instruction in favor of teaching only visual rhetoric is perilous because it reproduces the binary logic of the verbal bias. I argued instead that what we need is an instructional paradigm that helps students weave multiple content forms together. What we need, I suggested, is a "new sociology of knowledge" that takes multiplicity of media for granted (Delaney & Landow, 1993, p. 18), but nonetheless integrates written forms of expression. Jay David Bolter and David Grusin (1999) made a similar case for the integration of media, arguing that

> No medium today ... seems to do its cultural work in isolation from other media any more than it works in isolation from other social and economic forces. What is new about new media comes from the particular ways in which they refashion older media and the ways in which older media refashion themselves to answer the challenges of new media (p. 15).

Bolter and Grusin's concept of *remediation,* also called *repurposing information* (Heba, 1997) or *expansionism* (Stroupe, 2000) suggests that new media forms

From *Computers and Composition* 18 (2001): 123–35.

appropriate the literate conventions and the content of older media forms to build new, hybrid literacies that simultaneously rely on both "older" literacy skills and "new" literacy skills for the composition of texts. Like the verbal compositions that Mikhail Bakhtin (1981) wrote about in *Discourse in the Novel*, new media offers "a syntactic structure utterly specific to it: in it . . . two potential utterances are fused, two responses are, as it were, harnessed in a potential dialogue" where the hybrid structure is an "organized system for bringing different languages in contact with one another" (p. 361; also quoted in Stroupe, 2000, p. 219).

Helping students develop skills that allow them to engage with this hybrid, expansionist literacy requires a complicated curriculum occurring in a digital environment. I must offer one caveat, though, before discussing the pedagogy: Integrating technology into the classroom does not guarantee that composition instruction will begin to reflect an expanded view of literacy. To suggest that simply adding technology to a classroom will promote an expanded view of literacy ascribes agency to the technology, overlooking the fact that technology succeeds or fails as an instructional tool because of the ways people and institutions use it. Further, although computers assist with certain reading and writing tasks, they cannot fully duplicate by themselves the human tasks of rhetorical construction and critical commentary (Snyder, 1998).

With this notion that people are responsible for what computers do as a baseline, I examine below what might characterize an integrated composition pedagogy that places responsibility for rhetorical action more upon humans than on computers. Specifically, I argue that composition instruction should be based upon a *design model* that mirrors process-based pedagogy. I also argue that the pedagogy should include both verbal and visual instruction in a hypertextual environment in order to help students develop facility with an expanded set of literate practices. I conclude by arguing that in addition to helping students acquire skill with a new literacy, this pedagogy that asks students to compose multimodal arguments encourages students to recognize that multiple perspectives always attend any issue under discussion. This, in turn, develops students' agency because students become the ones responsible for educating their teachers.

2. TOWARD AN INTEGRATED COMPOSITION PEDAGOGY IN HYPERTEXT

In a pedagogy designed to teach an integrated form of composition, students' analyses of others' arguments is subordinate to the construction of their own arguments—although analysis and construction cannot be separated because learning the integrated form of writing asks students to connect others' ideas (in whatever medium) with their own ideas (in whatever medium) to build meaningful compositions. An integrated composition pedagogy encourages students, therefore, to build not only by adequately representing and including other viewpoints, but also by bringing multiple media forms into contact with one another. As Raymond L. Paquin (1999) noted, rich combinations of media produce the most effective texts. In this type of composition, students weave together disparate but connected bits of information to form an argumentative hypertext that combines images, words, and sounds, rather than selecting compositional parts from a single medium (Shelley, 1996). An integrated composition pedagogy, that is, allows students the opportunity to compose with an *interaction of media forms and content* because it is the interaction that moves us away from reproducing the limitations of arguing in one medium.

Visual rhetoric, one of the most significant aspects of this integration, is relatively new to those of us from English departments, although its importance was discussed at least as early as 1969 by Rudolf Arnheim in his work *Visual Thinking.* However, not until technological advances made computers widely available did technical writing scholars such as Edward Tufte (1990, 1997) and Charles Kostlenick (1989) begin charting the importance of visuals in solving rhetorical problems. According to Kostlenick, visual rhetoric means

> the ability of the writer to achieve the purpose of a document through visual communication at any level: for example, through the choice of a typeface (Courier, Helvetica) of graphic cues (bullets, lines, icons), of textual arrangements (lists, flow charts, trees), of data displays (a pie chart, line graph), even of the color, shape, and size of a page (p. 77).

Does this article in *Computers and Composition* seem "serious" because it uses the font that it does? Would the quotation above stand out were it not set apart by indenting it as a text block? These are rhetorical decisions based, for better or worse, upon my assessment of the ways that a particular group of imagined readers judge the credibility of an argument based—at least in part—upon the argument's visual appearance. After all, we see verbal text *before* we read it. Visuals are, therefore, both functional and persuasive (Boling, 1994).

Because visuals *act* rhetorically in a text, and outside the classroom "visual images from television, videos and magazines" assault students (Glasgow, 1994, p. 494), instruction in visual rhetoric, like the verbal rhetoric we currently teach, requires that students acquire the skills necessary both to construct and to unravel visuals utilizing technology (Barton & Barton, 1985). A visual rhetoric pedagogy essentially has two parts, theory and practice: how and when visuals should be used and how visual arguments are constructed. These two items can be taught simultaneously, though, by guiding students through inductive observation of visual forms, discussing the conventions they exhibit, and asking students to reproduce and manipulate them in their own work. The process parallels what Paquin (1999) called the "competencies of visual literacy:" the ability to manipulate visuals, construct visuals, abstract from visuals and combine visuals with verbal text (p. 245).

However, if we in composition seek to move beyond simply teaching visual rhetoric as an adjunct to verbal rhetoric, we should ask students to build integrated compositions in hypertext. Jane Yellowlees Douglas' (1998) article, "Will the Most Reflexive Relativist Please Stand Up," points the way here. She argued that hypertext allows for more sophisticated compositions because hypertext can represent "a complex web of factors, influences, and forces so dense that no one can arrive at a single interpretation" (p. 147). Authoring hypertexts that integrate the verbal and the visual, then, helps students to see that argumentation is a dialogue on a given issue because integrated compositions contain links among alternate viewpoints and media. The links that characterize hypertext cause alternative positions and media simultaneously to modify, complicate, or deconstruct one another because this *heteroglossia,* to use Bakhtin's (1981) term, occurs in a single text.

3. The Design Model

The design model is a composing process that teaches students how to see themselves as "assemblers" of the complex interactions (the heteroglossia) that Douglas referred to. Specifically, the design model resembles composition's emphasis on process, focusing on the four primary skills of "planning," "transformation," "evaluation" and "revision." However, the model distills these four major areas into nine smaller stages and encourages their integration with technology to help students see composition (in the sense of composing, not the discipline) as *assemblage.* The resulting text, most easily represented in hypertext, models *accrual* of knowledge, not Aristotelian logic, as pieces of information, but do not necessarily demonstrate logical constructions. The design model, then, encourages students to see composition as a process that occurs through making connections among disparate, yet related texts in contingent contexts where several possible conclusions can coexist.

Richard Lehrer, Julie Erickson, and Tim Connell (1994) introduced the design model and simultaneously emphasized the importance of placing "students in the role of developing rather than receiving knowledge" (p. 227). The table on the next page, adapted from Lehrer, Erickson, and Connell, summarizes the relationships among the four major skill areas listed above ("planning," "transformation," "evaluation" and "revision"), subdivides these four areas into nine more specific design skills, and lists the educational outcomes of the nine design skills. This model assumes that students will be able to author hypermedia documents in a collaborative, electronic environment.

The design model demonstrates several assembly stages in the composition process and works particularly well in hypertext. In the planning stage, students work collaboratively to identify the separate positions on an assigned issue that they wish to represent; to analyze the audience; to develop questions that they will need to answer to solve the problem; and to divide the work in order to manage the process more effectively. In transformation, the second stage, students utilize whatever means necessary to investigate and represent the problem. Students use a combination of sources, including visual texts, the World Wide Web, traditional print sources, interviews, or virtually any other source of information to build an electronic database of possibilities from which they can then select information relevant to the rhetorical problem at hand. Students include all possible information and represent each separate bit of information on a separate Web page.

To select information from the complete database they have compiled, students analyze the quality or appropriateness of the information in terms of

TABLE 29.1   The Design Model

Major Skill Area	Design Skill	Educational Outcome
Planning	Defining the problem Decomposing the problem Managing the project	• Posing questions • Dividing complex questions into parts • Analyzing audiences • Collaborating • Assigning tasks
Transformation	Discovering information	• Improving research skills (electronic, print-oriented, interviews, etc.)
	Selecting information	• Improving data analysis skills • Note-taking • Summarizing • Eliminating • Improving semantic mapping skills
	Organizing information	• Grouping • Dividing • Ordering • Improving associative thinking skills
	Representing information	• Linking representations • Creating multiple representations • Interweaving media • Producing graphics and video
Evaluation	Testing the design	• Soliciting feedback • Articulating intentions • Analyzing audience
Revision	Revising the design	• Analyzing reader response • Hypothesizing improvements • Generating potential repairs

Note: Table adapted from Lehrer, Erickson, & Connell (1994, p. 230).

the context they identified in the planning stage. Unnecessary information and links are eliminated and students can then organize the remaining information by grouping it and ordering it according to the subdivisions of the problem.

Students begin to transform information into argument by organizing the information (Bergeron & Bailin, 1997). Specifically, students link bits of information together in chains representing meaningful associations. Students are encouraged to recognize that arguments are highly contextual and are created through the association of *potentially* related information in a knowledge structure rendering the claims of a text probable. So, for example, an image of a building that collapsed during an earthquake, killing some and stranding others, might be effective as proof of the awesome power of nature, or it might be effective proof of a certain surviving family's triumph over disaster. The same image, framed differently by the pages to which it is linked, reveals that solutions to complex problems are not so much solutions as they are the accrual of possible propositions that derive from the way information is linked and presented. Allowing students to build hypertexts in this way demonstrates that composition is a process of recognizing multiple perspectives and building probable contexts from that multiplicity by selecting which bits of information occur in what order.

The final two steps in the design model, evaluation and revision, likewise encourage students to recognize the contingency of knowledge by soliciting feedback from their peers to see how effectively the proposed solutions answer the concerns of a real audience. In these final stages of constructing a composition, designers articulate to their peers what goals they attempted to accomplish in the hypertext to see if those goals were met. After soliciting feedback, analyzing the responses, and hypothesizing ways to improve the representation, students return to the hypertext and generate repairs. The repairs make the content and structure more useful for the anticipated audience while more effectively accomplishing the composition's goals.

The design model, as the description above suggests, creates a space where composition can maintain its historical concerns with process, critical thinking, and production, but expands composition beyond teaching students how to build print compositions. The design model extends beyond verbal composition because students must make choices in order to transform an associative database of multimedia information into a hypertextual, node-link structure. Students see that information, by itself, does not create arguments, but that ordering information comprises arguments. Based upon this recognition, students are more likely to see that multiple perspectives always characterize any issue and that a single composition—or more accurately a collection of links—is one among countless possible ways of representing a particular issue.

4. Sample Assignment Using the Design Model to Teach Integrated Composition

An assignment sequence that helps students begin to see themselves as the assemblers privileged by the design model begins by posing a problem complicated enough to allow students to develop several equally well-supported positions—exploring representations of masculinity, for example. The students then collaboratively research the issue by examining digital forms like the Web, and more traditional forms like magazine images, billboards, and television shows. Students then compile a multimedia database that includes screen captures, photographs, video tape, newspaper clippings, and their own thoughts recorded in a document created with word-processing software. These items are then digitized (if not already digital) so they can be easily manipulated, grouped, and ordered in the transformation stage according to the students' hypotheses about the argument present in each text. All of

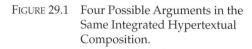

FIGURE 29.1 Four Possible Arguments in the Same Integrated Hypertextual Composition.

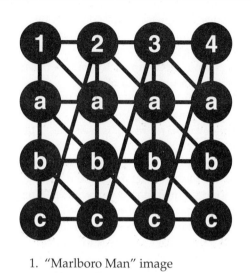

1. "Marlboro Man" image
2. "Gay Professional" image
3. "Suburban Dad" image
4. "Rap Musician" image

a. photograph from magazine
b. screen shot from Web site
c. quotation from academic journal

these digitized representations, once coded as HTML documents, whether taken from the Web or from other media, comprise the preliminary database from which students begin to build their arguments in the transformation stage.[1]

During the transformation stage, the students construct several parallel arguments. First, they simply group together each of the separate representations (now Web pages) that loosely argue the same point; second, they place each of these groupings into discrete Web sites linking among related representations on a single theme (note the distinction between "Web sites" and "Web pages:" a Web site is a collections of Web pages); and last, they create hyperlinks among the separate, thematically-related Web sites. If the node–link structure of a Web site on the topic of masculinity were combined into one Web text and represented visually, it would look something like Figure 29.1.

In Figure 29.1, each of the circles represents a node, a collection of media that comprises a single Web page, and the lines represent links among nodes.

Each column has a number in the top node representing a particular position (the "Marlboro Man," the "Gay Professional," the "Suburban Dad," and the "Rap Musician") on masculinity supported by the material contained in the nodes labeled a–c under the numeral, each of which represents evidence taken from a different medium. Each of the columns, then, represents a single viewpoint on the issue of masculinity demonstrated—not argued for—by the multimedia evidence included.

But each column is also cross-linked to the other perspectives (although this matrix link structure should by no means be viewed as ideal). In other words, the image of the "Marlboro Man" is linked to the image of the "Gay Professional" at several places and could potentially be linked to the other positions on masculinity as well. The result is that the "Marlboro Man" image complicates and deconstructs the image of the "Gay Professional" and vice versa because the two positions, although internally consistent within their separate columns, are linked to each other. In this case, to take one possible example, the visual evidence presented in node b from the "Marlboro Man" column could be a counter proof to the verbal text of node c in the "Gay Professional" or vice versa. There are countless other possibilities that designers could code among the columns and the different types of information included.

Each column, then, represents a single perspective or argument on an issue, but each of those separate positions are linked together to form a larger, integrated composition in hypertext. Students place the visual representations into dialogue with verbal ones, for example, juxtaposing competing representations by positioning them adjacent to one another in a single digital document utilizing link structures to subtly encode relationships among the separate columns or arguments. As Nicholas C. Burbules (1998) argued, links express specific argumentative intentions by subtly guiding users to recognize or intuit the connection between specific pages in a Web site. Users must ask themselves, for example, "what is the implied meaning that the juxtaposition of two pages connected through a link suggests?" (Burbules, p. 110).

However, because links "simply carry the reader with them to inferences that could just as well be drawn quite differently, or could be criticized and rejected" (Burbules, 1998, p. 115), users might not be able to articulate exactly how links encourage them to make meaning. Therefore, students who compose integrated compositions need to compose a separate master document or storyboard that records the intended relationships or assumptions that each link encodes. The "meaning" of these links recorded on the storyboard then guides composition of two more nodes: an introductory node that frames the issue under consideration and metacommentary node that discusses the social and ideological implications made visible by linking the different representations (Forman, 1994; Glasgow, 1994; Kress & van Leeuwen, 1996). Figure 29.2 modifies the structure represented in Figure 29.1 to demonstrate how adding an introductory node and a metacommentary node changes the composition's link structure (although the complete complexity can't be demonstrated in a two-dimensional image) and consequently complicates the representation of masculinity that a reader might get from the argument because more paths are now available to readers.

FIGURE 29.2   Four Integrated Arguments with Introduction (I)
and Metacommentary (M) Nodes.

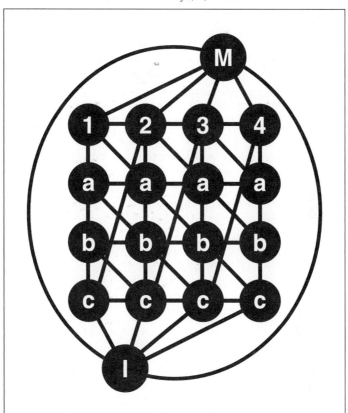

We see in Figure 29.2 that two nodes have been added, one labeled with
an "I" for the introduction and another labeled with an "M" for the metacommentary. Each of these additional nodes are then linked to the four columns
indicating that their purpose is to reflect on the contents of each of the representations contained with the separate columns (not necessarily on the specific node to which they are connected). Also, the metacommentary and the
introduction are linked in a way that circumscribes or contains the four separate arguments, showing that the additional nodes comment on the global nature of the hypertext about masculinity. Finally, in this visual representation
of a possible node–link structure of an integrated composition, the metacommentary is on top of the visual not because it is first in a temporal sequence
but because the contents of the metacommentary rely on the context created
by the interaction of the positions presented in the four columns.

Adding the introductory node and the metacommentary node is the final
transformation from information to argumentation, then, because the students verbally juxtapose the sequences, asking questions in verbal text about
the multimedia sequences or positions that they constructed: How are the

positions different? How are they similar? What do the differences and similarities suggest about the topic? Does one position appeal to a unique audience? Does one position utilize a particular visual technique? What are the sources of the images? Authoring these two framing devices—the introductory and the metacommentary nodes—causes students to evaluate each perspective in terms of the others, identifying points of association and contradiction among the positions. The resulting introduction and metacommentary are, therefore, pages that synthesize in our case four different perspectives on masculinity while simultaneously allowing each of the separate perspectives to maintain its autonomy.

After building a structure in this way—moving from planning the composition, to transforming and organizing the data gathered into discrete perspectives, to interweaving media with each representation, to linking the representations, to articulating the meaning of links, to composing reflections on the whole hypertext—each group submits its integrated composition to peer groups for review. Each group project is evaluated based upon the internal cohesion of each separate perspective as represented in Figure 29.1 by the numbered columns; the meaningfulness of links; whether or not the hypertext as a whole substantiates the claims offered in the introductory and metacommentary nodes; and whether or not verbal and visual texts were integrated effectively. Finally, evaluators determine whether users were encouraged to explore the hypertext in order to build their own conclusion about the issue or whether the hypertext was overly directive and therefore limited possible user interpretations. Based upon the successes and failures that the review illuminates, each group revises its argument.

This design process certainly complicates the process associated with composing verbal texts because the mingling of the verbal, the visual, and the hypertextual causes slippages in meaning: Associations are not necessarily classifications or logical proofs, yet the designer must be able to train the slippages into a form revealing their authorial purpose. The added complexity, then, produces a more thorough engagement with rhetorical, critical, and technological skills, and approximates the linked, multimedia structure of problem solving more effectively than either verbal or visual compositions alone do. Students develop critical, rhetorical, and technological facility because they compose their arguments from the distillations of others' verbal and visual arguments, combining those reconstituted arguments into a hypertext where each of the positions literally decomposes the others in the same hypertext.

In sum, this integrated composition paradigm encourages students to combine media and to create both linear and associative linked structures—the cornerstones of the expanded literacy for new media—thereby introducing them to the complexity of composing with the multiplicity inherent to hypertext while maintaining an association with more conventionally recognized forms of composition. Students begin to learn a far more sophisticated and integrated form of composition utilizing multiple media, reinforcing the notion that arguments are constructs, and literally making visible the multiplicity of a given issue.

5. CONCLUSIONS

Ultimately, empowering students is the goal of teaching an integrated form of composition: Teaching students to compose integrated arguments in a digital environment helps students realize that they command both the new forms of literacy that technology enables as well as the old forms of literacy that technology makes more accessible. And, to return to Moulthrop's (1991) question, "do rhetoricians see themselves as advocates of an endangered literacy or as pathfinders for new modes of information exchange?" our answer, if we teach such an integrated form of writing, is "both." An integrated composition pedagogy overcomes the verbal bias (and the binary logic it privileges) by making old and new expressive and critical resources available to students. This, in turn, develops students' abilities to reason about an issue based upon the context of associations in which a position appears because multiplicity of approach or position moves to the foreground in hypertext. This integrated, hypertextual approach therefore allows students to say "both" are true and encourages them to accept the ambiguity and often frustrating complexity of acknowledging the validity of multiple representations and viewpoints simultaneously.

Teaching integrated argumentation, then, moves in the direction of reconceptualizing literacy as a composite of skills and representative tools by enabling students to exploit multiplicity and by giving them access to the digital tools they need to create complex representations of issues. There is, of course, no guarantee that integrating technology into the classroom or teaching an integrated form of composition will produce students well-equipped to harness and tame the play among viewpoints, the ambiguity, and the fluid shifts of knowledge that digital media encourages (Tergan, 1997). Yet, building a pedagogy on a combination of the design model and on the possibilities that verbal text, visual text, and hypertext uniquely and in concert allow encourages students to make connections among disparate, yet related texts and enables students to recognize that knowledge is always contingent on its context. It emphasizes process, motion, recursion, and collaboration at each separate stage by concurrently developing rhetorical, critical, and technological skills that can be applied both to "traditional" forms such as print texts, and to digital forms such as the Web. The final stage of collaboratively producing networked, interactive, Web-based arguments synthesizes these skills and ultimately demonstrates to students that they control the means of representation, that they command the multiple literacies that act on them.

Although we can question whether students do in fact have increased agency because access to literacy by itself does not change existing arrangements of power (Bowen, 1994), the increased access to literacy does encourage students to compose longer, more collaborative texts. Through collaboration and hypertextual composition, students acquire familiarity with the dialogic nature of argument (Duin & Hansen, 1994; Ess, 1991), and they compose more extensive, media-integrated documents because they become the experts responsible for educating their teachers. Admittedly, teachers define the problems that students investigate, and teachers who define problems narrowly will probably receive the answers they expect. Nonetheless, the knowledge that students present in their integrated arguments derives from their selection, evaluation, and interpretation of discrete pieces of information according to their individual argumentative goals. The students' integrated compositions carry authority through the students' own assemblage of a context against which their claims can be analyzed. We as teachers, therefore, learn what the students present, and the quality and reliability of that information depends upon the complexity of the context students have constructed around the issues at hand. Students, in this case (albeit ideal) generate knowledge. They don't just write to us.

However, when we as teachers become learners, we also become better composition instructors. When the teacher's role is to broadly define problems for students to investigate and not lecture on grammatical rules or subject matter (Leonard, 1996), the teacher becomes a resource that individual students can call upon for their own needs within the context of their projects. A teacher's role in a class based upon this integrated composition pedagogy becomes *primarily*[2] one of supporting student goals by offering advice on research tools or rhetorical strategies or expressive options.

This action of empowering students by teaching them how to command new literacy forms, therefore, requires a significant shift in the teacher's role in writing education. Teachers create the space for students to become active constructors of knowledge by relinquishing an equal proportion of authority—an authority largely grounded on our verbal skill. Nevertheless, this does not mean that we as composition teachers should divorce ourselves from familiarity with the verbal literacy skills that we and the students in our classes have struggled to acquire. Quite the contrary. We must model for students literacy habits that demonstrate our willingness to acknowledge alternatives and possibilities for new types of expression. We must model our engagement with the multiple forms of literacy that constitute students' lives because those literacies also constitute our lives. We must, in short, make integrated composition and expanded literacy our own before we can ask students to value the skills and way of thinking that this new literacy promotes.

NOTES

1. This process must be accompanied by instruction on the skills necessary to manipulate graphics, HTML, and perhaps video and audio files effectively, with the goal of equipping students with a basic set of skills they can develop through practice. Also, issues of plagiarism and intellectual property need to be addressed because digital media make assuming others' work very easy.

2. I emphasize "primarily" because some direct instruction is usually necessary when teaching with technology. The teacher must also know when to intervene in projects that risk going awry or do not fit within the constraints of the proposed problem or when personalities conflict.

REFERENCES

Arnheim, Rudolph. (1969). *Visual thinking.* Berkley, CA: University of California Press.

Bakhtin, Mikhail M. (1981). Discourse in the novel. In Michael Holquist (Ed.), *The dialogic imagination* (pp. 259–422). Austin: University of Texas Press.

Barton, Ben F., & Barton, Marthalee S. (1985). Toward a rhetoric of visuals for the computer age. *The Technical Writing Teacher, 12,* 126–145.

Bergeron, Bryan P., & Bailin, Michael T. (1997). The contribution of hypermedia link authoring. *Technical Communication, 44,* 121–128.

Bolter, Jay David, & Grusin, David. (1999). *Remediation: understanding new media.* Cambridge, MA: MIT Press.

Boling, Elizabeth (1994). Meeting the challenge of the electronic page: extending instructional design skills. *Educational Technology, 34,* 13–18.

Bowen, Betsy. (1994). Telecommunications networks: expanding the contexts for literacy. In Cynthia L. Selfe & Susan Hilligoss (Eds.), *Literacy and computers: the complications of teaching and learning with technology* (pp. 113–129). New York: Modern Language Association.

Burbules, Nicholas C. (1998). Rhetorics of the web: hyperreading and critical literacy. In Ilana Snyder (Ed.), *Page to screen: taking literacy into the electronic era* (pp. 102–122). New York: Routledge.

Delaney, Paul, & Landow, George P. (1993). Managing the digital word: the text in an age of electronic reproduction. In George P. Landow & Paul Delaney (Eds.), *The digital word: text-based computing in the humanities* (pp. 3–30). Cambridge, MA: MIT Press.

Douglas, Jane Yellowlees. (1998). Will the most reflexive relativist please stand up: hypertext, argument and relativism. In Ilana Snyder (Ed.), *Page to screen: taking literacy into the electronic era* (pp. 144–162). New York: Routledge.

Duin, Ann Hill, & Hansen, Craig. (1994). Overview: reading and writing on computer networks as social construction and social interaction. In Cynthia L. Selfe & Susan Hilligoss (Eds.), *Literacy and computers: the complications of teaching and learning with technology* (pp. 89–112). New York: Modern Language Association.

Ess, Charles. (1991). The pedagogy of computing: hypermedia in the classroom. *Hypertext 91, third ACM conference on hypertext proceedings* (pp. 277–291). Baltimore: ACM.

Forman, Janis. (1994). Literacy, collaboration, and technology: new connections and challenges. In Cynthia L. Selfe & Susan Hilligoss (Eds.), *Literacy and computers: the complications of teaching and learning with technology* (pp. 130–143). New York: Modern Language Association.

Glasgow, Jacqueline N. (1994). Teaching visual literacy for the twenty-first century. *Journal of Reading, 37,* 494–500.

Heba, Gary. (1997). HyperRhetoric: multimedia, literacy, and the future of composition. *Computers and Composition, 14,* 19–44.

Kostlenick, Charles. (1989). Visual rhetoric: a reader-oriented approach to graphics and designs. *The Technical Writing Teacher, 16,* 77–87.

Kress, Gunther, & van Leeuwen, Theo. (1996). *Reading images: the grammar of visual design.* New York: Routledge.

Lehrer, Richard, Erickson, Julie, & Connell, Tim. (1994). Learning by designing hypermedia documents. *Computers in the Schools, 10,* 227–254.

Leonard, David C. (1996). Using the web for graduate courses in technical communication with distant learners. *Technical Communication, 43,* 388–400.

Moulthrop, Stuart. (1991). Beyond the electronic book: a critique of hypertext rhetoric. *Hypertext '91, Third ACM Conference on Hypertext Proceedings* (pp. 291–298). Baltimore: ACM.

Paquin, Raymond L. (1999). The competencies of visual literacy. In Robert E. Griffin, William J. Gibbs, & Beth Wiegman (Eds.), *Visual literacy in an information age* (pp. 245–248). Blacksburg, VA: International Visual Literacy Association.

Shelley, Cameron. (1996). Rhetorical and demonstrative modes of visual argumentation: looking at images of human evolution. *Argumentation and Advocacy, 33,* 53–68.

Snyder, Ilana. (1998). Beyond the hype: reassessing hypertext. In Ilana Snyder (Eds.), *Page to screen: taking literacy into the electronic era* (pp. 125–143). New York: Routledge.

Stroupe, Craig. (2000). Visualizing English: recognizing the hybrid literacy of visual and verbal authorship on the web. *College English, 62,* 607–632.

Tergan, Sigmar-Olaf. (1997). Multiple views, contexts, and symbol systems in learning with hypertext/hypermedia: a critical review of research. *Educational Technology, 37,* 5–18.

Tufte, Edward R. (1990). *Envisioning information.* Cheshire, CN: Graphics Press.

Tufte, Edward R. (1997). *Visual explanations: images, quantities, evidence and narrative.* Cheshire, CN: Graphics Press.

30   Some Notes on Simulacra Machines, Flash in First-Year Composition, and Tactics in Spaces of Interruption

ANTHONY ELLERTSON

Anthony Ellertson's multimedia article in the Fall 2003 issue of *Kairos,* an online journal of rhetoric, technology, and pedagogy, offers one example of new media writing in the composition classroom while demonstrating the ways digital technology can transform both students' writing and our own scholarly work. The piece explains many aspects of Flash, software that allows for interaction and animation in digital documents. Ellertson explains a case study in which composition students used the software in their own writing and argues for new rhetorical approaches to students' thinking and writing processes based both in theories of technology and classical rhetoric. And, most obviously, Ellertson creates his own piece using Flash, integrating text, still images, tickers, and even video to produce a dynamic and interactive reading experience.

Whether or not Flash itself is a technology that will survive in the rapid advancement of new media tools, this innovative piece offers an example of the possibilities of new media writing. Moreover, Ellertson's thoughtful insights about multimedia, rhetoric, and composition pedagogy will continue to inform researchers and teachers long into the future.

We have captured the opening screen and one additional screen (of ten) to give you an overview of the content of the article. We encourage you to go online and read Ellertson's article. The Web address is <http://kairos. technorhetoric.net/8.2>.

From *Kairos* 8.2 (2003), <http://kairos.technorhetoric.net/8.2/binder.html?features/ ellertson/home.html>.

FIGURE 30.1   Title and Introduction.

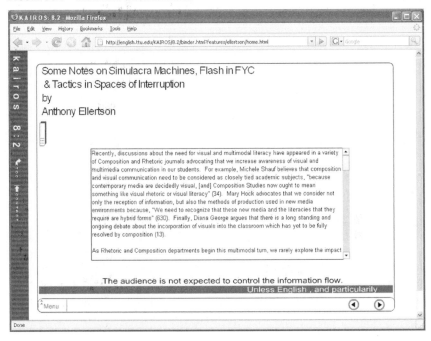

Source: Kairos 8.2 (2003), <http://kairos.technorhetoric.net/8.2/binder.html?features/ellertson/home.html>.

FIGURE 30.2   Page Introducing Flash.

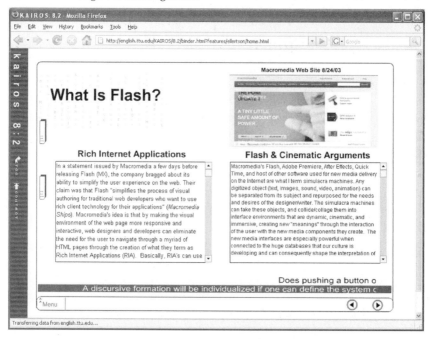

Source: Kairos 8.2 (2003), <http://kairos.technorhetoric.net/8.2/binder.html?features/ellertson/home.html>.

*Re: The Future of Computers and Writing: A Multivocal Textumentary**

BILL HART-DAVIDSON
AND STEVEN D. KRAUSE
(DIRECTORS/PRODUCERS/EDITORS)

Camera cuts back and forth between close-ups of writing activity in what appears to be a classroom computer space. Shots (e.g., of hands typing, mousing; screens with text editors, email, web browsers open; groups viewing documents on an overhead screen, etc.) don't allow us to see exactly where we are. From opening-sequence montage, fade to Ball State University in Muncie, Indiana, site of the 2001 Computers & Writing Conference; fade to Normal, Illinois, site of the 2002 Computers & Writing Conference; fade to West Lafayette, Indiana, site of the 2003 Computers & Writing Conference.

SCENE 1: CONTEXT FOR THE QUESTION

(Steve Krause, Bill Hart-Davidson, Nick Carbone, Trish Harris, and Ted Nellen sit on folding chairs at Computers & Writing 2001, at the front of a large and generic lecture-hall style classroom. Krause stands up.)

> KRAUSE: The resolution for our debate today goes like this (Carbone, Harris, Hart-Davidson, Krause, & Nellen, 2001): Resolved: In the near future, the field/interest/sub-discipline of computers and writing will cease to be different from the field/interest/larger discipline composition and rhetoric because all composition specialists shall be expected to understand the importance of using computers and other technologies to teach writing. All right, let's begin . . .

---

*Starring: Nick Carbone, Michael Day, Joel English, Trish Harris, Bill Hart-Davidson, Johndan Johnson-Eilola, Steven D. Krause, Ted Nellen, Mike Palmquist, Rich Rice, Rebecca Rickly
From *Computers and Composition* 21 (2004): 147–60.

(Jump-cut to a page of text — Gail Hawisher's (1987), "Research and Recommendations for Computers and Writing Instruction"; zoom in on a passage:)

> Those of us who taught with computers and studied the influence of computers on writers and their products approached our research with high expectations. It is not a surprise, then, that in our ebullience, we sometimes expected so much of the computers and word processing that our research became "technocentric." (p. 44)

> HART-DAVIDSON: Worries about being technocentric — a term Hawisher attributed to Seymour Papert (1993) — echo throughout the history of computers and writing. Are we so focused on the technology itself that we fail to see the people involved? Questions like this one came, and still come, from a desire to understand computers as tools for doing and teaching writing.

(Jump-cut to another text — John Theismeyer's (1989), "Should We Do What We Can?" Zoom in on:)

> We can help students attend more to composing than computing by writing our own operating instructions, paring down the user's manual to the functions students most need ... We can learn to teach effectively with open-topic prewriting aids by making sure students understand their purpose and by analyzing effective and ineffective models of completed exercises. In short, we can show students when, why, and how to use these programs. Even the computer's most benign features require such instructor intervention ... We need to remember that the computer is an additional tool in the classroom, not necessarily the primary one. (pp. 88–89)

SCENE 2: THE QUESTION BEGINS

(Fade back to the session and to the speakers at front of room.)

> HART-DAVIDSON: In 2003, the assertion that computers are merely a tool among others rather than an overwhelming force to be reckoned with not only in the writing classroom, but in all areas of communication, has become more and more difficult to defend. Because the identity of the field of computers and writing hinges upon the status of the machine relative to the activity and study of writing, the rise of the computer as a writing tool is as troubling as it is vital to the continuing relevance of the field.

(Nick Carbone addresses the crowd, which we see for the first time; we recognize many of the faces as Computers and Composition contributors.)

> CARBONE: Technologies become invisible quickly. Before computers we talked about writing atechnologically, as an act that primarily happened in the writer's brain, whether that brain be cognitively determined or socially constructed. Studies of composing processes — the research that tried to figure out what the process was/is in process writing — never paid much attention to the role technology played in

that process. Computers changed that, because people behaved differently when they wrote with computers, and the change startled us. The technology of writing was no longer fixed and invariable; it was/is/will be a factor in writing processes. Computers and writing exists, in part, to emphasize the roles of technology—for teachers, scholars, and writers—in the acts of writing. That's the essence of this field, and I think it's still distinct from composition and rhetoric as a whole.

(Six months later, Mike Palmquist typing at his computer. Through the window of his office, the Colorado woods in the distance.)

PALMQUIST: I've been thinking that rhetoric and technology might be a useful name to consider. It's been proposed before, by Eric Crump among others, and it seems apt. It covers communication and writing, and it allows us to think productively about other sorts of technology coming around the bend—or even so far down the road that we can't yet conceptualize it. I'm working with video more and more these days—mostly in the service of web-based instruction materials for writers. Even though most people today will read the materials via computer, others will perhaps soon read the materials on personal digital assistants (PDAs).

CARBONE: *(typing at his machine)* I think, on an institutional organizational level, English departments will want to keep the teaching of writing in their units, if only for the funding a required course brings; this might mean that we'll have to lose the word writing—although I hate to let it go. It's a good word, and its connotations grow with technology. If writing is as much mental as it is technological, if it is as much a way of seeing and organizing, whatever the tools at hand, then there's no reason to lose the word. I like the idea of being a writer better than I do the idea of being a technical communicator. So maybe we're back to the arguments Richard Lanham (1993) put forth: Rhetoric will once again underlie all instruction and study.

It may be that computers and writing, broadly and elegantly construed, with all that computer comes to mean and all that writing—with its mental, emotive, rhetorical and technological root systems already contain—will remain, for the field, such as it is: a small offshoot that we entered via compositions. For now.

(Back to Carbone a year earlier at the front of the lecture halls.)

CARBONE: The future of computers and writing isn't just related to the future of computers and the evolution that more changes in computer technologies and learning will bring. In fact, if we as a field tie ourselves only to studying and writing about and trying to understand only the latest thing to ooze from the broadband, we might just evolve ourselves out of being and break apart. To stay a field, we should be in those niches to be sure, in overlapping kinds of ways, but we really need to get better at understanding the writing technologies we've had and used for a while: Do we really know how word-processing software changes the way people write? What have been the effects on writing as a composing process now that we've had a generation or two of students who may have barely ever seen a typewriter let alone typed with one? Do we teach word-processing techniques more effectively as part of writing than we did 14 years ago, or 10 years ago, or even 8 years ago?

KRAUSE: Where is the boundary? With so many key terms in contention—writing, rhetoric, computers, composition—each becomes a point of departure for further reflection and research. But how far afield can we go before we are in another field altogether?

SCENE 3: DEBATING, TALKING, AND TYPING WITH OUR MOUTHS FULL

(Spring 2002. A nondescript restaurant, recognizable as being in Chicago only because of a few local posters and pieces of sports memorabilia on the walls. The restaurant is deserted, except for the cast of this textumentary gathered around a large table. The group is having a good time—eating, drinking, talking, laughing, and even writing. Cut to Rich Rice, who has his laptop open and is fervently typing. He responds to Krause's question.)

RICE: I've been reading a lot of Lanham (1993), Ilana Snyder (1998), Jay David Bolter (1991), Marshall McLuhan (1964), Peter Lunenfeld (1999) and the like while I'm reading about the history of portfolios. I wanted to look at meaningful learning and teaching differences between fixed media portfolios and digital portfolios. Focusing just on the electronic now, I've been thinking about computers and writing. Paper portfolios. Electronic portfolios. What I'm coming up with, well, is kind of simple, but here it is: Most people generally teach composition or technical communication by moving through stages, like reflection → reflexion → action. The idea is that you use writing or composing to learn, to make a change in how you see yourself, and then to make a change in society: reflection → reflexion → action. Now add Jay David Bolter and Richard Grusin (2000): immediacy → hypermediacy → remediation. Immediacy is when technology becomes transparent; hypermediacy is when you highlight the technology to learn something specific about the content, the writing. Then there's remediation, when you choose to use one technology over another to compose or present something. Usually this is something like choosing chalk over Microsoft POWERPOINT—remediating back to some tool.

I'm trying to think about digital portfolios in terms of combining the computer and the writing, because that's what electronic portfolios are. So here are some terms, combined: *reflective immediacy, reflexive hypermediacy,* and *active remediation.* Basically—because what I'm coming up with is a way of looking at portfolios, a rubric, really—I've been thinking about how this rubric might work with everything. Every kind of composing.

SCENE 4: IS IT WRITING? IS IT COMMUNICATION? IS IT OVER?

(Hart-Davidson, typing an email message on a laptop in a hotel room. He chuckles as he writes.)

HART-DAVIDSON: Blasphemy alert: Increasingly, I find myself arguing that writing, per se, is beside the point. Writing as a collective term for a fairly diverse set of technologies and practices associated with—to quote Bolter (1991), "the arrangement of discrete signs on or in a surface" (p. 45)—is a name for an implementation of a set of activities better described by the five canons of rhetoric. We use writing to invent, arrange, style, remember, and deliver information—and it's a damn fine platform for engaging these acts. But it's just an implementation. I think computers and writing can be about developing extensions to the writing platform. These extensions would, of course, build on the foundational implementation of the arrangement of discrete signs on or in a surface. We might seek to develop new technologies that optimize the way these signs move or change for specific kinds of purposes.

Johndan Johnson-Eilola's (1996) argument that technical communication's relationship with text has always been shaky can be extended, I would suggest, to just about everybody who uses (makes, reads) texts as resources to help them do other things. I'm not only talking about software manuals or directions for putting together a new vacuum cleaner. I also mean texts that help us make decisions, help us write other texts, and help us learn. These are things we hope writing will help us to do: We don't often want to write—writing is not our end goal, although we often do it because it is powerful way to support other aims. We don't often want to focus on making a good text, but rather on doing something else.

(Switch to the front of the room at Computers and Writing 2001.)

HART-DAVIDSON: I think our field will, of course, continue to pioneer discussions regarding how best to teach writing with computers. But I don't think our discussion here, for example, will be a discussion that differs in major ways from the one going on at, say, the Conference on College Composition and Communication. I believe our field will continue to push beyond the boundaries of the question "why teach writing with computers?" to engage a question like how might literate activity—the things people want, need, and love to do with reading and writing—be better supported given the network of technologies we now have available?

This question, I submit, would place the folks whose research interests have been computers and writing more squarely with academic and industry fields such as human–computer interaction or information technology. And it wouldn't be a radical shift in the focus of most folks who attend and present at the Computers & Writing conferences, and who are already routinely teaching, researching, and otherwise behaving as if writing is an information technology—if not the information technology upon which most others are based. What would constitute a shift, though, would be the degree to which we become the chief visionaries of, designers of, and patent holders for communication technologies that support literate activity.

The challenge all of us are faced with, I would contend, is to begin to dream and invent beyond the limits of the formidable implementation we have of the five conceptual features of written communication represented by the canons of rhetoric: invention, arrangement, style, memory, and delivery. It has been a successful implementation, to be sure. And we have all heard and agreed with the histories of writing technologies that explain why it is so difficult for us to uncouple the fundamental powers of a shared system of signs with the powerful feature-set of print. But we must do this.

KRAUSE *(who hums an REM song):* It's the end of computers and writing as we know it (and I feel fine). I think that the end of our subdisciplinary status and entrance into the mainstream of composition studies is a good thing. I believe the distinction between computers and writing and composition-in-general is largely over, because our colleagues—once uninterested or even against the use of computers in the teaching of writing—have come over to our side. Essentially, the battle that has been fought for the last 20 or so years and that has been so clearly documented is over. We won.

Even those compositionists who don't incorporate computer technology in their teaching acknowledge the value of it and the connection of it to the teaching of writing. It's a bit like teachers who don't use the chalkboard in their classes but acknowledge that chalkboards are an acceptable and even useful teaching tool: Today, those who would say that computers are harmful or not useful in the teaching of writing are few and far between, and, I would argue, considered to be crackpots. This might seem like common sense, but I think this shift is a significant one indeed. About seven years ago, Bill Hart-Davidson and I were in graduate school together at Bowling Green State University. Shortly after we set up an email discussion list between our two sections of first-year composition, we were hauled into the writing program administrator's office. I don't recall the conversation exactly, but we were asked something along the lines of "what the hell are you doing?" No one's asking that now; in fact, I suspect this same administrator is encouraging her current teaching assistants and adjuncts to use email lists in their classes.

When the field of computers and writing ceases to be different from the larger discipline of composition and rhetoric because all compositionists will be expected to understand the importance of using computers and other technologies to teach writing, we should celebrate rather than feel threatened. It is not so much the end of the subdiscipline of computers and writing as it is the beginning of the awareness of technology for all of us invested in the teaching of writing.

(The restaurant, Chicago, Spring 2002. Rice reads from the passage he has just composed.)

RICE: In the context of my study, theoretically it is the juxtaposition of the potentialities of digital portfolio presentation and assessment alongside traditional linear text composing or compilation processes that provides perceptual growth. Reflective immediacy is a core category that signifies teaching and learning properties that do not consider the impact of the digital medium, but focus on self-awareness or individual growth. The reflexive hypermediacy core category includes phenomena I observed, which focus on the medium and in so doing enable the teacher or learner a perspective that reflects on the self objectively. Active remediation denotes instances in which the teacher and students view one media construction, presentation, and/or assessment type as decisively better than another and indicates that a digital format directly impacts writing content.

SCENE 5: LOOKING AT COMPOSITION, AGAIN

TRISH HARRIS *(at Computers & Writing 2001):* I stray from the subtext of the resolution. It's true that technological ubiquity will become reality. Our classroom and scholarly practices—no longer wholly print- or classroom-bound—will become more expressive, pliant, creative, and thoughtful. The assumption that all composition and rhetoric faculty use computers in the classroom will be the standard. We struggle with ways of naming our discipline and our professional work at a time when we still have old paradigmatic practices in our sights. The luxury of such a struggle will footnote the variety of practices possible when technological ubiquity has become reality.

The names of our departments will probably change. But will we be more closely allied in practice and theory with human–computer interaction and information technology? I don't think so. We will still be teachers of writing, growers and encouragers of budding and practicing writers; we will simply all use technologies and tools to mediate those practices. Our focus will remain composition and rhetoric; yes, a few of us may dissolve into the mists with the artificial intelligence folks. But the bulk of us will still study composition and rhetoric, will be more generalist in our coursework as we prepare to teach writing, and will maintain writing and its related pedagogies and practices as our center.

Will the everywhereness of instructional technology mean the end of computers and writing scholarship, and composition and rhetoric scholarship, as we know it? Yes. Will the scholarship, however, end? Of course not. The next era of scholarship in our field will be less schismatic and more diverse, will reflect the emerging range of practice as it informs theory. Composition and rhetoric professionals might use but not study the new technologies, and my fear is that we will, as a body, stop studying technological literacy, electronic pedagogies, and digital divide politics.

The moment of resistance is past, and in the not-too-distant future we will be defined by our activity and practice rather than the soon-ubiquitous level of technical proficiency as composition and rhetoric becomes infused at every level with ubiquitous, invisibly functional technology. But when will this happen? In the near future? Around the corner? I'd argue that next is *now*, that each new hire represents a profound shift in the direction of ubiquitous skills, that each evolved practice informs and revises each of the old ones, that we have been for some time reinventing—and that we continue to reinvent—our departments and discipline.

I see a future in which we return to job postings that do not list technical skills or computer-mediated teaching experience—not because they are not important or not expected, but because it's understood that *all* candidates will have those skills and experiences. I unhappily see a future in which composition and rhetoric as a discipline will have subsumed computers and writing as a subdiscipline because the perceived need for separation, and a separate scholarship, will no longer exist.

(Cut to Becky Rickly. We see her at home; she types deliberately and with the fluency of a concert pianist.)

RICKLY: First, the naming—I recall participating in the multi-user, object-oriented domain (MOO) transcript at the end of *Computers and the Teaching of Writing in American Higher Education* (Hawisher, LeBlanc, Moran, & Selfe, 1996), and in that MOO Eric Crump and colleagues (1996) suggested that computers and writing didn't fit anymore—that what we did was *technology and rhetoric*. I remember thinking "that's it!" and I honestly believe that since then, I've translated computers and writing to technology and rhetoric in my head. But it's actually through the experience of immersing myself in rhetoric again and being part of a wonderful technical communication and rhetoric program that has helped me to see how this all fits—at least in my mind.

What I find interesting is how much of the initial thrust of the field was based on pedagogy, but also on production, of sorts—I remember papers and conferences on writing and word-processing, often emphasizing a how-to approach. We then started to look at how word processors seemed to enhance the writing process (and later, several scholars, notably Gail Hawisher, 1987, looked at how they might actually hinder the writing process). We don't hear or see those papers much anymore, because computers as tools in the writing, thinking, and production process are a given—aside from access and literacy issues, which are issues, albeit marginalized ones now.

But in the tiny slice of evolution I cited before, I see a pattern of sorts that makes me come back to rhetoric. James Kinneavy (1990) used to say that anyone studying rhetoric should look at five areas: history, pedagogy, administration, critical analysis, and production. And that's a lot of what we do in this field: study the applications of rhetoric. That's what I did, too, as a technical writer at AT&T. That's what I do as a teacher. Heck, I'd even go so far as saying that's what I do as a parent. But all of these ideas, to me, come back to the source: rhetoric.

Although I don't locate my rhetoric in the idealism of Plato or pragmatics of Aristotle, I do embrace the rhetoric of Isocrates (and I just saw yet another book championing his work, this time in technical communication; Whitburn, 1999)—a very practical, pedagogically oriented rhetoric based around the concepts of *phronesis* or practical wisdom, of *philosophia* or savvy critical judgment, and the ultimate goal of helping folks to become responsible participants in a democratic society. Isocrates spoke of a rhetoric of production, announcing that we need to produce texts/information/people as well as merely talk/critique.

What computers and writing or technology and rhetoric (C&W/T&R) does well is allow for boundary pushing; create redefinitions; establish (some) inclusion; lend a sense of rhetorical application; apply nicely to pedagogy; offer great potential for administration and publishing; encourage critical enthusiasm; make collaboration easy(ier); and make us re-think concepts such as human–computer interfaces, usability, and the cyclical nature of history, pedagogy, administration, critique, and production. What C&W/T&R doesn't do well is establish a more evident interplay of rhetorical areas—permeable boundaries with conscious overlap. C&W/T&R doesn't lend itself to traditional assessment—we should find ways to assess and value what we do in terms of what others also value. Bottom line: Rhetoric is vast, and it contains multitudes. Composition, technology, pedagogy, administration, critique, and production are all *applied* rhetoric. So are the different areas of technical communication: usability, human–computer interaction, production, etc.

SCENE 6: LOOKING AT WRITING AND COMMUNICATING, AGAIN

KRAUSE: What the field is becoming is always embedded within a larger, perhaps more important question, what writing—as activity, as artifact—is becoming. What is writing?

TED NELLEN (*at Computers & Writing 2001*): Writing is incorporating other technologies: hypertext, color, art, graphics, video clips, sound. Composition got sidetracked from the original forms of communication—orality, drama, and visual arts—to focus just on the alphabet and text. Books made the slow transition from words to include illustrations and the like—just look at the growth of multimedia in textbooks in the last couple of decades. Writing became too refined a discipline with spelling, grammar, and form. With the growth of technologies in the classroom, teachers of all disciplines are able to better utilize word-processing to incorporate the rigors of English conventions, and to incorporate other forms of communication in their classes—storyboarding, hypercard, hypertext, Macromedia FLASH and DIRECTOR.

I attended a conference in New York City for art teachers, and it opened my eyes to how middle school art teachers are teaching writing skills through high-end technologies and are getting reluctant students who wouldn't want to write to caption their art, and to thus move to a higher level; the technologies expand the horizons of composition and rhetoric. After all, what is the function of composition and rhetoric but to communicate? New technologies are allowing us to widen options for students, and thereby allow for a more inclusive and expanded field of composition and rhetoric.

Our word writing connotes letters and words, whereas the Greeks and Romans had *gram* and *graph,* which roughly translate into writing and drawing; these terms were interchangeable for the Greeks, but not for us. Composition and rhetoric became the tools of scholars and as such became a restricted area at the end of one's academic career and only if chosen—the PhD, of course. But if we bring the practices of our scholarship—make it public, peer-reviewed, and shared—back into schools at, let us say, the kindergarten class, we will be opening up composition and rhetoric. That we have restricted composition and rhetoric to the alphabet and to words is too bad, and has limited us. Now we have the opportunity to open up and be more inclusive.

(Cut to Joel English working in a home office.)

ENGLISH: At Old Dominion University, we have a collegial relationship with communications. And get this: We offer a distance-education degree program shared between communications and professional writing. All classes are offered over satellite, and students decide an emphasis—either professional writing or communications—while taking required classes in both. The degree is called Professional Communications, and is a morph of writing and communications. I'm thinking about this fusion of communications with composition and rhetoric, and dang it if it isn't the most natural-feeling curriculum combination I've ever found myself teaching. Whether students emphasize writing or communication, they all study common foci: rhetoric, technical communications, technology, composition.

JOHNDAN JOHNSON-EILOLA *(hunched over a keyboard. Through a window near his computer, we see snow blowing and drifting)*: This is something I've thought about a lot recently (over the last couple of years), as I've edged slowly out of computers and writing and toward technical communication (and at this point, I think I've even edged out of technical communication and into something else, maybe Johndan Studies or something).

I agree in general with the shift that Bill and Steve are positing. Computers and writing (and, for that matter, composition and rhetoric) have increasingly seemed of limited use to me. The most applicable work, as Bill has suggested, comes from an interdisciplinary amalgam of human–computer interaction and usability, along with more obviously culturally aware areas including postmodern geographies and architectures, advanced design theory (of the Lupton and Miller school, 1999), etc. This seems like an obvious — probably too obvious — nit to pick, but the inclusion of the term "writing" in computers and writing rather than "communication" strikes me as part of the problem. Communicating with/across/within a computer is no longer about writing as a primary activity — even though we're often largely locked into it — but about *design* in the broadest sense of the term: not just graphic design or visual design, but architecture, product design, video, audio, and more. That's not to say that there might not continue to be a field of computers and writing, but I think that field will continue to be an increasingly small subset of composition and rhetoric.

Scene 7: Rallying Cries?

KRAUSE: Although significant questions remain, there seems to be no shortage of rallying cries, but which should we heed? The technological ones?

HART-DAVIDSON *(at Computers & Writing 2001):* It's time to pay attention to the ways information technologies are all built upon what is, to us, a familiar operating system — the same system that drives the strategic use of written discourse. Our expertise, our passion, and our experience is, at this historical moment, the very set of competencies that can drive further innovation in information technology. What was once the study of computers and writing is bound, I predict, to become a host of other important endeavors — all of which advance the design of information technologies meant to support literate activity.

RICE *(In the restaurant again, he keeps typing away):* What's important isn't the computers in computer and writing. What's important is that we deconstruct or reflect on the tools used, whatever they are, to communicate something. I did a course to few years ago with Carole Clark Paper where we had students do crazy things like write clay, cuneiform business cards and illuminated manuscript lesson plans on deer skin. The medium isn't the message. The medium and the message is the message. You can have state-of-the-art ideas with old media types or communication modes like those in oral or chirographic cultures — active remediation. Writing isn't about computer technology. It's not about computers. It's about technology in the sense that all tools are technologies, and it's about composing. Or, decomposing. Deconstructing. Rather than computers and writing, how about technology and composing, or just plain old composing? I compose . . . therefore I am.

HART-DAVIDSON: And as rallying cries go, what about well-reasoned hedges? Part of paying attention — thank you for the enduring anthem, Cindy Selfe (1999) — means knowing when *not* to use computer technologies. Consider these three questions Michael Day posed.

(Cut to Michael Day, standing in front of a large projector screen.)

DAY: For me, it's a question of balance, the balance between the technical efficiency of job training and the expressivist free-ranging exploration of writing that has been a hallmark of the liberal arts education. So I pose these three questions:

1. Some of us still believe that the liberal arts education can and maybe even should provide a learning environment protected from the exigencies of business and industry, all of which would call for practical writing skills, of course using the machines of efficiency. Could we imagine some value in allowing a computer or Internet-free space for some writers? Or, because most writers will have grown up using word-processing software on computers, in showing them alternative composing methods?

2. The dot-com downturn may be showing us that the move into a work world populated with computer and Web jobs might not occur on such a grand scale; we cannot expect every student will be working with computers and the Internet. Therefore, is it really necessary that they get computer training in our classes? More and more of them learn it on their own, anyway.

3. We also need to think about the consistency of computer and Internet training as we prepare students for practical writing tasks versus the need for balance, variety, different approaches for different learning styles, and the freedom to escape from computers. Just how much should program administrators dictate specific uses of technology in writing classes?

   When I think of how we are saying that computers and writing has been subsumed by or is subsuming composition and rhetoric, I wonder how we might begin to rethink our answers to the questions about required computer labs, required online writing, job training, and electronic literacy on a programmatic level.

SCENE 8: NEW TECHNOLOGIES, NEW RESOLVE, FAMILIAR QUESTIONS

(The corridor of an inner-city high school in New York City, although from the looks of the building, we could be at just about any school, anywhere in the United States. A large multi-purpose room buzzes with conversation.)

KRAUSE: If Michael Day's questions sound a familiar note, it is no doubt because questions like these have been asked, more or less emphatically, throughout the last 20 years. We might say, in fact, that a defining feature of the scholarship in computers and composition is the raising of such questions, the continued problematization of the relationships between writing technologies, writing pedagogy and curricula, writing theories and practices.

(In the multi-purpose room, we see groups of writing teachers scattered around the room in twos and threes, sitting at large desks haphazardly clustered in what is one of several ad hoc arrangements of the space. We are looking at a teaching-with-

*technology workshop at the 2003 Conference on College Composition and Communi-
cation annual convention in New York City [Benninghoff, Day, Hart-Davidson,
Krause, Nellen, Rehberger et al., 2003]. On each desk, illuminating the faces of the
teachers, sits a laptop computer; we see the LCD screens and recognize wireless web
browsing going on. And that isn't the only network in the room—Michael Day
works with a group of three teachers; he is pointing to something on one of the screens
while one of the teachers glances rapidly back and forth between the screen and the
touchpad that moves the mouse pointer. As the camera fades on this scene of tech-
norhetoricians working and talking, Bill is overheard saying: "Does this wireless network change everything or what?!")*

FINIS

REFERENCES

Benninghoff, Steven, Day, Michael, Hart-Davidson, Bill, Krause, Steven, Nellen, Ted, Rehberger, Dean, et al. (2003). *Web design for composers: A workshop for composition teachers who want to create usable web sites.* Workshop at the Conference on College Composition and Communication, New York, NY. Retrieved from <http://matrix.msu.edu/~comp/>.

Bolter, Jay D. (1991). *Writing space: The computer, hypertext, and the history of writing.* Hillsdale, NJ: Lawrence Erlbaum.

Bolter, Jay D., & Grusin, Richard. (2000). *Remediation: Understanding new media.* Cambridge, MA: MIT Press.

Carbone, Nick, Harris, Trish, Hart-Davidson, Bill, Krause, Steven D., & Nellen, Ted. (2001). *The end of computers and writing: Benefactors and victims of success.* Panel discussion at the Computers & Writing Conference, Muncie, IN. Retrieved from <http://www.rpi.edu/~hartdw/cw2001blog.html>.

Crump, Eric, Carter, Locke, Day, Michael, Johnson-Eilola, Johndan, Rickly, Becky, & Takayoshi, Pamela. (1996). Our colleagues interact on a MOO. In Gail E. Hawisher, Paul LeBlanc, Charles Moran, & Cynthia L. Selfe (Eds.), *Computers and the teaching of writing in American higher education, 1979–1994: A history* (pp. 287–304). Norwood, NJ: Ablex.

Hawisher, Gail. (1987). The effects of word processing on the revision strategies of college freshman. *Research in the Teaching of English, 21,* 145–160.

Hawisher, Gail E., LeBlanc, Paul, Moran, Charles, & Selfe, Cynthia L. (1996). *Computers and the teaching of writing in American higher education, 197–1994: A history.* Norwood NJ: Ablex.

Kinneavy, James. (1990). *Theory of discourse.* New York: W. W. Norton.

Johnson-Eilola, Johndan. (1996). Relocating the value of work: Technical communication in a post-industrial age. *Technical Communication Quarterly, 5,* 245–270.

Lanham, Richard A. (1993). *The electronic word: Democracy, technology, and the arts.* Chicago: University of Chicago Press.

Lunenfeld, Peter. (Ed.). (1999). *The digital dialectic: New essays on new media.* Cambridge, MA: MIT Press.

Lupton, Ellen, & Miller, J. Abbot. (1999). *Design writing research: Writing on graphic design.* New York: Phaidon Press.

McLuhan, Marshall. (1964). *Understanding media: The extensions of man.* Cambridge, MA: MIT Press.

Papert, Seymour. (1993). *The children's machine: Rethinking school in the age of the computer.* New York: Basic Books.

Selfe, Cynthia L. (1999). Technology and literacy: A story about the perils of not paying attention. *College Composition and Communication, 50,* 411–436.

Snyder, Ilana. (Ed.). (1998). *Page to screen: Taking literacy into the electronic era.* New York: Routledge.

Theismeyer, John. (1989). Should we do what we can? In Gail E. Hawisher & Cynthia L. Selfe (Eds.), *Critical perspectives on computers and composition instruction* (pp. 75–93). New York: Teachers College Press.

Whitburn, Merrill. (1999). *Rhetorical scope and performance: The example of technical communication.* Norwood, NJ: Ablex.

SUGGESTED READINGS

FOUNDATIONAL WORKS

DeVoss, Dànielle, and Heidi McKee, eds. 20th Anniversary Spec. Double issue of *Computers and Composition* 20–21, (2003–2004).

Gruber, Sybille. *Weaving a Virtual Web: Practical Approaches to New Information Technologies.* Urbana: NCTE, 1999.

Hawisher, Gail, Paul LeBlanc, Charles Moran, and Cynthia L. Selfe, eds. *Computers and the Teaching of Writing in American Higher Education, 1979–1994: A History.* Greenwich: Ablex, 1996.

Hawisher, Gail, and Cynthia L. Selfe, eds. *Passions, Pedagogies, and 21st Century Technologies.* Logan: Utah State UP, 1999.

Inman, James. *Computers and Writing: The Cyborg Era.* Mahwah: Erlbaum, 2004.

Selfe, Cynthia L., and Susan Hilligoss, eds. *Literacy and Computers: The Complications of Teaching and Learning with Technology.* New York: MLA, 1994.

Selfe, Cynthia L. *Technology and Literacy in the Twenty-first Century: The Importance of Paying Attention.* Carbondale: Southern Illinois, 1999.

Takayoshi, Pamela and Brian Huot. *Teaching Writing with Computers: An Introduction.* Boston: Houghton, 2003.

LITERACY AND ACCESS

Faigley, Lester. "Literacy after the Revolution." *College Composition and Communication* 48 (1997): 30–43.

Grabill, Jeff. "Utopic Visions, the Technopoor, and Public Access: Writing Technologies in a Community Literacy Program." *Computers and Composition* 12 (1998): 297–315.

Gurak, Laura J., and Johndan Johnson-Eilola, eds. *Intellectual Property*. Spec. issue of *Computers and Composition* 15 (1998).

Haas, Christina. "On the Relationship between Old and New Technologies. *Computers and Composition* 16 (1999): 209–28.

Hawisher, Gail E., and Cynthia L. Selfe, eds. *Global Literacies and the World-Wide Web*. New York: Routledge, 2000.

Hawisher, Gail E., and Cynthia L. Selfe, eds. *Literate Lives in the Information Age*. Mahwah: Erlbaum, 1998.

Heba, Gary. "HyperRhetoric: Multimedia, Literacy, and the Future of Composition." *Computers and Composition* 14 (1997): 19–44.

Kemp, Fred O. "The User-friendly Fallacy." *College Composition and Communication* 38 (1987): 32–9.

Porter, James E. *Rhetorical Ethics and Internetworked Writing*. Greenwich: Ablex, 1998.

Reinking, David, Michael C. McKenna, Linda D. Labbo, and Ronald D. Kieffer. *Handbook of Literacy and Technology: Transformations in a Post-typographic World*. Mahwah: Erlbaum, 1998.

Reynolds, Thomas J., and Charles P. Lewis. "The Changing Topography of Computer Access for Composition Students." *Computers and Composition* 14 (1997): 269–78.

Tyner, Kathleen. *Literacy in a Digital World*. Mahwah: Erlbaum, 1998.

United States Copyright Office. "Digital Millennium Act." 1998. 2 June 2006 <http://copyright.gov/legislation/dmca.pdf/>.

United States Copyright Office. "Sonny Bono Copyright Term Extension Act of 1998." 1998. 2 June 2006 <http://www.loc.gov/copyright/legislation/s505.pdf>.

TECHNOLOGY AND IDENTITY

Alexander, Jonathan, and Will Banks, eds. Sexualities, Technologies, and the Teaching of Writing. Special issue, *Computers and Composition* 21 (2004).

Banks, Adam. *Race, Rhetoric, and Technology: Searching for Higher Ground*. Mahwah: NCTE/ Erlbaum, 2005.

Barber, Margaret M., Laura L. Sullivan, and Janice R. Walker. Diversity and Multiculturalism. Special issue, *Computers and Composition* 14 (1997).

Knadler, Stephen. "E-racing Difference in E-space: Black Female Subjectivity and the Web-based Portfolio." *Computers and Composition* 18 (2001): 235–55.

McKee, Heidi. "YOUR VIEWS SHOWED TRUE IGNORANCE!!!: (Mis)Communication in an Online Interracial Discussion Forum." *Computers and Composition* 19 (2002): 411–36.

Monroe, Barbara. *Crossing the Digital Divide: Race, Writing, and Technology in the Classroom.* New York: Teachers College, 2004.

Nakamura, Lisa. *Cybertypes: Race, Ethnicity, and Identity on the Internet.* New York: Routledge, 2000.

Regan, Alison. "'Type Normal Like the Rest of Us': Writing, Power, and Homophobia in the Networked Composition Classroom." *Computers and Composition* 12 (1993): 61–78.

Romano, Susan. "The Egalitarian Narrative: Whose Story? Which Yardstick? *Computers and Composition* 10 (1992): 5–28.

Slatin, John. "The Art of ALT: Toward a More Accessible Web." *Computers and Composition* 18 (2001): 73–81.

Takayoshi, Pamela. "Building New Networks from the Old: Women's Experiences with Electronic Communications." *Computers and Composition* 11 (1994): 21–35.

Warshauer, Susan Claire. "Rethinking Teaching Authority to Counteract Homophobic Prejudice in the Networked Classroom: A Model of Teacher Response and Overview of Classroom Methods." *Computers and Composition* 12 (1995): 97–111.

Woodland, Randal. "Queer Spaces, Modem Boys, and Pagan Statues: Gay/Lesbian Identity and the Construction of Cyberspace." *The Cybercultures Reader.* Ed. David Bell and Barbara M. Kennedy. London: Routledge, 2000.

COMPOSING

Bruffee, Kenneth. "Comment on 'Computer Conferences and Learning: Authority, Resistance, and Internally Persuasive Discourse.'" *College English* 53 (1991): 950–52.

Cooper, Marilyn M., and Cynthia L. Selfe. "Computer Conferences and Learning: Authority, Resistance, and Internally Persuasive Discourse." *College English* 52 (1990): 847–69.

Gruber, Sybille. "Re: Ways We Contribute: Students, Instructors, and Pedagogies in the Computer-mediated Classroom." *Computers and Composition* 12 (1995): 61–78.

Haas, Christina. *Writing Technology: Studies on the Materiality of Literacy.* Mahwah: Erlbaum, 1996.

Hart, Betty, and Margaret Daisley. "Computers and Composition in Japan: Notes on Real and Virtual Literacies." *Computers and Composition* 12 (1994): 37–47.

Hawisher, Gail E., and Cynthia L. Selfe, eds. *Global Literacies and the World-Wide Web*. New York: Routledge, 2000.

Moran, Charles." Notes Towards a Rhetoric of Email." *Computers and Composition* 12 (1995):15–21.

Rodrigues, Raymond L., and Dawn Wilson Rodrigues. "Computer-based Invention: Its Place and Potential." *College Composition and Communication* 35 (1984): 78–87.

Shauf, Michele S. "The Problem of Electronic Argument: A Humanist's Perspective." *Computers and Composition* 18 (2001): 33–7.

Sirc, Geoffrey M. "The Twin Worlds of Electronic Conferencing." *Computers and Composition* 12 (1995): 265–78.

Sullivan, Patricia, and Jennie Dautermann, eds. *Electronic Literacies in the Workplace: Technologies of Writing*. Urbana: NCTE, 1996.

Institutional Programs

Berge, Zane L., and Mauri P. Collins, eds. *Computer Mediated Communication and the Online Classroom*. Cresskill: Hampton, 1995.

Blakelock, Jane, and Tracy E. Smith. *Distance Learning: Evolving Perspectives*. Spec. issue of *Computers and Composition* 23 (2006).

Blythe, Stuart. "Networked Computers + Writing Centers = ? Thinking About Networked Computers in Writing Center Practice." *The Writing Center Journal* 17 (1997): 89–110.

Braine, George. "A Study of English as a Foreign Language (EFL) Writers on a Local-area Network (LAN) and in Traditional Classes." *Computers and Composition* 18 (2001): 275–92.

Coogan, David. "Towards a Rhetoric of Online Tutoring." *The Writing Lab Newsletter* 19.5 (1994): 3–5.

"Cover Story: Online Writing Labs." *Kairos* 1.1. 1996. 1 June 2006 <http://english. ttu.edu/kairos/1.1/index.htm>.

Hobson, Eric. ed. *Wiring the Writing Center*. Logan: Utah State UP, 1998.

Inman, James A., and Donna Sewell, eds. *Taking Flight with OWLs: Examining Electronic Writing Center Work*. Mahwah: Erlbaum, 2000.

Kinkead, Joyce, and Christine A. Hult, eds. *Writing Centers Online*. Spec. issue of *Computers and Composition* 12 (1995).

Lang, Susan. "Who Owns the Course? Online Composition Courses in an Era of Changing Intellectual Property Policies." *Computers and Composition* 15 (1998): 215–28.

Mullin, Joan A., ed. *WAC, WID, ECAC, CAC, CXC, LAC—VAC? Incorporating the Visual into Writing/Electronic/Communication/Learning Across the Curriculum.* Spec. issue of *Across the Disciplines.* 2005. 2 June 2006 <http://wac.colostate.edu/atd/visual/>.

Pennington, Martha, ed. *Writing in an Electronic Medium.* Houston: Athelstan, 1999.

Petersen, Patricia Webb, and Wilhelmina Savenye, eds. *Distance Learning: Promises and Perils of Teaching and Learning Online.* Spec. issue of *Computers and Composition* 18 (2001).

Reiss, Donna, Dickie Selfe, and Art Young. *Electronic Communication Across the Curriculum.* Urbana: NCTE, 1998.

Trimbur, John. "Multiliteracies, Social Futures, and Writing Centers." *The Writing Center Journal* 20 (2000): 29–32.

WAC Clearinghouse. 1998–2006. 2 June 2006 <http://wac.colostate.edu/>.

New Media Writing

DeVoss, Dànielle Nicole, Ellen Cushman, and Jeffrey T. Grabill. "Infrastructure and Composing: The *When* of New Media Writing." *College Composition and Communication* 57 (2005): 14–44.

Gee, James Paul. *What Video Games Have to Teach Us about Learning and Literacy.* New York: Palgrave Macmillan, 2004.

George, Diana. "From Analysis to Design: Visual Communication in the Teaching of Writing." *College Composition and Communication* 54 (2002): 11–39.

Hocks, Mary E. "Understanding Visual Rhetoric in Digital Writing Environments." *College Composition and Communication* 54 (2003): 629–56.

Kress, Gunther. *Literacy in the New Media Age.* London: Routledge, 2003.

———. *Multimodal Discourse: The Modes and Media of Contemporary Communication.* London: Hodder/Arnold, 2001.

Manovich, Lev. *The Digital Dialectic: New Essays on New Media.* Cambridge: MIT, 2000.

———. *The Language of New Media.* Cambridge: MIT, 2002.

Stroupe, Craig. "Visualizing English: Recognizing the Hybrid Literacy of Visual and Verbal Authorship on the Web." *College English* 62 (2000): 607–32.

Sullivan, Patricia. "Practicing Safe Visual Rhetoric on the World Wide Web." *Computers and Composition* 18 (2001): 103–21.

The WIDE Research Center Collective. "Why teach digital writing?" *Kairos* 10.1. 2005. 2 June 2006 <http://english.ttu.edu/kairos/10.1/binder2.html?coverweb/ wide/index.html>.

Williams, Sean D. "Part 1: Thinking Out of the Pro-verbal Box." *Computers and Composition* 18 (2001): 21–32.

THEORY

Beavis, Catherine, and Ilana Snyder. *Page to Screen: Taking Literacy into the Electronic Era.* London: Routledge, 1997.

Bolter, Jay David. *Turing's Man: Western Culture in the Computer Age.* Chapel Hill: U North Carolina P, 1984.

_____. *Writing Space: Computers, Hypertext, and the Remediation of Print.* Mahwah: Erlbaum, 2001.

Bolter, Jay David, and Richard Grusin. *Remediation: Understanding New Media.* Cambridge: MIT, 2000.

Braun, M.J. "The Political Economy of Computers and Composition: 'Democracy Hope' in the Era of Globalization." *JAC: A Journal of Composition Theory* 21 (2001): 130–62.

Faigley, Lester. "The Achieved Utopia of the Networked Classroom." *Fragments of Rationality: Postmodernity and the Subject of Composition.* Pittsburgh: U of Pittsburgh P, 1992. 163–99.

Gilbert, Pamela K. "Meditations upon Hypertext: A Rhetorethics for Cyborgs." *JAC: A Journal of Composition Theory* 17 (1997): 23–38.

Haraway, Donna J. *Modest_Witness@Second_Millennium.FemaleMan©_Meets_Oncomouse™.* New York: Routledge, 1996.

Haraway, Donna J. "A Cyborg Manifesto: Science, Technology, and Socialist-feminism in the Late Twentieth Century." Ed. Donna J. Haraway. *Simians, Cyborgs and Women: The Reinvention of Nature.* New York: Routledge, 1991. 149–81.

Johnson-Eilola, Johndan. "Control and the Cyborg: Writing and Being Written in Hypertext." *JAC: A Journal of Composition Theory* 13 (1993): 381–400.

Landow, George P. *Hypertext: The Convergence of Contemporary Critical Theory and Technology.* Baltimore: Johns Hopkins, 1992.

_____. *Hypertext 3.0: Critical Theory and New Media in an Era of Globalization.* Baltimore: Johns Hopkins, 2006.

Lanham, Richard. *The Electronic Word.* Chicago: U of Chicago P, 2005.

Reynolds, Nedra. "Composition's Imagined Geographies: The Politics of Space in the Frontier, City, and Cyberspace." *College Composition and Communication* 50 (1998): 12–35.

Welch, Kathleen. *Electric Rhetoric.* Cambridge: MIT, 1999.

ABOUT THE EDITORS

Michelle Sidler is Associate Professor of English and Coordinator of Composition at Auburn University, where she teaches various undergraduate courses in writing and rhetoric as well as graduate courses in composition, rhetoric, and professional communication. Sidler has published articles in journals such as *Computers and Composition, Rhetoric Review, The WAC Journal, Kairos,* and *JAC: A Journal of Composition Theory.*

Richard Morris received his Ph.D. in English from Purdue University. He has worked at Parkland College in Champaign, Illinois, since 1997, where he teaches composition, reading, literature, and the liberal arts and sciences seminar LAS 189, working both in the classroom and online. Morris has served as the Director of Composition, Coordinator of LAS 189, and coordinator of the college-wide mentoring program. With Michelle Sidler, he published an article in *JAC,* "Writing in a Post-Berlinian Landscape."

Elizabeth (Betsy) Overman Smith is Associate Professor in the Department of Languages, Literature, and Philosophy at Tennessee State University in Nashville, Tennessee. She teaches technical communication and first-year composition courses. While on the faculty of Auburn University, she served as the Coordinator of Instructional Technology for the English department and built or upgraded computer classrooms every year for seven years. She coauthored *How to Write for the World of Work,* 6th and 7th editions, and has published research on technical communication using citation analysis in the *Journal of Business and Technical Communication, Journal of Technical Writing and Communication,* and *Technical Communication Quarterly.*

Acknowledgments *(continued from page iv)*

INDEX

Abrams, Robin, 194
Administrators, CCCC on role of,
    17–18
African Americans
    poor schools, lack of technology,
        101–4
    See also "Persistence of Difference
        in Networked Classrooms:
        Non-negotiable Difference and
        the African American Student
        Body" (Taylor); racial/ethnic
        minorities
Agre, Phil, 443
Alexander, Jan, 338
Alexander, Jonathan, 207
Alliance for Computers and Writing
    (ACW), 463–66
America Reads Challenge, 99
Analytic induction strategy, 280
Annas, Pamela, 196
Anson, Chris M., 46, 391
Anxiety, computer, 254, 264,
    391
Arnheim, Rudolf, 471
Aronowitz, Stanley, 56
ASCII (American Standard Code
    for Information Interchange),
    foreign language, limited
    support for, 73–74
Ashton-Jones, Evelyn, 191
Assessment of writing
    adequacy model, 289–90
    authentic assessment, 278–79
    deep assessment, 279–86
    deep viewing approach, 282

Assessment of writing *(continued)*
    Dynamic Criteria Map (DCM), 286
    heuristic for, 300–304
    human versus machine scoring, 18
    Intelligent Essay Assessor, 277–78
    Online Learning Record (OLR),
        282–83
    on-line surveillance by teacher, 42–43
    outcomes assessment, 291–92
    self-assessment, 440
    team approach, 281–82
    TOPIC/ICON program, 284–85
    validity/reliability in. *See*
        "Rethinking Validity and
        Reliability in the Age of
        Convergence" (Penrod)
    of writing portfolios, 275–79
Asynchronous conferencing. *See*
        bulletin boards; discussions,
        electronic
Authentic assessment, 278–79
Authoring, in hypertext, 171–72

Baig, Edward, 59
Bailey, Carol A., 439
Barker, Thomas, 436
Barnouw, Eric, 26
Baron, Dennis, 116, 390
Barron, Nancy Guerra, 111
Barthes, Roland, 154
Basic Books v. Kinko's, 140
Bateson, Gregory, 168
Batson, Trent, 64, 240, 430
Bauman, Marcy, 378

Bell, Alexander Graham, 126
Berge, Zane L., 376
Berlin, James, 319, 458
Bernstein, Mark, 170
"Best of Both Worlds: Teaching Basic
        Writers in Class and Online,"
        (Stine), 370–71, 389–402
    hybrid environment, use of,
        397–401
    negative aspects, 390–93
    positive aspects, 394–96
Best practices, CCCC position paper
        on, 12, 15–19
Birkerts, Sven, 335, 444
Bizzell, Patricia, 219, 245, 297, 460
BlackBoard, 278
Blythe, Stuart, 385
Boden, Margaret, 114
Body language
    African American students, 225–26
    common gestures, 224
    spontaneous engagement, 224
Bolter, Jay D., 70, 120, 350, 469, 488
Bono, Sonny, 146
Bourdieu, Pierre, 96
Boyle, James, 136
Brady, Matthew, 137
Brand, Stewart, 169
Braverman, Harry, 24
Bricolage
    defined, 75
    women, benefits to, 75–76, 195
Bridwell-Bowles, Lillian, 198
Broad, Bob, 285–86
Brooke, Collin Gifford, 358
Bruffee, Kenneth, 288, 454–55
Bruner, Jerome, 171
Bulletin boards
    ESL students use, 412
    teachers/students use, 241–42
    See also discussions, electronic
Burton, Vicki Tolar, 158
Butler, Judith, 75

Campbell, Peter, 439
Capitalism
    computer interface and inequality,
        69–71

Capitalism (continued)
    desktop, corporate culture
        expressed in, 69–70
    monopoly capitalism,
        23–24, 32
Carbone, Nick, 485, 486, 487
Caruso, Domenick, 338
Cayton, M. K., 196
"CCCC Position Statement on
        Teaching, Learning, and
        Assessing Writing in Digital
        Environments"
    focus of, 12
    text of, 15–19
CD-ROM, lecture material
        on, 51
Center for Computer-Assisted
        Instruction, 430
Chadwich, Scott, 158
"Champing at the Bits:
        Computers, Copyright,
        and the Composition
        Classroom" (Logie), 90–91,
        135–50
    copyright law, development of,
        137–46
    fair use exemptions, 139–40
    Internet information resources on,
        147–49
Chandler, Alfred D., 23
Cheek, Madelon, 430
Childers, Pamela, 436
Chodorow, Nancy, 188, 200
Cicognani, Anna, 58
Clanchy, Michael, 122
Clinton, Bill, 89, 116
    education expenditures, 99
    Global Information Infrastructure
        (GII), 105–7
    and intellectual property rights
        laws, 142, 144–45
    National Information Infrastructure
        (NII), 105, 116, 142
    Technology Literacy Challenge,
        89, 93
Cognitive mapping
    functions of, 460
    and Web research, 356–58,
        360–61

Coherence of text. *See* "Looking for Sources of Coherence in a Fragmented World: Notes toward a New Assessment Design" (Yancey)

Collaborative activities, 435
ESL students, 411–16
peer teaching, 41
positive aspects, 37–38, 53–54, 241–42
software design by educators, 79–80
student power inequalities, impact on, 191–92, 241, 244–45
surveillance by teacher, 42–43
teacher as moderator, 242
technologies available for, 240–43, 436–37
See also discussions, electronic

Comment, 394

CommonSpace, 394, 436

Communication across the curriculum (CAC), 426
See also "WAC Wired: Electronic Communication across the Curriculum" (Reiss and Young)

Composition teachers. *See* teachers/instructors

Computational linguistics, 311–12

"Computer and the Inexperienced Writer" (Hult), 236, 326–32
revision strategies, 326–30

Computer-Assisted Composition Journal, 198

Computer industry
development of, 187
men versus women in, 186–87

Computers and Composition, 36, 198

Computers and writing instruction
African Americans. *See* "Persistence of Difference in Networked Classrooms: *Non-negotiable Difference* and the African American Student Body" (Taylor)
Alliance for Computers and Writing (ACW), 437–39
assessment of work. *See* assessment of writing

Computers and writing instruction *(continued)*
for basic writers. *See* "Best of Both Worlds: Teaching Basic Writers in Class and Online" (Stine)
body language, student, 223–26
collaboration. *See* collaborative activities; discussions, electronic
college programs in, 430–31, 437–39, 493
common formats for, 40–41
computer interface, ideological implications, 68–82
distance learning, 51–54
ESL students. *See* "Impact of the Computer in Second Language Writing" (Pennington)
future view, 61–62, 440–45, 485–96
and instructional enhancement, 48–54
instructors of. *See* teachers/instructors
Internet, writing-related resources, 418–19
and multimedia, 51–54, 56
rhetoric of technology concept, 36–39, 67
compared to traditional instruction, 252–53
and Web literacy. *See* "Web Literacy: Challenges and Opportunities for Research in a New Medium" (Sorapure, Inglesby, and Yatchisin)

Computers in classroom, early use of, 29

Concordance programs, 419

Condon, William, 457

Conference on College Composition and Communication (CCCC) position statement. *See* "CCCC Position Statement on Teaching, Learning, and Assessing Writing in Digital Environments"

Conference on Computers in Writing
and Language Instruction
(1988), 36
computers and writing survey,
38–39
Conference on Fair Use (CONFU),
142–43
Conferences, online. *See* discussions,
electronic
Confidence, about writing, 264–65
Conklin, Jeff, 170
Connection
as creative act, 461–62
versus production, 459–60
Connell, Tim, 472
Connors, Robert, 319
Contact zones. *See* "Politics of the
Interface: Power and Its
Exercise in Electronic Contact
Zones" (Selfe and Selfe)
Conté, Nicholas-Jacques, 123–25
"Contrasts: Teaching and Learning
about Writing in Traditional
and Computer Classrooms"
(Palmquist, Kiefer, Hartvigsen,
Goodlew), 234–35, 251–70
classmate interactions, 258–59
computer anxiety, 254, 264
computer versus traditional
classroom, 252–53, 267–70
curricular issues, 255–56
students in study, differences
among, 253–55
student-teacher interactions,
258–59, 265–66
teaching roles, 256–58
technology, student introduction to,
262–64
workshop versus traditional
atmosphere, 259–62
writing confidence, 264–65
writing performance, 266–67
Conversational learning, 431, 433
Cooper, Marilyn, 218, 319, 457
Copeland, Regina, 111
Copyright law. *See* "Champing at the
Bits: Computers, Copyright,
and the Composition
Classroom" (Logie)

Corporate culture, desktop as
reflection of, 69–70
Coyle, Karen, 194
Creativity, hierarchical systems as
barrier, 74
Creed, Tom, 54
Cronbach, L. J., 272
Cross, K. Patricia, 393
Crow, Steven, 375
Crowley, Sharon, 378–79
Crump, Eric, 487
Cuba, literacy campaign, 30–32
Cultural maps. *See* "Politics of the
Interface: Power and Its
Exercise in Electronic Contact
Zones" (Selfe and Selfe)
Curriculum. *See* "WAC Wired:
Electronic Communication
across the Curriculum" (Reiss
and Young)

Daedalus Interchange, 413, 436
Day, Michael, 485, 494–95
"Debate about Online Learning: Key
Issues for Writing Teachers"
(Webb Peterson), 370,
373–84
educational goals, 377–79
student learning, effects on, 379–82
teacher goals, 374–77
De Certeau, Michel, 94, 114
Dede, Christopher, 168
Deep assessment, 279–86
analytic induction strategy, 280
assessment programs, 282–86
trustworthiness, steps in, 281–82
See also assessment of writing
Deleuze, Gilles, 287
De Mandeville, Barnard, 22
Democracy, and rhetoric of
technology concept, 36–39,
67–68
Design model, elements of, 472–78
DeVoss, Dànielle, 151
Dibble, Vernon, 20
Discursive privilege, computer
interface, ideological
implications, 71–74

Discussions, electronic
and collaboration. *See* collaborative
activities
conferencing software, 394, 436
and egalitarian relationships,
191–92, 241, 244–45
ESL students, networking, 411–16
and gender. *See* "Feminist Research
in Computers and
Composition" (Gerrard)
participation, teaching students. *See*
"Pedagogy in the Computer-
Networked Classroom"
(Eldred)
privacy and sexual orientation,
208–10
rhetoric of technology concept,
37–38, 42–43
student self-absorption, 246
technologies available for, 240–43,
436–37
writing instruction, unique aspects,
37–38
Distance learning, 373–82
educational goals, 377–79
global, and English language use,
72–73
independent study courses, 54–56
interactive aspects, limitations,
57–58, 391
learning institution interest in,
56–59, 378
and lifelong learning, 377–78
limitations of, 380–81, 390–94
positive aspects, 53–54, 57, 394–96
reading online, required skills, 392
student learning, effects on, 379–82
teachers' roles, 374–77
writing assignment, example of,
51–54
"Distant Voices: Teaching and Writing
in a Culture of Technology"
(Anson), 13, 46–63
collaborative activities, benefits,
53–54
distance learning, 51–58
instructional enhancement, 48–54
issues for exploration, 61–62
multimedia tools, 50–56

Douglas, Jane Yellowlees, 471–72
Dreamweaver, 417
Drop-outs, white versus racial/ethnic
minorities, 66
Duin, Ann Hill, 210
Dunbar, Charles, 125
Dunn, Patricia A., 228
Dunn De Mers, Kathleen, 228
Dynamic Criteria Map (DCM), 286

Eagleton, Terry, 108
Egalitarian relationships, and
electronic discussions, 191–92,
241, 244–45
Elbow, Peter, 389
Eldred, Janet M., 239
Electronic communication across the
curriculum (ECAC), 426
See also "WAC Wired: Electronic
Communication across the
Curriculum" (Reiss and Young)
Electronic conferences. *See*
discussions, electronic
Electronic mail (e-mail)
coherence of text, 301–2
ESL students' use of, 411–12,
415–16
uses, by teachers/students,
240–41, 245
Ellertson, Anthony, 482
E-mail. *See* electronic mail (e-mail)
Empowerment, technology, effects on,
60, 72
ENFI classrooms, 243
English, Joel, 485, 493
English as a second language (ESL).
See "Impact of the Computer in
Second Language Writing"
(Pennington)
English language
ASCII support for, 73–74
as computer-related default
language, 71–74
in global distance learning, 72–73
Erickson, Jane, 472
Ericsson, Patricia, 308
ERROR 404 essay, 465–66
Ewell, Barbara, 434

Facilitator-graders, 57
Factory educational model, 54–55
Faigley, Lester, 95, 211, 218, 245, 374–75, 378, 455
Fair use (exemptions to copyright), 139–40
Feenberg, Andrew, 76
Feist v. Rural Telephone Service, 136–37
"Feminist Research in Computers and Composition" (Gerrard), 182, 185–206
  collaborative activities and sense of status, 191–92
  composition studies, men versus women, 198–99
  computer industry, women pioneers, 187
  feminist pedagogy, goals of, 190–91
  feminist software, 189, 193–94
  gendered writing styles, 196
  Internet, hostility to women, 187, 192–93
  learning styles, male versus female, 194–96
  online discourse, gendered, 197–98
  social class issues, 201–2
  use of technology and gender, 199–200
  video games, for boys versus girls, 188–90
Ferris, Pixie, 341
File-sharing, teachers'/students' use of, 241
Fish, Stanley, 171
Flaming, gender differences, 193
Flash, composition and writing, use of, 482–84
Flynn, Elizabeth, 185, 187
Folsom v. Marsh, 139
Forbes, Cheryl, 297, 305
Foucault, Michael, 40, 42, 154, 207, 223
Fraud
  and digitized text, 129–30
  intellectual property. *See* " 'It wasn't me, was it?' Plagiarism and the Web" (DeVoss and Rosati)
Freire, Paulo, 55

"From Pencils to Pixels: The Stages of Literacy Technologies" (Baron), 90, 116–34
  humanists and technology, 118–19
  pencil, 118, 123–25
  telephone and communication technology, 126–27
  word-processing technology, 127–29
  writing, historical development, 119–22
FrontPage, 417
Fulwiler, Toby, 242, 430, 441
Fuss, Diana, 216

Gabler, Hans-Walter, 167
Gaines, Jane M., 137
Games, design and gender, 188–89
Gannett, Cinthia, 196
Gateways, evaluation of, 360
Gee, James Paul, 100, 114
Gender differences
  computers, male image of, 186–88
  and computers and writing. *See* "Feminist Research in Computers and Composition" (Gerrard)
  learning styles, 194–96
  male versus female language, 196
Gerrard, Lisa, 185, 198
Getting America's Children Ready for the Twenty-first Century, 98–100
Giddens, Anthony, 96
Gilbert, Steven W., 430
Gillespie, Paula, 434
Gilligan, Carol, 195, 200
Girl Games, 189
Giroux, Henry, 76, 77, 81–82, 460
Global Information Infrastructure (GII), 105–7
Goldstein, Paul, 144
Gomez, Mary Louise, 66, 71
Goodlew, Barbara, 251
Gordon, Nicholas, 430
Gore, Al, and Global Information Infrastructure (GII), 105–7
Graff, Harvey, 100, 103, 114
Grammar checker. *See* MS Word Grammar Checker

Greene, Wendy Tibbetts, 198
Groppe, Laura, 189
Grumet, Madeleine, 195–96
Grusin, David, 469, 488
Guattari, Felix, 287

Haefner, Joel, 308, 311, 313
Hairston, Maxine, 457
Haist, Caroline, 309, 312, 320
Halliday, Michael K., 295
Hamp-Lyons, Liz, 457
Hansen, Chris, 210
Hara, Noriko, 381–82
Harding, Sandra, 200
Harman, David, 31
Harris, Leslie, 430
Harris, Muriel, 430
Harris, Trish, 485, 490–91
Harris, William, 121
Hart-Davidson, Bill, 485, 486,
    488–89, 490, 494
Hartvigsen, James, 251
Hartwell, Patrick, 309
Hasan, Ruqaiya, 295
Haswell, Richard, 295
Havelock, Eric A., 168
Hawhee, Debra, 319
Hawisher, Gail E., 12, 35, 67, 198, 218,
    239, 379, 438, 444, 486, 492
Hayles, N. Katherine, 223
Hearing-impaired students,
    synchronous conferencing,
    243
Heba, Gary, 353
Henderson, Bill, 118–19
Herring, Susan, 197, 199
Herzberg, Bruce, 219, 457
Hesse, Douglas, 278
Heuristic, for assessing writing,
    300–304
Hierarchical systems
    alternatives to, 75
    as barrier to creativity, 74–75
    versus bricolage, 75–76
    of computer interface, 74–76
Hilligoss, Susan, 211
Hillocks, George, 40
Himley, Margaret, 279
Hofstadter, Douglas, 169, 172

Holdstein, Deborah, 61, 198
Home computers
    and income level, 102
    whites versus ethnic minorities,
        102
Homosexuality. See "Out of the Closet
        and into the Network: Sexual
        Orientation and the
        Computerized Classroom"
        (Alexander)
Hopper, Grace, 187
Howard, Rebecca Moore, 154
Hult, Christine A., 326
Huot, Brian, 276, 300, 304
Hybrid space, cyberspace as, 58
Hybrid writing class, practice
        principles, 397–401
HyperCard, 175
Hypertext, 172–76
    defined, 171
    ESL students, writing of, 416
    links, student assessment of,
        343–45
    male versus female compatibility
        with, 196
    reading and writing in. See
        "Reading Hypertext: Order
        and Coherence in a New
        Medium" (Slatin)
HyperTIES, 174

Illiteracy
    technological illiteracy, 107–8
    use of term, historical view,
        20–22
Images, 341–43, 471–72
"Impact of the Computer in Second
        Language Writing,"
        (Pennington), 371, 398–401,
        404–22
    hypertext, creating, 416
    Internet as information resource,
        418–19
    networking methods, 411–16
    positive/negative aspects, 408–10,
        419–21
    word processing, use of, 405–7
    writing, student planning for, 407
Independent study, 54–56

Inequality
  computer interface, ideological
      implications, 68–82
  English as computer-related default
      language, 71–74
  and gender. *See* "Feminist Research
      in Computers and
      Composition" (Gerrard);
      women
  home computer ownership, 102
  literacy and technology, Marxist
      view, 22–32
  poor schools, lack of technology,
      101–4
  technological underclass, 67
Inglesby, Pamela, 160, 333
Intellectual property
  copyright law, development of,
      137–46
  Internet information resources on,
      147–49
  student plagiarism, approach to,
      159–60
Intelligent Essay Assessor, 277–78
Intermedia, 174
Internet
  plagiarism from. *See* " 'It wasn't me,
      was it?' Plagiarism and the
      Web" (DeVoss and Rosati)
  writing-related resources, 418–19
Iser, Wolfgang, 171
" 'It wasn't me, was it?': Plagiarism
      and the Web" (DeVoss and
      Rosati), 91, 151–64
  examples, 152–53
  intellectual property issue, 159–60
  online plagiarism, complications of,
      156–57
  plagiarism, reasons for, 155–57
  school policies, types of, 154
  suggestions for dealing with,
      157–62

Jameson, Frederic, 460
Jessup, Emily, 198–99
Johnson, Eric, 313–14
Johnson-Eilola, Johndan, 355, 454, 485,
      489, 493–94
Jones, Robert, 430

Kane, M. T., 273
Kaplan, Nancy, 198, 375
Keller, Evelyn Fox, 200
Kemp, Fred, 198, 243, 284, 310, 313,
      318, 320, 436, 464
Kendall, Lori, 193
Kiefer, Kate, 198, 251, 430
Kies, Daniel, 295
Kinneavy, James, 492
Kitalong, Karla, 159
Kling, Rob, 381–82
Kolich, Augustus, 155
Kolko, Beth, 223
Kopple, William J. Vande, 317
Kostlenick, Charles, 471
Kozol, Jonathan, 31, 457
Kraft, Paul, 28
Krause, Steven D., 485, 487, 489–90,
      492, 494, 495
Kremer, Brenda, 305

Landow, George, 344
Langsam, Deborah, 434
Lanham, Richard, 167, 168, 296, 487
Latour, Bruno, 94, 113
Learning institutions
  cost-cutting, interest in, 57–59
  distance learning, benefits to,
      56–57, 378
  teachers as telecommuters, 59
  technology sharing, 57
Learning styles, gender differences,
      194–96
LeBlanc, Paul, 218
Lecture material, on CD-ROM, 51
Lehman, Bruce, 142–43
Lehrer, Richard, 472
Lesson plans, traditional versus
      computer-supported class,
      255–56
Lifelong learning, and distance
      learning, 377–78
LINGUIST, 197
Lists, ESL lists, 412
"Literacy, Technology, and Monopoly
      Capital" (Ohmann), 12, 20–34
  computers and control of labor,
      26–28
  Cuba, literacy campaign, 30–32

Lists, ESL lists *(continued)*
  literacy, historical view, 20–22, 30
  monopoly capital, 22–24
  and social organization, 30
  technological determinism, 24–26
Literacy and technology
  CCCC position paper on, 12,
    15–19
  Marxist view. *See* "Literacy,
    Technology, and Monopoly
    Capital" (Ohmann)
Literacy education, 97–109
  developing countries, 30–32
  literacy myth, 100–104
  as political action, 104–8
  and technological literacy, 98–100
  violence of literacy concept, 76–77
Literacy testing, historical view, 22
Litvak, Joseph, 207
Logie, John, 135
Logocentric privilege, computer
    interface, 71–74
"Looking for Sources of Coherence in
    a Fragmented World: Notes
    toward a New Assessment
    Design" (Yancey), 235,
    293–307
  assessment heuristic, 300–304
  digital portfolio, 298, 302–4
  digital text, 296–300
  e-mail, 301–2
  print text, 295–97
Lovelace, Augusta Ada, 187
Lunenfeld, Peter, 488
Lyden, Peter, 56
Lyon, Marsha, 439

Malinowitz, Harriet, 208
Malloch, A. E., 153, 154
Mansfield, Susan, 430
Maps, cultural. *See* "Politics of the
    Interface: Power and Its
    Exercise in Electronic Contact
    Zones" (Selfe and Selfe)
Markussen, Randi, 60
Martin, Reginald, 219
Marxist view
  computer interface, ideological
    implications, 68–82

Marxist view *(continued)*
  literacy and technology. *See*
    "Literacy, Technology, and
    Monopoly Capital"
    (Ohmann)
McCorduck, Pamela, 50
McCormick, Kathleen, 196
McGee, Tim, 308
McLuhan, Marshall, 171, 488
Men. *See* gender differences
Menu miscue, 224
Messick, Samuel, 272–73
Meyer, Paul, 197
Microsoft Chat, 413
Miller, Susan, 187, 223
Milroy, Lesley, 313
MindNet, 316
mIRC, 413
Missingham, Roxanne, 197
Moderator, teacher as, 242, 247
Monitor hypnosis, 224
Monopoly capitalism, 23–24, 32
MOOs (multi-user object-oriented
    domains), 299, 413–14,
    436–37, 491
Moran, Charles, 56, 218, 390
Morse, Samuel, 118, 126
Moss, Pamela A., 277
Moxley, Joseph, 437
MS Word Grammar Checker
  computational linguistics, 311–12
  development of, 311–12
  differences and versions of Word,
    314–17
  limitations of, 311–20
  minimizing influence of, 320–22
  and natural language processing
    (NLP), 312–16
MUDs (multi-user domains), 299,
    413–14
Mullin, Joan, 430
Multimedia
  and classroom instruction, 56
  and independent study, 55–56
  instructor commentary, 52
  literature instruction, 50
  production of writing, changes to,
    50–51
  writing assignment, example of use,
    51–54

Munroe, James P., 21
Murray, Donald, 457

National Information Infrastructure
    (NII), 105, 116, 142
Natural language processing (NLP),
    and grammar checker, 312–16
"Negative Spaces: From Production to
    Connection in Composition"
    (Johnson-Eilola), 451–52,
    454–68
  computers and writing information
    sources, 463–66
  connection as creative act, 461–62
  connection versus production,
    458–60
  writing as product, 456–58
Negroponte, Nicholas, 49, 50
Nellen, Ted, 485, 492–93
Nelson, Ted, 74, 171, 308
Networked discussions. See
    discussions, electronic
Neuwirth, Christine, 198
Newman-James, Stephanie, 434
Newsgroups, ESL students' use, 412
New Teachers Study. See "Contrasts:
    Teaching and Learning about
    Writing in Traditional and
    Computer Classrooms"
    (Palmquist, Kiefer, Hartvigsen,
    Goodlew)
Noble, David, 26, 28, 444
Nodes, hypertext, 172–76
  integrated hypertexual composition
    linkages, 475–78
  types of, 174
Non-negotiable difference. See
    "Persistence of Difference in
    Networked Classrooms: Non-
    negotiable Difference and the
    African American Student
    Body" (Taylor)

Object-oriented programming
    systems (OOPS), and bricolage,
    75–76
Ohmann, Richard, 11, 12, 20, 103

Oliver, Mary Beth, 440
Olson, C. Paul, 76
Ong, Walter, 26, 168
Online databases, researching. See
    "Web Research and Genres in
    Online Databases: When the
    Glossy Page Disappears"
    (Sidler)
Online writing labs (OWLs), 385–88
Oppenheimer, Todd, 98
O'Shea, Tim, 29
"Out of the Closet and into the
    Network: Sexual Orientation
    and the Computerized
    Classroom" (Alexander),
    182–83, 207–17
  heterosexual students, benefits to,
    210–11
  Internet as information source, 208
  networked discussions and privacy,
    208–10
  "normalcy" and social pressure,
    214–16
  postmodern argument, 211–12
  role-playing exercises, 212–13

Pailliotet, Ann Watts, 279
Palmquist, Mike, 251, 430, 485, 487
Panopticon, 42
Paper, Carol Clark, 494
Papert, Seymour, 49, 74–76, 195,
    313, 486
Paquin, Raymond L., 470
"Part Two . . ." (Williams), 452, 469–81
"Pedagogy in the Computer-
    Networked Classroom"
    (Eldred), 234, 239–50
  audience, student awareness of,
    246–47
  ease of use of system, 243–44
  egalitarian effect, 244–45
  student participation, teacher
    direction, 245
  technology, choice of, 240–43
Peer teaching, 41, 414–15
Pencil
  development of, 123–25
  and Thoreau family, 119, 123–25

Pennington, Martha C., 404
Penrod, Diane, 271
Perelman, Leslie C., 392
"Persistence of Difference in
    Networked Classrooms: *Non-
    negotiable Difference* and the
    African American Student
    Body" (Taylor), 183, 218–27
  difference, research limitations,
    220–22
  negotiating difference online,
    223–26
  non-negotiable difference, meaning of,
    219–20
Petroski, Henry, 119, 125
Pew Roundtable, 46–48, 57
Photography, copyright
    protection, 137
Piller, Charles, 67
Plagiarism. *See* " 'It wasn't me, was
    it?' Plagiarism and the Web"
    (DeVoss and Rosati)
Pogrow, Stanley, 29
"Politics of the Interface: Power and
    Its Exercise in Electronic
    Contact Zones" (Selfe and
    Selfe), 13, 68–82
  capitalistic implications of interface,
    69–71
  class/race/gender, messages of, 70
  desktop as virtual reality, 69–70
  domination/colonialism aspects,
    69
  English as default language, 71–74
  interface as text revision, 80–81
  maps, power of, 68
  new interface, necessity of, 76–82
  rationality/logocentric privilege,
    74–76
  technology critique versus
    technology use, 78–79
  technology design needs, 79–80
  text as commodity, 70–71
"Politics of the Program: MS Word as
    the Invisible Grammarian,"
    (McGee and Ericsson), 236,
    308–25
  See also MS Word Grammar
    Checker

Polylog, 243
Porter, Jim, 382, 462
Porter, Lynette R., 377
Portfolios, writing
  assessment of, 275–79
  digital portfolio coherence, 298,
    302–4
  posting on Web, 441
  social/political context, 458
Postman, Neil, 335
Pratt, Mary Louise, 65, 67
*Princeton University Press v. Michigan
    Document Services,* 140
Privacy
  sexual orientation discussions,
    208–10
  versus signed responses, 245
Process approach
  design model, 472–78
  writing-across-the-curriculum, 58
  writing instruction, 457–58
ProQuest, 352–53, 355, 357, 359, 363
Puccio, Paul, 395
Pula, Judy, 304

Racial/ethnic minorities
  collaborative activities, benefits, 53
  computer interface as other-reality,
    70–73
  drop-out rates, 66
  instructional focus for, 67–68
  poor schools, lack of technology,
    101–4
  represented in graphics, 81
  school population, increase in,
    66, 71
  as technological underclass, 67
Rape, virtual, on Internet, 192–93
Rationality, computer interface, 74–76
Readability index, 166–67
Reading, online, required skills, 392
"Reading Hypertext: Order and
    Coherence in a New Medium"
    (Slatin), 91–92, 165–78
  authoring in hypertext, 171–72
  coherence, level of, 176–77
  conventional text compared to
    hypertext, 168–72

"Reading Hypertext: Order and Coherence in a New Medium" (Slatin) *(continued)*
links/nodes, 172–76
special effects to hypertext, 176
ReadPlease, 394
Real-Time Writer, 436
Recitation coordinator, 51
Redd, Teresa M., 434–35
Regan, Alison, 219, 457
Reich, Robert B., 459
Reiss, Donna, 425, 440
Reliability
defined, 271
See also "Rethinking Validity and Reliability in the Age of Convergence" (Penrod)
Repurposing information, 469–70
Research, online
databases. *See* "Web Research and Genres in Online Databases: When the Glossy Page Disappears" (Sidler)
instructions to student, 151–53, 161–62
and plagiarism. *See* " 'It wasn't me, was it?' Plagiarism and the Web" (DeVoss and Rosati)
unique issues, 156–57, 160–61
"Re: The Future of Computers and Writing: A Multivocal Textumentury" (Hart-Davidson and Krause), 453, 485–97
"Rethinking Validity and Reliability in the Age of Convergence" (Penrod), 235, 271–92
assessment difficulties, 274–76
concurrent and construct validity, 290–91
equivalence reliability, 274
reliability/validity defined, 271–72
and scientific approach, 272–73
validity/reliability, new approach to, 286–91
variable errors, 273–74
"Reversing Notions of Disability and Accommodation" (Dunn and Dunn De Mers), 183, 228–30

Revision
new versus experienced writers, 326–30
text-analysis programs, 328–30
Reynolds, Nedra, 356
"Rhetoric of Technology and the Electronic Writing Class, The" (Hawisher and Selfe), 12–13, 35–45
and computer-supported writing instruction, 38–41
and electronic conferences, 37–38, 42–43
rhetoric of technology, meaning of, 36, 67
teaching practices, survey of, 38–39
writing class, observations of, 39–41
Rice, Rich, 485, 488, 490, 494
Rickly, Rebecca, 485, 491–92
Ricoeur, Paul, 171
Riley, Richard, 98–99, 101–2
Rodrigues, Dawn, 198, 242, 246, 337
Role-playing, sexual orientation as focus, 212–13
Romano, Susan, 457
Rosati, Annette C., 151
Rose, Mike, 96, 114, 309, 457
Rudenstein, Neil L., 443
Russell, David R., 429, 441

Sadler, Lynn Veach, 198
Salinger v. Random House, 140
Sanchez, Raul, 223
Schools. *See* learning institutions
Schryer, Catherine, 352
Schwalm, Karen, 430
Schwartz, Helen, 198
Schwartz, Mimi, 198
Scoring. *See* assessment of writing
Search engines, teacher evaluation of, 358–60
Selber, Stuart, 391
Self, John, 29
Selfe, Cynthia L., 12, 35, 64, 89–90, 93, 194, 197, 198, 211, 218–219, 308, 379, 382, 390, 429–30, 438, 444, 457

Selfe, Richard J., Jr., 64, 194, 218, 308, 390, 430
Selinger, Michelle, 380
Sexual orientation. *See* "Out of the Closet and into the Network: Sexual Orientation and the Computerized Classroom" (Alexander)
Shaughnessy, Mina, 457
Sherman, Lawrence, 434
Sherry, Lorraine, 376, 380
Shires, Peter, 439
Shneiderman, Ben, 174
Sidler, Michelle, 350
Simic, Marjorie, 389
Simon, Linda, 338
Slatin, John M., 165, 282
Sledd, Andrew, 132
Smith, Adam, 22
Smith, Charles, 430
Smith, William L., 289
Snyder, Ilana, 488
Social class
    and minorities. *See* racial/ethnic minorities
    women and computer use, 201–2
Software programs
    for assessing writing, 277–78, 282–86
    concordance programs, 419
    conferencing software, 394, 436
    design by educators, 80
    ease of use, 243–44
    female software developers, 198
    feminist software, 189, 193–94
    interactive writing program, 413, 436
    presentation software, 298–99
    text-analysis programs, 328–30
    text-conferencing programs, 413
    Web page creation, 417
Soja, Edward, 459
Sokal, Alan, 129
"Some Notes on Simulacra Machines, Flash in First-Year Composition, and Tactics in Spaces of Interruption" (Ellertson), 452–53, 482–84

Sommers, Elizabeth, 327, 330
Sommers, Nancy, 338
Sorapure, Madeleine, 160, 333
Sosnoski, James, 392
Spatial orientation, and Web research, 354–57
Spitzer, Michael, 198
Stallings, W. Dees, 278
Star, Susan Leigh, 59–60
Stetson, George R., 21
Stine, Linda, 389
Stoll, Clifford, 54
Stone, David, 146
Strassmann, Paul A, 26–27
Straub, Richard, 389
Street, Brian, 100, 102–3, 114
Stuckey, Elspeth, 76, 77, 96, 114
Sullivan, Patricia, 218–19, 382
Sumerians, writing of, 120
Summerfield, Geoffrey, 212
Summerfield, Judith, 212
Synchronous conferencing
    ENFI classrooms, 243
    ESL students, 413–14
    hearing-impaired students, 243
    methods, 299, 413–14, 437
Systers, 193
Syverson, Margaret, 282

Tamosaitis, Nancy, 186
Tannen, Deborah, 197
Tate, Marsha, 338
Taylor, Frederick W., 24, 27
Taylor, Todd, 218
Teachers/instructors
    computer versus traditional classroom. *See* "Contrasts: Teaching and Learning about Writing in Traditional and Computer Classrooms" (Palmquist, Kiefer, Hartvigsen, Goodlew)
    and distance learning, 56–57, 374–77
    hybrid environment, best practices, 398–401
    instructional staff, positions of, 51, 57, 59

Teachers/instructors *(continued)*
  Internet, writing-related resources,
    418–19
  moderator role of, 242, 247
  on-line surveillance by, 42–43
  technological literacy of. *See*
    "Technology and Literacy: A
    Story about the Perils of Not
    Paying Attention" (Selfe)
  as technology critics, 68, 78–79
  technology design, contributions to,
    79–80
  as telecommuters, 59
Technological determinism, 25–26
Technological literacy, 98–114
  of basic writers, 391
  in computer-based communication
    facilities, 112
  and curriculum committees, 110
  defined, 98
  educator attention to. *See*
    "Technology and Literacy: A
    Story about the Perils of Not
    Paying Attention" (Selfe)
  and in-service educational
    programs, 113
  and poor/rural students, 112
  and professional organizations, 110
  in research/scholarship, 111
  technological underclass, 67
  U. S. initiative, 98–100, 105–7
  Web literacy. *See* "Web Literacy:
    Challenges and Opportunities
    for Research in a New
    Medium" (Sorapure, Inglesby,
    and Yatchisin)
"Technology and Literacy: A Story
    about the Perils of Not Paying
    Attention" (Selfe), 89–90,
    93–115
  composition teachers, technological
    literacy, importance of, 95–97,
    109–10
  ignoring technology, reasons for,
    94–95
  literacy education, 97–109
  technological literacy, 98–114
Technology Literacy Challenge,
    89, 93

Telecommuting. *See* distance learning
  teachers as telecommuters, 59
Telephone
  communication, changes to, 126–27
  male versus female use, 201
Text-conferencing software, 413
Thaiss, Chris, 442
Theismeyer, John, 486
Thoreau, Henry David
  family and pencil production, 119,
    123–25
  on telegraph, 118, 125–26
Thoreau, John, 119, 123–25
Thoreau Pencil Company, 119
TOPIC/ICON program, 284–85
"Toward an Integrated Composition
    Pedagogy in Hypertext"
    (Williams), 452, 469–81
  design model, 472–78
  integrated composition pedagogy
    concept, 470–72
  integrated hypertexual
    composition, node-linkage,
    475–78
Townsend, Martha A., 438
Trachsel, Mary, 54
Transitions Study. *See* "Contrasts:
    Teaching and Learning about
    Writing in Traditional and
    Computer Classrooms"
    (Palmquist, Kiefer, Hartvigsen,
    Goodlew)
Trimbur, John, 455
Tuell, Cynthia, 187
Tufte, Edward, 471
Turkle, Sherry, 74–76, 195
Typewriter, 127–28

Ulmer, Gregory, 456, 462
Unicode, versus ASCII, 73–74
Universal design, 228–30
URLs (Web addresses), analysis and
    Web research, 353–54

Validity
  concurrent, 290
  construct, 290–91

Validity *(continued)*
    defined, 271–72
    See also "Rethinking Validity and
        Reliability in the Age of
        Convergence" (Penrod)
Violence of literacy concept, 76–77
Visual literacy, 341–43, 471
Visual rhetoric, 471–72
Von Blum, Ruth, 198

"WAC Wired: Electronic
        Communication across the
        Curriculum" (Reiss and
        Young), 371–72, 425–47
    collaborative activities, 435–37
    college programs related to, 430–31,
        437–39
    ECAC, history of, 428–31
    future issues, 440–45
    WAC and classroom discourse,
        432–33
    writing to learn concept,
        431–35, 439
Waggoner, Zach, 391
Wahlstrom, Billie, 198
Walvoord, Barbara, 429–30
Warshauer, Susan, 219
Wax, Robin, 437
Webb Peterson, Patricia, 373
WebCT, 278
"Web Literacy: Challenges and
        Opportunities for Research in a
        New Medium" (Sorapure,
        Inglesby, and Yatchisin), 237,
        333–49
    home pages, assessment difficulty,
        338–39
    interactive aspects, 345–47
    links, assessment of, 343–45
    visual literacy, 341–43
    Web as extension of library, 337–38
    Web evaluation criteria, 336–37
Web pages, ESL students,
        creating, 417
"Web Research and Genres in Online
        Databases: When the Glossy
        Page Disappears" (Sidler), 237,
        350–65

"Web Research and Genres in Online
        Databases: When the Glossy
        Page Disappears" (Sidler)
        (continued)
    cognitive mapping, 356–58, 360–61
    geographic metaphors, 360–63
    online documents, 351–53
    retrieval mechanisms, evaluation
        of, 358–60
    spatial orientation, necessity of,
        354–57
    URL addresses, analysis of, 353–54
Weeks, Jeffrey, 211
Weidenborner, Stephen, 338
Weiser, Mark, 114
Weisser, Christian R., 437
Weizenbaum, Joseph, 68
West, Candace, 197
White, Andy, 438
White-Smith Co. v. Apollo Co. , 137–38
Whithaus, Carl, 296–97, 300, 305
"Why OWLs? Value, Risk, and
        Evolution" (Blythe), 370,
        385–88
Willard, Tom, 223
Williams, Joseph, 316–17
Williams, Patricia, 438
Williams, Raymond, 25
Williams, Sean D., 469
*Williams and Wilkins Co. v. National
        Library of Medicine*, 138
Williamson, Judy, 430
Woest, June, 435
Women
    bricolage, benefits to, 75, 195
    feminist research. *See* "Feminist
        Research in Computers and
        Composition" (Gerrard)
    inequality, and technological
        innovation, 59–60
    women-only lists/services, 193
    See also gender differences
Wood, Denis, 68, 76–77
Woodward, Jeanette, 337
Word-processing software
    development of, 127–29
    grammar checker. *See* MS Word
        Grammar Checker
    revision, 240, 326–30

Word-processing software *(continued)*
   student instruction in use,
      331–32
Workshop atmosphere, of computer-
      supported writing class,
      259–62
World Intellectual Property
      Organization (WIPO), 143–45
Wright, Janet, 212
Writing, historical view, 119–22
   compared to speech, 122
   technologies, development of. *See*
      "From Pencils to Pixels: The
      Stages of Literacy
      Technologies" (Baron)
Writing across the curriculum (WAC).
      See "WAC Wired: Electronic
      Communication across the
      Curriculum" (Reiss and Young)
   and process approach, 58

Writing instruction
   computer-assisted. *See* computers
      and writing instruction
   connection versus production,
      459–60
   interactive aspects, 57–58
   process approach, 457–58
   writing across the curriculum
      programs, 58–59
Writing styles, gendered, 196

Yancey, Kathleen Blake, 293, 300
Yatchisin, George, 160, 333
Yena, Lauren, 391
Young, Art, 425, 441

Zimmerman, Don H., 197
Zuboff, Shoshana, 43, 355–56